EDEXCEL AS/A LEVEL HISTORY

Active Book included

Paper 1&2 Student Book:
Religion and state in early modern Europe

Dr Alison Gundy | Hilary Brash | Adam Kidson
Series editor: Rosemary Rees

ALWAYS LEARNING

PEARSON

Published by Pearson Education Limited, 80 Strand, London, WC2R 0RL.

www.pearsonschoolsandfecolleges.co.uk

Copies of official specifications for all Edexcel qualifications may be found on the website: www.edexcel.com

Text © Pearson Education Limited 2015

Designed by Elizabeth Arnoux for Pearson

Typeset and illustrated by Phoenix Photosetting, Chatham, Kent

Produced by Out of House Publishing

Original illustrations © Pearson Education Limited 2015

Cover design by Malena Wilson-Max for Pearson

Cover photo/illustration © Getty Images: Palace of Westminster, London, UK/Frank Cadogan Cowper

The rights of Hilary Brash, Alison Gundy and Adam Kidson to be identified as authors of this work have been asserted by them in accordance with the Copyright, Designs and Patents Act 1988.

First published 2015

18 17 16 15

10 9 8 7 6 5 4 3

British Library Cataloguing in Publication Data

A catalogue record for this book is available from the British Library

ISBN 978 1 447 985310

Copyright notice

Printed in the UK by Ashford Colour Press Ltd, Gosport, Hampshire

Websites

Pearson Education Limited is not responsible for the content of any external internet sites. It is essential for tutors to preview each website before using it in class so as to ensure that the URL is still accurate, relevant and appropriate. We suggest that tutors bookmark useful websites and consider enabling students to access them through the school/college intranet.

A note from the publisher

In order to ensure that this resource offers high-quality support for the associated Pearson qualification, it has been through a review process by the awarding body. This process confirms that; this resource fully covers the teaching and learning content of the specification or part of a specification at which it is aimed. It also confirms that it demonstrates an appropriate balance between the development of subject skills, knowledge and understanding, in addition to preparation for assessment.

Endorsement does not cover any guidance on assessment activities or processes (e.g. practice questions or advice on how to answer assessment questions), included in the resource nor does it prescribe any particular approach to the teaching or delivery of a related course.

While the publishers have made every attempt to ensure that advice on the qualification and its assessment is accurate, the official specification and associated assessment guidance materials are the only authoritative source of information and should always be referred to for definitive guidance.

Pearson examiners have not contributed to any sections in this resource relevant to examination papers for which they have responsibility.

Examiners will not use endorsed resources as a source of material for any assessment set by Pearson.

Endorsement of a resource does not mean that the resource is required to achieve this Pearson qualification, nor does it mean that it is the only suitable material available to support the qualification, and any resource lists produced by the awarding body shall include this and other appropriate resources.

Contents

How to use this book

STRUCTURE

This book covers Route B of the Edexcel A Level and AS Level History qualifications. Route B consists of three papers which are linked by the theme '**Religion and state in early modern Europe**'.

- Paper 1: England, 1509–1603: authority, nation and religion
- Paper 2a: Luther and the German Reformation, c1515–55
- Paper 2b: The Dutch Revolt, c1563–1609

To take Route B, you must study Paper 1, plus **one** of the two Paper 2 options. You do not need to study the other Paper 2 topic for your exam, but you might like to read it for interest – it deals with similar themes to the topics you are studying.

If you are studying for A Level History, you will also need to study a Paper 3 option and produce coursework in order to complete your qualification. All Paper 3 options are covered by other textbooks in this series.

AS LEVEL OR A LEVEL?

This book is designed to support students studying both the Edexcel AS Level and A Level qualifications. The content required for both qualifications is identical, so all the material in the papers you are studying is relevant, whichever qualification you are aiming for.

The questions you will be asked in the exam differ for the two different qualifications, so we have included separate exam-style questions and exam preparation sections. If you are studying for an AS Level, you should use the exam-style questions and exam sections highlighted in blue. If you are studying for an A Level, you should use the exam-style questions and exam sections highlighted in green.

> **AS Level Exam-Style Question Section A**
>
> Reformers such as Thomas Cromwell were influential at court in the 1530s.
>
> Was the influence of Thomas Cromwell the main reason for reforms to the English Church in the period 1529–40? (20 marks)
>
> **Tip**
> *You will need to consider both Cromwell's role and other reasons for reform, such as the role of Henry VIII.*

> **A Level Exam-Style Question Section B**
>
> How significant was the challenge posed by the Puritans to Elizabeth's Religious Settlement in the years 1558–88? (20 marks)
>
> **Tip**
> *You need to think carefully about the word 'significant' and how this relates to Puritan activities across the period. Consideration of the changing level of significance over the period would also help in this answer.*

The 'Preparing for your exams' section at the end of each paper contains sample answers of different standards, with comments on how weaker answers could be improved. Make sure you look at the right section for the exam you are planning to take.

FEATURES

Extend your knowledge

These features contain additional information that will help you gain a deeper understanding of the topic. This could be a short biography of an important person, extra background information about an event, an alternative interpretation, or even a research idea that you could follow up. Information in these boxes is not essential to your exam success, but still provides insights of value.

> **EXTEND YOUR KNOWLEDGE**
>
> **John Calvin**
> John Calvin was a radical Protestant thinker whose ideas were adopted in the Swiss town of Geneva. He emphasised the importance of reading the Bible. He also supported the idea that salvation could be achieved solely through faith (justification by faith alone) as well as belief in predestination, the idea that God had decided who would go to heaven. Calvin also rejected the traditional hierarchy of the Catholic Church.

Knowledge check activities

These activities are designed to check that you have understood the material that you have just studied. They might also ask you questions about the sources and extracts in the section to check that you have studied and analysed them thoroughly.

ACTIVITY
KNOWLEDGE CHECK

Becoming Protestant

1 Read Source 9. What criticisms are made of the Catholic Church? Why would these criticisms have been particularly helpful to Henry in his attempts to annul his marriage to Catherine of Aragon?

2 Compare Anne Boleyn's role to those of Cromwell, Cranmer and Henry VIII. Who was the most important in bringing about the break with Rome?

3 What evidence is there that England had become Protestant by 1553?

4 Why was England not completely Protestant by this date?

Summary activities

At the end of each chapter, you will find summary activities. These are tasks designed to help you think about the key topic you have just studied as a whole. They may involve selecting and organising key information or analysing how things changed over time. You might want to keep your answers to these questions safe – they are handy for revision.

ACTIVITY
SUMMARY

1 Draw a graph showing how the religion of England changed from Catholic to Protestant during the period.

2 Make a spider diagram called 'The causes of religious change in the period 1509–88'. Use the following headings to summarise what you have learned: 'Role of individual monarchs'; 'Role of other individuals' (for example Cromwell, Anne Boleyn); 'Role of popular belief'; 'Role of new ideas'.

3 Make a list of examples of resistance to religious change. How successful were they?

Thinking Historically activities

These activities are found throughout the book and are designed to develop your understanding of history, especially around the key concepts of evidence, interpretations, causation and change. Each activity is designed to challenge a conceptual barrier that might be holding you back. This is linked to a map of conceptual barriers developed by experts. You can look up the map and find out which barrier each activity challenges by downloading the conceptual map from this website: www.pearsonschools.co.uk/historyprogressionapproach.

conceptual map reference

 THINKING HISTORICALLY Evidence (4a&b)

Methods for dealing with poverty

Sources 8 and 9 could be used by a historian to build up a picture of the methods used to deal with poverty in Tudor England.

Use Sources 8 and 9 to answer the following:

1 Explain why Sources 8 and 9 offer different views of Tudor methods of dealing with poverty. How might this affect their value as pieces of evidence in appraising methods of dealing with poverty in the 16th century? Explain your answer.

Discuss the following in groups.

2 Suppose the historian had ten more accounts that agreed broadly with Source 8 and only four that agreed with Source 9. What would that tell him about Tudor methods of dealing with poverty?

3 How far should the balance of the evidence play a role in constructing written history? What else must a historian consider about the evidence being used before drawing conclusions?

Getting the most from your online ActiveBook

This book comes with three years' access to ActiveBook* – an online, digital version of your textbook. Follow the instructions printed on the inside front cover to start using your ActiveBook.

Your ActiveBook is the perfect way to personalise your learning as you progress through your AS/A Level History course. You can:

- access your content online, anytime, anywhere

- use the inbuilt highlighting and annotation tools to personalise the content and make it really relevant to you.

Highlight tool – use this to pick out key terms or topics so you are ready and prepared for revision.

Annotations tool – use this to add your own notes, for example links to your wider reading, such as websites or other files. Or, make a note to remind yourself about work that you need to do.

*For new purchases only. If the access code has already been revealed, it may no longer be valid. If you have bought this textbook secondhand, the code may already have been used by the first owner of the book.

Introduction
AS/A Level History

WHY HISTORY MATTERS

History is about people and people are complex, fascinating, frustrating and a whole lot of other things besides. This is why history is probably the most comprehensive and certainly one of the most intriguing subjects there is. History can also be inspiring and alarming, heartening and disturbing, a story of progress and civilisation and of catastrophe and inhumanity.

History's importance goes beyond the subject's intrinsic interest and appeal. Our beliefs and actions, our cultures, institutions and ways of living, our languages and means of making sense of ourselves are all shaped by the past. If we want to fully understand ourselves now, and to understand our possible futures, we have no alternative but to think about history.

History is a discipline as well as a subject matter. Making sense of the past develops qualities of mind that are valuable to anyone who wants to seek the truth and think clearly and intelligently about the most interesting and challenging intellectual problem of all: other people. Learning history is learning a powerful way of knowing.

WHAT IS HISTORY?

History is a way of constructing knowledge about the world through research, interpretation, argument and debate.

Building historical knowledge involves identifying the traces of the past that exist in the present – in people's memories, in old documents, photographs and other remains, and in objects and artefacts ranging from bullets and lipsticks, to field systems and cities. Historians interrogate these traces and *ask questions* that transform traces into *sources of evidence* for knowledge claims about the past.

Historians aim to understand what happened in the past by *explaining why* things happened as they did. Explaining why involves trying to understand past people and their beliefs, intentions and actions. It also involves explaining the causes and evaluating the effects of large-scale changes in the past and exploring relationships between what people aimed to do, the contexts that shaped what was possible and the outcomes and consequences of actions.

Historians also aim to *understand change* in the past. People, states of affairs, ideas, movements and civilisations come into being in time, grow, develop, and ultimately decline and disappear. Historians aim to identify and compare change and continuity in the past, to measure the rate at which things change and to identify the types of change that take place. Change can be slow or sudden. It can also be understood as progressive or regressive – leading to the improvement or worsening of a situation or state of affairs. How things change and whether changes are changes for the better are two key issues that historians frequently debate.

Figure 1 Fragment of a black granite statue possibly portraying the Roman politician Mark Antony.

Debate is the essence of history. Historians write arguments to support their knowledge claims and historians argue with each other to test and evaluate interpretations of the past. Historical knowledge itself changes and develops. On the one hand, new sources of knowledge and new methods of research cause *historical interpretations* to change. On the other hand, the questions that historians ask change with time and new questions produce new answers. Although the past is dead and gone, the interpretation of the past has a past, present and future.

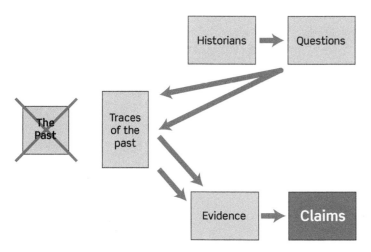

Figure 2 Constructing knowledge about the past.

THE CHALLENGES OF LEARNING HISTORY

Like all other Advanced Level subjects, A Level and AS Level history are difficult – that is why they are called 'advanced'. Your advanced level studies will build on knowledge and understanding of history that you developed at GCSE and at Key Stage 3 – ideas like 'historical sources', 'historical evidence' and 'cause', for example. You will need to do a lot of reading and writing to progress in history. Most importantly, you will need to do a lot of thinking, and thinking about your thinking. This book aims to support you in developing both your knowledge and your understanding.

History is challenging in many ways. On the one hand, it is challenging to build up the range and depth of knowledge that you need to understand the past at an advanced level. Learning about the past involves mastering new and unfamiliar concepts arising from the past itself (such as the Inquisition, Laudianism, *Volksgemeinschaft*) and building up levels of knowledge that are both detailed and well organised. This book covers the key content of the topics that you are studying for your examination and provides a number of features to help you build and organise what you know – for example, diagrams, timelines and definitions of key terms. You will need to help yourself too, of course, adding to your knowledge through further reading, building on the foundations provided by this book.

Another challenge is to develop understandings of the discipline of history. You will have to learn to think historically about evidence, cause, change and interpretations and also to write historically, in a way that develops clear and supported argument.

Historians think with evidence in ways that differ from how we often think in everyday life. In history, as Figure 2 shows, we cannot go and 'see for ourselves' because the past no longer exists. Neither can we normally rely on 'credible witnesses' to tell us 'the truth' about 'what happened'. People in the past did not write down 'the truth' for our benefit. They often had clear agendas when creating the traces that remain and, as often as not, did not themselves know 'the truth' about complex historical events.

A root of the word 'history' is the Latin word *historia*, one of whose meanings is 'enquiry' or 'finding out'. Learning history means learning to ask questions and interrogate traces, and then to reason about what the new knowledge you have gained means. This book draws on historical scholarship for its narrative and contents. It also draws on research on the nature of historical thinking and on the challenges that learning history can present for students. Throughout the book you will find 'Thinking Historically' activities designed to support the development of your thinking.

You will also find – as you would expect given the nature of history – that the book is full of questions. This book aims to help you build your understandings of the content, contexts and concepts that you will need to advance both your historical knowledge and your historical understanding, and to lay strong foundations for the future development of both.

QUOTES ABOUT HISTORY

'Historians are dangerous people. They are capable of upsetting everything. They must be directed.'

Nikita Khrushchev

'To be ignorant of what occurred before you were born is to remain forever a child. For what is the worth of human life, unless it is woven into the life of our ancestors by the records of history?'

Marcus Tullius Cicero

England, 1509–1603: authority, nation and religion

The period from the accession of Henry VIII in 1509 to the death of his daughter Elizabeth I in 1603 was one of great political, religious, social, economic and cultural change. In 1509, the Tudor dynasty had been established for just 24 years and it was by no means certain that it would survive. After 30 years of political instability during the Wars of the Roses, Henry VIII's father, Henry VII, had taken the throne by force, and was considered by some to be a usurper. The reigns of Henry VIII and his children Edward VI, Mary I and Elizabeth I not only fully established the Tudor dynasty, but also extended the Tudors' power and authority throughout England and Wales.

The main themes of this Paper are the changes that happened during the Tudor period. Influenced by the birth of new cultural, religious and political ideas of the European Renaissance, the Tudor monarchs were able to extend their power more completely across their kingdom. In an age of personal monarchy, each monarch's beliefs and style of rule left its mark on English politics, society and culture. Henry VIII's desire for a legitimate son and heir to secure the Tudor dynasty led to unintended long-term consequences for religious belief in England. In 1509, England was a uniformly Catholic country that owed allegiance to the pope; the countryside was dominated by monasteries that acted as landlords and farmers. By 1603, the Protestant Church of England had been established for 45 years, the monasteries had been dissolved and England was at war with its Catholic enemies. Henry VIII's actions also created a new political role for the English parliament, whose powers increased considerably during the period.

The period from 1509 also saw enormous social and economic change. A growing population led to rising unemployment and falling living standards for those on the margins of society. As a result, the Tudor authorities were faced with the growing problem of poverty and what to do about it. Radical religious change and social and economic hardship also contributed to serious popular rebellions such as the Pilgrimage of Grace (1536) and the rebellions in the south-west and East Anglia in 1549. In the reign of Elizabeth, economic and political developments led to the beginning of English exploration and the colonisation of the New World.

Although the poorest in society suffered increasing hardship, the wealthier members became increasingly prosperous. The Tudor monarchs and their nobility used their money and power to become patrons of art, poetry, music and architecture. New technologies such as the printing press enhanced the spread of new religious and political ideas – some of them dangerously radical – and the growth of literacy and education for those who could afford it. By Elizabeth's reign, there was a flowering of a new self-consciously English culture, fostered by the queen herself through her cult of Gloriana, where writers such as Shakespeare could flourish.

By the 1590s, however, the Tudor period was reaching crisis point. England was ruled by an ageing queen who refused to name an heir and whose court was increasingly riven by political faction; the demands of war were stretching the economy to breaking point; parliament's new-found confidence led it to challenge the queen's prerogative powers directly; and social and economic crises led to severe hardship among her people. But Elizabeth was able to survive these challenges. This was a testament to the enormous power of the Tudor monarchy and the respect and fear that it imbued among the English people.

1509	1509 – Accession of Henry VIII
1529	1529 – The Reformation parliament meets for the first time
1536	1536 – Dissolution of the monasteries and the Pilgrimage of Grace; publication of the English Bible
1547	1547 – Death of Henry VIII and accession of Edward VI
1553	1553 – Lady Jane Grey rules for nine days and is defeated by Mary Tudor
1559	1559 – Creation of the Elizabethan Church Settlement
1577–80	1577–80 – Francis Drake circumnavigates the globe
1588	1588 – The Spanish Armada is defeated
1601	1601 – The monopolies debates in parliament and Elizabeth's 'golden speech'

1527	1527 – Beginning of Henry's annulment proceedings against Catherine of Aragon
1534	1534 – The Act of Supremacy is passed
1537	1537 – Birth of Henry's son and heir, Edward
1549	1549 – The 'commotion time' rebellions in the south-west and East Anglia
1554	1554 – Thomas Wyatt's rebellion
1569	1569 – The Northern Revolt
1585	1585 – Outbreak of war with Spain
1594	1594 – Outbreak of Tyrone's revolt in Ireland
1603	1603 – Death of Elizabeth I

SOURCE 1

The Family of Henry VIII: An Allegory of the Tudor Succession, by Lucas de Heere, painted c1572. This was painted during the reign of Elizabeth I and shows the symbolic figure of War, Philip and Mary I, Henry VIII, Edward VI, Elizabeth I and the symbolic figures of Peace and Plenty.

SOURCE 2

'Beggars All': Beggars' bush, a wandering beggar and a gallant beggar, from the title page of *The Praise, Antiquity and Commodity of Beggary, Beggars and Begging*, an English 16th century woodcut. This shows Tudor attitudes towards the poor and problems associated with dealing with poverty.

1.1 Monarchy and government, 1509–88

KEY QUESTIONS

- What was the role of the monarchy in Tudor England, 1509–88?
- How did the role of parliament change between 1509 and 1588?
- What were the roles of the principal servants of the Crown?

INTRODUCTION

In 1509, when Henry VIII came to the throne, the Tudors were still a relatively new dynasty and faced threats from rival claimants. Nevertheless, they survived and created a period of political stability. Henry VIII and his children Edward VI, Mary I and Elizabeth I ruled in an age of personal monarchy when the ruler was still in charge of government. While Henry VIII inherited the throne as a young adult, his children faced particular challenges in governing the country. Edward VI became king at the age of nine, while his half-sisters were the first women to rule England in their own right since the 12th century. The period was also important for the contributions of the Tudors' chief ministers Thomas Wolsey, Thomas Cromwell and William Cecil. Finally, the actions of the monarchs and the changes that were made had important repercussions for the power and role of parliament, which grew considerably from the 1530s.

SOURCE

1 The Great Chain of Being from *Retorica Christiana* by Didacus Valades, printed in 1579.

ACTIVITY
KNOWLEDGE

Society and status

Look at Source 1.

What does it suggest about how 16th century people viewed society and status?

How might an image such as this be used by the Tudor monarchs to reinforce their position?

1533 – Henry VIII marries Anne Boleyn; birth of Elizabeth I

1509 – Accession of Henry VIII

| 1505 | 1510 | 1515 | 1520 | 1525 | 1530 |

1529 – Fall of Wolsey; first session of the Reformation parliament

WHAT WAS THE ROLE OF THE MONARCHY IN TUDOR ENGLAND, 1509–88?

Tudor society was hierarchical in nature, with emphasis placed on the importance of obedience to the monarch as the pinnacle of society and God's representative on earth. One common way in which this was expressed was in the 'Great Chain of Being', which depicted all members of society having their place and being dependent on each other. This idea emphasised that God had created an ordered society and that obedience was owed to those higher up the social scale.

SOURCE

2 From Sir Thomas Smith, *De Republica Anglorum*, 1583. Smith was a noted scholar and diplomat who wrote this book in the reign of Elizabeth I to describe the government of England.

The Prince is the life, the head and the authority of all things that be done in the realm of England.

Between 1509 and 1588, the rule of the monarchy was personal and it was accepted that kings ruled 'by the Grace of God' (*Dei Gratia* – abbreviated to D.G. on coins even today). This meant that, in the 16th century, monarchs were still in control of government and that the monarchy passed by the rule of **primogeniture** from father to son. For example, monarchs made the decision whether to go to war or to make peace. They could also summon and dismiss parliament at will. Under their coronation oath, they were responsible for upholding justice and the law, which was carried out in their name. However, to be successful, an English monarch could not ignore the customs and traditions of England or the laws made by parliament. Monarchs who tried to rule entirely as they pleased risked being labelled tyrants and could face rebellion and usurpation. This had happened to Richard II in 1399 and would later happen to Charles I in the 17th century. It was expected that, while a monarch would be able to choose their own friends and counsellors, they would also listen to their advice, though the monarch would not necessarily have to act on it.

This personal style of monarchy required the ruler of England to be physically able to run the country. In 1509, this meant that they needed to be adult (technically, 21 years old), male, physically strong, able to lead an army into battle, and with enough intelligence to make decisions and have some involvement in the day-to-day running of the country. A ruler who did not possess these qualities might well lead the country to the brink of disaster, as the rule of Henry VI had shown in the 15th century. The role of the monarch was vital to the smooth running of the country and remained so throughout the Tudor period. This helps to explain why Henry VIII was so determined to produce a living son and heir to carry on Tudor rule; it also explains why the Tudor succession was, at times, in doubt. First, Henry VIII was succeeded in 1547 by his son and heir Edward VI, who was just nine years old and could not be expected to rule on his own. Edward was then followed by his two half-sisters, Mary Tudor (1553–58) and Elizabeth I (1558–1603). This was the first time that a woman had ruled in her own right since the 12th century, yet the Tudor dynasty survived.

KEY TERM

Primogeniture
The system of inheritance by which property and titles passed from father to eldest son or the eldest surviving male relative.

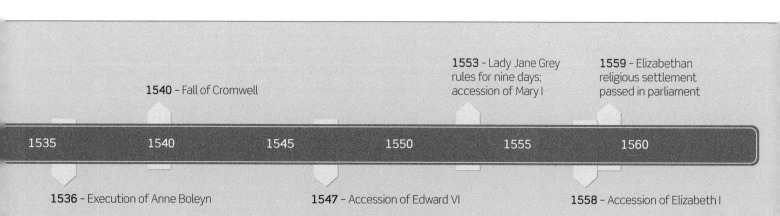

1540 – Fall of Cromwell

1553 – Lady Jane Grey rules for nine days; accession of Mary I

1559 – Elizabethan religious settlement passed in parliament

| 1535 | 1540 | 1545 | 1550 | 1555 | 1560 |

1536 – Execution of Anne Boleyn

1547 – Accession of Edward VI

1558 – Accession of Elizabeth I

EXTEND YOUR KNOWLEDGE

Henry VI and the Wars of the Roses, 1455–85

Although this Paper focuses on the period from 1509, an understanding of the events of the 15th century helps to explain the actions and preoccupations of Henry VIII. Henry VI was king of England from 1422 to 1461 and from 1470 to 1471. He was indecisive and easily influenced, allowing powerful nobility to control him. His mental breakdown in 1453 led to disputes over who should be protector. The outbreak of civil war between the rival houses of York and Lancaster followed in 1455, which became known as the 'Wars of the Roses'. Henry was deposed by the Yorkist claimant, Edward IV, in 1461. He was briefly reinstated to the throne in 1470–71, but was defeated and died in suspicious circumstances. Edward IV ruled until his death in 1483. There was further political instability between 1483 and 1487. Edward's sons were usurped by their uncle, Richard III. In turn, Richard was killed at the Battle of Bosworth by the only surviving Lancastrian claimant, Henry Tudor, who became Henry VII. However, Henry faced challenges in turn as his claim to be king was weak, culminating in the Battle of Stoke in 1487. Yorkist claimants to the throne were still viewed with suspicion under Henry VIII.

Personal and political qualities of the Tudor monarchs

As long as monarchy remained personal, the personality, strengths and weaknesses of a monarch mattered, as they could have an impact on how effectively that monarch was able to rule the country. An indecisive or weak king like Henry VI could create serious political instability, while a charismatic ruler with strong leadership and military skills, such as Henry V (1413–22), would be more likely to be seen to rule successfully.

Henry VIII, 1509–47

Henry came to the throne at the age of 17. Until 1502, he had been brought up as a second son who was not expected to become king, but this changed when his elder brother, Arthur, died. As the son of a king, Henry was well educated. He could speak four or five languages, and he could sing and dance. Henry was clearly intelligent. He wrote poems and songs, including 'Pastime with Good Company'. He even wrote a book in Latin, *Assertio Septem Sacramentorum* ('Defence of the Seven Sacraments', 1521). As a king, Henry was forceful and sometimes cruel, as his treatment of his wives, chief ministers and even close friends shows. He also disliked writing state papers, which he described as 'both tedious and painful'. Instead, he preferred to leave the details of day-to-day government to his ministers, although he always remained in charge.

Henry was influenced by **Renaissance** ideas of 'honour', which required him to defend England's rights abroad. For Henry, this meant going to war to regain English territory lost in France in the 1440s and 1450s. In this, he was inspired by his namesake, Henry V, who had won famous victories against the French in the early 15th century. A Renaissance prince was supposed to be an accomplished fighter. This appealed to Henry, who also enjoyed military sports such as jousting.

Edward VI, 1547–53

Edward was just nine years old when he came to the throne and for much of his short reign he remained a political figurehead controlled by his protectors. As heir to the throne, Edward was educated by the best **humanist** thinkers in the country, such as the brilliant Cambridge scholar John Cheke. Edward was an able child – at the age of seven he was already learning to read Latin. By 1550, he was also fluent in French, Spanish and Italian, and in 1551 he started to learn ancient Greek.

As a king he was also expected to lead an army, and he both watched and participated in tournaments. Edward also kept a Chronicle, a form of journal, which shows that he was also learning how to rule and was becoming increasingly involved in government. Edward's Chronicle and letters also reveal something of his personality. The longest and most detailed passages of his journal are related to military matters such as descriptions of jousts. Following a visit to Portsmouth in 1552, he wrote in a letter that the defences of the castle there were not as strong as they should be and he suggested some designs to improve them.

Edward's letters also reveal a tendency to priggishness and a growing Protestant faith. At the age of eight, he wrote to his stepmother, Catherine Parr, to ask her to persuade his elder half-sister Mary (who was nearly 30) 'to attend no longer to foreign dances and merriments [at court] which do not become a most Christian princess'. Unfortunately, Edward died at the age of 16, before he had an opportunity to fully take power.

KEY TERMS

Renaissance
Meaning 'rebirth', this is the term used to describe the renewed intellectual interest in ancient Greek and Roman culture. From the late 14th century, this led to experimentation in writing, art, architecture and thought.

Humanism
Renaissance humanism emphasised the importance of education for men and women and particularly the need to speak and write well. Students were taught Greek, grammar, rhetoric, logic, history, poetry and moral philosophy. Famous humanist thinkers and writers included Desiderius Erasmus and Sir Thomas More.

Mary I, 1553–58

Born in 1516, Mary was 37 when she became queen. Like her younger half-brother and half-sister, she was intelligent and had been well educated, especially as for many years it was assumed she would inherit the throne. Although Mary's childhood was happy, her teenage and adult years were overshadowed by Henry VIII's attempts to annul his marriage to her mother, Catherine of Aragon. Made illegitimate and excluded from the royal succession by the Act of Succession (1534), she was restored as second in line to the throne in 1544, but her illegitimacy was not reversed. Mary was personally pious and loyal to her Roman Catholic faith. During the reign of the Protestant Edward VI, she came under considerable pressure to renounce her beliefs, but she consistently refused. This stubbornness was later to cause problems during her own reign as she was determined to restore the English Church to full Catholicism. Politically, this was not an astute move as she failed to realise the complexity of the situation in England after 20 years of reformation.

This same stubbornness also drove her to believe that marriage to the Spanish king, Philip II, was the best way to achieve her religious aims. Her failure to realise the extent of opposition to this marriage and the English hatred and suspicion of foreigners led to open rebellion in 1554. Mary's health also affected her ability to rule effectively. She suffered from anxiety and depression, and her desperation to bear a son and heir led to phantom pregnancies, which kept her closeted in her chambers.

Elizabeth I, 1558–1603

Elizabeth (born in 1533) was the daughter of Henry VIII and his second wife, Anne Boleyn, for whom he divorced his first wife, Catherine of Aragon, and broke with the Roman Catholic Church in the process. Elizabeth was therefore the embodiment of the break with Rome and the movement towards a more Protestant Church.

Like her brother, she was brought up and educated by the best scholars available, including John Cheke's pupil, Roger Ascham. In 1536, Anne Boleyn was executed for treason and Elizabeth was made illegitimate in the second Act of Succession, but she was reinstated in the royal succession in 1544. Elizabeth was clever and quick-witted. She also learnt the harsh realities of politics at an early age. In 1549, she was caught up in the plans of Thomas Seymour, one of the uncles of Edward VI, to marry her without the king's consent. To marry a member of the royal family without the permission of the monarch was a serious offence that could even be classed as treason. This was what happened to Seymour, who was executed. Elizabeth's servants were arrested and questioned in the Tower of London and Elizabeth herself was questioned about her role.

In 1554, during Mary's reign, Elizabeth was arrested and sent to the Tower as it was suspected she had played a part in encouraging rebellion against Mary. She was questioned but would admit to nothing and eventually she was released to live under house arrest.

In 1558, Elizabeth became queen, and she had learned caution. As queen, this caution became indecisiveness – in a crisis, she would sometimes refuse to make a decision, much to the frustration of her counsellors. She also had a fearsome temper. In 1587,

for example, she wavered over whether she should execute her cousin, Mary, Queen of Scots, despite the threat that Mary posed to Elizabeth's life. She was eventually persuaded to sign Mary's death warrant, but then demanded that it should not be sealed or sent. In desperation, Elizabeth's Council ignored this order and Mary was executed – Elizabeth was furious.

Elizabeth also had considerable strengths as a ruler. She was a **politique**, who preferred compromise and moderation (especially over matters of religion) to the hard-line approach of Edward or Mary. This moderation, combined with stubbornness and a talent for man-management, allowed her to survive successfully despite her illegitimacy in the eyes of some.

KEY TERM

Politique
A moderate who believed that the unity of the country could be achieved through allowing some religious toleration.

EXTEND YOUR KNOWLEDGE

Mary, Queen of Scots (1542–87)
Not to be confused with Mary Tudor, Mary Stuart (also known as Mary, Queen of Scots) was the daughter of James V of Scotland and the French Princess Marie de Guise. Mary was also descended from Henry VII via his elder daughter, Margaret, and so had a claim to the English throne, though she was passed over in Henry's Acts of Succession and will. Mary became queen of Scotland at six days old. She was sent to France to avoid English attempts to capture her and marry her to Prince Edward. Mary married the French heir to the throne, Francis, and was briefly queen of France (1559–60), but she was sent back to Scotland on Francis' death. She then married her first cousin, Henry Stuart (Lord Darnley) and they had a son, James, in 1566. The marriage was unhappy and Darnley was found murdered in 1567. Mary's Catholic faith had already caused disquiet among her Protestant nobles, but her marriage to the chief suspect in Darnley's murder, the Earl of Bothwell, shocked Catholics too. After a short civil war, Mary was forced to abdicate in favour of her son. In 1568, she fled to England, where she was kept in comfortable imprisonment by her cousin, Elizabeth. From 1569, Mary became the focus of several Catholic plots to assassinate Elizabeth and put Mary on the throne instead. Eventually, Mary was executed, but her son, James, became king of both Scotland and England in 1603.

What were popular attitudes to the Tudor monarchy?

With the personality of the monarch so vital to the running of the state, it should come as no surprise that the attitudes of their subjects towards the Tudor monarchs would impact their ability to govern. Although monarchs such as Henry VI had been forced to abdicate or had been murdered, this was still considered a last resort and respect for the monarchy as an institution remained high. When rebellions did occur in this period, they were usually aimed at the ruler's policies or at their 'evil counsellors', those who had given the monarch poor advice. For example, the rebels involved in the Pilgrimage of Grace (1536) complained explicitly about 'persons of low birth and small reputation' in Henry VIII's council, as well as the religious and economic policies being pursued by the king and his advisers.

The Western Rebellion of 1549 was a reaction against the religious policies of Edward VI's government, while the noble leaders of the 1569 Northern Rebellion against Elizabeth I called themselves her 'most true and lawful subjects' and ended their proclamation with the words 'God save the queen'. To remove forcibly or kill a monarch, however inept they were, was considered to be acting against God's will. As Henry VIII put it in his response to the Lincolnshire rebels of 1536: 'How presumptuous are ye, the rude commons of one shire, and that one of the most brute and beastly of the whole realm and of least experience, to take upon you, contrary to God's law and man's law, to rule your Prince, whom ye are bound to obey and serve.' (See Chapter 3 for further information on the Pilgrimage of Grace.)

However, there were strong popular beliefs and traditions associated with the power and role of the monarchy. For example, Tudor monarchs could not raise taxation without the agreement of parliament. When Wolsey tried to do this in 1525 on Henry VIII's behalf with the non-parliamentary Amicable Grant, it led to a serious rebellion. Nor could a monarch, or his advisers, simply ignore the laws of the realm made in conjunction with parliament, especially those protecting property and inheritance. In 1553, when Edward VI, with the connivance of the Duke of Northumberland, attempted to alter the succession to the throne and to bypass the Catholic Mary Tudor in favour of the Protestant Jane Grey, the result was a successful rebellion in favour of Mary. Although Mary was a woman, the third **Act of Succession** (1544) had made her second in line to the throne after Edward and there was a mass popular rising in her support.

KEY TERM

Acts of Succession
These were passed by Henry VIII's parliaments and made changes to the line of succession and to the legitimacy of his daughters, Mary and Elizabeth. The Act of 1534 reinforced the judgement of Thomas Cranmer, Archbishop of Canterbury that Henry's marriage to Catherine was invalid and that Mary was illegitimate. The Act made Henry and Anne's children the legitimate heirs.

The 1536 Act, passed after Anne's execution, declared that Elizabeth was illegitimate as well and replaced her in the line of succession with the as yet unborn heirs of Henry and Jane Seymour.

The Act of 1544 named Edward as Henry's heir, but it also restored Mary and Elizabeth to the royal succession, although it did not explicitly make them legitimate again. The 1544 Act also made provision for a regency council should Henry die while Edward was still a minor; under the terms of the Act, the council was to be nominated by Henry in his will.

These Acts were significant because it was the first time that parliament had been used in this way to give legal standing to the royal succession. This shows the growing importance of parliament in this period as well as the political confusion created by Henry's marriages and the need to clarify who Henry's heirs were. However, in each case the Acts were made to reinforce the king's actions; parliament did not have the power on its own to dictate the royal succession.

Tudor propaganda

Although there was popular acceptance of the role and powers of the monarchy, the Tudor monarchs used a range of methods to reinforce popular obedience and loyalty. It was common for the royal courts of Tudor monarchs to put on 'disguisings', such as tournaments, which were open to all spectators. There were also more private court plays and banquets. The purpose of these often extravagant displays was to emphasise the power, wealth and legitimacy of the Tudor dynasty. As religious changes took effect in the 1530s, propaganda was also used to spread the beliefs adopted by the monarch. For example, Henry VIII's reign saw a staged battle on the Thames between two barges representing the king and the pope, in which the actors playing the pope and his cardinals were ducked in the river. Tudor monarchs also increased their visibility through progresses around the country, which were an opportunity for the monarchs to show themselves and be seen by their people. Elizabeth I, in particular, used this method and went on progresses with her entire court nearly every summer, staying in the houses of leading local nobility and gentry to save money. For example, in 1560 and 1569 she visited Hampshire, in 1572 she went to the Midlands and in 1578 she visited East Anglia.

Before Henry VIII became too old and ill to travel, he, too, used progresses, though to a lesser extent – in 1535 he visited Salisbury and the Bristol Channel, and in 1541 he went on a progress to the North of England, which included a stay at York. This latter progress was partially a response to the northern-based rebellion, the Pilgrimage of Grace (1536), and further unrest in 1541, but it shows the importance of the physical presence of the monarch to both impress and intimidate the local population. Although the reigns of Mary I and Edward VI saw fewer progresses as a result of illness and youth, they still used plays, masques and other displays to reinforce their rule. Edward's protector, the Duke of Northumberland, erected huge temporary banqueting houses in Hyde Park in London to entertain and impress the visiting French ambassadors and the Londoners alike.

Although Tudor monarchs did occasionally face popular rebellion, this was not usually aimed at removing them from their throne. Instead, rebellion was a response to unpopular policies. Evidence that the monarchy was genuinely popular is hard to find, though it is possible to argue that the absence of unrest is in itself evidence of acceptance. However, genuine popular reaction can be seen in the fact that the day of Henry VIII's death was commemorated every year by solemn mourning until the 1560s. Similarly, Elizabeth I's accession also became a day of national celebration – albeit one encouraged by the queen – when there was bell-ringing, prayers, bonfires, firing of guns and sports.

ACTIVITY
KNOWLEDGE

Successful monarchy

1 Make two lists under the headings 'Qualities of a successful monarch' and 'Qualities of an unsuccessful monarch'.

2 Write down three ways in which Tudor monarchs attempted to increase their popular support.

3 Discuss with a partner why it might be difficult for a historian to establish how popular the Tudor monarchy was.

What challenges did the Tudor monarchy face between 1509 and 1588?

How strong was the Tudor claim to the throne in 1509?

Although Henry VIII succeeded his father Henry VII to the throne peacefully and without incident in 1509, this could not disguise the fact that the Tudors were a new dynasty with a weak claim to the throne. The period from 1455 to 1487 had been disrupted by civil war between two rival families who claimed the throne – the Yorkists and the Lancastrians. Henry Tudor, the Lancastrian representative, had won the crown at the Battle of Bosworth where he had beaten the last Yorkist king of England, Richard III. Although it was commonly accepted at this time that victory in battle meant that God had given his blessing to the winner, the Tudor claim was not strong.

Henry Tudor, now Henry VII, inherited his claim to the throne from his mother, Margaret Beaufort, who was descended from King Edward III (1427–77). However, the Beaufort line was descended from the illegitimate children of Edward III's third son, John of Gaunt. They had only been made legitimate on the proviso that they, and their descendants, would not lay claim to the crown. Added to this, the remaining Beaufort descendant was Margaret, a woman. The succession at this time was determined by the theory of primogeniture. This meant that a woman could transmit a claim to the throne, but that it would not be as strong as a claim transmitted by a man. Thus, Henry VII's survival as king was by no means guaranteed and he faced a series of challenges from rival claimants who were related to the Yorkist kings he had replaced. However, Henry VII survived, aided by a marriage to Elizabeth, the eldest surviving daughter of the Yorkist king, Edward IV. Henry and Elizabeth's children had a stronger claim to the throne because of their combined Yorkist and Lancastrian blood. Furthermore, Henry VII enhanced his children's claim through a series of international alliances. His eldest son Arthur (who died in 1502) had married the daughter of the Spanish monarch, Catherine of Aragon. The death of Arthur was a blow to the new dynasty, but Henry's remaining son, the future Henry VIII, did survive and succeeded his father in 1509 without opposition.

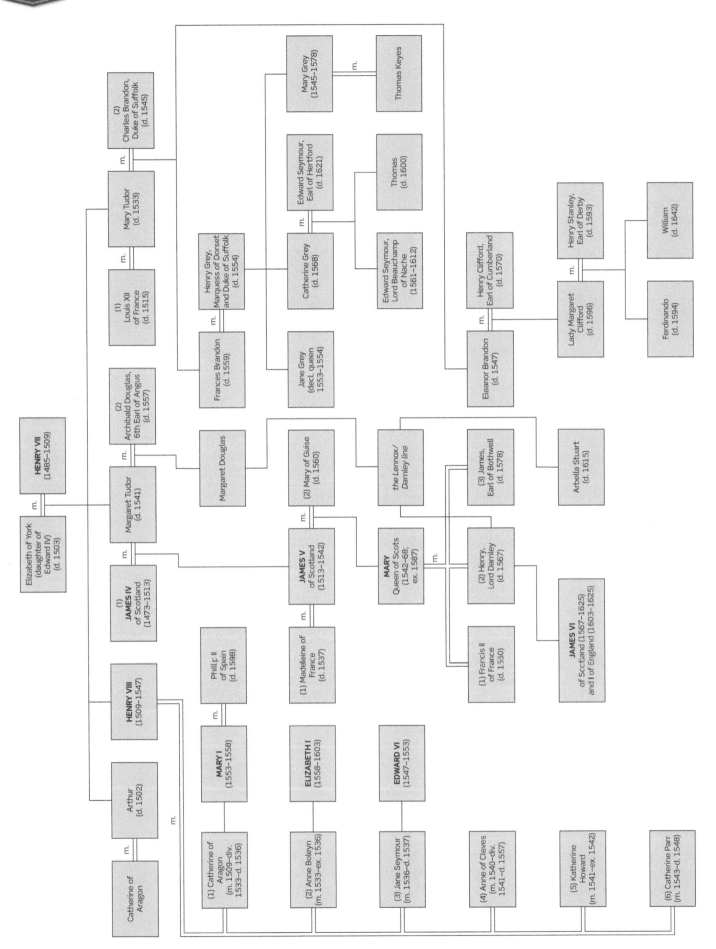

Figure 1.1 The Tudor family tree.

What problems did Henry VIII face in securing the Tudor succession?

As the son of a usurper, Henry VIII still needed to consolidate the dynasty by marrying and having a surviving son of his own. Given the prevalence of diseases that could kill children and teenagers, it was advisable for the monarch to have more than one living son. Henry himself was the second son of Henry VII; his elder brother Arthur (the original heir to the throne) had died at the age of 15 in 1502. Failure to produce a son would not only jeopardise the survival of the Tudor dynasty after Henry VIII, but also create speculation as to who would be king after he died. This speculation was dangerous as it could lead to political instability and plots focused on possible rival claimants, something that had happened repeatedly in the reign of Henry VII. These rival claimants from the Yorkist line (sometimes known as the **White Rose Party**) were often harshly dealt with, mostly because they had a good claim to the throne while Henry VIII struggled to produce a living male heir.

KEY TERM

White Rose Party
The term given to those descended from the 15th century Yorkist claimants to the throne such as the de la Poles and the Poles. The White Rose was the badge of the Yorkists.

Henry VIII married his brother's widow, Catherine of Aragon, as soon as he inherited the throne in 1509. Although Catherine at 24 was nearly seven years older than Henry, there was no reason to expect that she would not be able to fulfil her main duty as queen, providing Henry with a male heir. Unfortunately, between 1510 and 1518, she suffered a series of miscarriages and infant deaths. On 1 January 1511, Catherine did give birth to a living son also named Henry, to national rejoicing and the king's delight, but the child died just three weeks later. Catherine's only surviving child, born in 1516, was a girl, Princess Mary. Catherine's last pregnancy was in 1518, when she again gave birth to a girl who lived for just a few hours. In an age when it was accepted that only a man could rule, this lack of a male heir was potentially disastrous for Henry and his dynastic hopes. Women were not thought fit to rule and the only precedent for a woman ruling in her own right was the 12th century Queen Matilda, whose reign had led to a vicious civil war. Although Princess Mary was brought up and educated as a future queen of England, the lack of a surviving and legitimate male heir contributed to Henry's decision to annul his marriage to Catherine and his eventual decision to break from Rome. It also explains his treatment of Anne Boleyn, his second wife.

Henry's search for a son and heir

Henry married Anne in 1533 when she was already pregnant by him. The hope was that she would bear the son and heir Henry desired, but instead she gave birth to a healthy daughter, Princess Elizabeth. This series of events only served to fuel uncertainty over the succession. In annulling his marriage to Catherine, Henry had argued that it had never been legal in the first place and thus his daughter Mary was illegitimate and could not inherit the throne. This situation, and the position of the Princess Elizabeth as the new heir, was confirmed by the Act of Succession (1534). However,

Anne's subsequent miscarriages, including that of a deformed male foetus in January 1536, helped to bring about her own downfall.

Significantly, Henry was determined that his next marriage could not be challenged. Catherine of Aragon had died in 1536 and he wiped the slate clean by annulling his marriage to Anne Boleyn and passing a second Act of Succession (1536). Anne Boleyn was executed on the charge of adultery and Henry promptly married Jane Seymour. In 1537, Jane gave birth to Henry's only surviving son and heir, Edward, but unfortunately she died shortly after.

At the age of 46, Henry had finally succeeded in securing a son and heir, some 28 years after his first marriage, and the succession looked more secure. However, Henry had no more children after Edward despite three more marriages. Furthermore, his reign was rocked by serious rebellion in 1536, and it is no accident that, in the aftermath of this instability, the remaining Yorkists were either executed or, in the case of Reginald Pole, forced to flee the country. Henry himself acknowledged the continuing uncertainty in the third Act of Succession (1544) in which he restored both Mary and Elizabeth as heirs to the throne after Edward, although he never reversed their illegitimacy. This was an attempt to shore up the Tudor succession in the case of the early death of Edward. As Henry himself knew from his own experiences, it was by no means certain that Edward would survive, and he had no second son to fall back on. While there were no signs that Edward was anything other than a healthy child, the ageing Henry needed to ensure the continuation of the Tudor dynasty to his children.

EXTEND YOUR KNOWLEDGE

Yorkist claimants to the throne in 1509 and their eventual fates

Edmund and Richard de la Pole
- Nephews of Edward IV and Richard III.
- Edmund was imprisoned by Henry VII and executed by Henry VIII in 1513. Richard died in exile at the Battle of Pavia (1525).

Margaret Pole (Countess of Salisbury) and her sons Henry and Reginald Pole
- Descended from George, Duke of Clarence, brother of Edward IV and Richard III.
- The Poles were closely connected to the conservative faction at court. Margaret and Henry were arrested as part of the 'Exeter Conspiracy' (1538). Henry was executed in 1539, Margaret was executed in 1541. Henry's son remained in prison until Mary's reign. Reginald was forced into exile abroad where he remained in the service of the pope. In 1538, the pope gave him the task of organising a Franco-Spanish crusade against England. Pole also survived several assassination attempts by Cromwell's agents. He returned to England in 1554 after Mary came to the throne.

Henry Courtenay (Marquess of Exeter) and his son Edward (Earl of Devon)
- The son of Catherine, a daughter of the Yorkist king, Edward IV.
- Henry was arrested for allegedly conspiring with Reginald Pole to create a Catholic rebellion (1538). He was executed in 1539. Edward remained in prison until Mary's reign.

Edward Stafford (Duke of Buckingham)
- Descended from Edward III.
- Buckingham was executed for treason in 1521.

The role of faction at the Tudor court

Because Tudor monarchs had personal control over government, one route to power and influence was to gain personal access to the ruler. As a result, it became common for **factions** to form. In the later part of Henry's reign, during the 1530s and 1540s, factions often formed along religious lines. The conservative faction at court that favoured a return to traditional, Catholic forms of worship, was led by the Duke of Norfolk, his son the Earl of Surrey, and the bishop of Winchester, Stephen Gardiner. The reformer faction, which favoured more reform to make the English Church more Protestant, included Jane Seymour's brother, Edward Seymour, Earl of Hertford, and Thomas Cranmer, Archbishop of Canterbury. These competing factions attempted to influence Henry by placing their supporters in positions where they could influence him, often in the Privy Chamber or Council. An active adult monarch, as he was for most of his reign, Henry would not be undermined by these factions as he was able to control them by balancing the competing the groups and playing them off against each other. In Henry's last years and in the reign of his son (a young boy), factions did at times destabilise politics.

Henry VIII's will, 1547

The 1540s were increasingly dominated by the uncertainty caused by the fact that the ageing Henry VIII was in increasing ill-health caused by his lack of activity as the result of a jousting injury to his leg, which had led to an infected sore. As the 1540s progressed, it became apparent that the king was likely to be succeeded by a minor, an underage child, who would not be old enough to rule in his own right and who would need a form of protectorate or regency council until he was of age. The precedents for such a situation were not promising. The last minor to succeed to the throne in 1483, Edward V, had been usurped by his uncle, Richard III, and had disappeared without trace. It was vital, therefore, for Henry to ensure that his young son succeeded him without challenge.

However, by 1546, Henry's declining health meant that he was no longer able to control the rival factions in his Chamber and Council. This led to political instability that was a potential threat to the Tudor succession and the power of the Tudor monarchy. The balance of power between the rival factions had swung in favour of the reformer faction led by the Earl of Hertford. Hertford ensured that men loyal to him were placed in key positions in the Privy Chamber, where they had direct access to the king – these men included Sir John Gates and Gates' brother-in-law Sir Anthony Denny, who between them controlled access to the **dry stamp**. Influenced by this dominant faction, Henry was persuaded to change his will in December 1546 to make provisions for a regency council of 16 men who would rule on behalf of his son. In making this decision, Henry clearly wanted to avoid naming one protector who would rule the country, preferring instead rule by committee. However, in January 1547, as Henry lay dying, a series of political manoeuvrings took place through which Hertford was able to enhance his control over the future boy king.

- The will was changed to give the regency council 'full power and authority' to make any decisions necessary to the government of the realm.

- A further addition to the will was the 'unfulfilled gifts' clause that allowed the council to make gifts after Henry's death which he had 'granted, made… or promised'.

- Henry's death on 28 January 1547 was kept secret for three days while behind-the-scenes negotiations took place. These included getting custody and control of the young King Edward.

- The regency council named by Henry voted to make Hertford Edward's protector.

- Hertford's supporters were then rewarded under the 'unfulfilled gifts' clause. Hertford made himself the Duke of Somerset; Lisle became the Earl of Warwick; William Parr (Queen Catherine's brother) was made Marquess of Northampton. In total, Crown lands worth £27,053 were granted to Hertford and his supporters.

KEY TERMS

Faction
An informal grouping whose members have shared aims, for example to promote religious reform. Faction members would seek to gain power and access to the monarch – both informally through the Chamber and through formal positions in the government, such as the Council. Membership of factions fluctuated and was not stable.

Dry stamp
The holder of the dry stamp could use this to put Henry VIII's signature to documents. The stamp had a raised impression of the signature. This could be used to make an imprint of the signature, which could then be inked in.

Although there was no suggestion that Edward VI should not inherit the throne, these changes to Henry's will show how easily the political situation could be manipulated when there was a minor on the throne rather than an adult capable of running the country for himself.

Edward VI and the question of the succession, 1553

Historians of Edward's reign, such as A.F. Pollard, used to believe that Edward was a sickly child whose early death was no surprise. In fact, as Jennifer has shown, Edward was in generally good health, taking part in the usual childhood sports and games of a prince such as swordfighting, hunting and riding. But in early 1553, Edward fell ill with a feverish cold that rapidly developed into incurable pulmonary tuberculosis. The king, aged 16, had not yet married or had a son of his own. Even worse, Edward had no close male heir to whom the throne could pass – all his surviving closest relatives were women. In the event of Edward dying without children, under the terms of the Act of Succession (1544) and Henry VIII's will, the throne was supposed to pass first to Mary and her heirs, then to Elizabeth. The next heirs after this were the daughters of Henry VIII's youngest sister Mary and her husband Charles Brandon – Frances and Eleanor. Edward's actions in 1553 reveal the attitudes typical of the Tudor period – that women were not fit to rule, though they could transmit their claim to the throne to their sons. However, Edward's decision-making process regarding the succession was also influenced by John Dudley, Duke of Northumberland, who had taken Hertford's place as Edward's protector in 1550.

As Hertford had done with Henry VIII, Northumberland surrounded the king with members of his faction. For example, Edward's tutor Sir John Cheke was loyal to Warwick. Similarly, Sir John Gates, who had previously served Hertford, had by now transferred his loyalties to Northumberland, and remained in control of the dry stamp.

Another factor that encouraged both Edward and Northumberland to undermine the succession was the issue of religion. By 1553, England had undergone a rapid and radical series of religious changes that had created a fully Protestant Church. Edward, a committed Protestant, knew that if the throne were to pass to his sister Mary, a committed Catholic, the reformation would be reversed. In addition, under the terms of the 1534 Act of Succession, Mary had been bastardised. This had never been formally reversed, though Henry VIII had revised the succession to include her in 1544. This explains why Edward in 1552 chose to pass over Mary. However, his younger sister, Elizabeth, had more Protestant leanings, yet Edward chose not to leave the throne to her either. This was because Edward believed that she too was illegitimate as a result of the 1536 Act of Succession. At this time, a monarch's birth and parentage had to be unquestionably legitimate. Suspect legitimacy could be manipulated by potential rivals to the throne and lead to political instability. As it turned out, both Mary and Elizabeth were able to overcome this disadvantage, but in 1553 Edward did not know that and so he passed over both of his half-sisters in his plans. Instead, Edward turned to his cousins, the descendants of Henry VIII's sister, and especially the children of Frances Brandon, the Duchess of Suffolk, who had married Henry Grey and had three daughters: Jane, Catherine and Mary.

Edward's 'device for the succession'

In early 1553, with the help of Northumberland and his advisers, Edward began to draw up the document known as 'the device for the succession'. This document was written and altered by Edward himself and shows how, as his illness progressed, Edward's plans changed. Initially, Edward was still hoping to marry and have sons of his own, but he still outlined his plans for the succession if he were to die childless. When he originally wrote his 'device', Edward assumed that there would be time for either the Duchess of Suffolk or her eldest daughter Jane to have a son and heir. In his 'device' he left the crown to 'the Lady Fraunceses heirs males' or 'for lack of such issue to the Lady Janes heirs males.' Edward's plan, therefore, was that if he did not have a son and heir, the throne would pass to the son and heir of either Frances or Jane. By late May 1553, however, it had become clear that Edward was dying and that there would be no time for either Frances or Jane to produce a male heir to the throne. Edward, again with the advice of Northumberland and his supporters, changed his 'device'. He now left the throne to 'the Lady Fraunceses heirs males, *if she have any* such issue *before my death* to the Lady Jane *and her* heirs males.' The addition of the words 'and her' after 'Lady Jane' made it clear that Jane would inherit the throne first if there was not time for Frances or Jane to produce a son of their own. As Frances had not had a child for some years, at a stroke of the pen, Edward had left the throne to her eldest daughter, Jane, disinheriting both his half-sisters and overturning both an Act of Parliament and Henry VIII's will.

SOURCE 3   Edward's device for the succession.

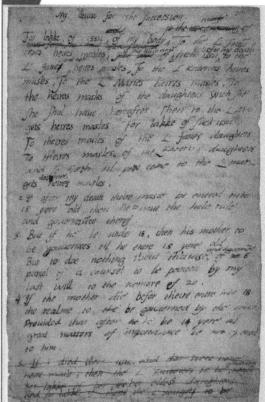

The Duke of Northumberland and the disputed succession

Although the 'device' was Edward's own work, there is some debate about the amount of influence brought to bear on him by Northumberland and his allies. Northumberland was careful to control access to Edward though the Privy Chamber. It is possible that the 'device' was dictated to Edward by Sir John Gates. Northumberland also had a good deal to lose if Edward died and either Mary or Elizabeth became queen. Northumberland's power rested on his relationship with Edward. Moreover, the Duke was also responsible for overseeing the final stages of the Protestant reformation. Northumberland's motives in 1553 were to retain his power and political position after Edward's death. This meant that he was unlikely to support the claim of either Mary or Elizabeth. Under the rule of the Catholic Mary, a grown woman who would be likely to reverse the religious changes that had occurred, the best that Northumberland could hope for was to be removed from power. At worst, he would be vulnerable to attacks from his political opponents. Nor could the duke hope to retain power under Elizabeth who, at nearly 20, would be equally likely to reject any attempts to control her as he had done her younger brother. On 21 May 1553, Northumberland enhanced his potential grip on power through the marriage of his fourth son, Sir Guildford Dudley, to Lady Jane Grey. Loach has suggested that Edward's alterations to the 'device' took place after this date, which meant not only that Lady Jane Grey would be queen, but that Northumberland would be her father-in-law. However, while Northumberland was motivated by the desire to keep hold of his power and position, it was ultimately Edward's decision to make Lady Jane Grey his successor.

Why did Mary Tudor become queen in 1553?

Despite the fact her brother had written her out of the succession, Mary Tudor gained popular support in 1553 because under the laws of the kingdom and by Henry VIII's will, she was the next in line to the throne. Mary herself took an active role in the crisis of July 1553. Northumberland had told her that he would support her claim to be queen after Edward, but spies at court informed her that he was lying. Mary, with the help of her advisers, then made sure that Northumberland would not be able to capture her. Instead of riding to London, Mary travelled to her estates in East Anglia, arriving at Kenninghall in Norfolk, where she heard the news of Edward's death.

At this point, it did not look likely that Mary would be able to claim the throne because Northumberland had control of London, the central offices of government and the navy. However, Mary was determined to declare herself queen and she was able to do this because she attracted popular support to her cause. She already had loyal supporters in her own household who hoped to see the return of the Catholic faith to England. To these were added other members of the religiously conservative East Anglian gentry such as Sir Henry Bedingfield, who had loyally served Mary's mother Catherine of Aragon. Members of the nobility also came to support her such as the Earl of Sussex. These men all brought money, provisions and armed men. On top of this, word began to spread of Mary's defiance. Although many towns and local officials followed Northumberland's orders and proclaimed Jane as queen, they began to buckle and change allegiance to Mary. Thomas Cornwallis, the sheriff of Norfolk and Suffolk was one such official. Initially, he followed orders and declared for Jane, but when he saw that popular support lay with Mary, he changed his mind. The result was that Northumberland himself was forced to leave the relative safety of London to deal with the threat. In his absence, the Privy Council, who had supported Jane, also began to change its mind. On 18 July, it issued a proclamation for the arrest of Northumberland and the following day it declared openly for Mary. The news was greeted with joy by Londoners and on 20 July Northumberland surrendered at Cambridge.

Mary was successful because of popular support for her legal claim to the throne. Ultimately, in mid 16th century England, this mattered more than the gender of the claimant. But for the first time in 400 years, a woman was queen in her own right, and she faced a whole new set of problems in asserting her rule.

What were 16th century attitudes towards female rulers?

Sixteenth-century attitudes to women meant that people commonly believed them to be inferior to men. John Knox, the evangelical opponent of Mary, wrote that the 'regiment' (rule) of women was 'monstrous' (unnatural). Knox argued that, according to the Bible, women were inferior to men, firstly because women had been created from man (Eve had been made from one of Adam's ribs) and secondly because in the Garden of Eden, Eve's temptation of Adam had led to man's fall. Women, according to Knox, could not be trusted.

While English law did not actually forbid a woman from becoming queen in her own right, there were no strong precedents for this.

THINKING HISTORICALLY Causation (3a&b)

The might of human agency

1 'Our lack of control'.
   Work in pairs.

Describe to your partner a situation where things did not work out as you had intended. Then explain how you would have done things differently to make the situation as you would have wanted. Your partner will then tell the group about that situation and whether they think that your alternative actions would have had the desired effect.

2 'The Tyranny of failed actions'.
   Work individually.

The Duke of Northumberland tried and failed to make Lady Jane Grey queen of England.

   a) Write down three ways that Northumberland could have acted differently in that situation.

   b) Now imagine that you are Northumberland. Write a defence of your actions. Try to think about the things that you would have known about at the time and make sure that you do not use the benefit of hindsight.

3 'Arguments'.
   For questions 3–5 work in groups of between four and six.

In turn, each group member will read out their defence. Other group members suggest ways to reassure the reader that they were not a failure and that in some ways what happened was a good outcome.

4 Think about Mary Tudor and her defeat of Northumberland in 1553.

   a) In what ways were the consequences of Mary's victory over Northumberland not anticipated by Mary herself?

   b) In what ways did Mary's seizure of the throne turn out better for her than their intended consequences?

5 Think about the decision of Edward VI and Northumberland to change the line of succession in favour of Lady Jane Grey.

   a) In what ways were the consequences of changing the line of succession not anticipated by Edward and Northumberland?

   b) In what ways did changing the line of succession turn out worse for Edward and Northumberland than their intended consequences?

6 Work individually.
   To what extent are historical individuals in control of the history they helped to create? Explain your answer with reference to specific historical examples from this topic and others you have studied.

The only time that a woman, Queen Matilda, had inherited the throne and attempted to rule in 1135, she had been challenged by her male cousin Stephen and the result was 18 years of civil war. The anarchy was only resolved by an agreement that allowed Matilda's son Henry to rule after Stephen's death, but not Matilda herself. Similarly, in the 15th century, Henry VII had become king, even though his mother, Margaret Beaufort, from whom he had inherited his claim, was still alive. However, in 1553, the circumstances were different in that there was no alternative male Tudor heir. Even Edward VI and Northumberland had accepted this fact in 1553 when they created the 'device' that was to put Lady Jane Grey on the throne.

SOURCE 4

John Knox, *First Blast of the Trumpet against the Monstrous Regiment of Women* (1558).

... to promote a woman to bear rule, superiority, dominion or empire above any realm, nature or city is repugnant to nature, contumely to God, a thing most contrarious to his revealed will and approved ordinance, and finally it is the subversion of good order, of all equity and justice.

In the age of personal monarchy, the king and queen had clearly defined roles. The king was supposed to rule his country, dispense justice and defend the realm by leading his troops into battle. The queen consort's role was to be his wife, to intercede with king for peace and mercy, and to provide him with a son and heir. When first Mary then Elizabeth came to the throne, it was expected that they would need a husband to take on the traditional kingly functions, which it was thought a woman could not perform. As the Holy Roman Emperor Charles V wrote to his ambassadors in England: 'You will point out to her that it will be necessary, in order to be supported in the labour of governing and assisted in matters that are not of ladies' capacity, that she soon contract matrimony with the person who shall appear to her most fit from the above point of view.' Mary also took this view as she began negotiations for a marriage to Charles' son, Philip. At 37, Mary would need to marry quickly if she was to stand any chance of bearing a son and heir to carry on the Catholic reformation she was planning.

How did Mary approach the issue of marriage?

Mary's decision to marry Philip was driven by a combination of dynastic and religious considerations. In many ways he was the obvious choice. If she were to marry a member of the English nobility, such as her distant relative Edward Courtenay, there was the potential for jealousy and rivalry at court. Choosing a foreign husband who was already a king would avoid these internal tensions and meant that she would be marrying her equal in rank. In addition, Philip, the heir to the Spanish throne, was an obvious choice. Mary was half Spanish herself and Philip was her cousin. In foreign policy, England tended naturally to look to Spain as an ally because Spanish power in Europe was a useful counterbalance to French dominance. Spain also controlled the Netherlands, which was a vital partner in the English cloth trade. In addition, Philip was a devout Catholic who would help Mary to restore Roman Catholicism to England. Although Mary was determined to marry Philip, she faced opposition both from within her Council, especially from Gardiner, who supported the Courtenay marriage, and also from her own parliament. When parliament met in 1553, the Speaker expressed the concerns about the marriage to Philip, which demonstrates the particular difficulties faced by Mary as a female ruler. Attitudes of the time concerning the role and capabilities of women led to the assumption in parliament that if Mary married a foreigner, her husband would automatically rule England and might even decide to take Mary abroad. Mary and her Council attempted to calm these fears by drawing up a marriage treaty (in 1554) that protected her power in England. The terms stated that:

- Philip would have the title of king, but he would not rule. He would only be allowed to assist Mary.

- If Mary were to die first, Philip would not be able to rule as king of England on his own. Philip's son by an earlier marriage, Don Carlos, would also have no claim to the English throne.

- Any children of the marriage would inherit the English throne.

- Philip was not allowed to appoint foreigners to positions in the English government.

- England would not be drawn into wars between Spain and France.

However, popular fears about the Spanish marriage were partly responsible for a rebellion led by Sir Thomas Wyatt in January 1554. The concerns raised by parliament, the Council and the rebels, as well as the terms of the marriage treaty, were brought about entirely because Mary was a woman. While suspicion of foreigners might lead to general opposition to a foreign marriage for any monarch, there would have been no fears about a queen consort taking over power in the way that there was for Philip as king consort.

How did Elizabeth I approach the issue of marriage?

Unfortunately for Mary, her marriage to Philip did not produce any children and she was succeeded by her half-sister Elizabeth in 1558. At 25, Elizabeth was young enough to have children and, like Mary before her, it was expected that she would marry in order to produce an heir and also so that she could have a husband to help her govern. There was extra pressure on Elizabeth as she was the last of the Tudor dynasty, which would end with her unless she produced an heir. The political instability that this would cause was brought home to her councillors when Elizabeth fell dangerously ill with smallpox in 1562.

Unlike Mary, Elizabeth seems to have been more than wary of marriage because of the problems it presented to a female ruler. In 1566, she angrily berated a parliamentary delegation who had requested that she marry. Elizabeth could have married Robert Dudley, Earl of Leicester (the son of the Duke of Northumberland), but this would have created tensions at court. She also had foreign suitors, including her former brother-in-law Philip of Spain, Archduke Charles of the Holy Roman Empire, and the French prince, Henry, Duke of Anjou. The Anjou marriage was given serious consideration as late as 1581, when Elizabeth was already in her late forties and too old to bear children, but it, like all the previous negotiations, came to nothing. Elizabeth was not prepared to marry, but the prospect of marriage was a useful tool in diplomatic negotiations.

Instead, Elizabeth remained single. As a woman in a man's world, Elizabeth used her gender to her advantage. In particular, she encouraged the notion of courtly love and the development of the image of the 'Virgin Queen' from the late 1570s. Ambitious young courtiers could attract Elizabeth's attention through personal attraction and flirtation. These 'male favourites' included Robert Dudley, Sir Christopher Hatton and Sir Walter Raleigh. However, these relationships were managed carefully. As the 'Virgin Queen',

Elizabeth was able to pose as desirable, yet beyond reach, and so control her male courtiers who might otherwise have controlled her. She also employed clever rhetoric in order to rally support and present herself as a leader of men, even if she could not fight herself. The best example of this is her famous speech at Tilbury in 1588 when, as England faced the threat of a Spanish invasion, she addressed her army, wearing a silver breastplate over her dress. Elizabeth and Mary both made use of the idea of that, as queens, they were 'married' to their country. In her speech at the London Guildhall in 1554, Mary rallied the Londoners against the threat of Wyatt's rebellion using this image, and Elizabeth used a similar analogy in her response to parliament's request for her to marry in 1559.

Although Tudor attitudes to female rulers made it harder for both Mary and Elizabeth to assert their authority, ultimately both were able to do so. Both faced challenges to their rule – Mary faced rebellion in 1554, and Elizabeth faced both rebellion and plots against her life – but both survived, even though the problematic issue of marriage and the succession created enormous difficulties, especially in the 1590s.

SOURCE 5 Mary's speech to her troops at the London Guildhall, 1554. In this speech, she was rallying her troops against a rebellion by Thomas Wyatt.

I am your queen, to whom at my coronation, when I was wedded to the realm and laws of the same (the spousal ring whereof I have on my finger, which never hitherto was, not hereafter shall be, left off), you promised your allegiance and obedience unto me.

SOURCE 6 Elizabeth's reply to parliament, 1559, following a request that she marry.

Now that the public care of governing the kingdom is laid upon me, to draw upon me also the cares of marriage may seem a point of inconsiderate folly. Yea, to satisfy you, I have already joined myself to an husband, namely, the Kingdom of England.

SOURCE 7 Elizabeth's speech to her troops at Tilbury before the attempted invasion by the Spanish Armada, 1588.

I know that I have the body but of a weak and feeble woman, but I have the heart and stomach of a king, and of a king of England, too.

ACTIVITY
KNOWLEDGE

Female rulers

1 Read Source 4. What were John Knox's arguments against female rulers?

2 Read Sources 5–7. How did Mary and Elizabeth use language and ideas to enhance their power as queen?

3 Write down three problems facing Mary and Elizabeth as queens.

4 Discuss with a partner how they tried to solve these problems. How successful do you think they were?

Fill in the following table to show the main strengths and weaknesses of the Tudor monarchs.

	Strengths	Weaknesses	Overall judgement
Henry VIII			
Edward VI			
Mary I			
Elizabeth I			

HOW DID THE ROLE OF PARLIAMENT CHANGE BETWEEN 1509 AND 1588?

The power of parliament

Parliament was an ancient medieval institution that had gained important powers by the Tudor period. These included the sole right to grant taxation, and the sole right to pass laws (Acts of Parliament). When a monarch needed taxation to supplement their income (usually for war or another emergency), it was usual for them to summon parliament. However, monarchs also retained the right to veto any laws they did not like, and to summon and dismiss parliament at will. In fact, there were long periods when parliament did not meet at all, and unlike parliament today, it was not involved in day-to-day government. Nevertheless, most monarchs would call parliament periodically. It was an important opportunity for them to test the mood of the country and to communicate their policies to the Members of Parliament (MPs) and thus to the localities.

How was parliament organised?

Parliament had two chambers, the unelected House of Lords, where hereditary peers and bishops sat, and the House of Commons, which was filled with elected MPs. Two MPs were elected to represent each county of England, and some boroughs (towns) also had the right to send MPs to parliament. To vote in a county, it was necessary to own property that brought in an income of at least 40 shillings (£2) per year. This meant that voting, when it happened, was restricted to those wealthy enough to own property outright. In many cases, however, MPs were elected uncontested – there was no competition for the seat. It was also common for members of the nobility to exercise patronage to ensure their clients were elected. The powerful dukes of Norfolk could usually influence the return of MPs in up to eight boroughs. In 1584, the Earl of Leicester wrote to the town of Andover: 'I make so bold heartily to pray you that you would give me the nomination of one of your burgesses [members of the town].' Parliament, therefore, tended to represent the interests of the landed gentry and nobility. To pass an Act of Parliament, a bill had to be heard in both the Commons and the Lords before being given royal assent by the monarch. While parliament was usually on the same side as the monarch, this did not mean that it could always be relied upon to do what the monarch wanted, and, as the century progressed, the Commons became more confident and needed careful managing.

Henry VIII's parliaments before 1529

Under Henry VII, parliament met just seven times in a reign lasting 24 years. This trend continued under Henry VIII. Parliament met only four times between 1509 and 1529: in 1510, 1512–14, 1515 and 1523. Its role in this period was mainly to grant taxation to fund the king's wars. When the wars were going well, especially in 1513, it was usually not too difficult to persuade parliament to grant taxation for the defence of the realm.

However, by 1517 Henry's foreign policy had become costly and ineffective. As the burden of taxation increased, with little to show for it, parliament became less keen to grant increasing amounts of money. This was partly because, as landowners, the MPs feared that too much taxation would lead to rebellion. As members of local society, they were well aware of the amount of grumbling and resistance. In 1523, this led to Wolsey meeting stiff opposition from the Commons to extract the amount of taxation he wanted. By this date, £288,814 had been raised in taxation, not to mention the 'loans' raised totalling £260,000. Given this burden, it is not surprising that when Wolsey tried to persuade the MPs by addressing them personally he was met with silence.

Although it is dangerous to judge later events with the benefit of hindsight, the parliament of 1512–14 showed some **anti-clerical** feeling. In 1512, it passed an Act to limit '**benefit of clergy**'. This anti-clerical feeling re-emerged in the 1515 parliament when it was exacerbated by the Hunne affair, in which a rich London merchant accused of heresy had been found dead while in the Bishop of London's prison. The Church claimed that he had committed suicide, but murder was rumoured. This anti-clerical feeling would later be exploited by Thomas Cromwell.

> **KEY TERMS**
>
> **Anti-clericalism**
> Criticism of the Church, often aimed at its apparent corruption and wealth. It also helped to fuel reformer demands for radical change, but not all those who were anti-clerical supported Protestantism.
>
> **Benefit of clergy**
> This allowed churchmen charged with a serious crime to be tried in the Church courts rather than in secular courts. Church courts gave more lenient sentences than the secular courts – clergymen (or those who claimed to be clergymen) could thus avoid the death penalty.

> **EXTEND YOUR KNOWLEDGE**
>
> **The Hunne affair**
> Richard Hunne was a London merchant. In 1511, his infant son died, and the local parish priest asked for the usual mortuary fee (payment for burial). Hunne refused to pay and was sued in the Church courts, which found against him. Hunne was then accused of heresy and sent to the Bishop of London's prison. In December 1514, Hunne was found hanged in his cell. The Church claimed it was a case of suicide. Despite his death, Hunne was still put on trial for heresy. He was found guilty and his corpse was ceremonially burned. This case caused considerable anger and resentment in London and fuelled anti-clericalism in parliament.

From 'king and parliament' to 'king-in-parliament'

In 1529, the parliament that became known by historians as the 'Reformation parliament' was summoned. Again, it is important to realise that in 1529 when this parliament was summoned no one knew that they were sitting in a parliament that would change the power of the monarchy and the religion of England so dramatically. Indeed, the term 'Reformation parliament' was not used before the 19th century.

The 1529–31 sessions

When parliament met in 1529, Wolsey had fallen from power and the king was still searching for a way to achieve the annulment of his marriage. Furthermore, Cromwell had not yet risen to power. As in 1512–14 there was some anti-clerical sentiment, but only three out of the 26 statutes passed in the first session of 1529–31 dealt with religious matters. Parliament met again for a second session in January 1531. By this time, Henry was threatening to use his parliament as a method to put pressure on Pope Clement VII to act. He told the pope that he planned to refer his divorce case to parliament. However, at this point, this seems to have been more of an attempt to blackmail the pope than a real threat.

The 1532 session

The third session of parliament began in January 1532 and lasted until May. By this point, Cromwell had been appointed to the king's Council, and was starting to use his power to enable Henry to divorce Catherine. Cromwell used parliament to pass laws that would reinforce the king's claim to supremacy over the Church and to make the divorce a reality. The Act in Conditional Restraint of Annates applied pressure on the Church by threatening to forbid newly appointed bishops from making customary payments to the pope. However, this was not a straightforward process as there was opposition in both the Commons and the Lords. This is why the Act was made 'conditional' (delayed for a year). Anti-clericalism in the Commons was also manipulated by the production of a petition known as the Commons' Supplication against the Ordinaries, which was a list of complaints against the Church to which Convocation (the Church's version of parliament) was forced to submit.

The 1533–34 sessions

When parliament met again in February 1533, it was with some urgency. Henry VIII had married Anne Boleyn, who was already pregnant, but any annulment from Catherine could still be challenged in Rome. Henry needed to ensure that the new baby, which he hoped would be his longed-for son, would be legitimate and that his marriage and the succession would be unchallengeable under English parliamentary law. At this point, Cromwell drafted the Act in Restraint of Appeals, which would cut off any attempt by Catherine of Aragon to appeal her case in Rome. Cromwell took particular care in the drafting of this bill and referred specifically to the idea of England as an empire, independent from foreign intervention, and of which the king was in sole charge. This Act allowed Thomas Cranmer, the Archbishop of Canterbury, to declare Henry's first marriage void under English law.

In 1534, parliament was used once again to confirm and enhance the new Royal Supremacy and the break with Rome. The Act of Annates was made permanent. However, the original plans to transfer these payments from the pope to Henry faced serious opposition in the Lords and had to be changed so that they were stopped completely. The Act of Succession made Princess Mary illegitimate and confirmed Princess Elizabeth as the new heir and included an oath, which meant that Henry and Cromwell could monitor carefully any opposition to the new order. The Act of Supremacy confirmed Henry's new position as supreme head of the Church, and the Treason Act widened the definition of treason. Under this Act, treason could be committed not only by deeds against the king or his family, but also by words.

The use of parliament from 1536 to 1547

Once the break with Rome was completed, Henry and Cromwell continued to use parliament throughout the 1530s. The smaller monasteries were dissolved by an Act of Parliament in 1536 and a second Act in 1539 dissolved the larger monasteries as well. parliament was also used to pass Acts that dictated religious belief. The Act of Ten Articles (1536) promoted a more 'reformed' version of faith, while the Act of Six Articles (1539) reflected Henry's reversion to a more conservative doctrine. Meanwhile, the second and third Acts of Succession (1536 and 1544) rewrote the line of succession twice more.

The consequences of the Reformation parliament

Although Henry was always careful to say that parliament was only acknowledging his supremacy rather than granting it to him, the use of parliament in this way set a precedent that would have unforeseen consequences. Once parliament had been used to create the Royal Supremacy and break with Rome, subsequent monarchs were forced to return to it whenever they wanted to alter the religious and political settlement enforced in the 1530s.

The events of the 1530s also created the notion of 'king-in-parliament'. This was the idea that the most powerful institution in the country was the king acting in conjunction with parliament rather than without it. The 'king-in-parliament' also had authority over the Church, but the king alone did not. Again, Cromwell seems to have been behind this idea. The theory was that God had granted Henry the Royal Supremacy, but the people had given Henry VIII the authority to assume the supremacy through parliament. The reigns of Mary and Elizabeth reinforced this idea. Mary had to repeal the supremacy through parliament and Elizabeth reasserted it again through another Act of Parliament. Each time this happened, parliament gained more power, though it was never more powerful than the monarch.

These new powers also meant that monarchs were forced to call parliament more frequently. Before 1529, parliament had met just four times in 20 years. Between 1526 and 1536, there were sessions nearly every year. As Extract 1 shows, the Reformation parliament in some ways marked a turning point in the frequency with which parliament met. The result of this was that the Commons in particular became increasingly confident. More frequent meetings meant that groups with particular agendas, such as the Puritans under Elizabeth, began to use parliament as a means of achieving their aims. More meetings also meant that local MPs became more confident in expressing their views, and were less easily intimidated by the presence of their monarch. These developments meant that the later Tudor monarchs, especially Elizabeth, had to develop new tactics for managing parliament.

EXTRACT
1

Parliamentary sessions under the Tudor monarchs, 1509–88. From J. Loach, *Parliament under the Tudors* (1991).

Monarch	Number of parliamentary sessions held	Dates of sessions
Henry VIII	9	1510, 1512–14, 1515, 1523, 1529–36, 1536, 1539–40, 1542–44, 1545–47
Edward VI	2	1547–52, 1553
Mary I	5	1553, 1554, 1554–55, 1555, 1558
Elizabeth I	6	1559, 1563–67, 1571, 1572–81 (only called in 1572, 1576, 1581),1584–85, 1586–67

Parliament and freedom of speech

One privilege claimed by the Commons was freedom of speech within parliament. MPs feared that without the guarantee that they would be able to speak freely while debating, they could face arrest and imprisonment. Before Elizabeth's reign, the privilege of parliamentary freedom of speech was usually respected by the government. But this did not mean that parliament could choose its subject for debate; usually, it had to wait for the topic to be introduced by the Crown. This settlement was usually effective in promoting harmony between Crown and parliament, but there were occasions when the Tudors faced opposition from their parliaments. For example, supporters of Catherine of Aragon attempted to stop the parliamentary process that would lead to the break with Rome. In 1532, opposition to the Annates bill forced Henry to come to parliament himself so that his presence would intimidate the Commons to support the legislation.

TIMELINE – KEY ACTS OF THE REFORMATION PARLIAMENT

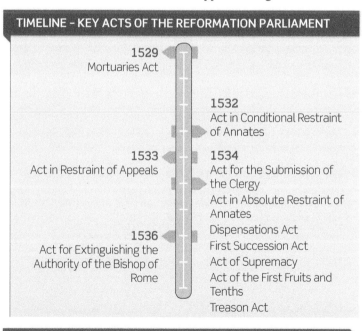

- **1529** Mortuaries Act
- **1532** Act in Conditional Restraint of Annates
- **1533** Act in Restraint of Appeals
- **1534** Act for the Submission of the Clergy
  - Act in Absolute Restraint of Annates
  - Dispensations Act
  - First Succession Act
  - Act of Supremacy
  - Act of the First Fruits and Tenths
  - Treason Act
- **1536** Act for Extinguishing the Authority of the Bishop of Rome

KEY TERM

Puritan
Described by the historian Patrick Collinson as 'the hotter sort of Protestant', the term 'puritan' was originally a term of abuse. Puritans saw the reformation as incomplete and wanted further reform. They tended to emphasise the importance of preaching and the Bible.

Parliament under Edward and Mary

Under Edward, parliament was used to continue and accelerate the Protestant reformation. Mary's parliaments of 1553–54 reversed the religious changes seen under Edward and Henry, and returned England to Rome. It used to be thought by historians such as Sir John Neale that Mary's parliaments saw a growth in an organised Protestant opposition led by independent MPs in the Commons. Certainly, Mary's parliaments were less easy to manage. For example, in 1555 there was serious opposition to two proposed bills. The first bill proposed that payments to the Church known as 'First Fruits and Tenths', which had been seized by Henry VIII, should be returned to the Church. This bill caused such opposition in the Commons that it was only passed by the queen's supporters keeping the House sitting until 3p.m., which was unusually late for parliamentary business. By this time, the bill's opponents seem to have given up and gone to lunch. The second bill, known as the 'Exiles bill', proposed that the lands and property of Englishmen who had gone into exile and refused to return could be seized. This bill was defeated in a very unusual incident in which Sir Anthony Kingston, MP for Gloucestershire, locked the doors of the House and forced the Speaker to put the bill to a vote before its supporters could arrive.

Neale used these incidents to argue for an organised Protestant opposition, which would become more apparent in Elizabeth's reign. However, Loach has shown that both of these incidents were the result of fears surrounding property rights, something that would have particularly concerned the representatives of the land-owning elites in parliament. If the Crown gave up its income from the First Fruits and Tenths, then the level of taxation might have to be raised, something that was never popular. Similarly, although many of those who had gone abroad in Mary's reign had Protestant leanings and wanted to avoid persecution, the Commons was more concerned about protecting property rights in general, especially for anyone who simply happened to go abroad and might face confiscation of their property through no fault of their own.

The growing confidence of parliament under Elizabeth I, 1558–88

Like Mary and Edward, Elizabeth was forced by precedent to use her parliament to reverse the changes undertaken by Mary and to restore the Royal Supremacy. In 1559, however, she faced some difficulties in achieving this, mainly because of religiously conservative peers and bishops in the House of Lords. This opposition may have led to more of a compromise than Elizabeth had originally intended. However, the problems that Elizabeth encountered from her parliaments were more the result of an increasingly confident Commons.

The Puritan choir

Neale argued for the existence of a '**Puritan** choir' in Elizabeth's parliament. This 'choir', Neale argued, consisted of a small group of religiously radical Protestants who had returned from exile under Mary and were determined to use parliament to create a more extreme religious settlement than Elizabeth wanted. However,

Neale's argument does not fit the available evidence. Norman Jones has shown that there were at most 25 Puritan MPs and that only four of these had returned to England in time for the 1559 parliament. Michael Graves' research on some of the key individuals of the choir has shown that most were not religious radicals at all and nor were they as organised as Neale claimed. For example, the supposed leader, Thomas Norton, was a moderate Puritan who had close links to William Cecil as well as other Protestants on the Council such as Francis Walsingham. Research has shown that Norton was actually acting as a parliamentary manager for Cecil. As Norton himself said, 'All that I have done I did by commandment of the House, and specially of the queen's Council there, and my chiefest care was in all things to be directed by the Council.'

Developments in parliament under Elizabeth

Even without a determined and organised opposition to Elizabeth, led by a group of Puritans, the role of parliament did change under Elizabeth. For example, the number of MPs in the House of Commons had grown from 302 in 1512 to 402 in 1559 and 462 by 1586. This growth in numbers helps to explain why the Council felt the need to 'manage' parliamentary business more. In some areas of policy, parliament was also growing more assertive. Encouraged by the Council, in 1563 and 1566 the Commons dared to raise the issue of marriage and the succession with the queen, something that would have been unimaginable in Henry VIII's reign. This led to some conflict between the queen and her parliaments concerning their right to freedom of speech. Elizabeth argued that parliament was free to discuss matters of the 'commonweal' (concerning the common good of the country), such as poverty, but that it did not have the right to discuss 'matters of state', such as her marriage, the succession and religious policy. The parliamentary Commons tended to ignore Elizabeth's wishes and this led to tensions. For example, in 1566 the Council was forced to allow parliament time to debate marriage and succession. In return, parliament agreed to discuss a grant of taxation, which it had threatened to withhold. There were also attempts by a minority of religious radicals, such as Anthony Cope, to introduce more radical Puritanism via parliament, but Cope and his allies were promptly imprisoned in the Tower of London by the Speaker.

Although there were some areas of dispute, it should be emphasised that Elizabeth and parliament were on the same side. Elizabeth did try to restrict parliament's claims to freedom of speech in 1566 and 1576, but this was as much to do with her views on her **royal prerogative** as an attempt to reduce parliament's powers. Where parliamentary pressure was apparently brought to bear on Elizabeth, such as the discussions about the succession and her marriage in 1563 and 1566 or debates over the fate of Mary, Queen of Scots in 1572 and 1586–87, these were the result of the Council having used parliament to force the indecisive Elizabeth into making a decision. However, in the 1590s, the relationship between monarch and parliament did become strained as a result of the political tensions of the last decade of Elizabeth's reign.

KEY TERM

Royal prerogative
The customary rights and privileges claimed by the Crown. These included rights as a landlord and rights to claim traditional feudal payments. Monarchs exploited the prerogative to raise money, such as the right to sell monopolies.

A Level Exam-Style Question Section A

How accurate is it to say that there were major changes in the role of parliament in the years 1529–88? (20 marks)

Tip

You will need to consider what the role of parliament was in this period in order to decide whether there were major changes to it. Are there certain periods in which there was more change?

ACTIVITY
KNOWLEDGE

Powers of parliament

1 Draw a graph to show the changing powers of parliament from 1509 to 1588. Write on the key events.

2 Choose the three events that you think show the most significant changes to parliamentary powers. Explain why you have chosen these events.

3 Make a list of ways in which you think the powers of parliament had not changed by 1588.

THE PRINCIPAL SERVANTS OF THE CROWN, 1509-88

The role of Wolsey, Cromwell and Cecil in Tudor government

Thomas Wolsey (c1472–1530), Thomas Cromwell (c1485–1540) and William Cecil (1520–98) all played a crucial role in Tudor government as the 'chief ministers' of Henry VIII and Elizabeth. All three men were responsible for enhancing the power of the monarchs they served, but there were crucial differences in their relationship with the Tudor rulers they served, which ultimately had very different effects on their careers.

Both Wolsey and Cromwell rose from humble beginnings. This meant that they were both reliant on Henry VIII for their promotion and for their power, especially because they lacked the traditional landed estates, wealth and rank that other servants of the Crown possessed.

Wolsey was the son of an Ipswich butcher. He was clearly a clever boy since he was sent to Magdalen College, Oxford and then embarked on a career in the Church. In this period, advancement through the Church structure was a common method used by those from the lower ranks in society to rise. Wolsey did just this. By 1509, he became almoner (someone who distributed money to the poor) to Henry VIII, and under the patronage of Richard Fox he became a member of the king's Council in the same year. Wolsey was a clever administrator and rapidly rose further because he pleased the king by co-ordinating the war effort against France in 1512–14. In 1514, he was made archbishop of York, in 1515 the pope made Wolsey a cardinal, and in the same year he became Lord Chancellor of England, which meant he was in charge of the judicial system. In 1518, he received the title from the pope of **legate a latere**. However, Wolsey's career and rise were entirely dependent on the king's will. From 1525, his relationship with Henry began to unravel, especially once he was unable to secure the annulment of Henry's marriage to Catherine. Wolsey's fall was as dramatic as his rise had been meteoric. By 1529, he had outlived his usefulness to the king. Wolsey was accused of **praemunire**, stripped of his possessions and banished from court. A year later, on his way to trial, Wolsey died.

Cromwell's career path and final fate closely mirrored Wolsey's. Cromwell was a self-made man. His background is shadowy, but he was born in London in about 1485 and was the son of a cloth maker. He left England in his teens and served as a soldier in the French army. He learned about accountancy and the law, though he had no formal training as a lawyer. By 1516, he was working for Wolsey and in 1523 he became an MP. Cromwell was highly intelligent, hard-working and almost entirely self-taught. He was also a political survivor. When Wolsey fell from power, Cromwell was able to recover quickly and by 1531 he had become a member of Henry's Council. Influenced by reformer ideas, he also developed strong religious convictions. Working with the faction that formed around Anne Boleyn, Cromwell was able to manipulate proceedings in a way that allowed Henry to achieve his annulment from Catherine of Aragon but also steered England towards a reformed Church.

However, Cromwell's power, influence and religious convictions meant that he had enemies at court. Like Wolsey, he was also entirely reliant on Henry's support, which could only be sustained by pleasing the increasingly volatile king. In 1536, Cromwell was able to survive Anne Boleyn's fall because he still had the king's support. But in 1539–40, Cromwell's attempt to create a Protestant alliance in Europe against the threat of a united Franco-Spanish invasion by negotiating a marriage with Anne of Cleves was a serious tactical error that angered Henry. Cromwell's enemies among the conservative faction at court saw their opportunity to remove Cromwell permanently by accusing him of treason and heresy. The king was angry enough at Cromwell to listen to them. Cromwell was tried and executed because his policies no longer suited Henry.

The relationship between Henry VIII and his two chief ministers was dictated by Henry's personality and style of rule. Similarly, the working relationship that formed between William Cecil, Lord Burghley and Elizabeth I was also conditioned by Elizabeth's own personality and style, but in contrast to Cromwell and Wolsey, Cecil was able to sustain his position from 1558 until his own peaceful death in 1598. Cecil came from a higher social rank than either Wolsey or Cromwell – he was a member of the gentry and had spent his entire career in royal service. Cecil had a chequered political past, serving the Duke of Somerset until his fall in 1549 and then transferring his service to the Duke of Northumberland. By 1548, Cecil was already in contact with Elizabeth.

KEY TERMS

Legate a latere
A representative of the pope who was given full powers to act on the pope's behalf.

Praemunire
A legal charge used against those who were suspected of appealing to a foreign power outside the English monarch's authority. In particular, it could be used against those who attempted to appeal to the pope. The charge was used against Wolsey in 1529 and against all the English clergy in 1530.

Despite his close connection with both Somerset and Northumberland's regime, Cecil survived under Mary and, in 1558, was perfectly placed to advise Elizabeth. Cecil's career under Elizabeth was so long and successful because they both were naturally cautious and pragmatic in their approach. As Cecil's career progressed, he did attract enemies. In 1569, there was a court-based plot in which those of the nobility with Catholic sympathies, such as the Duke of Norfolk, sought to remove Cecil from power. Ironically, Norfolk was supported by the Protestant Earl of Leicester, who also distrusted Cecil's power. Even more seriously, in 1569, the northern rebels wanted to remove him from power because he was pro-Protestant and they resented the amount of influence he had with the queen. Crucially, however, Elizabeth supported Cecil rather than his critics. She also rewarded him with the title Lord Burghley in 1571, and in return for his unwavering loyalty to her she allowed him to build up a network of supporters through patronage. This meant that Cecil never became politically isolated and was not completely dependent on the queen's whims for political survival, unlike Wolsey and Cromwell. This does not mean that Cecil was more powerful than the queen, however; their working relationship was built on trust and understanding that was mutually beneficial.

Wolsey's successes

Wolsey's main contributions were in his organisational abilities, which allowed Henry first to afford foreign war and then to play international peacemaker. He introduced a new form of taxation, the subsidy, which allowed the king to collect more taxation from his subjects. In his role as chancellor, Wolsey also attempted legal, social and economic reform. He attempted to improve the administration of justice by prosecuting in Star Chamber local officials who were accused of corruption. For example, in 1519, he prosecuted a prominent member of the Cheshire gentry, Sir John Savage, on suspicion that he had been using his local influence to protect his son from murder charges. Wolsey's aim was to teach Savage 'the new law of Star Chamber'. Savage was pardoned, but he lost many of his local offices and had to pay a fine of 4,000 marks to the Crown. More generally, Wolsey used Star Chamber and the court of Chancery to encourage ordinary men to seek justice for their grievances, which led to a huge increase in the workload of these courts. Wolsey also launched a national enquiry in 1517–18 to investigate the practice of illegal **enclosure** by landlords. On the basis of this enquiry, 264 landlords were prosecuted and 188 verdicts were reached.

KEY TERM

Enclosure
This was a social and economic trend, common in the 15th and 16th centuries. It involved landlords taking over areas of common land and enclosing them with hedges or fences. This was often associated with the move away from arable farming to sheep farming. Tudor theorists often blamed enclosure for poverty, unemployment and vagrancy.

Wolsey's failures

Wolsey's personality and ambition led to criticism. He held multiple church offices – he was not only Archbishop of York, but also the Bishop of Lincoln and Tournai. He used the profits of his office to live in a grand style. His household numbered 500 men, nearly as big as the king's, and his building at Hampton Court was so magnificent that contemporaries called him an 'alter rex' – another king. Wolsey's grand schemes were too ambitious. Although he encouraged cases to be brought into Star Chamber, this led to a backlog that Wolsey, distracted by war and diplomacy, failed to clear. He also used his power and position to prosecute personal feuds: Sir Robert Sheffield, who, as Speaker of the House of Commons in 1512 had been critical of Wolsey, was sent to the Tower and fined £5,333 for 'opprobrious words'. Wolsey also managed to upset the support of the very group he needed, the landed nobility and gentry. In 1523, he had to reverse his policy on enclosure as part of a deal with parliament, which tended to represent the interests of the landed elites. He also mismanaged the financial crisis of 1522–23, haranguing parliament in an attempt to get a higher rate of taxation from them, before turning to the non-parliamentary Amicable Grant.

The relationship between Wolsey and Henry VIII

As long as Wolsey was able to fulfil the king's wishes, he remained in power. As John Guy has argued, Wolsey did not usurp power from Henry; he was only allowed to wield it for as long as he was useful. Wolsey's contemporary critics used his social background to accuse him of undermining the power of members of the traditional nobility and gentry, such as the Duke of Buckingham, merely because he resented them. In fact, Buckingham was executed because he appeared to be plotting treason and raising a private army. It was the king who wrote to Wolsey: 'I would you should make good watch… on the duke of Buckingham… and on others which you think suspect.' In addition, Wolsey had rivals for his power, particularly from the gentlemen of the Privy Chamber. In 1519, Wolsey expelled the 'minions' (the young men friendly with Henry) from the household who had too much influence with the king. The Eltham Ordinances in 1526 can also be seen as an attempt to control the Chamber as a rival source of power. Ultimately, however, it was only from 1527 when Wolsey was unable to give Henry his divorce from Catherine of Aragon that his position came under threat.

EXTEND YOUR KNOWLEDGE

The Duke of Buckingham

Edward Stafford, Duke of Buckingham, was descended from Edward III and so had a claim to the throne. The Stafford family were particularly powerful on the border of Wales, where they had extensive lands that they could use to raise a private army. Stafford's father had used these powers to mount a rebellion against Richard III in 1483. Buckingham saw himself as a member of the traditional nobility who based his powers on his landed estates, not at court through service to the king; he resented what he saw as attempts to restrain his traditional powers. Buckingham's servant, Sir William Bulmer, was prosecuted in Star Chamber in 1519 for wearing the duke's livery (uniform) in the presence of the king. In 1521, Buckingham requested a licence to visit his lands in Wales with 400 armed men. This alarmed Henry because his actions seemed to threaten potential rebellion. Shortly afterwards, Stafford was arrested, tried and executed for treason.

Cromwell and parliament

Cromwell's genius was to realise that he could use parliament to give the king his annulment. By using parliament, Cromwell and Henry were able to present the laws that were made as the will of the people (since parliament represented them). By passing Acts of Parliament, the break with Rome was made legal under English law and anyone who broke the law could be punished. It also created a precedent. Any further changes to these laws would also need to be passed by parliament, as happened under Edward, Mary and Elizabeth.

By 1531, all attempts to persuade the pope to grant a divorce had failed, largely because the pope was under the control of Charles V, Catherine of Aragon's nephew. In 1532, Cromwell exploited the anti-clerical feeling in parliament, which led to the first steps in breaking from the pope and Rome. In 1533, he drafted the Act in Restraint of Appeals, which created the mechanism that would stop Catherine appealing to the pope over Henry's head. This Act is particularly famous because of its preamble, which defined Cromwell and Henry's vision of the Royal Supremacy for the first time.

Cromwell further extended his role in government when he was named vicegerent (deputy) in spirituals by Henry in late 1534. Although Cromwell was not a churchman, this unprecedented role gave him power to shape the religion of the country. As vicegerent, Cromwell used propaganda and a preaching campaign in churches to introduce reformer ideas more widely across England. He was also the architect of the dissolution of the monasteries in the period 1536–39.

SOURCE

8 Preamble to the Act in Restraint of Appeals, 1533. This introduction to the Act may have been written by Cromwell himself.

Where by divers[e] sundry old authentic histories and chronicles, it is manifestly declared and expressed that this realm of England is an Empire, and so hath been accepted in the world, governed by one Supreme Head and king having the dignity and royal estate of the imperial Crown of the same, unto whom a body politic compact of all sorts and degrees of people divided in terms and by names of Spirituality and Temporalty, be bounden and owe to bear next to God a natural and humble obedience: he being also institute and furnished, by the goodness and sufferance of Almighty God, with plenary, whole, and entire power, pre-eminence, authority…

Cromwell's role in government and fall from power

Alongside these religious reforms, Cromwell also enhanced royal power in 1536 through changes to the government of England and Wales, although most historians now agree that he should not be credited with creating a 'Tudor revolution in government'. The changes to the Privy Council happened despite not because of him, and the Council that emerged in 1537 was full of his political enemies such as the duke of Norfolk. Like Wolsey, Cromwell was only able to act while he had the king's support. From 1532 to 1536, their interests converged: Henry wanted a divorce and Cromwell, who was a convinced religious reformer, wanted to advance changes to the Catholic Church. But in 1536, the dissolution of the smaller monasteries created the most serious rebellion of the reign, with some 30,000 rebels involved who named Cromwell personally in their complaints. Henry himself was also no religious reformer, and by 1538, Cromwell was forced to end his preaching campaign.

Cromwell eventually fell from power in 1540 for two main reasons. First, he had arranged Henry's fourth marriage to the Protestant Anne of Cleves. Henry disliked Anne on sight, calling her 'the Flanders mare' and only went through with the marriage reluctantly. By this point the king had already fallen for the young and pretty Katherine Howard, the niece of the conservative duke of Norfolk. Norfolk and the conservative faction took advantage of this and the Cleves marriage to influence Henry against Cromwell. The final nail in Cromwell's coffin was the accusation that he had been protecting Protestants who had been accused of heresy. All these circumstances conspired against Cromwell, and on 10 June 1540 Cromwell was arrested. On 28 July he was executed for treason.

William Cecil's role in government and relationship with Elizabeth

Elizabeth and Cecil had a close partnership that lasted until his death in 1598. Until 1572, Cecil held the position of secretary of state, which meant he had great influence because it gave him access to Elizabeth and her correspondence. When he was created Lord Burghley in 1571, he was able to sit in the House of Lords, from where he could influence events in the Commons. In 1572, he became Lord Treasurer, a post he retained to his death.

Cecil was one of the most active members of Elizabeth's government. As treasurer, he organised the Council, managed parliament, controlled the exchequer, and was a Justice of the Peace (JP) in five counties. Like Elizabeth herself, Cecil was a politique. They both recognised the need for stability and compromise, and this formed the basis of their political relationship. Cecil was probably behind the document produced in 1559, the 'Device for the Alteration of Religion', which set out the religious problems faced by Elizabeth and proposed a settlement as soon as possible.

He was also responsible for negotiating a peace treaty with Scotland in 1560, which removed the presence of French troops (and therefore the threat of a hostile invasion from the North), and for setting up a Protestant government in Scotland, thus neutralising the threat from England's traditional enemy. Cecil achieved this despite Elizabeth's initial reluctance to intervene in foreign affairs – he even threatened to resign to persuade her to change her mind.

Cecil remained dominant in government from this time. A committed Protestant, in the 1570s and 1580s he was one of the chief architects of attempts to tighten controls on English Catholics, despite Elizabeth's reluctance to follow this policy. In 1587, he supported the execution of Mary, Queen of Scots and was in disgrace for weeks, but he recovered. However, he was also cautious regarding religion and, unlike his fellow councillor Francis Walsingham, he did not wish to see the establishment of a more radical religious settlement.

ACTIVITY
KNOWLEDGE

Royal Supremacy

1 Read Source 8. How did Cromwell justify the Royal Supremacy? Why was his use of an Act of Parliament to do this significant?

2 Use the section on the servants of the Crown to help you complete the following table.

	Thomas Wolsey	Thomas Cromwell	William Cecil
Background			
Position in government			
Successes			
Failures			
Extent to which he increased royal power			

3 In your opinion, which minister did the most to enhance royal power? Write a paragraph justifying your view.

4 Discuss with a partner: Why did both Wolsey and Cromwell fall from power when Cecil did not?

Changes to the structure of government

By the Tudor period, a complex system of government had evolved that could both help and hinder monarchs in their rule. These systems included formal institutions such as the Council, and financial and judicial systems. During the period 1509–88, the chief ministers of the Crown, especially Wolsey and Cromwell, sought to change the structure of Tudor government in order to increase its efficiency and extend its power. While some of these changes were more permanent, others were temporary, or frustrated by the monarchs or parliament. Above all, Tudor government remained personal and was dependent on the whims of the monarchs and the informal structures that evolved to serve them, such as the court, the household and the privy chamber. This meant that the chief ministers found that their powers were limited and were reliant ultimately on the will of the monarch, and that any changes they made would only succeed with the Crown's support.

EXTEND YOUR KNOWLEDGE

The court, the household and the privy chamber

Not to be confused with the legal Courts of Justice, the royal court served the monarch; wherever the monarch was, the court would follow. The court was important for display and entertainment and was an informal source of power. Under the Tudors, those who wanted power or influence would tend to come to the court in search of patronage. Those who succeeded in gaining patronage at court could then build up enormous power and wealth, though they remained dependent on access to the court in order to secure this. The court was also important for display. It was important for the Tudor monarchs to emphasise their power and wealth to important visitors, and the court allowed them to do this through elaborate and expensive displays such as tournaments and plays.

The household was usually responsible for the ruler's domestic needs. Monarchs and their families were served by a wide range of people who moved about the country with them. Hundreds of people were employed in the kitchens, laundries and gardens and were mostly menial servants, though they were controlled by high-level officials known as the board of the green cloth. The household could grow or shrink according to the personal needs of individual monarchs and their families.

The privy (private) chamber was actually a series of rooms where the royal family lived. David Starkey's work has shown that under Henry VIII, the privy chamber became an important political hub. The chamber had its own staff – the gentlemen of the privy chamber. The most important of these was the groom of the stool, in charge of the royal commode or toilet. Under Henry VIII, these positions were filled by Henry's most trusted friends, who were usually men from the nobility or gentry. These men were not simply servants. Because of their intimate and daily physical contact with Henry, they also became his advisers and were often employed in more formal areas of government. For example, between 1520 and 1525, gentlemen of the privy chamber were sent on diplomatic missions to France and on a military expedition against the Scots.

What was the role of the Council?

The Council was a more formal body that had existed since medieval times to advise ('counsel') the monarch. The monarch chose who should be on the Council and did not have to take their advice, though it was often in the king's or queen's best interests to at least listen to the Council's views. It also helped the monarch with the day-to-day running of the country and could act as a judicial court. The Council could also be divided by faction, especially in the 1540s and 1550s when the Crown was in the hands first of the ageing Henry VIII, then his young son Edward. The political importance of the Council varied depending on the style of rule adopted by different monarchs. However, the role of the Council changed during the Tudor period, becoming increasingly formal and 'professional'.

The role of the Council under Henry VIII

Until the 1530s, the Council was still a fairly large institution of perhaps 40 members, most of whom would not attend on a regular basis. In 1526, Wolsey was planning the **Eltham Ordinances** to reduce this to 20 men who would meet daily. Although Wolsey's plans initially came to nothing, by 1537 a council such as the one he had planned for had emerged. This became known as the 'Privy Council', and by Elizabeth's reign it was responsible for much of the daily running of the country, especially administration and legal matters. The Privy Council that emerged by 1537 did so without Cromwell's planning. Initially, the new-style Privy Council appeared as an unplanned response to the political crisis of 1536 when Henry VIII was faced with serious rebellion and needed a small council of trusted men to give rapid and clear advice.

KEY TERM

Eltham Ordinances
These were a series of reforms introduced by Wolsey in 1526. They included plans for the council and household, as well as a reduction of the number of men serving in the privy chamber. Wolsey claimed that these reforms were an attempt to improve royal finances, but in reality they were an excuse for him to purge the chamber of men whom he considered to be his enemies.

SOURCE 9 The size of the Council, 1509–88.

1509-29 (under Wolsey): 120

1536-37: 19

1540: 19

1548: 22

1552: 31

1553-58: 50

1559: 19

1586: 19

The role of the Council, 1547–88

Under Edward VI, the Council became less important politically as government and politics were dominated by the king's protectors who used control of the privy chamber to achieve this. Mary's Council continued the trend seen in Henry's reign. Although she had 50 named councillors, only 19 of these were 'working' councillors who were meeting three or four times a week. Mary's councillors were particularly involved in advising her over her marriage and the return to Catholicism, although they did not always agree on these issues. Under Elizabeth, the role of the Privy Council reached its peak. Its membership was honed down to about a dozen key individuals, and by the 1590s these men were meeting nearly every day, sometimes in both the morning and afternoon. By this period, the Council had become an essential part of government, which handled much of the day-to-day business of the realm. This did not mean that the monarch was sidelined, because he or she appointed the councillors and could dismiss them at will.

Changes to the Crown's finances

A constant theme of the Tudor period was the tension between the Crown's income and expenditure. Both Wolsey and Cromwell attempted to put the Crown's finances on a more secure footing, but they were only partially successful. In theory, the monarch was supposed to be financially independent, 'to live of their own' as contemporaries put it. The Crown had two main sources of income: 'ordinary revenue', which came from the royal lands and the monarch's status as a landlord, and 'extraordinary revenue', which was usually taxation granted by parliament for the monarch's special needs, usually the costs of war. 'Ordinary' income could come from rents or the sale of lands. But even with some considerable boosts to the Crown's income, the monarchy rarely had enough money and was often reliant on parliamentary taxation and other more legally dubious source of income. In 1521, for example, royal officials were so short of money that they had to resort to loans to pay the royal servants. The situation was not helped by extravagant expenditure. Henry VIII spent more than £100,000 on building at Hampton Court and Whitehall, while the royal household in the 1550s was costing £75,000 a year to run. Even Elizabeth, who avoided the costs of war until 1585, found it difficult to balance the royal books and died owing £350,000.

Changes to royal finance under Henry VIII

Financial policy under Henry VIII was driven by the king's desire to go to war and the costs that this entailed. It has been estimated that the income from Crown lands in 1515 was £25,000 per annum, but Henry's war against France in 1512–14 cost about £1 million. The king's chief ministers, Wolsey and Cromwell, were responsible for funding Henry's ambitions. Wolsey was prepared to try new methods to achieve this, such as the introduction of a **subsidy**, a new form of parliamentary taxation in 1513 that was based on an assessment of each individual's wealth. This raised £322,099 between 1513 and 1523. A further £117,936 was raised through the traditional form of taxation, the **Fifteenths and Tenths**. However, this was still not enough to fund Henry's wars and Wolsey was forced to resort to less legal methods, in particular the Amicable Grant (1525), which was in effect a forced loan from his taxpayers. As this loan was on top of the high levels of taxation already demanded and 'loans' extracted in 1522–23 that had raised £260,000 but had not been repaid, the result was rebellion. Wolsey was forced to take full responsibility and withdraw the grant, while Henry claimed no knowledge of his minister's plans.

KEY TERMS

Subsidy
The subsidy, introduced in 1513, was a more flexible form of taxation than Fifteenths and Tenths because it was based on an assessment of each individual's wealth by local officials.

Fifteenths and Tenths
Introduced in 1334, Fifteenths and Tenths were the traditional medieval form of taxation, which raised a fixed sum of money.

In the 1530s, Cromwell tried to solve these problems by the acquisition of former monastery lands for the Crown. This temporarily raised Crown income to a peak of £126,296 in 1541, but this did not last, as by the end of Henry's reign two-thirds of these lands had been sold off. Cromwell also created four specialised **financial courts** to handle the increased flow of money to the Crown. These were the Courts of Augmentation, First Fruits and Tenths, Wards and Liveries, and General Surveyors. However, of these innovations, only the Court of Wards and Liveries lasted beyond the end of the Tudor period. The other three courts were all amalgamated into the **Exchequer** under Edward and Mary.

KEY TERMS

Financial courts
The Court of Wards and Liveries was set up to deal with the estates and heirs of tenants of the monarch. Under Elizabeth I it was run by William Cecil; the position allowed him to build up enormous personal wealth. The Courts of Augmentations, First Fruits and Tenths, and General Surveyors were set up to deal with the estates and incomes acquired by the Crown as a result of the break with Rome and the dissolution of the monasteries.

Exchequer
This was the institution responsible for collecting the Crown's income. It was medieval in origin and by the Tudor period it had become increasingly slow, but reforms under Edward and Mary meant that it became more efficient.

Financial developments under Edward, Mary and Elizabeth

Under the protectorate of Northumberland and then the rule of Mary, some attempts were made to put the Crown on a more sound financial footing. More Crown lands were sold off to reduce debt, and under Mary, Crown income from customs, which had remained the same since 1507, was reformed, increasing income from duties on imports and exports from £25,900 in 1550–51 to £82,797 in 1558–59. Elizabeth reaped the benefits of these reforms but did little to change the financial system. Her main contribution was to end the **debasement of the coinage**, which had begun under Mary. Elizabeth's natural caution also meant that she avoided costly warfare before 1585, but after this, war with Spain led to high levels of taxation. The situation was made worse because Elizabeth and her advisers did nothing to reform the system of taxation. The result was decreasing returns – a subsidy yielded £140,000 in 1558 but only £80,000 by 1603. This in turn led to Elizabeth's controversial exploitation of her royal prerogative, which soured the last years of her reign.

KEY TERM

Debasement of the coinage
From the 1540s, the Tudor regime began melting down the gold and silver coinage and mixing it with other metals. This was to create more ready money for Henry VIII to spend on warfare. This practice had serious effects for the economy, causing price rises (inflation), and it was reversed under Mary and Elizabeth.

Changes to the legal system by Wolsey and Cromwell

The Tudor legal system was comprised of a series of national and local courts of law where most cases were heard. However, there were also 'special' courts of equity, which were used to try cases where there was no legal precedent or where circumstances surrounding the case made it difficult to get a fair hearing in one of the main courts. Examples of these equitable courts included the court of Star Chamber, Chancery (run by the Lord Chancellor) and the king's Council. They had the advantage of being much more flexible than the common law courts. Under Wolsey, the role of Star Chamber expanded considerably. In comparison with the reign of Henry VII where on average 12 cases per year were heard in Star Chamber, under Wolsey this grew to 120 cases per year. Wolsey used Star Chamber to prosecute over-powerful members of the nobility and to pursue his campaign against illegal enclosure, but he faced considerable opposition from parliament and this use of Star Chamber did not outlast his fall. By Elizabeth's reign, Star Chamber was used as a convenient court for trying cases of riot and abuses of the judicial system.

Further changes to the legal system were carried out by Cromwell in the 1530s. In 1536, an Act of Parliament abolished **franchises**. Also in 1536, parliament passed an Act that brought Wales into line with the English judicial system. These permanent changes helped to enhance royal power because they meant that the monarch now had more control over the legal system in the more remote areas of England and Wales, and there were fewer opportunities for the nobility to build up power bases where they could rival the Crown. Coupled with the changes to the Marcher Councils (see page 63) these developments meant that the local and legal power of the Tudor monarchy was more extensive by 1588.

KEY TERM

Franchise
Franchises were regions where the local lord had complete control over the law courts. These had developed in the Middle Ages and meant that there were areas of the country where the monarchy could not intervene in legal cases, giving the local lord enormous power. An example of a franchise was that controlled by the Bishop of Durham, who since 1066 had only implemented royal laws in the region under his control when he agreed with them.

THINKING HISTORICALLY Change (5a)

How did the role of parliament change in the period 1509–88?

Changes leading to the increasing role of parliament

Strands	Explanation of how the strand links to the increasing role of parliament, 1509–88
Henry VIII's desire for a son and heir	Henry's marriage to Catherine of Aragon had produced no male heir. By the 1520s she was too old to have more children. The belief that a woman could not rule in her own right meant it was thought Mary Tudor would not be able to rule. Henry was desperate for a son due to the fear of challenges to the Tudor dynasty from rival claimants. Anne Boleyn refused to become Henry's mistress. She was young enough to have children and Henry was determined to marry her. The international situation between 1529 and 1532 meant that Henry was not able to persuade the pope to grant an annulment, so he needed another way to end his marriage to Catherine, which parliament provided.
The role of Thomas Cromwell as the king's minister, 1532–40	Cromwell recognised the role that parliament could play in securing the annulment. He manipulated anti-clerical feeling in the Commons to put pressure on the papacy. He was the first to use parliament to define the powers of the monarchy (Act in Restraint of Appeals, 1533) and to legalise the Royal Supremacy (Act of Supremacy, 1534). This created a precedent for future monarchs because they would need to use parliament to make religious change. Cromwell helped to introduce the idea of the 'king-in-parliament', which enhanced parliament's role.
The use of parliament by Edward, Mary and Elizabeth to enforce religious change	Edward's advisers used parliament to create a Protestant reformation in the Acts of Uniformity (1549, 1552). Mary reversed the break with Rome via parliament. Elizabeth created her religious settlement through parliament (Acts of Uniformity and Supremacy, 1559).
The increasing frequency with which parliament was called and the growing confidence of MPs	Parliament sat with increasing frequency from the 1530s and 1540s. MPs became more confident in challenging the monarch's prerogative and policies, e.g. opposition to the Exiles bill (1555) under Mary; attempts to introduce a more radical religious settlement under Elizabeth; parliament's determination to discuss matters of state such as the queen's marriage and succession (1563, 1566) and the fate of Mary, Queen of Scots (1572, 1586–87).

Make two copies of the graph below. On the first, plot the individual strands from the first column of the table against the y-axis. Use a different colour for each. You do not need to label it with the events in the second column. On the second graph plot a single line that is a combination of all four strands (for example, at a given point two of the four strands are plotted high up on the y-axis while two are plotted lower; the combined strand would have to be plotted somewhere in the middle to represent a summary of those four individual strands).

Changes to the role of parliament likely

Changes to the role of parliament unlikely

1509-19 1520-29 1530-39 1540-49 1550-59 1560-69 1570-79 1580-88

AS Level Exam-Style Question Section B

William Cecil was Elizabeth's most powerful minister in the years 1559–88. To what extent did royal power grow in that period? (20 marks)

Tip

Make sure that you cover ways in which royal power increased and decreased.

Answer the following questions:

1 How have the strands combined to make change less or more likely?

2 Why did the role of parliament change so much by Elizabeth's reign but not before?

ACTIVITIES
SUMMARY

1 Draw a graph showing the changing power of the monarchy, 1509–88. Mark on it the key events that strengthened or weakened its power.

2 Create your own spider diagram called 'Why did the power of the monarchy change, 1509–88?' Use the following headings: 'Role of individual monarchs'; 'Role of chief ministers'; 'Role of parliament'. Use two colours to highlight changes that increased and decreased the power of the monarchy.

3 Use the information in this chapter to complete the following table.

	Situation in 1509	Situation in 1588
Role and powers of the monarch		
Role of parliament		
Financial position of the monarchy		
Role of the nobility		

4 Write a summary paragraph to answer the question: To what extent had the power of the Tudor monarchy grown by 1588?

 WIDER READING

Castor, H.R. *She-Wolves*, Faber & Faber (2011)

Graves, M.A.R. *Tudor Parliaments, the Crown, Lords and Commons, 1485–1603*, Longman (1985)

Loach, J. *Edward VI*, Yale University Press (2002)

Randell, K. and Turvey, R. *Henry VIII to Mary I: Government and Religion, 1509–1558*, Hodder Education (2008)

Starkey, D. 'Wolsey and Cromwell: continuity or contrast?', *History Today*, November 1985

Warren, J. *Elizabeth I: Meeting the Challenge: England 1541–1603*, Hodder Education (2008)

1.2 Religious changes, 1509–88

KEY QUESTIONS

- How and why did religious change happen, 1527–63?
- To what extent did Catholicism survive in England?
- How and why did Protestantism grow, 1509–88?

INTRODUCTION

The Tudor period saw radical shifts in national religion. Unlike the European religious changes, which were often the result of popular pressure from below, the English Reformation was mostly the result of pressure from above, and especially the personal preferences of the Tudor monarchs. Successive Tudor monarchs subscribed to the idea *cuius regio eius religio* (whose realm, his religion) – that the religious beliefs of the ruler should dictate those of their country. In a country where there was no police force or standing army, ensuring that the population conformed to the same religious beliefs was an important method of political and social control. As a result, religious views that differed to those imposed by the monarchs were usually treated as a threat.

The national Tudor Church – its **doctrine**, **liturgy** and appearance – underwent a series of radical changes from the break with Rome under Henry VIII, to more radical Protestantism under Edward VI, to Catholicism under Mary, and finally to the establishment of the Church of England under Elizabeth. In comparison to the European experience, where conflict erupted, the changes in England did not lead to wars of religion, although there was opposition through popular rebellion, plots and passive resistance. However, there is considerable debate among historians about the relative popularity and strength of Protestantism and Catholicism and popular attitudes to religious change.

HOW AND WHY DID RELIGIOUS CHANGE HAPPEN, 1527–63?

Why did the break with Rome happen?

The break with Rome, which ended the pope's power in England, was primarily the result of Henry's desire for a male heir. The king himself tended to have orthodox Catholic beliefs. In 1521, Henry had written a book (*Assertio Septem Sacramentorum* – 'Defence of the Seven Sacraments'), which attacked Martin Luther's beliefs. The pope even awarded Henry the title *Fidei Defensor* (Defender of the Faith) for his support of the Catholic faith. But Henry's marriage to Catherine of Aragon had produced one daughter and no son. By the 1520s, Catherine was past childbearing age and Henry had a series of mistresses, at least one of whom – Elizabeth Blount – had an illegitimate son by the king. In addition, Henry had fallen for Anne Boleyn, who refused to become his mistress. By 1527, therefore, Henry was prepared to end his marriage to Catherine.

1511–14 – The Hunne case creates anti-clerical feeling in parliament

1521 – First burnings of Lutheran books in England

1534 – Act of Supremacy and Treason Act confirm the break with Rome

1545–63 – Council of Trent attempts reform within the Catholic Church

1510	1515	1520	1525	1530	1535	1540	1545

1517 – Martin Luther publishes his Ninety-Five Theses, criticising the Catholic Church

1529 – First use of the word 'Protestantism'

1536–40 – Dissolution of the monasteries

TIMELINE – EVENTS LEADING TO THE ANNULMENT OF HENRY'S MARRIAGE AND THE BREAK WITH ROME

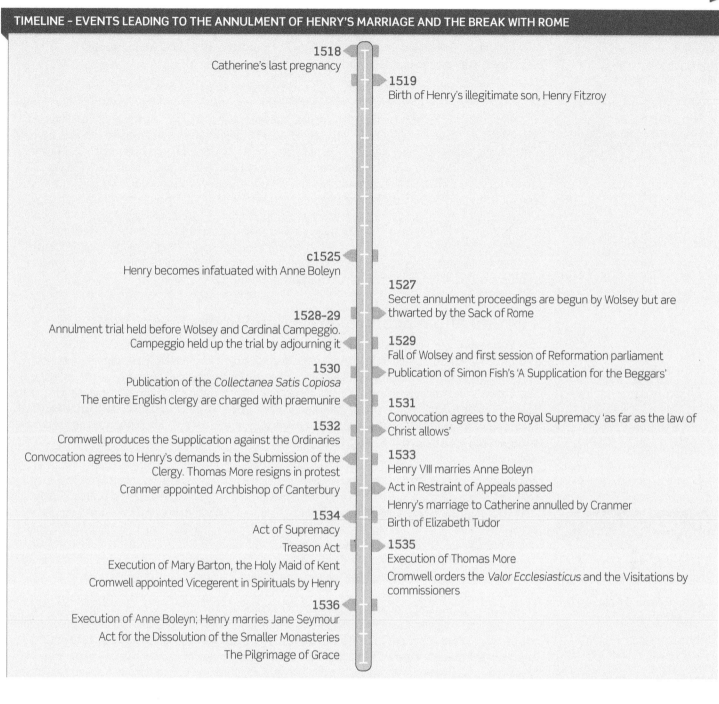

1518
Catherine's last pregnancy

1519
Birth of Henry's illegitimate son, Henry Fitzroy

c1525
Henry becomes infatuated with Anne Boleyn

1527
Secret annulment proceedings are begun by Wolsey but are thwarted by the Sack of Rome

1528–29
Annulment trial held before Wolsey and Cardinal Campeggio. Campeggio held up the trial by adjourning it

1529
Fall of Wolsey and first session of Reformation parliament

1530
Publication of the *Collectanea Satis Copiosa*

The entire English clergy are charged with praemunire

Publication of Simon Fish's 'A Supplication for the Beggars'

1531
Convocation agrees to the Royal Supremacy 'as far as the law of Christ allows'

1532
Cromwell produces the Supplication against the Ordinaries

Convocation agrees to Henry's demands in the Submission of the Clergy. Thomas More resigns in protest

Cranmer appointed Archbishop of Canterbury

1533
Henry VIII marries Anne Boleyn

Act in Restraint of Appeals passed

Henry's marriage to Catherine annulled by Cranmer

Birth of Elizabeth Tudor

1534
Act of Supremacy

Treason Act

Execution of Mary Barton, the Holy Maid of Kent

Cromwell appointed Vicegerent in Spirituals by Henry

1535
Execution of Thomas More

Cromwell orders the *Valor Ecclesiasticus* and the Visitations by commissioners

1536
Execution of Anne Boleyn; Henry marries Jane Seymour

Act for the Dissolution of the Smaller Monasteries

The Pilgrimage of Grace

1559–63 – The Elizabethan Church Settlement creates the Protestant Church of England

1570 – Elizabeth I excommunicated by the pope

1584 – Assassination of the Dutch Protestant leader, William of Orange

1588 – Spanish Armada defeated

1550 — 1555 — 1560 — 1565 — 1570 — 1575 — 1580 — 1585

1555 – The English Church returns to Rome

1566 – Start of the Protestant Dutch revolt against Spanish rule

1572 – St Bartholemew's Day massacre in France; Protestants are killed by Catholics

1585 – England goes to war with Spain

KEY TERM

Annulment
If a marriage is annulled, it means that it has never been legally valid. Any children of an annulled marriage are illegitimate. A divorce ends a marriage, but it acknowledges that it was legal while it lasted.

Using a passage from the Old Testament book Leviticus, Henry convinced himself that his marriage had never been valid in the first place because Catherine had previously been married to his elder brother Arthur. This argument might have allowed Henry to seek a papal **annulment**, which had been used in the past to end other inconvenient royal marriages.

In 1527, Wolsey was given responsibility for overseeing the king's 'Great Matter'. Unfortunately for Henry, a combination of circumstances meant that he was unable to get what he wanted. Catherine was prepared to fight the proceedings, especially because she feared for the status of her daughter Mary if the marriage was annulled. Catherine also had powerful allies both at court and abroad. In 1527, she appealed to her nephew, Charles V, for help. Charles had been dominant in European politics since his victory over the French at the Battle of Pavia (1525), but in May 1527 Charles' troops attacked Rome itself. The result was that the pope, Clement VII, was directly under Charles' control and would be very unlikely to grant an annulment that would upset not only Catherine but Charles as well. In 1528, Clement sent his legate (representative), Cardinal Campeggio, to England to help Wolsey hear the case. But Campeggio was under instructions to delay the proceedings. In the period 1527–29, these problems meant that Wolsey's attempts to find a solution were frustrated. By 1529, he had lost Henry's confidence and fell from power, but Henry had still not achieved his annulment. The eventual solution was to break with Rome and the pope.

The end of papal power in England under Henry VIII

By 1534, Henry VIII had created the Royal Supremacy. This meant that he denied the authority of the pope over the Church in England and claimed this right for himself. This outcome was not inevitable, however. Instead, it was a solution to Henry's desire to annul his marriage to Catherine and marry Anne, which was brought about through the interventions of those advising the king. Some of these advisers, such as Cromwell, Cranmer and Anne herself, had sympathies with Protestant reforming ideas, but Henry himself remained suspicious of these views. He supported the creation of the Supremacy because it allowed him to marry Anne Boleyn, with whom he hoped to have a legitimate male heir, and also because it enhanced his power in England.

KEY TERMS

Erastian kingship
Influenced by the ideas of the Swiss theologian, Thomas Erastus, this theory argued that the ruler of the state should also control the Church.

Act of Supremacy
This Act declared that the king was 'the only supreme head on earth of the Church of England'. However, the wording of the Act made it clear that parliament had not made the king the head of the Church (which would have implied that parliament had the power to give and take power from the monarch). Instead, it was claimed that the monarch had always had this power and the Act was confirming this.

Convocation
The assembly of archbishops and bishops that would meet to discuss theology and church matters. It would often meet at the same time as parliament.

Henry was very interested in his own powers as king, though this interest was undoubtedly fuelled by his need to find a way to end his marriage to Catherine. He commissioned leading scholars, including Thomas Cranmer, to research an intellectual justification for his annulment. This led to Cranmer's publication of the *Collectanea satis copiosa* (1530), a collection that used English chroniclers, some dating back to the Anglo-Saxon period, to argue that the kings of England were not subject to papal power. Henry himself read this work thoroughly and even annotated it. Meanwhile, other scholars toured European universities, looking for legal and theological arguments to support Henry's case. These were presented to parliament in 1531. The outcome of this research was the development of the theory of 'imperial' kingship – the idea that English kings had no superior except God. This meant that the king was the ultimate source of power in the kingdom and that any attempt to appeal to other foreign powers was illegal. The result of this process was to enable Henry to justify his increasingly **Erastian view of kingship** and to claim supremacy over the Church. These ideas were made law through a series of Acts of Parliament, including the Act in Restraint of Appeals (1533) and the **Act of Supremacy** (1534).

The development of the theory that supported Henry's supremacy allowed him, with the help of Cromwell and Cranmer, to attack the legal and financial powers of the pope. Anti-clerical criticism of the privileges of the Church, such as holding multiple positions at the same time, was exploited to put pressure on the English clergy and the pope. For example, the entire English clergy were charged with praemunire in 1530 and fined £100,000. In 1531, **Convocation** was also forced to recognise Henry as 'Supreme Head of the Church of England', although they added the phrase 'as far as the law of Christ allows'. Cromwell pushed home this advantage in 1532 by drawing up the Supplication against the Ordinaries, a parliamentary 'petition' to Henry complaining about the clergy's abuses of their power and asking Henry to act. Henry enhanced his control over the English Church still further in late 1532. On the death of William Warham, the Archbishop of Canterbury, Henry appointed Thomas Cranmer. By this time, Anne Boleyn had finally given in to Henry and was now pregnant. Desperate for a legitimate male heir, Henry increased the speed of change still further. Henry and Anne were married in secret in January 1533, but the problem of Henry's first marriage to Catherine remained. In April 1533, Cranmer led Convocation in discussions over the validity of the king's first marriage and the pope's authority; unsurprisingly, they supported the king.

These events allowed Cranmer to annul Henry's marriage to Catherine, while the Act in Restraint of Appeals meant that she could not make a legal appeal to the pope.

Thomas Cranmer (1489–1556)

Much of Cranmer's early career remains obscure, yet he became a central figure in the Reformation. Cranmer was educated at Cambridge, where he achieved a doctorate in divinity. He travelled in Wolsey's household to Europe and came up with the idea of asking European universities for their opinions on the annulment. This led to him travelling widely in Europe on the king's behalf and to his work on the *Collectanea Satis Copiosa*.

During his travels, he seems to have come into contact with reformist thinkers and was influenced by their ideas to the extent that he got married, something a Catholic priest was not supposed to do.

Cranmer was appointed Archbishop of Canterbury at the end of 1532 while he was still abroad in northern Italy. His appointment caused considerable surprise because he had only ever held minor positions in the Church and he held reformist views different from Henry's own. It may be that Cranmer's connection with the Boleyn family helped his appointment because he could be relied upon to follow orders as they held reformist views. In May 1533, he annulled Henry's marriage to Catherine of Aragon.

Cranmer's main contribution to the Reformation came in the period after 1536. He survived the deaths of both his allies Anne Boleyn and Thomas Cromwell and was eventually able to find allies at court in Catherine Parr and the reformist faction. Cranmer's survival suggests that he was a clever political operator, able to compromise and bend to the king's will.

Under Edward VI, he became the architect of the Reformation, writing books of homilies and two books of common prayer, the second of which remained in use for centuries. Under Mary, Cranmer was imprisoned and tried for heresy. He recanted his beliefs, thinking that this would save him from the flames, but Mary was determined to get revenge because she blamed Cranmer for the annulment of her mother's marriage. At his burning in 1556, Cranmer famously put his right hand into the flames first because it had signed his recantation.

The road to the break with Rome

Draw a diagram called 'The road to the break with Rome'. This could be a flow chart or mind map. Alternatively, you could choose to represent the break with Rome through a series of cartoons or a road map. The diagram should be annotated to show the key events, causes and roles of individuals such as Cromwell and Cranmer.

The consequences of the break with Rome under Henry VIII

The initial break with Rome meant that Henry replaced the pope as the head of the Church in England. It did not mean that the English Church would automatically become reformist (or 'evangelical') in its doctrine. However, those close to the king – Cromwell (as Vicegerent in Spirituals) and Cranmer (as Archbishop of Canterbury) – had reformer sympathies and were sometimes able to persuade the king to alter the religious beliefs and practices to fit a more evangelical approach. The main changes to religious practice between 1536 and 1539 were in three key areas: the dissolution of the monasteries, an attack on pilgrimages and other practices that the reformers saw as sacrilegious, and the promotion of an English Bible.

The dissolution of the monasteries was masterminded by Cromwell. For the reformers, the monasteries represented the wealth and corruption of the Church. They were also felt to be promoting what the reformers considered a 'superstitious' belief in **purgatory**. In 1535, *Valor Ecclesiasticus* valued all Church property and revealed to Henry the wealth of the monasteries – between 1536 and 1547 their dissolution raised £1.3 million. *Valor* was followed by visitations of the monasteries undertaken by commissioners appointed by Cromwell, such as Thomas Legh and Richard Layton. As Source 1 on page 41 suggests, part of the commissioners' mission was to find evidence of corruption in the monasteries to use as evidence against them. The evidence of the *Valor*, coupled with that of the commissioners, was used by Cromwell to justify the 1536 Act of Parliament that authorised the dissolution of the smaller monasteries, defined as worth less than £200 per annum.

KEY TERM

Purgatory
In the Catholic faith, this was the place to which a person's soul went after their death. It was believed that the soul would be purified in purgatory so that it could enter heaven. The Catholic Church preached that the soul's time in purgatory could be reduced in several ways, including by saying prayers for the dead. This became one of the primary roles of monasteries. Reformers denied the existence of purgatory because there was no reference to it in the Bible.

The process of dissolution involved the destruction of the monasteries' buildings – lead was stripped from the roofs and melted down, and stained glass and images were smashed. The abbots were either given pensions, if they co-operated, or threatened with execution for treason if they resisted, something that happened to the abbots of both Glastonbury and Reading.

Despite the Pilgrimage of Grace, which was a reaction to the dissolution, Cromwell was able to continue with the dissolution of the larger monasteries, even though they had been praised in the 1536 Act. This time, the monasteries were dissolved using a combination of persuasion, bribes and threats, and the 1539 Act that followed was simply a confirmation of what had already taken place.

The dissolution proved to be irreversible, mainly because two-thirds of monastic property was sold by the Crown. Much of this land was bought by members of the nobility and gentry such as the Cecil and Spencer families. This meant that they had a vested interest in the reformation and dissolution and were unlikely to surrender their estates, as Mary was to discover.

ACTIVITY
WRITING

Widening vocabulary

Use five of the words in the box to complete these sentences so that they best describe the nature of the causes of the Pilgrimage of Grace.

triggered	latent	nurtured
encouraged	inevitable	
dependent	incipient	

The dissolution of the smaller monasteries _____ the series of events that led to war.

_____ resentment against religious reform _____ resentment in the religiously conservative north of England.

Anger at government intrusion in their day-to-day lives _____ the people of Lincolnshire to rebel in 1536.

Noble and gentry sympathies for the rebels' cause meant that their involvement in the rebellion was _____.

THINKING HISTORICALLY   Causation (5a)

Interrelations

Causes never simply come one after another. They are often present simultaneously and have an effect on one another. Sometimes new causes develop and interact with existing ones.

Causes of the dissolution of the monasteries

1 Henry's need for money	2 The creation of the Royal Supremacy	3 The growth of Protestant ideas	4 The reported wealth and corruption in monasteries	5 Cromwell's religious beliefs	6 Anti-clericalism

Work in groups to produce a diagram of causes and the links between them.

1 On an A3 piece of paper, write all of the causes of the dissolution of the monasteries. Write these in boxes, the size of which will reflect how long they were a relevant factor. For example, if you argue that 'anti-clericalism' had been an important factor since the late 15th century, then this will be quite a big box, whereas the 'creation of the Royal Supremacy' would be a lot smaller. Spread these boxes over the page.

2 Then make links between all of the causes. Draw lines between the boxes and annotate them to explain how the causes are connected and in what ways each affected and altered the other. For example, between 'the growth of Protestant ideas' and 'Cromwell's religious beliefs' you could write something like, 'without the growth of Protestantism, Cromwell would not have been convinced that the monasteries were unbiblical and needed to be dissolved.'

Answer the following questions:

3 How do the causes differ in their nature? (Think in terms of events, developments, beliefs, states of affairs, etc.)

4 How do the causes differ in the roles they played in causing the dissolution of the monasteries? (Think about whether each cause created the right conditions, was a trigger for events, or acted in some other way.)

5 Write a 200-word paragraph explaining how important it is to recognise the relationships between causes. Give examples from your diagram. Try to include connective phrases such as: 'this created conditions conducive to...', 'this triggered an immediate reaction...', 'this made the development of that situation more/less likely'.

SOURCE 1

Letter from one of Cromwell's commissioners, Richard Layton, to Cromwell. Writing in 1535, Layton was reporting on the Priory of Maiden Bradley (Wiltshire).

By this bringer, my servant, I send you relics, first two flowers wrapped in white and black sarcenet that on Christmas Eve, at the very hour when Christ was born, will spring and burgeon and bear blossoms, which has been proved, says the Prior of Maiden Bradley. Ye shall also receive a bag of relics, wherein ye shall see strange things… as God's coat, Our Lady's smock, part of God's supper from the Lord's Supper, part of the rock on which Jesus was born in Bethlehem – belike there is in Bethlehem plenty of stones and some quarry, and make their mangers of stone. The scripture of everything shall declare you all; and all these of Maiden Bradley, where as is an holy father Prior, and hath but six children, and but one daughter married, yet of the goods of the monastery trusting shortly to marry the rest. His sons be tall men waiting upon him, and he thanks God he never meddled with married women, but all with maidens the fairest could be gotten, and always married them right well. The pope, considering his fragility, gave him licence to keep an whore…

The dissolution of the monasteries led to far-reaching and unforeseen consequences, but Cromwell was also keen to promote other doctrinal changes. New bishops were appointed who shared Cromwell's religious views, such as Hugh Latimer, who was made Bishop of Worcester. The Act of Ten Articles (1536) was the first attempt to define the doctrine of the new English Church. These were mostly in line with Catholic belief, but the article on the Eucharist was deliberately ambiguous in its language, while the number of **sacraments** considered necessary for the salvation of the soul was decreased from seven to three, which was in line with reformer views. As vicegerent, Cromwell also issued two sets of injunctions (instructions) to the English clergy in 1536 and 1538. These discouraged practices that were seen as superstitious by reformers such as pilgrimages, the emphasis placed on relics and the worship of saints. The injunctions also encouraged the use of an English Bible, which was fundamental to evangelical thought. The move towards a Protestant Church reached its peak in 1538–39. In 1538, the shrine to Thomas Becket at Canterbury Cathedral, the most famous saint's shrine in the country, was destroyed. Finally, in 1539, Henry authorised the English 'Great Bible', a copy of which was to be placed in every parish church, although it still took five years for most of them to get a copy.

After 1539, however, the pace of religious change under Henry slowed and was even reversed. Henry himself was not a reformer and was particularly suspicious of reformer views on the **Eucharist**. Conservative influence had never gone away at court. The *Bishops' Book*, published in 1537 and written by a committee of clergy, had restored the four sacraments left out in the Ten Articles. Also, as Cromwell's influence began to waver, the conservative faction at court regained the upper hand. In 1538, Henry was **excommunicated** by the pope, who was encouraging the Catholic countries of France and Spain to launch a crusade against England. Henry's reaction was to move away from evangelical reform. In November 1538, he presided in person over the trial of the evangelical John Lambert, who was sentenced to death for heresy. In 1539, the Act of Six Articles was passed, which reinforced Catholic doctrines such as **transubstantiation** and celibacy for priests. Following Cromwell's execution in 1540, the king continued to move back towards a more Catholic doctrine with the publication in 1543 of the *King's Book*. This book, which was also known as *The Necessary Doctrine and Erudition of a Christian Man*, emphasised traditional beliefs in Masses for the dead and rejected reformer beliefs such as the idea that faith alone would lead to salvation. However, evangelical influences at court and in royal policy did not disappear. In 1543, Henry married Catherine Parr, who had Protestant sympathies. The reformer faction at court still existed, led by Edward Seymour, while Prince Edward and Princess Elizabeth were being educated by the best scholars in the country, who also had reformist views.

EXTEND YOUR KNOWLEDGE

John Lambert and Sacramentarianism

Sacramentariansim was a belief inspired by more radical Protestants in Switzerland. Sacramentarians did not believe in the real presence at Communion, something that Henry VIII considered heresy. Lambert was connected to other radical preachers from Cambridge and had been in trouble several times on suspicion of heresy. In 1538, he publicly challenged a sermon and was arrested on suspicion of denying the real presence. His trial was a show trial in which Henry was determined to demonstrate that radical thinkers had gone too far, and this was a signal for the conservative changes in religion that followed. Cromwell also had links with Sacramentarians. In 1539, he was accused of protecting Protestants at Calais who had been found guilty of heresy. This charge helped to bring about his downfall.

KEY TERMS

Sacrament
This is a ceremony within the Christian Church that is seen as God's forgiveness of sinners ('grace'). In the Catholic Church there are seven sacraments: Eucharist, baptism, confirmation, penance, marriage, ordination and extreme unction. In the 16th century Protestant view there were three: Eucharist, baptism and penance.

Eucharist
Sometimes known as Holy Communion or the Lord's Supper, this is a sacrament that represents the Last Supper of Jesus and his followers before his trial and crucifixion. All Christians recognise the importance of this sacrament although they differ about how it should be interpreted.

Excommunication
Expulsion from the Catholic Church. This meant that the person who was excommunicated could not receive any of the sacraments. It was particularly serious for a monarch to be excommunicated because it meant that their subjects were no longer expected to obey them.

Transubstantiation
The Catholic belief that in the Eucharist the bread and wine become the body and blood of Christ. This was known as the 'real presence'. Martin Luther criticised this belief, and a key feature in the evangelical doctrine was denial that transubstantiation took place. The most radical Protestants denied the real presence altogether and argued that the Eucharist was simply a commemoration of the Last Supper.

ACTIVITY
KNOWLEDGE CHECK

Key roles in the break with Rome

1 Look at the picture of the front page of the Great Bible in Source 2. Consider what this suggests about:

  a) Henry's role in Tudor society

  b) the role of the Bishops and Cromwell

  c) the role of ordinary people

  d) the role of Tudor propaganda.

2 Annotate a copy of the timeline of the break with Rome on page 37. Use two different colours to show changes that would have pleased the reformers and changes that would have pleased the Catholics.

3 Make four headings: 'Henry VIII', 'Cromwell', 'Cranmer', 'Parliament'. Under each heading write down what their role was in creating the break with Rome. Who played the largest role?

AS Level Exam-Style Question Section A

Reformers such as Thomas Cromwell were influential at court in the 1530s.

Was the influence of Thomas Cromwell the main reason for reforms to the English Church in the period 1529–40? (20 marks)

Tip

You will need to consider both Cromwell's role and other reasons for reform, such as the role of Henry VIII.

What were Edward VI's religious beliefs?

Although he had inherited an ambiguous religious situation, Edward was taught by some of the finest scholars in England, who also happened to have reformist sympathies. It is perhaps unsurprising, therefore, that he would grow up to hold Protestant beliefs himself. His journal and the observations of those at court reveal that he was genuinely interested in Protestant ideas. He listened to sermons every Sunday and appears to have been noting them down to put in his journal. In 1551, he took a personal interest in Mary's refusal to stop hearing the Mass privately and wrote to her to tell her to obey. He was also Supreme Head of the Church even though he was still a child.

SOURCE 3

Thomas Cranmer writing about Edward VI to Martin Micronius, a minister in London for European Protestants exiled from the continent, in May 1549.

Our king is a youth of such godliness as to be a wonder to the whole world. He orders all things for the advancement of God's glory. He has on every Lord's day a sermon... I wish the bishops and nobility were inflamed with the like zeal.

SOURCE 2

Frontispiece of Henry VIII's Great Bible, published in 1539. It shows Henry VIII handing the Word of God to his bishops, who are handing it to the people. The people are shouting '*Vivat rex*' or 'Long live the king'.

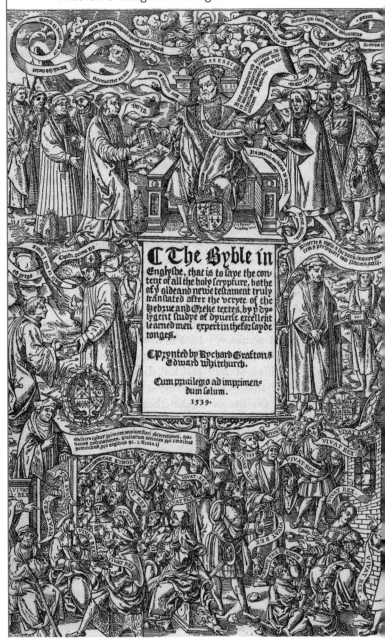

Religious change under Edward VI

Although Edward was a minor, this did not stop his regents, Somerset and Northumberland, from making changes to the English Church in the king's name. These changes moved the Church in a more Protestant direction. Even before parliament could meet to repeal the later Acts of Henry's reign, religious change had begun.

In July 1547, Cranmer published his *Book of Homilies* (sermons), which had a moderate Protestant slant. These were to be used throughout the Church and were to be read from the pulpit by clergy who were less able at preaching. In the same month a new series of injunctions was issued. Its aim was to remove all remaining Catholic practices in parish churches. The injunctions ordered that all images were to be removed from churches, no candles were to be allowed except for two on the altar, and clergy were told to encourage their congregations not to leave money for Masses in their wills. Religious conservatives such as bishops Gardiner and Bonner were imprisoned when they tried to protest.

When parliament met in late 1547, the conservative changes made by Henry VIII, such as the Act of Six Articles, were repealed. Parliament also passed an Act to allow the dissolution of **chantries**. In 1548–49, the pace of change increased and became more radical. Cranmer issued an English form of wording for the Mass (which had always been in Latin) and in January 1549 the Act of Uniformity imposed his new English *Book of Common of Prayer* on the country. Also in 1549, clergy were given the right to marry. The spread of Cranmer's writings was aided by the use of the printing press, which allowed widespread and rapid distribution of his ideas. By 1549, therefore, the liturgy and appearance of the English parish church was fundamentally different from that of 1547 and led, in part, to the serious rebellions of 1549.

These changes were continued by Northumberland after Somerset's fall. In January 1550, parish churches were ordered to surrender all Catholic service books. Thousands of these books were burnt in what Richard Rex has called 'probably the greatest episode of book-burning in English history'. By 1552, Cranmer had produced a more Protestant version of the *Book of Common Prayer*, which was influenced by the work of Martin Bucer, who had escaped persecution abroad and arrived in England in 1549. This second prayer book required that the Catholic stone altar was replaced with a wooden table and told the clergy to wear a plain surplice rather than their traditional, more decorated vestments. The prayer book also moved further away from the idea of transubstantiation and towards an even more Protestant interpretation, which denied the real presence. Finally, in 1553, Cranmer published the 42 articles, which clarified the English faith as Calvinist Protestant and would form the basis for Elizabeth's 39 Articles.

KEY TERM

Chantry
This was a side chapel in a larger church or a separate building for the sole purpose of providing a chapel where priests would pray for the souls of a benefactor and his family.

TIMELINE – RELIGIOUS CHANGE UNDER EDWARD AND MARY, 1547-58

1547
Publication of Cranmer's *Book of Homilies*
Act for the Dissolution of the Chantries

1549
First Act of Uniformity and publication of the first *Book of Common Prayer*
The Western Revolt
Act allowing the marriage of priests

1552
Second Act of Uniformity and the second *Book of Common Prayer*

1553
Publication of the 42 articles
Death of Edward VI; succession crisis; accession of Mary Tudor

1554
Wyatt's Rebellion; marriage of Mary to Philip
Reginald Pole arrives in England

1555
Burning of Protestants begins

1555-56
Synod meets to discuss Church reform

1558
Death of Mary and Pole

Religious change under Mary

Mary's strong Catholic faith meant that she was determined to restore the English Church to Rome. During Edward's reign she had obstinately refused to stop hearing Mass, despite considerable pressure from the king and his Council. Her marriage to Charles V's son, Philip, was an important part of this process. The first moves towards Catholicism were in 1553 when some prominent Protestant bishops, including Cranmer, Latimer and Ridley, were imprisoned.

At this stage, Mary seems to have hoped that there would be a popular and spontaneous return to Catholicism, but this did not happen. This was partly because she underestimated the determination of English Protestants. In addition, the reaction to news of the Spanish marriage led to Wyatt's Rebellion in 1554. This meant that Mary had to be more cautious in her approach. Finally, Mary realised that it would not be possible to demand the return of former monastic land that had been sold to new owners. Helped by Philip, she had to negotiate with the pope and his legate, Reginald Pole, who wanted to take a more hard-line approach. The result of these problems was that it was not until the second parliament of November 1554 that the full return to the Catholic faith began. In that month, Pole finally arrived in England and offered complete papal absolution (forgiveness) in return for the repeal of all religious laws passed since 1529. Pole also finally agreed that former church lands would not have to be returned, a compromise that kept parliament and landed society happy.

Apart from the issue of the former monastic lands, Mary and Pole did have some success in restoring England to full Catholicism. They appointed six educated and loyal Catholic bishops such as Thomas Goldwell, Bishop of St Asaph. Of these Catholic bishops, five later resigned in protest at Elizabeth's policies, showing their commitment to their faith. To challenge the Protestant use of the printing press, Pole also encouraged the publication of Catholic literature. Between 1554 and 1558, 64 Catholic titles were published. Pole also called a Church synod (1555–56), whose aim was to improve the education of the clergy and the running of the Church through a top-down approach. The synod recommended the establishment of seminaries (training colleges for priests) though only one was set up before the end of Mary's reign. Pole also encouraged his bishops to set good examples for their clergy and he ordered all clergy to live in their parishes to improve the quality of care that their congregations would receive. Mary and Pole also had other successes, such as the founding of six new monastic institutions. In addition, 800 Protestants were either encouraged or forced to leave the country. They remained in exile until Elizabeth's reign.

Unfortunately for Pole and Mary, this return to Catholicism would not last beyond her reign. This was partly because Mary did not live long enough to enforce the changes and partly the result of the tactics used by Pole and Mary. Pole had been out of the country for 20 years and did not fully understand the extent or nature of the changes that had taken place. In addition, he quarrelled with Pope Paul IV, which meant that appointments to seven bishoprics were held up in 1557–58, which frustrated his attempts to renew the leadership of the Church. Pole's top-down approach was undermined by the fact that there were not enough well-educated priests to serve all of the parishes, so Pole had to grant 200 exemptions allowing **pluralism**. While Catholic publications increased, they were no match for Protestant works, 98 of which were published in Mary's reign. Pole also believed that the best way to reintroduce Catholicism was to concentrate on the clergy, not their congregations. As a result, he rejected the offer of help from the **Jesuits**, whose emphasis on preaching might have encouraged congregations to embrace the changes more completely.

The most notorious aspect of Mary's policy was the burning of nearly 300 Protestants between 1556 and 1558. While these executions mirrored punishments of heretics in Europe, but on a much smaller scale, this policy was used by Protestant writers such as John Foxe for propaganda purposes. Some of the burnings were of high-profile victims, such as the Edwardian Protestant bishops Latimer, Ridley and Hooper in 1555. The most famous victim was Thomas Cranmer. Under examination, Cranmer had recanted his Protestant views in the hope that this would save him. Mary, however, was determined that Cranmer should be executed, and in 1556 he was burnt at the stake. Most of the victims of the burnings were from much humbler backgrounds, mostly artisans, labourers or yeomen. While some of the burnings did seem to attract a popular outcry, there was also acceptance or even support for these punishments, with some members of local government, such as the Earl of Derby, helping to hunt heretics. While Mary lived, therefore, it seemed likely that Catholicism would remain dominant, but Protestantism had not been completely destroyed.

KEY TERMS

Pluralism

This was a common problem in both the Protestant and Catholic churches caused by a shortage of qualified clergy. Pluralism occurred when a clergyman was responsible for more than one parish and its congregation. This also led to the related problem of absenteeism and poorly qualified or semi-literate priests tending to the needs of the parishioners.

Jesuit

A member of the movement founded in 1540 by Ignatius Loyola to spread Christianity by way of missionary work. The movement was not specifically set up to deal with Protestantism but became a powerful tool for the Catholic Church during the Counter-Reformation. The Jesuits used a technique known as 'spiritual exercises', a form of meditation, which when done properly could lead to new commitment to Catholicism.

SOURCE

4

A woodcut illustration from John Foxe's *Book of Martyrs* depicting the execution, by burning at the stake, of Archbishop Thomas Cranmer.

EXTEND YOUR KNOWLEDGE

John Foxe and the *Book of Martyrs*

John Foxe (c1516–87) was educated at Oxford. He became a Protestant in the 1540s and was ordained as a priest in Edward's reign. During Mary's reign, he went into exile to escape persecution. While there, he wrote his *Book of Martyrs*, which is sometimes known as the 'Acts and Monuments'. This was a book recording the martyrdom of Protestants burnt for their faith, which often included gruesome pictures of their deaths. The book was a form of Protestant propaganda. First published abroad in 1554, it was published in England in 1563, by which time Foxe had added to it using the burnings under Mary. Foxe dedicated his book to Elizabeth I and pursued a career in the English Church. The *Book of Martyrs* remained in print throughout Elizabeth's reign and beyond. It has sometimes been accused of presenting a one-sided picture of the burnings under Mary.

ACTIVITY
KNOWLEDGE CHECK

Successes and failures of Edward VI and Mary Tudor

Fill in the following table using the information from the chapter so far.

	Edward VI	Mary Tudor
Religious changes made in their reign		
Successes		
Failures		
Overall summary: how successful were they in implementing religious change?		

The Elizabethan Church Settlement, 1558–63

On Elizabeth's accession to the throne she faced a dilemma. On the one hand, as the daughter of Anne Boleyn she was the embodiment of the break with Rome, and she had been educated by tutors with reformer sympathies. Protestants who had been persecuted under Mary expected her to break with Rome. Some of the Protestant exiles who returned to England had been radicalised by their experiences abroad and hoped to see reform of the Church along more Puritan lines. However, if Elizabeth broke with Rome and made England Protestant again, she would face the potential threat of invasion from hostile Catholic countries coupled with Catholic rebellion in England. In the view of the Catholic Church, she was also illegitimate and could face deposition if she allowed religious reform to progress too far.

Elizabeth's personal beliefs

As well as these political considerations, Elizabeth's own approach to religion and politics shaped the settlement that emerged between 1558 and 1563. Elizabeth was naturally cautious and preferred compromise to a hard-line approach. Her own religious beliefs seem to have been a mixture of a more traditional liking for decoration, music and ceremony with a Protestant view of doctrine, although she had no sympathy for the views of radical Puritans. For example, Elizabeth favoured the music of Catholic composers such as Thomas Tallis and William Byrd, and supported their careers through her patronage. She also kept crosses and candles in her private chapel, despite the opposition of her own bishops, and she resisted attempts by more radical Protestants to modify the settlement of 1559. On the other hand, in 1558 she walked out of Mass at the elevation of the Host, the representation of the Catholic belief in transubstantiation, something that Protestants rejected. Elizabeth's personal faith was ambiguous, perhaps deliberately so as she famously said that she 'did not wish to make windows into men's souls'. Her aim was to create a compromise settlement that would be acceptable to as many of her subjects as possible and which would allow her political survival. By presenting a religiously ambiguous front, she could aim to appeal to as wide a range of people as possible.

How was the Elizabethan religious settlement reached, 1558–59?

Like her predecessors, Elizabeth had to use parliament to legalise her religious settlement. However, she faced some problems, mainly in the House of Lords where there were influential Catholic sympathisers among the nobility – about half of whom were Catholic – and all of the bishops appointed by Mary. As a result, Elizabeth's first parliamentary bill of 1559, which attempted to enforce her Royal Supremacy and create a Protestant religious settlement, was defeated by the Lords in March 1559. Elizabeth and Cecil realised that if they were to get a more Protestant religious settlement, they would need to undermine the Lords' power. They did this in several ways during a parliamentary break for Easter:

- A debate was held between Catholic and Protestant supporters. This was organised by Protestants such as Cecil and led to a Catholic walkout.

- Bishops White of Winchester and Watson of Lincoln were arrested and sent to the Tower for their refusal to take part in the debate, thus decreasing the influence of the bishops in the Lords.

- On 2 April, the peace treaty of Cateau-Cambrésis was signed with France. This decreased the likelihood of a French-led Catholic invasion.

On parliament's return, instead of one bill, two separate bills were introduced: the bills for Supremacy and for Uniformity. The aim was to ensure that even if the more controversial Uniformity bill ran into trouble, the restoration of the Supremacy would not be affected. But even in the Supremacy bill there was compromise, since Elizabeth took the title 'Supreme Governor' rather than 'Supreme Head' of the Church. This was an attempt to appeal to both Catholics, who only recognised the pope as supreme head, and some Protestants who did not like the idea of a woman as head of the Church. This bill also ensured that Elizabeth's governorship would be accepted by including an oath of loyalty to be taken by all officials; the penalty for refusing to take the oath was to be loss of office. The bill was passed by both the Commons and the Lords without problem.

However, the bill of Uniformity still faced problems from the Lords because it was more Protestant than the Catholic peers were prepared to allow. The bill was actually a compromise in terms of the doctrines it aimed to enforce. For example, although it reimposed the more radical 1552 prayer book with a fine of 12d (pence) for those who refused to attend weekly church services, two sentences were added to the Communion service from the more moderate 1549 prayer book. These were 'The body/blood of our Lord Jesus Christ which was given for thee, preserve thy body and soul unto everlasting life'. This meant that Catholics could still believe that transubstantiation had taken place, while Protestants could interpret the wording differently. Another compromise in the bill was that Church decoration and the clergy's vestments were to be returned to their 1548 state, that is, before the most radical Protestant changes of 1549. Again, this was an attempt to moderate the settlement to appeal to the Catholic lords, but even so the bill only narrowly passed the Lords vote by 21 to 18. Arguably, Elizabeth and Cecil's careful management of the situation, and in particular the absence of the two imprisoned Catholic bishops plus the Abbot of Westminster (who mysteriously missed the vote) was decisive in the eventual passing of the Act of Uniformity.

Following the successful passing of the two acts, Elizabeth was able to enforce her settlement through the new Oath of Supremacy. All but one of Mary's bishops (the aged Bishop of Llandaff) refused to take the oath and were deprived of their posts. This allowed Elizabeth to appoint Protestant sympathisers in their place, including Matthew Parker (Anne Boleyn's chaplain) as Archbishop of Canterbury. The initial acceptance of the settlement among the lower clergy can be seen in the fact that only about 300 out of 8,000 refused the oath and were deprived of their offices. Although some of these bishops and other reformers put pressure on Elizabeth for more Protestant reform, the initial settlement created in 1559 was to last for the rest of the reign, and became the basis for what is known as the Elizabethan Church of England.

The Elizabethan Settlement, 1559–63

Although Elizabeth I was determined to accept no changes to the 1559 Settlement, she did issue a set of injunctions in 1559 that further defined the operation of the Church. These injunctions included instructions on what the clergy were to wear: 'seemly habits, garments and such square caps', which had been used in Edward's reign. Elizabeth's own dislike of clerical marriage was reflected in how difficult it was made for a priest to take a wife – he needed the permission of two JPs and his bishop. Clergy were also ordered to preach at least four times a year, and all parish churches were to have an English copy of the Bible.

However, after the 1559 Settlement, Elizabeth preferred to leave matters of doctrine to Convocation, but she was still prepared to intervene when she was unhappy with what they were doing. In 1563, Convocation met to discuss the 42 articles of faith introduced in Edward VI's reign; these were to become the 39 Articles. At this meeting, a group of Puritans tried to continue what they saw as further and necessary reform of the Church, which they considered had not gone far enough. Under Puritan pressure, the Convocation passed article 29, which denied the real presence in the Communion; this was unacceptable to both Catholics and moderate Protestants. Elizabeth was forced to step in. She ordered the article to be left out, so in fact only 38 were originally published. She also refused to allow the 39 Articles to be passed by parliament until 1571. Nor did the Puritan challenge end there. At the same Convocation, they put forward six articles that would have made the appearance of the Church and its services much more radical. These articles included the demand that the minister should wear a simple surplice and that those receiving Communion should not be made to kneel. Although the articles were defeated in Convocation by 59 votes to 58, they showed that the Puritans could represent a potential challenge to the Elizabethan Settlement.

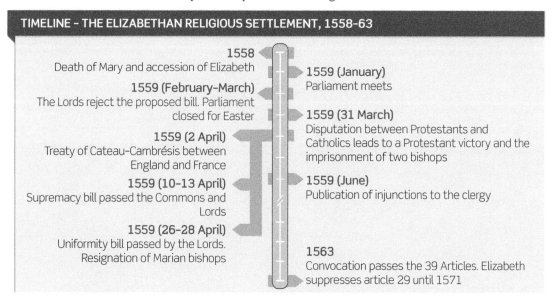

TIMELINE – THE ELIZABETHAN RELIGIOUS SETTLEMENT, 1558–63

1558
Death of Mary and accession of Elizabeth

1559 (January)
Parliament meets

1559 (February–March)
The Lords reject the proposed bill. Parliament closed for Easter

1559 (31 March)
Disputation between Protestants and Catholics leads to a Protestant victory and the imprisonment of two bishops

1559 (2 April)
Treaty of Cateau-Cambrésis between England and France

1559 (June)
Publication of injunctions to the clergy

1559 (10–13 April)
Supremacy bill passed the Commons and Lords

1559 (26–28 April)
Uniformity bill passed by the Lords. Resignation of Marian bishops

1563
Convocation passes the 39 Articles. Elizabeth suppresses article 29 until 1571

SOURCE

5   Speech by Viscount Montagu (an opponent of the Supremacy) to parliament on the Supremacy bill and its likely consequences, 1559.

In changing of religion we condemn all other nations, of whom some be our friends and many our enemies, open and ancient, who long time have, and no doubt do expect, an opportunity to annoy us. If the pope hearing us by schism divided from the Church do proceed to the excommunication of the realm... how enjoyeth the king of Spain? And thereby authority given to him to possess the same that could by strong hand obtain it? This may be of right feared in ourselves, being environed [surrounded] and, as it were, set about in one of two so potent enemies, who as you know would be loath to lose such opportunity... And add to this our own weakness and poverty at home: men's minds discontented, great sums of money due, and more of necessity demanded; and chiefly remember the evil nature of our people that always upon a little liberty are ready to rebel... who seeth not the peril of the realm almost inevitable?

SOURCE
6   D.M. Loades, on the years after the 1559 Act of Supremacy , in *Politics and the Nation, 1450–1660* (1974).

Apart from the dwindling number of the bishops, there was little opposition to these measures. Fewer than a dozen lay peers dissented, and there was no organised resistance in the Commons... The price was paid in the decade from 1558 to 1568, when the new and precarious Anglican settlement was challenged, not by a solid body of the Catholic faithful, but by a few individuals... The vast number of the parochial [parish]clergy conformed. Like their parishioners, most of them probably preferred the Mass to Protestant Communion, but they were not prepared to make any sacrifices for their preference and resorted to grumbling and evasion.

AS Level Exam-Style Question Section B

Mary I attempted to restore the English Church to Catholicism.

To what extent did Mary I succeed in changing the English Church in the years 1553–58? (20 marks)

Tip

Make sure that you consider both sides of the argument – Mary's successes as well as failures.

THINKING HISTORICALLY   Change (4a)

The significance of the establishment of the Royal Supremacy under Elizabeth I, 1559.

1 In what ways does Viscount Montagu think that the Supremacy Act might be significant?

2 How significant does Montagu seem to think the Supremacy Act might be in the long run?

3 Compare this to historian David Loades. What significance does Loades ascribe to the Supremacy Act?

4 Why do you think these views might differ so greatly?

A Level Exam-Style Question Section A

How far was religious change in the years 1547–63 driven by the personal religious beliefs of successive monarchs? (20 marks)

Tip

You will need to consider the role of the personal beliefs of Edward, Mary and Elizabeth as well as other reasons for religious change.

ACTIVITY
KNOWLEDGE CHECK

The Elizabethan Settlement

1 Find aspects of the Elizabethan Settlement that might please:

   a) Catholics

   b) Protestants

   c) Elizabeth.

2 Were there any parts of the Settlement that could cause potential problems for Elizabeth?

3 Explain how far you would agree with the view that 'the Elizabethan Settlement was a compromise which pleased nobody'.

THINKING HISTORICALLY Change (4b&c)

What were the consequences of the break with Rome?

The development	Medium-term consequences	Long-term consequences
The English Reformation 1532–43	People demanded that power was held by members of the Church of England rather than non-conformists or Roman Catholics	Technically, the monarch must still be a member of the Church of England, but not many people really care one way or the other. The English Reformation still has some effect on the arrangements that the British have for their government, i.e. a parliament rules with a monarch as head of state

Imagine you are looking at the whole of history using a zoomed-out interactive map like Google Maps. You have a general view of the sweep of developments and their consequences, but you cannot see much detail. If you zoom in to the time of the English Reformation, you can see the event in detail but will know nothing of its consequences in the medium or long term. If you zoom in to look at the medium- or long-term consequences, you will know about them in detail but will know very little about the events that caused them. For example, the growth of Puritanism led to the rise of a determined group of opponents to the monarchy in the reign of Charles I. It was this group, led by Puritan MPs such as John Pym, which was prepared to challenge the royal prerogative; the growth of radical religious and political ideas in the 1640s eventually led to the execution of Charles. Looking even further into the 17th century, fear of Catholicism and its links to tyranny led to the deposition of the legal heir, the Catholic James II, in favour of his daughter Mary and her husband William of Orange, who were Protestant; this was known as the Glorious Revolution (1688).

Look at the table above and answer the following questions:

1 What were the immediate consequences of the development?

2 In what ways are the medium-term consequences different to the long-term consequences?

3 Work in groups of three.
  Each student takes the role of the teacher for one of the above (the development, medium-term consequences or long-term consequences) and gives a short presentation to the other two. They may comment and ask questions. After each presentation, the other two group members write a 100-word paragraph showing how the presentation links to their own.

Answer the following questions individually:

4 What happens to the detail when you zoom out to look at the whole sweep of history?

5 What are the advantages and disadvantages of zooming in to look at a specific time in detail?

6 How could you use the map in order to get a good understanding of history as a whole?

TO WHAT EXTENT DID CATHOLICISM SURVIVE IN ENGLAND?

What were popular attitudes to Catholicism?

Until the break with Rome in the 1530s, Catholicism was the sole faith in England and had been for hundreds of years. The Roman Catholic Church was an integral part of every stage of ordinary people's lives, from cradle to grave. Local churches and monasteries were also often the sole providers of education, health care and help for the poor. However, when the Reformation occurred in England, it was assumed by historians such as A.G. Dickens that this was an inevitable result of the Catholic Church becoming too wealthy, corrupt and distant from its congregation. Certainly, there was criticism of the Church, but as the historians Eamon Duffy, Richard Rex and Christopher Haigh have emphasised, there is also considerable evidence that suggests the Catholic Church was still popular and even growing in its popularity.

English Catholics believed that salvation of the soul lay through belief in God and thought that through God's grace (mercy), there could be forgiveness for sins. When a person died, it was thought that their soul would spend time in purgatory as penance for their wrongdoing during their lives, but that this time could be reduced by their actions on earth. Forgiveness could be achieved in a number of ways, for example through receiving sacraments such as baptism, attending the Eucharist (Mass), and the confession of sins and doing penance for them. Because everyone would sin regularly, it was important to keep seeking forgiveness; it was not uncommon to go to Mass every day. The soul could also be helped by the purchase of indulgences issued by the pope or bishops, which were believed to reduce the time spent in purgatory. The very wealthy could leave money in their wills to build chantries where priests would be employed to pray for the souls of the benefactor. Those with less money would still pay for a priest to say Masses for their soul. There were also other ways to reduce the soul's time in purgatory, for example prayer to the saints and pilgrimages. It was thought that those closer to God and Jesus – the saints – could intercede for sinners on earth and could also perform miracles such as curing serious illness. As a result, saints, and the shrines where their relics were kept, were venerated. The most famous of these included the shrine of St Thomas Becket at Canterbury, the shrine to Our Lady (Jesus' mother) at Walsingham (Norfolk), and the Holy Blood (of Jesus) at Hailes Abbey (Gloucestershire). All of these shrines, together with many others, drew hundreds if not thousands of pilgrims who would visit the shrines to pray to the saints. Such was the continuing popularity of pilgrimages that many of these centres of pilgrimage suffered economic decline when the shrines were destroyed in the 1530s.

Saints' days were also celebrated and helped to mark the passage of the year. These were often known as 'holy days' (or 'holidays'). The most popular of these marked the life of the Blessed Virgin Mary. Living holy men and women also attracted popular attention, such as Elizabeth Barton (the Holy Maid of Kent), whose prophesies and preaching while in a trance-like state drew large audiences in the early 1530s. Popular Catholicism can also be seen in a new trend, the building of pulpits in churches, which began in the late 14th century. Pulpits were used for preaching, and their addition in many parish churches shows that sermons were an increasingly popular method of spreading understanding about the Catholic faith. Ironically, the use and importance of sermons is usually associated with Protestantism, but they were also being used by the Catholic Church long before the English Reformation. Catholicism was still very much alive in the early 16th century, and the Church was a fundamental part of ordinary peoples' lives. This helps to explain why there was at least some resistance to religious change, such as the Pilgrimage of Grace, and why Catholicism survived throughout the Tudor period.

The extent of the religious changes, 1529–36

Henry VIII's break with Rome in the 1530s led to a top-down process of change that altered the appearance, liturgy and doctrine of local churches to a considerable extent in that decade.

The first significant changes began with the enforcement of the Royal Supremacy. Under the Supremacy Act and the Treason Act of 1534, it became an offence punishable by death to deny that Henry was the Supreme Head of the English Church. All adult men were required to take an Oath of Supremacy, which was administered by specially appointed commissioners. These Acts were used to target those who opposed the Supremacy and Henry's marriage to Anne Boleyn, and there were some high-profile victims, such as Sir Thomas More (the former chancellor) in 1535 and Elizabeth Barton (the Holy Maid of Kent) in 1534. The Maid had been encouraged by opponents of the Supremacy to prophesy an early death for the king if he married Anne Boleyn. On a local level, all parish clergy were also required to take an oath renouncing the power of the pope and to remove all references to the pope from the prayer books. As the king's vicegerent, in 1534, Cromwell encouraged a preaching campaign in parish churches, which reinforced the message that the Royal Supremacy was legal, as was Henry's marriage to Anne. However, it appears that not all parish clergy obeyed Cromwell's orders, as in 1535 he issued orders to bishops and JPs telling them to arrest and imprison clergy who were still preaching in support of papal supremacy.

Cromwell's reforms, 1535–36

Cromwell's attempts to alter the English Church continued throughout 1535 and 1536, though they did not reach their height until 1538. Indulgences were discouraged because they were considered an unnecessary superstition, and they disappeared very rapidly during the 1530s. Similarly, belief in purgatory was attacked, especially through the dissolution of the monasteries. Even before the break with Rome, there had been criticism of the Catholic Church's use of false relics. The visitation of the monasteries carried out by Cromwell's commissioners in 1535 aimed to expose these abuses, and many relics were destroyed in 1538.

Some further changes to the appearance and ordinary people's experience of worship occurred as a result of Cromwell's first set of injunctions (1536) and the passing of the Act of Ten Articles. The Act enforced a moderate form of Protestantism and allowed for the interpretation of the Eucharist to remain ambiguous. However, Cromwell followed this by pushing Convocation to pass an Act that removed many of the traditional feast days, especially those that fell during the harvest period of July to September. The reason given was that the existence of so many feast days and 'holidays' was damaging the economy, but this was also an attack on traditional Catholic beliefs and practices. Cromwell then published his first set of injunctions to the clergy. These required all clergymen to preach the Supremacy and follow the doctrine put forward in the Ten Articles. The injunctions also ordered that children should learn the Lord's Prayer and the Ten Commandments in English, not the traditional Latin; every priest was to purchase a copy of the English and Latin Bible, which was to be placed in the parish church for anyone who wished to read it. Finally, the injunctions attacked 'superstitions' such as pilgrimages and the worship of images.

However, the most important change to popular religion was the dissolution of the smaller monasteries in 1536. Monasteries such as Hailes were often important centres for the cult of saint worship and pilgrimages. A key focus of the monastic life was also to pray for souls of the dead, lessening their time in purgatory.

For reformers such as Cromwell, they represented a form of religious belief that encouraged superstition and worship of saints and images rather than God. Indeed, some smaller monasteries that had been found to be corrupt had been shut down by Wolsey. Monasteries also often had links with foreign Catholic powers and with the pope himself; their continued existence represented a threat to Henry's supremacy. The Act passed in 1536 was to close the monasteries that made less than £200 a year. This affected 372 monasteries in England, though some gained an exemption.

The popular reaction in Lincolnshire and Yorkshire, known as the Pilgrimage of Grace, was swift and serious and was the largest of Henry's reign. The rebels demanded the return of the traditional Catholic religion, the papal supremacy and the reinstatement of the monasteries. They even called their rebellion a 'pilgrimage', a sign of their commitment to traditional forms of worship. This rebellion was eventually put down, and it did not stop Henry and Cromwell from dissolving the larger monasteries as well, but it is evidence of the popular anger caused by the attack on Catholic religious practices up to 1536.

To what extent were Cromwell's changes effective and lasting?

By 1536, some permanent changes had been made to the English Church. Indulgences disappeared, traditional concepts such as purgatory, the worship of saints and images, and pilgrimages were under attack. The smaller monasteries were closed down, and a moderately Protestant form of worship had been introduced. However, Catholicism had not yet disappeared and Cromwell found it difficult to stamp out popular practices that had been in place for centuries. For example, his campaign against purgatory in 1535–36 met with opposition from the Bishop of London, who openly preached at St Paul's in defence of prayers for the dead. Cromwell also had to issue a second set of injunctions to the clergy in 1538, which suggests that the first set did not have the desired effect. Similarly, his campaign to introduce a copy of the English Bible to every church in England only became properly effective in 1539 when the Great Bible was authorised by Henry VIII himself. Before that date, parish clergy had been told to buy a copy themselves, but copies had not been readily available for purchase. Finally, evidence from wills suggests that there was still strong popular belief in traditional Catholic doctrine and especially what would happen to someone's soul after death. Even in London, where Protestantism took root more quickly, 85 percent of wills made in the 1530s were using traditional references to saints and prayers for the soul. These references would gradually decline during the rest of the Tudor period, but for the 1530s they are strong evidence that the extent of religious change was still limited.

SOURCE

From the will of Joan Brytten, of Wood Street, London, dated 1540.

I bequeath my soul to almighty God and unto our Blessed Lady. I bequeath unto the high altar of Saint Michael's for my tithes negligently forgotten – 8d. For the rest of my goods, I will that a priest shall sing for my soul, my master Milard's soul, his wife's soul, and all Christian souls within the church of Saint Gregory's for six months.

How and why did Catholicism survive in the regions?

English Catholicism had first been undermined in Henry VIII's reign but came under serious attack under Edward VI. Between 1547 and 1553 there was a move to radical Protestantism, which saw fundamental changes to the doctrine, liturgy and appearance of local churches. These changes led partly to a rebellion in Cornwall and Devon in 1549, triggered by the government's order for all clergy to use the new prayer book. The rebels demanded among other things a return to the religiously conservative Act of Six Articles of 1539, prayers for the dead and services in Latin. Although this rebellion was suppressed, resentment of changes imposed by Edward's government can be seen in Duffy's famous study of the parish of Morebath (Devon). Duffy found that, although the villagers usually conformed to government orders, they resented the Edwardian changes to the extent that in 1552 they concealed the priest's traditional vestments from government officials rather than surrender them as they had been ordered to do. This evidence of both open and passive resistance suggests that popular Catholicism in regions such as the west of England remained strong. The west was particularly remote from the London central government; as a result, it was harder for the Tudor monarchs to enforce their will directly on the region. So the west remained a Catholic stronghold to the extent that attempts to introduce Protestant reforms by government officials led to the serious rebellion in 1549.

Under Mary, the restoration of England to papal control encouraged the recovery of Catholicism, although Mary's short reign meant that her success was limited and temporary. However, under Elizabeth, Catholicism in the regions came under increasing pressure, but still survived at the end of the reign, albeit as an increasingly underground movement among those who could afford it. Apart from the west, the north of England, especially Yorkshire and Lancashire, remained Catholic. This survival of Catholic traditions was made possible partly by Elizabeth's own approach. In the 1560s, Elizabeth's policy was to create a settlement that would allow most moderate Catholics to conform. The 1559 Settlement and the 39 Articles (1563) kept the doctrine of the Church of England as moderate as possible. In particular, the liturgy of the Communion was made deliberately ambiguous so that both moderate Protestants and Catholics would be more likely to accept it. This policy led to the development of a group known as 'Church papists', a moderate majority of Catholics who conformed outwardly to the Church of England. In addition, until the threat of a Catholic rebellion became serious from 1568, the authorities were often prepared to turn a blind eye to Catholic recusant activity. This allowed the Catholic faith to remain strong. Even when the government tightened controls on **recusants**, it was still unable to stop recusant activity. In Lancashire, there were 304 identified recusants in 1578; in Yorkshire there were 750 in 1582. Survival of Catholic traditions and practices was also supported by the existence of conservative clergy who had received their training before 1559 and who continued to cling to older traditions well into the 1580s. This was partly because there were not yet enough educated Protestant clergy to minister to every parish.

In 1583, for example, the preacher Thomas Gibson complained about the old priests' influence: 'the people are still in ignorance and blindness and kept still in their popish errors… they know not the use of the sacraments… they hold still to papistical transubstantiation.' Even worse for the government, Catholic priests who had been deprived of the posts after the 1559 settlement continued to serve as private tutors and priests for Catholic families. Again, this trend was particularly strong in the north; it has been estimated that there were 150 deprived priests active in Yorkshire in the 1560s and 1570s.

The survival of Catholicism was not just limited to the outlying regions of England. Haigh has shown that some Church of England congregations still clung to Catholic practices not just because of their priests, but because they preferred them. For example, there were parishioners in Berkshire who in 1584 were still refusing to receive the Protestant version of **Communion in both kinds**, and in 1569–70, 132 recusants were identified in Hampshire. This evidence suggests that varying practices still continued within the Church of England and were tolerated to some extent under the Elizabethan compromise. However, the longer that Elizabeth survived, the longer her compromise became widely accepted and it became harder to remain openly Catholic. This decline can be explained by a combination of the increasingly hard-line approach of Elizabeth's government together with the difficulties ordinary Catholics faced in maintaining their faith.

KEY TERMS

Recusant
A term applied to those who refused to attend Church of England services.

Communion in both kinds
Protestants believed that communicants should receive both the bread and the wine ('both kinds'). In Catholic tradition, communicants received only the bread.

ACTIVITY
KNOWLEDGE CHECK

Catholic influences

1 Read the will in Source 7. What does this suggest about this person's faith? What does it suggest about the influence of the Catholic Church?

2 From what you have read so far, which of the changes made by Henry were likely to be permanent? Which were likely to be temporary?

3 What evidence is there that England was still predominantly a Catholic country by 1540?

Recusancy and the Jesuit missions under Elizabeth I

In 1559, the Act of Uniformity required everyone to attend a Church of England service each Sunday, but the punishment for non-attendance was set at 12d (1 shilling). This was affordable for wealthier members of society such as members of the gentry and nobility. This meant that wealthier recusants at least continued to worship in private Masses, with government authorities often turning a blind eye. However, in the late 1560s, political circumstances changed, meaning that Catholics came under increasing suspicion of being possible rebels and traitors because their loyalties were potentially divided between Elizabeth and the pope.

These circumstances included:

- the arrival of the Catholic Mary, Queen of Scots in England in 1568; she had a claim to the throne and became a figurehead for Catholics who wanted to overthrow Elizabeth

- the deterioration of English relations with Spain caused by tensions over the Netherlands (where Dutch Protestants were revolting against Spanish Catholic rule) and English piracy in the New World that targeted Spanish shipping

- the Revolt of the Northern Earls (1569), which aimed to marry the Duke of Norfolk to Mary, Queen of Scots, to restore Catholic practices and to get Mary recognised as heir to the throne

- the papal excommunication of Elizabeth in 1570; this could have led all loyal Catholics to rise up against the 'heretic' queen and overthrow her.

Although the majority of Catholics chose national loyalty to their queen and country rather than to a foreign power, the result of these increased tensions was that Elizabeth came under pressure from her Council and parliament to enact harsher punishments against Catholics. At the same time, the Catholic threat seemed to be increasing as a result of the arrival of English Catholic priests in England from 1574. These priests had been trained in a Catholic seminary specially set up in Douai (in the Netherlands) in 1568 by the English Catholic William Allen, who had fled England. Allen's example was followed in Rome, Valladolid and Seville with the intention that Catholicism could be reintroduced to England through their trainees' work. During Elizabeth's reign, these seminaries sent about 800 priests to England, who were supported in secret by Catholic recusants. English-trained Jesuit priests also began to arrive in England, including Cuthbert Mayne, Edmund Campion and Robert Parsons. These highly trained and educated men and those who sheltered them were seen by Elizabeth's government as a threat to political stability and were dealt with harshly when caught.

The Catholic plots against Elizabeth and the government response

Encouraged by Elizabeth's excommunication and the presence of Mary, Queen of Scots, a few Catholic recusants and their sympathisers became involved in plots to assassinate Elizabeth and replace her with Mary. In 1571, the Duke of Norfolk was implicated in a plot by a Florentine banker, Roberto Ridolfi, to use a Spanish invasion force to remove Elizabeth and replace her with Mary. Norfolk was executed in 1572 and parliament attempted to pass an Act of Parliament that would have banned Mary from the English succession. Elizabeth would not agree to this and prorogued (suspended) parliament until 1576, but she did agree to other Acts that tightened control on English Catholics. These included a law that made it treason to bring the bull of excommunication into the country. Further threats followed, however, with the arrival of the seminary and Jesuit priests.

In 1577, Cuthbert Mayne was the first to be captured and executed, and his host was imprisoned for life. In 1581, Elizabeth agreed to stricter laws against recusants, including a huge increase in the fine for non-attendance of church services to £20 a month and a strengthening of the Treason Act. However, the pressure for Elizabeth to act against the recusants increased still further when her spymaster, Walsingham, discovered another plot to put Mary on the throne in 1583. This time, the plot was even more of a threat because it involved a group of English Catholic gentry including Francis Throckmorton, the Spanish ambassador Mendoza and the French Catholic Duke of Guise. This plot led to the Bond of Association, a document circulated by Elizabeth's Council. Those who signed the Bond pledged to put to death anyone who tried to gain the throne by harming Elizabeth. The parliament of 1584–85 once again sought to tighten controls on Catholic priests and their recusant supporters. This led to the Bond being made law.

An Act against Catholic priests also ordered them to leave the country within 40 days or be executed for treason. Anyone found guilty of helping them would also face the death penalty. By now, fears of assassination had gained new strength following the assassination of the Protestant Dutch leader by a Spanish Catholic sympathiser in 1584. Also, in 1585, England was finally being drawn into a war with Spain after years of increasing tension. This meant that there was a strong possibility of a foreign Catholic invasion force combining with Catholic recusants and Mary Stuart to remove Elizabeth. The situation was made even worse by the existence of an alliance between Philip II and French Catholics, known as the Catholic League. In 1586, these fears became justified when Walsingham discovered another plot to assassinate Elizabeth involving Mary (an English Catholic), Anthony Babington and the French ambassador who supported the League.

Unlike previous plots, Mary was directly implicated by letters she had written to Babington. Pressure from parliament and her Council forced the reluctant Elizabeth into signing Mary's death warrant, though she was furious when she found that her orders had been carried out.

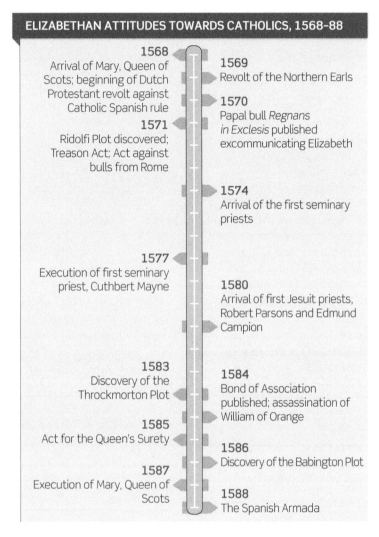

ELIZABETHAN ATTITUDES TOWARDS CATHOLICS, 1568–88

1568
Arrival of Mary, Queen of Scots; beginning of Dutch Protestant revolt against Catholic Spanish rule

1569
Revolt of the Northern Earls

1570
Papal bull *Regnans in Exclesis* published excommunicating Elizabeth

1571
Ridolfi Plot discovered; Treason Act; Act against bulls from Rome

1574
Arrival of the first seminary priests

1577
Execution of first seminary priest, Cuthbert Mayne

1580
Arrival of first Jesuit priests, Robert Parsons and Edmund Campion

1583
Discovery of the Throckmorton Plot

1584
Bond of Association published; assassination of William of Orange

1585
Act for the Queen's Surety

1586
Discovery of the Babington Plot

1587
Execution of Mary, Queen of Scots

1588
The Spanish Armada

What was the impact of the Jesuit and seminary priests?

Seminary and Jesuit priests played a role in keeping alive Catholic recusancy, even as the laws against them became harsher. John Bossy has argued that the arrival of the priests transformed low-level and disorganised Catholic resistance in the 1560s into something more organised and determined. Certainly, the numbers of recusants recorded by the government went up rather than down during Elizabeth's reign. The number of Lancashire recusants had increased to 3,516 by 1603. However, the rise in recusants was not actually the result of the missionary priests' successes. In fact, the increased numbers were because the authorities were keeping better records and a closer eye on possible threats.

Many priests were courageous and were prepared to die for their faith, such as Cuthbert Mayne and Robert Campion, thus setting an example for their followers. Yet by the end of the reign, actively practising Catholics were a minority. It has been estimated that by 1603 only 50,000 Catholics, including Church papists, remained in a population of about four million.

This was partly the result of the harsher government response to recusancy. However, the seminary and Jesuit priests themselves were not completely effective and their activities led to the survival of a particular type of Catholicism. This is because most priests came into England via the ports in the south-east such as Dover and Rye. Most did not then move very far beyond this region, which was an area where there were fewer practising Catholics and where Protestantism had taken root. Haigh has found that in 1580, half of the missionary priests in England were working in Essex, London and the Thames Valley, where only one-fifth of recusants lived. Meanwhile, only one-fifth of the priests had gone to the north of England, where 40 percent of known recusants lived. These geographical variations meant that for some practising Catholics, however loyal they were, there was no practising priest. The result was that many ordinary Catholics moved back into the Church of England. The recusants who did continue to practise were from the nobility and gentry.

What was the role of the Catholic nobility?

The support of the Catholic nobility and members of the gentry allowed Catholicism to survive in England. At the start of the reign, some members of the nobility were openly Catholic, such as Thomas Percy (Earl of Northumberland), while Thomas Howard (Duke of Norfolk) was Protestant in name but Catholic in his sympathies. Northumberland and Norfolk were both eventually executed for treason. Although most Catholic nobility and gentry were not prepared to go this far, it was their status, power and wealth that allowed them to protect the missionary priests and led to the development of what Haigh has called 'seigneurial Catholicism', which was particularly strong in the north; in the 1560s, about 75 percent of the leading families of Yorkshire were Catholic. The reasons for this are partly because many of the missionary priests were themselves from landed families. Also, because so many of the missionary priests remained in the south and east of England where Catholicism was less dominant and the threat of arrest higher, they turned naturally to those with the money and position to protect them – the Catholic gentry and nobility. Two Catholic priests, William Weston and Henry Garnet, even organised a type of employment agency for fellow priests, which placed them in the households of sympathetic gentry and nobility. This meant that many missionary priests became the equivalent of family chaplains rather than serving a whole community. Poorer Catholics could not afford to house a priest or regularly access Catholic services and tended to conform to Church of England practices as a result. These developments help to explain both the survival of Catholicism and the recusancy figures during Elizabeth's reign, but the Catholicism that survived was a minority religion practised by members of landed society who could more afford to do so.

SOURCE

8 Account of Thomas Stanney (a missionary priest in Hampshire, 1590) of the response of poorer Catholics.

We still have a great many hungry souls that want bread, and there is no one to give it to them; we have many also that would be glad to shake off the yoke of bondage, heresy and embrace the Catholic faith, and I can find none to help them and receive them into the Church.

ACTIVITY
KNOWLEDGE CHECK

Key events

1 Use what you have read so far in this chapter to fill in this table.

Event	Who was involved?	What happened?	How much of a threat to Elizabeth?
Arrival of Mary, Queen of Scots			
Revolt of the Northern Earls			
Elizabeth's excommunication			
Ridolfi Plot			
Throckmorton Plot			
Babington Plot			

2 From what you have read, find three examples of Catholic survival under Elizabeth I.

3 On a blank map, record where Catholicism remained strong and where it declined.

4 Make a list of reasons why Catholicism began to decline by the end of the reign of Elizabeth I.

HOW AND WHY DID PROTESTANTISM GROW, 1509–88?

Protestant influences in England before 1527

Although Protestantism was a term not generally in use before the 1520s, the influences that helped to create English Protestantism were present before the break with Rome. However, without the king's desire for a male heir, which created the circumstances for Protestantism to grow, it is unlikely that the English Church would have developed in the way that it did.

Although the Catholic Church was by no means weak by the early 16th century, it had its critics. Early forms of criticism dated back to the late 1300s when a preacher named John Wycliffe and his followers the Lollards attacked the Church for its corruption and promoted an English version of the Bible. The Lollards were swiftly dealt with, but the tradition that they created remained and fed later anti-clerical and Protestant feeling. By the early 16th century, the English Catholic Church was dominated by the clergy; the lay congregations had little part to play in church services, which were in Latin, not English. The congregation was cut off from the priest quite literally by the rood screen, which placed a physical divide between the laity and the clergy and meant that the congregation could see little of what was going on during the Mass. Although attendance at Mass was common, the congregation would only receive Communion three times a year and this was Communion of one kind only (the bread, not the wine).

The quality of the clergy was also varied and it was still common for many of them not to be university graduates. In London, two-thirds of the clergy had a degree, but in more rural areas it was possible that some of the congregation would be better educated than their priest. In the diocese of Norwich, for example, only 256 clergy had a degree out of 1,454 appointed in the years 1503 to 1528. This meant that the quality of care and preaching their parishioners might receive was varied. In addition, some clergy had multiple positions, which meant that they were absent from their parishes. The most famous example of this was Cardinal Wolsey, who was Archbishop of York as well as Bishop of Lincoln and Tournai. Wolsey did not even visit York until his fall in 1529.

Some clergy were also criticised for their morals. Catholic priests were supposed to be celibate, but sometimes this vow was broken and priests not only kept 'concubines' but had illegitimate children as well. Wolsey himself had an illegitimate son.

Some monasteries were open to criticism for their wealth and low moral standards. Wolsey investigated and closed down about 30 institutions between 1524 and 1529 for these reasons, though his own personal wealth and arrogance also led to criticism.

However, before 1529, popular criticism of the Church was not linked to attempts to overthrow its power. There were outbursts of anti-clerical feeling, such as that provoked by the Hunne case of 1511–15, but the Protestant reformation that followed was not inevitable.

AS Level Exam-Style Question Section B

To what extent did English Catholicism decline in the years 1558–88? (20 marks)

Tip

To answer this question you need to consider both strengths and weaknesses in popular Catholicism. This might include geographical and social differences.

A Level Exam-Style Question Section A

How accurate is it to say that Catholicism remained a serious threat to Elizabeth I's security throughout the years 1558–88? (20 marks)

Tip

You will need to cover the whole period and consider what is meant by a 'serious threat' to security.

Protestant influences from the 1520s

In the early 16th century, the Catholic Church came under criticism from humanists such as Erasmus who wanted to see reform of the corruption and wealth of the Church but did not wish to break away from it. However, the actions of Martin Luther in 1519 led to the movement eventually known as Protestantism, which criticised not only Catholic corruption but also its appearance, doctrine and liturgy. Luther's ideas began to arrive in England in the 1520s, spread by the import of printed books. The first burnings of heretic books took place in 1521. The first known Lutheran was the friar Robert Barnes, who preached his controversial views at Cambridge in 1525 and was executed for heresy in 1540.

Other Cambridge academics were also influenced by Luther's ideas at this time. They included important thinkers and writers such as William Tyndale and Miles Coverdale (who both translated and published versions of the English Bible), Hugh Latimer (who was famous for his preaching), and the future Archbishop of Canterbury, Thomas Cranmer. Lutherans were also discovered at the Oxford college founded by Wolsey himself in 1528. These men argued for greater emphasis in the role of the Bible which they thought should be accessible to all, a return to a simpler and less corrupt Church, and they challenged the Catholic Church's teaching on transubstantiation and the supreme role of the pope, claiming that there was no biblical precedent for either. These ideas gained some supporters at Henry's court, including Thomas Cromwell, Sir Anthony Denny and Anne Boleyn.

What was the role of Anne Boleyn?

As Henry's potential mistress, Anne Boleyn did not have direct power over government, but she did have considerable behind-the-scenes influence with the king. Having spent much of her youth in France, where she had been well educated, Anne came to the English court in 1521 and by 1524–25 had already attracted Henry's attention. However, because Anne steadfastly refused to sleep with the king and become his chief mistress, her role, and the king's interest in her, became more significant as he fell in love with her, and by early 1527 he had promised to marry her. Anne continued to hold Henry's interest throughout his attempts to annul his marriage to Catherine and her own marriage to him until her fall in 1536, though her influence was increasingly shaken by her apparent inability to produce a living son and heir.

Anne was an influential figure at court who held religiously reformist views. Starkey argues that she was influenced by French thinkers with similar ideas to Luther, whom she read during her time abroad. In particular, Anne was interested in the study of the Bible and owned a copy written in French, not the traditional Latin. She also owned a psalter that contained a new, radical and French translation of the psalms. The ownership of such books was illegal, but Anne's influence meant that she was immune from prosecution. Anne's involvement went beyond an interest in reformer thought. Using their influence at court, she and her father Thomas supported the rise of Thomas Cranmer in 1529. Cranmer also had reformist sympathies and used his academic background to explore theological and historical arguments to challenge the papal supremacy.

Anne's promotion of reformers did not stop with Cranmer, who became Archbishop of Canterbury in 1532. She also employed Hugh Latimer, Nicholas Shaxton and William Barlow as chaplains in her household. All three men held reformist views and all three were promoted to bishoprics by Henry between 1534 and 1536. Another chaplain, Matthew Parker, was to become Elizabeth I's first Archbishop of Canterbury.

The development of Protestant influences, 1529–47

Although Henry was never a Protestant, and indeed burnt reformers for heresy, the break with Rome did encourage the development of Protestantism in England. The key years for these developments were 1529 to 1539, when those with reformist sympathies were able to influence the king. From late 1538, there was a conservative backlash, but by this time, popular Protestantism had taken hold in some regions, although Protestants were still a minority in 1547.

The ideas and actions of reformist sympathisers such as Cranmer and Cromwell were vital in allowing Henry to get his annulment and marry Anne. This is because they were prepared to encourage the idea that the pope had no authority in England and had usurped Henry's power. Henry was happy to believe this because it suited his own ideas about the power of the monarchy and allowed him to increase his control over the Church through the Supremacy. Cromwell also played on anti-clerical feeling in the Reformation parliament as a way to put pressure on both the pope and the English Church, for example in his drafting of the Supplication against the Ordinaries. He also shaped the Royal Supremacy, destroyed the legal power of the pope and pushed the Church in a Protestant direction.

Popular Protestantism also began to flourish, but only with the encouragement of the government. In 1529, anti-clerical feeling was stirred up by Simon Fish's publication 'A Supplication for the Beggars'. This pamphlet, which Anne Boleyn is said to have supported, criticised the wealth and corruption of the Catholic Church. It also challenged the key Catholic beliefs of purgatory and the sale of indulgences. Protestant ideas were also spread through the preaching campaign and religious changes enforced by Cromwell between 1534 and 1538. In London in particular, Protestant ideas gained a stronghold. London was the centre of a trade in heretical and illegal books and its trading links with the continent encouraged the exchange of more radical ideas. When the religiously conservative Act of Six Articles was passed in 1539, several hundred Londoners were interrogated by the bishop because they were suspected of breaking the law through their religious beliefs. From London, reformer beliefs spread to counties in the south-east such as Kent and Essex, where copies of the English Bible were being used. Reformist sympathisers such as Cranmer and Catherine Parr were also still present at court, although they had to be careful about what views they expressed. However, the Protestants remained a minority during Henry's reign. The fall of Cromwell in 1540 and the influence of a conservative faction at court led to a religious clampdown in which radicals such as Robert Barnes, who had previously been given a licence to preach, were burnt. It is estimated that in 1547, even in London, only one-fifth of the population were Protestant, which means that the majority of citizens still subscribed to traditional Catholic views.

Outside the capital city, the South East and centres of learning such as Oxford and Cambridge, Protestantism was still uncommon. The radical changes that occurred under Edward VI were the result of top-down pressure from the regents Somerset and Northumberland, not popular pressure from below.

SOURCE

9 Simon Fish, 'A Supplication for the Beggars', 1529.

The yearly exactions from the people taken by this greedy sort of sturdy idle holy thieves. They have a tenth part of all produce, wages and profits. What money pull they in by probates of testaments, privy tithes, men's offerings to their pilgrimages and at their first masses; by masses... by mortuaries, hearing of confessions (yet keeping thereof no secrecy)... by extortion &c.; ...These locusts own also one third of the land. Or in all more than half of the substance of the realm. Yet they are not in number, one to every hundred men, or one in every four hundred men women and children.

How did Protestantism develop under Edward VI?

Under the rule of Somerset and Northumberland, England took a dramatic step towards Protestantism. The changes that were imposed by the government between 1547 and 1553 completely altered the appearance and doctrine of parish churches and cathedrals alike. While these steps caused a Catholic reaction in the Western Revolt in 1549, in other parts of the country Protestantism began to take a hold, with the result that Mary found it difficult to turn the religious clock back to 1529.

One way in which the Edwardian reforms encouraged the growth of Protestantism was through the repeal of the Act of Six Articles and laws controlling the censorship of books. The result was a huge increase in the publication of books, including 159 radical Protestant works and just one Catholic work. This apparent openness to radical views also led to the formation of a group of radical thinkers who had been exiled from their own countries. These included two prominent theologians, Italian Peter Martyr and the Swiss Martin Bucer. Bucer was appointed professor of divinity at Cambridge, while Martyr held the rival position at Oxford. These men's lectures and writings attracted large audiences and influenced two future Elizabethan archbishops, Parker and Grindal. The abolition of the chantries in 1547 was also achieved without any opposition because popular belief in purgatory had been undermined to such an extent under Henry. After the outbreak of rebellion in 1549, there was no further unrest despite the fact that Northumberland's reforms were even more radical than those of Somerset.

By Edward's death in 1553, England's churches and services were undoubtedly Protestant, but does this mean that the population had embraced Protestantism as well? Although chantries had gone, services were in English and followed Protestant doctrine, and parish churches had lost most of their decoration and ornaments, this did not mean that England was now a fully Protestant country. Although nearly 300 men and women were prepared to martyr themselves for their faith under Mary, and a further 800 went into exile, this was a minority of the population.

As in Henry's reign, the effects of government policy were felt differently in different regions. In London and Kent, Protestantism gained in popularity, but in Sussex, 40 percent of the gentry remained Catholic until well into Elizabeth's reign. The north of England, especially Lancashire, also remained mostly Catholic. Historians also point to the number of priests who took advantage of the freedom to marry, something that Protestants promoted. In London, nearly one-third of the clergy got married, but in Lancashire just 10 percent of the clergy took a wife. As Penry Williams has argued, 'The general impression given by the Church in 1553 was that it contained some stalwart Catholics and Protestants, but that these men and women were in a minority. Most were confused and uncertain, acquiescent in any lead from above.'

ACTIVITY
KNOWLEDGE CHECK

Becoming Protestant

1 Read Source 9. What criticisms are made of the Catholic Church? Why would these criticisms have been particularly helpful to Henry in his attempts to annul his marriage to Catherine of Aragon?

2 Compare Anne Boleyn's role to those of Cromwell, Cranmer and Henry VIII. Who was the most important in bringing about the break with Rome?

3 What evidence is there that England had become Protestant by 1553?

4 Why was England not completely Protestant by this date?

What was Puritanism?

Puritans wanted to live a 'pure' or 'godly' lifestyle. They were Protestants, but they tended to have more radical beliefs. Under Elizabeth I, this group first emerged from among those who had gone into exile to avoid religious persecution under Mary. While abroad, they had been influenced by more extreme religious ideas, particularly those of John Calvin. All Puritans thought that the Elizabethan religious settlement was a starting point for further reform. However, the Puritans were not a united group. While some were able to accept and work within the structure and liturgy of the Church of England, others tried to change the Settlement, and a minority tried to reject it all together. These beliefs, even among the most moderate Puritans, brought them into conflict with Elizabeth herself, who was determined that the 1559 Settlement should not be altered. Puritans tended to emphasise the importance of the Bible as the centre of their faith.

EXTEND YOUR KNOWLEDGE

John Calvin
John Calvin was a radical Protestant thinker whose ideas were adopted in the Swiss town of Geneva. He emphasised the importance of reading the Bible. He also supported the idea that salvation could be achieved solely through faith (justification by faith alone) as well as belief in predestination, the idea that God had decided who would go to heaven. Calvin also rejected the traditional hierarchy of the Catholic Church.

This led them to reject beliefs and practices to which there was no reference in the Bible. They also tended to prefer churches and services that were simpler in their style and decoration since they believed that ornamentation was a distraction from their worship. Puritans emphasised the Word of God and the role of preaching. This meant that they favoured better education for clergymen. There were also disagreements about doctrine, particularly the interpretation of the Communion service and what happened to the bread and wine.

Moderate Puritans who were prepared to accept most elements of Church of England practice included men such as Edmund Grindal, a former exile under Mary who became Archbishop of Canterbury in 1570. Puritans like Grindal were prepared to work within the Church in order to change it for the better. They justified this using the idea of **adiaphora**. But even Grindal found that Elizabeth asked him to make one compromise too many and was suspended from his post as Archbishop of Canterbury.

KEY TERM

Adiaphora
This was the belief that some religious practices were not necessary for the salvation of the soul. Elizabeth thought this meant that she could pronounce on these issues, including clerical vestments and ornaments in the church, and that it would not harm anyone's soul. Some Puritans thought adiaphora meant that because something was not vital for the salvation of their soul, they did not have to do it.

The role of Calvinists

Some Puritans supported the Calvinist system of worship and organisation. Although they did not deny the role of the monarch, they thought that there was no biblical precedent for the traditional Church structure of archbishops and bishops. Instead, they favoured a system in which individual congregations could run themselves, led by the 'presbyters', the church elders and ministers. However, Calvinists also feared social disorder and so did not believe that each congregation should be allowed complete independence. They wanted England to adopt a national framework that would include regional and national meetings ('synods') of representatives from each congregation. These synods would then impose discipline on local congregations.

Although elements of Calvinist thought were present in the Elizabethan Settlement, the queen was not prepared to let the Church of England go further down this route. This was partly because her own religious tastes did not make her inclined to support these beliefs, but mostly because she feared that a more radical settlement would alienate moderate Lutherans and Catholics alike and thus destabilise her reign. Similarly, she was not prepared to allow individual congregations to run themselves because she feared the spread of dangerous religious and political ideas that might challenge her power. Unfortunately for Elizabeth, the moderate and Presbyterian Puritans, although a minority, were very determined and had powerful support from among her own bishops and nobility, which made it hard for her to defeat them quickly or completely.

How did Puritanism develop during Elizabeth's reign?

The Puritans tried several different methods to alter the Settlement. These included challenges through Convocation, through parliament and through local 'grass-roots' activities.

The Puritan challenge to the Settlement through Convocation emerged in 1563 with discussions over the 39 Articles and a Puritan attempt to introduce six articles to reform the Church. As we have seen, these were narrowly defeated and Elizabeth herself had to step in to suppress article 29, albeit temporarily. However, after this date, the government was more careful to control who was elected to sit in Convocation and the Puritans found that they were not able to manipulate this system any more.

Radical members of the clergy caused further debate within the Church between 1564 and 1566 over the issue of clerical vestments. While to the modern eye what a clergyman wears might not seem important, to some Puritans vestments represented something that was unbiblical. Once again, Elizabeth was determined to uphold the injunctions she had issued in 1559, which instructed clergymen on what to wear. The debate persisted, however, and in 1565 Elizabeth was forced to write to the Archbishop of Canterbury, Matthew Parker, complaining about bishops who permitted 'varieties, novelties and diversities' in clerical dress. Parker responded by ordering the bishops to make their clergy conform to Elizabeth's demands, but this had limited effect because in 1566 Parker had to issue the 'Advertisements', which ordered all clergy to wear the appropriate vestments. Parker then targeted the London clergy where Puritanism was particularly strong, and ordered 110 to appear at Lambeth dressed in the appropriate clothing. Thirty-seven refused and were suspended. Although this was a victory for Elizabeth in that she got her way, the Puritan challenge continued through both parliament and grass-roots activities of local congregations and clergy.

The Puritan challenge in parliament

Although Neale's thesis of a 'Puritan choir' in parliament can no longer be given credence, there were some MPs in Elizabeth's parliaments who were prepared to change the Settlement through parliamentary bills, which they hoped would become Acts. The first example of this was in 1571, when the moderate Puritan bishops tried to introduce the 'Alphabetical bills', so called because the bills were arranged and listed from A to F. These bills were an attempt by the bishops to improve clerical standards by attacking abuses such as pluralism. Unfortunately for the bishops, a Puritan MP, William Strickland, attempted to add his own version of the *Book of Common Prayer* to the Alphabetical bills. If Strickland had succeeded, he would have replaced the moderate prayer book enforced under the Act of Uniformity (1559). Elizabeth would not allow this to happen and used her royal veto to stop both of the bills. She was prepared to make one concession to the moderates, however, which was to allow the 39 Articles to become law.

Puritan pressure on parliament did not stop in 1571. There were further attempts to create a more Presbyterian system in the sessions of 1584 and 1587. The Puritans were helped by illegal printing presses that were used to produce pamphlets and books.

In 1584, there were Puritan attempts to advance a 'bill and book', which would have introduced a national Presbyterian Church and replaced the Elizabethan *Book of Common Prayer* with one based on services in Geneva. The attempt in 1584 was defeated as a result of a speech by one of Elizabeth's councillors, Christopher Hatton. In 1586, Elizabeth's response was to have the MPs responsible sent to the Tower.

The Puritan challenge from below

Puritan theologians and preachers often received powerful protection from sympathisers on Elizabeth's Council. These included Robert Dudley (the earl of Leicester) and Ambrose Dudley (the earl of Warwick). Reformers seeking to 'purify' the Church were also supported by Edmund Grindal (the archbishop of Canterbury) from 1575. This support, coupled with the difficulties in controlling the activities of local preachers, made it difficult for Elizabeth to completely stamp out support for Presbyterianism.

Two important leaders of the Puritan challenge were the theologian Thomas Cartwright and the clergyman John Field. In 1570, Cartwright gave a series of lectures at the University of Cambridge, which supported a Calvinist system. He lost his post as a result and spent much of his life abroad, but he was protected by the Earl of Leicester, who made him Master of the Lord Leicester Hospital (Warwick) in 1585. Cartwright also expressed support for John Field, who in 1572 published his *Admonitions to Parliament*, which was a vicious attack on the bishops. Field followed this up with *A View on the Popish Abuses Yet Remaining in the English Church*, which criticised the *Book of Common Prayer* and claimed that it was 'an unperfect book, culled and picked out of that popish dunghill, the Mass book of all abominations'. Field was imprisoned for a year, but this did not stop him promoting a Presbyterian structure. In the 1580s, he encouraged the growth of the **classes system**, informal meetings to which representatives of local congregations would send representatives, and which were often used for study and prayer by the clergy. However, this had little effect because of government action.

KEY TERM

Classes system
This was similar to, but not the same as, the Genevan model. The 'classes' or 'classical system' were informal meetings involving clergymen but not laymen, but there was no attempt to organise these on a national level.

An important Puritan challenge to the Elizabethan Settlement in the 1570s was 'prophesyings'. The emphasis placed by Puritans on sermons and reading the Bible led to informal meetings of clergy and their congregations, whose aim was to improve the quality of preaching. Clergy would preach in front of a mixed audience of lay members and 'moderators', other clergy whose role was to listen to the sermons and then give feedback to the preacher. For moderate Puritans such as Edmund Grindal, these prophesyings could be reconciled with membership of the Church of England. Grindal believed that there was a need to improve the quality of the clergy and as appointed Archbishop of Canterbury from 1575 he was prepared to support their continuation. However, Elizabeth wanted the prophesyings stopped. She feared that these meetings were a cover for the establishment of a Calvinist system, especially as it was difficult to control exactly what was being discussed at the meetings. Moreover, some prophesyings seemed to have got out of control. In the village of Southam (Warwickshire), for example, prophesyings were being held without the local bishop's knowledge but with the backing of the local gentry. In 1576, Elizabeth demanded that Grindal put a stop to all prophesyings. Grindal refused and was suspended from office until his death in 1583. In that year, Elizabeth wrote to all of her bishops instructing them that anyone caught participating in prophesyings should be imprisoned and their name sent to her Council. Elizabeth's actions stopped the prophesyings; however, she was not successful in stopping Puritans meeting in other ways.

How did the government respond to the Puritan challenge?

As her actions show, Elizabeth herself was not willing to allow any challenges to her Settlement. This meant that she was also prepared to enforce harsh punishments on Puritans who challenged her. Elizabeth's tactics were often to suppress or veto something she did not like, such as article 29 in the 39 Articles or the Alphabetical bills. She was also prepared to suspend her own Archbishop of Canterbury when he would not obey her and to send the supporters of Cope's 'bill and book' to the Tower. However, as the potential threat from Catholics increased in the late 1560s, Elizabeth found that she needed her Protestant supporters to back her against possible rebellion or invasion. This explains why she eventually allowed the 39 Articles to be made law in 1571, although on other issues, such as clerical dress and prophesyings, she remained firm.

Elizabeth was supported by the actions of government. When the prophesyings in Warwickshire got out of control, the Earl of Leicester attempted to calm the situation down, though he also continued to protect Puritan clergy. Members of the Council such as Christopher Hatton were used as Elizabeth's mouthpiece in parliament to discourage debate on religious matters. Elizabeth's bishops and archbishops also had a part to play. Although Grindal defied the queen, Matthew Parker (archbishop from 1559 until his death in 1575) and John Whitgift (archbishop from 1583 until the end of Elizabeth's reign), both supported her. Parker's 'Advertisements' in 1566 were written to the bishops on Elizabeth's instructions. He also used Convocation to control licences to preach. All clergy were asked to 'subscribe' completely to the 39 Articles before they were allowed to have their licences renewed. Preachers such as John Field were even summoned in person to swear not only to uphold the articles but also the prayer book and to wear the proper vestments. When Field would not do this he was suspended from preaching.

Whitgift's work against the Puritans went even further. Like Elizabeth, he was deeply unsympathetic to their aims and fully supported the terms of the 1559 Settlement. Whitgift tightened controls on Puritan clergy with the introduction of the Three Articles in 1583. All clergy were ordered to take an oath subscribing to all three articles. These articles required clergymen to support the Royal Supremacy, the *Book of Common Prayer* and the 39 Articles, and to subscribe to the view that there was nothing in any of these that was against the Word of God. Whitgift did not stop with this oath, however. He ordered that any clergymen suspected of Puritan activity were to take an *ex officio* oath. This meant that they had to swear to answer all questions truthfully before they knew what the questions were. The result of this harsh measure was that 300 clergymen in the diocese of Canterbury were suspended for refusing to take the oath. Under Whitgift, the challenge from the Calvinists died down considerably, although it did not disappear completely.

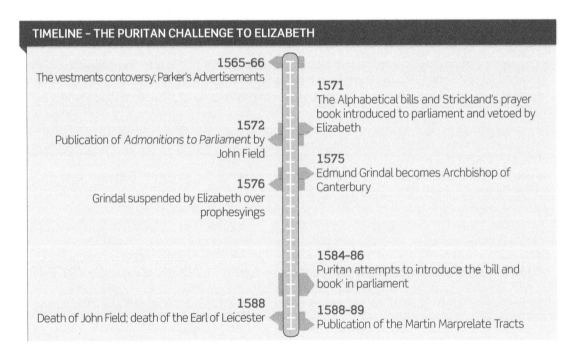

TIMELINE – THE PURITAN CHALLENGE TO ELIZABETH

1565–66
The vestments contoversy; Parker's Advertisements

1571
The Alphabetical bills and Strickland's prayer book introduced to parliament and vetoed by Elizabeth

1572
Publication of *Admonitions to Parliament* by John Field

1575
Edmund Grindal becomes Archbishop of Canterbury

1576
Grindal suspended by Elizabeth over prophesyings

1584–86
Puritan attempts to introduce the 'bill and book' in parliament

1588
Death of John Field; death of the Earl of Leicester

1588–89
Publication of the Martin Marprelate Tracts

How significant was the development of Puritanism?

In some ways, the development of Puritanism has been overemphasised by historians who were looking for a long-term explanation for the 17th century English Civil Wars, where Charles I went to war against Puritan opponents in his own parliament. Although Puritanism was important, its supporters remained a minority and they failed to change any aspect of the 1559 Settlement. Nor did the 'Puritan choir' exist. After 1587, attempts to create a Calvinist national church through parliament died away, while grass-roots movements such as prophesyings were suppressed. By 1589, many leading supporters and protectors of Puritans had died, including Walsingham and the Earls of Leicester and Warwick. This meant that there was less protection for Puritan preachers. The publication of the controversial 'Martin Marprelate Tracts' in 1588–89 also damaged the Puritan movement. These were a series of vicious and foul-mouthed attacks on the English Church and its bishops.

At a time when many believed the English Church and its queen had been awarded a victory over Spanish Catholics by God, such an attack was seen as close to treason. Puritans such as Thomas Cartwright were quick to claim that they had nothing to do with it, but the Marprelate Tracts show that there were considerable divisions within the Puritan movement – they did not agree over methods or beliefs.

Puritanism was a significant movement in other ways, however. Its emphasis on evangelism (spreading God's word) through preaching led to growing support for Puritan ideas in some southern counties. When Whitgift tried to enforce the Three Articles, gentry from southern England sent him protests and petitions; 38 landowners from Kent sent letters complaining about the lack of preaching in their county. Meanwhile, in Suffolk, Norfolk, Essex and Northampton, leading members of the gentry had become converted to a more Puritan approach. As landowners, they often had control over appointments of parish clergy on their estates. This meant that they could appoint and protect 'godly' clergy. Sir Walter Mildmay, a member of Elizabeth's Council, even founded Emmanuel College, Cambridge to train Puritan ministers. The Puritan impact on printing of cheap and readily available pamphlets and religious tracts was also important. The English Bible published in 1560 went through 130 editions during Elizabeth's reign. Those who could not afford a Bible could purchase a Protestant catechism, a version of a Catholic teaching aid to teach religion through learning a series of questions and answers. About 100 catechisms were published during Elizabeth's reign. The printing presses were also used to promote Protestant propaganda, which was increasingly linked to national pride and the idea that Englishmen were God's chosen people. This included pictures and songs set to popular tunes and were both anti-papal and xenophobic. Despite their differences with the monarch, Puritans recognised that they were on the same side. But the true significance of the growth of Puritanism was that, apart from a few radicals, most of the godly were able to find a way to remain within the Elizabethan Church of England, rather than becoming enemies of it.

ACTIVITY
KNOWLEDGE CHECK

Threats to Elizabeth's security

1 On a blank map (or the one used in the activity on page 55), mark the regions where Protestantism was strong.

2 Discuss with a partner: Why did Protestantism develop more in some parts of the country than in others?

3 Make a spider diagram showing the different methods used by the Puritans to challenge the Elizabethan Settlement. In a different colour, show how the government responded to each challenge.

4 Write a page answering the question: Who was more of a threat to Elizabeth's security on the throne, the Puritans or the Catholics? Explain why you think this.

ACTIVITY
SUMMARY

1 Draw a graph showing how the religion of England changed from Catholic to Protestant during the period.

2 Make a spider diagram called 'The causes of religious change in the period 1509-88'. Use the following headings to summarise what you have learned: 'Role of individual monarchs'; 'Role of other individuals' (for example Cromwell, Anne Boleyn); 'Role of popular belief'; 'Role of new ideas'.

3 Make a list of examples of resistance to religious change. How successful were they?

WIDER READING

Doran, S. *Elizabeth I and Religion, 1558-1603*, Routledge (1994)

Harper-Bill, C. *The Pre-Reformation Church in England 1400-1530*, Routledge (1996)

MacCulloch, D. *The Later Reformation in England 1547-1603*, Palgrave Macmillan (2000)

Pendrill, C. *The English Reformation 1485-1558*, Heinemann (2000)

Rex, R. *Henry VIII and the English Reformation*, Palgrave Macmillan (2006)

AS Level Exam-Style Question Section A

The Puritans wanted to change the Elizabethan Settlement in the years 1558–88.

Was Elizabeth's opposition the main reason for the Puritans' lack of success? (20 marks)

Tip

Elizabeth's role must be compared with other reasons for Puritan failures.

A Level Exam-Style Question Section B

How significant was the challenge posed by the Puritans to Elizabeth's Religious Settlement in the years 1558–88? (20 marks)

Tip

You need to think carefully about the word 'significant' and how this relates to Puritan activities across the period. Consideration of the changing level of significance over the period would also help in this answer.

1.3 State control and popular resistance, 1509-88

KEY QUESTIONS

- How did Tudor monarchs control the country?
- Why was there increasing poverty in Tudor England?
- How serious was the resistance to Tudor rule?

INTRODUCTION

Tudor monarchs had no standing army or police force to help them control their realm. This meant that they were reliant on local members of the nobility and gentry to act in voluntary and often unpaid roles to enforce local order and keep control. Normally this system worked well because members of landed society had a vested interest in maintaining social order – they had the most to lose if riots or rebellions broke out. However, because this system was so dependent on the co-operation of those with land and power locally, Tudor monarchs faced two big problems. First, if popular rebellion did break out, it was very difficult to put down, particularly in more remote parts of the country where communications were poor. Second, there was always the possibility that members of landed society might join the rebellion rather than support the monarch. This threat of rebellion and social disorder meant that Tudor monarchs developed various systems to control the more remote parts of England and Wales and enhance royal power there. It also meant that they needed to find ways to deal with problems caused by social and economic tensions. Poverty was increasing at this time and there were several periods of severe crisis. Poverty also led to homelessness and rising numbers of beggars and vagrants who were a potential threat to social order. These problems drove attempts by the government to control the situation through a system of punishments and also the development of local provision for poor relief.

HOW DID TUDOR MONARCHS CONTROL THE COUNTRY?

What were the Marches?

The Marches was the name of a militarised zone on the English borders with Wales and Scotland. In the Middle Ages, the Marcher regions had developed their own laws and customs because they were the first line of defence against hostile invasion. The nobility who controlled these areas thus gained enormous legal and military power and were quasi-kings in their dominance of the Marcher regions. In the 16th century, the Tudor monarchs sought to undermine these traditional powers by creating systems that allowed them more direct control of these regions.

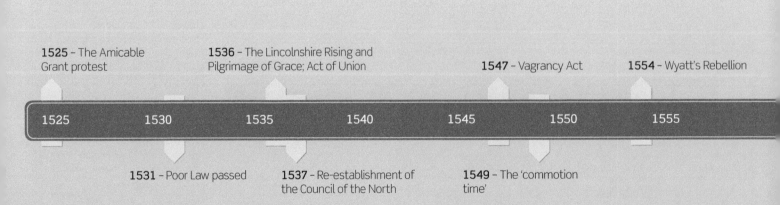

1525 – The Amicable Grant protest

1536 – The Lincolnshire Rising and Pilgrimage of Grace; Act of Union

1547 – Vagrancy Act

1554 – Wyatt's Rebellion

| 1525 | 1530 | 1535 | 1540 | 1545 | 1550 | 1555 |

1531 – Poor Law passed

1537 – Re-establishment of the Council of the North

1549 – The 'commotion time'

The Marcher Council

By the early 16th century, the Welsh Marches' role had changed because Wales had been conquered by England in the 1290s and so there was no longer a threat of a hostile Welsh invasion. However, the government of Wales and the Marcher regions of Gloucestershire, Herefordshire and Worcestershire remained out of step with the government of England. Although the Crown controlled the **Principality of Wales**, before the 1530s Wales had its own legal system, which still depended on the local Marcher lords' powers and control. This meant that in Wales and its Marcher regions it was possible to commit a crime in one lordship and then escape justice by fleeing into another one. As a result, the area was hard to control and had a tendency to lawlessness.

Wolsey had made an unsuccessful attempt to strengthen royal control in the region by creating a Council of the Marches with the nine-year-old Princess Mary acting as a figurehead. In doing this, Wolsey was following the precedent created by Henry VII and Edward IV of using their prerogative rights to create councils to govern remote areas, but his experiment failed.

In 1534, Cromwell began a series of permanent changes to the government of Wales. He began by appointing Rowland Lee to act as the Lord President of the Council of Wales. Lee was given sweeping powers to tackle crime and disorder in the region. In 1536, parliament passed Cromwell's Act of Union. This transformed the structure of Welsh government. The Principality of Wales and the Marcher lordships were abolished and replaced with 13 English-style counties that used the English legal system. This meant that the Council could now control Wales and the Marches more easily as they were no longer faced with varying laws and practices.

In the 1540s, the Marcher Council was reorganised to take account of Cromwell's changes. It became a more formal body with a president and vice-president who were appointed by the monarch. Under a Parliamentary Act of 1543, which reorganised the Welsh legal system still further, the Council was given specific powers for the first time. These powers were strengthened because they now rested on the authority of the king and parliament, not solely the royal prerogative. They included the right to hear legal cases in a manner similar to the English Star Chamber and to oversee law and order in both Wales and the former Marcher counties. By Elizabeth's reign, the Marcher Council had adapted further to include the Lord Lieutenant.

It is a measure of the success of the Marcher Council that there was little trouble from this region during the Tudor period. The reforms of the 1530s successfully extended the power of the Tudor monarchs into a region that had previously been potentially problematic.

The Council of the North and its role

Controlling the north was a more challenging problem for the Tudor monarchs. Geographically remote with poor communications, it was also under threat of invasion from Scotland. The threat of invasion and the border with Scotland were so large that the northern Marches were split into three: the Western, Middle and Eastern Marches. These were controlled by wardens, who were responsible for their defence and keeping order. Control of this militarised zone, where houses were still fortified and cross-border raids were common, was not easy.

> **KEY TERM**
>
> **Principality of Wales**
> This was made up of Welsh lands conquered in the 13th century, that were traditionally given to the heir of the English throne, the Prince of Wales. These lands belonged to the English Crown as a result of the conquest, and included Anglesey, Caernarvon, Flint and Carmarthen. They were distinct from the Marcher regions, which had technically always been in England but formed a buffer zone with Wales.

1569 – The Revolt of the Northern Earls

1585 – Lord Lieutenants become permanent

| 1560 | 1565 | 1570 | 1575 | 1580 | 1585 | 1590 |

1563 – Statute of Artificers

1572–76 – Poor Laws passed

Before 1525, Henry VIII relied on the powerful regional nobility to act as wardens; the key families were the Dacres, the Cliffords, the Percy Earls of Northumberland and the Neville Earls of Westmorland. These families were involved in complex feuds with each other and could not always be relied upon to keep the peace. In 1525, for example, Lord Dacre was fined £1,000 in Star Chamber for his tolerance of disorder in the north. However, as long as there remained the threat of invasion from Scotland, these men were needed to provide the first line of defence.

In 1525, however, Wolsey decided that the north needed to be brought under stricter control. He re-established the Council of the North, which had first been used in the late 15th century. Like the Marcher Council, the Council of the North had both a legal and an administrative role and worked alongside the wardens to promote the authority of the Tudor monarchs. Its authority was enhanced because the president was either a bishop or a member of the nobility who often came from the south or the Midlands. This meant that they had no vested interests in the decisions they were making. The rest of the Council was made up of local gentry, lawyers and clergy. Many of these men served for long periods of time, such as Sir Thomas Gargrave, a lawyer from Wakefield who was a councillor from 1545 to 1579. Although the president was usually not a northerner, the rest of the Council came from the region. These arrangements encouraged a consistent approach to the government of the north, although the promotion of these men also caused resentment and feuds. Councillors were given further power and knowledge of the region under their control because they were also appointed as Justices of the Peace (JPs). As a result, the Council of the North developed as a body that could oversee the administration of the north, control border reivers (raiders) and manage local order through hearing court cases as a northern version of Star Chamber.

Development of the Council of the North from 1537

The existence of the Council of the North was not enough to prevent the most serious rebellion of the Tudor period breaking out in 1536 (see pages 76–78). As a result of the Pilgrimage of Grace, Cromwell remodelled the Council in 1537 in order to strengthen its powers. He gave it wide powers to hear and decide cases of treason, murder and **felony**. The Council took a leading role in denouncing those who had been involved in the rebellion. It also became the voice of the government in London, responsible for passing on and enforcing all royal proclamations and orders made to sheriffs and JPs. It oversaw food supplies, regulated trade, organised local musters for military campaigns, and heard private cases between individuals.

Under Elizabeth I, the Council became responsible for combatting recusancy. The north was the least Protestant and most openly Catholic region of England. There was a danger, therefore, that northerners would not accept the Elizabethan religious settlement or would attempt to rebel against the queen as they did in the Northern Revolt of 1569. Although the president and the vice-president, the Earl of Sussex and Thomas Gargrave respectively, had played a leading role in putting down the rebellion, the 1569 revolt led to the Council being reconstructed in order to strengthen Elizabeth's power. In 1572, the Puritan Henry Hastings, the Earl of Huntingdon, who was also Elizabeth's cousin, was made president. Huntingdon was a complete outsider with no lands or power in the north. This was not a disadvantage, however, because he had the support of Elizabeth and the Privy Council. Huntingdon remained in his post until 1595. During this time he enforced a rigorous crackdown on recusancy that not only included punishment of Catholics but also the appointment of Protestant preachers to spread the religious settlement approved by the government. The result of these changes was that the north became much more stable. There was no further rebellion and the power of the traditional noble families there was much eroded while the control of the monarchy was enhanced through the Council.

> **KEY TERM**
>
> **Felony**
> This was a capital crime that did not include treason. A capital crime was punishable by death. Capital crimes included offences such as murder, arson, witchcraft and heresy.

> **ACTIVITY**
> **KNOWLEDGE CHECK**
>
> **The Councils**
> 1 Summarise in your own words the reasons why the Marcher Council and the Council of the North developed.
>
> 2 List the powers of the Councils. For each power, explain how this helped to increase the power of the Tudor monarchs.

THINKING HISTORICALLY — Causation (4a&b)

The causes of the Northern Revolt, 1569

Nothing that happens is inevitable. There are causes of change that did not have to develop as they did. Something could have altered or someone could have chosen differently. What actually occurred in the past did happen, but it did not have to be like that.

Work on your own and answer the questions. When you have answered the questions, discuss the answers in groups.

Perceived reasons for the outbreak of the Northern Revolt in 1569

Development	Event	State of affairs	Event	Trigger event
The rise in distrust between the northern earls and Elizabeth I	Elizabeth I put Henry Hastings in charge of the Council of the North	Tension between the Protestant queen who was Head of the Church of England and northern Catholics	The arrival of Mary, Queen of Scots in England (1568)	Elizabeth I summoned the Earls of Northumberland and Westmorland to court

1 Consider the introduction of the prayer book and the religious tensions of the time.

   a) How did the appointment of Henry Hastings affect the tension between the queen and the northern earls?

   b) Had there been no tension, would Hastings' appointment still have been important?

   c) What other aspects of the situation existing in 1569 would have been affected had there been no political tension?

2 Consider the tension between Protestants and Catholics, the arrival of Mary, Queen of Scots and Elizabeth's order to the Earls of Northumberland and Westmorland.

   a) How important is the tension between Protestants and Catholics as a causal factor of the two events?

   b) What might have happened if Elizabeth had not summoned Northumberland and Westmorland to court?

3 What other consequences came about as a result of the information in the table? Try to identify at least one consequence for each.

4 Choose one factor. How might the Northern Revolt have developed differently if this factor had not been present?

What was the role of the nobility in maintaining control?

At the beginning of Henry VIII's reign, the nobility were an integral part of government. In the regions, they performed their traditional medieval feudal functions. As major landowners, they were responsible for upholding law and order in the regions where they were most powerful. In this role, they were often the first line of defence against rebellion, although occasionally they joined the rebels instead. At the centre of government, they were the king's friends and advisers, serving on his Council, in parliament and at court. In some ways, the role of the nobility did not change greatly during the Tudor period; they remained important as a link between the centre and the localities. However, the basis of their power changed considerably. Increasingly, the nobility drew their power from access to the monarchs at court. The Tudor monarchs began to recruit their own personal followers, a royal version of the medieval noble affinity, through grants of local office such as Justice of the Peace. They also 'planted' leading councillors and members of their household into specific regions, regardless of whether they already had lands and influence there or not. For example, Charles Brandon (the Duke of Suffolk), who was Henry VIII's close friend, was moved by the king from East Anglia to Lincolnshire in the late 1530s to control a region where there had been serious unrest. Elizabeth I appointed the Earl of Huntingdon as president of the Council of the North for exactly the same reason. As a result of this changing relationship, the power of the nobility increasingly rested on their ability to gain grants of land and office for themselves and their followers. This meant that their role in maintaining control in the localities changed as well.

EXTEND YOUR KNOWLEDGE

The medieval feudal nobility and the development of the royal affinity

In the Middle Ages, the nobility were responsible for maintaining law and order and for raising an army when the monarch needed it. Their ability to do this came from the ownership of land. Members of the nobility were allowed to maintain their own followers, known as an 'affinity', to help them. The affinity formed the core of a noble's fighting force, but would also serve him in times of peace. Noble affinities could help keep the peace, but they could also cause trouble in the localities and even be used against the monarch. Edward, Duke of Buckingham was an example of this feudal tradition; he was also a Marcher lord, owning land in Gloucestershire. This may have made the government particularly nervous about his actions and led to his execution for treason in 1521. Kings such as Henry VII tried to restrict these private armies with Acts of Parliament and severe punishments. However, the monarchs also began to adopt their own version of the affinity as a method of extending royal control further into the localities, undermining the power of the feudal nobility. This policy was adopted more widely by Henry VIII and his successors.

The nobility were vital to maintaining control, and although the Tudor monarchs sought to make them more dependent on the Crown they never tried to take this role from them. The rank and social status of a member of the nobility meant that they could command respect locally. This is why members of the nobility were usually appointed to local offices and positions such as membership of the Council of the North or the Marches, or as a Justice of the Peace. A nobleman's links with court and the monarch were also important in passing useful local information to the ruler through the Council or Chamber. In times of crisis they were often those with an ear to the ground who could best advise the monarch about what to do. They also acted as the monarch's representatives and mouthpieces locally. This can be seen on numerous occasions.

For example, in 1525 the Dukes of Norfolk and Suffolk were the on-the-spot witnesses to the local protests over the Amicable Grant. Not only did they speak to the rebels, but they also reported what they had heard to Wolsey. In 1536, the Duke of Norfolk was sent at the head of an army to deal with the Pilgrimage of Grace and he played an important role in negotiating with the rebels and advising the king on how to approach the situation. Similarly, the monarchy relied on members of the nobility to suppress the rebellions of 1549, 1553 and 1569. The nobility also played a role in implementing other government policies, especially religious changes. The Catholic Earl of Derby helped to investigate Protestants in Mary's reign, and the Puritan Earl of Huntingdon helped to enforce Protestantism in the north in Elizabeth's reign. By Elizabeth's reign, it was members of her Council and household who dominated the running of local government. Elizabeth granted her trusted inner circle of advisers both local office and land. For example, her Treasurer William Cecil was a JP in Lincolnshire and Northampton. Robert Dudley (the Earl of Leicester) controlled Cheshire, Wales and the Marches and was also a JP in several counties. The role of these courtier-noblemen was further extended through their role as Lord Lieutenants, but they owed their power and position entirely to the queen.

Letter from Henry VIII to the Earl of Derby, 19 October 1536.

We lately commanded you to make ready your forces and go to the earl of Shrewsbury, our lieutenant to suppress the rebellion in the North; but having since heard of an insurrection attempted about the abbey of Salley in Lancashire, where the abbot and monks have been restored by the traitors, we now desire you immediately to repress it, to apprehend the captains and either have them immediately executed as traitors or sent up to us. We leave it, however, to your discretion to go elsewhere in case of greater emergency. You are to take the said abbot and monks forth with violence and have them hanged without delay in their monks' apparel, and see that no town or village begin to assemble. We shall remember your charges and service. We send a commission under the Privy Seal as your authority.

However, the nobility could also be the root of trouble and local disorder, which is why the Tudor monarchs tried to control them more closely. Wyatt's revolt and the Northern Revolt both had their roots in court-based plots involving members of the nobility, and there was noble involvement in the Pilgrimage of Grace. The nobility could also be the cause of local disorder. This was particularly the case in the marcher regions where royal authority was weaker and the traditional feudal power of the nobility was stronger. The setting up of the Councils of the Marches and the North was a response to this problem, and the power of traditional Marcher lords such as the Duke of Buckingham (who was powerful in Gloucestershire), the Nevilles, Percys and Dacres declined as a result. However, they were replaced by a new breed of nobility, such as William Cecil, Robert Dudley and the Earl of Huntingdon. The nobility were, however, still prominent in government during Elizabeth's reign. This can be seen in the fact that the Bond of Association (1585), which was drawn up to defend Elizabeth from assassination, was the work of noble members of her Council.

Justices of the Peace

What was the role of the Justices of the Peace under Henry VIII?

The role of Justice of the Peace (JP) had first emerged in the 14th century and they had been gathering increasing power and influence locally ever since then. JPs were appointed for each county (this was known as the county bench) and their powers were wide ranging by the start of the Tudor period. They could hear and decide cases of felony and **trespass**; they could arrest potential suspects; they supervised the regulation of weights and measures and the fixing of prices and wages; they also had to attend sessions four times a year (quarter sessions) to perform their role. Increasingly, JPs were not just active at quarter sessions, they were using their powers more widely to monitor and control local society. Being a JP was hard work, but it was also an excellent opportunity to influence local affairs. The Tudor monarchs tried to monitor carefully who became a JP. They also used the county benches to insert members of their court into local government to enhance royal control.

KEY TERM

Trespass
The term for less serious crimes that did not attract the death penalty.

JPs were usually drawn from those with the most local status – the nobility and gentry. However, they did not have to be resident in a region to become a JP. The qualification for selection was the ownership of land that brought in income of at least £20 a year, a sizeable amount. Some JPs were appointed because they were lawyers. These men formed the 'quorum', the group of JPs who had to be present at meetings.

At the beginning of Henry VIII's reign, most county benches had between 20 and 35 members. Appointment as a JP was usually for life. Occasionally, however, the government would remove a JP from the county bench. This was usually because the JP was suspected of not following government orders or of misusing his position to increase his local power. Wolsey was particularly keen to improve local justice and the quality of JPs. In 1526, for example, he summoned the JPs to hear a speech before asking them to fill in a 21-section questionnaire on law and order in their regions. Cromwell was also careful to check who was appointed as a JP, particularly since he expected them to enforce the Supremacy and the Reformation.

How did the role of the JPs develop under the later Tudors?

DEVELOPMENT OF THE ROLE OF JP UNDER THE LATER TUDORS

1549
JPs ordered to take inventories of parish goods and prosecute anyone found to have stolen them

1552
Act of Parliament lays down that all alehouses have to be licensed by JPs

JPs ordered to enforce the second *Book of Common Prayer*

1563
Act for the Relief of the Poor makes JPs responsible for supervising the collection of poor-relief donations

Statute of Artificers makes JPs responsible for fixing local wages

1572
Parliament makes JPs responsible for listing the poor in each parish

During the reigns of Edward, Mary and Elizabeth, the trend for placing more responsibility on the JPs continued. The social and economic crisis of the early 1550s led to fears of social disorder, leading to Acts of Parliament that placed responsibility on JPs to oversee local alehouses and religious changes at a local level.

By Elizabeth's reign, both the amount of business conducted by the JPs and the size of the county benches needed to oversee this business had increased. The average size of the county bench had grown from 25 under Wolsey to between 40 and 50 under Elizabeth. Members of the local gentry had also realised that becoming a JP was the key to social advancement. As a result, Cecil had to keep an increasingly close eye on the membership of the benches, but he was reliant on the reports of royal judges who only visited the counties twice a year. As a result, there was an element of corruption, though royal control over the county benches was strengthened by the appointment of leading councillors and Lord Lieutenants to county benches.

By 1603, there were 309 Acts of Parliament that placed responsibility on the JPs. These responsibilities included their traditional role from the start of the period, but also new ones brought about by religious, political and social change.

Elizabethan JPs had acquired powers to deal with new felonies introduced by the government including riots, damage to property, witchcraft and recusancy. They also had to deal with a wide range of more minor offences such as damage to crops, swearing, drunkenness and abduction of heiresses. In addition, they were responsible for the administration of the Tudor Poor Laws (see pages 70–74). By the 1580s, therefore, the role of the JPs in administering Tudor law and controlling the regions had expanded enormously. Through them, the power and control of the Crown expanded as well.

SOURCE 2

From Edward VI's Licensing Act, 1552. This shows the changing role of the JPs' powers and the increasing role they played in enforcing social order.

Forasmuch as intolerable hurts and troubles to the common wealth of this realm doth daily grow and increase through such abuses and disorders as are had and used in common ale-houses and other houses called tippling-houses; It is therefore enacted... That the Justices of Peace within every shire, city, borough, town corporate, franchise, or liberty within this realm, or two of them at least, whereof one of them to be of the Quorum, shall have full power and authority... where they be Justices of Peace to remove, discharge and put away common selling of ale and beer in the said common ale-houses and tippling-houses in such town or towns and places where they shall think meet and convenient; And that none... shall be admitted or suffered to keep any common ale-house or tippling-house but such as shall be thereunto admitted and allowed in the open Sessions of the Peace, or else by two Justices of the Peace, whereof the one to be of the Quorum...

SOURCE 3

Report from a Leicestershire JP to Francis Walsingham, 1582, showing the relationship between local JPs and the Privy Council and the JPs' role in surveillance.

At our last assizes... a fellow suspiciously wandering about our county was taken... I find him so subtle that my advice was that the lords of her majesty's Privy Council should be advertised [told].

SOURCE 4

From a letter written by Edwin Sandys, Archbishop of York, to William Cecil, 1587, showing the problems the government faced in appointing reliable JPs.

I have noted in a paper, herein enclosed, such as in my opinion may be well put out of the commission [dismissed as Justices of the Peace]... I assure you some of them be the baddest sort, unworthy to govern, being so far out of order themselves. And to speak truth, although there be many gentlemen in Yorkshire, yet it is very hard to choose fit men for that purpose.

Robert Lee. He is a notable open adulterer, one that giveth offence and will not be reformed. He useth his authority as well to work private displeasure as to serve other men's turns.

Peter Stanley. A man noted to be a great fornicator. Of small wisdom, and less skill.

Thomas Wentworth. A very senseless blockhead, ever wronging his poor neighbours. He bought grain in the beginning of last year in every market, and heaped it up in his houses to sell at the dearest.

Francis Alford. This man liveth much in London. A man of small living, less skill and no countenance.

The role of the Lord Lieutenant under Elizabeth I

As the traditional feudal role of the nobility declined under the Tudors, a replacement was needed for their role in providing the monarch with an army. This replacement was the system of Lord Lieutenants, which first appeared as an experiment in the late 1540s and 1550s and became a permanent feature of Tudor government in 1585 when England went to war with Spain.

The Lord Lieutenants were given responsibility to oversee the war effort of a specific county. Once appointed, most of these men remained in post for life. They were usually either the most powerful nobleman living in the region or a member of the Privy Council who had estates locally. Often, these people were one and the same thing. The Lord Lieutenants were given far-reaching powers. They were ordered to arrange the defence of their counties and the muster of all men who were available and eligible to serve in the army, to ensure that these men were armed and trained and to impose discipline. All other local officials, including the JPs, were instructed to obey and assist the Lieutenants. Because the Lieutenants were also Privy Councillors, members of the Councils of the North and the Marches and senior noblemen, they also provided an important link between the regions and the central government and were ultimately answerable to the monarch, who could dismiss them at will. The result of these developments was an improved system of military organisation, with better records, recruitment and communication. However, the system was to come under increasing strain in the 1590s as the war with Spain continued.

AS Level Exam-Style Question Section B

To what extent did the Tudor state increase its control of local government in the years 1536–88? (20 marks)

Tip

Note the date range of this question. Your evidence should be drawn from within these dates.

A Level Exam-Style Question Section A

How far were the Tudor monarchs able to extend and sustain their control of local government in the years 1536–88? (20 marks)

Tip

Did the Tudors both maintain and extend control throughout the entire date range of the question?

ACTIVITY
KNOWLEDGE CHECK

Monarch and nobility

1 Read the letter from Henry VIII to the Earl of Derby (Source 1). What does this suggest about the relationship between the monarch and the Tudor nobility?

2 Make a list of the main responsibilities of the nobility in keeping control in 1509 and again in 1588. Highlight in two colours the main changes and continuities in their role.

3 Read Sources 2, 3 and 4 on page 67. What do they suggest about the strengths and weaknesses of the system of JPs?

4 Write an extended paragraph to answer the question: To what extent did the Tudor monarchs increase their control over the regions between 1509 and 1588?

Why did population growth lead to increasing poverty?

The main cause of poverty in Tudor England was the increase in the population in the 16th century beyond a level that could be supported. There was steady growth across the period, apart from in the 1550s when bad harvests and an influenza epidemic in Mary's reign led to a temporary decline in numbers. In 1525, the population of England was about 2.26 million; by 1551 it was 3.01 million and by 1591 it was 3.89 million.

The result of this growth was rising prices and falling wages. This was because of the basic economic principle of supply and demand. As the population grew, more pressure was placed on resources, particularly food. The more people there were to feed, the more the demand for food grew, meaning that farmers and merchants could charge higher prices for their goods and expect them to be paid, leading to price inflation. Furthermore, it was not easy for landlords to increase food production as they lacked the necessary technology to turn less fertile land into ground suitable for arable farming. The situation was made worse in some periods because the Tudor government did not have the ability to ensure that its population could always be fed. In particular, harvests could be affected by bad weather, which reduced the crop yield and led to a shortage of foodstuffs. When this happened, for example in 1519–21, 1527–29, 1549–51, 1554–56 and 1586–87, as grain became scarcer, prices soared still higher. It was not just grain prices that rose; prices for goods such as butter, eggs, cheese and wool rose too, as the agricultural economy struggled to keep pace with the increase in population.

Population growth also led to declining wages, as with more young people entering the job market there was more competition for work and employers did not have to pay higher wages in order to attract workers. The result of higher prices coupled with lower wages can be seen in Source 5. During the period, the cost of living rose dramatically, reaching a peak in the 1580s and 1590s. For those people who had sufficient land and property to exploit this trend through agricultural production the situation did not present a challenge, but for those lower down the social ladder the effects hit hard.

The dissolution of the monasteries in the late 1530s may also have exacerbated the spread of poverty, because the monasteries were a traditional source of support and **alms** for the poor.

The result of these conditions was that unemployment rose and more people fell into poverty with little or no support on hand to help. As Source 5 shows, the purchasing power of an agricultural labourer in Tudor England was already on the decline at the start of the period and reached a low during the 1550s, from which it never fully recovered. For those who struggled to find any work, the situation was even worse.

SOURCE

The Phelps-Brown Index showing the cost of living in the 16th century. To get an idea of long-term price movements, the economist Henry Phelps-Brown chose a region, southern England, where the records on price movements were especially rich and continuous, and then determined the average price in a given year of a fixed set (or 'basket') of consumable goods. For wages, Phelps-Brown turned to typical wage rates of building artisans and established how much they would have purchased in those 'baskets' of consumable goods. The base index is set at 100. Numbers above 100 mean that average prices/wages have exceeded the base. Numbers below 100 mean that prices/wages have declined below the base.

Date	Average price index of a basket of essential food (period 1451-75 = 100)	Purchasing power of an agricultural labourer (1450-99 = 100)
1510–19	111	89
1520–29	148	80
1530–39	155	80
1540–49	192	71
1550–59	289	59
1560–69	279	66
1570–79	315	69
1580–89	357	57

Land and the growth of poverty

For those without land, or just enough land to subsist, the changes caused by population growth and inflation were more extreme. The situation was made worse by ambitious landlords who enclosed the **common land** on which the poorest in society were reliant, though this problem was not as much of a cause of poverty as contemporaries like Thomas More thought. Other problems were linked to attempts by landlords to increase their profits by **rack-renting** and **forestalling**. Like enclosure, these problems were blamed by contemporaries as the main cause of poverty, but were not as important as population growth. It is possible, however, that after the dissolution of the monasteries in the 1530s, the former monastic land passed into the hands of lay landlords who were less scrupulous in their dealings with the tenants they had inherited.

Monetary causes of poverty

There were also other factors that exacerbated the growth of poverty. These were the result of changes to the coinage and the amount of money in circulation.

One factor was the influx of gold and silver into Europe from the New World. This led to a **price revolution** and more inflation. As more gold and silver was turned into currency, so prices rose further.

In England, inflation was made even worse by the government's debasement of the coinage between 1542 and 1551. Debasement involved the melting down of the coinage, which contained large amounts of valuable gold and silver, and mixing these metals with less valuable metals. The coins were then recast. Because more metal was used there were more coins for the government to spend, each containing a smaller amount of precious metals. These developments meant that there was more money in circulation, which in turn led to more inflation. Merchants were likely to charge more for their goods if there was more coinage to pay for it.

In addition, the debasement of the coinage meant that its face value decreased. This led to traders charging more money for the same goods. The impact of this was felt most by those whose wages were declining or who did not have regular employment.

The 16th century saw the creation of a wider gap between the rich and the poor. However, Tudor politicians and economists did not yet fully understand the reasons for this. In particular, they tended to blame the poor themselves, assuming that they were too lazy to find work.

SOURCE

6 *A Remedy for Sedition* by Richard Moryson, 1536.

How much ground is lost in England? How much corn might we carry into other countries if we would use the commodities of our own realm? How many heaths be there that would bear other fruits than shrubs, brakes, broom and fern if they were well handled? How many cities are decayed, how many towns that are now hamlets, quite down, that would stand if the third part of England did not live idly? Towns would up again if crafts were set up. There are few nations, but many be idle. Yet I think there is not two greatest nations in Christendom that hath half so many that live without crafts as little England hath.

SOURCE

7 A declaration of the citizens of London to the Privy Council, 1552.

And first, may it please your honours to understand, that it was too evident to all men that beggary and thievery did abound. And we remembering how many statutes from time to time have been made for the redress of the same, and little amendment hath hitherto followed, thought to search the cause hereof, and after dire examination had, we evidently perceived that the cause of all this misery and beggary was idleness: and the means and remedy to cure the same must be by its contrary, which is labour. And it hath been a speech used by all men, to say unto the idle, work! Work! Even as though they would have said, the means to reform beggary is to fall to work.

And we considered also that the greatest number of beggars fallen into misery by lewd and evil service, by wars, by sickness, or other adverse fortune, have so utterly lost their credit, that though they would shew themselves willing to labour, yet are they so suspected and feared of all men, that few or none dare, or will receive work them to work: wherefore we saw that there could be no means to amend this miserable sort, but by making some general provision of work, wherewith the willing poor may be exercised; and whereby the forward, strong and sturdy vagabond may be compelled to live profitably to the commonwealth.

EXTRACT

1 From S. Brigden, *New Worlds, Lost Worlds: The Rule of the Tudors, 1485–1603* (2000).

The Tudor century saw a terrible growth of impoverishment. A huge population rise from the early century; agricultural transformations; and the operation of the land market in favour of the aggrandizing [those who wanted to increase their wealth or status], left many homeless, landless, destitute. Even in what passed for good times there was never enough work to go around; what work there was was seasonal and increasingly badly paid, and the poor were often driven on to the road to look for it. In bad times, those who lived on the edge of subsistence were especially vulnerable. Failing harvests drove up prices beyond the ability of the poor to buy, and destitution followed. At times, the desperation of the poor cried out. At a dole of bread in Southwark in 1533 there was such a press of people that four men, two women and a boy were crushed to death. Some in their terrible poverty abandoned their children in the doorways of the rich.

Vagrancy and punishment

Why were vagrants and beggars punished?

Increasing levels of poverty led to another problem for the Tudor state: vagrancy and begging. Because it was assumed that there were jobs available but the unemployed were too lazy to work, the Tudor authorities tended to use punishment to try to control the problem. Vagrants and beggars, those who wandered from place to place, were treated with suspicion because this practice made it harder to control the population, particularly in times of political and social unrest. This is why many Tudor laws concerning vagrancy and the poor made vagrants return to their own parishes to seek help, where they would be known to the local authorities. Instability and the spread of seditious ideas that might undermine the Tudor state could then be more easily avoided. In addition, vagrants and beggars did not have a master. In the Tudor mind, which saw society as a hierarchy, this was perceived as a threat to social order, and those who were found wandering were liable to be arrested simply because they had no master.

How were vagrants and beggars punished?

The belief that poverty was a choice of the idle led successive Tudor governments to pass increasingly harsh laws that set out a series of controls and punishments for those found begging or wandering without a master. Until the 1570s, Tudor laws distinguished between the **impotent poor** and the able-bodied poor, supporting the former, but punishing the latter. The impotent poor were to be cared for, but the able-bodied poor were considered to be 'idle' or 'sturdy beggars', who could work but chose not to.

KEY TERM

Impotent poor
This term was used for people who suffered physical disability or illness that made it impossible for them to work.

Laws concerning the control and punishment of vagrants and beggars had been in place since the late 15th century. In 1495, a law had been passed which ordered that beggars and the idle poor were to be put in the stocks for three days, whipped and returned to their original **parish**. In this period, poor relief in the parishes was still based on voluntary contributions by wealthier parishioners to the church alms fund. As poverty grew, so punishments became more severe. In 1531, a Poor Law was passed that ordered vagrants and beggars to be whipped. Beggars who were classed as impotent poor were to be licensed by the JPs and allowed to beg.

KEY TERM

Parish
This was the area under the organisation and control of a local church. Each parish had its own priest who looked after the needs of his congregation. The parish became the centre of administration for poor relief.

In 1547, the most severe laws of the period were passed, which reflected the rising social and economic tensions of the time. Under the Vagrancy Act, a vagrant was defined as someone who was able-bodied and who had been without a master or employment for three days. The punishments for vagrants were harsh. A first offence would lead to a 'V' being branded on the person's chest. The vagrant would also be forced to work as a slave for two years for the person who had informed against them. If someone was found guilty of vagrancy for a second time they would be branded with the letter 'S' on their face and would be enslaved for life. The final punishment for persistent vagrants was execution as a felon. Under the Vagrancy Act, impotent beggars were to be sent back to the parish where they were born, to be looked after in a house for the disabled poor. This was to be funded by donations in church.

However, the Vagrancy Act was so harsh that the local authorities found it impossible to enforce. It was repealed in 1550 and replaced in 1552 by a new Poor Law. This Act required the impotent poor to be registered for the first time. It also required parish priests and bishops to place more pressure on those who were reluctant to make voluntary contributions to alms in the parishes.

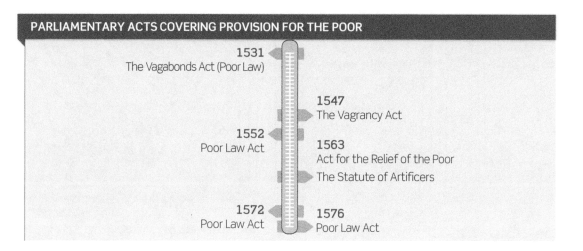

PARLIAMENTARY ACTS COVERING PROVISION FOR THE POOR

1531
The Vagabonds Act (Poor Law)

1547
The Vagrancy Act

1552
Poor Law Act

1563
Act for the Relief of the Poor

The Statute of Artificers

1572
Poor Law Act

1576
Poor Law Act

How did provision for poor relief change?

Under Elizabeth I, attitudes towards poverty and provision for the poor began to change. Parish funds for poor relief received a considerable boost under the Act of Uniformity. The 12*d*.-per-week fine, which was paid by recusants for non-attendance at church services, was put towards parish poor relief. In 1563, the Act for the Relief of the Poor moved towards making payments to poor relief in the parish almost compulsory. Special collectors of alms were to be appointed, and according to the Act they were to 'gently ask and demand of every man and woman what they of their charity will be contented to give weekly towards the relief of the poor'. Refusal to contribute could lead to imprisonment, but the contributor could choose how large or small their payments were.

The Statute of Artificers (1563) also attempted to address some of the issues caused by vagrancy. It ordered that all males between the ages of 12 and 60 below the rank of gentleman should look for work and were not to leave their employment without permission. All unmarried people under the age of 30 were to be forced to serve any employer at times of harvest, but they were also to be trained in a craft.

However, under the 1572 Poor Law, attitudes towards the able-bodied poor began to change. Punishments for unlicensed beggars remained severe: they included boring a hole through the right ear with a hot instrument or whipping for those under 14. It also became harder to get a licence, as it now had to be signed by two JPs. This would not have been easy for someone of low social status to achieve. Despite this, for the first time, the government recognised that there was not enough work available for the able-bodied poor. The 1572 Act encouraged parishes with extra poor-relief funds to build 'houses of correction' for vagrants and beggars. In 1576, a second Poor Law ordered that there should be one house of correction per county and that supplies of wool, flax and iron should be stockpiled for the poor to work on.

The 1570s and 1580s were a period of relative economic stability, with few bad harvests, so the government did not need to pass further laws, although the social and economic crisis of the 1590s would bring about further significant changes. By 1588, although vagrants and beggars were still forced into houses that aimed to 'correct' their behaviour, the Tudor government had moved some way towards supporting the poor and away from punishing them for laziness. There was also an increased expectation, enforced by parliamentary law, that local parishes would provide for their poor and that this provision would come from contributions from local parishioners, which were almost compulsory. This move was influenced by the development of voluntary and local initiatives, especially in the larger towns.

SOURCE 8

A 16th century English woodcut showing a vagrant being whipped through the streets.

SOURCE 9

From the 1572 Poor Law.

Where all the parts of the realm of England and Wales be presently with rogues, vagabonds and sturdy beggars exceedingly pestered, by means whereof daily happeneth in the same realm horrible murders, thefts and other outrages, be it enacted...

That all persons above the age of fourteen years, being rogues, vagabonds or sturdy beggars, shall upon their apprehension be brought before one of the justices of the peace or mayor or chief officer of cities... and if such persons be duly convict of his or her roguish or vagabond trade of life, that then immediately he or she shall be grievously whipped and burnt through the grissle of the right ear with a hot iron of the compass of an inch about.

And forasmuch as charity would that poor, aged and impotent persons should as necessarily be provided for, it is enacted that the justices of the peace, mayors, sheriffs, bailiffs and other officers make diligent search and inquiry of all aged, poor, impotent and decayed persons; and shall also number [count] all the said poor people; and that done, they shall assess all the inhabitants dwelling within the said limits [of the parish or town] to such weekly charge as they and every one of them shall weekly contribute to the relief of the said poor people. And if any person being able to further this charitable work will obstinately refuse to give towards the relief of the said poor people, the said obstinate person shall be brought before two justices of the peace and abide such order therein as the said justices shall appoint.

What was the importance of the role of charities and local authorities in poor relief?

In an age before the welfare state, provision of relief for the poor rested largely on charitable contributions. Both the Catholic and Protestant Churches preached that it was a Christian's duty to help the poor and vulnerable in society. Before the Reformation and the dissolution of the monasteries, the Catholic Church supported the poor through charity; monks and nuns would give their leftover food to the poor, and monasteries provided hospitals to care for the sick.

Before the Reformation, most of the charitable giving that occurred was via the Catholic Church. Contributions to poor relief were often left in wills. The wealthier in society would leave money to found almshouses where the poor could be cared for. These pre-Reformation almshouses often included a chapel and were counted as chantries, which meant that many were lost when the chantries were dissolved in 1547. However, new almshouses were still set up later in the period, such as the Lord Leycester Hospital in Warwick, founded by Robert Dudley to support old soldiers.

After the Reformation, donations to charity went directly to poor relief in the parishes where they were administered by local churches. Merchants in the larger towns were particularly involved in charitable giving. It has been estimated that their contributions formed about 60 percent of all 16th century charity.

These contributions helped not only the relief of the poor, but also supported funds to help those who wished to set themselves up in business, and education for the children of the poor. For example, Stephen Jenyns, a wealthy merchant and Mayor of London from Wolverhampton, left money to set up a school for 12 poor boys in his hometown. In London, where there was even greater wealth, larger bequests could be found. William Lambe, a cloth maker, left almost all of his huge fortune of £5,695 to charity, including £6 to buy 120 pails so that 60 poor women could earn their living as water carriers. Private charity remained important throughout the period. It is estimated that private contributions (not including payments to poor relief) rose from £227,000 in the period 1541–60 to £634,000 by 1601–20.

Because the problem of poverty was felt most acutely in the towns, voluntary schemes for poor relief tended to be developed there first. London was a special case because it was so much larger than any other town in England. In 1500, it had a population of about 60,000; this had grown to 200,000 by 1600. The divide between the rich and the poor was particularly extreme in London, where it is estimated that about five percent of the population owned 80 percent of the total wealth. London's rapid growth led to severe poverty, and the London authorities were forced to act. In 1547, London introduced compulsory poor rates.

Practical help for the poor was enhanced by co-operation with the Crown. Edward VI encouraged this process because he was concerned about the provision for the poor following the Reformation. Encouraged by a sermon by the Bishop of London,

The Lord Leycester Hospital in Warwick, founded by Robert Dudley, Earl of Leicester, in the 1570s as an almshouse for former soldiers. It still retains its function today.

Nicholas Ridley, who preached that the poor should be shown mercy, Edward arranged for the grant of several Crown properties to a group of London merchants for the specific purpose of setting up help for the poor. These properties included Bridewell Palace, which became a house of correction for the able-bodied poor, Christ's Hospital for orphans in 1552 and St Bartholomew's Hospital for the sick poor. They also acquired Bethlehem Hospital, known as 'Bedlam', which was used as a hospital for the insane. St Bartholomew's was run by an unpaid alderman (member of the city council), aided by other unpaid governors who oversaw the accounts and general running of the hospital. There was also a matron, 12 nurses and three surgeons, all of whom were paid. By 1588, the hospital could take 120 patients, but it often let in more. As well as medical treatment, there were prayers twice a day to which all patients had to listen. If a patient was cured, the hospital would give that person money to get home, clothes and a 'passport' to show that he or she was not an unlicensed vagrant. These initiatives were mirrored in other large towns such as Norwich and York where compulsory contributions to poor relief were set up in 1549 and 1551, respectively. As in London, town authorities took over the running of former church foundations. In York, the town council took over the running of several hospitals including St Thomas' Hospital, where in 1574 the authorities decided to pay for 18 people to stay.

ACTIVITY
KNOWLEDGE CHECK

Causes of poverty

1 List the main causes of poverty in Tudor England.

2 In what ways do Richard Moryson (Source 6) and the citizens of London (Source 7) agree about the causes of poverty? In what ways do they disagree?

3 Use the material in this section to fill in the following table.

Response to poverty and date	Response to impotent poor	Response to able-bodied poor	What does this response reveal about attitudes to poverty?
1531 Poor Law			
1547 Vagrancy Act			
1547–52 measures in London for poor relief			
1552 Poor Law			
1563 Act for the Relief of the Poor			
1563 Statute of Artificers			
1572, 1576 Poor Laws			

AS Level Exam-Style Question Section B

Between 1531 and 1576, there were many attempts by the government to deal with the problem of poverty.

To what extent did government methods of dealing with poverty change in the period 1531–76? (20 marks)

Tip

What evidence is there of government attitudes to poverty? What evidence is there that these changed or stayed the same?

THINKING HISTORICALLY Evidence (4a&b)

Methods for dealing with poverty

Sources 8 and 9 could be used by a historian to build up a picture of the methods used to deal with poverty in Tudor England.

Use Sources 8 and 9 to answer the following:

1 Explain why Sources 8 and 9 offer different views of Tudor methods of dealing with poverty. How might this affect their value as pieces of evidence in appraising methods of dealing with poverty in the 16th century? Explain your answer.

Discuss the following in groups.

2 Suppose the historian had ten more accounts that agreed broadly with Source 8 and only four that agreed with Source 9. What would that tell him about Tudor methods of dealing with poverty?

3 How far should the balance of the evidence play a role in constructing written history? What else must a historian consider about the evidence being used before drawing conclusions?

A Level Exam-Style Question Section A

How far were Tudor attempts to deal with poverty in the period 1531 to 1576 the result of the fear of social disorder? (20 marks)

Tip

Attempts to deal with poverty do not need to include only Acts of Parliament; they can also include attempts by individuals and local communities.

HOW SERIOUS WAS THE RESISTANCE TO TUDOR RULE?

Why was rebellion a potential threat to the Tudor monarchs?

Any popular rebellion that got out of hand was a threat to any monarch of this period. If the local gentry and nobility who were the first line of defence were overwhelmed, it was very difficult for the local authorities to deal with revolts. Although those men and women who joined popular rebellions were poorly armed and lacked military training and discipline, the sheer number of people involved in Tudor protests was often larger than the forces mustered by local landowners or even the government. Even when the rebels' protests were peaceful, stopping them posed serious difficulties for the Tudor monarchs.

In assessing the level of threat posed by Tudor rebellions it is important to consider a number of factors:

- the numbers of rebels involved
- the geographical extent of the rebellion
- the role of local gentry and nobility
- the rebels' demands
- the ability of the government to respond to the threat.

What was the significance of resistance to Tudor subsidies and taxation?

Opposition to high levels of taxation or attempts by the government to introduce new methods of taxation was a common cause of popular revolt. The first-ever large-scale peasants' revolt had been against unpopular methods of taxation as far back as 1381, and that had created a precedent for popular protest.

Taxation was at the root of most of the popular protest seen in the period 1509–25. Because Henry VIII had an ambitious foreign policy involving wars in France and Scotland, he needed to raise money through taxation. To do this he needed the support of parliament, which was the only institution that could grant taxation. However, Henry had inherited an outdated taxation system that struggled to meet the demands he placed on it. In addition, parts of his country were relatively poor, especially the north of England, which struggled to pay the amounts asked of it. In 1513, Henry demanded a particularly high level of taxation, which led to some passive resistance in Yorkshire. Research has shown that money raised from taxation of the West Riding of Yorkshire that should have been paid in the summer of 1513 was not actually paid until 1515, and the king was forced to remit (cancel) the payments from 19 towns and villages from that area. This cancellation then created a precedent for the future; after some communities had received a cancellation of their taxation once, they would expect it again, and the government would struggle to reinstate its demands.

Why was there resistance to the Amicable Grant in 1525?

More serious problems for Henry occurred in the period 1523–35. Once again, he wanted to fund a foreign campaign, but by now the country had been bled dry of money. In 1523, Wolsey found that parliament would not agree to his demands for £800,000, though they did agree to a subsidy to be collected over four years, which had raised £136,578 by 1525. This was not enough for Henry's needs, so Wolsey turned to a less legal and more experimental method, the Amicable Grant. The Grant was not a parliamentary tax, and so Wolsey was already on shaky legal ground. To make matters worse, despite its name, the Amicable Grant was actually a forced loan, known as a benevolence. Benevolences had been declared illegal by a 1483 Act of Parliament, but this did not stop Wolsey. Wolsey compounded the problem by ordering local commissioners to collect most of the money in a three-month period between March and June 1525. This was a very short time period, which put more pressure on local communities who were also paying the second instalment of the 1523 subsidy. The result of this financial pressure was at first passive resistance across wide areas of the country; there was widespread non-payment and resistance in Warwickshire, East Anglia, Berkshire, Wiltshire and Kent. Even more seriously for local order, large groups began to gather in protest, though these remained mostly peaceful. The most famous of these was at Lavenham (Suffolk), where about 4,000 people gathered. Lavenham had a group of wealthy landowners who had been able to afford the government's financial demands, but a large proportion of people in the region were out of work and unable to pay. Popular protest did not stop at anger over high rates of taxation; it also included more general criticism of the king's wars, which had achieved very little. The events at Lavenham were particularly dangerous because such a large gathering would have been hard to control or disperse and represented a direct challenge to the royal policy.

The protest over the Amicable Grant was successful in that Wolsey was forced to give up the idea. The threat of the large gathering in Lavenham was enough for the local nobility, the Dukes of Norfolk and Suffolk, to use cautious negotiation in their approach because they feared provoking the rebels into violence. The four ringleaders of the revolt were pardoned and there was no further attempt by the government to raise taxation until 1534. Henry had to abandon his plans to go to war and instead had to pursue a peace policy. Significantly, the protest over the Amicable Grant shows that the Tudor monarchs were not able to raise money from their subjects by non-parliamentary methods. Nor were they able to demand as much money as they liked. Their subjects knew this and were prepared to use tactics such as non-payment and open protest in order to make their views heard.

SOURCE

11 From a letter written by the Archbishop of Canterbury, William Warham, to Cardinal Wolsey, 5 April 1525.

It will be hard to raise the money, especially as other parliamentary grants are still to be paid. Reports, for the secret ear of the Cardinal, show the dissatisfaction prevailing. People say they shall never have rest from payments as long as some liveth. Some of the commissioners only announce the king's command without pressing it further through fear of the people.

Although the later Tudor revolts were not focused on the issue of taxation in the same way, it was still a contributing factor to the rebellion in 1536. The demands of the Pilgrims of Grace in 1536 included economic grievances and concerns over taxation. The 1534 Subsidy Act had created a parliamentary precedent because it was granted in a time of peace and not because of the traditional reason which was the need to fund the king's wars and the defence of the realm.

ACTIVITY
KNOWLEDGE CHECK

Problems and protests

1 What does Warham's letter (Source 11 on page 75) reveal about the problems facing the commissioners in 1525?

2 Make a list of the reasons why the protest against the Amicable Grant succeeded.

The nature and threat of popular risings, 1536–69

What were the causes of the Lincolnshire Rising and the Pilgrimage of Grace?

The rebellions that broke out in Lincolnshire and the north of England during 1536 were caused by the reaction to the rapid and radical changes that were being imposed by Henry VIII and Cromwell in the period 1535–36. This is clear from the actions of the Lincolnshire rebels. The trigger for the rising in Lincolnshire was the presence of no less than three sets of government commissioners in the region, overseeing the dissolution of the smaller monasteries, the collection of the 1534 subsidy, and assessing the standard of education among the clergy. Such a high level of government intervention focused on one region was bound to cause tension and rumours. The spark for the rebellion was the arrival of the Bishop of Lincoln's official at Louth on 2 October to carry out a visitation of the clergy. The official was seized by the guards and made to swear an oath of loyalty to them. His papers were burnt in an act of defiance against government intervention. The men of Louth then showed their anger at the dissolution of the smaller monasteries by marching to the nearby Legbourne nunnery and capturing the commissioners who were there to dissolve it. The following day, tensions increased as the government commissioners tried to continue with their work. The result was that 3,000 people met together at Louth and the government commissioners who had planned to negotiate with the angry rebels were forced to flee.

The rebel petition that was drawn up on 9 October makes it clear that the rebels' main grievances were over the dissolution of the smaller monasteries, the 'evil counsel' that Henry was receiving from men of 'low birth', such as Cromwell and Chancellor Richard Rich, and the promotion of men with reformer sympathies such as Cranmer. There were also other concerns, however. One article complained about the **Act of Uses (1535)**, a grievance that was echoed in the articles of the Pilgrims of Grace. The inclusion of this article reflects the concerns of the gentry who joined the rebellion. A final article complained about the 1534 subsidy and the inability of the Lincolnshire men to pay, mirroring the concerns of those who joined the rebellion.

The petition reflects the fact that gentry, landlords and the rebels joined the revolt. Although the evidence is not clear as to whether the gentry joined willingly or were coerced, as some later claimed, the preoccupation with government intervention in their lives and especially the religious changes that were occurring was a factor that united them. This was significant because it shows the level of threat this rebellion posed to Henry's government. The gentry were supposed to put down any local trouble; by joining in, they were adding considerable support, power and leadership to the revolt.

The causes of the larger and more serious Pilgrimage of Grace were also linked to the dissolution of the smaller monasteries and religious reform. There has been debate about the extent to which there was genuine popular anger at the dissolution and the extent to which the grievances of the clergy and leaders such as Aske were imposed on the rebels. However, research by historians such as Michael Bush has revealed the genuine anger felt by the rebels about the dissolution. The rebels tried to restore 16 of the 55 monasteries that had been suppressed. The rebels also feared the social and economic consequences of the dissolution, and especially the impact on the poor who relied on the alms provided by the monasteries, as the pilgrims' ballads circulating in 1536 suggest. There were also wider social and economic concerns, which reflected the hardship faced in the north of England. The wide-ranging Pontefract Articles complained about enclosure, unfair rises in rent imposed by landlords, and the corrupt activities of local officials. They also asked for remission from the 1534 subsidy, which had hit the impoverished north particularly hard. The views of members of the clergy who joined the rebellion are also reflected in the articles in complaints about government attacks on the traditional privileges of the Church such as benefit of clergy. The leader of the Pilgrimage of Grace, Robert Aske, an educated lawyer, was able to articulate the rebels' fears more clearly and it was he who encouraged the idea that the rebellion was a traditional 'pilgrimage'. However, the rebels' actions and the majority of the complaints made by the rebels were about the religious changes imposed by the government. The rebels wanted an end to the heresies of Luther and other thinkers, the restoration of the powers of the pope and the reversal of the dissolution of the smaller monasteries.

KEY TERM

Act of Uses (1535)
This was an attempt by Henry and Cromwell to stop gentry landowners avoiding the financial demands made by the king as their feudal overlord. Technically, the monarch was the feudal landlord for all of England and the landowners were his tenants. This meant that the monarch had the right to the guardianship of the tenants' lands and heir when the heir was a minor, which was potentially a very profitable source of income. Landowners had tried to get round this by creating a legal device known as an 'enfeoffment to uses', which created a group of trustees for their lands and heir. The Act of Uses restricted these enfeoffments in an attempt to raise more money for the Crown and was resented by landowners.

SOURCE 12 From the Pilgrims' Ballad, 1536, one of many that were circulating at the time.

Alack! Alack!
For the church sake
Poor commons wake,
And no marvel!
For clear it is
The decay of this
How the pore shall miss
No tongue can tell

How serious were the rebellions of 1536?

The Lincolnshire rising was potentially serious because some local Lincolnshire gentry became involved. As the rebellion gathered momentum, numbers swelled to 10,000 and the rebels were able to march on Lincoln as members of the local nobility such as Lord Hussey fled. The local clergy also became involved, including some monks. However, Henry took swift action, threatening the rebels with harsh punishment if they did not disperse. The threat was backed up by a royal army, which had quickly marched to Lincolnshire and was led by the Duke of Suffolk. When a herald arrived on 11 October, he was able to persuade the rebels to go home. While their actions up to that point had been mostly peaceful, if they had chosen to fight the royal army they would have been committing treason. As a result of decisive action by the government, a battle had been avoided and the Lincolnshire rebellion collapsed in less than two weeks. However, the fact that the rebellion had spread so quickly and attracted such widespread support from all sections of society showed that it was a potential threat. The reason that the government was able to deal with it so quickly was because at this stage it was only the Lincolnshire rebels that had risen – the rebels of Yorkshire had sent a message to their Lincolnshire counterparts to say that they were not yet ready to rise. The relative ease with which the rising was put down may have lulled Henry into a false sense of security, because on 19 October he disbanded a second army he had sent north to deal with the Lincolnshire rebels, leaving the Duke of Suffolk and his army to finish suppressing the trouble in Lincolnshire on their own.

The Pilgrimage of Grace began on 10 October in the East Riding of Yorkshire and was closely connected to events in Lincolnshire. Representatives of the rebels in Yorkshire were communicating with the Lincolnshire rebels as early as 2 October, and the leader of the Pilgrimage of Grace, Robert Aske, had been involved in the Lincolnshire risings. By 16 October, the rebellion in the East Riding had attracted 10,000 followers and the rebels were able to take over the city of York. On 19 October, the rebels captured the port of Hull and Pontefract Castle. Lord Darcy, who had been trying to defend Pontefract, wrote letters to the king asking for help, but he did little else to stop the rebels and was eventually persuaded to join them. While the rebels in East Yorkshire were making great gains, the North Riding of Yorkshire also rose up. Again they had support from leading members of the local nobility and gentry, Lord Latimer and Sir Christopher Derby. The North Yorkshire rebels captured Barnard's Castle before meeting up with Aske's rebels at York. Further afield, but encouraged by the rebels in Yorkshire, rebels were mustering in Westmorland and Cumberland. By late October, there were nine well-armed and organised rebel hosts (armies), many of whom had converged on York. The geographical extent of the rebellion covered most of the north and north-east of England. The only region where they were less successful was in Lancashire, where the Earl of Derby remained loyal to Henry despite his religiously conservative beliefs. This was because Henry had given Derby huge powers over Lancashire, Cheshire and North Wales, which convinced Derby to remain loyal and put down the rebels instead.

How did the government suppress the Pilgrimage of Grace?

The Pilgrimage of Grace was extremely serious for the government. The rebel army was 30,000 strong, and had in its ranks well-trained fighters who had recent military experience in the wars against Scotland. By contrast, Henry's military resources were overstretched. The Duke of Suffolk was still restoring order in Lincolnshire, and Henry had sent a second army home. The result of this was that the rebels had three weeks in which to gather and prepare a strategy. The situation was made worse because so many of the northern gentry had joined the rebellion.

Eventually, on 23 October, the Duke of Norfolk and the Earl of Shrewsbury marched north with an army of about 8,000 men. Because they were so outnumbered by the rebels they had little choice but to negotiate, so Norfolk sent a letter to the rebels asking for a meeting. Aske agreed and the meeting took place on 27 October. At this meeting, the rebels presented a list of five articles, and it was agreed that two representatives would take it to the king and that a truce would be called. When Henry was presented with the rebel articles, his initial response was to write an angry reply. Norfolk persuaded him that it would be better to offer the rebels further negotiations in the hope that the longer these were extended, the more momentum the rebellion would lose. The rebels accepted the king's offer and drew up a second set of 24 complaints to give to Norfolk. The second meeting between Norfolk and the rebels took place at Doncaster on 6 December when the rebels asked for the king's pardon, which Norfolk was able to grant, together with a promise of a parliament and further negotiations on the fate of the monasteries. When news of the king's pardon reached the rebel camp on 8 December, many of them started going home, as Norfolk had hoped.

However, the king had no intention of keeping his side of the agreement. Gradually, some of the former rebels began to realise that Henry had tricked them. In January 1537, there was a short, unsuccessful rising led by Sir Francis Bigod and a former pilgrim, John Hallam, who briefly captured Beverley (East Yorkshire). There was also renewed unrest in the West Riding of Yorkshire, Cumberland and Westmorland, which was put down near Carlisle. This unrest gave Henry the excuse he needed to punish the rebels. At least 144 people were executed, including the gentry and noble leaders such as Aske, Sir Thomas Percy, Bigod and Hussey. As a longer-term response, Henry also reorganised the Council of the North. Resentment of his policies continued in the north, however. In 1541, there was a plot to kill the president of the Council of the North and capture Pontefract Castle, but this was quickly discovered and put down by the Council itself. Henry had learnt his lesson when it came to the management of the north and there would not be another rebellion there until 1569.

TIMELINE – THE LINCOLNSHIRE RISING AND THE PILGRIMAGE OF GRACE, 1536-37

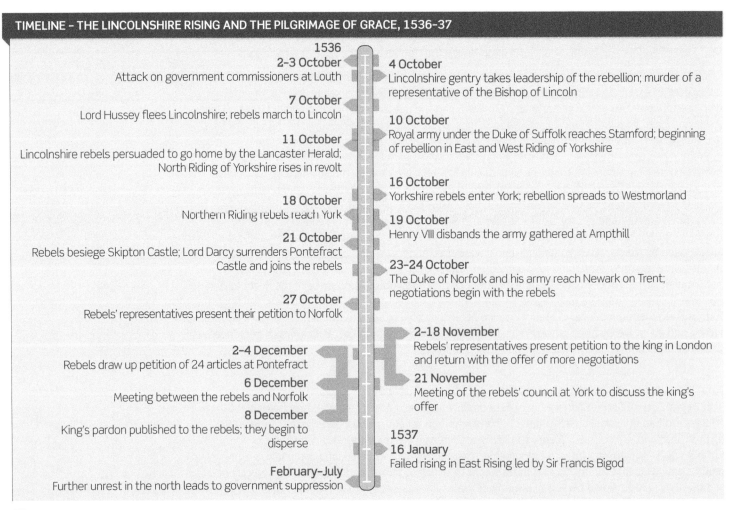

1536

2-3 October
Attack on government commissioners at Louth

4 October
Lincolnshire gentry takes leadership of the rebellion; murder of a representative of the Bishop of Lincoln

7 October
Lord Hussey flees Lincolnshire; rebels march to Lincoln

10 October
Royal army under the Duke of Suffolk reaches Stamford; beginning of rebellion in East and West Riding of Yorkshire

11 October
Lincolnshire rebels persuaded to go home by the Lancaster Herald; North Riding of Yorkshire rises in revolt

16 October
Yorkshire rebels enter York; rebellion spreads to Westmorland

18 October
Northern Riding rebels reach York

19 October
Henry VIII disbands the army gathered at Ampthill

21 October
Rebels besiege Skipton Castle; Lord Darcy surrenders Pontefract Castle and joins the rebels

23-24 October
The Duke of Norfolk and his army reach Newark on Trent; negotiations begin with the rebels

27 October
Rebels' representatives present their petition to Norfolk

2-18 November
Rebels' representatives present petition to the king in London and return with the offer of more negotiations

2-4 December
Rebels draw up petition of 24 articles at Pontefract

21 November
Meeting of the rebels' council at York to discuss the king's offer

6 December
Meeting between the rebels and Norfolk

8 December
King's pardon published to the rebels; they begin to disperse

1537
16 January
Failed rising in East Rising led by Sir Francis Bigod

February-July
Further unrest in the north leads to government suppression

THINKING HISTORICALLY Causation (3c&d)

Causes of the outbreak of the Pilgrimage of Grace

1 Work on your own or with a partner to identify as many causes of the outbreak of the Pilgrimage of Grace as possible. Write each cause on a separate card or piece of paper.

2 Divide your cards into those causes that represent:

a) the actions or intentions of people

b) the beliefs held by people at the time

c) the contextual factors or events (that is, political, social or economic events)

d) states of affairs (long- or short-term situations that have developed in particular ways).

3 Focus on the intentions and actions of the key people in the run-up to the outbreak of the rebellion. For each person draw on your knowledge to fill in the table below, identifying:

a) their intentions

b) the actions they took to achieve these

c) the consequences of their actions (both intended and unintended)

d) the extent to which their intentions were achieved.

Key figure	Intentions in 1536	Actions taken	Consequences	How far intention achieved
Henry VIII	To dissolve the monasteries to raise money To reinforce the Royal Supremacy and the break with Rome To extend royal control across England	Allowed Act of Parliament ordering the dissolution of the smaller monasteries Allowed Cromwell and his commissioners to investigate the state and wealth of the monasteries	The dissolution of the smaller monasteries (intended) Triggering of revolts in Lincolnshire and the north (unintended) Involvement of gentry and nobility in the revolt (unintended)	Short term – dissolution of the smaller monasteries achieved Long term – a more cautious approach to the dissolution of the larger monasteries Long term – royal control extended in the north
Thomas Cromwell				
Robert Aske				
The Percy family				
The Duke of Norfolk				

4 Discuss the following questions with a partner.

a) Did any one party intend for the Pilgrimage of Grace to break out in 1536?

b) How important are people's intentions in explaining the outbreak of the Pilgrimage of Grace?

What were the causes of the Western Rising in 1549?

The Western Rising was part of a wider crisis in Tudor government in 1549. Known as the 'commotion time', this also included Kett's Rebellion in East Anglia and wider unrest in 25 counties. Part of the reason that these rebellions were so serious for the government was because they stretched resources to the limit.

The Western Rising was the result of tensions that had been building in Cornwall since at least 1547. These tensions were due to government intrusion into the county and resentment over the religious reforms that were being imposed. The government was represented by William Body, who was closely connected to Cromwell. In 1547, Body summoned the clergy to hear the new injunctions, only to be met with demonstrations. At the same time, government commissioners were surveying the chantries, creating even more tension. In 1548, when Body returned to oversee government orders that all images in churches be destroyed, a mob led by a parish priest attacked and killed him.

The spark for the serious rebellion that followed in 1549 was the news that the new prayer book was to be enforced. In Cornwall this led to a rebellion that began in Bodmin and attracted the support of a gentleman, Humphrey Arundel. By 6 June, the Cornish rebels had formed a camp at Bodmin.

At the same time there was a rising in Devon following a service using the new prayer book. This rising began at Sampford Courtenay and quickly spread. By 20 June, the Cornish rebels had joined up with the Devon rebels in the town of Crediton. The set of articles produced by the rebels reveals their concerns about religious change. They wanted a return to the Six Articles (1539), the Mass to be celebrated in Latin, the Eucharist to be of one kind not two, images in churches, prayer for souls in purgatory, the recall of the English Bible and prayer book, and the partial restoration of the monasteries and chantries.

The rebels showed their contempt for the new English liturgy, calling it 'a Christmas game'. However, there was also a social and economic element to the rebellion. The Duke of Somerset had ordered a new tax on sheep and woollen cloth, and that would have hit Devon particularly hard as the economy of that county was based on sheep farming. Rumours were also going round that there were plans for other new taxes on geese and pigs. These complaints appeared in earlier versions of the rebels' articles but were omitted from the final version, which was shaped by the clergy who became involved in the rebellion such as Robert Welsh, a parish priest from Exeter. However, the initial motivation for the risings and the rebels' early actions show that the clergy represented the popular anger against religious change accurately. The seriousness of the rebellion was clear by early July, when 2,000 rebels besieged Exeter.

What challenges did Edward's government face in suppressing the Western Rising?

One problem faced by the government was that the remoteness of the region hampered communications with local gentry and led to delays and misunderstandings. Lord John Russell, a major landowner in Devon thanks to the dissolution of the monasteries, was sent by the Duke of Somerset to deal with the rebellion. But Somerset was unaware that the Cornish and Devon forces had united. He could only provide Russell with a very small army because of riots in the Midlands, Kett's Rebellion in East Anglia and fears of a French invasion. These problems meant that Somerset did not act properly to suppress the rebellion until 10 July, when he gave Russell more troops. But Russell's army of about 1,700 men was still outnumbered by the rebels. He was not able to lift the siege of Exeter until 3 August, when he received help from Lord Grey, who arrived with reinforcements. By this time the number of rebels had swelled to about 6,000. Some 300 were killed in the lifting of the siege, but many more fled and re-established their camp at Sampford Courtenay. By now, France had declared war on England and there was a possible threat of French intervention on behalf of the rebels. It took Russell until 16 August to gather enough men and supplies to deal with the rebels once and for all. The royal army defeated the rebels at Sampford Courtenay and it is estimated that about 4,000 rebels were killed.

The Western Rebellion, however, had been a threat in several ways. The inability of government forces to deal with it effectively allowed it to grow and it took a sizeable royal army to suppress it. Luckily for the government, the rebels preferred to stay in the West Country rather than march to London. This meant that they did not spread the rebellion still further at a time when the country was seriously disturbed.

The causes of Kett's Rebellion

Kett's Rebellion was centred around the important town of Norwich, but historians have shown that it was far bigger than one camp of rebels. Trouble had been brewing in the Norfolk area since at least 1548. Norwich itself was a rich town, but about 6 percent of the population owned 60 percent of the land and goods. The gap between rich and poor was widened by the abuses of local government officials, especially John Flowerdew, who had begun enclosing common land.

Riots against illegal enclosure of common land broke out in May 1549 and spread quickly through Essex and Norfolk in early July, with angry villagers uprooting hedges. A leader soon emerged in Robert Kett, who was a tanner by trade but who was also wealthy enough to own land in Wymondham, Norfolk. Kett himself had enclosed some common land, but when confronted by the rebels he agreed that his actions were illegal and that he would return the land.

The demands of the rebels were particularly worrying for the government because they came dangerously close to class warfare and emphasised popular anger against gentry wealth and privilege. The rebels complained about the corruption of local government officials such as John Flowerdew, who used their office for personal gain. The petition also included complaints about illegal enclosures and rack-renting. The rebels' anger was stirred up further by the actions of Somerset, who in 1548 had begun to investigate illegal enclosures. Somerset made the situation worse by making promises of reform to the rebels. He even sent out a new commission of enquiry into enclosure in early July, which gave the commissioners the power to act as well as inquire. Somerset's actions did not pacify the rebels; they only encouraged them to continue.

The actions of the rebels show the strength of feeling against the local gentry. Kett set up a 'commonwealth', an alternative form of government, which raised money and collected food and supplies in the king's name. Kett's commonwealth was a direct challenge to the power of the local gentry and might even have challenged the national government as an 'alternative' source of power and authority. There were also attacks on the property of unpopular members of the gentry such as Flowerdew. Unlike the West Country rebels, however, Kett's rebels actively supported the government's religious policies, even demanding the dismissal of priests who could not preach properly, to be replaced with those who could. The rebels also used the new English prayer book at their daily services in the Mousehold Heath camp. Ironically for the government, which had introduced these religious reforms in the first place, the rebels were inspired to take them further than had been intended. This posed a threat to the power and stability of the Church and the national government.

How did the government respond to Kett's Rebellion?

Kett decided to march on Norwich, which at this time was the second-largest city in England. By 12 July, the rebels had set up a camp at Mousehold Heath outside the city walls, which was estimated to have attracted 16,000 people. Other camps were also set up at Downham Market (Norfolk) and Bury St Edmunds (Suffolk). The rebellion spread well beyond East Anglia to Kent, and there was trouble in Surrey and Sussex.

Ironically, many of the local gentry were not present when the rebellion began because they had been summoned to Windsor on 1 July to form an army to deal with the Western Rising. Those who were left behind were overwhelmed by the sheer scale and speed of the rising.

Initially the government offered a truce, but this failed. On 22 July, the rebels attacked and overran Norwich. William Parr, the Marquess of Northampton, was sent with an armed force. His offer of a pardon led to just 20 rebels giving themselves up and his attack on Norwich on 31 July failed completely. The government was forced to raise more troops under the command of the Earl of Warwick. This new force of about 12,000 men reached Norwich on 23 August and a stand-off between Warwick and the rebels began. But it was not until the arrival of 1,000 mercenaries on 26 August that the leadership of Kett started to waver as his supply lines were cut off. The rebels moved to Dussindale where they were attacked by Warwick's horsemen and professional soldiers. Kett was captured and up to 3,000 of the rebels were killed. Kett himself was executed for treason in November 1549.

Once again, it had taken the government a considerable amount of time and military might to put down rebels who were determined and organised. The severity of the situation was made worse because so many risings happened across such a wide geographical area at the same time, stretching government resources dangerously. The government also struggled to deal with the rebels because in both the south-west and East Anglia there was a power vacuum. This was because in both regions the dominant noble families – the Courtenays in the South West and the Howards in East Anglia – had been destroyed in the last years of Henry VIII's reign.

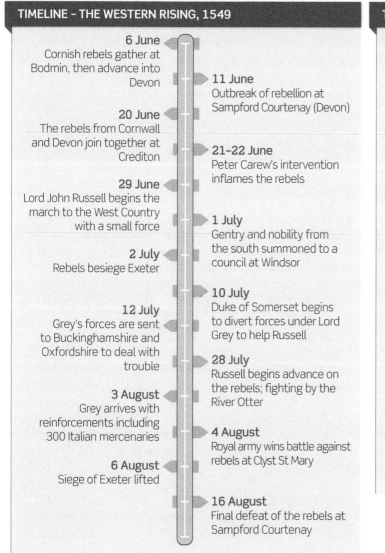

TIMELINE – THE WESTERN RISING, 1549

6 June
Cornish rebels gather at Bodmin, then advance into Devon

11 June
Outbreak of rebellion at Sampford Courtenay (Devon)

20 June
The rebels from Cornwall and Devon join together at Crediton

21–22 June
Peter Carew's intervention inflames the rebels

29 June
Lord John Russell begins the march to the West Country with a small force

1 July
Gentry and nobility from the south summoned to a council at Windsor

2 July
Rebels besiege Exeter

10 July
Duke of Somerset begins to divert forces under Lord Grey to help Russell

12 July
Grey's forces are sent to Buckinghamshire and Oxfordshire to deal with trouble

28 July
Russell begins advance on the rebels; fighting by the River Otter

3 August
Grey arrives with reinforcements including 300 Italian mercenaries

4 August
Royal army wins battle against rebels at Clyst St Mary

6 August
Siege of Exeter lifted

16 August
Final defeat of the rebels at Sampford Courtenay

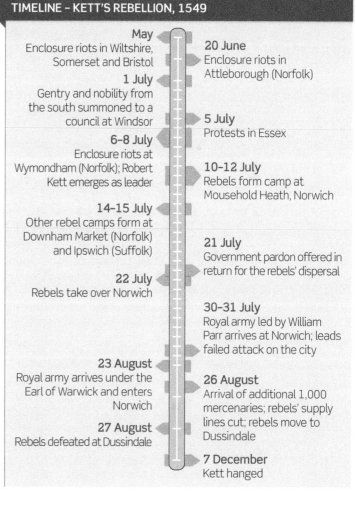

TIMELINE – KETT'S REBELLION, 1549

May
Enclosure riots in Wiltshire, Somerset and Bristol

20 June
Enclosure riots in Attleborough (Norfolk)

1 July
Gentry and nobility from the south summoned to a council at Windsor

5 July
Protests in Essex

6–8 July
Enclosure riots at Wymondham (Norfolk); Robert Kett emerges as leader

10–12 July
Rebels form camp at Mousehold Heath, Norwich

14–15 July
Other rebel camps form at Downham Market (Norfolk) and Ipswich (Suffolk)

21 July
Government pardon offered in return for the rebels' dispersal

22 July
Rebels take over Norwich

30–31 July
Royal army led by William Parr arrives at Norwich; leads failed attack on the city

23 August
Royal army arrives under the Earl of Warwick and enters Norwich

26 August
Arrival of additional 1,000 mercenaries; rebels' supply lines cut; rebels move to Dussindale

27 August
Rebels defeated at Dussindale

7 December
Kett hanged

Change (5b)

Causes of the 'commotion time', 1549

Changes in the years leading up to the outbreak of popular rebellion in 1549

Radical religious change since 1547 under Edward led to a rapid move to Protestantism	An ageing king (Henry VIII) had been replaced by a minor (Edward VI)	Social and economic change had led to increased poverty, rising prices, unemployment and a gap between the rich and poor
Local government official William Body had attempted to enforce religious reform in the West Country	The introduction of the new prayer book in 1549 led to protest at Bodmin	Government commissioners were investigating illegal enclosures in 1548
There were enclosure riots across the Midlands, south and east in 1549	Resentment of corrupt local officials such as William Cavendish	Attacks on Robert Kett's land in 1549 turned him into a rebel leader

Patterns of development consist of changes that at given times converge and have a bearing on one another and at other times diverge and have little in common. In the above example, the changes come together to form a pattern of development that tends towards rebellion.

Group work.

Write each change on a small piece of paper and arrange the pieces on a large A3 sheet of paper as you think best. Then link them with lines and write along the line what it is that links those changes. Think about how those links may have changed over time.

Answer the following questions individually or in pairs:

1 Why is 1547 an important year in changing approaches to religious reform?

2 Which changes were significant in the rebels' growing anger in 1549?

3 What changes were important in drawing rioters from across the Midlands, south and east into the rebellion that began in Norfolk?

4 The actions of which member of the central government represent a divergence from the general pattern of 1548-49?

Why did Sir Thomas Wyatt rebel in 1554?

Wyatt's Rebellion of 1554 was very different from the popular rebellions of 1536 and 1549. The 1554 rebellion began as a plot at court by men who were concerned about Mary's proposed marriage to Philip of Spain instead of the English candidate, Edward Courtenay. The main plotters were all Protestant and included Sir Peter Carew (the Devon gentleman who had failed to put down the 1549 Western Rising), Henry Grey (the Duke of Suffolk and father of Lady Jane Grey) and Sir Thomas Wyatt (an influential member of the Kentish gentry). They feared that the marriage would lead to England becoming a Spanish satellite state that would be dragged into Spanish wars. The growth of English nationalism also led to the fear of foreign interference. The Spanish marriage meant that Mary planned to restore Catholicism, which for Protestants like Wyatt and Suffolk represented a serious threat.

Their initial plan was to persuade the Protestant Princess Elizabeth to marry Courtenay and to place them on the throne instead of Mary, with the support of the Council. However, the Council backed Mary's decision to marry Philip, and so the conspirators began to plot what they hoped would be a national uprising. The idea was for the rebels to lead simultaneous risings from the west, Midlands and Kent, but news of their plot got out. The imperial ambassador Simon Renard informed the queen, and Courtenay was easily persuaded to admit what he knew. The planned rebellions failed except in Kent, a county in which Protestant sympathies were strong, where Wyatt was able to gain a considerable armed following very quickly.

Why was Wyatt's rising a threat to Mary's government?

Wyatt used anti-Spanish propaganda to attract supporters, but he concealed his ultimate plan, which was to depose Mary. Wyatt was successful in his methods; he took up arms on 25 January 1554 and by 28 January had attracted about 3,000 supporters.

To make matters worse, the government was finding it difficult to raise an army, especially because there was considerable sympathy for Wyatt's views. When the 80-year-old Duke of Norfolk arrived at Gravesend with 500 Londoners, he found that they deserted him for the rebels and Norfolk was forced to retreat to the safety of the Tower of London.

Wyatt's Rebellion also posed another threat. Its proximity to London meant that there was a danger that the capital city with all of its institutions of government could be captured, not to mention the queen herself.

Twice the queen offered to negotiate, but these offers were rejected by the rebels. At this point, Mary took matters into her own hands, making a speech at London's Guildhall to rally the crowds behind her. She also refused to leave London or even move to Windsor or the Tower where the defences were strong; instead, she insisted on staying at the Palace of Westminster.

Between 3 and 6 February, Wyatt and his men tried to enter London, but initially they found the defences barred against them. However, the rebels were encouraged by the ambivalent attitude of the Londoners; some Londoners stood back and let Wyatt pass. They did not turn decisively against Wyatt until he and his depleted army reached Ludgate, which was locked. At this point, the Earl of Pembroke was able to capture the remaining rebels, which brought the revolt to an end.

The involvement of members of the court, Suffolk and Wyatt, was a threat to Mary because they were powerful leaders of local and national politics. Courtenay and Elizabeth were both imprisoned in the Tower on suspicion of involvement in the plot. Elizabeth had probably been in touch with the conspirators, but there was no firm evidence that she or Courtenay had been directly involved in the plot, so neither was charged. Mary's government was still suspicious of them, however, so Elizabeth was placed under house arrest and Courtenay was exiled. The most important victims of the rebellion were two people who had played no part in it: Lady Jane Grey and her husband, Guildford Dudley. Both were executed on 12 February 1554.

Wyatt's Rebellion was serious because, although relatively brief, it exposed the problems facing Mary in restoring Catholicism through her Spanish marriage. It also revealed that some members of her court could not be trusted. In addition, Wyatt and his men got very close to capturing Westminster – at one point they reached Hyde Park, which is only a short distance from Westminster. However, Mary's leadership and the loyalty that was felt towards her was enough to put down the rebellion, although the rebels' poor planning also played a part. If all of the rebellions had happened as planned, Mary might have been facing a much more serious crisis.

Why was there a rising led by the northern earls in 1569–70?

The revolt in the north in 1569 was the last serious revolt in the Tudor period. The rebellion was partly the result of the arrival and imprisonment of the Catholic Mary, Queen of Scots, in England in 1568. Her presence meant that she was a potential figurehead for any Catholics who wanted to restore their religion by putting Mary on the throne. Among those who were sympathetic to Mary were two Catholic noblemen from the north, Thomas Percy (Earl of Northumberland) and Charles Neville (Earl of Westmorland). These noblemen felt alienated from court not only because of religious policy but also because Elizabeth had promoted her Protestant nobility into positions normally held by the Percys and Nevilles. For example, Elizabeth's cousin, Lord Hunsdon, had been put in charge of the Eastern March. Moreover, the north in general still had strong Catholic sympathies. For example, William Cecil estimated that in 1566 two-thirds of the northern JPs were Catholic. Surviving sympathy in the north helped to bring about popular rebellion. Meanwhile, Mary herself was encouraging her supporters in her letters and was in contact with both Northumberland and the pope.

One solution to the problem of what to do with Mary was for her to marry the leading member of the English nobility, the Duke of Norfolk. Supporters of this idea at court thought that this alliance would secure the English succession and control Mary through marriage to someone who was at least nominally Protestant. However, Elizabeth was not prepared to consider this option and began to suspect Norfolk of being involved in a plot against her. Norfolk was not only powerful, he was also the brother-in-law of Westmorland. Norfolk left court on 26 September but did not go to the north, remaining instead at his manor of Kenninghall, in Norfolk, while he decided what to do. On 1 October, he wrote to Westmorland telling him not to rebel. Norfolk then surrendered himself to the queen.

To what extent did the Revolt of the Northern Earls pose a threat to Elizabeth?

Although Norfolk had surrendered, rumours of a potential revolt were still circulating. Elizabeth remained suspicious of Westmorland and Northumberland and summoned them to court. This forced the earls into open rebellion on 9 November, although Westmorland was more enthusiastic than Northumberland, who had to be persuaded to act by some of his supporters.

On 14 November, the earls marched to Durham Cathedral where they celebrated Catholic Mass. By 22 November, the rebels had marched to Bramham Moor; by this time they had attracted around 3,800 foot soldiers and 1,600 horsemen. The horsemen were a particular threat since this meant that the rebels were well equipped.

Meanwhile, officials who remained loyal to the queen found it difficult to act. Sir George Bowes had to defend Barnard's Castle in County Durham from the rebels, as by the first week in December he was under siege from nearly 5,000 rebels. Bowes' own men began to change sides and eventually handed him over to the rebels. Similarly, the Earl of Sussex, who as president of the Council of the North was in charge of maintaining order, was trapped in York with only 400 horsemen. The rebels controlled so much of the north that Sussex stopped sending letters to London because he feared they would fall into the wrong hands.

The rebels even managed to capture the port of Hartlepool, hoping that the Spanish King Philip II would send troops to help them, though this hope turned out to be false because Philip did nothing.

Despite the rebels' apparent strength, their rebellion began to collapse. Instead of marching further south from Bramham Moor in an attempt to release Mary from prison, they turned back on 24 November. It is unclear why the rebels changed their minds, but it might have been because they had heard that the government had moved Mary from Tutbury Castle and she was out of their reach. As the rebels retreated, some began to leave, but it was not until 16 December, when a royal army of 10,000 men was approaching, that the rebel earls disbanded their army and fled. Northumberland fled over the border into Scotland; he was handed over by the Scottish authorities in 1572 and beheaded. Westmorland remained in exile abroad. Eight other leaders of the rebellion who were captured were executed.

The rebellion failed partly because it lacked co-ordination and the rebels themselves were never fully clear about what they were trying to achieve. They also lacked support from other members of the conservative northern nobility and gentry. For example, Henry Lord Clifford supported Mary, but he was not prepared to join the rebellion. Another potential supporter, Lord Dacre, was in London when the rebellion took place, but he probably would have joined it. In 1570, Dacre used an army of 3,000 men to attack the government representative Lord Hunsdon, before fleeing to Scotland. Another reason why the rebels did not succeed was because the foreign intervention that they hoped for did not materialise. Philip of Spain was reluctant to help Mary because she had too many connections with France, who was his enemy.

Helping Mary to become queen of England would have strengthened French power, particularly in the English Channel. The rebels also hoped that Scottish supporters of Mary might invade from the north, but this was prevented by the pro-English regent of Scotland. However, Elizabeth herself clearly saw the rebellion as a threat because she ordered that 800 rank and file rebels should be executed. Even if not all of these executions were carried out, Elizabeth's reaction showed that, in a climate of increasing political instability, the Northern Revolt was a threat to her position as queen.

SOURCE 13

Sir Ralph Sadler writing to Sir William Cecil from York, 6 December 1569, explaining why the Earl of Sussex would not be able to trust his forces to fight the rebels.

I perceive her Majesty is to believe that the force of her subjects of this country should not increase, and be able to match with the rebels; but it is easy to find the cause. There are not ten gentlemen in all this country that favour her proceedings in the cause of religion. The common people are ignorant, superstitious, and altogether blinded with the old popish doctrine, and therefore so favour the cause which the rebels make the colour of their rebellion, that, though their persons be here with us, their hearts are with them. And no doubt all this country had wholly rebelled if, at the beginning, my Lord Lieutenant had not wisely and stoutly handled the matter. If we should go to the field with this northern force only, they would fight faintly, for if the father be on this side, the son is on the other; and one brother with us and the other with rebels.

Figure 3.1 The major centres of revolt in the period 1525–69.

Map key:
- Northen Rebellion (1569)
- Western (Prayer Book) Rebellion (1549)
- Pilgrimage of Grace (1536)
- Amicable Grant Revolt (1525)
- Kett's Rebellion (1549)

Locations: Carlisle, Durham, Brancepeth, Barnard Castle, Hartlepool, Richmond, Skipton, York, Pontefract, Lincoln, Norwich, Lavenham, Sampford Courtenay, Crediton, Exeter, Bodmin

TIMELINE – THE REVOLT OF THE NORTHERN EARLS, 1568–69

1568–69
Arrival of Mary, Queen of Scots in England

1569 16 September
Norfolk leaves court and takes up residence at Kenninghall

1 October
Norfolk sends a message to Westmorland telling him not to rebel; Norfolk surrenders to the queen

9 October
The Earl of Sussex (President of the Council of the North) questions Northumberland and Westmorland

24 October
Elizabeth demands that the earls appear at court

Early November
Westmorland's supporters mass at Brancepeth Castle

9 November
Northumberland joins the rebellion openly

13 November
Sussex begins to raise royal forces

14 November
Rebels march to Durham then begin to march south

22 November
Rebels reach Bramham Moor

24 November
Rebels turn back to the north

Early December
Rebels besiege Barnard's Castle

14 December
Rebels overrun Barnard's Castle

16 December
Rebels disband their army and flee

January 1570
Elizabeth orders Leonard Dacre to court

February 1570
Dacre defeated and captured by Lord Hunsdon

EXTEND YOUR KNOWLEDGE

Thomas Howard, fourth Duke of Norfolk (1536–72)

Thomas Howard was the grandson of Thomas Howard, third Duke of Norfolk, who died in 1554. Although his grandfather had been Catholic, the fourth duke was at least in theory Protestant, but in reality he was semi-Catholic. This is why Elizabeth was suspicious of the plan to marry Norfolk to Mary, Queen of Scots. Norfolk was also sympathetic to the resentment of the northern nobility over Elizabeth's preference for 'non-traditional' councillors such as Cecil and Robert Dudley.

Norfolk threw himself on Elizabeth's mercy in 1569 together with several other members of the nobility who had been involved in the marriage plan, including the Earls of Pembroke and Arundel. Norfolk was sent to the Tower. He was released in August 1570 but was implicated in the Ridolfi Plot to assassinate Elizabeth and replace her with Mary, Queen of Scots (1571), although the evidence against him was circumstantial. Norfolk's previous track record ensured that he was re-arrested, tried and executed for treason in January 1572.

How serious was the threat posed by popular rebellions, 1536–70?

Undoubtedly, popular rebellions posed a considerable threat to the Tudor regime. The sheer numbers involved in 1536, 1549 and 1569 caused problems because the local authorities and even royal armies struggled to suppress them and resorted to negotiation instead. The geographical location of the rebellions also made it harder for the authorities to act. The rebellions of 1536, 1549 and 1569 took place in the north and west, regions that were hard to get to and hard to communicate with. It is no surprise that, given their remoteness from the centre of government, both the north and the west remained religiously conservative and so a challenge to government policies. The situation was made worse in 1536 and 1569 because the very people who were supposed to suppress the rebellions, the nobility and gentry, joined in instead.

The length of time these rebellions lasted shows how difficult it was for the government to act against them. Because communications between the monarch in London and these regions took so long, events often overtook government attempts to react, as happened in the Western Rebellion in 1549. Even the rebellions in more accessible regions, Kett's and Wyatt's, posed a threat because of their proximity to the central government. Although Kett's Rebellion was of the 'camping' variety, with rebels forming large settlements rather than marching, Wyatt's Rebellion got very close to the heart of government at Westminster.

However, there were limits to the extent of the threat posed by popular rebellion. None of the rebels openly claimed that they wanted an end to the monarchy. Tudor propaganda was very effective in imposing the acceptance of a social hierarchy, which meant that to get rid of the monarchy was unthinkable. Two rebellions did come close to challenging the right of specific monarchs to rule – Wyatt's in 1554 and the northern earls' in 1569. However, these rebellions, like those of 1536 and 1549, were eventually defeated by the government. Ultimately, the government was always able to play on the natural sense of loyalty and obedience among the people to persuade them to disperse. In addition, enough of the nobility and gentry did remain loyal during the outbreak of popular rebellion to ensure continuing support for the Tudor monarchs.

On most occasions, the professional armed soldiers employed by the Tudor monarchs were no match for the amateur and poorly equipped rebels. Where fighting was not an option, as in 1536, the government could play for time and negotiate, trusting that the promises of a monarch would be enough to pacify the rebels.

Why was there a decline in popular resistance in the years 1570–88?

After the Northern Revolt there were no more large-scale popular rebellions in England and Wales in the period 1570–88. Although there were several Catholic plots and smaller disturbances and riots, none of them reached the scale of the earlier Tudor rebellions.

There are several reasons for this. First, Elizabeth I was adept at using propaganda to present herself as the champion of English Protestantism against the invasion of foreign Catholic powers who posed a threat to English independence. Events such as the St Bartholomew's Day massacre in France (1572), in which Protestants were killed by Catholics, and the assassination of the Protestant leader of the Dutch revolt (William of Orange (1584)) by a Catholic, helped to reinforce this fear of Catholicism and promote loyalty to Elizabeth as the defender of the realm. The combination of propaganda and events abroad played on increasing feelings of English nationalism and pride, as the *Armada Portrait*, painted in the aftermath of the English victory over the Spanish fleet, shows (see Source 14). Her propaganda also emphasised that all subjects should be obedient to her. In addition, the growth of the 'Gloriana' cult surrounding Elizabeth and the use of celebrations such as Elizabeth's 'Accession Day' reinforced her popular appeal to her subjects and promoted loyalty to her.

At the same time, those who appeared to support Mary, Queen of Scots or Catholicism were presented as dangerous traitors. The result of this was that most Catholics saw themselves as English first and Catholic second and preferred to support Elizabeth and England rather than the foreign powers who were trying to assassinate her. This helps to explain why Catholic plots were carried out by a Catholic minority and did not lead to another popular rebellion as had happened in 1569; in 1588, there was no Catholic uprising in support of the Spanish Armada. After the popular rising in the north in 1569, the plots against the queen did not progress further than the planning stage. The leaders of the plots were a minority of nobility and gentry such as the Duke of Norfolk (1571), Sir Francis Throckmorton (1583) and Sir Anthony Babington (1586). None of these plots gained wider support. In each case, Francis Walsingham's spy network helped to implicate and catch the plotters before they could get very far with their plans. When they were caught, they were tortured and punished.

Increasingly harsh punishments for those who did rebel also played their part in encouraging loyalty and obedience. Elizabeth sent out a stern message in 1569–70 in her punishment of the rebels. From 1571, parliament passed increasingly severe Acts against those who missed Church services, held private Masses, aided priests or owned a copy of the bull excommunicating Elizabeth.

Elizabeth's council also took action against possible rebels by writing the **Bond of Association** (1584) which was reinforced by the **Act for the Queen's Safety** (1585). These harsh punishments not only acted as a deterrent, they also showed the level of support for Elizabeth as they were introduced and backed by her nobility and gentry.

The development of the powers of the Justices of the Peace as a first line of defence against rebellious activity also helped to suppress potentially dangerous situations.

In addition, the longer that Elizabeth remained on the throne, the less likely it was that challenges to her religious settlement would emerge. The older generation of committed Catholics gradually died out and were replaced by those who had known only the Elizabethan Settlement. This was coupled with more effective Protestant propaganda through preaching and pamphlets.

However, the absence of rebellion can also be explained by Elizabeth's lack of action and by social and economic forces that were driving change. The earlier rebellions of the Tudor period had been sparked by grievances over heavy taxation. Elizabeth avoided this problem in two ways. First, she avoided commitment to major warfare before 1585. This meant that she did not have to ask parliament for taxation on a regular basis. Second, she avoided making any changes to how taxation was assessed. This meant that the contributions made by taxpayers fell during the reign and nothing was done to increase them. As a result, Elizabeth avoided tax rebellions, though she was storing up problems for her successors.

The relatively stable social and economic situation in the 1570s and 1580s also reduced the possibility of a popular revolt like those seen in 1525, 1536 or 1549 which were partially caused by lack of food or work.

Finally, Elizabethan society itself was changing. Rebellions such as the Amicable Grant and the 1536 and 1549 troubles had been led mostly by the **yeomen**, or **middling sort**. However, by Elizabeth's reign, this group had become increasingly literate. In the diocese of Norwich, for example, it is estimated that illiteracy had fallen from 60 percent to 30 percent by the 1580s. Instead of being left out of local government, this group was now included within it, taking on roles such as the administration of the poor law and voting in elections. As they became part of the political system, so they became more likely to defend it rather than attack it through rebellion. They were also more likely to use the legal system to resolve disputes rather than resorting to violence. Similarly, with the increasing use of parliament, members of the gentry became more likely to voice their grievances through this forum rather than resorting to violent protest.

All of these factors led to fewer popular rebellions in England. This does not mean that there was no discontent or social and political instability, but from 1570 this was managed very effectively by Elizabeth and her government.

KEY TERMS

Bond of Association
The Bond was drawn up by Francis Walsingham and other members of the Privy Council in response to the plot to assassinate Elizabeth known as the Throckmorton Plot (1583). Those who signed the Bond pledged to protect the queen and to take revenge on anyone who attempted to harm her. A further clause stated that if Elizabeth was killed, anyone profiting from her death would be killed in revenge and would not be allowed to claim the throne. This was a reference to Mary, Queen of Scots and an attempt to stop any assassination attempt in her name, even if she was not involved.

Act for the Queen's Safety
The Act made provision for a council of 24 peers to investigate any invasion or rebellion attempt made against the queen and to disbar those responsible from inheriting the throne.

SOURCE 14 The Armada Portrait of Elizabeth I, painted c1588.

KEY TERM

Yeomen (or 'middling sort')
This was a social group formed of wealthier peasants who were usually landowners in their own right, but who were below the rank of gentry. Yeomen were sometimes craftsmen with skills that allowed them to be self-sufficient, for example, weavers, tanners and brewers. Examples of yeomen involved in rebellion include Robert Kett.

ACTIVITY
KNOWLEDGE CHECK

Rebellions

1 Use the information above to fill in the following table.

Rebellion	Causes	Geographical location	Who was involved?	How did the government respond?	Level of threat to the Tudor monarchy
Lincolnshire Rising/ Pilgrimage of Grace					
The Western Rebellion					
Kett's Rebellion					
Wyatt's Rebellion					
The Revolt of the Northern Earls					

2 Look back at the section in Chapter 1 on Mary Tudor's successful campaign to claim the throne in 1553. Historians have sometimes described these events as a 'successful Tudor rebellion'. How far do you agree with this claim?

3 Summarise in your own words why there was less popular protest after 1570.

AS Level Exam-Style Question Section A

From 1525 to 1569, the Tudor monarchs made reforms to local government including the role of JPs and the marcher councils.

Was the desire to decrease the power of the nobility the main motive for changes to local government (1525–69)? (20 marks)

Tip

You will need to consider other reasons for the reform of local government, such as concerns about local disorder and rebellion.

A Level Exam-Style Question Section B

How accurate is it to say that economic problems were primarily responsible for the discontent with Tudor rule in the years 1536–69? (20 marks)

Tip

Note the word 'primarily'. What does this mean and is this the best word to use for describing the causes of discontent throughout the period of the question?

ACTIVITY
SUMMARY

1 Look back to the section on the government's response to the Catholic threat and the role of Protestant propaganda under Elizabeth I. How does this response help to explain the decline in popular rebellion after 1570?

2 Make a spider diagram called 'How did the Tudor government control the localities?' Use the following headings to build up a set of revision notes: 'Role of the nobility'; 'Control of border territories'; 'JPs and Lord Lieutenants'; 'Social control of vagrants'.

3 Make a list of reasons why popular rebellion failed.

WIDER READING

Fellows, N. *Disorder and Rebellion in Tudor England*, Hodder Education (2002)

Heard, N. and Turvey, R. *Change and Protest, 1536–58: Mid Tudor Crises?* Hodder Education (2009)

Mervyn, B. *Enquiring History: Tudor Rebellions 1485–1603*, Hodder Education (2014)

Thomas, P. *Authority and Disorder in Tudor Times, 1485–1603*, Cambridge University Press (1999)

1.4 Economic, social and cultural change, 1509–88

KEY QUESTIONS

- How much did patterns of domestic and foreign trade change during the period?
- How far did Tudor society change?
- What was the significance of changes to Tudor culture, 1509–88?

INTRODUCTION

The Tudor period saw considerable developments in economy, society and culture. Before 1551–52, London and small rural towns benefited from the growth of the profitable cloth trade. After this period, when the cloth trade saw a temporary decline, exploration and the opening up of new trading routes, together with innovation and diversification within the cloth trade, led to new opportunities for both London and other English towns. The growth of towns in turn led to the development of new industries, but it also intensified the problems caused by poverty and unemployment. There was also rapid and radical cultural change. The spread of grammar schools and changes to university education were linked to the increasing use of the printing press. The result was a rise in literacy rates, the spread of new ideas and the growth of Tudor culture in art, drama, music and poetry.

HOW MUCH DID PATTERNS OF DOMESTIC AND FOREIGN TRADE CHANGE DURING THE PERIOD?

What was the significance of the English wool and cloth industries?

The income generated from the wool and cloth trade with the continent made some parts of England and particular individuals very wealthy. In the Middle Ages, English sheep farmers had produced fine-quality wool that was exported to Antwerp in the Netherlands, where it was turned into cloth. The proximity of Antwerp just across the North Sea encouraged this trade to flourish. Sheep farming was therefore a profitable occupation for large and small landowners alike; in particular, monastic foundations such as the Cistercians built much of their wealth on sheep.

By the 15th century, English manufacturers had started to produce their own cloth as well. The English cloth trade grew enormously in the Tudor period and was reliant on cheap rural labour for its success. Wealthy cloth merchants (known as clothiers) would buy the raw wool and then use local craftsmen working in their own homes to turn the wool into cloth, a process known as 'putting out'.

1509 – First grammar school founded in London

1536–40 – Dissolution of the monasteries

| 1505 | 1510 | 1515 | 1520 | 1525 | 1530 | 1535 | 1540 | 1545 |

1517 – Commission of enquiry into enclosure

1548 – Commission of enquiry into enclosure

The cloth would then be sold either direct to foreign merchants or via the **Merchant Adventurers**, based in London. The production of cloth was a very labour-intensive process. It would take 15 people one week to produce one medium-quality undyed cloth measuring 12 yards by 1¾ yards (about 11 metres by 1.6 metres). This meant that the industry grew in regions where there was ready access to both supplies of raw wool and the labour to turn it into cloth. This led to the growth of villages whose main industry was cloth making. The main cloth-making regions were in Kent, East Anglia, Gloucestershire, the West Country and the West Riding of Yorkshire, and key rural villages in these regions included Trowbridge (Wiltshire), Sudbury, Lavenham and Long Melford (Suffolk).

KEY TERM

Merchant Adventurers
This was a regulated company. All members were regulated by an agreed set of rules, but they traded as individuals. If an individual made a loss or went out of business, the company would be under no obligation to help them. The Merchant Adventurers were dominated by the members of the London livery trades but did include members from other towns such as York.

SOURCE

1 Lavenham Guildhall, built c1530 with money generated from the wool trade. The size and scale of this building reflects the significant wealth of the merchants of Lavenham.

The importance of the wool and cloth trade to the English economy can be seen both from its growth in the Tudor period and from the income that it generated. English cloth exports to Europe increased from an average of 55,000 cloths in the mid-15th century to 130,000 by the middle of the 16th century.

1551 – Collapse in English cloth trade

1560s – Start of migration of Dutch textile workers

1579 – Eastland Company set up

| 1550 | 1555 | 1560 | 1565 | 1570 | 1575 | 1580 | 1585 | 1590 |

1555 – The Russia Company set up

1566 – Unrest in Antwerp

1585 – Barbary Company set up

In Elizabeth's reign, exports averaged 100,000 cloths and brought in £750,000 a year. By this time, 90 per cent of the trade was done via London merchants. However, the cloth trade was vulnerable to booms and slumps. In the 1540s, the government's policy of debasement made English exports cheaper, leading to an artificial increase in profits for the cloth trade. The revaluation of the coinage from 1551 to 1552 led to a temporary decline in profits, although this stabilised in Elizabeth's reign. More seriously, the cloth trade was reliant on access to Antwerp. If this access was disrupted, then exports of cloth suffered. From c1566, the outbreak of the Dutch Revolt meant that it became increasingly difficult for English merchants to trade in Antwerp. This led to two developments: the arrival of Protestant refugees with new cloth-making techniques, and increased English interest in exploration and opening up new markets.

How did the new draperies change the English cloth trade?

The immigrant Dutch cloth weavers had developed new, lighter-weight fabrics that involved mixing woollen and **worsted yarns**, or woollen yarn with silk. This new cloth was cheaper and more colourful than the traditional English broadcloth, and it sold well in Mediterranean markets in southern Europe where the climate called for cooler, lighter materials. These were markets that had been neglected by English cloth merchants, who focused on Antwerp, but with the decline of Antwerp as a centre for trade, partly as a result of the Dutch Revolt, the arrival of new cloth-making techniques was a boost to the cloth industry because it opened up new markets. The new lighter cloths also tended to last less well than the traditional English cloths. This increased the demand for replacements. Furthermore, the new draperies needed large amounts of labour to sustain them, which at a time of high poverty and unemployment provided new opportunities for workers.

Associated industries also sprang up alongside the new draperies. Foreign silk-weavers arrived in London in the 1570s. Some Dutch migrants also introduced the technique of starch-making from wheat. Starch was vital to the production of fine materials like lawn and cambric, and was used for making the fashionable ruffs of the period. Such was the success of starch production that it became one of the monopolies sold by Elizabeth I to raise money in the 1590s. The importance of the new draperies was that they encouraged the English cloth trade to diversify its products beyond broadcloth to new textiles such as 'says' (serge), 'grosgrains' (a corded material) and 'mockadoes' (mock velvet). By the end of the 16th century, the new draperies were bringing in £250,000 per annum.

EXTEND YOUR KNOWLEDGE

The economic decline of Antwerp
Antwerp was dominant as a northern European trading port during the 15th and 16th centuries, but its importance began to decline from the early 1560s. Access to Antwerp and its trade had been an important consideration in Tudor foreign policy, especially as it was controlled by the Habsburgs, who also ruled Spain. In 1563, English reliance on Antwerp was exposed when its Spanish rulers imposed an embargo on the English cloth trade. This was lifted in 1564, but in 1566 there was widespread rioting in Antwerp, partly as a result of Protestant discontent in the town. In 1567 the Spanish sent a force under the Duke of Alba who put down the unrest with great brutality. England was forced to become involved in the revolt of the Netherlands to protect its trading interests as well as to protect Dutch Protestants. In the 1570s, Antwerp's position as a trading port was damaged further by the 'Spanish fury' in 1576, when Spanish troops sacked the port.

What was the impact of the migration of foreign textile workers?

The foreign textile workers who began to arrive in England from the 1560s were, like all foreigners, known as 'aliens'. As this name suggests, migrants were usually viewed with suspicion and dislike in Tudor England and their activities were closely monitored and controlled. However, the reception of the Dutch cloth workers was unusual in that they were actively welcomed by the English government. They were highly skilled, more so than the English cloth workers, and the government went out of its way to encourage them to settle in towns across the south and east of the country. Most of the migrants arrived via the ports in London, Southampton and Bristol, but communities were soon established in towns such as Maidstone, Canterbury and Sandwich (all in Kent), as well as Norwich (Norfolk) and Colchester (Essex). Such was the demand for these skilled workers, and the stimulus they could bring to urban economies, that the town council of Maidstone asked for 60 families with skills in making 'mockadoes' and 'says' to move there, but the government only allowed them 30.

The activities of these textile workers in the town were carefully regulated in that they were only allowed to employ English apprentices and unskilled workers, but the arrival of the Dutch migrants created a whole new industry in Maidstone – the making of linen thread. This in turn encouraged the growing of flax in the region around Maidstone in order to make the linen. Gradually the linen industry grew as ordinary people started to wear linen clothes rather than woollen ones. The Dutch migrants also had a similar impact in Norwich, helping to revive the worsted cloth industry there. By the mid-1580s, there were 4,600 'aliens' living in Norwich alone. However, the impact of the foreign textile workers was only felt in the regions and communities where they settled, in the south and east. In other places, there was no real change to the cloth industry.

ACTIVITY
KNOWLEDGE CHECK

The wool and cloth trade

1 Make a list of reasons why the wool and cloth trade was important to the English economy.

2 Make a flow chart or diagram to show the impact of the arrival of the new draperies in England. What was the role of Antwerp in the wool and cloth trade? How did this change?

The role of London as a market for goods

London was not just the largest city in England, it was also the largest city in Europe. In Henry VIII's reign, its population was about 60,000, and by 1570 it had risen to between 86,000 and 100,000. No other English town had a population of more than 20,000; the second-largest town was Norwich, which had 18,000 inhabitants by the 1570s. Because London was such a large city, it could not feed its population without supplies from other regions. The demand for grain, vegetables, meat, fish and dairy products grew steadily during the period, and encouraged the development of these agricultural industries in the regions around London such as East Anglia and Kent, produce from which was sold in the large London markets. Cattle were driven in from Essex, Suffolk, Kent and Bedfordshire and were sold at the Smithfield market. The Cornhill and Cheapside markets provided flowers, vegetables, poultry and dairy products, while Eastcheap market had its own slaughterhouses where butchers sold meat. Noble families also built houses in London, mostly along the Strand. These included Somerset House (built for Edward Seymour, Duke of Somerset) and Russell House. The presence of this wealthy elite, not to mention the monarch (who was usually based at the London palace of Whitehall or at Hampton Court in Middlesex), stimulated the demand for exotic and luxury goods from abroad such as silks, velvets and furs.

London was also a trading port for imports and exports, and during the Tudor period its importance grew rapidly. The Thames was vital for London's role as a place where a wide variety of goods could be bought and sold. Improvements to the navigation of the Thames in the 1540s meant that London began to overtake and undermine the trade of other ports such as Bristol and Southampton, known as 'outports'. Increasingly, both domestic and foreign traders used London as the base for their activities.

London was also a centre for manufacture. The main trades were organised into 12 major guilds or 'livery companies', which controlled and monopolised both the manufacture and sale of their goods. These guilds included the Grocers, the Mercers, the Fishmongers and the Merchant Taylors. The wealthiest merchants in each of these guilds organised themselves into 'liveries', a governing body for each guild. These men dominated not only their own trade, but also the social and political life of London. The Merchant Adventurers, which had a monopoly on the export of cloth, was closely linked to the livery companies; it was common for the senior members of the companies to be a member of the Adventurers as well. Earlier in the period, the livery companies and Adventurers had some competition from foreign merchants, especially the German Hanseatic League. The Hanse had special trading privileges, including the fact that they were exempt from taxation, and they specialised in the import of timber and grain from northern Germany and the Baltic states. Not only did they come under the general suspicion aimed at all foreigners, but they also faced criticism for making profits from imported grain at times of poor harvests. From the 1550s, the Hanse's privileges were gradually eroded by government legislation. This allowed the new **joint-stock companies** to seize the initiative in creating new trading links with the Baltic states. However, despite the monopolisation of the cloth trade and the increasing use of London as a port, the wealth generated only benefited those who controlled the London companies and the clothiers. Beyond this, London remained a city in which high levels of poverty existed.

KEY TERM

Joint-stock companies
Unlike regulated companies, these allowed investors to share both the risk and the profit among themselves. They were open to anyone with the money to invest and thus attracted a wider membership, including members of the English nobility.

SOURCE 2

Map of London: Southwark and part of Westminster, dated 1572. There was only one bridge across the river, London Bridge, which can be seen clearly. The artist was Franz Hogenburg, a Dutch artist and mapmaker who was expelled from Antwerp in 1568 and spent several years in London.

What were the consequences of exploration for the development of English trade?

Although there had been some English exploration in the reign of Henry VII, there was little under Henry VIII. Spain and Portugal were dominant in leading exploration and they had conquered vast areas of land in the West Indies and South America. By Elizabeth's reign, Spain had a virtual **monopoly** on trade in the New World. Interest in English exploration began to revive in Edward VI's reign, perhaps because of concerns over the English reliance on Antwerp, which were proved accurate by events in the 1560s and 1570s. The main focus of English exploration, which occurred from 1553 to the end of the period, was to find a sea route to Asia (through the 'north-western' and 'north-eastern' passages thought to be found to the north of Europe and north of Canada). Although this failed, there were other consequences for the development of English trade through the establishment of new trading links overseas.

The first major voyage of discovery set off in 1553 to search for the north-east passage. Its patron was the Duke of Northumberland, and it was led by the soldier Hugh Willoughby and the navigator Richard Chancellor. Chancellor eventually reached the Baltic and the White Sea; from there, he made his way overland through Russia to Moscow, where he set up a trading post. This led to the setting up of a joint-stock company, the Russia (or Muscovy) Company, in 1555. Although trade with Russia remained limited, Chancellor's success, combined with the weakening power of the Hanseatic League in the Baltic states, led to improved trade with the region especially in timber and tar. The Eastland Company was set up in 1579 to oversee this trade, which especially benefited York and Hull as they traded English cloth for flax and corn. In the Mediterranean there were attempts to expand English trading links with Muslim states. In Morocco from the 1550s, English cloth was

KEY TERM

Monopoly
This was control of a trade or industry by one person or group, which meant that there was no competition in that market. English governments could grant monopolies on particular goods or trades. For example, the Merchant Adventurers had a monopoly on the sale of English cloth abroad. The sale of monopolies became particularly controversial in the 1590s.

traded for sugar. Trading was formalised in 1585 with the creation of the Barbary Company, a regulated company led by the Earl of Leicester, which failed to make a profit. More successful was the deal made in the 1570s between English merchants and the sultan of Turkey, which led to the creation of the Turkish Company in 1581. The English gained Turkish exotic goods such as carpets, while the Turkish wanted English lead and tin, and this trade was the most profitable one for England other than the traditional cloth trade with Europe.

More controversially, English explorers and **privateers** tried to challenge the Spanish and Portuguese monopoly on trade. Between 1553 and the early 1570s, there was a series of English expeditions to the Guinea Coast, between Ghana and Sierra Leone, which aimed to bring back gold and pepper. These expeditions were violent because they led to confrontations with the Portuguese, who controlled trading rights there. They also led to the beginning of the African slave trade, which was developed by the activities of the pirate and explorer John Hawkins who, in 1562, began transporting slaves captured in Africa to the West Indies. Hawkins was confronted and defeated by the Spanish navy in 1568, but his activities encouraged those of Francis Drake in the 1570s. Drake launched a series of attacks on Spanish shipping in the early 1570s and in 1577 began what was to become the circumnavigation of the globe. Apart from attacking Spanish shipping, Drake's mission between 1577 and 1580 was also to try to find the north-west passage. He failed in this but was successful in creating the beginning of English trade with Asia when he made contact with the sultan of Ternate in Indonesia. This contact was to lead eventually to the formation of one of the most famous and successful of the companies, the East India Company, in 1600.

Drake's success encouraged further exploration by Martin Frobisher and John Davis to North America, where they hoped to find the north-east passage. This exploration failed but led to the establishment of the first English colonies at Roanoke Island in 1585 and Chesapeake Bay in 1587; both settlements were in Virginia, which was named after Elizabeth I, and were masterminded by Sir Walter Raleigh. Although both of these colonies were failures, they paved the way for English colonisation in the 17th century, while the beginning of the Atlantic trade benefited Exeter and Bristol. This was because a trading 'triangle' developed between Africa, the Americas and England – English ships transported slaves from Africa to work in the English colonies in America. The slave ships were then loaded with goods that would be imported into England and sold there.

Nevertheless, the English export trade was still dominated by cloth, but the consequences of expansion meant that there was a wider market than there had been at the start of the period.

SOURCE

3 Richard Hakluyt, *The Principal Navigations, Traffics and Discoveries of the English Nation*, 1589.

It can not be denied, but as in all former ages there have been men full of activity, stirrers abroad, and searchers of the remote parts of the world, so in this most famous and peerless government of her most excellent Majesty, her subjects through the special assistance and blessing of God, in searching the most opposite corners and quarters of the world, and to speak plainly, in compassing the vast globe of the earth more than once, have excelled all the nations and people of the earth.

EXTEND YOUR KNOWLEDGE

John Hawkins and deteriorating relations with Spain
The activities of John Hawkins in the West Indies were a direct threat to Spanish trading interests in the region. He managed to trade successfully with local authorities in the Caribbean because they were short of labour, but the Spanish Crown was angered by this attack on the Spanish trade monopoly. In 1568, Hawkins and his fleet were harboured at San Juan de Ulua (Mexico) when they were attacked by a Spanish fleet commanded by the newly appointed viceroy of New Spain. Three of Hawkins' six ships were lost and the rest limped home having lost most of their profits. This attack symbolised the deteriorating relationship between England and Spain in this period.

Hawkins' activities were also funded partly by Elizabeth I, who took some of the profits.

ACTIVITY
KNOWLEDGE CHECK

Economy and exploration

1 Why was London so important in the English economy?

2 Make a list of the main successes and failures of English exploration. What do you think was the most important success? What was the most important failure?

AS Level Exam-Style Question Section B

From 1551, the English cloth trade went into a temporary decline.

To what extent did the decline in the cloth trade damage the English economy between 1551 and 1588? (20 marks)

Tip

You need to look at ways in which the cloth trade did damage the economy and ways in which it did not. This may include looking at the recovery of the cloth trade.

A Level Exam-Style Question Section A

How accurate is it to say that there were major changes to English industry and trade in the period 1551 to 1588? (20 marks)

Tip

This question requires you to consider the extent of change but also continuities across the whole date range.

HOW MUCH DID TUDOR SOCIETY CHANGE?

Population increase and the impact on Tudor society

As Source 4 shows, population increase happened gradually throughout the Tudor period. The most rapid increases were in the 1520s and 1530s and the 1570s and 1580s.

The causes of population increase are complex, but most historians agree that it was the stable conditions of the 15th century that encouraged the first signs of growth. After the Black Death in the 14th century, which killed between one-third and half of the population, England's population recovered very slowly in the 15th century. This was partly because of disease, but also because many people were marrying later – in their mid-twenties, when they could afford it. This led to them producing fewer children. Coupled with a high death rate, this meant that the population was slow to recover before the early 16th century.

The smaller population created an artificially high standard of living. A smaller population drove up wage rates, while food prices were low. Rents were also low. These developments occurred because the smaller population meant that there was less demand for rented land, so landlords were forced to keep rents low in order to attract tenants. A smaller work force also meant that employers found it harder to find workers and had to pay higher wages to attract employees.

Gradually, as this prosperity continued, the marriage age began to drop again and the birth rate began to increase, while better standards of living may have improved fertility rates. Although there were bad harvests in 1519–21, 1527–29 and 1544–45, these were not bad enough to stop the upward trend of growth.

As Source 4 suggests, the population recovered fairly rapidly under Elizabeth. The stable social and economic conditions of the middle years of Elizabeth's reign meant that the annual death rate never increased to more than 2.68 percent of the population. High birth rates, better life expectancy and low death rates all contributed to increased population.

There was one exception to this trend, however. The years 1555–59 saw the worst economic crisis of the period. There was a series of poor harvests between 1555 and 1557, and an influenza epidemic broke out in 1555, peaking in 1557–59. A malnourished population was no match for the severity of the epidemic. The population dropped by six percent during those years, causing a temporary overall decline, although the improved conditions under Elizabeth led to recovery and renewed growth from the 1570s.

The results of this steady population growth were that more pressure was placed on local and national resources. The Tudor state was not equipped to deal with the impact of a bigger population. The outcome of this was that levels of poverty increased, towns began to fill with migrants looking for work, and there was more pressure on resources like food. Developments such as the dissolution of the monasteries and enclosure may well have contributed to this pressure on resources.

SOURCE 4 Population growth in Tudor England, based on the research of E.A. Wrigley and R.S. Schofield in *The Population History of England, 1542–1871: A Reconstruction* (1981).

Date	Population in millions
1525	2.26
1541	2.77
1551	3.01
1561	2.98
1571	3.27
1581	3.59
1591	3.89

What was the impact of the dissolution of the monasteries?

Some sections of society gained from the dissolution of the monasteries. The Crown itself gained temporarily because it acquired the former monastic lands, worth £1.3 million. In 1536, Cromwell even set up a special financial office – the Court of Augmentations – to deal with the lands, money and treasure that were taken from the monasteries. Two-thirds of the monastic lands were sold off in the 1540s to pay for Henry's wars, raising about £800,000 for the king; the rest had been sold by the end of the Tudor period. Those who bought this land, the nobility and gentry, also benefited from the dissolution, such as the Russell family in the south-west and Bedfordshire. The Russells used this land to establish themselves as important landowners; the former monastery of Woburn Abbey (Bedfordshire) was turned into their family home.

Abbots and priors who did not resist the dissolution were either given pensions or found another role within the Church as bishops or clergy. The Abbot of Romsey, for example, received a pension of £266 a year. Ordinary monks were also given smaller pensions of about £5 a year, which was about the same as the annual wage of an unskilled worker, but the monks were able to seek alternative employment.

Although the change of land ownership from Church to lay landlords may have brought about additional hardship for the tenants and employees of the monasteries, the evidence is that in most cases there was continuity of employment because the new owners needed the labour to keep the estates running.

There were negative consequences of the dissolution, however. About 7,000 ex-monks and nuns had to find a new life and way to support themselves after the dissolution. Nuns and friars received smaller pensions than monks. Former nuns were particularly badly hit because Henry insisted that they were not able to break their vow of chastity. This meant that they could not get married. Without a husband it was difficult for a woman with no independent means to survive or to make a living.

Monasteries had also been sources of learning, education and charity. The destruction of monastic libraries, together with the beautiful and richly decorated monasteries, has been described by historians such as Richard Rex as an act of cultural vandalism. Henry did found six new bishoprics using former monastic lands and buildings; these included Peterborough, Gloucester and Chester. He also re-established cathedral churches that had once been attached to monasteries such as Canterbury, Winchester, Ely and Durham. Wolsey's college at Oxford, Cardinal College, was refounded by the king as Christ Church College, while King's Hall Cambridge became Trinity College.

However, these high-profile foundations did not disguise the fact that Henry had promised to fill the gap left by the monasteries, but most of these promises were broken because the money was needed to fund Henry's wars against France and Scotland. Many former monastic buildings were left to decay. Schemes to fund preachers, schools, hospitals and poor relief were dropped. Because many schools and hospitals had been attached to monasteries, they were lost when the monasteries were destroyed unless they were given a special exemption by the Crown. It was left to private individuals to refound these or to start new ones later in the Tudor period. In some cases, individuals such as Robert Dudley, Earl of Leicester stepped in, but this was not always the case.

In a period of increasing poverty, the removal of the safety net provided by the monasteries undoubtedly led to increased hardship among those who relied on them the most. The impact was felt most in those areas that were poorest, particularly the north of England, where the Pilgrimage of Grace began as a protest against the dissolution of the smaller monasteries.

SOURCE

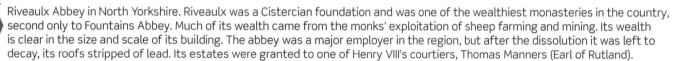

5 Riveaulx Abbey in North Yorkshire. Riveaulx was a Cistercian foundation and was one of the wealthiest monasteries in the country, second only to Fountains Abbey. Much of its wealth came from the monks' exploitation of sheep farming and mining. Its wealth is clear in the size and scale of its building. The abbey was a major employer in the region, but after the dissolution it was left to decay, its roofs stripped of lead. Its estates were granted to one of Henry VIII's courtiers, Thomas Manners (Earl of Rutland).

What was the impact of the spread of enclosure on the rural population?

Enclosure was blamed by many contemporaries for the growth of poverty and vagrancy in Tudor society. The practice of enclosure was most common in areas that could be used for either arable or sheep farming in the south-east and the Midlands.

Under the medieval open-field system of agriculture, land was divided among the inhabitants of the village and used for subsistence farming of crops and animals. The common land was shared by all and was often used to graze animals. The practice of enclosure aimed to create larger profits from the land. Landlords saw the financial opportunities that rearing sheep for the cloth trade could bring. They were also under pressure from rising inflation, which meant that they needed to increase their income. Sheep farming needed little manpower but could bring vast profits and led to large-scale enterprises, such as those of Sir William Fermour of Norfolk, who owned 17,000 sheep.

Enclosure could take several different forms and had been taking place since at least the 15th century. Sometimes, enclosure was a response to depopulation, where the tenants had left or died and had not been replaced. More seriously, some landlords enclosed village common lands, which affected the poorest members of the community as they were most reliant on these lands to graze their animals. This type of enclosure could have a knock-on effect because common grazing provided manure for the village crops; without this, it became harder to grow enough food to survive. Some landlords also used the practice of 'engrossing' – amalgamating two or more farms into one. The buildings on these farms might then be left to decay while their former occupants were forced to move elsewhere. Other practices by landlords such as deliberately raising rents to force tenants out also attracted criticism from contemporaries such as Thomas More.

Enclosure certainly caused some social and economic hardship. The most vulnerable were **copyhold tenants** (whose leases were most open to challenge) and the landless (who were reliant on the common lands for survival). It was these groups who were most likely to find themselves forced out of their homes and into poverty. Contemporary thinkers such as Thomas More and John Hales blamed enclosure for many of the social problems of the time. Their writing, combined with more general concerns about the damage enclosure appeared to be causing, led to government action. In 1517, Wolsey issued a commission of enquiry into illegal enclosures, and in 1548 the Duke of Somerset did the same, with disastrous results for the social and political stability of the country when rebellion broke out in East Anglia in 1549.

Successive Tudor governments also tried to regulate enclosure and sheep farming. The 1533 Sheep and Farms Act tried to restrict the number of sheep kept per farmer to 2,400; engrossing was allowed, but only for a maximum of two farms. From March to November 1549, a tax on sheep was introduced, and an Act of 1555 ordered farmers who kept more than 120 sheep to also keep two cows and rear a calf in order to encourage pastoral farming.

Under Elizabeth, however, enclosure became less of an issue for the government until the 1590s. This was because after 1551 the cloth trade suffered a temporary decline and landowners turned to arable farming instead, which meant that there was a drop in the trend for farmers to enclose land for sheep farming. Improved economic stability in the 1570s and 1580s increased standards of living and reduced the levels of visible poverty. The result of these changes was that there was less need to blame enclosure for social problems than there had been under the earlier Tudor monarchs.

However, enclosure was not the root cause of poverty. Poverty in the period was caused by population growth and inflation, although enclosure made these problems worse. But because enclosure was blamed by contemporaries such as Thomas More, it was a source of discontent and potential unrest, especially in the period 1548–49 when widespread riots against enclosure were seen across the Midlands and the South East, and caused serious difficulties for the Duke of Somerset's government in the South West.

KEY TERM

Copyhold tenants
Copyhold tenants were supposed to keep a copy of their lease, and a copy was also kept in the rolls of their manor. Copyhold leases could vary. Some were inherited; others were for life or for a number of years; some were 'by the will of the lord of the manor'. Those tenants who inherited the lease were generally the most secure, though they could still be forced out due to the fines that they had to pay when they inherited. The least secure were those who had no fixed terms to their lease, but any copyholder was vulnerable to eviction if the records that proved their right to the lease were lost or destroyed.

EXTEND YOUR KNOWLEDGE

Thomas More's *Utopia*

Utopia was first published in Latin in 1516. The title of the book refers to the invented island of Utopia, which More used as a way of commenting on the social and political realities of England. It is also very revealing about how early Tudor thinkers approached social, economic and political problems. More placed Utopia in the New World and used it to describe what he thought would be a perfect society. Utopia was ruled by a prince who was elected and could be removed if he was corrupt; there was no private property – goods were stored in a warehouse and distributed centrally, while the inhabitants did not own the houses they lived in. The economy of Utopia was based on agriculture, but More wrote that all inhabitants were expected to learn a craft as well. More's famous attack on the evils of sheep farming should be seen in the context of his work. It should also be noted that the word 'utopia' comes from the Greek; translated into English, it means 'nowhere'. *Utopia* in some ways was an extended intellectual joke.

SOURCE

6 From Thomas More, *Utopia* (1516).

But yet this is not only the necessary cause of stealing. There is another, which, as I suppose, is proper and peculiar to you Englishmen alone. What is that, quoth the Cardinal? Forsooth my lord (quoth I), your sheep that were wont to be so meek and tame, and so small eaters, now, as I heard say, be become so great devourers and so wild, that they eat up, and swallow down the very men themselves. They consume, destroy, and devour whole fields, houses, and cities. For look in what parts of the realm doth grow the finest, and therefore dearest wool, there noble men, and gentlemen... yea much noying [injuring] the weal public, leave no ground for tillage: they inclose all into pastures, they throw down houses, they pluck down towns, and leave nothing standing, but only the church to be made a sheephouse... Therefore that one covetous and unsatiable cormorant and very plague of his native country may compass about and inclose many thousand acres of ground together within one pale or hedge, the husbandmen be thrust out of their own, or else either by coveyne [collusion] and fraud, or by violent oppression they be put besides it, or by wrongs and injuries they be so wearied, that they be compelled to sell all: by one means therefore or by other, either by hook or crook they must needs depart away, poor, silly, wretched souls, men, women, husbands, wives, fatherless children, widows, woeful mothers, with their young babes, and their whole household small in substance and much in number, as husbandry requireth many hands. Away they trudge, I say, out of their known and accustomed houses, finding no place to rest in.

ACTIVITY
KNOWLEDGE CHECK

Growing poverty

1 Draw a spider diagram showing the main reasons for population growth.

2 Which groups in society benefited from a) the dissolution of the monasteries, and b) enclosure?

3 Why did More in Source 6 criticise the practice of enclosure?

4 Write a summary paragraph to explain how the dissolution of the monasteries and enclosure together contributed to the problem of poverty.

What was the impact of growing urbanisation?

Compared to London, whose population size expanded quickly and continuously during the Tudor period, the growth of other towns was less dynamic and more prone to depopulation caused by disease or migration. By the end of Henry VIII's reign, towns other than London were in a state of decline both in terms of population and industry, but the situation began to recover from the 1550s with new growth and the development of some new settlements.

SOURCE

 The growth of towns in the Tudor period based on the research of E.A. Wrigley and R.S. Schofield in *The Population History of England, 1542–1871: A Reconstruction* (1981).

	Estimated population in Henry VIII's reign	Estimated population by the end of Elizabeth's reign
London	60,000	215,000
Norwich	12,000	15,000
Bristol	10,000	12,000
Exeter	8,000	9,000
York	8,000	11,500
Newcastle	4,000	9,000

In the 1520s and 1530s, some towns that had been significant in the medieval period were facing depopulation and decay. These towns included Coventry, York, Canterbury, Ipswich, Leicester and Bristol. It is estimated that the population of Coventry fell from between 8,000 and 9,000 in 1500 to 6,000 in 1523, and that there were 565 empty houses, representing about a quarter of its domestic buildings. Representatives of towns complained to the king and parliament, though some of these complaints were also attempts to reduce the tax burden of local communities.

The reasons for the decline were varied. The most important cause was the growth of the cloth industry in smaller towns like Lavenham and rural areas, coupled with the clothiers' methods of 'putting out' (subcontracting) work. The growth of London and its ports also undermined the trade of other cities such as York and Bristol before exploration under Elizabeth opened up new trade routes. The dissolution of the monasteries had an economic impact on urban centres, which were reliant on the income brought in by pilgrimage to shrines; this affected both Canterbury and York.

Tudor governments attempted to solve these problems through Acts of Parliament. In the 1530s and 1540s a series of Acts ordered town authorities to rebuild derelict properties. Under Mary, there were attempts to restrict the growth of the cloth industry in the countryside and smaller towns and to encourage clothiers back to larger towns. An Act of 1556 attempted to impose a fine of £5 per cloth on anyone starting up a rural cloth business. However, none of these government measures were very effective while the cloth industry remained profitable. But from the 1550s, with the temporary decline of the cloth trade, towns started to recover and grow.

The main reasons for increased urbanisation in the second half of the 16th century were linked to the growing population, the pressure on jobs and changes in trading patterns. Towns such as York, Bristol and Exeter all benefited from the new trading routes that were being opened up in the Baltic and Atlantic. The cloth trades of Norwich, Colchester, Ipswich and Canterbury were rejuvenated by the arrival of migrant Dutch workers and the 'new draperies'. Norwich in particular also benefited from more diversification into industries such as clothes and hat making. Other towns that had also begun to grow included Bristol and Exeter. The results of this growth were to stimulate migration into the towns by those looking for work. Gentry families also started to buy town houses where they would spend the winter months. Increased population led to increased work for the building trade and for those supplying both essential foods and luxuries such as sugar and wine. A new occupation that developed in Tudor towns was that of vintner, a wine-merchant. Other towns developed their own specialisations: the rapid growth of Newcastle was the result of its profitable coal trade, which supplied the growing London market. New settlements were also springing up such as Birmingham and Manchester. Birmingham had a flourishing trade in iron manufacture while Manchester was specialising in linen and textile manufacture.

Towns were particularly sensitive to the social and economic crises that affected Tudor England. Conditions in the towns were cramped and dirt and disease could spread quickly. In 1579, for example, Norwich's population fell from 18,000 to 15,000 as a result of a plague.

Although some residents of towns were very wealthy, the wealth was not equally divided among the population, meaning that there was a large gap between the wealthy minority and the poorer majority. Many town residents owned little or no property because they could not afford it. This meant that they were not self-sufficient as they could not grow their own food. The result of these problems was that in times of food shortages, many inhabitants were not able to fend for themselves. Although there was considerable wealth in the towns, there was also poverty and destitution as the rural unskilled poor moved to the towns to look for work. Tax returns, although not always reliable, suggest that about 30 percent of the population in most towns paid no tax. In some cases this was because of tax dodging, but in other cases this was because of genuine poverty. In times of poor harvest or disease, it was this group that would be reliant on poor relief or might resort to begging and vagrancy. As early as 1547, the city of London had made contributions to poor relief permanent, and it is significant that it was soon followed by other major towns such as Ipswich, Norwich and York.

Those coming to towns to look for work could also create problems. Between 1532 and 1542, over 1,400 apprentices migrated from the West Country into Bristol, putting pressure on house prices. The poor harvests and influenza epidemic of the late 1550s also made the situation in towns more tense. Poor living conditions and lack of food led to the spread of disease and caused high mortality rates that led to temporary labour shortages in the early years of Elizabeth's reign. This then drove increased demand for workers and some workers demanding higher wages.

The Statute of Artificers (1563) was the government's attempt to deal with the problems of unemployment, wages and poverty. For the first time, JPs were ordered to set maximum rates for wages in each county. The collection of the harvest was prioritised and apprenticeships were regulated so that unqualified people could not enter skilled jobs for which they were not trained. However, tensions within towns remained whenever there were poor harvests or disease.

SOURCE 8 An Elizabethan street scene, from *A Book of Roxburghe Ballads*. Published in the 17th century, this was a collection of songs from the Tudor and Stuart period, accompanied by illustrations like this one.

SOURCE

9 A letter from an unemployed craftsman, John Baker, to Henry VIII, written in 1538.

I am a poor craftsman who has travelled and gone through most parts of your realm to earn my living. I have been in most of the cities and large towns in England. I have also gone through many little towns and villages, but alas it did pity my heart to see in every place so many monuments where houses have been and now there is nothing but bare walls standing. Which I think is very dishonouring unto your highness and causes much inconvenience among your people. It causes men to lie by the highwayside there to rob and it also causes much murder.

THINKING HISTORICALLY — Evidence (3a)

The value of evidence

Read the evidence from Thomas More (Source 6) and John Baker (Source 9), then work through the following tasks.

1 Write down at least three ways in which More's account is useful for establishing the causes of poverty in England and three ways in which Baker's letter is useful.

2 Compare your answers with those of a partner, then try to come up with at least two limitations of each source for establishing why there was increased poverty in England in the reign of Henry VIII.

3 Discuss with a partner whether you think that More or Baker is more useful for establishing the causes of poverty in Tudor England.

4 What if the sources were used to answer the question: What was the role of wealthy landlords in the growth of poverty in Tudor England? Complete the diagrams below to show the usefulness and limitations of the two sources for this question and for two questions of your own.

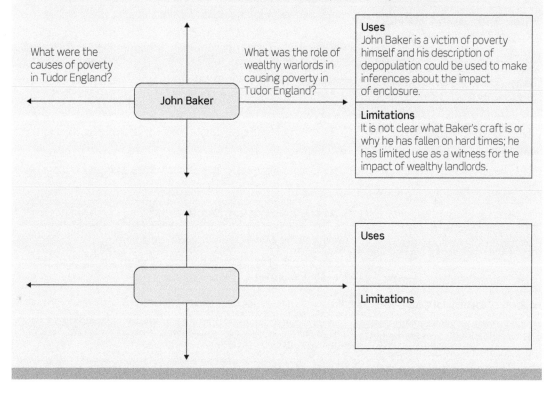

The growing professional classes

The main professions in Tudor England that required a form of education or university education were in the Church, the law, medicine or the civil service, where the right financial, legal or political skills could lead to great rewards. The growth in the professional classes was the result of increasing literacy and opportunities to receive an education at grammar schools and universities.

Although employment in the Church is in many ways not strictly a 'profession' in the modern sense of the word, those who worked within the Church had received some form of education. A boy who wanted a career in the Church would usually be educated at a **grammar school** or a school attached to a cathedral or monastery, where they would learn Latin. It was not necessary for a potential priest to go to university, which explains why Tudor governments were keen to improve the standard of clerical education. Some clergy were employed at low rates of pay in chantries; some became parish priests and others became tutors or teachers in private households or schools. However, a few of the most fortunate or able students were able to rise high in the Church, teaching at Oxford or Cambridge, becoming bishops, or entering royal service. The career of Thomas Wolsey shows what an ambitious and clever boy from a relatively lowly background could achieve.

Newer and increasingly popular professions were also available to the ambitious and able. The growth of the law courts in London and in the localities created a demand for trained lawyers. The study of law was also a route into royal service, which could be very lucrative. Unlike a career in the Church, where little formal training and only basic literacy were needed, those who became lawyers could not practise without years of study beforehand. Potential lawyers might study civil law at Oxford or Cambridge or they might receive training through the London **Inns of Court**, which were known by contemporaries as the 'third university'.

KEY TERMS

Grammar school

As the name suggests, grammar schools were originally designed to teach Latin grammar to boys who planned to enter the Church. Gradually, the curriculum was widened to include Greek, logic and rhetoric. Grammar schools were used as a training ground for university. From the later Middle Ages, some grammar schools were founded that were not connected to the Church (for example Eton, founded in 1440). After the Reformation, some of the former Church grammar schools were refounded. Edward VI played an important role in this process.

Inns of Court

These were the bodies that trained lawyers. Prospective lawyers would live and study at one of the 'Inns' (called Lincoln's Inn, Middle Temple, Inner Temple and Gray's Inn). By the 16th century, the Inns provided both a formal education and organisation for the profession.

Entry to the Inns was competitive; potential entrants would need a good standard of education and some form of financial support, as students would have to support themselves while they were training. At the top of the profession were judges and barristers who worked in the largest and most important central courts; below them were attorneys who worked in the localities and who provided advice and represented their clients in court; solicitors were more lowly, but still had professional training. Such was the growth in the law courts that the number of working barristers rose from 10 to 85 between 1510 and 1569; by 1590, there were 411. Similarly, in 1560 there were 200 attorneys; by 1606 there were 1,050.

An increasing number of men with a legal education also began to act as MPs, mainly because their expertise was particularly valued by local communities; in 1563, there were 140 MPs with legal training in parliament; by 1603 there were 253. This increase was the result of the professional training and legal expertise that lawyers had, which meant that they were elected by local communities to promote the region's interests in parliament by formulating laws. Lawyers were also well paid enough to be able to afford to become an MP, which was an unpaid role.

As royal government grew, there was also more demand for legal expertise in royal service, and some men with legal training and the right contacts rose high. William Paget was the son of a London craftsman, read civil law at Cambridge, and rose through the service of such powerful men as Thomas Cromwell and Edward Seymour. Paget became first an MP, then a member of the Privy Council and finally he was ennobled by Somerset. Similarly, Sir Walter Mildmay, a councillor of Elizabeth I, was educated at Gray's Inn and employed in the Court of Augmentations. His financial and legal gifts meant that he rose rapidly in royal service. Although Paget and Mildmay were examples of those who rose to the very top, law as a profession was a way to earn both wealth and increased status in Tudor society.

Another profession that grew in the Tudor period was that of physician (doctor). The Royal College of Physicians was founded by the Crown in 1518 and was intended to protect medical practitioners with qualifications from those who claimed to have medical skill and knowledge but who had no formal training. The college was able to license physicians across England and punish those who practised without a licence. Doctors were trained at Oxford and Cambridge but also in the European universities; the foundation of the college allowed them professional status for the first time.

ACTIVITY
KNOWLEDGE CHECK

Urbanisation

1 Summarise, in your own words, why some towns were declining in the early Tudor period.

2 Make a list of the advantages and disadvantages of urbanisation.

3 Explain how and why some professions grew in the Tudor period.

AS Level Exam-Style Question Section B

Towns grew from the start of Elizabeth's reign.

Was the growth of towns the main cause of poverty in the Tudor period, 1558–88? (20 marks)

Tip

This question is about the causes of poverty in the later part of the Tudor period. You will need to consider other reasons for the causes of poverty as well.

A Level Exam-Style Question Section B

How accurate is it to say that the most significant cause of poverty in the years 1509–88 was population growth? (20 marks)

Tip

A good answer will compare or link population growth to other reasons for poverty.

WHAT WAS THE SIGNIFICANCE OF CHANGES TO TUDOR CULTURE, 1509–88

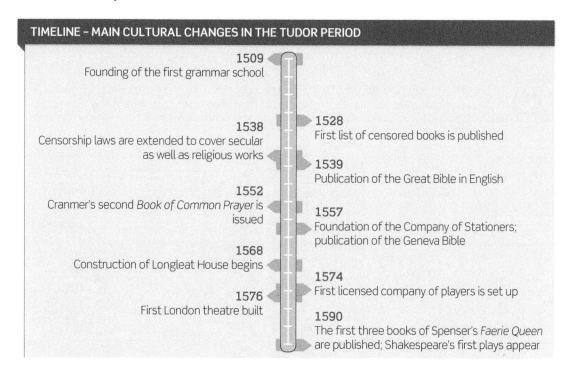

TIMELINE – MAIN CULTURAL CHANGES IN THE TUDOR PERIOD

1509
Founding of the first grammar school

1528
First list of censored books is published

1538
Censorship laws are extended to cover secular as well as religious works

1539
Publication of the Great Bible in English

1552
Cranmer's second *Book of Common Prayer* is issued

1557
Foundation of the Company of Stationers; publication of the Geneva Bible

1568
Construction of Longleat House begins

1574
First licensed company of players is set up

1576
First London theatre built

1590
The first three books of Spenser's *Faerie Queen* are published; Shakespeare's first plays appear

The impact of the growth of grammar schools and universities

During the Tudor period there was a considerable increase in the growth of grammar schools and the provision of university education. Before the Reformation, education was provided mainly by the Church, but the growth of humanist ideas, which emphasised the role of education for all, led to the foundation of grammar schools. In 1509, John Colet, the Dean of St Paul's (London) and a renaissance humanist, founded St Paul's School, the first grammar school to be based on humanist ideas. By 1530, there were 124 grammar schools. Although some schools run by monasteries were closed during the dissolution, they were sometimes refounded by private charitable donations. Edward VI also took a keen interest in education, and a series of grammar schools were founded in his name. Encouraged by the Protestant reformers' emphasis on a Bible in English that should be available to all, and the need to educate those who could not read the Bible for themselves, the trend of founding grammar schools continued from the 1540s to the 1580s; 136 new grammar schools were founded during Elizabeth's reign. However, these schools were only for boys. Girls from noble and gentry families would be educated at home and in the households of other wealthy families. The impact of the Renaissance meant that some aristocratic girls such as Anne Boleyn and her daughter Elizabeth I were educated to a high standard. Despite these new ideas, it was still expected that a girl's education would equip her to run her own household when she was married rather than be used in a profession.

At the same time, university education was expanding. Although there were still only two universities in England – Oxford and Cambridge – the number of students increased, while teaching methods and the subjects taught also evolved. At Oxford, student numbers increased from 1,150 in 1550 to about 2,000. Cambridge saw similar growth. It is estimated that just under half the students at university were the sons of the gentry or nobility. The rest came from those below gentry status. Not all students would end up with a degree. In this period, it was still common for gentry families to send their sons to university to acquire further education and polish, but they would leave before they took their degree.

At both grammar schools and university, the influence of humanist thought encouraged a wider range of subjects to be studied. Although grammar schools were still primarily focused on the teaching of Latin, which was needed for entry to university and the professions, some taught Greek or arithmetic.

At university, this led to a wider curriculum: it became possible to study Greek and rhetoric as well as other humanist interests such as languages and music. The development of the universities' college and tutorial system in this period enhanced the standard of education. Colleges provided a base for students to live where they could also receive one-to-one tuition from their tutors rather than simply attending voluntary lectures and debates. New colleges were also founded or refounded: Trinity and Emmanuel in Cambridge in 1546 and 1584 and Christ Church and Trinity in Oxford in 1546 and 1554.

SOURCE 10

An English 16th century picture of a grammar school classroom from that time. Students of different ages were taught in the same room. Often the older ones taught the younger pupils. Corporal punishment was common, though humanist scholars such as Roger Ascham disapproved of it.

The result of the growth of grammar schools and universities was to raise levels of literacy and the standards of education in England and Wales. Because children were taught to write only after they could read, it is possible to measure literacy rates by the number of people who could sign their own names in church court records. The work of David Cressy has shown that illiteracy rates for men and women were at about 80 percent and 98 percent respectively in 1550. By 1600, they were at 72 percent and 92 percent, which suggests more people could sign their own names by 1600 than in 1550. However, literacy rates varied according to region and social status. In 1530, illiteracy rates among gentlemen were higher in the north of England than in the Midlands, east and south. As a result of increasing education opportunities, this gap had narrowed; by the end of Elizabeth's reign, only 17 percent of northern gentlemen could not sign their name. Between 1550 and the end of the period, more yeomen and merchants also became literate, but there were still high rates of illiteracy among labourers and the poorest in society.

Grammar schools and universities were in theory open to all male students, but the gentry, yeomen and merchants benefited from this system the most. Attendance at school was not compulsory and the poorest in society needed their children to work to increase the family income. In these circumstances it was likely that only boys would receive some, if any education; girls would not have been given these advantages. However, literate neighbours with access to their own Bibles, plus increasing numbers of printed pamphlets and ballads, meant that political and religious ideas could still spread.

What was the impact of the printing press?

The relationship between the production of printed books, pamphlets and ballads, ideas about education and the growth of literacy is complex, but the impact of the printing press certainly played its part.

The first printing press was introduced to England by William Caxton in 1476. To begin with, the press was used to print copies of books that were already in existence in monastic libraries, but gradually a wider range of texts was published. Because printing presses could print books and pamphlets so quickly, and because they were outside the control of the Church, it was harder to control what was published. In the period 1520–29, approximately 800 books were published. By the start of Elizabeth's reign, the number had risen to an average of about 1,800 books per decade.

SOURCE

11 From a 1568 woodcut by the Swiss artist Jost Ammans showing printers at work in a printing house in the late 1500s.

The Tudor government responded by tightening the censorship laws. In 1529, the first list of censored books was created, and in 1538 censorship laws were extended to include secular as well as religious works. In 1557, a new London company, the Stationers, was founded by the government. It was given a monopoly on licensed presses apart from those at Oxford and Cambridge. In return, it was to monitor and prevent unlicensed printing.

However, it was not just English printing that caused problems for the government. European printing presses also produced large numbers of books, some of which were imported to England. As early as 1521, books with Lutheran ideas were discovered and burnt in London. During Mary's reign, the English Protestant exiles used foreign printing presses to publish at least 98 books or tracts of propaganda. These included radical works such as John Knox's *First Blast of the Trumpet against the Monstrous Regiment of Women*. Although ownership of a book that was heretical or treasonous was punishable by death, Mary's government found it impossible to suppress these works completely. In Elizabeth's reign, the Puritans used the printing presses to publish their own propaganda, the most notorious of which were the vicious 'Martin Marprelate Tracts' (see pages 60–61). The press was also used to criticise Elizabeth's policies. In 1579, the Puritan John Stubbs published a pamphlet called 'The Discovery of a Gaping Gulf', which was an attack on Elizabeth's planned marriage to the French Duke of Anjou. Stubbs' punishment was to have his right hand cut off, showing that Elizabeth was concerned about the role the press could play in spreading popular challenges to her rule. This did not stop illegal books being imported from Europe, however. Printing presses in France and the Netherlands supplied at least 223 works to English Catholics during Elizabeth's reign.

The power of the printing press was also harnessed by Tudor governments to spread their own propaganda. Cromwell used the printing press from 1534 to justify the break with Rome and spread reformist ideas. The publication of the English Bible (1539) was made possible because of the printing press. Three thousand copies were printed in London and Paris in November 1539 and another 3,000 were printed in London in March–April 1540. Most English parishes had acquired a copy within five years.

Protestants under Edward and Elizabeth also used printed tracts to spread their ideas. This was strongly linked to the Protestant emphasis on education so that worshippers could read the Bible for themselves. However, despite the government's best intentions, this policy could backfire. The New Testament of the Geneva Bible was first published abroad in 1557 by English Protestant exiles. It appeared in full in 1560 and included notes and headings designed to explain the text more fully to the reader. Unfortunately, these notes encouraged a Calvinist theology that was too radical for Elizabeth. Archbishop Parker was forced to publish a rival 'Bishops' Bible' in 1568 but the Geneva version remained popular until the 17th century, and went through 130 editions, showing how difficult it was to control effectively the printing press and what people read.

However, the printing press was not just used for religious publications. As literacy increased, so did the appetite for reading, which in turn encouraged more interest in education. In the Middle Ages, book production had been the job of monastic scribes, who would copy out a book by hand. This meant that production of books was slow and expensive and that ownership of books was confined to monasteries and a very few wealthy members of the nobility. The arrival of the printing press meant that books could be printed much faster and more cheaply. The result was that book ownership increased, especially among the gentry and nobility, but even those further down the social scale were keen to buy and read the printed word. Printers also responded to popular demand for all kinds of reading material such as ballads, plays and almanacs. They also printed chapbooks, which were small, easily transported books sold by travelling salesmen.

SOURCE 12 A sixteenth century woodcut showing scribes at work during the Tudor period in England.

ACTIVITY
KNOWLEDGE CHECK

The printing press and education

1 Draw a diagram to show how the introduction of the printing press and the expansion of education were linked.

2 Make a list of the main results of the growth of grammar schools and universities.

3 Discuss the following questions with a partner:

   a) Did the growth of education and the printing press affect all parts of society equally?

   b) Which groups benefited the most?

   c) Which groups benefited the least?

   d) Why were the effects not felt by everyone?

How did religious change affect English culture?

Religious change had a profound effect on the language, politics and way of life of England. Before the Reformation, any notion of the English 'state' was vague and English literature was not yet widely read or published because it was considered inferior to Latin. Popular culture was based around the feast days of the Catholic Church, and Catholic art and imagery dominated the popular imagination.

In political terms, the development of the Supremacy and the justification for it created a new sense of nationalism. Henry VIII's theory that England was an empire and that the ruler should not be subject to any outside intervention led to anti-Catholic xenophobia (fear of foreigners) and an increased sense of what it meant to be English. This helps to explain the negative reaction in 1553–54 to Mary I's proposed marriage to Philip II of Spain, who was both a Catholic and a foreigner. Anti-Catholic and anti-Spanish propaganda under Elizabeth heightened this sense of England as 'God's country' with Elizabeth as the 'godly queen'; Catholic Spain was presented as tyrannical, with its Inquisition persecuting Protestants, an image aided by John Foxe's reports of gruesome massacres by Catholics of Protestants.

Following the Reformation, this growth of 'Englishness' was accompanied by an increased emphasis on the use of the English language. As Protestant reformers encouraged the translation of the Bible and church services into the native tongue, so the English language became more valued. The work of translators such as William Tyndale and Miles Coverdale, who produced English editions of the Bible in 1526 and 1535, introduced the Bible and its language to a wider audience. Thomas Cranmer's revised *Book of Common Prayer* of 1552 was used for hundreds of years, partly because of his sensitive and beautiful use of English. Scholars and teachers such as Roger Ascham emphasised the importance of the use of plain English in teaching. Grammars and dictionaries were published and the vocabulary of the English language increased. Although English had been widely spoken and used since the 14th century, it was in the 16th century that English culture and law became identified with English nationhood. The use of English became compulsory in legal business, and reformers demanded (but did not get) the translation of all Acts of Parliament from Latin to English. The native Welsh- and Irish-speaking populations were only granted the same rights as Englishmen if they used the language and law of England, not of their own countries. In the 1570s, this development of English led to the emergence of important poets such as Edmund Spenser and Philip Sidney, and eventually William Shakespeare, whose masterly use of language was employed in his play *Richard II* to describe English patriotism.

The English Reformation was also a destructive force. With the end of the Catholic Church in England came the end of a culture that had lasted hundreds of years. English churches had been highly decorated with paintings, statues and images. These were either destroyed or painted over. Instead of learning about the Christian faith through pictures and images, congregations were now expected to listen to sermons. Rood screens – highly decorated wooden or stone screens that separated the clergy from the priest – were removed. Crucifixes, which were the visual representation of Christ's suffering and sacrifice on the cross, were also removed and were often replaced by the royal coat of arms. Wealthy and highly decorated shrines such as Thomas Becket's at Canterbury were destroyed; the tradition of pilgrimage was destroyed with them. Many traditional holy days were banned by the reformers, who thought that they encouraged idleness and rowdiness. Popular medieval traditions such as miracle or morality plays, which enacted scenes from the Bible or battles between vices and virtues, survived until early in Elizabeth's reign, but the last one in York was shut down in 1574. Within 50 years, the Reformation had changed popular culture beyond recognition.

The traditional medieval forms of entertainment such as art and poetry had been replaced by a culture that emphasised the new Protestant religion, the increasing use of the English language and sense of an English nation-state.

Patronage and the development of drama, music and poetry

Tudor drama, music and poetry were largely dependent on the support of the monarch and nobility. A patron might pay an annuity to a writer, musician or artist in order to fund them. They might also give them employment at court or in their household and subsidise performances. All of the Tudor monarchs were particularly keen on supporting portrait artists, provided those artists depicted the Tudor monarchy in a way that was politically acceptable. Most of the artists that they patronised came from Europe, which allowed the introduction of some new techniques such as miniature painting. Henry VIII paid Hans Holbein, one of the most famous and accomplished artists of the period, to be the court painter. He also employed members of the Hornebolte family, who introduced the art of miniature painting. Holbein was paid £30 a year for his services. Holbein first came to England under the patronage of Thomas More. Mary and Elizabeth employed the female artist Levina Teerlinc, who also doubled up as gentlewoman of the chamber. Elizabeth continued to employ artists who would portray her as she wanted, for example Nicholas Hilliard, the first English miniaturist. Under the patronage of the Tudor monarchs, there was some development of new styles and techniques of painting, but this is not what the artists were employed for. Their careers depended on showing the Tudor monarchy in the best light possible. Noble patrons also sometimes employed artists to paint them and their families. However, the Tudor nobility were more interested in other forms of patronage and culture, although some were art collectors. Robert Dudley, Earl of Leicester had a collection of about 220 pictures.

Developments within drama and poetry as a result of patronage from both the monarchy and the nobility were much more obvious. It was common for the monarchs and nobility to maintain a troupe of 'players' (actors) who would spend some of the year touring the countryside and giving performances. Both Thomas Howard, the third duke of Norfolk, and his wife patronised their own troupes and Henry VIII also had his own players. The main role of the patron was to provide protection against arrest as vagabonds, which for travelling players was an occupational hazard. In return, the players would provide entertainment for their patron and his guests. Being a patron was a way that a nobleman could show both his wealth and his influence. Poets and writers also sought noble patronage.

Although Elizabeth I was too careful with money to spend much on patronage, her nobility took a keen interest in sponsoring players, playwrights and poets. A writer would try to attract potential patrons with a panegyric – a text that praised the patron. If the writer was successful, a patron would promote his career and hope to gain fame and prestige through his writing. Although patrons were often not prepared to give much financial support to writers, the exception was the Earl of Leicester, whose wealth and status meant that he could act as a patron of the arts on a grand scale. At Leicester House on the Strand, he gathered together a group of poets who would go on to be very influential in the development of English literature. These men included Leicester's own nephew, Sir Philip Sidney, and Edmund Spenser, who in 1590 produced the first three books of his poem *The Faerie Queen*. The informal meetings between these men, which were encouraged by Leicester's patronage, led to a 'golden age' of poetry. Leicester also patronised actors and theatre companies.

After the Poor Law of 1572 introduced even harsher penalties for vagabonds, it became more essential than ever for travelling actors to find a patron to protect them. In the same year, James Burbage wrote to Leicester asking for his protection for Burbage's company of players. Leicester agreed, and obtained authorisation from the queen in 1574. From then on, all of the main player companies had a noble patron after whom they were named. These included the Lord Admiral's company and the Lord Chamberlain's company.

SOURCE

13 Puritan criticism of the theatre from a sermon preached at St Paul's Cross by Thomas White in London, and published in 1578.

Look but upon the common plays in London, and see the multitude that flocketh to them and followeth them. Behold the sumptuous theatre houses, a continual monument of London's prodigality and folly. But I understand that they are now forbidden because of the plague. I like the policy well if it hold still, for a disease is but lodged or patched up that is not cured in the cause, and the cause of the plagues is sin, if you look to it well: and the cause of sin are plays: therefore the cause of plagues are plays.

Patronage of music also led to some important developments. All of the Tudors were fond of music, but Elizabeth I's patronage of music was particularly important in its development. Following the Reformation, Church music in particular was in decline; music even came under attack from Puritans. Elizabeth, however, was fond of music and employed about 60 musicians in her Chapel Royal and company of the Queen's Musick. The musicians she employed included major composers and performers such as Thomas Tallis and William Byrd, who made significant contributions to English music despite the fact that both were Catholic. Members of the nobility also acted as musical patrons including Leicester, Christopher Hatton and William Cecil. These men encouraged the development of both sacred and secular music.

What was the significance of royal and noble patronage of the arts?

Royal and noble patronage of the arts had both political and cultural significance. For the Tudor monarchs, patronage of the arts was particularly important because it allowed them to control their popular image and spread propaganda. For this reason, all of the Tudor monarchs took a particular interest in court entertainment, both private 'disguisings' and the public tournaments.

Part of Holbein's job was to use his talents as a painter to project the image of kingship and the Tudor dynasty that Henry wanted. Holbein's most famous work was a huge mural at the Palace of Whitehall, representing the version of Henry and his family that the king wanted to show to the world.

Under Elizabeth, the role of painters such as Nicholas Hilliard was to project the correct image to England and Europe. As Elizabeth grew older and was still unmarried, the issue of the succession became harder to avoid, especially from the 1580s when the queen was past childbearing age and there were increasing threats from Catholic plots and foreign invasion. To preserve the myth of the ageless Gloriana, the 'Virgin Queen', Hilliard was prepared to use the 'mask of youth', the template of Elizabeth's face designed in the 1580s, which all painters had to use in their portraits of her and which bore little resemblance to the ageing queen.

However, because the Tudor monarchs were keen to control their image so closely, this could lead to the suppression of new methods and styles if they were not fit for purpose. Hilliard, although talented, was considered very backward by European standards, especially in his use of perspective. His rival, a miniaturist called Isaac Oliver, had trained overseas, but his work may have been rejected by Elizabeth because it was too realistic. Royal patronage was a way for painters to advance, but it also reinforced England's cultural conservatism and isolation.

SOURCE

The mural at Whitehall painted by Hans Holbein c1537, which survives as a copy after the original was destroyed by fire. It shows Henry VIII and his third wife, Jane Seymour; behind them are Henry's parents, Henry VII and Elizabeth of York. The painting may have been commissioned to celebrate the birth of Edward VI. Henry had acquired the Palace of Whitehall from Thomas Wolsey after his fall and spent a huge amount of money decorating it.

SOURCE 15 Miniature portrait of Elizabeth I painted by Nicholas Hilliard c1588 using the 'mask of youth'. Elizabeth was in her mid-50s by this time, but the image represents a much younger-looking queen.

Royal and noble patronage also helped to fill the gap left by the Catholic Church as a patron of the arts after the Reformation. Wolsey, for example, had huge personal wealth and used it to fund the rebuilding of Hampton Court Palace from 1514. Before their dissolution in the 1530s, monasteries were also important centres of learning, while the Church was also a major employer of artists and musicians. Royal and noble sponsorship of musicians, artists, writers and actors ensured that these cultural traditions survived and developed in new directions. The musician Thomas Tallis was sponsored in turn by Henry VIII, Edward VI, Mary and Elizabeth despite his Catholicism. Similarly, noble patronage of poets such as Sidney and Spenser allowed new styles of poetry to flourish such as the sonnet and blank verse. Noble sponsorship of companies of players and the playwrights they employed protected them from arrest and led to the writing and staging of the greatest Elizabethan plays. Companies built their own theatres in London and performed there. The Lord Admiral's company performed the early plays of Christopher Marlowe in the late 1580s and the Lord Chamberlain's company performed Shakespeare's plays from about 1590.

However, there were limits to the effects of royal and noble patronage. Experimentation with the sonnet and blank verse had begun in the reign of Henry VIII with the work of Sir Thomas Wyatt and Henry Howard, Earl of Surrey, themselves members of landed society. In addition, developments in music, poetry and drama were also the result of wider social change.

The Renaissance, with its focus on ancient Greek and Roman culture, encouraged new interest in polyphonic music and in poetic styles such as the sonnet. The reformation added to these changes. As the Catholic Church no longer dominated and controlled art and culture, more experimentation could take place. The increasing use of the printing press allowed a range of music and literature to be published, both religious and secular, as long as it passed the increasingly strict censorship laws. This fed popular demand that in turn created the conditions for further experimentation and change. The development of the famous Elizabethan London theatres from 1576 was not funded by noble patrons, but by the managers of the companies, such as James Burbage, who were theatrical entrepreneurs.

What were the main developments in drama, music, poetry and architecture?

Tudor drama developed rapidly under Elizabeth I despite the criticisms of the Puritans, who thought that plays encouraged sin and immoral behaviour. However, even before Elizabeth's reign, there was a long tradition of drama. Medieval miracle and morality plays were performed by amateurs in English in centres such as Coventry and York, and continued into Elizabeth's reign, when they were finally suppressed. English grammar schools followed a humanist tradition of putting on plays in Latin. The court also put on 'disguisings', elaborate performances that might involve music and dancing. However, the break with Rome, the increasing use of the printing press and noble patronage encouraged Elizabethan drama to reach new heights. The growth of the English language and vocabulary, plus the humanist emphasis on the study of classical Greek and Roman texts, history and languages encouraged home-grown playwrights to produce their own versions of classical stories or to rewrite English history for the Tudor propaganda machine.

In 1576, the first London theatre (called the 'Theatre') was built and opened by James Burbage. It was followed by the Rose, which opened in 1587. This innovation replaced the use of temporary stages and allowed playwrights to use more complex staging. The theatres had no roof and were built in the round, but usually they had a pulley system to raise and lower actors, and a trapdoor. Poorer members of the audience (the groundlings) could pay one penny to stand, while wealthier visitors could pay to use the seating provided in the balconies. Using the company of professional actors patronised by the Earl of Leicester, Burbage was able to provide entertainment to rich and poor alike. These conditions encouraged playwrights such as Christopher Marlowe to produce plays such as *The Jew of Malta* (c1589).

The main developments in Tudor poetry occurred throughout the Tudor period. An early Tudor poet who wrote in English was John Skelton. Skelton was Henry VIII's tutor and he later pursued a career within the Church and as a writer of satirical poetry in English, which often mocked the wealthy and powerful. The most famous example was 'Why came ye not to court?', a vicious attack on Wolsey. Wyatt and Howard came from the ranks of landed society and were both courtiers and poets. In writing poetry, their aim was to improve the English language and the quality of English poetry. Both were influenced by humanist 'new learning', and in particular by reading Latin and Italian verse.

Wyatt and Howard translated the **sonnets** of Petrarch, a 14th century Italian writer, but also began to write their own poetry. They are credited with inventing what became the most common form of sonnet in England. One of Wyatt's most famous works, 'Whoso list to hunt' is a love sonnet, which may have been about Anne Boleyn. Howard was the first person to use **blank verse** in his translation of the work of the Roman writer, Virgil.

The sonnet and blank verse became the most widely used literary forms by the Elizabethan playwrights and poets. Shakespeare wrote 154 sonnets during his career and used blank verse throughout his plays. In many ways, Shakespeare's career sums up the impact of humanist thought and the Renaissance on English culture and society. Although not much is known of his early life, we know that he was the son of a successful glover from Stratford-upon-Avon (Warwickshire) and was born in 1564. Shakespeare went to school at one of the new grammar schools established by Edward VI, where he would have learnt to read and write and would have studied Latin. At some point in the 1580s, Shakespeare moved to London and became involved with the theatre companies, eventually turning to playwriting by the early 1590s. In Shakespeare's work, innovations in poetry, English and drama were combined to create propaganda for the Tudors.

KEY TERMS

Sonnet

A form of poem that has 14 lines. It was used by classical poets and during the Renaissance. Wyatt and Howard contributed to the formation of the structure of the English sonnet by inventing the three sets of four rhyming lines followed by two rhyming lines at the end (a couplet).

Blank verse

This does not rhyme, but every line has the same rhythm, known as iambic pentameter. It was a form common in classical literature. Howard's translations introduced this form to England.

SOURCE

16 'Whoso List to Hunt', a love sonnet in the new English style written by Thomas Wyatt the elder. In the poem, Wyatt is an exhausted deer hunter who has found that his quarry has not only outrun him but belongs to someone else. The deer is thought by some to symbolise Anne Boleyn, with whom Wyatt had fallen in love. The reference to Caesar may be a reference to Henry VIII and his relationship with Anne.

Whoso list to hunt, I know where is an hind,
But as for me, alas, I may no more;
The vain travail hath wearied me so sore,
I am of them that furthest come behind.
Yet may I by no means my wearied mind
Draw from the deer, but as she fleeth afore
Fainting I follow; I leave off therefore,
Since in a net I seek to hold the wind.
Who list her hunt, I put him out of doubt,
As well as I, may spend his time in vain.
And graven with diamonds in letters plain,
There is written her fair neck round about,
'Noli me tangere, for Caesar's I am,
And wild for to hold, though I seem tame'

[Noli me tangere means 'Do not touch me']

EXTEND YOUR KNOWLEDGE

Sir Thomas Wyatt (senior) and Anne Boleyn

Thomas Wyatt senior was the father of the Thomas Wyatt (1521–54) who rebelled against Mary. Wyatt senior was a diplomat and courtier, and was educated at Cambridge. His marriage to the daughter of Lord Cobham, a Kent landowner, was unhappy, but it did produce his son and heir.

Around 1525, Wyatt was pursuing Anne Boleyn. She was already engaged to Henry Percy, the son of the Earl of Northumberland, and had attracted the attention of the king. Anne toyed with Wyatt, but ultimately she was not interested in becoming his mistress. Wyatt's poem, 'Whoso list to hunt' is thought to be about Anne. He compares her to a deer who flees from the hunter and who belongs to another, 'Caesar' – that is, Henry VIII.

In 1536, Wyatt was among the courtiers arrested and sent to the Tower for their alleged adultery with Anne, but he escaped execution. His career did partially recover. He was friendly with Cromwell and in 1537 was sent to Spain as an ambassador. But in 1541 he was in trouble again following Cromwell's fall. Wyatt was sent once more to the Tower, but he survived having begged forgiveness of the king.

Music

Developments in music were also influenced by the Renaissance and European interest in polyphonal music (music with several parts or lines). English composers under the patronage of the Church or the monarchs experimented with this form both in the production of religious works and, increasingly, of secular works. Henry VIII liked the medieval tradition of grand, lengthy music, with a high (treble or descant) line, but this began to change during the Reformation when musical pieces became shorter and plainer. Under Edward VI the high treble part was removed, and English texts were used instead of Latin. Mary's reign saw a return to the longer, more complex pieces in Latin, with a high descant. Music under Elizabeth was, like her religious settlement, a compromise: Latin could still be used but the length of pieces again became shorter.

Composers' musical styles and careers were highly influenced by the religious changes that took place. Early composers included John Taverner and Christopher Tye. Taverner was appointed to be choirmaster and organist at Wolsey's Cardinal College, Oxford, in 1526. He produced a series of Latin Masses and other religious works in Latin, using polyphonal techniques. Tye, working a generation later, had Protestant sympathies and was employed at Edward VI's court to give advice on music. His works were still secular but used English translations; his work *The Actes of the Apostles* (1553), a translation of the New Testament book set to music, was dedicated to Edward VI.

The work of earlier composers reached its peak in the Elizabethan musicians and composers Tallis and Byrd. Tallis' career lasted from the 1520s to the 1580s despite his Catholicism. His survival was probably due to his ability to adapt. Under Elizabeth, his compositions reached new heights with the ambitious *Spem in Alium* (c1570), an unaccompanied piece for 40 separate voices and parts, but he also branched out from the Latin, using English texts and composing some secular pieces.

Architecture

Architecture and building also changed and developed during the Tudor period. Although the changes are most obvious in the many surviving stately homes built by the Tudor nobility, the houses of those of lower social status also underwent considerable alterations.

The only Tudor monarch to build new palaces was Henry VIII. In the 1530s, he began the building of Nonsuch Palace (Surrey). He also embarked on ambitious and expensive rebuilding plans at Whitehall and Bridewell.

The later Tudor monarchs did not build, partly because their finances were so limited. However, their nobility, influenced by humanist and European ideas on architecture, built extravagantly. The earliest example was Somerset House, built on the Strand for the Duke of Somerset. From the 1570s, members of the nobility began to build country houses on a grand scale. The first example was at Longleat (Wiltshire), owned by Sir John Thynne. Construction began around 1568 and he used the stonemason Robert Smythson to help him design and build the house. Smythson later became known as one of the earliest architects, although it was not really considered to be a profession until the 17th century. Smythson went on to build another famous Tudor house at Wollaton (Nottingham) for Sir Francis Willoughby. Other anonymous builders and designers constructed famous mansions, such as Cecil's country house Theobalds, and the Earl of Leicester's renovation of the medieval Kenilworth Castle.

The style of these houses, known as 'prodigy houses', was strongly influenced by humanist interest in Roman and Greek classical architecture. They were designed for comfort and privacy, and employed the use of light and space to create a pleasant living environment. These houses were very different from the medieval stone castles and fortified manors of the early 16th century, whose main purpose was defence. Increasingly, brick was used as a building material rather than stone. The emphasis on light and space meant the use of multiple windows. The late Tudor mansion was not built for defence, reflecting the increasing political stability of the period. Inside the house a series of private rooms for the family's use was constructed. Although most houses still incorporated the medieval great hall, the family would use a parlour for relaxation and a separate dining parlour for meals. The formal or 'state' rooms were on the first floor and included a series of bedchambers and a long gallery. The gallery was first seen in the palaces of Henry VII and VIII and it was used for exercise and private conversations. Galleries were then adopted by Tudor courtiers for use in their houses; having a long gallery added prestige to the house's owner.

SOURCE 17

A description of Kenilworth Castle in the reign of Elizabeth I written in 1575 by Robert Langham, a mercer, to Humphrey Martyn, the son of a wealthy London merchant. The letter describes Elizabeth's progress in Warwickshire in the summer of 1575.

Every room so spacious, so well belighted, and so high roofed within; so seemly to sight by due proportion without; in day time, on every side so glittering by glass; at nights, by continual brightness of candle, fire and torchlight, transparent through the lightsome windows.

SOURCE 18

Wollaton Hall, Nottingham, designed by Robert Smythson, built between 1580 and 1588.

EXTRACT

1 John Guy writing about architecture in *Tudor England* (1988).

Architecture was the field where Gloriana's impact was least conspicuous. Between Henry VIII's death and 1603, not a single new palace was constructed or acquired... [Elizabeth's] annual progresses shifted the responsibility for housing her court during the summer on to her subjects. In the wider sense that courtiers therefore rivalled each other to build magnificent houses for her entertainment, she exercised residual influence on architecture. But the aesthetic initiative passed to the nobility and gentry: the finest examples of Elizabethan style were Burghley's house at Theobalds, Leicester's at Kenilworth Castle... Sir France Willoughby's at Wollaton... Size and symmetry were especially valued in Elizabethan architecture. Great houses were seen as 'lanterns': light inside, glittering outside.

THINKING HISTORICALLY　Evidence (3b)

It depends on the question

When considering the usefulness of a piece of evidence, people often think about authenticity in the case of artefacts, reliability in the case of witness statements or methodology and structure in the case of secondary accounts. A better historical approach to the usefulness of a piece of evidence would be to think about the statements that we can make about the past based on it. Different statements can be made with different degrees of certainty, depending on the evidence.

Work in small groups and answer the following questions:

1 Look at Source 18.

  a) Write three statements that you can reasonably make about the development of Elizabethan architecture based solely on Source 18.

  b) Which of the statements can be made with the greatest degree of certainty? Why is that? Which statement can be made with the smallest degree of certainty?

  c) What else might you need to increase your confidence in your statements?

2 Source 18 is an artefact and Source 17 is a witness statement. Which is more useful to the historian studying the development of Elizabethan architecture?

3 Look at Extract 1. How would the historian have gone about constructing this piece? What kinds of evidence would he have needed?

Building was not just confined to the Tudor nobility and gentry. Surviving wills suggest that the average number of rooms in a house went from three in Henry VIII's reign to between four and five by Elizabeth's reign. Prosperous yeomen in Elizabeth's reign might have as many as six to eight rooms, while husbandmen (a tenant farmer or small landowner) might have two to three rooms. Wealthier farmers tended to build a second floor and would include a fireplace and chimney rather than an open hearth. Those with less money extended their houses on the ground floor and would often build a separate kitchen to reduce the risk of fire.

By the end of Elizabeth's reign, Tudor culture had changed considerably as a result of the Reformation, humanist ideas and royal and noble patronage. The growth of English drama and poetry led to the first theatres and a distinct English style of verse. Art was harnessed by the Tudor monarchs for propaganda purposes, while music also developed into something that was recognisably English in style. Architecture and building experienced rapid growth and the results can still be seen today.

SOURCE

19 William Harrison, *The Description of England* (1577). Harrison was a Church of England clergyman and writer whose work described the political, geographical and social features of Elizabethan England.

The ancient manors and houses of our gentlemen are yet, for the most part, of strong timber, in framing whereof our carpenters have been and are worthily preferred before those of like science among all other nations. Howbeit, such as be lately builded are commonly either of brick or hard stone or both, their rooms are large and comely...

The furniture of our houses also exceedeth and is grown in manner even to passing delicacy; and herein I do not speak of the nobility and gentry only but likewise of the lowest sort in most places of our South Country that have anything at all to take to... In noblemen's houses it is not rare to see abundance of arras, rich hangings of tapestry, silver vessel, and so much other plate as may furnish sundry cupboards, to the sum oftentimes of £1,000 to £2,000 at the least, whereby the value of this and the rest of their stuff doth grow to be almost inestimable. Likewise in the houses of knights, gentlemen, merchantmen, and some other wealthy citizens, it is not geason [uncommon] to behold generally their great provision of tapestry, Turkey work [Turkish tapestry], pewter, brass, fine linen, and thereto costly cupboards of plate, worth £500 or £600 or £1,000, to be deemed by estimation.

ACTIVITY
KNOWLEDGE CHECK

Cultural change in Tudor England

1 Research the careers and works of these Renaissance figures: Thomas Kyd, Henry Howard, Philip Sidney, Christopher Marlowe, William Byrd, Christopher Tye. What contributions did they make to the development of new techniques? What role (if any) did patronage play in their careers? What was their most lasting contribution to the development of English culture?

2 Make a spider diagram called 'The causes of cultural change in Tudor England'. Use the following headings to summarise the main causes and give examples of each change: Education; The printing press; Growth of the English language; Humanism; Royal and noble patronage.

The impact of the cult of Gloriana

The 'cult of **Gloriana**' emerged in the 1570s and was a form of propaganda that encouraged the 'worship' of Elizabeth I.

KEY TERM

Gloriana

She was the Faerie Queen in Spenser's poem of the same name. Spenser made it clear in a letter to Walter Raleigh that Gloriana symbolised Elizabeth I: 'In that Faery Queen I mean glory in my general intention but in my particular I conceive the most excellent and glorious person of our sovereign.'

Its emergence was the result of increasing political instability: the threat of Catholic plots; rebellion and invasion; the arrival of Mary, Queen of Scots; and Elizabeth's excommunication in 1570 meant that her throne was under threat. In addition, as a female ruler who in the eyes of many was illegitimate, Elizabeth needed to find a way to encourage obedience to her. As it became clear in the early 1580s that Elizabeth was not going to marry and have a child, she had to find alternative methods to enhance loyalty to the Tudor dynasty and distract from the issue of the succession. The result of these political circumstances was the cult of Gloriana.

The cult of Gloriana emerged from a combination of ideas and influences. The medieval royal tournament, where knights would joust to earn rewards from the monarch, had evolved under the Tudors. The tournament became an opportunity to honour royal power and enhance its prestige in England and abroad through a show of wealth and courtly culture. Under Elizabeth, the tournament evolved to celebrate and enhance the cult, with members of the court jousting to win her favour. From about 1570, under the guidance of Sir Henry Lee, the most important tournament celebrated Elizabeth's Accession Day, 17 November. This day was also celebrated throughout England when sermons in churches emphasised Elizabeth's role as the defender of the Protestant faith against hostile Catholic forces led by the pope, who was identified with the 'Antichrist' (the devil). The Accession Day celebrations also performed another important function in that they replaced the gap left by Catholic feast days abolished during the Reformation.

To distract from the fact that Elizabeth was not married and had no child, her status as the 'Virgin Queen' was celebrated. This drew on the traditional Catholic cult of the Virgin Mary, which had been the most popular cult in England before the Reformation. Elizabeth's virginity was emphasised as a positive; her chastity and purity were the things that would protect England.

The humanist interest in classical literature led to the development of 'courtly love', the idea that Elizabeth would be loved by her subjects, but that she herself would remain pure, and above corruption. Some poets, such as Sir John Davies, identified Elizabeth with the classical myth of the Greek goddess Astraea, who, according to legend, was the last immortal to leave earth. Astraea was portrayed as a virgin whose return to earth would bring a new period of peace and prosperity. In depicting Elizabeth as Astraea, Davies was promoting an image of her as the Virgin Queen whose rule had brought about a golden age.

The results of the cult of Gloriana were partly political and partly cultural. Elizabeth found a way to win the hearts and minds of her subjects even though she was a female ruler. The cult also distracted from her lack of heirs and the political instability that might result from this. Elizabeth herself encouraged her cult; she gave out miniatures of herself to her favoured courtiers, who would keep them as a reminder of their devotion to her. This helps to explain the popularity of English miniatures from this period, and especially the work of Hilliard who used the 'mask of youth'. Changes to Elizabethan art were also linked to the growth of the cult. At the start of the reign, Elizabeth's portraits were very similar to those of her predecessors, plain and lacking in any political imagery or symbolism.

From around 1570, artists began to paint Elizabeth as the Virgin Queen and relied heavily on symbolism to make a political point. Increasingly, Elizabeth was portrayed with a variety of objects drawn from classical stories, all of which the viewer was expected to interpret. For example, she was shown with a phoenix, which represented renewal and regrowth, and a sieve, which stood for chastity. Elizabeth's portraits were also designed to promote the image of the monarch as ageless. The introduction of the 'mask of youth' was an important part of this process.

The cult was celebrated by poets and writers, too. The first three books of Spenser's poem, *The Faerie Queen* were published in 1590 and Spenser made it clear that the main character, Gloriana, was Elizabeth I herself. By this time, images of Elizabeth were everywhere, on coins, woodcuts and on the front page of the Bible published in 1568, but these images were carefully controlled. The impact of the cult was to create an idealised image of Elizabeth and her rule and it was successful in that opposition to her rule declined. It was also successful in disguising the political problems of the reign and in particular the issue of the succession, but in the 1590s the cracks did start to appear.

SOURCE

20 The Sieve Portrait. This was painted by the Italian artist Federico Zuccari in 1579, but other versions of this portrait also exist. The sieve is a reference to the myth of Tuccia, a Roman virgin who proved her virginity by carrying water in a sieve.

AS Level Exam-Style Question Section B

English art, poetry, music, drama and theatre changed considerably during the reigns of Edward VI, Mary I and Elizabeth I.

To what extent were these changes the result of noble patronage? (20 marks)

Tip

You need to explain how noble patronage affected changes to Tudor culture before considering other reasons for these changes.

A Level Exam-Style Question Section B

How significant were alterations in religious belief in explaining cultural change in the years 1509–88? (20 marks)

Tip

You will need to consider whether changes in religious belief were the sole reason for changes to culture. Did the impact of religious change differ over time?

ACTIVITY
SUMMARY

In your own words, summarise the main developments in English culture.

1 Make a list of reasons why English culture developed during the Tudor period. Prioritise them and explain which reason you think is the most important.

2 Using the information from this chapter, fill in the following table.

	Trade	Culture
Evidence of change, 1509–88		
Evidence of continuity, 1509–88		
How much change was there overall?		

3 What do you think was the most important change to the economy, society or culture of the Tudor period? Justify your choice.

 WIDER READING

Lotherington, L. *The Tudor Years*, Hodder Murray (2003)

Picard, L. *Elizabeth's London*, Phoenix (2004)

Pound, J.F. *Poverty and Vagrancy in Tudor England*, Pearson (1986)

Strong, R. *Gloriana: The Portraits of Elizabeth I*, Pimlico (2003)

Williams, P. *The Later Tudors: England, 1547-1603*, Oxford University Press (2002)

Youings, J. *Sixteenth Century England*, Pelican (1984)

1.5 Was there a general crisis in government in the last years of Elizabeth I's reign, 1589–1603?

KEY QUESTIONS

- How significant were the threats to security from Spain and Ireland?
- How extensive was faction at court? What was the impact of the succession issue?
- What was the significance of growing conflict with parliament?
- How serious was the social and economic distress of the 1590s?

INTRODUCTION

A crisis in government could mean several things. For the last years of Elizabeth I's reign, it might mean a monarch who was no longer able to rule or manage government effectively. In the 1590s, Elizabeth certainly found it harder to manage her courtiers, her military captains and her parliaments, but did this lead to more serious problems such as revolt, civil war or other challenges to her authority? A crisis in government might also be taken to mean a situation where there was a breakdown between the central government and the localities it was supposed to control. The events of the 1590s might also suggest other ways in which there was a crisis. Long-lasting and financially crippling war fought on several fronts created social, economic and political tensions that grew during the last decade of Elizabeth's reign.

HOW SIGNIFICANT WERE THE THREATS TO NATIONAL SECURITY FROM SPAIN AND IRELAND?

The Anglo-Spanish conflict – background

England and Spain had been involved in a 'cold war' long before actual war broke out. The main issues were:

- the revolt in the Netherlands against Spanish Catholic rule, to which the English were giving unofficial support to protect English trading interests
- the growth of Spanish dominance in Europe which threatened the balance of power, aided by Spain's annexation of Portugal in 1580
- the threat to Protestant England and Elizabeth posed by Catholic plots and possible invasion
- Spanish intervention in the French Wars of Religion and their involvement in the Catholic League
- attempts by English privateers to challenge the Spanish monopoly on trade in the New World.

1585 – England goes to war with Spain

1589 – Henry IV becomes king of France

1585	1586	1587	1588	1589	1590	1591	1592	1593	1594

1588 – Spanish Armada

1590 – England sends troops to France

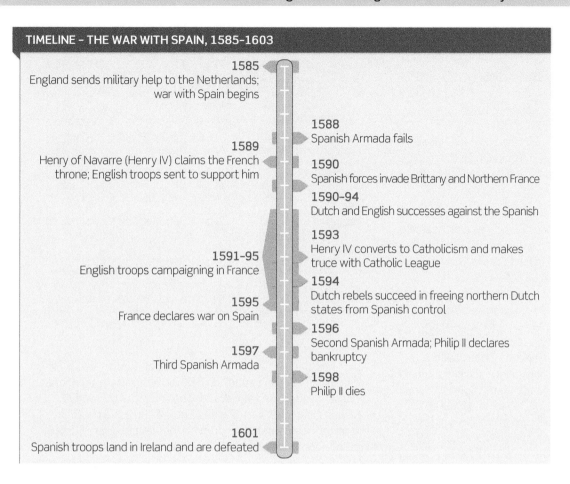

TIMELINE – THE WAR WITH SPAIN, 1585-1603

1585
England sends military help to the Netherlands; war with Spain begins

1588
Spanish Armada fails

1589
Henry of Navarre (Henry IV) claims the French throne; English troops sent to support him

1590
Spanish forces invade Brittany and Northern France

1590–94
Dutch and English successes against the Spanish

1593
Henry IV converts to Catholicism and makes truce with Catholic League

1591–95
English troops campaigning in France

1594
Dutch rebels succeed in freeing northern Dutch states from Spanish control

1595
France declares war on Spain

1596
Second Spanish Armada; Philip II declares bankruptcy

1597
Third Spanish Armada

1598
Philip II dies

1601
Spanish troops land in Ireland and are defeated

In 1585, Elizabeth was persuaded to intervene directly to help the Dutch rebels. This signalled the English entry into war with Spain, which would last until 1604. The war was characterised by Elizabeth's reluctance to commit money or troops to major campaigns – she preferred a defensive strategy, which would protect English trading interests in the Netherlands. At times, however, she was persuaded to send troops, ships or money to her allies. This was because her counsellors feared the Spanish Catholic dominance of the entire European coastline from Spain to the Netherlands and the invasion threat that would pose to England. The war was fought on several fronts. English troops were sent to the Netherlands and to France; there were also naval raids against Spain itself and against its shipping in the New World. Spain responded with several invasion fleets and by intervention in the Irish rebellion against English rule. The war with Spain was fought on several fronts, therefore. This stretched English resources to their limits, which in turn led to problems for Elizabeth's domestic government with both parliament and the rule of the localities.

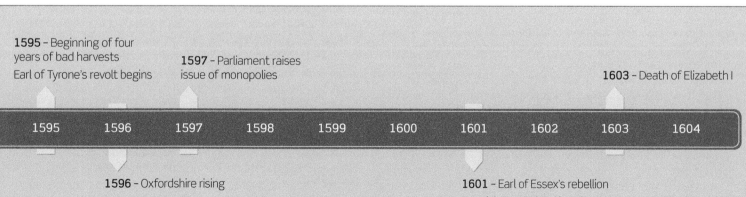

1595 – Beginning of four years of bad harvests
Earl of Tyrone's revolt begins

1597 – Parliament raises issue of monopolies

1603 – Death of Elizabeth I

| 1595 | 1596 | 1597 | 1598 | 1599 | 1600 | 1601 | 1602 | 1603 | 1604 |

1596 – Oxfordshire rising

1601 – Earl of Essex's rebellion
Spanish troops land in Ireland
Monopolies debate in parliament

The Anglo-Spanish conflict between 1589 and 1603

In 1589, the first Spanish Armada had already been defeated, partly by English tactics but mostly by the weather. Mary, Queen of Scots had been executed in 1587, which removed a possible rival to Elizabeth as well as a focus for Catholic plots. From 1589, the next few years of the war until 1595 saw Spain intervening directly in France, and English intervention in the Netherlands and France as well as attacks on Spain and its interests in the New World.

In 1589, the Protestant Henry of Navarre became King Henry IV of France. The accession of a Protestant king was unacceptable to the French Catholic League. Philip had already been subsidising the League, but in 1589 he decided to intervene directly in France. His aim was to help the League defeat Henry IV, who was allied with the Dutch Protestant rebels and with England. Philip hoped that if Henry was defeated, Dutch and English resistance would also collapse. He may even have been planning to put his daughter, the Infanta Isabella, on the French throne. If he had succeeded, the Spanish would have controlled the European coastline from Spain to the Netherlands. Philip sent 3,500 troops to Brittany in 1590 and ordered the Spanish troops in the Netherlands (led by the Duke of Parma) to gather on the border with northern France. Spanish troops launched major campaigns from there into Flanders between 1590 and 1596. The threat to Elizabeth and England was clear: if the Spanish controlled the French coastline, especially the coastline of Brittany and Normandy, they were ideally placed to launch an invasion of England over the Channel. Elizabeth was persuaded by her counsellors to send both financial and military aid to Henry IV and the Dutch. She sent £35,000 to Henry in 1589 and another £10,000 in 1590. Initially, 4,000 troops were sent to France in 1589, another 3,000 were sent to Brittany in 1591 and another 5,200 in 1592–93. A further 3,000 troops were sent under the Earl of Essex to besiege Spanish-held Rouen in 1591. At the same time, English troops under the command of Sir Francis Vere were helping the Dutch rebels.

English intervention was costly both in terms of life and money, but by 1595 the threat of Spanish European domination had declined significantly. Henry IV had converted to Catholicism and had defeated the resistance led by the Catholic League and Spanish troops. In 1595, he rallied French nationalism by declaring war on Spain. This helped England because it meant that the balance of power in Europe was restored and the Spanish were now fighting a united France. The Dutch did briefly intervene to help the French war against Spain in 1596 when the Spanish troops captured the key strategic port of Calais. By 1594, the Dutch had also had major successes against Spanish troops in the northern provinces of the Netherlands, although the war continued for the rest of Elizabeth's reign.

Although the Spanish had been beaten back in the northern provinces and in France, they remained at war with England and so posed a continuing threat to English security. When France and Spain agreed a peace treaty in 1598, England was excluded.

Henry of Navarre (Henry IV) and the French Wars of Religion
Henry of Navarre was a French Protestant who, from 1584, was also heir to the French throne. For some Catholics, such as the Guise family, the idea of having a Protestant on the throne was completely unacceptable. The king of Spain, Philip II, thought the same, and made an alliance with them (Treaty of Joinville, 1584) in which he provided funding for French Catholic troops.

In 1589, the French King Henry III was assassinated and Henry of Navarre claimed the throne. At this point, Spain became directly involved in the conflict, while Henry looked to England for help.

Although Elizabeth did provide both money and men, Henry did not always do what she wanted, especially regarding the defence of Normandy.

In 1593, Henry converted to Catholicism, famously declaring that 'Paris is worth a Mass'. This did not end the conflict in France, however, and Elizabeth continued to help him until 1595 when the Catholic League had finally been defeated.

Apart from intervention in the land wars of Europe, English ships were also involved in attacking Spanish interests on the Iberian Peninsula and in the New World. These attacks had varied success, mostly because the English government did not have the resources to fund them properly, but also because Elizabeth's cautious approach meant that she was not willing to commit all of her forces to an all-out attack. Instead, they were funded as a joint-stock enterprise, with the queen, members of the nobility and wealthy merchants all contributing to the costs, but all expecting a share of the profits. This meant that often profits were put before strategic advantage.

In addition, Elizabeth found that as a woman, her commands and wishes were often ignored by her military captains, who would do whatever they wanted. These combined problems meant that English military expeditions never fully achieved their aims. In 1589, for example, Essex joined the naval mission to Spain and the New World expressly against Elizabeth's orders. This expedition illustrates the problems that Elizabeth faced in defending England. She contributed £49,000 to the fleet, a gesture that had a mixture of military and financial aims: to attack the remnants of the Spanish Armada; to sail to Lisbon and encourage a Portuguese revolt against Spanish rule; and to sail to the Azores to attack the Spanish treasure ships. Nineteen thousand soldiers and 4,000 sailors were involved. The fleet sailed to Lisbon, but there was no revolt. Ignoring their orders to attack the Spanish fleet in their harbours, the English commanders sailed straight to the Azores instead, where they failed to capture any treasure ships. By the time the fleet returned empty-handed, 11,000 men had died. Other missions were more successful. Essex led a joint mission with the Dutch to attack Cádiz in 1596. Two Spanish ships were destroyed, two were captured and Cádiz itself was captured temporarily. These exploits made Essex a temporary hero, but it was a missed opportunity because no attempt was made to attack the main Spanish fleet at Lisbon, and nor were the treasure ships from the West Indies captured.

The problems of a joint-stock approach to warfare against Spain were clear, but this approach continued because Elizabeth's government was increasingly overstretched and under pressure. Elizabeth encouraged privateers to attack and loot Spanish shipping, but this was not overly successful. Individual ships were captured – £400,000 worth of treasure was captured between 1589 and 1591 – but there was no co-ordination between the English privateers. Spanish shipping, which was increasingly well guarded by warships, was able to slip through the net. Even the English successes were undermined by a lack of discipline. In 1592, £100,000 worth of goods from a Spanish ship were taken by the English sailors for their personal profit. There was still £141,120 worth of goods left over, but only £80,000 in goods reached the English government's treasury, not nearly enough to fund the high cost of war against Spain.

English tactics, which were largely the result of insufficient funds, meant that England could not mount a decisive challenge to Spain, although Elizabeth's cautious approach also meant that they did not lose the war completely because she never risked committing all of her troops or resources in any one campaign. Her tactics were enough to stop the English losing to Spain, but never enough to win decisively. However, the longer the war dragged on, the more damage it did to England's economy and society, as the escalating costs both in terms of money and loss of life led to increasing discontent and criticism of the regime.

The war with Spain undermined the social and economic stability of England, but it also led to the very real possibility of a Spanish Catholic invasion against Protestant England. The combination of attacks on Spain and its shipping by the English army and navy and the work of the English privateers led to counter-attacks by Spain. Although the defeat of the Armada in 1588 was celebrated as a great God-given victory by the English, this did not stop the Spanish rebuilding their navy and planning further invasion attempts in the 1590s. This led to invasion scares and panic in England, especially on the south coast. In 1595, a small Spanish force of about 400 men actually made a series of landing raids in Penzance (Cornwall), though they fled at the news that a fleet under Drake was approaching. More seriously, Philip II sent armadas in 1596 and 1597 that got as far as the English Channel; both were destroyed by bad weather rather than by English intervention. The 1597 mission was meant to give help to the Irish rebels, who at this point had the upper hand in their struggle against the English as the war escalated into new fronts. Although Philip II died in 1598, the war carried on under his successor Philip III. In 1601, a Spanish fleet reached Ireland and actually landed troops and guns there. Although this invasion was defeated, the linking of Spanish and Irish Catholic interests was a serious threat to English security, especially given Ireland's strategic importance.

Figure 5.1 Map of Europe in the 1590s showing some of the main areas of conflict in England, France, Spain and Ireland.

To what extent did the conflict with Spain present a threat to national security?

The war with Spain meant that English security was under threat of invasion in the period 1595 to 1601. Between 1589 and 1595, this threat was diminished to some extent because the first invasion force had been defeated in 1588, but during this time the Spanish were rebuilding their navy. The English attempted to disrupt the rebuilding process by attacking the Spanish treasure ships bringing gold and silver to fund the war effort and attempting harbour raids on the Spanish fleet. These attempts had some success, such as in 1596, but were undermined by the joint-stock funding of the English fleets, which meant that captains put commercial profit before military strategy. By 1595, the Spanish warships had been rebuilt and could threaten invasion once more. The fleets of 1595 and 1596 were unlucky in that they were dispersed by the weather, but they could easily have posed a threat if they had remained intact. Moreover, even during the period 1589–95, Spanish troops were active on the French coastline. Elizabeth's counsellors were concerned enough about this potential threat to persuade her to intervene directly in France.

However, the closest that Spain got to a successful invasion was in Ireland in 1601. Apart from this, their fleets did all fail. In addition, the Spanish war effort, like the English one, was coming under increasing strain. Philip was attempting to fight wars on three fronts and this led to the overextension of his resources. Spanish troops in the Netherlands mutinied every year from 1589 to 1602, and Spain actually went bankrupt in 1596. Military successes by the Dutch rebels and the French King Henry IV in the northern provinces of the Netherlands and in France itself meant that the Spanish did not achieve European dominance, and the balance of power between France and Spain was restored.

With hindsight, it is possible to argue that the threat posed by Spain to English national security was just that – a threat that did not become reality. Without the benefit of hindsight, however, Elizabeth, her counsellors and her people would only have seen the danger posed by Spain and were forced to act accordingly.

ACTIVITY
KNOWLEDGE CHECK

The Spanish threat

1 Make a timeline showing the Spanish threat to England's security during the period 1589–1603. Mark on it the key events.

2 Did Spain remain a consistent threat to English national security? Why?

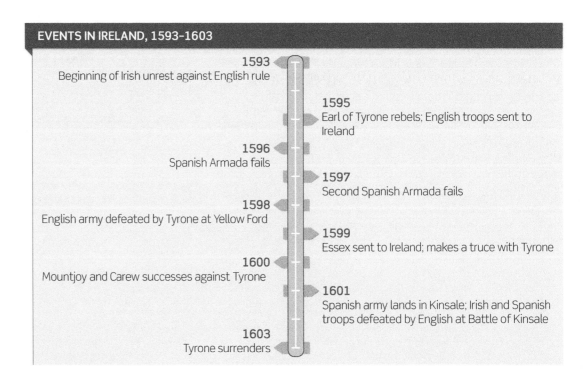

EVENTS IN IRELAND, 1593–1603

1593 Beginning of Irish unrest against English rule

1595 Earl of Tyrone rebels; English troops sent to Ireland

1596 Spanish Armada fails

1597 Second Spanish Armada fails

1598 English army defeated by Tyrone at Yellow Ford

1599 Essex sent to Ireland; makes a truce with Tyrone

1600 Mountjoy and Carew successes against Tyrone

1601 Spanish army lands in Kinsale; Irish and Spanish troops defeated by English at Battle of Kinsale

1603 Tyrone surrenders

Anglo-Irish relations under Elizabeth

Ireland was problematic for all English monarchs. England controlled Dublin and the area surrounding it through a Lord Lieutenant. This region around Dublin was known as 'the Pale', but most of Ireland and the Irish were outside this area, which is where the expression 'beyond the pale' comes from.

The situation outside the Pale was complex. Most of Ireland was controlled by Anglo-Irish members of the nobility, known as the 'Old English', who maintained their own private armies and acted as quasi-kings in the regions under their control. These men were the descendants of earlier English settlers who intermarried with the native Irish. Over hundreds of years the Old English had developed their own identity. Some spoke the native language of Ireland, Gaelic, and most were proud of their semi-independent status. The English government had a difficult relationship with these men; while some were happy to co-operate, others resented English attempts to extend control throughout Ireland, and rebelled. Elizabeth had already faced rebellions in Munster in 1569 and 1579. However, English monarchs could not simply leave Ireland to its own devices because its position off the west coast of England made it a perfect launch pad for hostile invasion. In addition, Ireland remained mostly Catholic despite the Reformation; English attempts to introduce Protestantism had met with little success. This meant that an Irish Catholic rebellion was a real threat, especially if it received support from sympathetic foreign powers such as Spain, who could use the situation in Ireland as a pretext to invade England.

By the 1580s, the Elizabethan government was taking a more hard-line approach to Ireland through the 'plantation' of English Protestant colonists. These colonists were often courtiers who bought up and took over lands forfeited by the Munster rebels. By the early 1590s, resentment was growing in Ireland, and in 1595 a serious revolt broke out which lasted until 1603.

Tyrone's revolt, 1595–1603

Hugh O'Neill, Earl of Tyrone, was a member of the Anglo-Irish nobility whose lands lay in the province of Ulster. O'Neill had been brought up in England in the household of the Earl of Leicester, but in the early 1590s his relations with the English government became increasingly tense. O'Neill felt under threat from the growing number of English Protestant colonists in Ireland who threatened to encroach on Ulster from the south, and he wanted Elizabeth to grant him the right to rule Ulster, but Elizabeth would not agree. There was already unrest in Ulster in 1593, but by 1595 Tyrone himself joined what became a full-blown revolt against English rule and in defence of Catholicism.

Tyrone's revolt was a serious challenge to England. His rebel army was large and well organised. He used English and Spanish captains to train his men, and he imported weapons and ammunition. He also had a steady source of income from Ulster that allowed him to fund his army properly.

In 1595, Tyrone led an army of 1,000 cavalry, 4,000 musketmen and 1,000 pikemen. The rebellion was not confined to Ulster, either: it spread rapidly to Sligo, Connaught, Munster and Leinster.

Boosted by large forces, Tyrone was able to take on the English army. In 1598 he won a major victory over the English at the Battle of Yellow Ford where around 830 English troops were killed and 400 wounded.

In 1599, Elizabeth was forced to send the largest army of her reign to deal with the Irish revolt. Led by Essex, the army had 16,000 infantry and 1,300 cavalry. Unfortunately, Essex failed miserably in his mission. He spent the summer moving through Leinster and Munster with his army without bringing Tyrone to battle. He only marched north when Elizabeth angrily ordered him to do so and even then he made a truce with Tyrone, rather than fighting him. Essex then deserted his post to rush back to England and justify his actions to the queen.

The only positive result for England was that Tyrone kept to the truce until it expired in 1600, but he then marched south to the fortress of Kinsale on the Cork coast. By now, Elizabeth had replaced Essex with Charles Blount (Lord Mountjoy) at the head of a force of 13,200 men. Mountjoy's tactics were ruthless but effective. In 1600, he pushed Tyrone's forces back north into Ulster, burning houses and killing the native Irish as he went. He also cut off Tyrone's supply lines in an attempt to bring his forces into submission. Tyrone was saved by the arrival in 1601 of the Spanish troops that had first been promised in 1597. Three thousand four hundred highly trained Spanish soldiers landed at Kinsale, bringing with them siege guns. Mountjoy was forced to besiege the Spanish at Kinsale using 7,000 men, but this freed Tyrone to march south to join his allies, gathering reinforcements as he went. Tyrone arrived at Kinsale in December 1601 with an army of 6,500. Thinking that he would be able to defeat the English, who were trapped between the Spanish and the Irish, Tyrone prepared for battle, but Mountjoy launched a surprise attack before the Irish forces were ready. The battle at Kinsale was the last of the rebellion. Tyrone retreated to Ulster and in January 1602 the Spanish troops surrendered.

Ironically, when Tyrone finally submitted to Mountjoy on 30 March 1603, he received very generous terms. He was pardoned and was recognised as the chief lord of Ulster under the English crown, almost the very title that he had been trying to get from Elizabeth in the first place. The reason for Mountjoy's generosity was linked to events at the English court. Elizabeth had died six days before and Mountjoy, who opposed the Cecil faction, was keen to return to England in order to ingratiate himself with James VI. Mountjoy may therefore have offered the concessions in order to reach a settlement as quickly as possible. These concessions were to cause problems for James in the future as he tried to control Ireland.

EXTEND YOUR KNOWLEDGE

Hugh O'Neill, Earl of Tyrone

Hugh O'Neill was a member of the O'Neill Anglo-Irish family of Ulster. His father, Shane O'Neill, had fallen foul of the English forces in Ireland and was killed in 1567. Hugh was brought up as an English Ward of Court in an attempt to anglicise him. The traditional Gaelic title was 'the O'Neill'. Shane, like other Anglo-Irish nobility, had been persuaded to surrender this title in return for an English one, the Earl of Tyrone. The first sign that Hugh was turning against English influence was when he was elected to the title of 'the O'Neill' in the traditional manner in 1593.

An account of Mountjoy's tactics in Ulster, written in 1600 by Fynes Moryson, secretary to Mountjoy.

[W]here other deputies used to assail the rebels only in summer time, this lord prosecuted them most in winter, being commonly five days at least in the week on horseback all the winter long. This broke their hearts; for the air being sharp, and they naked, and they being driven from their homes into the woods [which were] bare of leaves, they had no shelter for themselves. Besides that, their cattle were also wasted by travelling to and fro. Add to that they were... troubled in the seed time [and] could not sow their ground. And in the harvest time both the deputy's forces and the [English] garrisons cut down their corn before it was ripe, and then in winter time they [the English troops] carried away or burnt all the stores of food in the secret places where the rebels had conveyed them.

To what extent did Tyrone's revolt pose a threat to English national security?

If the Irish revolt had occurred in isolation, it would have created a problem for the English government but it would not have become a threat to English national security. Irish revolts in the past had been put down, though not without considerable money, manpower and loss of life on the part of the English. The English army was eventually successful in 1600–03 when Elizabeth was prepared to send a substantial force under competent leadership to deal with the revolt. Part of the reason it took so long for the Irish revolt to be suppressed was that Elizabeth appointed Essex to do the job, mainly because he was determined that any military glory that was achieved in Ireland would belong to him and not to the rival faction at court led by Robert Cecil. Essex's appointment was a mistake, but Mountjoy showed what a properly led English army could achieve and the revolt was suppressed.

However, the European context in which the Irish revolt took place made it a serious threat to English security. England's resources were already overextended as a result of ten years of war in the Netherlands, France, Spain and the New World. For Elizabeth, the timing of the revolt in 1595 could not have been worse, and she was both unable and unwilling to send enough troops to deal with the situation, which allowed the rebellion to gather momentum. Even worse, the religious element of the revolt meant that Spain could justifiably offer support to fellow Catholics. In 1597, it was lucky that the Spanish Armada, intended to provide support for Ireland, was dispersed by bad weather. In 1601, the Spanish did land a large and well-trained force in Ireland, which shows what was possible when the elements did not intervene. Mountjoy was very fortunate to win the battle at Kinsale – he was outnumbered and trapped between hostile Catholic and Irish forces. While it is possible to argue that Mountjoy made his own luck with a surprise attack, the consequences had he failed potentially would have been very serious for Elizabeth. If Mountjoy's army had been defeated, Ireland would have fallen under the control of a large and united Catholic Spanish and Irish force, which Philip III could have used as a base either for further operations against the English navy in the Atlantic or, even worse, from which to invade England.

To what extent did the threats from Spain and Ireland create a general crisis in government?

In some ways, the war against Catholic Spain and in support of the Protestant Dutch and French king (until 1593) helped to increase English patriotism and a feeling that God was looking favourably on English Protestants by granting them victories. Individual triumphs such as that of Essex at Cádiz were greeted with celebrations and gave English propagandists plenty of ammunition in their anti-Spanish, anti-Catholic pamphlets. Although the threat of invasion grew from 1595, none of these attempts by the Spanish were successful apart from the Spanish troops who arrived in 1601, and even they were defeated. Before 1595, the defeat of the Armada in 1588 created a breathing space during which the physical threat of invasion and the fear this caused were limited. The activities of the English privateers in the New World also had some positive results in the longer term. Although they could not stop the flow of bullion from the New World to Spain, they did succeed in capturing over 1,000 Spanish and Portuguese ships. By the end of his reign, Philip II had realised that Spain would not be able to maintain its monopoly over trade. The activities of the privateers paved the way for the establishment of the East India Company in 1600, formalising trade with Asia, but this was an unintended outcome and only really benefited the economy under the Stuarts in the 17th century.

However, the fact that England, a small country of just under four million people, remained at war for 18 years on more than one front meant that a financial and military crisis developed. Elizabeth's government had an income of about £300,000 per annum, which was not nearly enough to deal with the heavy financial demands of war. Elizabeth spent £144,786 on her campaigns in France in 1589–91 alone; maintaining English forces in the Netherlands cost £100,000 per year; providing warships to guard the Channel cost £1,000 a month, and the cost of garrisoning Ireland rose to £5,000 per month. All of these costs had to be borne by the English parliament and taxpayers. The longer the war went on, the more expensive it became and the more pressure was put on the English economy, leading to the discontent that was voiced both in parliament and in the country at large.

There was also the human cost of the conflict. Eleven thousand Englishmen were killed in France in just three years, mostly from disease, lack of supplies and insanitary conditions. Even worse for Elizabeth's government, those who did return spread more criticism and discontent, which was reflected in William Shakespeare's depiction of military hardship and the corruption in the **muster systems** in his play *Henry IV* Part II (written c1596–99).

KEY TERM

Muster system
This was organised on a county basis by the Lord Lieutenants and their deputies to muster the local militia. A list was kept of all eligible men, and every household was supposed to provide its own weapons. There were also supposed to be training sessions, but these rarely happened. This system led to poorly trained, poorly equipped and reluctant soldiers and led to the formation of the trained bands.

The demands of war also led to tensions within local government. Local officers were put under increasing pressure by the central government to meet its demands. Between 1585 and 1603, 105,810 men were forced into military service. Some local officials began to resist government demands, though their resistance was passive, not violent. For example, by 1592, local landowners were resisting attempts to send the county **trained bands** abroad. The bands were experienced and, as their name implies, were trained, but because of this training it was felt that they should be used for national defence and not sent abroad. Moreover, the trained bands were often from those of higher status within county society such as yeomen and artisans who could more easily avoid conscription through manipulation of the system. The deputy lieutenants of Essex admitted that they had been substituting men of lower status for those of higher status who had been chosen to serve abroad. During the 1590s, it was costing each county £2,000 a year to pay for and equip the men who were to serve abroad. In Suffolk and Norfolk, these demands led to resistance through non-payment. The financial shortfall meant that counties could not afford proper equipment for the soldiers, which led in turn to men being sent to serve abroad but not being properly equipped, and that decreased morale further. By 1600, when England was also trying to put down the Irish revolt, there was very nearly a mutiny of Kentish cavalry at Chester, where they were waiting to be sent to Ireland.

KEY TERM

Trained band
These were supposed to be elite forces drawn from the local militia who met regularly for training. They were funded by their local counties.

However, the resistance to the demands of war remained passive. Members of landed society certainly grumbled and tried to dodge the demands placed on them, but there was no full-scale, national campaign of resistance to government policies, and neither did local officials actively refuse to co-operate with the government's demands.

ACTIVITY
KNOWLEDGE CHECK

Threats and government responses

1 Fill in the following table to summarise what you have read.

	Key events	Response of English government	Level of threat to English national security
Spain			
Ireland			

2 With a partner, find evidence to support each of these challenge statements:

   a) The war did not create a serious crisis in government before 1595.

   b) The war created a serious crisis in government in the years 1589 to 1603.

   c) The war only created a serious crisis in government from 1595.

EXTRACT

1 From P. Williams, *The Later Tudors: England 1547–1603* (1995).

The pause [in 1595] between the ending of the civil strife in France and the beginning of the next phase of hostilities ... the rebellion in Ireland, and the naval expeditions to Cádiz and the Azores – allows us to assess the cost and the achievement of England's military endeavours since the Armada. ... The equipment and weapons of the levies were a continuous drain upon the resources of the shires and their collection was a source of discontent and irritation. ... Nevertheless, the subsidies were voted; a high proportion of the required men was levied; and mutinies were few. Up to the middle of 1595, there is not much sign of serious hostility towards the Crown either from the counties or from Parliament ... but more testing times for the government and the counties were to come in the second half of the decade.

However towards the end of 1595, the military situation was ... as threatening as ever ... In May 1595, Hugh O'Neill, Earl of Tyrone, began the most serious revolt of the century against English rule. At sea, the Spanish fleet had been rebuilt and Philip II was again capable of launching an Armada.

ACTIVITY
WRITING

Analysing language
Analyse Extract 1.

1 Identify words and phrases used to express degrees of doubt and certainty. Write them out: most certain to least certain.

2 Identify words and phrases used to describe the relationships between causes. Which are the most precise in their meaning?

3 Identify words and phrases that show the historian's attitude towards the impact of war with Spain. Write a short paragraph explaining the historian's views, using quotes from the extract to back up your points.

AS Level Exam-Style Question Section B

Analyse and evaluate Extracts 1 and 2 (overleaf).

To what extent did the problems created by war pose a serious threat to Elizabeth's power from 1589 to 1603? (20 marks)

Tip

Make sure that you think about what is meant by a 'serious threat', for example invasion or Elizabeth being overthrown.

EXTRACT

2 From R. Sloan in J. Lotherington (ed.), *The Tudor Years* (2003).

So, the purpose for which England went to war in 1585 was, by and large, achieved, as the spectre of overwhelming Spanish power was overcome. ... In this vital respect the war achieved much for England.

This is not to say that the foreign policy that led to war can be called a success. It was a war Elizabeth had long sought to avoid, and its occurrence must therefore be considered a policy failure ... it was a war that produced much disruption and unrest, causing as it did an oppressive level of taxation, dislocation of trade, enforced and bitterly resented military service, a profusion of detested monopolies, and widespread corruption in public life.

The war ... threatened her authority even more directly; so dominant at home, she found that commanders like ... Essex constantly disobeyed her orders – usually to ill effect.

THINKING HISTORICALLY — Interpretations (4a)

The weight of evidence

Work in pairs.

1 Read Extracts 1 and 2. Use highlighter pens to colour-code copies of the extracts. Use one colour for 'evidence', another colour for 'conclusions' and a third for language that shows the historian is 'reasoning' (for example, 'therefore', 'so'). Alternatively, draw up a table with three columns, headed 'Evidence', 'Conclusions' and 'Reasoning language' and copy the relevant parts of the extracts into the columns.

2 How do the extracts differ in terms of the way that the evidence is used?

3 Which of these extracts do you find more convincing? Which has the best supported arguments?

4 What other information might you want in order to make a judgement about the strength of these claims?

5 Write a paragraph of 200 words explaining the importance of using evidence to support historical claims.

THINKING HISTORICALLY — Interpretations (4b)

Method is everything

Bad history	Good history
• Based on gut feeling • Argument does not progress logically • No supporting evidence	• Based on an interpretation of evidence • Argument does progress logically • Evidence deployed to support argument

Work in pairs.

Historical writing can reveal much about the methods by which it was constructed. Read Extracts 1 and 2 and answer the following questions.

1 Look carefully at the spectrum of methodology above.

  a) Where would you place each extract on the spectrum of historical practice?

  b) What evidence would you use to support your choice?

2 Look at Extract 2. How would you change it to make it the same quality of historical writing as Extract 1?

3 Use a dictionary. Explain the following words in relation to historical writing: substantiation, deduction, inference, cross-reference.

4 How important is it that historians understand and evaluate the methods used by other historians?

THE IMPACT OF THE SUCCESSION ISSUE

The development of faction in the 1590s

Before about 1589, Elizabeth's court and Council had been relatively free of faction. But between 1588 and 1591, many of Elizabeth's trusted advisers and courtiers who had served her since the beginning of her reign died. These included the Earl of Leicester in 1588, Walter Mildmay in 1589, Francis Walsingham in 1590 and Christopher Hatton in 1591. Of the older generation of councillors, only William Cecil (Lord Burghley) was left, and he was ageing and in increasingly poor health; he died in August 1598. The old generation was replaced with an ambitious new group of courtiers who perhaps did not always possess the same sense of loyalty to, and understanding of, the queen as the generation who had grown up with her. Elizabeth was also ageing – she was in her mid-50s by 1589, which was already an impressive age by the standards of the time – but she was to survive for another 14 years.

Elizabeth had remained unmarried and childless. As she aged, the issue of who would succeed her became increasingly prominent in court politics. Elizabeth refused to name a successor (even on her deathbed), fearing that he or she would become a figurehead for plots against her. However, this did not stop those around her from planning what would happen after her death. Securing the succession for 'their' candidate became one source of rivalry between the factions that formed in the 1590s because it was a way to ensure their continuing power and influence at court after Elizabeth's death. The factions were also divided over the war with Spain: what tactics to follow, and even whether to continue fighting. The rival factions jockeyed for position at court and in the Council. Access to the queen was vital in the faction leaders' attempts to get key appointments for their followers. Elizabeth's natural cautiousness meant that she was often reluctant to commit herself, but this only led to more pressure being applied by those who wanted her favour and patronage.

The factions of the 1590s: Cecil versus Essex

The factions that developed in the 1590s coalesced around William Cecil and his son Robert on one side, and Robert Devereux (Earl of Essex) on the other. William Cecil was planning for his own succession as well as Elizabeth's; he hoped to pass his power and position to his younger son, Robert. Robert Cecil was small and had a deformed spine: Elizabeth called him her 'little elf'. He was a talented administrator, but also a shrewd and crafty politician and administrator who sought to secure his position as Elizabeth's chief minister and enhance his standing with her most likely successor, James VI of Scotland. Born c1563, Robert Cecil's main experience of office before the 1590s was as an MP. His father put pressure on Elizabeth to advance Robert's career; in 1591, the queen knighted the younger Cecil, and admitted him to the Privy Council, making him the second-youngest person in Elizabeth's reign to receive this honour.

SOURCE 2

Portrait of Sir Robert Cecil, painted by John de Critz the Elder, c1602.

It should not be assumed that Elizabeth lost control of her government and councillors in the 1590s. Although Elizabeth promoted Robert Cecil partly out of respect for his father, she was also prepared to advance him because he agreed with her about England's military strategy. Elizabeth favoured a cautious, defensive war against Spain, and both of the Cecils supported her on this. Moreover, she had always followed a strategy of balancing the views of her Council by appointing men with differences of opinion – in the 1570s and 1580s, Leicester and Cecil had disagreed about England's foreign policy. Moreover, Elizabeth was not prepared to give in to all of the demands that the Cecil faction placed on her. Robert Cecil was hoping to be appointed as the queen's secretary, a position that had been held by Walsingham until his death in 1590. Elizabeth, however, left the position vacant until 1596, when Robert Cecil finally achieved his aim. On the other hand, Elizabeth's caution and reluctance to make decisions did not reduce the rivalry between the factions as she had hoped. Instead, both sides tried to get their own man appointed to the position, increasing the tension between them.

The reason for some of the tension at court was the disruptive presence of Robert Devereux, Earl of Essex. Essex was a member of an old noble family and thus the representative of a dying breed, the feudal nobility. He was the stepson of the Earl of Leicester, and saw himself as the natural successor both to Leicester and to the poet and man of action Sir Philip Sidney, whose widow he married. Leicester had been Elizabeth's favourite, and both he and Sidney had advocated an offensive war against Spain in support of Protestant interests abroad.

SOURCE 3

Robert Devereux, second Earl of Essex, c1596, painted by Marcus Gheeraerts the Younger.

Roughly the same age as Robert Cecil (Essex was born in 1565), he was very different in both looks and temperament. Essex was tall, handsome and athletic, but also arrogant, impulsive and easily angered. He based his reputation on his military prowess; he was prepared to fight duels, built up a military following and sought military success abroad.

He also tried to court popular opinion as a 'man of the people', which got him into trouble, particularly when he appeared to be challenging Elizabeth's own popularity and power. As a favourite of Elizabeth, he was prepared to flatter and entertain her. Anthony Bagot, a friend of Essex, wrote: 'when she is abroad, nobody near her but my L. of Essex; and, at night, my L. is at cards, or one game or another with her, that he cometh not to his own lodging till birds sing in the morning'.

Elizabeth kept Essex under close control, however. Although he was a member of the nobility, he was not well off, and he was reliant on the queen for enough patronage to support himself and his followers. In 1588, he was given the lucrative monopoly on sweet wines, which had previously belonged to Leicester. Essex was appointed to the Council in 1593, which allowed him to argue for a more aggressive military policy. But crucially, Essex always remained reliant on the queen for his power and influence. He did not have the resources to build up a following in the localities and his power was based at court. The Cecils, however, were able to build up power much more effectively, mainly because William Cecil monopolised so many positions in government: until 1596 he was Lord Treasurer, Master of the Court of Wards (which controlled the estates and custody of minors and was a rich source of patronage), and acting secretary in the absence of a permanent appointment. After 1596, when Robert Cecil became secretary, the Cecils tightened their hold still further. Ironically, it was this dominance of key positions in government by the Cecils that led to Essex's increasingly desperate attempts to enhance his own power. In the 1590s, the balance of power between the factions was disturbed, although as John Guy argues in Extract 3 their positions only became polarised from 1595 to 1596.

Members of the nobility and gentry who wanted to advance their own careers attempted to seek the support of the Cecils or Essex as patrons. At the same time, the Cecils competed with Essex for power and influence and access to patronage. They needed to build up a following to support them in the Council, court and locally and so worked to attract potential clients by getting them the appointments they desired. This led to rival groupings forming at court, which was the centre of power and patronage because it allowed access to the queen, the ultimate source of all grants of land, office and power. These groupings began to form in the early 1590s, though they were still quite fluid until 1595, when positions began to polarise. Significantly, although Essex was able to attract some noble support, plus the talented Bacon brothers (Francis and Anthony), he lacked many supporters in the most influential positions of government – the Council, the household and the localities – especially compared with the Cecils. Essex liked to portray himself as a man of action who thought that it was legitimate for the nobility to use violence to defend their honour and achieve their political aims. He himself was a Lord Lieutenant, and he attracted at least 12 deputy lieutenants into his faction. He also had the support of the military men who served him during his campaigns abroad. This military support was potentially dangerous, but crucially Essex did not have the support of his fellow Lord Lieutenants, who were ultimately in charge of military musters. The Cecils, meanwhile, used their influence to gain supporters both in the Council and in the key positions in the Council of the North, which enhanced their military support base.

The Cecil faction	The Essex faction
William Cecil, Lord Burghley (d. 1598; Lord Treasurer, Master of the Court of Wards; acting secretary until 1596)	Robert Devereux, Earl of Essex (Master of the Horse from 1588; Privy Councillor from 1593)
Sir Robert Cecil (Privy Councillor from 1591; secretary from 1596)	Roger Manners, Earl of Rutland (son-in-law of Sir Philip Sidney)
Charles, Lord Howard of Effingham (Lord High Admiral from 1585; Earl of Nottingham from 1597)	Sir Robert Sidney (younger brother of Sir Philip Sidney)
Sir John Stanhope (Treasurer of the Chamber from 1596)	Charles Blount, Lord Mountjoy
Henry Brooke, Lord Cobham (Warden of the Cinque Ports from 1597)	Sir William Knollys (Privy Councillor from 1596)
Thomas Cecil (elder son of William; president of the Council of the North from 1599)	Roger, Lord North (Privy Councillor from 1596)
George Carey, Lord Hunsdon (Lord Chamberlain and Privy Councillor from 1597)	Anthony and Francis Bacon
Sir Thomas Heneage (Privy Councillor from 1587)	*Supporters in 1601:*
	Henry Wriotheseley, Earl of Southampton
	Edward Russell, Earl of Bedford

ACTIVITY
KNOWLEDGE CHECK

Faction

1 Explain in your own words how and why faction developed in the 1590s.

2 Find and print out pictures of the Earl of Essex and Robert Cecil. Annotate and draw links between each picture to show their relationship to each other, their strengths and weaknesses, roles in government and at court, and their key supporters. Use your annotations to decide which man had the stronger political position.

3 In what ways did Elizabeth's actions make faction worse?

How did the growth of faction lead to political instability?

Before 1595, at times the Cecils and Essex did co-operate. For example in 1591–92, they worked together to put pressure on Elizabeth to intervene in France to prevent the Spanish Catholic forces there gaining more territory and posing an invasion threat to England. Between 1593 and 1594, relations deteriorated to some extent, with both sides putting forward rival candidates for the secretaryship and the post of Attorney General. In the case of the secretaryship Elizabeth refused to make an appointment, but in reality the Cecils were doing much of the work associated with the post. In the case of the Attorney General's post, the Cecils managed to secure the appointment of their man, Sir Edward Coke. These events undoubtedly caused Essex to resent the Cecils' influence and power. However, Essex was able to prove his worth to Elizabeth in 1593 when the spy network he had been nurturing discovered a plot by the queen's doctor, Antonio Lopez, to murder her.

The rivalry between the factions began to develop into something much more dangerous in 1596. Essex was sent to Cádiz on a military expedition against the Spanish. He was largely successful, but he could have been more so. While he was away, the Cecils tightened their grip on the Council and government with Robert Cecil finally being appointed secretary. This shows the importance of having daily access to the queen. Essex then quarrelled with the queen over the division of the profits from his campaign. Not surprisingly, Essex came off worst and blamed Robert Cecil, who had been asked to make an inventory of the Spanish goods.

More tensions emerged in 1597 when the old Lord Cobham died and the offices he had held became available. These included the valuable and influential posts of Lord Chamberlain and the lord lieutenancy of Kent. Essex lobbied the queen on behalf of his follower Robert Sidney, but Sidney was passed over in favour of Cobham's son and heir. Essex planned another campaign against Spain in 1597, but this was unsuccessful and led to the queen's displeasure. Essex meanwhile was angered by the promotion of Charles Lord Howard, another Cecil supporter, to the rank of Earl of Nottingham. According to the rules of precedence, this meant that Howard now outranked Essex. Essex, as a member of the traditional nobility, was furious and challenged the earl to a duel before withdrawing from court in a rage. Although Essex's pride was soothed with the position of Earl Marshal, the incident showed both the tensions at court as a result of faction and Essex's tendency to react violently.

SOURCE 4

Sir Henry Wotton in 1641, the year before civil war broke out between Charles I and parliament, writing about Elizabethan faction. Wotton, like many commentators of the 17th century, tended to emphasise the successful nature of patronage under Elizabeth, but also the results of patronage badly managed and the dangers of a clique of courtiers dominating access to the monarch.

Francis Allen seeks a post at court and is supported by Essex, the Cecils are sure to have another candidate in the field. Sir Thomas Bodley loses the post of Secretary of State simply because Essex takes up his cause out of spite against Cecil, and because Cecil consequently feels himself bound in honour to oppose him. Standen, applying to Burghley for a reward for the valuable foreign correspondence with which he has supplied the queen, is frankly told by the Lord Treasurer that, since he has chosen to send his information through Essex, and not through him, he must look to Essex for support. Anthony Bacon supports a certain Mr. Trott in his suit for the clerkship to the Council of York, and procures for him the support of Essex. Immediately the opposite party at York sends word to Burghley, that Essex has put forward a candidate, and prays Burghley's support for a rival.

Essex's downfall came as a result of events in Ireland. The revolt that had broken out in 1595 led to increased tensions at court and between Elizabeth and Essex. In 1598, Elizabeth suggested that the Essexian William Knollys should be appointed Lord Deputy of Ireland, but Essex suggested the Cecilian George Carew instead, probably in an attempt to remove him from court. This led to a full-blown argument in the Privy Council. Essex turned his back on the queen, Elizabeth slapped him and Essex put his hand on his sword as if to draw it. The Earl of Nottingham had to intervene and Essex withdrew in a rage, with the parting shot that he would not have taken such an insult from any monarch, even Henry VIII.

With the death of William Cecil in 1598, the political situation deteriorated further. Despite his argument with the queen, Essex was appointed Lord Deputy of Ireland in 1599. He left England in March 1599. In his absence, Robert Cecil ensured that all of the key posts went to him, his friends and family. Cecil himself became Master of the Court of Wards; his brother Thomas became president of the Council of the North. Meanwhile, Essex's campaign in Ireland was unsuccessful; Essex's own mistakes were partly to blame, but the situation was made worse by the lack of support from Elizabeth's government. In September 1599, he left Ireland and returned to England, explicitly disobeying Elizabeth's orders. He burst into the queen's privy chamber where he found the queen only just awake and not ready to receive visitors. Elizabeth insisted that he face a full meeting of the Council to explain his actions. At the same time, London was filled with Essex's followers, including soldiers. Elizabeth decided to put Essex under house arrest. He remained there until June 1600 when he was put on trial. The charges against him were largely manufactured by Cecil and originally accused Essex of treason. Cecil was even prepared to accuse Essex of conspiring with the Spanish and the pope to gain the crown for himself. On this occasion, however, Essex was found guilty only of misconduct of his campaign in Ireland, but this was serious enough for him to be suspended from his offices. Even worse for Essex, in September, Elizabeth refused to renew his monopoly on sweet wines and Essex rapidly fell into debt.

By the end of 1600, Essex had lost most of his more moderate supporters such as Francis Bacon and William Knollys and was surrounded by men who like him had a grudge against the Cecils or Elizabeth (such as the Earl of Southampton) or who had accompanied him on military campaigns.

In February 1601, Essex and his supporters were planning to use an armed force to surround and capture the court and the queen. Essex was also prepared to use dangerous historical precedents to support his actions. It was arranged that the Lord Chamberlain's company would perform Shakespeare's *Richard II*, which is the story of how a tyrannical king was deposed by his cousin Bolingbroke. The deposition scene in the play had already been banned as too politically sensitive, but the performance went ahead and included the forbidden scene. Essex was sending out a message that he, like Bolingbroke, was justified in his actions. He was also implying that Elizabeth, like Richard, was surrounded by favourites who gave her false advice. The queen and the Council were alerted to Essex's plans and Elizabeth demanded that the earl come to court and explain. Essex felt that revolt was the only option. He took hostage the four councillors who were sent with the queen's message, and with about 140 followers he marched towards the City of London where he hoped to get the support of the trained bands and popular support. When this failed, he returned to Essex House, which was then besieged by the queen's men. Essex was forced to surrender and was tried and executed for treason. With his death, his faction disintegrated and Robert Cecil's remained dominant for the rest of the reign and beyond.

The succession issue and faction

Elizabeth's childlessness led to a problem for councillors since she consistently refused to name her successor. There were rumours that she had nominated James VI of Scotland on her deathbed, but whatever she may have indicated, the reality was that the decision lay with the Privy Council.

There were several possible candidates for the throne, including James VI, Arbella Stuart, Edward Seymour and the Infanta Isabella. (See the Tudor family tree in Figure 1.1, page 16.) James VI in many ways was the most obvious candidate, but there were barriers to his inheritance. Under the 1544 Act of Succession, Henry had been given the power to name his heirs in his will. He had named his children Edward, Mary and Elizabeth, then Frances Grey and Eleanor Clifford (the daughters of his younger sister, Mary Tudor) and their children, then the 'rightful heirs', a very vague phrase. Henry's will also demoted the claim of the Stuart heirs of his elder sister Margaret, who had married James IV of Scotland. This was a potential problem for Margaret's descendant, James VI. In addition, James' mother (Mary, Queen of Scots) had been executed for treason, and he was a Scottish foreigner. However, James was Protestant, which for the Protestants in England meant that he seemed the best candidate to protect their interests. James' supporters also argued that Henry VIII's will was not valid because it had been stamped with the dry stamp, not signed by the king in person.

The other candidates for the throne also had a claim, but received much less support. Like James VI, Arbella Stuart was descended from Margaret Tudor and had been brought up in England, but the Cecils seem to have favoured her cousin James and she was passed over, perhaps because she had Catholic sympathies.

Edward Seymour (Lord Beauchamp of Hache) was descended from Catherine, daughter of Frances Grey, but his claim was not secure because his mother had married without Elizabeth I's permission and her marriage had been annulled, making Seymour technically illegitimate. In addition, the accession of an adult male member of the English nobility might have not appealed to the Cecils, as this could have led to rival factions and jealousy. Finally, the Infanta Isabella was a Spanish princess and the daughter of Philip II. Her claim to the English throne was a very distant one (via John of Gaunt, son of Edward III) and her only real supporters were the Jesuit priests in England. Moderate English Catholics did not support the Infanta's claim because they hoped to get more religious toleration by accepting a Protestant monarch, James.

James VI thus emerged as the leading claimant to the throne and, ironically, he was supported by both Essex and the Cecils. However, the rival factions were both keen to ensure that they remained in power after Elizabeth's death and so tried to manoeuvre themselves into a position of trust with James while undermining their rivals. James, meanwhile, was unsure of Elizabeth's intentions and sought support and reassurance from her courtiers.

In 1599–1600, Essex and his friend Lord Mountjoy were both in secret correspondence with James. Mountjoy, who had replaced Essex as Lord Lieutenant in Ireland, wrote to James in 1599 suggesting that James, supported by Mountjoy in Ireland and Essex in England, should raise troops in Scotland and demand that Elizabeth name him as her heir. Technically, even entering into correspondence with a foreign monarch was treason; advising him to raise troops to challenge the English monarch was even worse. In December 1600, Essex himself wrote to James, complaining about 'this reigning faction', by which he meant the Cecilians. This time, Essex accused the Cecil faction of supporting the Infanta, not James. Luckily for Elizabeth, James responded cautiously; he would not commit himself to Mountjoy's offer and sent two ambassadors south to speak to Essex. When the ambassadors reached London they found that Essex had been executed, and he began negotiations with Cecil instead.

Despite Essex's claims, Cecil also supported James' succession as the best means to secure his own political future. Between 1600 and 1603, he too was in secret correspondence with James. Because Elizabeth would not commit herself, Cecil could not openly support James either without risking the queen's anger, but a secret correspondence was equally dangerous. Cecil's main aim after 1601 was to make sure that James was completely reliant on him. Although Essex was dead, there were other potential rivals at court, especially the queen's favourites Walter Raleigh and Henry Brooke (Lord Cobham). Cecil worked with his close ally Henry Howard, who wrote most of the letters, to ensure that James was given the impression that Cobham and Raleigh were not to be trusted and that Cecil was in charge at court.

In March 1603, Elizabeth entered her final illness. There are conflicting accounts as to whether she finally agreed that James should be her heir, but what really mattered was that James, a foreigner with a disputed claim, was able to inherit the throne peacefully thanks to the manoeuvrings of a faction who drew their power from their connection to the court, not from their military strength.

To what extent did court faction lead to a crisis of government?

In some ways, faction-fighting led to a very unsettled and volatile atmosphere at court that had not been seen before in Elizabeth's reign. The combination of an ageing queen, uncertainties about the succession, and the behaviour of the faction leaders led to tensions that exploded in 1601 with Essex's revolt.

The queen's management of the situation undoubtedly made the situation worse. Her refusal to make decisions regarding key appointments led to more faction-fighting, not less. She was also prepared to tolerate Essex's angry outbursts and sulking because he flattered and amused her.

At the same time, Elizabeth allowed patronage to come under the control of just one group, the Cecil faction. This was potentially dangerous because it created a group of 'haves' and 'have nots'. Resentment of the Cecil faction and its monopoly of patronage was not restricted to Essex and his followers. It was lucky for Elizabeth that this resentment lacked co-ordination and remained as grumbling, apart from Essex's rebellion. This could have been much more dangerous for Elizabeth than it turned out to be. Essex did have popular support in London, which he was careful to cultivate, and his original plan to use his small armed force to target the court at Whitehall could have worked if he had the element of surprise. In effect, Essex was planning a palace coup in which his ultimate goal was to remove Elizabeth, the most serious form of rebellion. In the sense that faction created political instability and a noble revolt, it did contribute to a sense of crisis in the 1590s.

However, it is easy to overstate the case for the instability caused by faction. Essex and the Cecils were both reliant on the queen to some extent for her favour and patronage, Essex more so than Cecil. She could have withdrawn her support for them at any time, as she did with Essex, leaving them without the source of their power, office and position at court. The fact that the nobility were now reliant on maintaining a presence at court in order to secure power and influence meant that their traditional feudal and military roles had been almost entirely undermined. Essex and his followers were completely reliant on their small armed followings in London in 1601; they simply did not have the ability to raise troops in the localities. The muster of troops was under the control of Elizabeth through the Lord Lieutenant system, and she chose these men carefully. Similarly, the court-based power of the nobility meant that James' succession in 1603 was established peacefully, albeit by some potentially treasonous diplomacy. In 1603, there was no return to the situation of 1485, when Henry VII had won the English throne on the battlefield with the military support of a few members of the medieval nobility. In this sense, the existence of faction did not create a succession crisis because the nobility were ultimately reliant on Elizabeth, not their military strength, for their power.

ACTIVITY
KNOWLEDGE CHECK

Effects of faction

1 List the evidence that faction caused a crisis in government in the period 1589–1603.

2 Why might some historians argue that faction did not lead to political instability?

EXTRACT 3 From John Guy, *Tudor England* (1988).

It can be argued that the Cecils in the 1590s surrounded themselves with second-rate men on whom they could rely, and on whom they bestowed office so that no rival might challenge their ascendancy. ... It was, however, the dazzling but paranoid Essex ... who self-consciously rivalled the Cecils for patronage and power. By the late 1590s their feud had escalated into a factional battle to control her policy. The atmosphere at Court deteriorated; for the first time in her reign the queen was on the sidelines ...

When Elizabeth realised that her favourite [Essex] sought to rule her Court, she granted Robert Cecil an authority not previously allowed to any other councillor. Cecil had the queen's ear throughout, while from July 1598 Essex was forbidden the royal presence. Indeed, Essex's brashness and presumption consistently won him enemies: when disgraced, he only had himself to blame ...When admitted to the Privy Council in 1593, he championed an offensive strategy, urging land campaigns in Europe. He also resumed Leicester's secret correspondence with James VI of Scotland in an effort to sponsor a Protestant coalition. But he lacked Leicester's private patronage, as well as failing to win royal patronage for his followers, the real test of a faction leader's credibility. His supporters increasingly complained that he could get anything for himself but nothing for his friends, though Essex's own view in the darkening weeks before his departure for Ireland was that he could do neither.

EXTRACT 4 From D. Loades, *Politics and Nation, England 1450–1660* (1999).

The grinding effort of the war, the parsimony and caution of an ageing ruler, and the inevitable feeling that the reign was drawing to a close had produced widespread restlessness and dissatisfaction. This feeling was particularly strong among the younger gentry, many of whom had attached themselves to Essex as the man of the future. Such men were only too willing to believe that their patron was the victim of factional malice – and those personal qualities which at one time had endeared him to his sovereign had also given him a popularity with the common people, especially in London, which survived his fall. Consequently, Essex House became the headquarters of a faction, and a resort for all those who felt deprived of office, favour or employment by the ascendancy of Cecil ...

... [Essex's] hatred for Cecil had become an obsession. He ... endeavoured to persuade Mountjoy to bring his Irish army into England to secure the Protestant cause. He expressed opinions of his enemies which stirred up some of his followers to plot murder, and opinions of the queen which went to the very brink of treason ... Essex had many of the makings of an 'overmighty subject', and had it been more efficiently managed, his stroke against Cecil could have caused a dangerous insurrection.

A Level Exam-Style Question Section A

Analyse and evaluate Extracts 3 and 4. In the light of differing interpretations, how accurate is it to say that the growth of faction led to genuine political instability in England? (20 marks)

Tip

What is meant by 'genuine political instability'? Did faction at Elizabeth's court pose this kind of threat consistently?

THINKING HISTORICALLY | Interpretations (3a)

Differing accounts

Carefully read Extracts 3 and 4, which are historical interpretations of the impact of faction in the 1590s. Then complete the following activities.

1 For each of the historians create a summary table of their views.

    a) Make a note of how they address the key issues outlined in the table below.

    b) Make a note of the evidence they give in support of this claim.

    c) Use your notes and knowledge to give evidence that supports or challenges their interpretation.

HISTORIAN:_____	Interpretation of the issue	Evidence given	Evidence that supports or challenges this view
How important was faction in creating political instability in England in the 1590s?			
How far did the actions of Elizabeth herself create a political crisis in England?			
To what extent was the existence of faction a threat to Elizabeth's power?			

2 In pairs discuss which historian's interpretation of England in the 1590s seems to best fit with the available evidence. Which seems the most convincing?

3 Make a note of any issues that made it difficult to compare the two interpretations directly.

4 Challenge: Seek out another historical interpretation of the impact of faction on England in the 1590s and compare this to the views you have explored already.

WHAT WAS THE SIGNIFICANCE OF GROWING CONFLICT WITH PARLIAMENT?

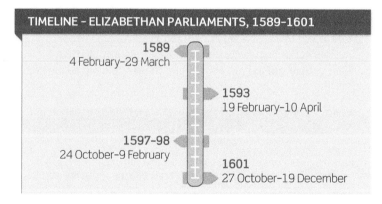

TIMELINE – ELIZABETHAN PARLIAMENTS, 1589–1601

- **1589** 4 February–29 March
- **1593** 19 February–10 April
- **1597–98** 24 October–9 February
- **1601** 27 October–19 December

What were the roles of the Crown and parliament, 1589–1603?

Both Crown and parliament had well-defined traditional roles by Elizabeth's reign. As monarch, Elizabeth had the sole right to summon and dismiss parliament at her will; she could also veto laws. Parliament was the only body that could grant taxation.

The House of Commons believed that they had the sole right to introduce taxation bills into parliament. Its members saw themselves as the representatives of their voters and local communities, who were the ones who would have to pay the tax. Although this apparent sense of accountability was sometimes less important to MPs than their private interests, they were still uneasy if they felt that the queen or her Council were trying to dictate to them on matters of taxation, as was the case in the 1593 parliament.

Other functions of parliament were to offer advice and to be a link between Elizabeth and her government and the localities that they governed. Parliament was summoned four times between 1589 and 1593, each time because the queen needed money to fund her wars. Grants of taxation were not parliament's only business, however. Acts were passed to deal with the increasing problems of poverty and vagrancy in 1597 and 1601, but most bills were initiated by private individuals rather than Elizabeth's government and were often on behalf of a particular community or trade. But MPs could also communicate with the queen when government policies were causing resentment or unrest. In the 1590s, the war was putting particular pressure on local communities, not only because of taxation but also because of payments levied for the trained bands and local defence. The queen's use of her prerogative powers was also causing resentment, and it was this that made the parliaments of 1597 and 1601 so restless.

SOURCE 5 Sixteenth-century engraving of Elizabeth I sitting in parliament.

As the demands of war increased, Elizabeth had less spare money for patronage. Granting monopolies was an easy way to reward her courtiers and raise ready money, as the courtiers would pay for the privilege. Some monopolies were relatively uncontroversial because they were the Tudor equivalent of a patent, which provided traders and merchants with protection from their rivals. The monopolies that caused the complaints were those that Elizabeth granted to her courtiers for profit. Walter Raleigh, for example, had monopolies in tin, playing cards and the licensing of taverns. In a bid to raise more money, Elizabeth was granting more and more monopolies on an increasingly wide range of goods – some luxury, others more basic. The system appeared corrupt, with greedy courtiers creating huge profits for themselves by raising prices. Because they had the monopoly on a particular product, there was no competition, so monopolies forced prices up. At a time of social and economic hardship, the price rises were particularly damaging, especially when commodities such as steel and salt were affected. Monopolies on these goods had resulted in the price of steel doubling; salt was 11 times more expensive. It was resentment over monopolies, and Elizabeth's and Robert Cecil's handling of the complaints in parliament, which created tension in 1597 and 1601.

The 1589 and 1593 parliaments

The parliaments of 1589 and 1593 both saw disagreements between the Commons, the queen and her councillors over her prerogative and parliamentary attempts to control it. In these parliaments, however, the issues under discussion were mostly resolved. In 1589, Elizabeth's councillors were keen for the Commons to agree to taxation to fund the defence of the realm; the Commons refused to grant the money until their grievances had been heard and redressed. Withholding taxation as a method to get the monarch to address parliamentary complaints was an old tactic, so there was nothing particularly unusual about the Commons using it. What concerned Elizabeth and her councillors in the Lords was that the Commons was planning a **parliamentary bill** to limit abuses of purveyance by royal officers.

Elizabeth I was very careful to protect her prerogative rights and regarded with suspicion any attempts to change them. Meanwhile, parliament was increasingly concerned about what it saw as abuses of the royal prerogative and used its position to challenge excessive royal demands. In the 1560s to 1580s, parliament had been most concerned about Elizabeth's marriage and succession and the question of religion. By 1589, these issues had mostly subsided, but new complaints and concerns had taken their place. The main concerns of parliament in the 1590s were the queen and her officials' misuse of **purveyance** and monopolies. Because purveyance was worth about £37,000 a year to Elizabeth, she had been reluctant to surrender her rights, though when faced with complaints in 1589, she was prepared to compromise. More serious were local and parliamentary complaints over the abuse of the royal prerogative to grant monopolies.

KEY TERMS

Purveyance
Purveyance was traditionally used to feed the royal household. Royal officials had the right to purchase food and other goods at between half and one-third of the actual market price. Local farmers and merchants were forced to accept this as part of the royal prerogative, but they would complain bitterly because the practice undermined their livelihood.

Parliamentary bill
A bill could be introduced in the House of Lords or Commons. It would be discussed in both Houses, and if agreed by both Houses and the queen would become an Act of Parliament. Bills were often introduced by the government, but they could also be introduced as 'private' bills by any member of parliament.

For Elizabeth, this was an attempt to control the royal prerogative by Act of Parliament and she ordered that the bill be dropped. The Commons agreed and was persuaded to grant the taxation that had been requested. In return, Elizabeth promised to make reforms to the purveyance system, a promise that she carried out. Elizabeth's actions defused the situation and her later parliaments did not complain about purveyance again.

In 1593, there were some further tensions. Before parliament even met, Peter Wentworth, the MP for Northampton, had tried to persuade several other MPs to introduce a **petition** and bill into parliament asking that the queen decide the royal succession. Wentworth had already been in trouble before for his defence of an MP's right to freedom of speech in parliament and for publishing a pamphlet on the issue of the succession. The Council heard about what he was planning and arrested Wentworth and his allies. Wentworth was sent to the Tower, where he died four years later. Four other MPs were put under house arrest for the duration of the parliamentary session.

KEY TERM

Petition
A petition was different from a bill in that it was a document addressed to the monarch complaining about a particular issue. Petitions could be made within parliament as a way to bring the monarch's attention to a complaint, but it was up to the monarch to read or listen to the petition and act on it. Using a petition was therefore a less aggressive tactic than introducing a bill, which could alter the law or prerogative.

However, a more serious dispute between Elizabeth's councillors, especially William Cecil, and the Commons then emerged over taxation. The Commons had agreed to a bill that would allow for two subsidies to be raised, but in a meeting with representatives of the Lords, the MPs were told by Cecil that this was not enough and they should reconsider the amount they were prepared to offer. This angered some of the MPs, who felt that the Commons should have the sole right to initiate a taxation bill and that the Lords should not intervene in the process. MPs such as Francis Bacon and Henry Unton argued that because they represented the majority of people who would pay the money, it should be they who decided whether taxation should be granted and how much should be levied. Eventually, the councillors in the Lords managed to calm down the MPs and they granted the subsidy that the Lords had requested. Although this incident was relatively minor in itself, it did demonstrate the increased confidence of the Commons, especially in asserting their own rights and privileges. It also demonstrated the need for the Commons to be managed carefully. However, the 1593 parliament ultimately did what it was asked, though with some grumbling.

SOURCE

Sir Henry Unton's response to the Lords' request for an increased subsidy, 1593.

In matters of subsidy and contribution we might not be governed or directed [by the Lords because] we are far more interested therein than they. They offer but a small portion for themselves, we both for ourselves and infinite thousands besides... we are stewards of many more purses than they.

EXTEND YOUR KNOWLEDGE

Peter Wentworth (1524–97)
Peter Wentworth was a Puritan MP in the parliaments of 1571, 1572, 1586, 1589 and 1593. He had powerful connections as he was brother-in-law to Sir Francis Walsingham and Sir Walter Mildmay, but these connections did not prevent him getting into trouble.

In the 1576 session of parliament, he made a speech in favour of parliamentary free speech in which he criticised the queen directly. The House of Commons was so embarrassed that it sent him to the Tower, where he remained for a month until the queen released him. In 1587, he was sent to the Tower again, this time for supporting the Puritan 'bill and book'.

Wentworth then turned his attention to the issue of the succession; he attempted to get his tract *A Pithie Exhortation to her Majestie for Establishing her Successor to the Crowne* published. This led to his imprisonment in 1591–92. Wentworth's final attempt to raise the issue of the succession led to his final arrest in 1593 and imprisonment until his death in 1597 because he would not apologise to the queen. Historians such as Neale see him as an early champion of modern notions of free speech and parliamentary privilege, but most contemporaries saw him as a troublemaker.

The 1597 parliament

The parliament of 1597 saw much more serious criticism of Elizabeth's government and particularly the abuse of monopolies. By 1597, the social and economic situation had deteriorated dramatically; the war with Spain was continuing, bringing increased fears of invasion, and Tyrone's rebellion in Ireland had broken out. The Commons' anxieties were first expressed in November 1597 when the MP Francis Moore initiated a discussion 'touching sundry enormities growing by patents of privilege and... the abuses of them', meaning monopolies. Some MPs wanted to introduce a parliamentary bill to tackle the issue, but they were eventually persuaded to petition Elizabeth instead, which meant that they were not challenging her prerogative directly. Elizabeth managed to defuse the situation by promising that all monopoly licences would be examined. The Commons then agreed to pass another substantial grant of taxation, ironically with much less opposition than in 1593. The 1597 parliament represented the first direct criticism of Elizabeth's policies, although there was no direct challenge to her prerogative. The situation might well have resolved itself if Elizabeth had kept her promise, but she did almost nothing. When parliament was summoned again in 1601, the Commons' simmering resentment exploded into outright anger.

What was the significance of the 1601 parliament?

The parliament of 1601 was the last of Elizabeth's reign and was dominated by the Commons' attack on the monopolies granted by the queen. The Commons' anger was much more extreme than in 1597, when their complaints had been neutralised by the queen's promises. By 1601, however, when Elizabeth was forced to call parliament to grant taxation, nothing had happened; most patents granting monopolies had not been cancelled, and worse, new monopolies had been created.

The 1601 parliament was unusual because it contained 253 barristers or gentry educated at the Inns of Court, the highest number of lawyers in any Tudor parliament. These men were not only well versed in legal procedure, they had also come across the problems caused by monopolies in the law courts, where those with grievances against the monopolies were unable to get justice. In addition, at least 157 MPs in this session of parliament had also been present in 1597, and were therefore likely to be sympathetic to complaints about monopolies.

The anger of the Commons was made worse because they had seen that petitioning the queen in 1597 had made no difference, so some MPs were prepared to introduce a parliamentary bill to restrict the royal prerogative on the issue. Robert Cecil also mishandled the situation; the Crown only wanted the grant of subsidies, not to discuss other issues. Cecil even told parliament that he wanted no 'fantastic speeches or idle bills'. This was not what the angry MPs wanted to hear. Even worse, a crowd of people who said they were '**Commonwealth men**', burst into the parliament lobby and stairs to beg MPs to do something about the abuses of the monopolists, and Cecil complained that 'Parleamente matters are ordinarye talke in the streetes'. These scenes were unprecedented in any Tudor parliament and showed the extent of popular anger and the danger of the situation deteriorating into riots.

Faced with such anger, Elizabeth responded cleverly. On 25 November 1601, she sent a message to the Commons by the Speaker of the House, promising that some monopolies would be cancelled and some would be suspended while they were investigated. On 28 November, she cancelled 12 monopolies that had been the subject of particular complaint in parliament including those on salt, vinegar and starch. She also authorised those with grievances against the monopolists to prosecute them in the common law courts. She then met with a delegation of about 140 MPs, where she gave her 'golden speech' (see Source 9), in which she admitted to some 'lapses of error', but still upheld her prerogative rights. The 'golden speech' was a triumph of political manipulation; Elizabeth managed to appear gracious, while in reality conceding very little. She also received the taxation for which parliament had originally been called.

KEY TERM

Commonwealth men
This was a term used in Tudor England to describe men who were interested both in the state as a whole and also the common good of the people.

SOURCE

Robert Cecil, speaking in the 1601 parliament.

I have been... a member of this House in six or seven parliaments, yet I never did see the House is so great a confusion. I believe there never was in any parliament a more tender point handled than the liberty of the subject, that when any is discussing this point, he should be cried and coughed down. This is more fit for a grammar school than a court of parliament.

SOURCE

From an account of the 1601 parliament by the MP Hayward Townshend, a lawyer. Mr Martin [MP for Barnstaple, Devon] said:

I speak for a town that grieves and pines and for a country that groaneth under the burthen of monstrous and unconscionable substitutes to the monopolitans of starch, tin, fish, cloth, oil, vinegar, salt and I know not what: nay, what not? The principle commodities both of my town and country are ingrossed into the hands of these bloodsuckers of the commonwealth.

SOURCE

Elizabeth I's 'golden speech' to a Commons deputation, 1601.

Though God hath raised me high, yet this I count the glory of my Crown, that I have reigned with your loves... I was never so much enticed with the glorious name of a king or royal authority of a queen, as delighted that God hath made me his instrument to maintain his truth and glory and to defend his kingdom from peril, dishonour, tyranny and oppression... Though you have had and may have yet many mightier and wise princes sitting on this seat, yet you never had nor shall have any that will love you better... And I pray... that before the gentlemen depart into their counties you bring them all to kiss my hand.

To what extent did the parliaments of 1589–1601 contribute to a crisis in government?

Historians such as Neale have depicted the events of the 1590s parliaments as the forerunner for the 17th century English civil wars. They argue that as parliament was called more often to deal with a wider range of business and contained increasing numbers of confident MPs, so it became more prepared to challenge the monarchy's power and prerogative. According to this view, the debates over purveyance, taxation and monopolies paved the way for more serious challenges to the rights of the Stuart kings, and ultimately to parliament being prepared to declare war on the monarchy. These views are based on the fact that because these events did occur they must have been caused by earlier events under the Tudors. Therefore, Neale tends to emphasise the amount of opposition to royal policy among the parliamentary Commons, as well as the Commons' growing confidence and organisation, and sees the 1590s as representing a crisis of government that would grow in the 17th century.

More recently, historians such as Geoffrey Elton, followed by Michael Graves, have argued that there was no 'high road to civil war' – that the events of the 17th century were not inevitable and were certainly not foreshadowed in the later Elizabethan parliaments. They emphasise the amount of co-operation between the monarchy and parliament and the general lack of disagreement between the two. For these historians, Elizabeth I and her parliament were mostly on the same side and disagreements between them had been exaggerated, although they would still argue that the 1590s represented a more general crisis in society and government.

In some ways, the parliaments of the 1590s did depart from the role of previous Tudor parliaments. The behaviour of the Commons was more rowdy and needed more careful management by Elizabeth's councillors, not all of whom had the necessary skills for this job. Robert Cecil made the situation in 1601 worse by his attempts to over-control parliamentary debates; he lost control of the Commons on several occasions and even had to apologise for his rudeness. Even William Cecil, usually the master of parliamentary management, irritated the Commons in 1593. Elizabeth's own actions also created a situation in which the Commons' resentment grew. Although her insistence on her royal prerogative was no different from preceding monarchs, her failure to act on the Commons' complaints in 1597 made the situation much worse in 1601. Perhaps Elizabeth had not fully realised that she was dealing with a group of men who were as convinced of their own rights and privileges as she was of hers.

The Commons' confidence had certainly grown. It is impossible to imagine any parliament before those of the 1590s being quite so determined and hard to manage. The later Elizabethan parliaments were very different in their nature and attitude to those under Henry VIII, and much less biddable. In addition, the social and political context in which Elizabeth's parliaments met exacerbated these tensions. The social and economic crisis that hit England from the mid-1590s had a profound effect on the mood both of ordinary people and the MPs who feared the effects of increasing and incessant taxation on a country that was already stretched to its limits. The continuation of the war with Spain and the start of Tyrone's revolt meant that Elizabeth remained reliant on parliament for grants of taxation, while the demands of war created additional tensions in the localities. Given these circumstances, it is not surprising that Elizabeth's later parliaments were particularly tension-filled, thus giving the impression of crisis.

However, it is easy to exaggerate the amount of tension caused by parliamentary sessions. There were just four sessions in the years 1589–1603, each lasting between two to four months. This means that for the majority of the period, parliament was not meeting at all because it was not yet an integral part of Tudor government. Government was carried out by Elizabeth and her Council, and it was they who made the decisions, not parliament.

In addition, every time that parliament met, Elizabeth got the taxation she had requested. Although in 1593 there was an attempt to link the supply of money to the redress of grievances, on other occasions parliament acquiesced to Elizabeth's demands; on no occasion did they ever refuse her a grant of taxation.

Although both Elizabeth and her councillors made mistakes in their management of parliament, these were not fatal and were easily solved. Elizabeth herself was the mistress of skilful speeches, which won the MPs over. Even Robert Cecil contributed to the management of parliament. Like his father, he was able to place 30 of his own clients into constituencies in 1597 (and 31 in 1601). These Cecil clients, like the clients of other members of the nobility, could be relied upon to vote the way Elizabeth wanted.

Although parliament raised concerns about government policies and appeared on occasion to be challenging the prerogative, this was a traditional part of monarch–parliament relations. Part of parliament's role was to act as a safety valve for local grievances. In airing these grievances, the Commons was alerting the queen to potential sources of tension before they could escalate. This process did not mean that the Commons was hostile to royal power or even wanted to challenge it; as long as Elizabeth listened and was seen to respond, there would be no political crisis. In 1597 and 1601, the queen came close to misjudging the Commons' mood, but she had the political awareness to stop the serious complaints in these parliaments from becoming anything worse.

ACTIVITY
KNOWLEDGE CHECK

Parliaments

1 Complete the following table.

Parliamentary session	Complaints made by the Commons	Elizabeth's response to the complaints
1589		
1593		
1597		
1601		

2 Why was the 1601 parliament potentially serious for Elizabeth and her government?

3 Which methods were particularly effective in managing the Commons? Which were least effective?

4 Write a summary paragraph to answer the question: How far did Elizabeth's parliaments contribute to a crisis in government, 1589–1601?

EXTRACT

Michael Graves, *Elizabethan Parliaments, 1559–1603* (1987) analysing the seriousness of the complaints regarding monopolies.

In the 1590s the financial pressures of war compelled Elizabeth to reduce direct material rewards, such as grants and leases of land and pensions to her servants, and replace them with benefits which cost the Crown nothing. So monopolies rapidly multiplied. Thus far she could hardly be blamed but when, in 1597, the Commons grumbled about the proliferation of monopolies, she promised reform and did nothing. In 1601 the pent-up anger of the governing class exploded in the Lower House. At last Elizabeth was obliged to act. She promised the immediate cancellation of some monopolies, the suspension of others, and that the rest would be examinable in the law courts. This parliamentary episode must be seen in its right perspective. Parliaments were occasions for the monarch to take counsel. Elizabeth had not heeded such counsel in 1597 and paid the price in 1601. But that was no more than the normal give-and-take of the parliamentary process. Just as the queen… could admonish a parliament to spend its time on public matters… and not meddle in questions of religion, so a parliament could warn her of public unrest. The monopolies agitations was not an example of a rising House of Commons, but of rising discontent. Nor was it the consequence of an organised parliamentary opposition… It was a spontaneous response to a common grievance, voiced by the governing class through its representatives.

None of this denies the presence of friction, disharmony, disagreement, even conflict in Elizabethan parliaments. This is hardly surprising, because parliaments were occasions when a formidable queen met the power-conscious elites of Church and state and a competitive, acquisitive, self-confident governing class… [Elizabeth] needed parliaments for money, if for nothing else. Elizabeth had no option but to call them. However, when she did, disagreements and differences of opinion rarely escalated into constitutional conflicts… Disagreements were normally brought to a satisfactory conclusion or kept within bounds by an essential harmony between Crown and governing class… As a last resort the queen could veto unacceptable bills or defuse an explosive situation with honeyed words or well-timed concessions, such as… her action on monopolies in 1601.

THINKING HISTORICALLY   Interpretations (5a)

What I believe is how I see

Below are three descriptions of the perspectives of very famous historians. They have been written for the purposes of this exercise.

Herodotus	Leopold von Ranke	Karl Marx
His research consisted of conversations Identified that accounts had to be judged on their merits Some believe that certain passages in his writing are inventions to complete the narrative	Believed in an evidence-based approach and relied heavily on primary sources Desired to find out the 'facts' and discover the connections between them Stressed the role of the individual in shaping history	Believed that history would go through stages leading to a state where everybody was equal Believed that historical changes were ultimately determined by changes to the economy Marx was often driven by political considerations and looked for evidence to support his point of view

Work in groups of between three and six. Each member or pair will take the perspective of one of the above historians and argue from that perspective. Work through questions 1–4 as a group and answer question 5 individually.

1 Herodotus did not use written evidence to construct his history. Does this mean that his history is less useful than the others?

2 Ranke based his writing almost exclusively on primary sources from the time he was investigating, rather than secondary sources. How might this affect his ability to see larger patterns in history as opposed to the other two?

3 Marx put his philosophy of history, and perhaps politics, first and research second. Would this make his history weaker than the others?

4 'Colourful' individuals populate the writing of Herodotus and Ranke, while Marx concentrates on the difference between classes. Write three historical questions that each historian might ask.

5 The three historians mentioned above all had different methods and motivations and yet their writing has been valued ever since it was created. Explain how the prior knowledge that we bring to the history that we write does not invalidate it.

HOW SERIOUS WAS THE SOCIAL AND ECONOMIC DISTRESS OF THE 1590s?

Before the 1590s, there had been a period of relative social and economic stability with mostly good harvests. The population, which had declined in the worst years of dearth and disease in the late 1550s, had recovered and was growing again. Although hunger and poverty were still very real problems, the relative stability of the first three decades of Elizabeth's reign had given local authorities the opportunity to stockpile supplies.

From 1594, however, the situation deteriorated rapidly. There was a series of poor harvests in 1594, 1595, 1596 and 1597, the worst years being 1596–97 when the harvests were ruined by too much rain. Because food supplies took more than a year to recover following a bad harvest, the effect of several bad harvests in succession meant that the problems associated with one bad harvest were multiplied over several years with no opportunity for the economy to recover. Moreover, the dearth was a European-wide one – areas of France, the Netherlands and Germany were also badly affected, which meant that there were fewer supplies of cheap imports from abroad.

The consequence of this in some regions was famine; other regions saw severe food shortages and riots, especially in urban areas. Death rates rose and the government feared that the social order would collapse. The situation was no doubt made worse by returning soldiers and sailors, some injured, others without employment, whose tales of hardship in England's wars spread discontent and worsened the problem of beggars and vagabonds. However, although the authorities certainly saw this is as a period of crisis, it is less clear that the socio-economic system was on the point of collapse.

Rising prices, food shortages and mortality rates

One result of the repeated harvest failures of the 1590s was that prices rose dramatically because of high demand and a shortage of food. As Source 10 shows, the average price of wheat more than doubled between 1593–94 and 1596–97. Wheat was used for making bread, one of the most important sources of cheap food for the poor. It was not just the price of wheat that rose. Agricultural prices were higher in the period 1594–98 than they had been at any other time in the Tudor period.

For those with little or no income, these rises meant that they struggled to buy the basic foods that they needed for survival, especially since the value of real wages was falling. In 1597, they reached their lowest level for any year between 1260 and 1950 according to the Phelps-Brown Index.

These problems were particularly severe in the towns, where a high proportion of the population were living on or below the poverty line. The situation was made even worse by migration from the countryside, as the rural poor moved to the towns in search of food and jobs. In London, it is estimated that the number of people living in poverty rose from 5 percent to 9 percent in the late 1590s. Although records are scarce, the situation was probably as bad, if not worse, elsewhere, especially in smaller towns. A survey for Ipswich in 1597 reveals that 13 percent of the population were classed as impotent or able-bodied poor.

As the price of wheat soared, those who could not afford it began to buy other, cheaper but less edible grains, such as barley, oats, peas and beans. This pushed up demand for those products as well, leading to further price rises.

In some parts of England, especially the north, the south-west and smaller towns, the impact of these problems was at its worst. Despite government attempts to ease the problems by banning grain exports and the feeding of peas to cattle, there was real starvation, especially in 1596–97, the worst years of shortage. One observer wrote in a letter to William Cecil in 1596: 'I greatly fear that this year will be the hardest year for the poor people that hath happened in any man's memory.' The writer was correct. In Cumbria and Newcastle upon Tyne there were deaths from starvation. As the food shortages got worse, so the death rate rose. In 1596 and 1597, the death rate was 21 percent above the national average; in 1597–98 that has risen to 26 percent above the national average. Those who were already weakened from malnourishment were more likely to become victims of disease. Plague was a particular problem in London, especially in 1593–94, when the theatres were closed because of an outbreak of the disease. It is quite likely that other towns, where conditions were cramped and unsanitary and there was increasing hardship, suffered in the same way.

By 1598, the level of social and economic distress was such that whole families were seeking poor relief, not just individuals. As a result, the system for poor relief, which had been set up in the 1570s, was put under an immense strain.

SOURCE 10 The price of wheat in the 1590s, quoted from P. Williams, *The Later Tudors: England, 1547–1603* (1995).

Date	Average price of wheat per quarter (in shillings)
1592–93	19.90
1593–94	23.00
1594–95	34.87
1595–96	37.09
1596–97	50.07
1597–98	46.18
1598–99	28.03

Riots and social tension

The combination of hunger, high prices and rising death rates also led to an increase in social tension. Crime rates rose in the 1590s, leading to more prosecutions in the law courts. In particular, the rate of theft rose considerably in the years 1596–98, probably as a result of social and economic hardship. It is likely that many of these thefts were the result of a genuine need for food and clothes and were impulse crimes.

There were other signs that Tudor society was under increased pressure. In 1595, food riots broke out in London, the South East and the South West. In London, 1,800 apprentices, soldiers and unemployed men were involved in two riots against fishwives, butter sellers and foreign merchants. They even assaulted some London officials and planned to steal armour and cut off the mayor of London's head. The London riots were put down, but unrest was reported in Kent and Norfolk in 1595–96. Worryingly for the government, there was talk in these regions of establishing 'camps' to protest against farmers and those who were stockpiling grain in order to make profits. The rebels in Norfolk even referred directly to Robert Kett's Rebellion (1549), which had taken the form of a series of rebel camps. This was alarming, because not only were there signs of unrest, but the agitators were looking back to one of the most serious popular rebellions of the 16th century which had come dangerously close to class warfare. In 1596–97, the sense of unrest continued with further food riots in East Anglia, the South West and on the border between Kent and Sussex.

The government and local authorities were very concerned about the level of tension. In particular, they feared bands of violent vagrants attacking their social superiors. These fears were probably fuelled by the widespread publication of pamphlets in the 1590s with lurid descriptions of the crimes committed by wandering bands of beggars. When the Oxfordshire rising broke out in November 1596 in protest over enclosures and food prices in the region, the authorities reacted swiftly and violently. Inspired by the news of the apprentices' riots in London the previous year, the rebel leaders planned to attack the house of the Oxfordshire Lord Lieutenant, Lord Norris, seize his weapons and march to London. However, only four rebels actually turned up; they waited two hours, then disbanded, and were arrested. The Privy Council reacted very strongly to the 'rising'. They ordered that the troublemakers should be brought to London to be examined under torture by the Council itself. The councillors seem to have been terrified that there was gentry involvement in the unrest, but none was uncovered. The rebel leader was a carpenter, Bartholomew Steer, and the other men involved were young unmarried artisans or servants, all of whom had nothing to lose. Nevertheless, the rebels were executed for treason on the grounds that they had waged war against the monarch. This was despite the fact that the rising had not been violent. The Council wanted to send a very clear message that this would be the fate of any other rebels. The Council's paranoia was also apparent in its response in Oxfordshire where there was a special charge made in the local assizes (law courts) against the perpetrators of enclosure. The rising may also have been the trigger for the Poor Laws that were passed in 1597 and 1601.

SOURCE

11 Edward Hext, a Justice of the Peace from Somerset, writes to Lord Burghley in 1596 about crime and vagabonds.

I do not see how it is possible for the poor countrymen to bear the burthens... laid upon him... There be [some] that stick not to say boldly that they must not starve, they will not starve. And this year there assembled 80 in a company and took a whole cartload of cheese from one driving it to a fair, and dispersed it among them... which may grow dangerous by aid of such numbers as are abroad, especially in this time of dearth...

[On vagabonds] of these sort of wandering idle people there are three or four hundred in a shire, and though they go by two or three in a company, yet all or the most part in a shire do meet either at fair or market, or in some alehouse, once a week... And they do grow the more dangerous in that they find they have bred that fear in the Justices [of the Peace] and other inferior officers that no man dares to call them into question.

The government response to the social and economic problems of the 1590s

Even before the mid-1590s, the Tudor central government was considering its response to poverty, disease and food shortages. As early as 1586–87, Books of Orders were printed and were regularly reissued in the 1590s. The Books were documents sent to all JPs telling them what actions they should take in the event of plague or famine. For plague, they were to quarantine houses where there was disease; these houses were to be guarded by watchmen to ensure that the sick remained in isolation. Orders for the measures to be taken in the event of famine were first issued in 1586 and republished in 1594 and 1595. These ordered JPs to make searches for grain (in an attempt to combat food hoarding), and set up the compulsory sale of food to those in need. In times of real shortage, however, it is unlikely that these measures were particularly effective, especially because there simply was not enough food in circulation.

In the parliaments of 1597 and 1601, however, real attempts were made to deal with the problems caused by the successive bad harvests of 1594–97. In 1597–98, 11 out of the 17 bills that were introduced were attempts to deal with poverty.

In 1597, a new Vagrancy Act was passed that ordered vagrants to be arrested, whipped and returned to their parishes where they were to be forced to work if they were able-bodied or sent to the almshouse if they were impotent poor. Persistent vagrants were to be sent to the houses of correction or even to work on the English galley ships. The final punishment was to be execution for felony.

Debates over enclosure also arose again, and particularly the effect that enclosure for sheep farming was having on arable farming and therefore on food supplies. The Tillage Act (1597) attempted to reverse the effects of enclosure by forcing pasture land that had been enclosed since 1588 to be restored to arable farming.

Most importantly, a new Poor Law was passed, the first since 1576. Although this did not introduce many new ideas, it did bring together in one Act the various aspects of poor relief that had been developing for the last 30 years. With minor corrections added in the Poor Law of 1601, it set up the system of poor relief that was to last into the 19th century. The position of the Overseer of the Poor, first introduced in 1572, was more clearly defined. Two unpaid overseers were to be elected every year for each parish, and their work was to be supervised by the JPs. The overseers had the power to put to work those without money or jobs. They were also responsible for assessing how much money was needed to support the poor, and for collecting and distributing poor relief. In addition, the overseers were to supervise the poorhouse. The Act also made provisions for parishes that might struggle to collect enough funds and to avoid corruption. Overseers were ordered to meet monthly and to submit their accounts to the JPs annually. If a parish could not meet its poor relief costs, then other parishes were to be asked to contribute. The impotent poor were to receive relief either in their own homes (known as 'outdoor' relief) or in almshouses. The able-bodied poor were to be given work to do in poorhouses, while persistent vagrants and beggars were to be sent to the houses of correction.

Although none of these government measures could do anything about the poor harvests and food shortages, which improved of their own accord after 1598, these laws do at least represent some attempt to respond to the problems of the 1590s. In particular, the government response in the 1597 parliament shows the level of concern that existed both in the central government and the localities about the possibility of social and economic breakdown. However, it is debatable whether the fears about social disorder were really justified.

To what extent did harvest failure and social distress lead to a general crisis in government?

The social and economic problems of the 1590s were in some ways very serious for Elizabeth's government. At a time of war and high taxation, with an ageing queen and an unsettled political environment, the social and economic hardship contributed to the sense of a general malaise (a feeling of unease) at the time. Although the levels of hardship were not felt as severely in all parts of the country, some areas such as the rural uplands of the north and the south-west suffered disproportionately. It was these regions where there was genuine dearth and starvation. Small towns also tended to suffer more because they lacked the trading routes and economic wealth to support their poor in times of hardship. The spread of riots and discontent, which were the result of food shortages, was also particularly worrying for the government, as the response to the Oxfordshire rising suggests. Rioters who looked back to the 'commotion time' of 1549 and who wanted to model themselves on Kett's Rebellion were also a concern because Kett's rebels had targeted their social superiors. The authorities feared that society would break down and the poor would rise up against the rich.

However, the governments' fears were the result more of paranoia and rumour than of a genuine risk of popular rebellion. An important difference between the problems of 1549 and those of the 1590s was that the wealthier husbandmen (farmers with small landholdings) who might once have sided with the rebels had become more prosperous and better educated and now tended to participate in local government rather than protest against it. The Oxfordshire rising and the riots of 1595–96 were the result of discontent among the very poorest in society; they were not joined by those of higher rank. This meant that the riots lacked leadership and were easily suppressed, though they certainly frightened the government into taking action.

Even the most severe effects of harvest failure were not as geographically widespread as they might have been. Although death rates increased and there was serious hardship in some regions, in others the effects were less badly felt. Although London saw food riots and plague, it escaped the very worst of the food shortages because it had access to grain imports from the Baltic that were not affected by the European dearth. Similarly, larger towns were more easily able to stockpile food, which could then be given to those most in need. Unlike the North and South West, the central Midlands and the parishes of eastern England and the South East were much less affected by starvation.

Moreover, although mortality rates rose, the deaths of the 1590s were nowhere near on the same scale as those of the 1550s, when about six percent of the population died. Whereas the crisis of the 1550s actually led to an overall decline in England's population, this did not happen in the 1590s, when the total population continued to grow throughout the decade. It has been suggested that this may have been because the poor were able to switch to other, cheaper, grains that meant that they were less prone to starvation, though this did have the effect of pushing up prices still further. Overall, the problems created by the string of poor harvests in the mid-1590s undoubtedly caused a temporary crisis in some parts of the country. However, the effects of these shortages were not felt equally everywhere and the situation did improve after 1598–99. Changes to the social structure tended to discourage the type of popular revolt seen earlier in the century. Elizabeth's government certainly thought that there was a crisis which might challenge social stability and its ability to govern, but the threat was nowhere near as serious as they believed it was.

Conclusion

In some ways, there was a crisis of government under Elizabeth, not as the result of any single event or issue, but as a combination of the problems that faced her. Her government came under increasing criticism for its corruption and greed. The monopolies debates of 1597 and 1601 were a symptom of a more general feeling of discontent with the power and the wealth of the court. This was made worse by the pressures of a long and costly war that lasted for the final 18 years of her reign. There is evidence that some local communities resented the money, equipment and men they had to contribute. Some historians have argued that this led to a divide between the 'court' and the 'country', the local communities, which ultimately would bring about civil war in the 17th century as resentment over government exactions grew. It is also no accident that the monopolies debate in parliament broke out at a time of social and economic hardship. Monopolies on basics such as salt were pushing up prices just at the time when food shortages were causing real hardship. The MPs who complained in parliament were not those affected directly by these shortages but they represented communities who were, and their fear of social unrest caused by such high levels of hardship explains why they attacked those men who were seen as the 'bloodsuckers' – parasites of the English economy and government. On top of this, the queen's own ability to manage her realm and her ministers was declining. She allowed the Cecils to dominate patronage, and Essex's ambition, arrogance and resentment to grow. She misjudged parliament's mood in 1597 and was faced with an outburst of anger in 1601 as a result. Her cautious tactics and general reluctance to commit a large amount of men and money to any one military campaign meant that the English had several important victories but were not able to retain the upper hand against Spain. Elizabeth's caution ensured that England did not lose, but also that it could not win, so the war dragged on.

Nevertheless, the case for a crisis in government can be overstated. There was no major popular rebellion in the 1590s, despite the severity of the economic conditions.

This was because the majority of England's population preferred to remain within the law and to make their voices and complaints heard through more legal channels, such as parliament. Although there were grumblings among local communities about the economic burdens of war, men and money were still raised; government did not grind to a halt, and nor did the leaders of local society (the Lord Lieutenants and the gentry) rebel against the government's demands.

Late-Elizabethan local government worked effectively because Elizabeth appointed the same people to positions of command locally as she did to her Privy Council. Even though she outlived all of her most trusted advisers, the system she had created continued to work because local and central government were linked together in men such as the Cecils. Further down the social scale, JPs such as Hext (Source 11) were busy keeping the government informed of their local concerns. This meant that there was less likelihood of revolt breaking out because the Privy Council knew what was happening, even if they did sometimes panic, as in the case of the Oxfordshire rising. In addition, Elizabeth had not completely lost her touch. She was able to soothe the parliament of 1601 by getting rid of the worst of the monopolies while keeping her prerogative intact. Even the complaints in parliament were an attempt to make the government aware of its failings and the anger in the country, rather than to seriously challenge the queen's power. Parliament was still happy to grant Elizabeth taxation. Finally, although faction and uncertainty over the succession existed, there were no serious plots to usurp Elizabeth, apart from Essex's attempted coup which attracted no popular or noble support outside his own small circle of friends. In 1603, James VI's accession to the throne was completely peaceful and widely accepted. The breakout of rebellion or civil war was avoided, suggesting that Elizabeth and her government remained ultimately in control of events.

ACTIVITY
KNOWLEDGE CHECK

The price of food

1 Summarise in your own words why food prices increased in the 1590s.

2 Make a list of the social groups and regions that you think would be most badly hit by price rises. Why were they more vulnerable?

3 What evidence is there that there was a genuine crisis of government caused by harvest failures?

4 Why were the problems of the 1590s not more serious?

ACTIVITY
SUMMARY

1 Make your own timeline of the events of the 1590s. Events should include the role of faction; the war with Spain and the Irish revolt; social and economic problems; and Elizabeth's parliaments.

2 Highlight any events that you think show that there was a crisis of government.

3 Was there a permanent state of crisis throughout the period, or were some years worse than others? If so, which years were they?

4 Were any of the factors you have studied enough to create a crisis of government on their own (e.g. war) or was it the combination of factors that presented more problems for Elizabeth's government?

WIDER READING

Adams, S. 'The succession and foreign policy', *History Today*, May 2003

Graves, M.A.R. *Elizabethan Parliaments 1559-1601*, Longman (1996)

Pound, J.F. *Poverty and Vagrancy in Tudor England*, Routledge (1986)

Saunders, W. 'Faction in the reign of Elizabeth I', *History Today*, March 2004

Preparing for your AS Level Paper 1 exam

Advance planning

1. Draw up a timetable for your revision and try to keep to it. Spread your timetable over a number of weeks, and aim to cover four or five topics each week.
2. Spend longer on topics that you have found difficult, and revise them several times.
3. Above all, do not try to limit your revision by attempting to 'question-spot'. Try to be confident about all aspects of your Paper 1 work, because this will ensure that you have a choice of questions in Sections A and B.

Paper 1 overview:

AS Paper 1	Time: 2 hours 15 minutes	
Section A	Answer 1 question from a choice of 2	20 marks
Section B	Answer 1 question from a choice of 2	20 marks
Section C	Answer 1 compulsory interpretations question	20 marks
	Total marks =	60 marks

You should familiarise yourself with the layout of the paper by looking at the examples published by Edexcel. The questions for each section are followed by eight pages of lined paper where you should write your answer.

Section A questions

Section A questions ask you to analyse and evaluate either cause or consequence. You should consider either the reasons for, or the results of, an event or development. You will be asked for coverage of a period of around ten years, possibly a little longer. For example, a question for Option 1F might be 'Was the involvement of President Truman the main reason for the changing status of black Americans in the years 1945–55?' Your answer should consider the reason(s) given in the question, then look at other relevant points and reach a conclusion.

Section B questions

Section B questions cover a longer timespan than in Section A, at least one third of the period you have studied. The questions take the form of 'How far…', 'How significant…', 'To what extent…' or 'How accurate is it to say…'. The questions can deal with historical concepts such as cause, consequence, change, continuity, similarity, difference and significance. Again, you should consider the issue raised in the question, consider other relevant issues, and then conclude with an overall judgement.

Section C questions

There is no choice in Section C, which is concerned with the historical interpretations you have studied linked to the question 'Was there a general crisis in government in the last years of Elizabeth I's reign, 1589–1603?' You will be given two extracts totalling around 300 words (printed separately) and the question will take the form 'How far do you agree with the view that…?' There is no need to use source analysis skills such as making inferences or considering provenance for Section C answers. You will need to use the extracts and your own knowledge to consider the view given in the question.

Use of time

This is an issue that you should discuss with your teachers and fellow students, but here are some suggestions for you.

1. Do not write solidly for 45 minutes on each question. For Section A and B answers you should spend a few minutes working out what the question is asking you to do, and drawing up a plan of your answer. This is especially important for Section B answers, which cover an extended period of time.
2. For Section C it is essential that you have a clear understanding of the content of each extract and the points that each extract is making. Read each extract carefully and underline important points. You could approach your answer by analysing the first extract, then the second, and then using your own knowledge before reaching an overall judgement. You might decide to spend up to ten minutes reading the extracts and drawing up your plan, and 35 minutes writing your answer.

Preparing for your AS Level exams

Paper 1: AS Level sample answer with comments

Section A

These questions assess your understanding of the period in breadth. They will ask you about the content you learned about in the four key themes, and may ask about more than one theme. For these questions, remember to:

- give an analytical, not a descriptive, response
- support your points with evidence
- cover the whole time period specified in the question
- come to a substantiated judgement.

The Puritans wanted to change the Elizabethan Settlement in the years 1558 to 1588.

Was Elizabeth's opposition the main reason for their lack of success? (20 marks)

Average student answer

Elizabeth I came to the throne in 1558. She was the third of Henry VIII's children to come to the throne and followed Edward VI and Mary I. Edward VI had tried to make England into a Protestant country, while Mary had turned England back to Catholicism. Elizabeth I was the daughter of Anne Boleyn and Henry VIII and so represented the break with Rome. She was educated by Protestants and had Protestant sympathies, but she was also very cautious and wanted to keep Catholics happy, so she introduced a religious settlement that was a compromise between Catholicism and Protestantism. Some people, known as the Puritans, did not like this settlement and tried to challenge it, but they were not very successful because Elizabeth refused to change it.

The Puritans wanted to change the Elizabethan Settlement because they disliked it as it was too much of a compromise and not radical enough for them. However, Elizabeth was not prepared to let them change the Settlement because she was very stubborn and believed that she was right to enforce a compromise as she wanted to avoid a rebellion by the Catholics. The Puritans tried on many occasions to change the Settlement but they were never successful as Elizabeth always stopped them. For example, some Puritan clergymen tried to challenge the Settlement by refusing to wear the right type of clothes. Elizabeth was furious and ordered Archbishop Parker to tell the clergy that they must wear the correct clothes. Parker did this and some clergy were dismissed when they would not co-operate.

This shows how the Puritans were unsuccessful because of Elizabeth's determination. But the Puritans were as stubborn as Elizabeth and they continued to challenge the Settlement throughout her reign. They did this by organising meetings where people could meet to study the Bible and clergymen could learn how to preach. The Puritans also used Convocation to get their views across, but they were stopped by Elizabeth. They also tried to challenge the Settlement through parliament by trying to change the prayer book and criticising Elizabeth's policy. They used these tactics repeatedly during Elizabeth's reign. But every time the Puritans tried to challenge the Settlement, whatever method they used Elizabeth remained firm and would not change her mind, so by 1588 the Puritans had achieved nothing.

> This is a weak opening paragraph because it does not analyse and define the question. It tends toward narrative and strays outside the date range. There is some attempt to address the question, but the main argument is not clear.
>
> It could be improved by starting with a sentence like 'The Puritans were unsuccessful in challenging the religious settlement in the years 1558 to 1588 partly because of Elizabeth's opposition.'

> Using the correct language is important; 'vestments' would be a better word to use than 'clothes'.

> This paragraph is generally relevant to the question and attempts to address the factor in the question. It describes what the Puritans tried to do and attempts to explain why they were not successful. The factual detail is correct, but there is not much detailed support. It could be improved with some precise, accurate examples.

The Puritans were also not very successful because they were not very organised and disagreed among themselves. There were lots of different groups in the Puritan movement and they all wanted different things. Some Puritans were more moderate and believed that they could change the Settlement by working within the Church. An example of this was Edmund Grindal, who was made Archbishop of Canterbury in 1575. Grindal was not very radical but he did have some sympathy with some of the more moderate reforms that some Puritans wanted, such as better education for the clergy. When Elizabeth ordered him to stop the Puritan meetings, which had become very popular, Grindal refused. Elizabeth was so angry that she put him under house arrest where he remained until his death. When Elizabeth appointed her next archbishop, Whitgift, she did not repeat her mistake with Grindal; Whitgift was very anti-Puritan in his beliefs. Other Puritans wanted more radical reform and tried to change the prayer book and alter the Settlement by making it more radical. An example of this was in 1563 when some Puritans tried to introduce six articles to Convocation that would have made the Settlement more radical, but these were defeated. A Puritan called William Strickland also made the situation worse by trying to introduce his own version of the prayer book by adding it to another bill that was already being considered by parliament. This upset the bishops and meant that they would not help the Puritans in the future. Other Puritans tried to introduce changes to the prayer book through parliament in the 1580s by introducing Anthony Cope's 'bill and book', but they were defeated and some of the MPs who supported them were sent to prison.

> These examples are all accurate, but they are in the form of a list; there is no explanation of how these events led to Puritan failures. It would be better to choose one example and then explain how this caused the Puritans to fail.

The Puritans also damaged themselves by publishing the 'Martin Marprelate Tracts' in 1588–89, which were very radical and vicious and made the movement look bad. By 1588, the Puritan challenge had nearly disappeared and they had lost many of their most influential supporters, who had all died. All of these things meant that the Puritans were not successful at all by 1588 as they were very disorganised.

> This paragraph has some accurate detail and examples, but it is not directly focused on the question. It describes what the Puritans did, but it could be improved with an explanation of how this led to their failure because they were not united in their aims.

The Puritans also failed because they were opposed very strongly by Elizabeth's archbishops, Parker and Whitgift, and by members of her Council. All of these men obeyed Elizabeth's instructions to stop the Puritans and to punish them severely. Parker did this in the 1560s when he would not allow Puritan clergymen to wear the clothes they wanted, and Whitgift was very severe on the Puritans in the 1580s, which meant that they were never able to succeed. The punishments used against the Puritans were very severe – clergymen were dismissed or were made to take an oath that they would support the Settlement. The Puritans did have some supporters in the Council but these men were never prepared to support disorder or instability because their loyalty was to the queen. These severe actions meant that many Puritans were discouraged from challenging the Settlement or were removed from positions of power where they could be a threat to the Settlement. This meant that they were not successful.

> This paragraph is focused on the question but needs some precise examples – such as the nature of the oath they had to swear under Whitgift and the actions of Councillors such as Leicester and Hatton – to support the points made.

To conclude, there were many reasons why the Puritans did not succeed in challenging Elizabeth's Settlement. These included Elizabeth's opposition as well as the lack of unity and the harsh punishments they faced. All of these factors were important in stopping the Puritans from succeeding. By 1588, the Puritan challenge had died away and they had not been successful at all.

> The concluding paragraph attempts to answer the question but lists the main reasons and does not reach an overall judgement. It would be a stronger conclusion if the main factor was addressed and it explained which reason was the most important for the Puritans' lack of success.

Verdict

This is an average answer because:

- it does not always explain its points fully
- it does not always use evidence to back up points
- it does not come to a strong, reasoned judgement.

Use the feedback on this answer to rewrite it, making as many improvements as you can.

Paper 1: AS Level sample answer with comments

Section A

These questions assess your understanding of the period in breadth. They will ask you about the content you learned about in the four key themes, and may ask about more than one theme. For these questions, remember to:

- give an analytical, not a descriptive, response
- support your points with evidence
- cover the whole time period specified in the question
- come to a substantiated judgement.

The Puritans wanted to change the Elizabethan Settlement in the years 1558 to 1588.

Was Elizabeth's opposition the main reason for their lack of success? (20 marks)

Strong student answer

Elizabeth's opposition to the Puritan challenge to her religious settlement was certainly a very important reason why they failed to achieve their aims. However, there were also other reasons why they were not more successful. These included their lack of unity and the severity of the punishments that they faced, which links back to Elizabeth's determination to oppose them. Because this was the age of personal monarchy, Elizabeth was ultimately in charge of all decisions, so her opposition to the Puritans can be said to be the most important reason for their lack of success.

The Puritans were a group who believed that the Elizabethan religious settlement of 1559 was only a starting point for further change. Sometimes known as 'the hotter sort of Protestant', Puritans focused on the importance of the Bible ('sola scriptura') and were strongly influenced by the ideas of Calvin such as predestination. From 1559, Puritans tried to put pressure on Elizabeth to make changes to her initial compromise Settlement so that it would reflect their ideas and beliefs. Elizabeth was determined that this would not happen. For Elizabeth, the compromise Settlement was the key to political stability; she could not afford to upset Catholics or more moderate Protestants with a radical Settlement that might potentially lead to rebellion. Moreover, Elizabeth herself disliked many aspects of Puritanism, especially long sermons. Both personally and politically, therefore, she was motivated to oppose the Puritan challenge in whatever form it took. Examples of Elizabeth's consistent and determined opposition to the Puritans can be seen throughout the period. When some Puritan sympathisers within the clergy started to challenge the Settlement by not wearing the correct vestments, Elizabeth instructed Archbishop Parker to clamp down on these activities. Parker obeyed and in 1566 he suspended 37 out of 110 London clergy who appeared before him without the correct clothing. A similar pattern emerged in the 1570s and 1580s when the Puritans changed their tactics. Successive attempts by Puritans in the 1570s and 1580s to introduce changes to the prayer book through parliament were met with determined opposition from Elizabeth herself. For example, in 1571, she vetoed most of the Alphabetical bills, a moderate attempt to introduce Church reform, simply because the Puritan MP William Strickland had attempted to attach an amended prayer book to the bills. Even Puritan attempts to improve the standard of clergy education and preaching through 'prophesyings' were opposed by Elizabeth. She even put her own archbishop, Grindal, under house arrest when he refused to suppress the prophesyings as she wanted. By 1588, the Puritans had failed to achieve any real change to the Settlement. Elizabeth's determined opposition played a key role in this because, as queen, it was she who decided on policy. She was not prepared to support the changes the Puritans wanted. As long as this was the case, the Puritans could never succeed.

However, it would not be accurate to say that the Puritans failed only because of Elizabeth's opposition to them. They also created problems for themselves because the movement as a whole lacked unity and cohesion. In addition, the very nature of Puritanism, which encouraged

---

The introduction is clearly focused on the demands of the question. The main factors are outlined and it is clear what the overall argument will be.

Although this paragraph does not appear to be focused at the start, the explanation of the nature of the Puritan challenge and Elizabeth's opposition is relevant. The evidence used is precise and well selected, and it covers the date range. Expert thinking is also apparent in the understanding of the patterns seen across the period.

This paragraph is well focused and considers a second factor. Although there is some repetition of points from the previous paragraph, they are being used to make a different, but related, point. The end of the paragraph returns to the main factor and makes an explicit comparison and judgement as to which factor was more important.

individual faith, meant that it was not a movement that could easily gain momentum or organise a national campaign. Puritans themselves were very divided both in their beliefs and tactics. Although they all tended to share an emphasis on the Bible and preaching, they varied in terms of how much change they wanted and even whether this could be achieved within the Church of England or not. Some more moderate Puritans, or Puritan sympathisers, held office within the Church and hoped to use their positions to achieve change. Other Puritans took a more radical view, however, and attempted to impose change on the Church through parliament or by setting up their own local groups to encourage better education for the clergy. The diversity of these approaches, which were not united under one leader and were trying to achieve very different things, meant that Puritanism was weakened as a movement and was less likely to achieve its aims. Furthermore, the behaviour of some Puritans discredited the movement and caused it to lose support. The publication of the 'Martin Marprelate Tracts' in 1588–89 damaged the Puritan cause. The tracts were so vicious that they did more harm than good to the reputation of the movement, weakening its likelihood of success still further. The tracts were so controversial because they were a personal attack on the Church of England's bishops and archbishops and, by extension, the queen as governor of the Church. This came dangerously close to treason and lost the Puritans support. However, while the disunity of the Puritan movement was an important factor in its lack of success, it does not fully explain why the Puritans failed. The opposition of the queen was a more important factor in explaining why the Puritans failed because as long as she did not support them they were never likely to succeed whatever tactics they used.

The Puritan challenge to Elizabeth also failed because it lacked support from the powerful men who advised the queen. Working with Elizabeth, these men were prepared to use harsh methods and punishments in order to stop the Puritans. Although there were men on Elizabeth's Council who were sympathetic to Puritan ideals, such as Cecil, Walsingham and Leicester, their loyalty lay with the queen and none of them were prepared to see her reign challenged by political or religious instability. For example, Leicester, although he protected men like Thomas Cartwright, was not prepared to allow prophesyings to get out of hand, and he stepped in when they looked like they were going to do so. Similarly, Archbishop Grindal took a very hard line with Puritan clergy from 1583. He introduced an 'ex officio' oath that made suspected Puritans swear to answer all questions truthfully before they knew what questions they were to be asked. Grindal's policy was so harsh that 300 clergymen were suspended in the diocese of Canterbury alone.

> This section shows a good level of detail and use of historical terminology.

In parliament, although Elizabeth was not able to control the introduction of Puritan bills, she was able to control what happened to them. She was also prepared to have Puritan sympathisers in the House of Commons arrested and sent to the Tower. The harsh attitude of the government towards Puritanism and its supporters was an important reason why the Puritans were unsuccessful. However, it was Elizabeth's attitude to Puritanism and determination to oppose it that set the tone for how her councillors and officers acted.

> This paragraph is brief, but it deals with a third key reason for the lack of success. There is clear evaluation of the importance of factors.

In conclusion, the main reason for the Puritans' lack of success in the period 1558–88 is undoubtedly because of Elizabeth's opposition to the movement. Without her opposition, the Puritans would have been able to introduce the changes they wanted via Convocation or parliament, but because Elizabeth refused to allow these changes to happen, the Puritan movement remained unsuccessful. Although the Puritan movement did have its own weaknesses that contributed to its lack of success, this was not as important as Elizabeth's own attitude and she made sure that she appointed to positions of power men who would support her in this (with the exception of Grindal).

> Although relatively brief, there is a clear overall judgement about which factor was the most important in explaining the Puritans' lack of success.

Verdict

This is a strong answer because:

- the focus and analysis of the question is sustained throughout the answer
- the use of knowledge is accurate and relevant to the question

- the demands of the question are well understood and the relative importance of different factors is evaluated
- the written communication in this answer is particularly strong; key vocabulary is well used and the logical structure enhances the overall argument.

Paper 1: AS Level sample answer with comments

Section B

These questions assess your understanding of the period in breadth. They will ask you about the content you learned about in the four key themes, and may ask about more than one theme. For these questions, remember to:

- give an analytical, not a descriptive, response
- support your points with evidence
- cover the whole time period specified in the question
- come to a substantiated judgement.

Between 1531 and 1576, there were many attempts by the government to deal with the problem of poverty.

To what extent did government methods of dealing with poverty change in the period 1531–76? (20 marks)

Average student answer

Poverty was a very serious problem in Tudor England. There were many different types of poor in England, such as those who were too old or ill to look after themselves, the urban poor, and those who were unemployed and who roamed the country looking for work. This group was known as 'vagabonds'. There were many causes of poverty in Tudor England such as rising population, enclosure, changes to the cloth trade and economy, and periods when there were epidemics or poor harvests. The Tudor government tried to deal with these problems, although not very successfully.

Poverty was a serious problem in Tudor England and the poor were often treated as criminals. The Tudor government feared that poor people who did not have masters would wander around the countryside and spread disease and dangerous ideas. This meant that the government was keen to stop such behaviour and took a very harsh line against the poor. In the early years of Henry VIII's reign, beggars and the idle poor could be put in the stocks, whipped and returned home. There was also no method of funding poor relief and contributions were entirely in the hands of the wealthy, who could donate if they felt like it. As the population and poverty grew in the 1520s and 1530s, the government realised that this system would no longer be enough to look after all the poor in Tudor society, so in 1531 they introduced a new Poor Law into parliament.

The Poor Law of 1531 laid out new punishments for vagrants, which included whipping and licensing by JPs that allowed the impotent poor to beg. There was still no attempt to make wealthier parishioners contribute to poor relief and there was still a distinction between the deserving and undeserving poor. In the 1540s, there was more social and economic crisis and so the punishments for vagrancy became even harsher in 1547 with a new law called the Vagrancy Act. This Act defined a vagrant as someone who had been out of work for three days and who was able-bodied. This was a very harsh definition, showing how worried the government and parliament were about vagrancy. Under the Act, vagrants could be branded, forced to work as slaves, or even executed. Any beggar who was found to be unable to work was to be sent back to their parish where they would be looked after. The terms of the Vagrancy Act were so harsh that they could not be enforced and it was eventually repealed in 1550. This shows that there was no real change to the government's policy and nor were they very successful in dealing with the problems caused by rising poverty.

The introduction is not well focused on the question. It appears to be answering a different question either on the causes of poverty or how successful government policy was. A better tactic would be to outline the methods used to deal with poverty and make an initial judgement on the extent to which they changed or stayed the same.

Although accurate, this section is outside the date range of the question, which asks about the period from 1531. It could be improved with an opening sentence such as: 'In 1531, the Tudor government's methods of dealing with poverty were still focused on punishing the idle and vagrant poor who roamed the country, as well as supporting the impotent poor who could not work'.

The detail in the paragraph is within the time frame, but the structure of the answer means that it is 'telling the story' by describing each Act. This means that although the detail is accurate, it is not well focused on the question of how much change there was.

In 1552, a new Act was passed to replace the 1547 Act. The 1552 Act made it a legal requirement for the impotent poor to be registered, and it gave permission for local authorities to put pressure on wealthier parishioners to make contributions to poor relief. This Act remained in place until Elizabeth's reign. There then followed some very important Acts in the 1560s that led to some major changes. For example, in 1563, there was an Act that made contributions to poor relief nearly compulsory. The Statute of Artificers tried to deal with vagrancy by making it compulsory for younger people to look for work and making it illegal to leave employment without permission. The 1572 Poor Law also brought in new ideas for dealing with the poor. It introduced new punishments for vagrants, but it also funded houses of correction where the able-bodied poor who had no jobs could go. This Act was reinforced with another Act in 1576 that ordered every county to provide one house of correction for the able-bodied poor. Local authorities were also ordered to make sure that there were good supplies of materials for the poor to work on.

After 1576, the government did not have to make as many changes to methods of providing for the poor and there were no more important Acts before 1588. This was because the economic situation improved and stabilised in this period, so poverty was less of a problem. By 1588, the government had created successful methods of dealing with poverty, though vagrancy still continued.

It was not just the national government that was concerned with poverty. Before the Reformation, poor relief was carried out by the monasteries who gave out alms to the poor and provided health care. After the Reformation, it was up to local authorities and individuals to help the poor.

Local authorities in the most important towns such as London, Norwich and York were also getting worried about the numbers of poor, unemployed people. Towns began to introduce their own methods of dealing with the poor, even before the national government did. For example, London made contributions to poor relief compulsory in 1547, many years before the national government passed laws that did the same thing. Norwich and York also introduced compulsory payments over the next few years. The system also relied on private individuals to make donations and set up foundations such as hospitals and schools to help the poor. This became even more important after the monasteries were dissolved in the 1530s.

In conclusion, government methods of dealing with poor relief changed considerably during the period 1531 to 1588. Methods of dealing with the able-bodied poor changed the most. In 1531, the able-bodied were still being punished for being poor by being forced back to their parishes or through physical punishments. These methods continued through the 1540s, 1550s and 1560s, but started to change in the 1570s when the government brought in more support for the able-bodied poor through houses of correction. Methods of dealing with the impotent poor did not change as much – they were still dealt with in local poorhouses. There were also changes to how poor relief was funded – more pressure was placed on the wealthy to make contributions. Local authorities and individuals also took on more of the responsibility of looking after the poor long before the government introduced its laws.

> There is a narrative start to this paragraph. A better opening sentence would be: 'From 1552, the government's methods of dealing with poverty began to change'. The following sentences begin to address the question of the extent of change, but the paragraph reverts to detailed narrative. It could be improved with an explanation of the significance of these changes; for the first time the government was not simply punishing the able-bodied poor and there was a move to compulsory poor-relief payments.

> This section shows signs of expert thinking because it is dealing with the period of stability and argues for continuities. There is a drift towards answering a different question: how successful was the government's policy towards poor relief?

> Although this paragraph deals with local authorities' responses, it could be made relevant as part of 'Tudor government'. The material could be made more relevant by an explanation of the changes that were happening in local towns, especially because the monasteries' traditional role in poor relief had ended by the 1540s, which put more pressure on other forms of support.

> The conclusion does offer a judgement on the question of how much change there was in methods of poor relief. It also attempts to argue that some changes were bigger than others and that there were some continuities, but it tends to describe the changes that occurred, rather than reach a final judgement on how much change there was.

Verdict

This is an average answer because:

- there is some material that falls outside the date range of the question
- the structure of the answer leads to detailed narrative rather than a clear focus on the extent of change
- the final judgement is not absolutely clear.

Use the feedback on this answer to rewrite it, making as many improvements as you can.

Paper 1: AS Level sample answer with comments

Section B

These questions assess your understanding of the period in breadth. They will ask you about the content you learned about in the four key themes, and may ask about more than one theme. For these questions, remember to:

- give an analytical, not a descriptive, response
- support your points with evidence
- cover the whole time period specified in the question
- come to a substantiated judgement.

Between 1531 and 1576, there were many attempts by the government to deal with the problem of poverty.

To what extent did government methods of dealing with poverty change in the period 1531–76? (20 marks)

Strong student answer

There were both changes and continuities in the Tudor governments' methods of dealing with poverty in the years 1531 to 1588. In some ways, there was very little change, for example in methods of dealing with those who were unable to work, known as the impotent poor. However, there was greater change in methods of dealing with vagrants and the able-bodied poor, which moved from punishment towards more practical methods. The methods of raising money for poor relief also altered considerably, especially from the 1560s. In addition, the impact of the dissolution of the monasteries and the growth of towns meant that there was a growing role for town authorities and even individuals to develop their own methods of managing poor relief, some of which then influenced the national government's methods. The least amount of change in the government's methods in dealing with poverty was how the impotent poor were dealt with. Throughout the period, there was always an assumption that those who were too old, ill or otherwise unable to work would be supported by their parishes, often in local poorhouses. There was little change to these methods throughout the period and the impotent poor continued to be looked after. It also remained the responsibility of the home parish of the poor to provide relief for them.

However, there were changes in the period regarding the funding of this support. At the start of the period in the 1530s, poor relief was funded by voluntary collections among the wealthier parish members and there was no suggestion that these contributions should be made compulsory. As the number of poor began to rise, these methods became unsustainable, and the national government began to pass laws that put increasing pressure on the wealthy to contribute to local poor relief. The first step towards a system of compulsory payment emerged as a result of Elizabeth's Act of Uniformity, as recusancy fines were diverted to parish poor relief. This was the first attempt at creating a more regular and permanent source of funding for poor relief, although it was by no means a guaranteed source of income. In 1563, the Act for the Relief of the Poor moved a step closer to forcing all those who could pay to make contributions to poor relief. The Act introduced the post of local collectors of alms, who were to put pressure on the wealthier members of the parish to make contributions to poor relief, and those who refused could be imprisoned. However, there was no attempt to enforce uniform levels of payment – it was left up to the individual to decide how much they wanted to contribute. Nevertheless, the changes in the early years of Elizabeth's reign were noticeable; at the start of the period, methods of funding poor relief had been disorganised and reliant on individuals' generosity. By the 1560s, there was an increased expectation that everyone would contribute and a framework in place that meant that contributions could be more easily collected and monitored.

Methods of dealing with the able-bodied poor also saw considerable change in the period, especially in the 1570s. At the start of the period, government methods of dealing with the able-bodied poor were based on the need to deter vagrancy and to force the able-bodied to work. In 1531, a new Poor Law was passed to deal with the increasing numbers of unemployed vagrants.

The introduction clearly addresses the question of how much change (and continuity) there was across the period. There is a clear sense of structure and the introduction prefigures the main argument without going into too much detail. The later sentences deal with continuity in the period. This helps to bring balance to the answer because it is dealing with the extent of change.

This paragraph is well focused on an important area of change in methods of funding for poor relief. The evidence is well selected and covers a 30-year period efficiently without slipping into narrative.

The structure of the answer helps to assess the different amounts of change in different aspects of government policy. There is a very good range and breadth of supporting material. The 1580s are not covered so well, but there is an attempt to do so, which in the time allowed is sufficient. The paragraph is well balanced, considering both change and continuity.

This replaced a previous Act that had also aimed to punish vagrants; the new Act made it legal for vagrants to be whipped. This was an attempt to control the number of beggars by making it harder for them to beg. As social and economic hardship increased, so the government methods of dealing with the able-bodied poor grew even harsher. The most severe punishments were introduced in the 1547, which allowed vagrants to be branded, enslaved and even executed. This Act did not last, however, as it proved to be too harsh, and it was replaced in 1552 by a new Act that introduced registration for the impotent poor. However, it was still the case that the able-bodied poor faced punishment if they were not registered or licensed. The real changes in methods of dealing with the able-bodied poor began in the 1570s. The Acts of 1572 and 1576 still made it illegal to be a vagrant and included such punishments as ear-boring and whipping. Nevertheless, for the first time, the government also tried to introduce other methods of dealing with the able-bodied. Houses of correction were to be set up where the able-bodied would be put to work on materials such as wool, flax and iron. Although there was still an emphasis on punishment in these methods by 'correcting' the behaviour of the poor, for the first time there was also an attempt to give the able-bodied poor who could not find work something to do rather than simply punishing them for being unemployed and masterless. These new methods were sustained in the 1570s and through to the end of the 1580s because the social and economic situation was relatively stable, which meant there was no great need for the government to introduce further measures.

There was also significant change in how local government authorities dealt with the problem of poverty across the period. Until the dissolution of the monasteries in the later 1530s, much of the provision for relief of the poor was carried out by monks and nuns who gave out alms and looked after the sick. With the destruction of the monasteries, new methods had to be found to deal with the rising numbers of poor in Tudor England, especially in the larger towns, where the growth of urban poverty was a particular problem. As the largest city in England, London took the lead. In 1547, long before the national government was to do so, the city of London had made contributions to poor relief a permanent expectation for its wealthier citizens. London was followed in this strategy by other large towns such as Ipswich and York. These earlier changes at a more local government level were then adopted and used by the national government. In some ways though, local methods of poor relief did not change that much. In particular, it remained the case that there was no guarantee that the poor would receive relief in a particular region and the system remained reliant on the generosity of private individuals who made charitable contributions to help the poor through setting up almshouses, hospitals and schools.

In conclusion, there were both changes and continuities in the methods used by the Tudor government to deal with the problem of poverty. The extent of change in methods for helping the impotent poor was very limited but there was considerable change in how poor relief was funded. In the 1530s, poor relief contributions were entirely voluntary; by the 1580s they were close to compulsory and there were systems in place to ensure that payments were collected and defaulters punished. The most significant amount of change in methods of dealing with the poor came in the 1570s, when there was the first attempt at some form of job creation rather than simply punishing the able-bodied poor. However, many of these changes that were described were first attempted at a local level by town authorities and then adopted by the national government. This meant that the extent of change in methods was slower to happen at a national level than a local one and was dependent on the organisation and determination of local individuals and governments.

This paragraph on the role of local authorities' methods is relevant because they are part of the 'Tudor government'. Although less well developed than the previous paragraphs, it adds a new dimension to the argument by showing that change happened in different places at different speeds. However, there could be a clearer overall focus on the extent of change.

The judgement is well developed and fits with the arguments made in the rest of the essay. The extent of change is well addressed here and the judgement includes a comparison of the amount of change that took place at local and national level.

Verdict

This is a strong answer because:

- the answer is balanced and considers the extent of change that took place

- the selection of detail mostly covers the whole period under discussion
- expert thinking is apparent in the focus on change, continuity, trends and patterns.

Paper 1: AS Level sample answer with comments

Section C

These questions require you to read the two extracts carefully to identify the key points raised and establish the argument being put forward. For these questions, remember to:

- read and analyse the extracts thoroughly, remembering that you need to use them together
- take careful note of the information provided about the extracts
- deploy your own knowledge to develop the points and arguments that emerge from the extracts and to provide appropriate context
- develop an argument rooted in the points raised in the extracts and come to a substantiated conclusion.

Historians have different views about the extent to which there was a general crisis in government in the last years of Elizabeth's reign. Analyse and evaluate the extracts and use your knowledge of the issues to explain your answer to the following question:

Study Extracts 1 and 2 in Chapter 5. How far do you agree that the problems created by war posed a serious threat to Elizabeth's power from 1589 to 1603? (20 marks)

Average student answer

War broke out between England and Spain in 1585. It was a war fought on several fronts, including in France, the Netherlands, Ireland and the New World. In 1589, Spain sent an armada to invade England but the fleet was destroyed by a storm and the English fleet. Other attempts by Spain to mount an invasion also failed. The war caused serious problems for Elizabeth's power. As Sloan argues, it led to her key military commanders disobeying her and it caused enormous problems in England with an 'oppressive level of taxation, dislocation of trade, enforced and bitterly resented military service, a profusion of detested monopolies, and widespread corruption in public life'. This suggests that war posed a serious threat to Elizabeth's power from 1589 to 1603.

The wars in which England was involved were a serious threat to Elizabeth. As Williams and Sloan mention, the scale of the wars was considerable. Williams mentions that the English had been involved in 'the rebellion in Ireland, and the naval expeditions to Cádiz and the Azores'. This suggests that Elizabeth's power was under threat because it was very difficult for England to fight a war on so many fronts at the same time. Sloan supports the view that the war was too expensive for England when he says, 'it was a war that produced much disruption and unrest, causing as it did an oppressive level of taxation'. This shows that war was far too costly for a country like England to sustain. The war led to serious problems with parliament, which began to criticise Elizabeth's financial policies such as monopolies and purveyance. MPs were already angry about the abuse of purveyance in the earlier parliaments; there were then further clashes with the Crown, which wanted more taxation than the Commons was prepared to grant. In the parliaments of 1597 and 1601, angry MPs demanded that the queen do something about the amount of corruption and the number of monopolies she was granting. These disputes were a threat to her power because the MPs were openly critical of the queen and challenged her prerogative, and Elizabeth was forced to make concessions by cancelling some of the most unpopular monopolies. The challenges that Elizabeth faced from her parliament were caused by her need to raise more money to fund the overseas wars, so war posed a serious threat to her power.

The introduction takes a narrative approach. It identifies one side of the debate – that war posed a serious threat to Elizabeth's power – and it introduces one of the sources, but it is unbalanced in its view of the impact of war. It could be improved by the use of both extracts to introduce the debate over whether war threatened Elizabeth's power.

The extracts are used together to support the view that the problems caused by war led to challenges to Elizabeth's power. There is some attempt to explain these views by use of own knowledge, but this is not developed very far. There could have been more explanation of the impact of sustaining the costs of war within a system that was not set up for such demands.

Another way in which wars caused a serious threat to Elizabeth's power was because finding the men, money and resources to support the war effort caused resentment in local communities, some of whom started to rebel. Williams says that 'The equipment and weapons of the levies were a continuous drain upon the resources of the shires and their collection was a source of discontent and irritation. The county levies almost always fell short of their quotas and nearly 20 per cent of the men were usually deficient in arms or equipment.' Sloan agrees with this when he talks about 'enforced and bitterly resented public service'. The war caused a serious threat to Elizabeth's power because local communities grew weary of having to find men, money and resources. For example, in Norfolk, Suffolk and Essex, there was corruption and resistance through the non-payment of levies. There was even a near-mutiny by Kentish soldiers who were going to be sent to fight in Ireland. The situation was made worse because there was no obvious sign that the money and resources were being well spent. The Spanish continued to be a threat in the 1590s, mounting several invasion forces and intervening in Ireland. Local communities were angry that their money, men and resources appeared to have been wasted. This resentment boiled over in parliament and threatened the queen's popularity. If her people were no longer prepared to support and follow her, her power was under threat as a result of the war.

> Both extracts are used here and there is some understanding of the interpretations they are offering, although there is no reference to Williams' point that before 1595 at least there was little open opposition to the demands of war. The claims in the sources are developed by some accurate own knowledge, though this could be more precise, especially the point about the Spanish invasion fleets.

Elizabeth's power also came under threat because her nobility would no longer obey her, especially her military commanders who 'constantly disobeyed her orders'. For example, the military commanders of the expedition to Lisbon completely ignored Elizabeth's orders (despite the fact that she had contributed considerable amounts of money to the fleet). Instead of trying to cause rebellion in Lisbon, they sailed on to the Azores in search of Spanish bullion ships to attack. This lack of discipline was reflected in other expeditions where the profits were dispersed among the sailors and not paid to Elizabeth. They failed in this and 11,000 men were killed. In 1599, the Earl of Essex disobeyed Elizabeth's direct order, and returned to England from Ireland. This led to a direct challenge to Elizabeth's power. Essex wanted to be treated as a war hero and thought that he had popular support behind him because of this, but Elizabeth saw him as a traitor. In 1601, Essex rebelled, showing how the wars made her military commanders have the confidence to challenge the queen directly. Although his rebellion failed, and all the Spanish attempts at invasion, these events show that her power was directly challenged as a result of war.

> The answer is still focused on the threats posed to Elizabeth's power as a result of war. It has some accurate and well-developed support, but apart from a brief mention of the counter-argument in the final sentence, there is no real consideration of the debate in the sources about the impact of war.

In conclusion, war posed a serious threat to Elizabeth's power from 1589. Both Williams and Sloan agree that the cost of war was too high for England to maintain, in terms of both money and resources. England was also too small to be able to fight a war against a military power as large and powerful as Spain. Elizabeth was also ageing and the war damaged her popular image and made commanders like Essex want to challenge her orders and even her throne. Although Williams argues that these problems were not as severe as some historians would like to argue, the wars from 1589 posed a serious threat to Elizabeth's power.

> The conclusion attempts to reach a judgement and there is some recognition that there are differences between the sources' claims. However, the judgement is not fully supported and has not considered both sides of the debate.

Verdict

This is an average answer because:

- the debate outlined in the extracts is not fully recognised, although there is some attempt to highlight differences
- both extracts are used, and there is some attempt to expand their views using own knowledge, but this is not always fully developed

- the overall argument and judgement lacks balance, but it is related to the debate in the extracts.

Use the feedback on this answer to rewrite it, making as many improvements as you can.

Paper 1: AS Level sample answer with comments

Section C

These questions require you to read the two extracts carefully to identify the key points raised and establish the argument being put forward. For these questions, remember to:

- read and analyse the extracts thoroughly, remembering that you need to use them together
- take careful note of the information provided about the extracts
- deploy your own knowledge to develop the points and arguments that emerge from the extracts and to provide appropriate context
- develop an argument rooted in the points raised in the extracts and come to a substantiated conclusion.

Historians have different views about the extent to which there was a general crisis in government in the last years of Elizabeth's reign. Analyse and evaluate the extracts and use your knowledge of the issues to explain your answer to the following question:

Study Extracts 1 and 2 in Chapter 5. How far do you agree that the problems created by war posed a serious threat to Elizabeth's power from 1589 to 1603? (20 marks)

Strong student answer

While both Williams and Sloan agree to some extent that the problems created by war posed a serious threat to Elizabeth's power between 1589 and 1601, there is also a debate in the extracts as to the extent of the problems caused as well as whether war caused a threat to Elizabeth throughout the whole period. Sloan argues that the war created challenges both for Elizabeth's leadership as well as for the country as a whole which then led to the declining popularity of her rule and challenges to her power. Williams, however, while not denying the severity of the problems caused by war from 1595, argues that before this period the war caused grumbling, but no 'serious hostility towards the Crown.' Undoubtedly, the wars from 1589 caused Elizabeth's rule at times to be questioned, but it is less certain that they ever posed a 'serious threat' to her power.

As Sloan argues, Elizabeth had tried to avoid war, mainly because England could not successfully engage with a world power like Spain, especially on several fronts for such a long period of time. In particular, England's finances were simply not able to cope with the demands of such a costly war and this led to serious challenges to Elizabeth's power, both within parliament and, to a lesser extent, in local communities. Although Williams downplays the political impact of the costs of the war before 1595, he still acknowledges the huge sums of money that were involved. Sloane takes this argument further, claiming that 'war … produced much disruption and unrest, causing as it did an oppressive level of taxation, dislocation of trade, enforced and bitterly resented military service, a profusion of detested monopolies …'. He also argues that the war caused a collapse in Elizabeth's popularity. If this claim is accurate, then a loss of popularity would have posed a serious threat to Elizabeth, and, as Sloan goes on to argue, it led to an attempt by Essex to overthrow her. There is considerable evidence to support these claims. For example, the annual income for Elizabeth's government was £300,000 per annum, but the costs of keeping the war effort going soon put huge pressure on Crown finances. But by the mid-1590s, the government's expenditure was £1,100,000. The costs of war only continued to rise after 1595, when the Spanish threat was renewed and the Irish revolt began. These costs put a huge strain on the government's finances, and Elizabeth was forced to turn to unpopular and only semi-legal methods in order to find more money, which led to increasing criticism in parliament that was a potential threat to her power.

Another problem caused by war was the supply of men and resources from the localities. In a country of 4 million people the continuing war placed huge demands on the localities, which Sloan argues led to 'bitterly resented military service'. Williams agrees that 'the equipment and weapons of the levies were a continuous drain upon the resources of the shires and their collection was a source of discontent and irritation'. However, the extracts disagree about the level of threat

The first paragraph sets up the debate between the two extracts and outlines the main arguments to be discussed.

This paragraph shows clear focus on the question. The extracts are used together to compare and discuss the issues raised. The use of contextual knowledge is accurate, it covers the date range and extends the points made by the extracts.

This section shows an understanding that the issue under discussion relates to interpretations of events, and that different historians can interpret the same events in different ways. Own knowledge is used to suggest which interpretation seems more plausible. The section uses own knowledge to show the validity of the historians' claims about the threat to stability posed by war.

to Elizabeth's power that these problems caused, at least before the mid-1590s. While Williams argues that 'up to the middle of 1595, there is not much sign of serious hostility towards the Crown either from the counties or from parliament.' However, Sloan emphasises the entirely negative results of the war on Elizabeth's popularity and, by extension, her power. There is certainly evidence to support Sloan's view that military service was 'bitterly resented'. In the localities, there were increasing attempts to avoid the demands placed on them by the government.

This was particularly true in counties with a coast. Local communities felt that they were at the risk of being overrun by foreign invaders and were therefore reluctant to commit their resources to overseas campaigns when they themselves were under threat. This reluctance gradually became open anger that boiled over in the parliaments of 1597 and 1601. The threat to Elizabeth's power was not restricted to a small group of troublemaking MPs, therefore. The crowds outside parliament and the increasing reluctance of local communities suggest that there was increasing resentment to her rule, which was caused to a great extent by the wars. However, this argument cannot be taken too far. Williams makes a valid point about the level of discontent before 1595 – the resistance seen in parliament before this date was indeed minimal. Furthermore, there was no popular rebellion against Elizabeth in these years. When Essex did try to mount a rebellion in 1601, he received no popular support from Londoners and his challenge to Elizabeth's power rapidly collapsed. Furthermore, Elizabeth handled the potential challenges very effectively. This meant that although war created tension and resentment among her subjects, ultimately they remained loyal to her and so the threat to her power was not as serious as it could have been.

The wars exposed a fundamental weakness in Elizabeth's rule – she could not command men on the battlefield and ultimately they could disobey her and even try to overthrow her, which was a serious threat to her power. However, it can be argued that Essex did not succeed and although her commanders' personal disobedience was an embarrassment, the wars actually helped to reduce the threat to Elizabeth. As Williams argues, before 1595 the wars had created serious challenges, but that these had been met. Sloan reinforces this point when he argues that 'the spectre of overwhelming Spanish power was exorcised.' The war created national pride and patriotism against a common threat, an invasion from a foreign, Catholic power. Furthermore, each of the attempts that the Spanish made to invade England were unsuccessful. It can be argued, therefore, that although the war caused many problems that led to some challenges to Elizabeth's authority, it did not lead to a serious threat. When the Spanish did try to mount invasion forces, there was no popular rising from English Catholics, who preferred to remain loyal to their queen. Apart from Essex's feeble attempt in 1601, there was no serious threat to Elizabeth's crown, although the war certainly led to many more criticisms of her rule.

This paragraph widens the debate suggested by the extracts to the issue of national security. There is a clear, balanced argument.

Therefore, the war certainly created some problems that made Elizabeth's rule less popular and led to protest in parliament, the localities and, in part, to Essex's revolt. As both Williams and Sloan agree, the main threats to her rule were the demands placed on the country by the government's need for resources and men. These demands led to unprecedented protests in parliament and the dangers of a more widespread revolt. However, the protests in parliament were carefully managed and popular revolt never materialised, which suggests that the threat was not as serious as it might have appeared. Sloan and Williams disagree about the extent of the threat and the seriousness of the impact of war before 1595. However, the debate in the extracts can be resolved by the fact that although Elizabeth's popularity was on the wane as a result of war, her position on the throne was never really under threat either from internal rebellion or external invasion. Ultimately, although the wars led to open criticism of Elizabeth, this was not the same as a 'serious threat' to her power.

The answer reaches a substantiated judgement based on the debate in the extracts and own knowledge, which is well-selected and has suitable range and breadth.

Verdict

This is a strong answer because:

- it identifies and illustrates the arguments of the two extracts
- it deploys a sound range of specific evidence to develop points emerging from the extracts

- it develops an argument that considers both interpretations and provides balance.

Preparing for your A Level Paper 1 exam

Advance planning

1. Draw up a timetable for your revision and try to keep to it. Spread your timetable over a number of weeks, and aim to cover four or five topics each week.
2. Spend longer on topics that you have found difficult, and revise them several times.
3. Above all, do not try to limit your revision by attempting to 'question spot'. Try to be confident about all aspects of your Paper 1 work, because this will ensure that you have a choice of questions in Sections A and B.

Paper 1 overview:

AL Paper 1	Time: 2 hours 15 minutes	
Section A	Answer 1 question from a choice of 2	20 marks
Section B	Answer 1 question from a choice of 2	20 marks
Section C	Answer 1 compulsory interpretations question	20 marks
	Total marks =	60 marks

You should familiarise yourself with the layout of the paper by looking at the examples published by Edexcel. The questions for each section are followed by eight pages of lined paper where you should write your answer.

Section A and Section B questions

The essay questions in Sections A and B are similar in form. They ask you to reach a judgement on an aspect of the course you have studied, and will deal with one or more historical concepts of change, continuity, similarity, difference, cause, consequence and significance. The question stems which will be used will include 'To what extent…', 'How far…', 'How significant was…' and so on. You should consider the issue raised by the question, develop your answer by looking at other relevant points, and reach a judgement in your conclusion.

The main difference between Section A and Section B questions will be the timespan of the questions. Section A questions will cover a period of ten years or more, while Section B questions will be concerned with at least one-third of the period you have studied.

A Section A question for Option 1E might read 'How far was high expenditure on the armed forces responsible for economic decline in the USSR in the years 1964–82?' Your answer should consider the issue of expenditure on the armed forces, look at other issues such as agricultural decline, falling productivity in industry, and Brezhnev's reluctance to undertake economic reforms, before reaching an overall judgement on the question.

A Section B question on the same paper will cover a longer period of time, but have a similar shape. For example, 'How successful were the government's social policies in improving the lives of the Soviet people in the years 1917–64?' Here you should consider various successes, such as full employment, education and healthcare, but also point out policies which were less successful, such as housing and different policies towards women over time. You should conclude by reaching a judgement on the question.

Section C questions

There is no choice in Section C, which is concerned with the historical interpretations you have studied linked to the question 'Was there a general crisis in government in the last years of Elizabeth I's reign, 1589–1603?' You will be given two extracts totalling around 400 words (printed separately) and the question will take the form, 'How convincing do you find the view that…?' There is no need to use source analysis skills such as making inferences or considering provenance for Section C answers. You should approach your answer by analysing both extracts separately, and then use your own knowledge to support, and to counter, the view given in the question, before reaching an overall judgement.

Use of time

This is an issue that you should discuss with your teachers and fellow students, but here are some suggestions for you.

1. Do not write solidly for 45 minutes on each question. For Section A and B answers you should spend a few minutes working out what the question is asking you to do, and drawing up a plan of your answer. This is especially important for Section B answers, which cover an extended period of time.
2. For Section C it is essential that you have a clear understanding of the content of each extract and the points that each extract is making. Read each extract carefully and underline important points. You might decide to spend up to ten minutes reading the extracts and drawing up your plan, and 35 minutes writing your answer.

Preparing for your A Level exams

Paper 1: A Level sample answer with comments

Section A

These questions assess your understanding of the period in breadth. They will ask you about the content you learned about in the four key themes, and may ask about more than one theme. For these questions, remember to:

- give an analytical, not a descriptive, response
- support your points with evidence
- cover the whole time period specified in the question
- come to a substantiated judgement.

How far was popular anger at religious policy the main reason for rebellion against the Tudor monarchs? (20 marks)

Average student answer

There were many rebellions in Tudor England against the monarchs and their policies. In 1525, there was the Amicable Grant revolt. The Pilgrimage of Grace was a very serious rebellion that took place in 1536 and posed a great threat to Henry VIII's government. There were also serious popular uprisings in 1549, which caused the Duke of Somerset to fall from power, and a smaller rising led by Thomas Wyatt against Mary I in 1554. Popular anger at religious policy was a very important reason, but there were also many other reasons why there was rebellion.

Popular anger at religious policy was a very important reason for rebellion against the Tudor monarchs. The first rebellion that had a religious focus was the Pilgrimage of Grace in 1536. This was a very serious rebellion for Henry VIII to face as it involved up to 30,000 rebels in the north of England who at one point were prepared to march south. Henry was very lucky that the rebels chose to negotiate rather than fight, since their army was much bigger than his own. The rebels were upset at Henry's religious policies because he had recently started to close down the smaller monasteries and they wanted him to restore these. There were even monks who armed themselves to fight, showing their anger. Henry was able to defeat the rebels by making them promises and then going back on them when some rebels became angry at the lack of change. Religion was therefore a very important cause of the Pilgrimage of Grace.

Another rebellion that had religious causes was the 1549 rebellion in the West Country. The rebellion kicked off because the locals in Cornwall and Devon were unhappy about the religious changes the government was planning. The Cornish rebels began to meet in large numbers at Sampford Courtenay before joining up with the Devon rebels at Crediton. The rebels disliked the new English prayer book and services in English and refused to back down. It was a particularly serious situation for the government because there was a child-king on the throne and in 1549 there were rebellions right across England, which meant the government's resources were stretched. It took two months for Lord Russell to get a big enough army together to put down the rebels, and Somerset fell from power as a result, showing how unpopular his religious policies were. There was also a religious element to Wyatt's rising against Mary I in 1554. Wyatt and his supporters were worried about Mary's proposed marriage to the Catholic Philip of Spain. Wyatt had Protestant sympathies and feared that the marriage would lead to persecution as Philip and Mary tried to restore England to Catholicism. This led Wyatt and his fellow plotters (who were all Protestants) to plan a rising to prevent the marriage happening and perhaps to put the Protestant Elizabeth on the throne instead.

This introduction attempts a focus on the question and is aware that it is a multi-factor question. However, it tends to list the main rebellions rather than introduce the main arguments. The other factors to be discussed later in the answer could be mentioned briefly. The question is open-ended regarding dates; this response does not appear to be considering the Northern Rising in 1569. The introduction could also be improved by explaining what is meant by 'popular anger'.

This paragraph has some implied focus on the question but it would be better if it explained how anger at Henry's policies caused mass rebellion. For example, it could look at the rebels' demands. There is also a tendency in this paragraph to stray from the original question, instead discussing how serious the rebellion was.

Wyatt and his rebels got a lot of sympathy – some soldiers even deserted to join them, but they were easily put down and beheaded. This evidence shows that popular anger at Tudor religious policy was very important in causing rebellion in the period, but it was by no means the only reason for revolt.

Another reason for rebellion against Tudor monarchs was economic discontent. The rebellion over the Amicable Grant (1525) could not have been caused by religious anger because at that point there was only one religion in England, Catholicism, and the controversial break with Rome had not yet happened. The Amicable Grant was the result of people's anger over high levels of taxation to pay for the king's wars. Wolsey had been putting more and more pressure on the people to pay increasing amounts of taxation and the people were fed up. The final straw came when Wolsey introduced the Amicable Grant. This had not been approved by parliament as was normal, and some felt that it was therefore illegal. Some 10,000 angry people met at Lavenham in Suffolk to protest about the grant and the nobility had great difficulty in putting them down.

Social and economic motives also played a part in the 1549 risings in East Anglia. The country was suffering from high levels of poverty and was under threat of attack from France. The Duke of Somerset also made the situation worse by seeming to encourage protest over enclosure. He did this by sending out commissioners to inquire into illegal enclosures. This sparked enclosure riots in East Anglia, especially Norfolk. In particular, a local dispute in the village of Wymondham got out of hand. A mob tried to uproot the hedges of Robert Kett. Instead of becoming angry, Kett sided with the rebels and quickly became their leader. The rebels set up a large camp outside Norwich and began to run their own 'commonwealth'. They were particularly angry about corrupt local officials who took advantage of their own power to make themselves rich. The rebels also sided with Somerset over his social, economic and religious policies and had to be put down by a force led by John Dudley.

To conclude, it is clear that popular anger over religious change was the most important reason for rebellion against the Tudor monarchs. This is because religious change threatened not only the people's day-to-day existence but also what would happen to their immortal souls. Anger over religious change is therefore the most important reason for popular rebellion.

This paragraph is partially focused on the question, though there is some drift to narrative. The response does link back to the question at the end, but this is an assertion. This could be avoided if the response explained why there was popular revolt over religious policy. There is also no reference here to the Northern Rising (1569), which needs to be covered in any discussion of discontent about religious policy.

This paragraph has better focus on the question, but it needs an overall explanation of what caused the rebellion to happen. The use of the word 'people' is very generalised – it could be improved by reference to the specific social groups such as unemployed textile workers who took part in this rebellion.

The conclusion reaches a judgement, but this is an assertion rather than a substantiated judgement.

The detail in this paragraph is accurate, but there is a drift into detailed narrative. It could be improved by a more detailed explanation of the causes of the rebellion which can be shown in the rebels' actions and demands. It would also be appropriate here to talk about the economic conditions in the 1530s that led to the outbreak of the Pilgrimage of Grace.

Verdict

This is an average answer because:

- it describes what happens in the rebellions rather than explaining their causes
- it does not cover the entire range of evidence – the 1569 rebellion is missing
- in places, the supporting detail could be more precise and well selected
- the final judgement is an assertion and is not fully explained or substantiated.

Use the feedback on this answer to rewrite it, making as many improvements as you can.

Paper 1: A Level sample answer with comments

Section A

These questions assess your understanding of the period in breadth. They will ask you about the content you learned about in the four key themes, and may ask about more than one theme. For these questions, remember to:

- give an analytical, not a descriptive, response
- support your points with evidence
- cover the whole time period specified in the question
- come to a substantiated judgement.

How far was popular anger at religious policy the main reason for rebellion against the Tudor monarchs? (20 marks)

Strong student answer

Popular rebellion against the Tudor monarchs occurred on a fairly regular basis throughout the period. In 1525, 1536, 1549, 1554 and 1569, there were serious uprisings that could be described as 'popular' because they attracted widespread support from a cross-section of society. The rapid and extreme nature of the religious changes sparked rebellions in 1536 and 1549; discontentment with Elizabeth's religious policies also played an important part in causing the Northern Rising in 1569. Underlying social and economic hardship was also a contributing factor in causing popular revolt, especially at the start of the period. Another cause of popular rebellion was resentment at increasing government centralisation and intervention in the localities. It can be argued that anger at religious policy played an increasingly important role in causing rebellion during the period, but it would be simplistic to argue that popular rebellions were solely fuelled by one cause.

> The response shows a clear understanding of the demands of the question and that other factors brought about revolt apart from religion.

Anger at Tudor religious policy was the most important cause of the Lincolnshire Rising and Pilgrimage of Grace (1536) and of the Western Rebellion (1549). These popular revolts were triggered by rapid and unprecedented changes to religious belief and worship. Both Henry VIII and the Duke of Somerset had caused enormous and rapid change. Following the break with Rome, in 1536, Henry VIII allowed Cromwell to begin the dissolution of the smaller monasteries. The monasteries represented hundreds of years of Catholic tradition in England. Furthermore, the role of the monks was a vital part of Catholic faith because they played a role in prayers for the souls of the dead. In attacking this tradition, Henry was attacking a fundamental part of Catholic belief. In both 1536 and 1549, these radical changes triggered popular uprisings in the most religiously traditional regions of England – both the north and west were strongholds of the Catholic faith and had not been as influenced by new, Protestant ideas that had infiltrated southern parts of England. Both sets of rebels were clearly motivated by anger over religious change. In 1536, the Pilgrims tried to restore monasteries that had been dissolved, while the Western rebels demanded a return to the religiously conservative Six Articles and the Latin Mass. These rebellions are the best examples of anger at religious change leading to popular rebellion.

> This paragraph is well focused on the question and has very good factual support of the argument that popular anger at religious policy was the main reason for rebellion.

To a slightly lesser extent, popular anger over religion also played a role in the rebellions of 1554 and 1569. While Thomas Wyatt's rebellion was in some senses the result of a court-based plot to overthrow Mary, the motivations of the rebels were religious. Wyatt and his fellow plotters such as Peter Carew and the Duke of Suffolk were all Protestant and feared the consequences of the Catholic Mary's marriage to Philip of Spain. The aim of the rebellion may have been to replace Mary with the Protestant Elizabeth, suggesting that the rebels were motivated by fear of persecution for their religious beliefs by Mary and Philip. The only region that actually rose in rebellion in 1549, Kent, also had strong Protestant traditions and would have been threatened by a return to Catholicism. Conversely, the Revolt of the northern Earls in 1569 was partly caused by dislike of the Protestant Elizabeth's religious settlement. In the 1560s, about two-thirds of the JPs in Northern England were still Catholic, and even though Elizabeth's settlement was deliberately aimed at

> There is a clear sense of argument and prioritising of causes here. It also shows awareness of the demands of the question in that it introduces other causes while still emphasising religious causes.

achieving a compromise that would be acceptable to Catholics, the arrival of the Catholic Mary, Queen of Scots in England created a figurehead for those who wanted a return to Catholicism and Elizabeth's removal. The religious resentment that fuelled the revolt was apparent in the actions of the rebels; on seizing Durham Cathedral, the rebels celebrated a Catholic Mass. However, it would be too simplistic to argue that these rebellions were solely caused by popular anger at religious policy. In 1554 and 1569, other causes also played a part. In addition, it would not be accurate to argue that religious policy was the main cause of all popular rebellion. Kett's rebels in 1549 actually supported the government's religious policy, while in 1525, the religion of England was still uniform; rebellion in this year was caused by social and economic grievances, not religious anger.

Social and economic grievances often played a role in causing rebellion against the Tudor monarchs. In 1525 and in Kett's Rebellion of 1549, social and economic tensions were the major cause of popular revolt, and were a contributing cause of the unrest in 1536, in the Western Rebellion and in 1569. The Amicable Grant revolt broke out as a result of Wolsey's increasingly unpopular attempts to raise money for the king's wars. Following in the wake of increasingly high and sustained levels of taxation, the Amicable Grant was collected at the same time as the second instalment of a subsidy granted in 1523. These demands led to widespread popular protest in the form of non-payment, which echoed an earlier protest seen in 1513–15. In Suffolk, where there was considerable economic hardship caused by a temporary slump in the cloth trade, 4,000 men gathered at Lavenham. These protests had nothing at all to do with religious policy, but followed a long tradition of popular protest over unreasonable government demands for wars that were seen to be wasteful or going badly. However, Kett's Rebellion (1549) was a very different type of revolt. Its causes were nothing to do with religion – in fact the rebels supported religious reform, especially the better education of clergy. Instead, Kett's Rebellion was sparked by social and economic grievances and was fuelled by Somerset's own policies. Kett's Rebellion actually challenged the social order in a way that no other rebellion did. It was not led by members of the gentry – in fact they were targeted by the 'middling sort' who resented their corruption and abuse of their power. Kett's rebels were in part encouraged by Somerset's commissions of enquiry into illegal enclosures, which targeted the traditional nobility and gentry. The rebels' demands included an end to illegal enclosures and rack-renting, and their actions showed that they were attempting to set up an alternative form of government that excluded the elites but was peaceful and loyal to the monarchy. Kett's rebels were motivated by a desire to restructure society and redress many of the social injustices of which they were victims. The causes of this rebellion were therefore very different to those of other revolts in the Tudor period and were not motivated by religious anger.

> This paragraph ranges across the whole period under discussion. It is clearly focused on the demands of the question because it addresses the importance of underlying social and economic tensions in causing popular rebellion and shows that not all rebellion was caused by religious change.

In conclusion, popular anger at religious policy was the most important cause of the Pilgrimage of Grace and the Western Rebellion and also played a very important part in the Northern Rising and Wyatt's revolt. However, it is not accurate to say that all rebellions in the Tudor period were caused by anger at religious policy. Before the 1530s, popular resistance took the more traditional form of revolt over high taxation and was often provoked by regional social and economic distress. Social and economic factors remained important in fomenting anger, but it was not the most important reason for the outbreak of rebellion in 1536, 1549, 1554 or 1569. Finally, all of the revolts were linked to resentment at increasing government intervention in local affairs. This was often a reason for members of the traditional nobility and gentry, especially in the north, to join rebellion as they were angry that their power was being undermined. However, it does not explain why these rebellions became so large or genuinely popular. This can be explained before the 1530s by social and economic causes and after the 1530s by anger at religious change.

> The final judgement is detailed. It addresses the question and reaches a substantiated conclusion that includes a consideration of the motivations of different social groups in joining the rebellion.

Verdict

This is a strong answer because:

- the evidence covers the whole period

- the argument is clear and well focused throughout
- there is evidence of expert thinking in the prioritisation of causes.

Paper 1: A Level sample answer with comments

Section B

These questions assess your understanding of the period in breadth. They will ask you about the content you learned about in the four key themes, and may ask about more than one theme. For these questions, remember to:

- give an analytical, not a descriptive, response
- support your points with evidence
- cover the whole time period specified in the question
- come to a substantiated judgement.

How accurate is it to say that there were major changes to English industry and trade in the years 1551 to 1588? (20 marks)

Average student answer

It is partly accurate to say that there were major changes to English industry and trade from 1551. There were important changes to the wool and cloth industry. The growth of London and other important towns also led to the growth of new trades, as well as exploration. However, there were also other causes for change to English trade and industry, such as the decline of Antwerp as a market and social and economic hardship, especially in the 1550s and 1560s.

Industry and trade did change to a great extent after 1551. The most important changes to English industry and trade were developments in the wool and cloth trade. Before the 1550s, most English wool and cloth had been exported to Antwerp to be sold in the markets there. This trading focus began to change, however. Starting in 1551–52, there was a temporary slump in the English cloth trade caused by the cloth market being oversupplied, leading to a disastrous fall in prices. Although this was only a temporary change, a more permanent alteration occurred in the 1560s. The start of the Dutch revolt against Spanish rule caused serious disruption to the traditional English trading routes with Antwerp. Because English merchants could no longer rely on trade with Antwerp, they began to explore new markets for their goods. This was combined with the arrival of new techniques in cloth making that led to more diversity in the products made and in the development of new centres of industry in England. An example of these developments can be seen in the arrival of Dutch Protestant refugees who brought new weaving techniques with them. The refugees settled around the south-east and East Anglia and were actively encouraged by local authorities because of their skills. The refugees helped the development of 'new draperies', which were lighter but less durable cloths that could be sold to southern, Mediterranean markets away from Antwerp. The presence of the refugees also led to other new industries and trades developing such as the growth of flax for the new linen market centred around Maidstone. The need to find new foreign markets for English goods also led to more overseas exploration. This exploration was aided by the declining power of the Hanseatic League, which had dominated trade with the Baltic states before the 1550s. From the 1550s, expeditions funded by the new joint-stock companies opened up new trading routes with Russia, the Baltic states and Africa. These brought about changes in English trade; there was now a wider market for English goods. Exploration also opened up the possibility of colonisation and new luxury imports such as furs and silks. Therefore, there was considerable change in English trade and industry.

Another reason for the change in trade and industry after 1551 was the growth of London. London was important throughout the period because it was the largest town in England. As a port, it was a major trading centre and it was dominated by important trading companies such as the Merchant Adventurers. London's population had grown enormously during the period.

The introduction starts off focused on the question, which is the extent of change after 1551. However, the question has been misread as a multi-factor question. It could be improved with an explanation of why 1551 was an initial turning point and a consideration of the amount of change that happened after that date.

This paragraph is focused on the question of the extent of change. The material is precise, though it tends to reflect change in the earlier part of the period under discussion. It could be improved by consideration of the continuities that also existed in the wool and cloth trade after 1551. This would make the answer more balanced.

As it grew, so it needed more supplies to feed its population. This encouraged the growth of pastoral and arable farming in the south and east in order to meet the demand for food. London was also increasingly dominated by foreign trade, especially after it became easier to navigate the Thames. However, other towns also began to profit from new trading opportunities from the 1550s. New trading routes with the Baltic states benefited towns such as York and Hull. Also, the beginning of the transatlantic trade with the New World led to new opportunities for towns such as Exeter and Bristol as trading ports. There was also growth of new trades in other towns. For example, in the later part of the 16th century, Newcastle's wealth grew as a result of the development of the coal trade with London. The results of these changes were that towns such as Coventry, which had been in decline, began to recover as the population started to grow again. After the sudden population decline of the 1550s caused by disease, the population began to grow again in the 1570s and more people moved into towns in search of work. Increased population meant that there were increased opportunities for trade and industry to grow. Therefore, there was considerable change in domestic trade and industry from the 1550s which was caused by population growth and the development of new trading routes overseas.

> Although this paragraph does deal with changes to domestic trade and industry, there is some drift from the focus of the question away from the extent of change and towards causes of change. It could be improved by more focus on the lack of change in domestic industries, for example the continued reliance on the wool and cloth trade outside the south and east.

However, there were also other reasons trade and industry grew in the period from 1551. One reason for this growth was the new increase in population from the 1570s onwards. After a slump in population caused by an influenza epidemic and a series of poor harvests in the late 1550s, the upward trend in growth began again in the 1560s. In 1561, the population was about 2.98 million; by 1581 it was 3.59 million. This growth in population had important effects on trade and industry. Firstly, with more workers available, there was a move back into the towns that had become depopulated in the earlier part of the period. This stimulated towns and their industries to grow again. The arrival of the Dutch Protestant refugees also led to a regrowth in towns such as Norwich and also to the development of new industries such as hat-making.

A final reason for the growth of trade and industry was changes to the cloth trade and government intervention. The cloth trade was so dominant in the first half of the century that the Tudor government became worried about the effects of sheep farming and tried to intervene in order to restrict its growth. For example, in 1533 and 1549, Acts were introduced to restrict the sizes of flocks and to tax. The real causes of change to industry happened after 1551, first of all because of the temporary decline in the cloth trade with Antwerp. As the trade declined, so farmers who had made their living from sheep farming reverted to arable farming instead. At the same time, the population of towns began to grow again because there was less focus on sheep farming and cloth making. This led to the regrowth of towns and new industries from the 1560s.

> The focus of the answer has now moved away from the extent of change and the question is being answered as if it were a multi-factored question on the causes of change, which is not what the question asked.

In conclusion, English trade and industry changed considerably from the 1550s. The biggest changes were the developments that took place as a result of new exploration. English trade became less reliant on the Antwerp cloth market and found new trade routes with eastern and northern Europe, the Mediterranean and the Americas. There was also change in the types of goods being traded, with the introduction of new technologies. In particular, the impact of the Dutch refugees was very important in causing these changes to happen. Also important in causing change was the slump in the cloth market and changing social and economic conditions that stimulated growth after 1551. These conditions all led to considerable change in English trade and industry from 1551.

> The paragraph does in part answer the question, but it lacks balance because it only considers changes to trade and industry. It could be improved by also considering the lack of change after 1551.

Verdict

This is an average answer because:

- there is some lack of range in evidence with the focus mostly on the 1550s and 1560s
- the argument is unbalanced because while change is covered, there is no consideration of the extent of this change
- the judgement is not substantiated and does not deal with the extent of change.

Use the feedback on this answer to rewrite it, making as many improvements as you can.

Paper 1: A Level sample answer with comments

Section B

These questions assess your understanding of the period in breadth. They will ask you about the content you learned about in the four key themes, and may ask about more than one theme. For these questions, remember to:

- give an analytical, not a descriptive, response
- support your points with evidence
- cover the whole time period specified in the question
- come to a substantiated judgement.

How accurate is it to say that there were major changes to English industry and trade in the years 1551 to 1588? (20 marks)

Strong student answer

In some ways, it is accurate to say that there were some changes in England's trade and industry after 1551. From 1551 there was a decline in England's cloth trade with Antwerp and the emergence of new techniques in cloth making. Exploration funded by new joint-stock companies opened up new trading routes and led to the growing importance of towns such as York and Bristol as trading centres. Domestic trade and industry also saw developments, especially after the population began to recover from the 1570s. However, it would not be accurate to say that England's trade and industry underwent major changes as there were still continuities from the earlier period, especially in the importance of London as a trading centre and the types of industries that predominated.

> The introduction outlines the key points and addresses the question of the extent of change directly.

The main changes that occurred to the wool and cloth industry after 1551 were partly caused by events on the continent. From the early 1550s, there was a disastrous but temporary slump in the cloth market. Although the cloth market did recover under Elizabeth's reign and brought in £750,000 per year, there were other, more permanent, changes to this industry that occurred. These changes began in the 1560s and were brought about by the combined impact of the decline in the importance of Antwerp and the beginning of the Dutch revolt. This led to the beginning of English exploration, funded by the emergence of new joint-stock and regulated companies. Explorers such as Chancellor opened up a trading route with Moscow in 1555. Other expeditions led to the formation of new trading links in the Mediterranean, with African states and in the New World. For example, in 1585, the Barbary Company was set up to oversee trade with Morocco, where the luxury commodity sugar was traded for English cloth. In the 1560s, the privateer John Hawkins began the trade in slaves from Africa. These new trading routes meant that there were now new markets for English cloth and that the traditional trade with Antwerp declined after 1551. These new markets also led to the import of new goods into England, which supplied the growing demand for luxury goods including sugar, carpets and furs. A further development in this area was the collapse of the dominance of the Hanseatic League, which had monopolised trade with the Baltic states. This allowed English traders to find new markets for their goods in northern Europe. For example, English cloth was traded for flax and corn. The growth of this northern European trade also led to the re-emergence of York as a trading centre, a town that had previously been in decline. This evidence suggests that there were considerable changes in the wool and cloth trade after 1551. However, it is possible to overstate the case as there were also many continuities. For example, London remained the centre of English trade. Furthermore, although England was beginning to expand its trade in other goods such as lead and tin, the market was still dominated by the wool and cloth trade. By 1588, very little diversification had taken place into the manufacture of other goods for the overseas markets, which shows that there was very little overall change.

> This paragraph is well focused on the issues raised by the question because it deals with both change and continuity in the cloth trade, providing a balanced argument. Its use of examples is precise and it covers the whole date range of the question.

Although the overseas cloth trade still dominated the focus of English manufacturing, there were changes within the cloth trade itself that were also linked to the Dutch rebellion. As Spain tried to suppress Dutch Protestant resistance from the 1560s, refugees began to arrive in England, seeing it as a safe haven from persecution. Many of these Dutch Protestant refugees had expertise in the new techniques for the manufacture of cloth. This led to the growth of the 'new draperies' in England, and the setting up of workshops that specialised in these new techniques. The techniques included mixing woollen cloth with silk to create a lighter, brighter, but less durable cloth that was particularly attractive to countries with warmer climates, where English traders were trying to expand. The Dutch refugees settled in small towns around

> This paragraph provides balance and shows expert thinking because it identifies changes and continuities through its evaluation of the extent of change throughout England.

the south and east of England, including places such as Norwich and Canterbury, where they stimulated the growth of the cloth industry. The impact of the new draperies on trade and industry can be shown in the fact that by the end of the period they were bringing in £250,000 per year. However, the new draperies only created limited change to English trade and industry. The Dutch migrants tended to stay in the south and east of the country, so while these areas saw some change in manufacturing patterns, the west and north were unaffected by these changes. These areas continued to produce the traditional types of heavy English worsted and woven cloth in rural or small-town centres. This meant that they were more affected by the decline of the traditional cloth markets after 1551 and were slower to recover because they were less able to diversify. Therefore, it would be accurate to say that there were some changes to the English cloth trade after 1551, but these changes were regional and were not felt equally across the country.

Change was accelerated in the south and east by the arrival of the new draperies. From the 1570s, the population of England began to grow again, further stimulating the revival of towns such as Norwich, Ipswich and Bristol. This population growth led to the development of new urban industries and trade. The demand for more housing led to the growth of the domestic building trade. Members of the gentry also began to purchase town houses where they could live in more comfort during the winter. This group was a key consumer of luxury goods and their presence stimulated the growth of new trades such as wine making. The exploration and discovery of new trading routes meant that some trading ports that had been overshadowed by London earlier in the period began to find new purpose. York, for example, benefited from the new trade routes with the Baltic states while Bristol profited from new links with the Americas. Some towns began to develop their own industries and trades in order to feed the London domestic market. For example, Newcastle began to develop as an important northern town because of the growth of the coal-mining industry nearby. This coal was mined and sent for domestic consumption in the capital city. London itself also saw changes to its trade and industry. As the population of London continued to grow – it had a population of between 86,000 and 100,000 by the 1580s – it needed improved supply lines in order to support its population. As it was impossible for London's citizens to grow the necessary food to survive, the agricultural industry in the surrounding regions of East Anglia and Kent began to grow to supply the capital with meat, fish, grains and other produce. However, although these changes were important, in many ways they cannot be described as 'major'. London still remained the most dominant city. Its population by the end of the period was close to 100,000 – the next-biggest town was Norwich, which by the 1580s had a population of just 15,000. The sheer size of London compared to other towns meant that it continued to dominate as a centre for trade and industry. Although other towns such as York and Bristol were starting to make gains as trading centres, they could not compete with London. Furthermore, although there were developments in some industries such as coal mining and building, these were still dwarfed by the wool and cloth trade, which despite its temporary decline, still dominated production within England and its export trade abroad.

> This paragraph repeats some earlier points but is focused on the development of domestic trade and industry as opposed to overseas trade, thus adding balance to the argument.

It is not completely accurate to say that there were major changes to trade and industry in England from the 1550s, therefore. There were certainly important developments to the cloth trade in terms of overseas markets and the types of cloth that were being made. Exploration opened up new opportunities for towns and merchants to explore, but not all of these were successful or fully developed by the end of the period. London remained the dominant trading centre throughout the period and other towns were left trailing in its wake in terms of their trade and industry. Furthermore the changes were not seen across England. The south and east saw the most developments particularly with the new draperies, but the cloth industry in the north and west remained relatively untouched. It would be more accurate to say that there was some change to trade and industry, especially in the cloth trade, but this cannot be described as major because the underlying trends remained the same.

> The final judgement is well substantiated; it deals with the word 'major' and thus directly answers the question.

Verdict

This is a strong answer because:

- it deals explicitly with change, continuity and trends, showing critical and expert thinking

- the evidence covers the whole date range of the question
- the argument is balanced and the conclusion substantiated.

Paper 1: A Level sample answer with comments

Section C

These questions require you to read two extracts carefully to identify the key points raised and establish the argument being put forward. For these questions, remember to:

- read and analyse the extracts thoroughly, remembering that you need to use them together
- take careful note of the information provided about the extracts
- deploy your own knowledge to develop the points and arguments that emerge from the extracts and to provide appropriate context
- develop an argument rooted in the points raised in the extracts, and come to a substantiated conclusion.

In the light of differing interpretations, how convincing do you find the view that the growth of faction led to genuine political instability in England? To explain your answer, analyse and evaluate the material in Extracts 3 and 4 in Chapter 5, using your knowledge of the issues. (20 marks)

Average student answer

In the 1590s, two factions developed at Elizabeth's court, one led by William and Robert Cecil and the other the Earl of Essex. The Cecils tended to want peace with England's European neighbours or at most a war that would not cost England too much in terms of money, men or equipment. The Earl of Essex, who was much younger than the elderly queen and was one of her favourites, wanted war. He saw himself as the political heir to his stepfather, the Earl of Leicester, as a protector of Protestantism. The Cecils and Essex also clashed over access to the queen and patronage as well as their power at court. They were constantly arguing and this created tensions and even led to Essex's rebellion because he was angry at his treatment. As Loades says, Essex became an over-mighty subject and so was very dangerous to Elizabeth.

In some ways, faction was very dangerous to Elizabeth. As she grew older, she was less able to control the men around her. Plus, all her trusted advisers, such as Walsingham and Leicester, had died and the new generation of councillors were more interested in planning for the succession and their own interests than in serving her loyally. William Cecil was one of the few councillors left to Elizabeth who had a long history of loyal service, but he too was growing old and was starting to focus on securing the position of his younger son, Robert, as Elizabeth's chief minister. Meanwhile, the young Earl of Essex, who was handsome, athletic and good at flattering Elizabeth, had started to rise to prominence. Elizabeth liked the attention and commentators noted that she would spend hours with Essex. Essex was ambitious, however, and wanted power at court, but Elizabeth was not prepared to oblige him. Instead, she increasingly focused her grants of patronage on the Cecils. This meant that Essex and his followers were left out and their resentment grew, which led to political instability, as Loades argues when he says that Essex's 'hatred of Cecil had become an obsession … his strike against Cecil could have caused a dangerous insurrection.' In 1600–01, Essex was so resentful of the power of the Cecils and the attitude of the queen that he first left Ireland without orders to do so, argued with the queen and drew his sword on her, and then tried to stage an armed uprising using his 'popularity among the common people'. This was very serious because it could have led to a more widespread uprising against the queen. Essex had the support of Southampton, Rutland and others who were also angry at being excluded from power. Their rebellion came dangerously close to treason and was only unsuccessful because they did not get any real support from the Londoners or other members of the court.

The introduction does not address the specific question of whether faction led to 'genuine political instability'. It tends to a narrative overview and only mentions one of the extracts at the very end. It could be improved by addressing the debate in the extracts and outlining the main arguments of the essay.

This paragraph is more focused on the threat to Elizabeth than to political stability – these are not quite the same thing. One of the extracts is mentioned, but its claims are not developed by reference to knowledge of events that might support Loades' views such as the idea that this court faction was angry to the point of rebellion because it was largely excluded from patronage and high office, while the Cecils dominated through their control of the secretaryship.

However, the extract presents a different view of how dangerous factions were to Elizabeth. Guy agrees with Loades that there were serious problems caused by the rivalry between Essex and the Cecils and that Elizabeth was no longer in a position to control the men around her. Guy also agrees that the rivalry was about religion. For example, Essex and his ally Mountjoy were keen to ensure a Protestant succession and reopened secret negotiations with James VI of Scotland, which was technically treason. They even suggested that Mountjoy raise an army in Ireland in support of James to force Elizabeth to name him as her heir. Essex and the Cecils also fell out over patronage, causing political instability as a result of their rivalry for power. The Cecils used their position of influence with the queen to ensure that their friends and supporters were appointed to key positions, such as the Bacon brothers. The Cecils also ensured that the rich Cobham inheritance was distributed to their clients, which angered Essex even more. But Essex was not without support; he had 12 deputy Lord Lieutenants in his faction. As Guy argues, however, there were limits to the threat that Essex posed. In reality, his power was based solely on access to the queen and her favour. He had little real power or influence in England apart from this, whereas the Cecils controlled the main offices at court and were also major landowners. Essex was further weakened by his financial situation. His finances were reliant on the queen's favour and when she withdrew his monopoly on sweet wine he was left in debt and without a proper income. Although Essex was able to gather supporters in 1601, such as Southampton, he was not actually very popular and was not able to rouse the Londoners to support him, meaning that his revolt was a fiasco and easily put down. In the end, as Guy argues, Essex was not really a threat to Elizabeth at all, and with him out of the way, Robert Cecil was able to dominate politics without any real rivals.

In conclusion, the development of faction in the 1590s did not really pose a threat to Elizabeth or to political stability. The Cecils had all the real power, as Guy argues, and their power and influence caused resentment, but not enough to cause the sort of 'political instability' that would lead to civil war. Also, while Essex appeared to be powerful, he was too reliant on the queen. When she withdrew her favour, he was left with nothing and his attempted rebellion did not attract widespread popular support, which meant that there was no real political instability even when there was a noble uprising.

> This paragraph has more relevant contextual detail to develop the point in the second extract, although some of this might have been better in the first paragraph. The evidence that the threat to political instability was not as serious as it might have been could be better developed by reference to Essex's lack of real landed power and that even his own allies deserted him when it came to the possibility of rebelling.

> There is an attempted judgement that does try to argue a point of view, but it is not well explained or supported. It also attempts to address the issue of the threat to political stability, but this has not been clearly defined or developed during the answer.

Verdict

This is an average answer because:

- it lacks sustained focus on the specific question
- it identifies some of the key points in the sources, but it lacks the specific illustration and explanation needed for a proper debate
- there is some development of the topic, but the evidence is not always well selected or fully developed

- there is an attempt to weigh up the argument and reach a conclusion, but the essay lacks the overall development to allow a substantiated judgement to be reached.

Use the feedback on this answer to rewrite it, making as many improvements as you can.

Paper 1: A Level sample answer with comments

Section C

These questions require you to read two extracts carefully to identify the key points raised and establish the argument being put forward. For these questions, remember to:

- read and analyse the extracts thoroughly, remembering that you need to use them together
- take careful note of the information provided about the extracts
- deploy your own knowledge to develop the points and arguments that emerge from the extracts and to provide appropriate context
- develop an argument rooted in the points raised in the extracts, and come to a substantiated conclusion.

In the light of differing interpretations, how convincing do you find the view that the growth of faction led to genuine political instability in England? To explain your answer, analyse and evaluate the material in Extracts 3 and 4 in Chapter 5, using your knowledge of the issues. (20 marks)

Strong student answer

Taken as a set, both sources agree to some extent that the growth of faction in the 1590s caused political instability. However, they disagree as to the extent and seriousness of this instability. There is therefore some doubt as to whether the instability was 'genuine' or merely superficial tensions. Both Guy and Loades agree that there were problems at court because an ageing queen could no longer manage the ambitious men around her who were looking to the future and the next monarch. They also agree that the Cecil faction was allowed to dominate at the expense of other groups such as Essex and his followers. However, they disagree about the extent to which these tensions led to genuine instability. Loades sees Essex's revolt as a very serious response to growing factional tensions that could have led to a 'dangerous insurrection' by a traditional 'over-mighty subject'. While not denying that tensions existed, Guy casts doubt on whether they would lead to 'genuine political instability' as Essex lacked any real power to cause trouble. Ultimately, the debate can be resolved by considering what is meant by 'genuine political instability', which can be defined as tensions serious enough to challenge the queen's power or throne or lead to popular rebellion throughout England.

> The extracts are considered together. The phrase 'genuine political instability' is defined and there is a clear sense that the response is engaging with the debate in the extracts.

In some ways, the growth of factions did lead to genuine political instability as a result of rivalry between the Cecils and Essex. As Guy argues, 'by the late 1590s their feud had escalated into a factional battle to control her policy. The atmosphere at court deteriorated; for the first time in her reign the queen was on the side-lines.' Loades supports this view in his claim that 'his [Essex's] hatred for Cecil had become an obsession'. Both authors also agree that part of the problem was that Elizabeth was growing older and was no longer able to manage potential rivalries as well as she had once been able to do. Most of her loyal councillors had died by 1589, for example Walsingham and Leicester. Only William Cecil was left, and he was growing old and preparing to hand over his power to his son, Robert. Elizabeth's personality also exacerbated the situation. Elizabeth was very vain and increasingly conscious of her age, so that she was easily flattered by ambitious young men such as Essex. Indeed, contemporaries commented on the amount of time Essex and the queen spent together, which would have caused jealousy among Essex's rivals, the Cecils, who were denied such intimate access. The queen's age and refusal to name a successor also added to the tensions between the factions. The race between the Cecilians and Essexians to secure their own candidate's claim to the throne led both sides to come dangerously close to treason as they negotiated behind the queen's back.

> This paragraph develops the claims in both extracts that there was serious instability caused by faction, which led to both sides committing treason. The paragraph is closely focused on the question and there is some development from own knowledge.

Faction had become a destabilising influence at court to the extent that both sides were more focused on securing their own future and destroying their rivals than they were on serving Elizabeth.

However, it is debatable whether the factional rivalry over the succession led to 'genuine' political instability. Loades claims that the dangerous nature of Essex's revolt in 1601 'went to the very brink of treason', which could have caused 'a dangerous insurrection' if it had been managed more effectively. Guy does not go as far as this, however, arguing that Essex 'lacked Leicester's private patronage', and failed 'to win royal patronage for his followers'. Guy is implying that Essex did not have any real power, and the influence he did have was superficial because it was based entirely on Elizabeth's favour and being continually present at court in order to win grants of patronage for himself and his followers. Guy's argument is convincing when the evidence is examined. Although Essex was a councillor from 1593 and was also a Lord Lieutenant, his actual power was limited, especially when compared to the Cecils. William Cecil had spent years building up a web of connections in the court and localities using his position as Lord Treasurer and Master of the Court of Wards. Robert Cecil was able to enhance the Cecils' power base when he became secretary. These positions gave the Cecils access to patronage in a way that Essex did not have. Furthermore, Essex's own interests as a military man meant that he was out of the country for long periods of time such as his expeditions to Cádiz and Ireland. So he could not use his personal influence at court to secure positions for his supporters. As Guy argues, 'His supporters increasingly complained that he could get anything for himself but nothing for his friends.' Essex's lack of ability to extend his support base meant that when he tried to rebel in 1601 he found himself lacking in support – he only had 140 men with him on his abortive march on Whitehall. He also failed to gain more popular support in London, which meant that his attempt to capture the queen was a failure. Essex's political weakness and lack of support in 1600–01 suggest that although faction had grown and was partly responsible for his attempted rebellion, ultimately the challenge posed by Essex was not an example of 'genuine' political stability.

> This paragraph develops Guy's counter-argument about the level of threat posed by Essex's rebellion. There is good support from own knowledge and an attempt to deal with the word 'genuine'.

In other ways, however, it could be argued that faction did lead to genuine political instability, although not to the point where it would lead to deposition of the queen or civil war. Both Guy and Loades recognise the impact that the growth of faction had on politics in the 1590s, although Guy argues that the tensions only really became apparent in the second half of the decade. Both extracts emphasise that the growth of faction led to the development of ideological differences at court and within the queen's Council and imply that these tensions were new to the 1590s, where previously, the Elizabeth's reign had been remarkably free from faction fighting. Loades supports this argument that Essex was keen 'to secure the Protestant cause', particularly in 1600–01. Meanwhile, the Cecils preferred a more cautious policy of defensive war, which was more in alignment with what the queen herself preferred. These disagreements had the potential to create political instability because it meant that the queen's councillors were not united behind her and would even disobey orders in an attempt to prove themselves and gain an advantage over their rivals.

Therefore, although Loades emphasises the potential threat to political stability caused by Essex's revolt, in reality Essex did not have the power or followers to mount a successful challenge to Elizabeth's power and so was not a 'genuine' threat. In other ways, however, the growth of faction did undermine the overall stability of the court and effectively turned Elizabeth into a 'puppet' of faction rather than the 'puppet-master'. As Guy argues, these tensions became much worse in the second half of the 1590s when William Cecil's influence diminished. The rivalries between factions caused genuine political instability in the sense that Elizabeth's power was undermined and she was no longer in control of politics and patronage to the extent that she had been earlier in the reign.

> The conclusion is substantiated by the evidence used throughout the argument. There is awareness of the similarities and differences between the extracts and an attempt to resolve the debate between them.

Verdict

This is a strong answer because:

- the extracts are used together and there is awareness of the similarities and differences between them
- own knowledge is deployed to expand or support the extracts' claims and is fully integrated in the answer
- it develops an argument that considers both interpretations and tries to provide balance
- there is a clear judgement.

Luther and the German Reformation, c1515–55

The German Reformation of the early 16th century is one of the key turning points in European history. It caused the disintegration of the religious unity of Europe that had lasted for a thousand years. In much of northern Europe Roman Catholicism lost ground to Protestant churches, while national identity and patriotism were soon defined in religious terms. Germany, Scotland, the Netherlands and France all descended into religious wars and political upheavals, and England experienced a roller coaster of religious change. The repercussions were not limited to religion and politics. Separate Catholic and Protestant traditions developed in scholarship, education, church architecture, literature, art and music.

SOURCE

1

Hans Holbein the Younger, *Luther as the German Hercules*, c1523. In this Protestant woodcut, a lean Luther is depicted as the hero Hercules, energetically slaying the enemies of Germany. He grips the pope with his teeth while he strangles the Dominican inquisitor Jacob van Hoogstraaten, who presided over the first-ever execution of Lutherans in 1523 in Cologne. On the ground, bludgeoned to death with his Herculean club, lie Luther's other victims – Aristotle, Thomas Aquinas, William of Ockham and Peter Lombard – men whose thoughts and works had dominated European thought for centuries.

Martin Luther writes the 95 Theses	1517
Charles V elected Holy Roman Emperor Leipzig Debates	1519
Edict of Worms *Loci Communes*	1521
Luther's New Testament published	1522
Recess of Speyer	1526
Siege of Vienna	1529
Schmalkaldic League formed	1531
Regensburg Colloquy	1541
Death of Luther	1546
Peace of Passau Siege of Metz	1552

The focus of this option is Martin Luther, the man who triggered the German Reformation. A German friar and university lecturer, Luther might have lived out his life in complete obscurity had he not ventured, in late 1517, to challenge one point of Catholic theology.

Quite why Luther's initial protest should have been so enthusiastically received is open to dispute. However, conditions in Germany were such that he had a remarkably receptive audience, and a very powerful weapon in the newly developed printing press.

The extraordinary response he experienced (coupled with some inept handling from those in authority) helped to turn Luther from a loyal son of the Church into a reluctant rebel, and pushed him to widen the scope of his protest and elaborate his ideas. In the ensuing soup of religious anarchy, a separate, reformed 'Lutheran' Church emerged in Germany during the 1520s and 1530s.

SOURCE

Luther as a Winesack, unknown Bohemian artist, c1620–30. This Catholic image of Luther portrays him as an obese drunkard who has lecherously married a nun. He carries as trophies the heads of those whom he has deceived into adopting his heretical views.

1518	Debate with Cajetan
1521	Excommunication of Luther Three pamphlets
1521-22	Luther in Wartburg Castle
1524-25	Peasants' Revolt
1527	Sack of Rome
1530	Augsburg Confession
1540	Philip of Hesse and the bigamy scandal
1545	First meeting of the Council of Trent
1546-47	Schmalkaldic Wars Battle of Mühlberg
1555	Peace of Augsburg Abdication of Charles V

2a.1 Conditions in early 16th century Germany

KEY QUESTIONS

- Why was central government so weak in Germany?
- How healthy was the economy?
- Was the German Catholic Church in need of reform?
- Why was there so much hostility towards the papacy?

INTRODUCTION

EXTRACT

1 From Henry J. Cohn, in *The European World*, edited by Beat Kümin (2009).

In the 'Holy Roman Empire of the German Nation' the Reformation took hold rapidly and with greater early popular support than in other European countries. This head start cannot be solely explained in terms of the charismatic popularity of Martin Luther. In all eras outstanding leaders require favourable conditions to persuade large populations to change their outlook on the world.

Luther made his initial protest in 1517; by 1521, one observer reported that, 'Nine out of ten cry Luther'. A key reason for his almost immediate success lies in the context – the 'favourable conditions' – in which he made his protest, rather than what he was actually saying. Politically, the lack of a strong central authority in the empire meant that Germany was more open than any other state in Europe to financial exploitation by Rome. This helps to explain the level of nationalistic, anti-papal anger that existed even prior to 1517, a situation that Luther was able to capitalise on. Anger at clerical abuses and the power and privileges of the Church added to the tension and was fuelled by humanist literature, deep piety and a belief that the world was about to end. A holy man was even expected. The inability of the Emperor Charles V to silence Luther can be explained by the political make-up of the empire: he did not have sufficient direct power to do much anyway, while to get elected he had been forced to make important concessions to the electors that effectively tied his hands even more. Indeed, conditions were so 'favourable' that it is doubtful whether Luther would have succeeded in any other place.

1480s – Reform of the Diet; creation of the Swabian League

1493 – Maximilian I becomes emperor

1495–1512 – Imperial courts are established and Germany is divided into 'circles'

| 1480 | 1482 | 1484 | 1486 | 1488 | 1490 | 1492 | 1494 | 1496 | 1498 | 1500 |

1490s on – Germans fear the imminent end of the world

1500 – Birth of Maximilian's grandson, Charles V

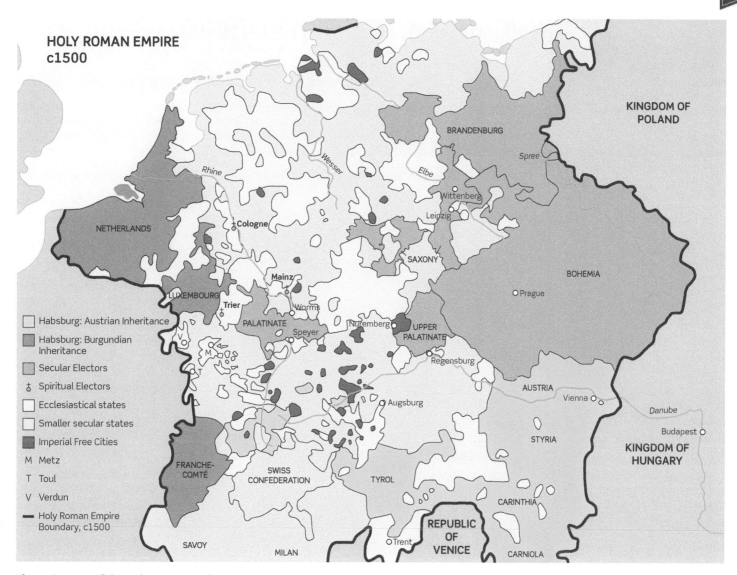

HOLY ROMAN EMPIRE
c1500

KINGDOM OF
POLAND

BRANDENBURG

Wesser   *Elbe*   *Spree*

Rhine

Wittenberg

Leipzig

NETHERLANDS

Cologne

SAXONY

BOHEMIA

Prague

Mainz

LUXEMBOURG

Trier

Worms

PALATINATE

Speyer   Nuremberg   UPPER
PALATINATE

Regensburg

AUSTRIA

Vienna

Danube

STYRIA

KINGDOM OF
HUNGARY

Budapest

Augsburg

☐ Habsburg: Austrian Inheritance
☐ Habsburg: Burgundian
     Inheritance
☐ Secular Electors
♟ Spiritual Electors
☐ Ecclesiastical states
☐ Smaller secular states
☐ Imperial Free Cities
M Metz
T Toul
V Verdun
— Holy Roman Empire
     Boundary, c1500

FRANCHE-
COMTÉ

SWISS
CONFEDERATION

TYROL

CARINTHIA

CARNIOLA

SAVOY

MILAN

Trent

REPUBLIC
OF
VENICE

Figure 1.1 Map of the Holy Roman Empire c1500.

1503 – Erasmus publishes *The Handbook of a Christian Soldier*

1503 – Julius II becomes pope

1515 – Leo X decides to raise money for the rebuilding of St Peter's by issuing an indulgence. He arranges for Albert of Mainz to organise the sale of the indulgence in the empire. Albert employs Johann Tetzel as his chief salesman

1515–17 – *Letters of Obscure Men* is published, ridiculing the Church

1517 – Tetzel reaches the border of Electoral Saxony

| 1502 | 1504 | 1506 | 1508 | 1510 | 1512 | 1514 | 1516 | 1518 | 1520 |

1509 – Erasmus publishes *In Praise of Folly*, attacking clerical abuses

1513 – Leo X becomes pope

1514 – *Julius Exclusus* is published, ridiculing the late pope

1516 – Erasmus publishes his Greek New Testament

1519 – The imperial election – Charles V becomes emperor

WHAT WAS THE HOLY ROMAN EMPIRE?

In 1500, the **Holy Roman Empire** was vast: it covered all of central Europe, including modern Germany, Austria, Switzerland, Luxembourg, Belgium, the Netherlands, the Czech Republic and Slovakia, as well as land that is now in eastern France, western Poland and northern Italy.

The empire was not a single country. Rather, it resembled an extremely challenging jigsaw puzzle, with over 390 pieces of different sizes and shapes. Excluding Switzerland (which had won independence in 1499), and Belgium, the Netherlands and northern Italy (which were all only nominally part of the empire by 1500), these pieces included:

- 46 ecclesiastical states, ruled by the 'prince bishops', the six archbishops and 40 bishops of the empire
- 26 large secular states, ruled by the 'princes', including one king (Bohemia), one archduke (Austria), one landgrave (Hesse), five margraves, one prince, and 17 dukes
- about 60 small ecclesiastical states ruled by lesser prelates
- about 150 small secular states ruled by counts and lesser lords
- about 65 imperial cities, run by city councils and owing allegiance directly to the emperor and not to any other prince.

The jigsaw was made even more complex by the fact that boundaries between these states and cities were seldom logical. An imperial city might be located within the borders of another state, for example. To add to the confusion, there were about 600 imperial knights. In the Middle Ages, these knights numbered over 10,000 and had played a crucial and proud role as the heavy cavalry of medieval armies. By 1500, the pride remained, but their military role was largely redundant and many led impoverished lives in dilapidated castles.

The structure of central government

These states and cities each ruled themselves and fiercely guarded their individual liberties and privileges. Some of the greater princes lived as kings and had developed extensive courts: the Margrave of Brandenburg had a court of 200, and the Elector of Saxony employed a court artist, Lucas Cranach the Elder. However, even the greatest of the princes did not want *total* independence, as most states were too small to be safe on their own. To provide defence against external threats (particularly from France or the Ottoman Empire) and to prevent internal conflict, they all accepted the need for some sort of central organisation and a single leader with an umbrella-like overview. In other words, they needed some imperial institutions and they wanted an emperor. However, what power these should hold was a source of ongoing debate and tension: central government had to be strong enough to fulfil its functions – defence, law and order – but not so strong that it undermined the autonomy of the states and cities.

The emperor

Leadership of the empire was provided by the Holy Roman Emperor. Unlike the kings of England or France, the emperor did not inherit his position: he was elected by the seven **electors**. In theory, any prince could stand for election. In practice, however, the position had gone to a member of the Habsburg family since 1437. This made sense: as the biggest landowners in the empire, the Habsburgs were the only family rich enough for the post, and their Austrian lands provided a buffer against threats from the Ottoman Empire.

From 1493 to 1519, Maximilian I was emperor. He had many great qualities: he was cultured, charming, brave and generous. Unfortunately he was also indecisive. According to the Venetian Ambassador, Maximilian was guilty of flitting from one scheme to another but settling on none. If he focused on anything it was improving the fortunes of his family, the House of Habsburg, through expensive wars in Italy and shrewd marriage alliances. At least the latter were successful: he had married Mary the Rich, heiress to the Duchy of Burgundy, in 1477. Then Maximilian organised for his son Philip the Fair to marry Joanna of Castile (the sister of Catherine of Aragon), and his grandchildren later married into the royal houses of Portugal, Hungary and Denmark. He established a dynasty that lasted 400 years. However, he failed to strengthen his position as emperor.

SOURCE

The Emperor Maximilian in about 1515, on the left, with his grandchildren Ferdinand, Charles (in the middle) and Mary (though this may in fact be an image of her betrothed, Louis of Hungary, who was the adopted son of Maximilian). Behind the children stand their father, Philip the Fair, who had died in 1506, and their grandmother, Mary the Rich, who had died in 1482. This was painted by Maximilian's favourite German artist, Bernhard Strigel.

What power did the emperor and the princes have?

The position of emperor came with a great deal of honour and status: in theory, the emperor was the secular head of Christendom, and was meant to use his political power to defend the Roman Catholic Church. The post commanded respect, and certainly all the middling princes, knights and cities looked to the emperor for protection against the great princes.

In reality, however, the post held remarkably little power. There was no salary. There was no imperial army. There was no effective system of imperial taxation or indeed any system of imperial coinage. The emperor could raise troops to defend the empire, but only with the electors' permission. He could raise the money he needed for those troops, but had to ask the diet (or parliament), which was dominated by the princes, for the right to tax. He could arbitrate in disputes between states, but only if asked by the princes. He could propose reforms, but he had no right to directly intervene in the internal affairs of any of the states or cities in the empire.

Lacking a central executive and a central army, and faced with almost insurmountable communication difficulties, the emperor had to rely on the princes to implement the decisions of the diets and to enforce law and order in the circles. The princes' willingness to co-operate was entirely self-interested: they were only helpful if a measure did not threaten their own power or their own territory.

The imperial diet

The key institution of central government in the empire was the imperial diet. This consisted of three 'colleges' or estates: one for the electors, a second (newly established in 1480) for the other ecclesiastical and secular princes, and a third (even newer, having only been established in 1489) for representatives from the imperial cities, though the latter did not achieve voting rights until 1648. The diet only met when it was summoned by the emperor. However, since the emperor could only raise taxes or troops or address national concerns by going through the diet, this happened reasonably frequently. Ten diets met between 1501 and 1521; 18 met between 1521 and 1555. The empire had no capital city, so each diet was known after the town or city where it met. Charles V's first diet, for example, met in the small town of Worms, which is why it is known as the Diet of Worms.

When a diet did meet, a standard procedure was followed.

- The emperor's propositions were read out.

- The colleges then met separately to discuss and vote on these (voting was as complex as the empire itself: the electors each had a single vote, for example, while lesser counts shared collective votes).

- The colleges then passed their views and recommendations back to the emperor, while also raising grievances or concerns of their own.

- If the emperor and the diet were in agreement, their conclusions were published as a 'recess', which, it was agreed in 1512, should be binding on everyone, even if they had not attended the diet or had no vote or had disagreed.

Decisions made by the diet were then transmitted to the circles to be implemented. That was the theory. Of course, it only worked if the interests of the emperor and the princes happened to coincide.

The circles

In the period 1500–12, the empire was divided into ten 'circles', each consisting of a number of states and cities. Five of the circles were dominated by just one or two territories: Bavaria dominated the Bavarian Circle, for example, while the Austrian Circle was composed only of Habsburg lands. Another of the circles was made up of the four electors with lands on the River Rhine (Mainz, Cologne, Trier and the Palatinate). A further four circles were made up of multiple states. The Swabian Circle, for example, was composed of the many tiny cities and states in the south-western corner of the empire.

The purpose of these circles was regional co-ordination. Each circle had an assembly with representatives drawn from all the member states, and this assembly was then meant to enforce decisions taken by the diet, to collect taxes and supervise coinage, and to settle disputes between member states. If a dispute could not be settled, it was referred up to the Imperial Cameral Court, the judges for which were drawn from all of the circles. The circles had another function: raising troops, which might be needed for local peacekeeping or might be requested by the emperor for national defence. Within a circle, a military force was raised on a quota system, with small states providing just a few soldiers, and large ones many.

The Swabian League

In practice, the only effective armed force in the empire was the Swabian League. Created in 1488 by Maximilian's father, the Swabian League originally had the function of securing law and order in the south-west. Its members were initially all local small rulers – Swabian nobles and knights, counts and 22 local imperial cities, but by the early 16th century some ten princes had joined. The Swabian League was the closest thing there was to an imperial army, and Maximilian used its 13,000 troops to crush expansionist attacks being made by Bavaria in 1504, and to evict Ulrich of Württemberg in January 1519.

EXTEND YOUR KNOWLEDGE

Duke Ulrich of Württemberg (1487–1550)
Duke Ulrich was an unpleasant, egotistical man. He taxed his people so oppressively that he caused a peasant revolt in 1514. His personal life was scandalous. In 1511, he had married Sabina, niece of the Emperor Maximilian and daughter of the Duke of Bavaria, but the marriage was an unhappy one. Ulrich then fell in love with the wife of a knight named Hans von Hutten (cousin of the humanist, Ulrich von Hutten), and in 1515 he killed Hans. Sabina fled, and Maximilian declared Ulrich an outlaw. In 1519, the Swabian League drove him from Württemberg, which was sold to Charles V. The entire episode was a rare example of princes working together. Ironically, some of the same princes helped to restore him to Württemberg in the 1530s.

Central courts

Every state and city in the empire had its own laws and there was no common legal system. Because of this, it made sense to have a supreme court of sorts to act as an ultimate arbiter in settling those disputes between states, or within a state between a prince and his subjects, that could not be settled at circle level. It is a measure of how much distrust there was between the princes and Maximilian that two rival courts of appeal existed by 1500, one dominated by the princes and the other by the emperor:

- The Imperial Chamber Court: established in 1495, this was based in Frankfurt. Although the emperor chose the chief justice and several deputies, the princes, via the circles, selected the 20 judges.

- The Imperial Aulic Court: established in 1498 (because Maximilian resented the amount of princely power in the Imperial Chamber Court), this was based in Vienna, in the heart of Habsburg territories.

Conclusion

In the four decades preceding Martin Luther's outburst in 1517, a great deal had been done to improve regional co-ordination and central government – the circles had been set up, the Swabian League and the central courts had been established, the diet was meeting regularly and included colleges for lesser princes and cities. Arguably, Germany was more politically united than it had been for centuries. Even a new title – the Holy Roman Empire 'of the German Nation' – had been adopted, reflecting a new sense of 'German-ness'. This new sense of national identity was helped by another political development, the loss in the previous 50 years of many of the non-German parts of the empire.

An incidental consequence of this was that German was increasingly used as the sole language for business and administration, while German history became a new focus for attention in universities, and the double-headed black eagle, symbol of the empire, was increasingly displayed with pride.

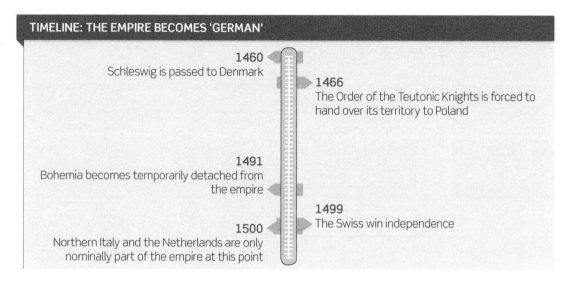

In a period of rapid change, however, one thing remained the same: the lack of a strong central authority in the empire. This mattered because it meant that Germany was more open than any other state in Europe to financial exploitation by Rome. It also mattered because it meant that the emperor lacked the power to implement change, or indeed to stop change.

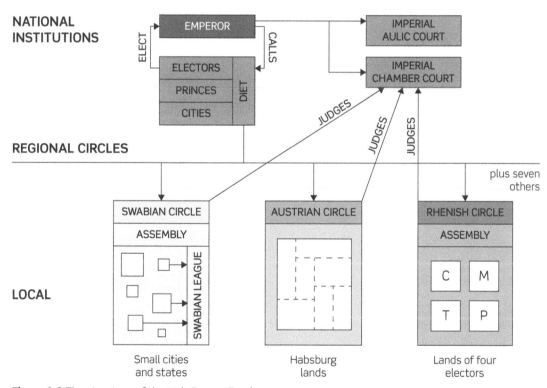

Figure 1.2 The structure of the Holy Roman Empire.

The imperial election of 1519

Maximilian died in January 1519. Characteristically, he had not pre-organised the election of his grandson Charles. He had not even finished his own tomb. The 19-year-old Charles was therefore forced to compete for the title of emperor against King Francis I of France.

Almost by accident, Charles was the most powerful man in Europe by 1519. As the oldest surviving male on both sides of his family, his inheritance at a young age was vast.

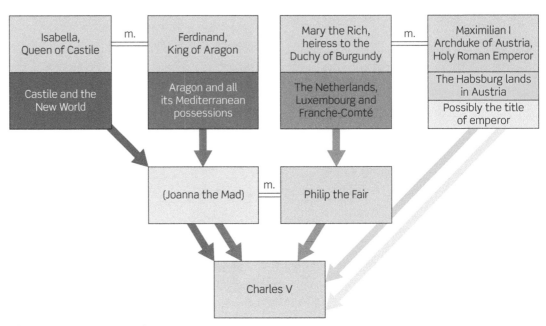

Figure 1.3 Charles' antecedents.

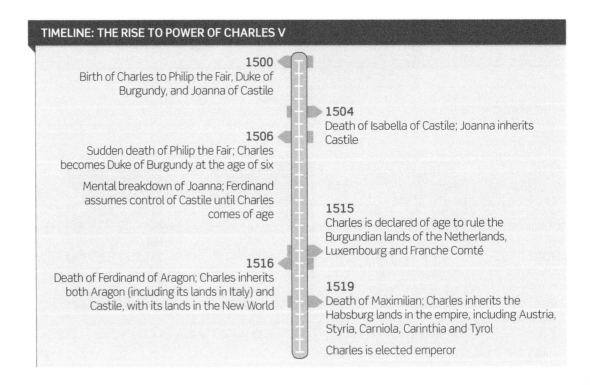

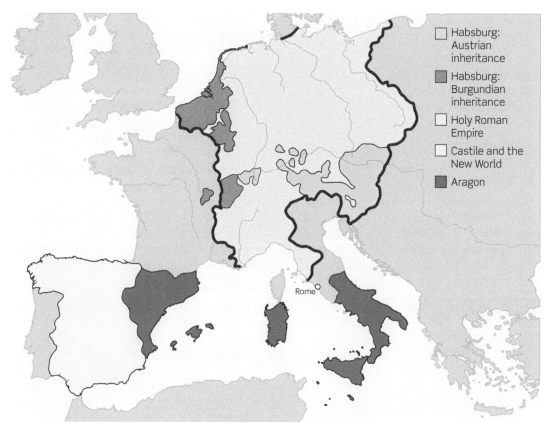

Figure 1.4 Map showing the location of Charles' inheritance in 1519. The areas within the bold black line make up the Holy Roman Empire.

Charles' success in the imperial election of 1519 was not a foregone conclusion. The electors were concerned. Would Charles use resources from his vast inheritance *outside* the empire to strengthen his position *inside* the empire? Would he use German resources to help him solve problems in his other territories? Spain was then in revolt, and such a thought was not out of the question. Pope Leo X was even more concerned because, if Charles added the empire to his Aragonese inheritance, Charles would dominate the Italian peninsula. Leo tried to persuade the elector Frederick the Wise of Saxony to stand as a sort of compromise candidate, but Frederick declined the honour.

Despite their reservations, the electors did finally decide on Charles, and he was formally elected in June 1519.

Why did the electors choose Charles?

- Because Charles handed out the largest bribes (850,000 florins), money he had to borrow.

- Because Charles was a Habsburg, and as the greatest landowner in the empire, he would be most likely to defend Germany against external threats, especially from the **Ottoman Empire**.

- Because, given the rest of his inheritance, Charles was likely to be absent most of the time, and therefore less likely to challenge the princes' power.

- Because a French candidate would be unwelcome in the empire, given its new sense of German national identity.

- Because the Swabian League surrounded the town where the electors were meeting and made it clear that it favoured Charles, and not the French king.

- Because Charles agreed to sign the **Capitulation of 1519**. Worried about Charles' potential strength, the electors made this a condition of election.

KEY TERMS

Ottoman Empire
By 1519, the Ottoman Empire covered much of what is now Turkey, the Balkans, the Middle East and the North African coast. The possibility of further Ottoman expansion alarmed Europe so much that it was gripped by a 'Great Fear'.

Capitulation of 1519
Charles promised:

- to respect the rights and privileges of the princes

- to consult the electors and the diet on all imperial matters

- to use only Latin or German when in the empire

- not to appoint foreigners to imperial positions

- not to bring any foreign troops into the empire

- not to declare war without the consent of the electors.

How did the imperial election help Luther?

As we shall see, the election of 1519 had three repercussions that help to explain Luther's survival.

- Hoping to win the goodwill of the elector Frederick the Wise, the pope had agreed that Luther did not have to travel to Rome for interrogation, where he might well have been executed.

- In signing the capitulation, Charles weakened the position of the emperor still further: he could only work through the electors and the diet to deal with Luther, and he was honourable enough to abide by that agreement for 30 years.

- In choosing Charles, the electors had selected someone they knew would be absent from the empire for lengthy periods of time. Charles' vast inheritance came with multiple problems and enemies, and he rarely had the time to focus on the empire's issues.

ACTIVITY
KNOWLEDGE CHECK

Unification and central government

1 How unified was Germany (the Holy Roman Empire) by 1519?

Tip: Balance your answer and consider factors that unified Germany, as well as those that kept it divided.

2 Was the weakness of central government in Germany a positive or a negative thing?

Tip: Consider those who benefited from a weak central government, but also any problems that ensued.

HOW HEALTHY WAS THE ECONOMY?

In all of the great political upheavals of the last 200 years, the state of the economy has played a decisive role. Hitler, for example, only achieved electoral success because of the Great Depression, while both the French and the Russian Revolutions were triggered by a collapsing economy and food shortages. It therefore makes sense to look at Germany's economy in the early 16th century, in case it too suggests that trouble was imminent. There were three main factors impacting on the economy in Germany in this period.

- **Population growth**. Germany's population rose from about 12 million in 1500 to 15 million in 1550, equivalent to about 0.7 percent growth per annum, or 25 percent over the period. This reflects relatively peaceful times in the empire and the absence of serious epidemics.

- **Growing towns and cities**. There were some 4,000 towns and cities in the empire. In 1500, only a few of these were of any great size, including: Cologne 45,000 (seat of the archbishop-elector); Nuremberg 38,000 (home of the artist Albrecht Dürer); Augsburg 20,000 (home of Jakob Fugger); and Vienna 20,000 (capital of the Habsburgs' Austrian lands). Some towns expanded exceptionally rapidly in the early 16th century: Augsburg's population had doubled from 20,000 to 40,000 by 1550.

- **Inflation**. From about 1530, prices started to rise steeply. Wages rarely kept up. For example, in the town of Speyer, wages trebled between 1521 and 1621, but at the same time the price of rye, wheat and beans – the staple foodstuffs – increased by between 13 and 15 times.

In fact, many sectors of the empire's economy were thriving in the early 16th century. The silver-mining industry located in Saxony, Bohemia and the Tyrol, for example, was particularly successful: output increased fivefold in the 70 years to 1530. Until the discovery of New World silver deposits, Germany's mining industry provided most of Europe's bullion, which enabled German banking to develop to the point that it even challenged that of Italy. By 1515, Jakob Fugger the Rich of Augsburg had moved from mine owning to being a financier and trader on an international scale – he even lent the money that Charles needed for the imperial election bribes in 1519.

Another positive development resulted from the rapid population growth experienced at the time. 'Germany is overcrowded,' complained Ulrich Hutten in 1518, but in fact the impact on the economy was very positive for some groups. Along the Rhine and in north Germany, demand for more food led to improvements in the agricultural sector. Ideas were imported from the Netherlands, including careful selection of seeds and breeding of animals, better tools and deeper ploughing. Landowner peasants prospered. Demand for consumer goods increased, which led to a boom in textile production and the manufacturing sectors of towns like Augsburg and Munich. This, in turn, led to a boom in trade along the great rivers that criss-crossed the empire – the Rhine, Danube, Elbe, Wesser and Spree. The most successful towns were located on these rivers.

For miners, manufacturers and merchants, these were good times. If they had economic frustrations, these were directed at their inept patrician city councils, which were often totally out of touch with the latest economic developments and yet thwarted all attempts by newly wealthy and upwardly mobile **burghers** to share their power. Equally frustrating were the myriad borders that had to be crossed as one traded in the empire, with customs duties to pay at each one. But otherwise, times were good.

KEY TERM

Burgher
A citizen of a town or city who was also a member of the trading or mercantile class.

However, not everyone would have agreed that the economy was thriving.

- North Germany's Baltic ports were in decline, victims of a strange circumstance. In 1473, the Baltic's herring shoals had moved to the North Sea. This was a complete disaster for the Baltic ports, which had depended on herring fishing for their livelihood. The Hanseatic League (an organisation of Baltic trading towns) went into a slow decline, made worse when Atlantic seaboard trade took off from the 1540s. Originally, 120 towns had been in the League; by 1557, the total had shrunk to 63.

- Peasants were also experiencing real hardship. Perhaps 70 percent of the empire's population of 12 million was peasants, living in isolated hamlets and tiny villages. Largely illiterate, their lives were dictated by the seasonal demands of agriculture. Population growth had a negative impact on this group: the custom of subdividing land equally between all sons led to smaller and smaller landholdings. Many peasants therefore lived increasingly on the margins. A poor harvest could mean hunger, and one in four harvests failed. A poor harvest also meant high food prices and inflation. Landlords naturally wanted their own incomes to keep up with inflation, but they employed some harsh solutions:

  - To the west of the River Elbe, landlords increased rents and restricted the ability of peasants to tap into traditionally free sources of food by declaring hunting and fishing illegal, and by enclosing land previously used for common grazing. Land fenced off in this way was often given over to sheep – wool made more profit than peasants' rents.

  - To the east of the Elbe, landlords reintroduced serfdom – they forced peasants to work longer and harder for no money, and forbade them to move.

- Unbelievable hardship, coupled with deep resentment of exploitative landlords, meant an increasingly explosive situation in the countryside. There were 18 significant peasant revolts between 1500 and 1525 – this compares with 21 revolts in the previous *hundred* years.

- Urban labourers were also suffering. Inflation had a negative impact on this group because their wages rarely kept up with food prices. Many towns became increasingly segregated, with the disadvantaged living in slums that surrounded a nucleus of wealthy residential areas in the centre. Tension between these classes could lead to rioting and anti-Semitic pogroms, because Jews were often blamed. The whole problem was then exacerbated as peasants streamed into towns to escape rural poverty. Failing to find work, many turned to begging, but were then accused of being troublemakers, criminals and carriers of diseases like the pox. Many town councils introduced laws to have beggars arrested, whipped and expelled. More rarely, a philanthropist might try to help: in Augsburg, Jakob Fugger built houses for the poor, the so-called 'Fuggerei'. It was a generous gesture, but not enough. By 1558, 47 percent of the population of Augsburg were too poor to pay taxes, and 10 percent were in receipt of poor relief.

This brief survey might suggest immediate support for change from the rural and urban poor, the dispossessed and the beggars. In fact, though, some of Luther's greatest support was to come from the educated elite of the towns and cities, the very people who were thriving in the early 16th century. Around 50 of the 65 imperial cities converted to Lutheranism.

One reason lay in their position. Those who lived by the great rivers had the advantage of knowing more quickly what was going on in the world. Travel in the early 16th century was achieved by three methods: on foot (slow), by horse (expensive) or by boat (also costly). Roads were not made up and were seldom more than tracks, potholed and potentially dangerous. Rivers were far safer, and quicker. Furthermore, elite town dwellers were far more likely to be literate, and (since the invention of printing) more likely to buy and read books and pamphlets and to absorb the ideas of the humanists.

SOURCE

2 This woodcut by Anton Woensam shows Cologne in 1531. The River Rhine is in the foreground, swarming with boats that carried goods from the heart of the empire down to the North Sea. The wealth and piety of the city can be seen from the large number of churches on the skyline. To the right, the cathedral is being built – a vast crane can be seen. It was intended to house the relics of the Three Wise Men, who can be seen in the skyline. Land inside the walls was expensive, so houses were often narrow, but high. Cologne had a thriving print industry, but it did not turn Lutheran – proof of the power of censorship.

WAS THE GERMAN CATHOLIC CHURCH IN NEED OF REFORM?

In 1500, one institution bound western Europe together: the Roman Catholic Church. Everyone was Catholic, and religion touched everyone's lives. Understanding what people thought about the Church's teachings, its clergy and its head (the pope) is crucial to understanding why Luther's protest was so successful.

ACTIVITY
WRITING

Extend your vocabulary

Understanding the early modern period will involve mastering what may be some new vocabulary. Start a glossary, and as you read through the rest of this Paper use the text to write definitions of the following words and phrases:

ad fontes, anti-clericalism, basilica, curia, cardinal, Eucharist, heresy, heretic, holy relic, indulgence, mass, non-residency, papacy, papal bull, penance, pluralism, purgatory, seven sacraments, simony, transubstantiation.

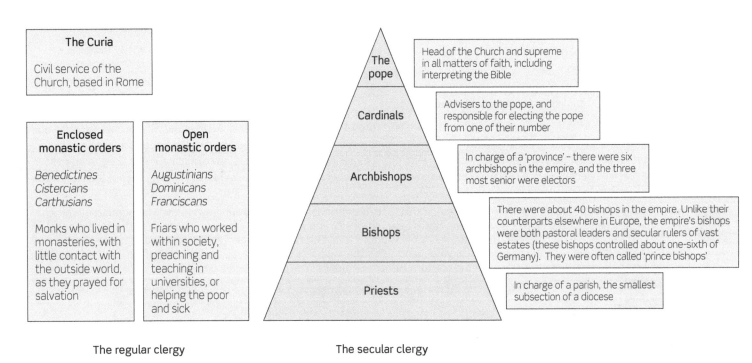

The Curia

Civil service of the Church, based in Rome

Enclosed monastic orders

Benedictines
Cistercians
Carthusians

Monks who lived in monasteries, with little contact with the outside world, as they prayed for salvation

Open monastic orders

Augustinians
Dominicans
Franciscans

Friars who worked within society, preaching and teaching in universities, or helping the poor and sick

The regular clergy

The pope — Head of the Church and supreme in all matters of faith, including interpreting the Bible

Cardinals — Advisers to the pope, and responsible for electing the pope from one of their number

Archbishops — In charge of a 'province' – there were six archbishops in the empire, and the three most senior were electors

Bishops — There were about 40 bishops in the empire. Unlike their counterparts elsewhere in Europe, the empire's bishops were both pastoral leaders and secular rulers of vast estates (these bishops controlled about one-sixth of Germany). They were often called 'prince bishops'

Priests — In charge of a parish, the smallest subsection of a diocese

The secular clergy

Figure 1.5 The structure of the German Catholic Church.

Key beliefs of the Catholic Church

Official doctrine in 1500 was underpinned by a belief in life after death, and the possibility of either eternal salvation in Heaven or eternal damnation in Hell. Before souls went to either, they first went to purgatory, which was not a pleasant place. Here, the souls of the dead suffered hideous tortures as they were cleansed of their sins on earth, possibly for millions of years. Those who could be cleansed of their sins went to Heaven; those whose sins were too great to be cleansed went to Hell.

The power of the Church lay in the fact that it claimed to be the only route to eternal salvation. Obedience to the teachings of the Church was therefore crucial in order to minimise the time spent in purgatory and to be saved. This obedience involved:

- attending church

- taking part in an annual cycle of religious ceremonies and rituals, like fasting for 40 days during Lent and celebrating the feast days of saints, during which it was forbidden to work

- obeying the Ten Commandments – Thou shall not steal, Thou shall not kill, etc.

- performing 'good works', like going on pilgrimages, being charitable or collecting holy relics

- showing devotion to the Virgin Mary and the saints, as well as believing in the power of their relics

- participating in the **seven sacraments**, religious events that were a crucial means to achieving salvation.

KEY TERM

Seven sacraments

Baptism: All babies were born with 'original sin', which could only be removed by being baptised by a priest. During the ceremony, the baby was received into the Christian community.

Confirmation: This ceremony confirmed the baptism and took place when a child was about nine.

Penance: In theory, there were four parts to penance: contrition, confession, satisfaction and absolution. First, a person had to feel sorry for their sins. Then, at least once a year and usually the day before Lent started, all Catholics had to confess their sins to their priest. He would absolve them (forgive them), but they also had to perform a 'work of satisfaction', a penance, the scale of which depended on the seriousness of the sins confessed. Penances might involve just saying prayers or fasting, but they might be expensive (like going on a pilgrimage) or public and humiliating.

Eucharist (or Communion): This sacrament was at the centre of worship. It was based on the Last Supper of Christ, when Jesus shared bread and wine with his disciples. The Catholic Church taught that when the bread and wine were 'consecrated' by a priest during the service called Mass, a miracle called transubstantiation happened, and they were transformed into the body and blood of Christ. Only priests could receive communion 'in both kinds' – that is, both the bread and the wine. Everyone else, the laity, could only receive the bread. This they had to do at least once a year, on Easter Day, and preferably three times a year, from about the age of ten. Simply gazing on consecrated bread and wine was almost as good as receiving communion.

Marriage: The Church determined who could and could not marry, and only a marriage presided over by a priest was acceptable.

Extreme unction (or last rites): Those who wished to shorten their time in purgatory had to make a final confession and be anointed by a priest before they died.

Ordination: A person who took holy orders became a priest, monk or nun. They committed their life to the Church and could not marry. They were thought to be superior to the laity and ahead on the route to salvation. Emphasising this, they wore special clothes and had special privileges, like not paying taxes. Priests played an important part in delivering the sacraments to their congregations.

SOURCE

3 An image of purgatory, from *The Last Judgement*, a triptych by Hieronymous Bosch. This was painted around the year 1500 for wealthy clients, who may possibly have been Philip the Fair and Joanna the Mad, since their respective patron saints are painted on the outside panels. On this central panel, Bosch shows sinners being tormented for the sins they have committed on earth. Gluttons (middle left) are being spit-roasted and pan-fried, for example, while those guilty of lust face a nightmarish red slide (middle right) that might end in bisection. The devils are terrifying, strange compounds of vaguely familiar insects. Only a very few are saved – they are the tiny lights in the top left. Bosch's images were based on a series of 'eyewitness reports' from mortal men who had returned to earth after a brief spell in purgatory.

Were people satisfied with these teachings?

Measuring levels of satisfaction is always difficult. The historian Euan Cameron suggests that one should distinguish between the religious needs of the majority – the illiterate peasant farmers and labourers who made up the bulk of the population – and the religious needs of the educated urban elite.

The majority

Most people were actually far more concerned about this life than they were about the afterlife. For them, the seven sacraments were a low priority. Four of them were once-in-a-lifetime events anyway, while penance was only an annual event, and Eucharist might be received just three times a year. Since services were in Latin, as was the Bible, most people did not understand official doctrine anyway.

Instead, the majority worried about everyday things, like how to avoid illness or crop failure, or how to attract a partner or get pregnant, or how to avoid fire. Their religious needs involved getting God's help now, and this was largely being met via 'sacramentals', a huge array of semi-magical practices, rituals and beliefs. For example, a loaf of bread baked and blessed on Good Friday would help to avert fire. Blessed candles ensured light through the year. Touching the altar cloth was thought to be a cure for epilepsy. Processing consecrated bread could help to ward off bad weather. Indeed, consecrated bread was so powerful that a fragment sown into clothing would ensure a safe journey.

People shaped and led this 'popular religion', and most parish priests helpfully delivered what was demanded. So the majority of the population was content: for them, the Church had the right answers and was meeting their needs by allaying their everyday anxieties. More than that, the celebrations that punctuated the ritual year were fun. They involved the whole community. Everyone looked forward to the 12 days of Christmas or carnival, for example, and the opportunity to dress up and have a feast.

The elite

The religious needs of the educated urban laity were more in line with official Church doctrine – they were far more concerned with the afterlife. They wanted to be reassured that their souls would achieve eternal salvation. Again, there is very little evidence that anyone in 1500 thought the Church was teaching the wrong thing. The seven sacraments were accepted, as were all the other official means to achieve salvation.

People were exceptionally devout. The Elector of Saxony, Frederick the Wise, for example, piously built up a huge collection of over 19,000 holy relics, which included a twig from the burning bush, a piece of bread from the Last Supper, and a hair from Jesus' beard, while Archbishop Albert of Mainz had 42 entire holy skeletons. The number of masses endowed by upper-Austrian gentry reached a peak by 1517. Church building flourished, paid for by wealthy patrons. If such people had any criticism about the Church's teachings, it was reserved for the sacramental, which they considered superstitious, pagan and misleading.

So, in 1500, almost everyone respected the core teachings of the Church and there had been almost no **heresy** trials in Germany since the 1470s. The spiritual energy of many wealthy, literate Germans can be seen in the high sales of books written by humanists. These books suggested ways to be a better Christian, and their popularity suggests that interest in religion had never been greater.

The influence of humanism

In the decades before the Reformation, an intellectual revolution took place in Europe: religious ideas and beliefs that had been accepted for centuries were questioned and reviewed by intellectuals and scholars, men whom we call Christian humanists.

The historian Bernd Moeller has argued that the work of these humanists was crucial to the later success of Luther: 'No Humanism, No Reformation'.

Why were the humanists so important?

Humanists played a key role before 1517 in three ways:

- They pioneered the practice of trying to create the purest translations possible of the Bible. They went back to the oldest sources they could find in their search for accuracy (a practice known as *ad fontes*). In doing so, they uncovered the fact that the Vulgate Bible then in use contained errors. For example, Erasmus produced a new translation of the Greek New Testament in 1516, and where the Vulgate (Matthew 4:17) had used the phrase 'do penance', Erasmus suggested that a more accurate translation would read 'be penitent', an inward emotion. Erasmus had no wish to challenge the Church; he wanted reform from within, and he was hurt when his Greek New Testament was condemned by Rome. Luther, on the other hand, was inspired.

- Humanists also promoted the idea that a good Christian life, worthy of Jesus, should be based on a deep personal understanding of the Bible rather than just relying on what the Church said. Ignorance was inexcusable: Erasmus wanted everyone to read the Bible. Study, inner spirituality, prayer and meditation were all more important to being a good Christian than mindless activities like going on pilgrimages and viewing relics. 'We kiss the shoes of saints and their dirty handkerchiefs, yet we leave their words, their most holy relics, neglected', wrote Erasmus. He wanted to encourage debate on current religious practices, but again, many saw him as challenging the authority of the pope.

- Humanists openly criticised and made fun of the Church. For example, the humanist Ulrich von Hutten co-authored a satirical volume of *Letters of Obscure Men*. The *Letters* mocked clerical ignorance, idleness, hypocrisy and immorality. Other humanists attacked the papacy and denounced the exploitation of Germany by Rome. In this way, humanists were partly responsible for the mood of **anti-clericalism**, anti-papalism and nationalism that existed in Germany in 1517. They had created a climate in which Luther's protest could thrive.

KEY TERMS

Heresy
A belief contrary to the official doctrine of the Church. Heretics were normally burned to death.

Anti-clericalism
Opposition to the clergy, on the basis of their 'abuses' and their power.

Desiderius Erasmus (c1466–1536)

Towering above the other humanists was Desiderius Erasmus. The illegitimate son of a priest, he was born in Rotterdam. His early education was at a school in Derventer, where the teachers belonged to the Brethren of the Common Life, a Dutch movement that believed in a simple life of prayer, poverty and piety, and it is possible to see their influence on his later life. Erasmus was originally destined to be a monk, but he rapidly decided that it was not the career for him. Instead, he went on to study at the University of Paris, where he was unimpressed with the quality of scholarship; he commented later that it was a time to catch up on his sleep. His enthusiasm, however, was captured by the then fashionable study of classical texts. He devoted the rest of his life to their study, focusing especially on those that cast light on Christianity. He travelled widely, lectured in Oxford, Cambridge and Louvain universities, and wrote over 30,000 letters, as well as books.

Erasmus' reputation was based in part on his biblical scholarship and mastery of Latin and Greek, and in part on his sense of humour. Much of his work was serious. In *The Handbook of the Christian Soldier* (1501), Erasmus advocated a return to a purer, simpler form of Christianity, focused on the Bible and free of all the unnecessary practices and ignorant superstitions that had accumulated over the centuries. His *Greek New Testament* (1516) was intended as a tool to help men achieve this.

Erasmus was also a very witty writer. In satires like his *In Praise of Folly* (1509) and the *Colloquies* (1518), he poked fun at clerical abuses and superstitious religious practices. The popularity of these works was extraordinary: by 1536, the *Colloquies* had run to over 300 editions. Erasmus expressed brilliantly what people were thinking – and 'educated Europe laughed. More than any other single man, he lowered the European reputation of popes and clergy, monks and friars, and (above all) of the theologians' (Owen Chadwick).

Erasmus wanted open debate and the papacy to lead a reform of the Church. To that end, he challenged ideas, institutions and practices. However, Erasmus did not want to cause a revolution, and he certainly did not want to split the Church. Though he might have been a vital influence on Luther, he eventually rejected Luther completely. In 1520, Cardinal Aleander reputedly said, 'Erasmus laid the egg which Luther hatched.' Erasmus replied: 'I laid a hen's egg, but Luther hatched a bird of quite different kind.'

Ulrich von Hutten (1488–1523)

Ulrich von Hutten was an imperial knight, a scholar and a poet. Like Erasmus, he advocated the importance of studying the Bible free from all the interpretations layered on by Rome. Also like Erasmus, he was a strong critic of clerical abuses and he was probably one of the co-authors of *Letters of Obscure Men* (1515–17), a series of satirical letters purporting to be written by clergy, which actually just exposed their shallowness, ignorance and mediocrity. The *Letters* were written in retaliation to an attack by Rome on a fellow German humanist, Johannes Reuchlin. Reuchlin had wanted to study Hebrew texts for academic purposes; Rome denounced this as heresy.

However, there were differences between Erasmus and von Hutten. Whereas Erasmus was European in his outlook, von Hutten was a fierce German nationalist. He was angered by the way, in his opinion, Rome took advantage of the fears and superstitions of ordinary Germans, and the way Rome bled Germany dry of funds. Where Erasmus remained a firm believer in the institution of the papacy, von Hutten's ideal was probably a German Church without the pope. Where Erasmus rejected Luther, Hutten soon supported him, though chiefly because of Luther's anti-papal stance. He backed Franz von Sickingen and other imperial knights in a demonstration of military support for Luther, an ill-judged attack on the lands of the Archbishop of Trier in 1522. The attack failed; von Hutten fled and died in obscurity the following year from syphilis, on an island in Lake Zurich. His great nephew, Philip Melanchthon, became a leading Protestant reformer in Wittenberg.

Conrad Celtis (1459–1508)

Conrad Celtis was a German humanist, historian and poet (in 1487, he was even made Poet Laureate by the emperor), who focused his attention on a study of the history of Germany. He was particularly excited by the rediscovery in 1455 of a text called *Germania* written by the Ancient Roman historian Tacitus in AD 98. *Germania* showed how most of ancient Germany – an allegedly honourable, brave, pure Germany – had avoided conquest by the Roman Empire.

To a nationalist like Celtis, it seemed logical to ask why Germany now seemed almost totally under the control of Rome. At his inaugural lecture at Ingolstadt University in 1492, he explained that the problem lay in Germany's barbarism: teaching poems and songs was needed to instil a love of the fatherland.

In 1497, Celtis translated into German and published a new edition of Tacitus' *Germania*. Though he had completely different motives for his protest, Luther's anti-Rome tone found a receptive audience already enthused with pro-German, anti-Italian feeling. Luther's success, therefore, was due in part to the groundwork done by Celtis.

SOURCE 4

The preface to Erasmus' translation of the New Testament, published in 1516.

I wish that all women might read the gospel, and the Epistles of Paul. I wish that they might be translated into the tongues of all people, so that not only the Scots and the Irish, but also the Turk and the Saracen might read and understand. I wish the countryman might sing them at his plough, the weaver chant them at his loom, the traveller beguile with them the weariness of his journey. Only a very few can be learned, but all can be Christian, all can be devout, and – I shall boldly add – all can be theologians.

Why was anti-clericalism so prominent in the empire?

Theory 1: Because of the level of clerical abuses

Given their importance in meeting people's religious needs, whether in this life or the afterlife, one might have expected high standards of professionalism among the clergy. However, such standards were often missing. As the historian Ann Laurence states, 'Enthusiastic lay piety was not matched by a comparable movement of spiritual renewal among the clergy.'

SOURCE 5

Written in 1509 and dedicated to his friend, Thomas More, Erasmus' most famous satire, *In Praise of Folly*, made fun of serious issues. It was an instant best-seller, and by 1536, it had run to 42 editions. Narrated by 'Folly', the book ended with a fierce attack on standards in the Church. In the text below from Chapter 54, monks were the subject.

The whole tribe is so universally loathed that even a chance meeting is thought to be ill-omened – and yet they are gloriously self-satisfied. In the first place they believe it's the highest form of piety to be so uneducated that they can't even read. Then they bray like donkeys in Church repeating by rote the psalms they haven't even understood, they imagine they are charming the ears of the heavenly audience with infinite delight. Many of them too make a good living out of their squalor and beggary, bellowing for bread from door to door, and indeed making a nuisance of themselves in every inn, carriage or boat, to the great loss of other beggars. This is the way these smooth individuals, in all their filth and ignorance, their boorish and shameless behaviour, claim to bring back the apostles into our midst!

There is a view that anti-clericalism existed because the Church was riddled from top to bottom with a number of abuses. Positions in the Church were sold to the highest bidder rather than awarded to the best candidate (a practice called simony), and it was possible to hold more than one position at a time (a practice known as pluralism). The result was often unqualified bishops, who saw the Church solely as a means to make money so that they could live like princes. Pluralists were often non-resident, and their indifference to their responsibilities could be shocking. At all levels, it was possible to criticise the clergy for scandalous living and immorality, including gambling, drunkenness and womanising. Absenteeism was rife, and ignorance of Latin, let alone doctrine, was commonplace. One could find evidence for all of this.

Furthermore, such criticism was not new. For several generations before Luther, there had been prophecies that a 'holy man' would appear to reform the Church and rid it of abuses, in preparation for the Last Judgement. It is a measure of how gripped Germany was by such thoughts that even old works criticising the clergy and advocating reform were popular best-sellers.

SOURCE 6

The *Reformatio Sigismundi* was written anonymously c1438. Using the printing press (invented in about 1440), Augsburg publishers issued eight editions between 1476 and 1522. Written in German, it was probably the most widely circulated reform paper of its time. It prophesied that one day, a simple priest would come to 'bring the Christian Church into the best possible order'.

The hour will come for all faithful Christians to witness the establishment of the rightful order. Let everyone join the ranks of the pious who will pledge themselves to observe it. It is plain that the Holy Father, the pope, and all our princes have abandoned the task set them by God. It may be that God has appointed a man to set things right. Let no one, neither princes nor cities, make excuses for not heeding God's warnings...

Take a good look at how bishops act nowadays. They make war and cause unrest in the world; they behave like secular lords, which is, of course, what they are. And the money for this comes from pious donations that ought to go to honest parish work, and not to be spent on war. I agree with a remark made by Duke Frederick of Austria to the Emperor Sigismund in Basel: 'Bishops are blind; it is up to us to open their eyes...'

It seems to me that great evils have arisen in the western part of Christendom since Pope Calixtus imposed the rule of celibacy. It may be a good thing for a man to keep himself pure, but observe the wickedness now going on in the Church! Many priests have lost their livings because of women. Or they are secret sodomites. All the hatred existing between priests and laymen is due to this. In sum: secular priests should be allowed to marry. In marriage they will live more piously and honourably, and the friction between them and the laity will disappear.

AS Level Exam-Style Question Section A

Read Source 6. Why is the *Reformatio Sigismundi* valuable to the historian for an enquiry into dissatisfaction with the Catholic Church in early 16th century Germany?

Explain your answer using the source, the information given about it and your own knowledge of the historical context. (8 marks)

Tip

Consider first what you can learn of value from the content. What sort of complaints are being expressed? Then consider the dates this was written and then repeatedly reprinted. Why do these make this such a valuable source?

However, abuses alone do not explain the level of anti-clericalism in Germany for several reasons.

- The level of abuses was often exaggerated in anti-clerical literature: scandal meant better sales.

- The situation was not uniformly bad. About half the priests in southern Germany had a degree, which was an exceptionally high proportion, given the rarity of university places. Furthermore, some monastic orders had already reformed themselves (including Luther's order, the Augustinians). Some bishops were conscientious: the Bishop of Basle in Switzerland warned his clergy 'not to curl their hair with curling tongs, nor to carry on trade in the churches, or to raise a disturbance there, nor to keep drinking booths or engage in horse trading, and not to buy stolen property'.

- Some 'abuses' were actually valued and in high demand: convents were used to 'dump' the excess daughters of the well-to-do, for example, which would explain any lack of vocation among nuns, while there was an open market in buying church positions.

- Most ordinary people did not mind if their priest lived with a woman, or could not understand Latin, or sometimes got drunk. The one abuse that they really resented was non-residency: they just wanted their priest to be there in order to provide them with the sacraments and sacramentals.

- Many of the fiercest critics were clergy themselves, and they had been openly criticising abuses for a long time without causing a crisis. They did not contemplate splitting the Church over the issue. Rather, like Erasmus, they hoped to promote reform from within the Church.

The chief cause of anti-clericalism was therefore not the level of abuses. However, attacking abuses had created a climate where it was acceptable to criticise and laugh at the Church.

Furthermore, Luther unquestionably benefited from the fact that a 'holy man' was expected. Many felt God's displeasure with man's sinfulness was reaching a climax – the warnings were clear. A terrible new disease, the pox or syphilis, had appeared in the 1490s. Other ill omens were eagerly lapped up by the public: broadsheets circulated showing comets and 'monstrous births' (babies or animals born with significant abnormalities). Adding to the mood of anticipation was the fact that 1500 was a half millennium. This passed disappointingly peacefully, but a Great Conjunction of the Stars was predicted to coincide in 1524 with a conjunction of all the planets in Pisces. This happens only once every 750 years and was interpreted as heralding the Second Coming of Christ, and the end of the world. So Luther succeeded in part because of a coincidence: reform (of some abuses, but not doctrine) was wanted, and he was 'expected'.

Theory 2: Because of the power of the Church and the privileges of the clergy

Almost everyone in Germany accepted the Church's teachings, and most could put up with the failings of their local parish priest and probably did not know about the excesses of their bishop. However, there was widespread resentment at the extent to which the Church interfered in everyday life and the way in which the Church abused its power and its privileges.

It would be hard to underestimate the Church's power in the empire in 1500. It was the largest landowner, controlling about one-sixth of German land. Three of the seven electors were members of the Church, while more than half of the second college in the diet were ecclesiastical princes. These prince bishops acted as secular rulers. The Church also had huge legal power: it processed everyone's wills for example, while members of the clergy had the privilege of only being tried in Church courts, where they invariably got off lightly. Clerical privileges were a source of real resentment: they were exempt from paying taxes and contributing to defence funds.

SOURCE

'Grievances and Demands' of Cologne's burghers, 1513. In 1513, the craft guilds and leading merchants of Cologne rose in revolt against their city council. It was a brave thing to do, since a previous revolt, in 1482, had ended with the ringleaders being tortured and executed. The guild leaders and merchants put together a list of 154 complaints, including corruption and financial mismanagement by the council, abuses of weights and the lack of regulation in trade. Many of their grievances were directed against the clergy, including the following.

Clerical persons should from now on bear the same civic burdens as burghers.

Let the clergy pay taxes on the wine they tap for themselves.

Let the clergy be asked to make a substantial loan to the city.

Every cleric, secular or regular, young or old, who has committed a felony against the Council is to be taken to the Dean of the Cathedral Chapter, who should punish the cleric as though he were a lay person.

Every pastor should be paid a fixed salary. In return for this the pastor shall perform his offices without making a charge.

No monk shall henceforth become a parish priest. [Monks should] stay in their monasteries [so that] the sacraments are not bartered to the faithful for money.

Most deeply resented were the financial demands made by the Church. Everyone resented the price put on the means to salvation: one had to pay for baptisms, marriages and burials, pay for confession, pay to see relics, pay to go on pilgrimages, pay for **indulgences**. The historian Alister McGrath explains that 'The clergy came to be seen as exploiting the new interest in religion without contributing to it.'

The Church made poor people even poorer. One-tenth of every person's income or produce had to go to the Church (the 'tithe'). The Church's lands were controlled by bishops, who behaved as secular rulers, and tenants on these lands resented the speedy way rents were put up by their uncaring, absentee ecclesiastical landlords, especially in a time of inflation.

Meanwhile, employers were angered by the economic power of the Church, and the increasingly large number (over 100 by 1500) of holy days and feast days during which work was forbidden. The Church even determined what one could eat: on three days a week, and on the eve of every holy day, and during the 40 days of Lent, no meat could be eaten, which made life difficult for those who lived far from rivers or the sea, and almost ruinous for butchers. Even a trivial matter could cause resentment: no butter could be eaten during Lent, for example – a rule that might have been easy to adhere to in Rome, but was almost impossible in Germany, where butter was the fat used to cook with, and olive oil had to be imported at huge cost. Of course, it was possible to buy a dispensation to eat butter – yet another irritating example of Church exploitation. Perhaps because of the vacuum of central authority in the empire, there was a feeling that the Church had more power in Germany than anywhere else in Europe, and that Rome was exploiting Germany. Anyone who challenged this exploitation would have a favourable reception.

ACTIVITY
KNOWLEDGE CHECK

The state of religion
Historians disagree about the 'state of religion' in Germany prior to the Reformation. In *The German Reformation* (2003), the historian R.W. Scribner suggests four different schools of thought:

- that the Church was healthy: there was a strong sense of devotion to the Church and a powerful revival of piety
- that the Church was unhealthy: it was riddled with abuses and failings that were openly criticised
- that there was too much religion: 'religious observance had become a spiritual burden, creating anxiety'
- that there was not enough religion: 'a thin veneer of Christianity overlaid essentially pagan beliefs'.

Which of these views do pages 178–184 support?

WHY WAS THERE SO MUCH HOSTILITY TOWARDS THE PAPACY?

Acceptance of the authority of the pope was a central point of Catholic teaching. However, by the early 16th century, attacks on the papacy were extremely popular. Any cartoon, book or pamphlet that mocked Rome and exposed decadence and scandal – the more luridly the better – became a best-seller in Germany.

There were three main reasons for this anti-papalism:

- the personal behaviour of the Renaissance popes, Alexander VI (1492–1503), Julius II (1503–13) and Leo X (1513–21), which was almost completely at odds with their claim to be the spiritual leaders of Christendom
- the condition of the Church in Rome, which was about as far from being an example for Christendom as it was possible to be
- a growing belief that these hypocritical 'foreign' popes and their scandal-ridden Roman Church were financially exploiting pious Germany, something that was deeply resented.

And it mattered. In the words of the historian John Lotherington, 'Anti papalism did not automatically mean the rejection of Catholic doctrine. But it did mean that the enemy of the Pope might well be seen as the friend of the German people.'

The Renaissance popes

Alexander VI was Spanish, which might explain the lack of respect he commanded in Italy. Poisoning, murder and extortion were all laid at his door, and his surname (Borgia) is even now a byword for scheming. His behaviour was remarkably 'unpapal': he had seven children and particularly adored his murderous (literally so) son Cesare and daughter Lucretia. On his death, wrote the Duke of Mantua, 'He was carried to the grave with little honour, his body being dragged from the bed… by a porter, who fastened a cord to his feet, because no one would touch him.' In 1503, Julius said of Alexander: 'He desecrated the Holy Church as none before. He usurped the papal power by the devil's aid, and I forbid under the pain of excommunication anyone to speak or think of Borgia again. His name and memory must be forgotten.'

Julius II's passions, meanwhile, were art and war. He commissioned Michelangelo to paint the Sistine Chapel ceiling, set in motion plans to restore Rome and established the Swiss Guard (which still does duty in the Vatican today). Acting more like a European prince, he made and unmade alliances with Maximilian and led his own troops into battle, a fact that shocked Europe almost as much as his rumoured homosexuality.

SOURCE 8

The reputation of Julius II, in *Julius Exclusus* ('Julius Excluded from Heaven'), 1514. This popular short satire was most probably written by Erasmus, though he never acknowledged the fact. (To do so would have been dangerous, though there might have been another reason: Erasmus was hoping that the new pope, Leo X, would legitimise his birth.) 'Julius Excluded from Heaven' was written as a dialogue between Pope Julius II, the 'warrior pope', who had recently died, and St Peter, who guards the gates to heaven. On arrival, Julius finds the gates locked: 'What the devil is this? The doors don't open? Somebody must have changed the lock or broken it.' In the following text, Julius is trying to persuade St Peter to let him in.

The invincible Julius ought not to answer to a beggarly fisherman. However, you shall know who I am and what I am. I have done more for the Church and Christ than any other pope before me. I have set all the princes of Europe by the ears. I have torn up treaties, kept great armies in the field; I have covered Rome with palaces. And I have done it all myself, too. I owe nothing to my birth, for I don't know who my father was; nothing to learning, for I have none; nothing to youth for I was old when I began; nothing to popularity, for I was hated all round. Spite of fortune, spite of gods and men I achieved all that I have told you in a few years, and I left work enough cut out for my successors to last ten years longer. This is the modest truth, and my friends at Rome call me more a god than a man.

Leo X was the last man to become pope before he became a priest. He was elected pope on 9 March 1513, ordained a priest on 15 March, consecrated a bishop on 17 March, and crowned pope on 19 March. Leo's vices were less vicious than those of his predecessors: he was a cultured, easygoing man and a significant patron of the arts. He employed the artist Raphael and reorganised Rome's university. However, he was also a spendthrift. On being made pope, he allegedly said to his brother: 'God has given us the papacy, let us enjoy it.' To replenish his treasury, he created and sold off to the highest bidders 1,353 offices in the Church, including 31 new cardinals on a single day in July 1517 alone. Simony on this scale scandalised Europe.

SOURCE 9

Leo X's elephant. This is from a popular book called *Letters of Obscure Men*, a collection of satirical letters that were published anonymously between 1515 and 1517. The authors may have been the humanists Crotus Rubeanus and Ulrich von Hutten. The *Letters* were banned in 1517, and Pope Leo said that the authors and all readers were excommunicated.

The elephant was real: it was an Asian elephant called Hanno, given to Leo by King Manuel I of Portugal when Leo became pope. It died in 1516 from complications following treatment for constipation with a gold-enriched laxative. The author has injected a subtle insult into this letter. Ancient Greek writers used to describe the language of foreigners they could not understand as 'bar bar', nonsense. From this we get the word 'barbarians'.

You have no doubt heard that the pope has a great animal, called Elephant, and that he holds it in great honour and loves it much. Now you must know that this animal is dead. When it was taken sick the pope was in great distress, and summoned several physicians and said to them: 'If it is possible, cure Elephant for me.' Then they did their best; made careful diagnosis and administered a purge that cost five hundred golden florins, but it was in vain, for the animal died. The pope grieved much for Elephant. They say he gave a thousand ducats for Elephant; for it was a wonderful animal, and had a long snout of prodigious size. When it beheld the pope, it knelt before him and cried with a terrible voice, 'Bar! Bar! Bar!' I believe there is no other animal of the kind in the world.

These popes were failing in their role as leaders of the Christian Church. In neglecting their duties and in allowing corruption and incompetence to occur, they laid the Church open to attack. They also failed to pay any attention to new ideas about faith coming from humanist writers like Erasmus, other than to condemn them. They failed to provide a decisive reaction to the growing waves of anti-papalism.

The condition of the Church in Rome

Lack of respect for the Renaissance popes was closely married to reports circulating in Germany about the behaviour of the clergy in Rome, said to be leading lives of luxury and making a mockery of Christianity. These reports were not just rumour, many were based on eyewitness accounts from pilgrims and scholars. Erasmus, Celtis and Luther all visited Rome.

SOURCE

10 Francesco Guicciardini's description of Rome. Guicciardini was a Florentine humanist and lawyer. In 1515, he went to Rome and began a 20 year career in papal administration. This is from his *Aphorisms*, written in 1529, probably just for himself rather than for publication.

No man is more disgusted than I with the ambition, the avarice and the profligacy of the priests. ... [My] position at the court of several popes forced me to desire their greatness for the sake of my own interest. But, had it not been for this, I should have loved Martin Luther as myself – not in order to free myself from the laws which Christianity lays upon us but in order to see this swarm of scoundrels put back into their proper place, so that they may be forced to live without vice or without power.

Rome's exploitation of Germany

By 1500, Rome exploited Germany more than anywhere else in Europe. The reason was political: the empire lacked a strong centralised government, the sort that had developed in England, France and Spain. Monarchs in the latter countries negotiated with Rome from a position of strength and were able to keep the pope at arm's length. The king of France, for example, could demand 'voluntary loans' from the French clergy, and controlled appointments to about 600 of the chief positions in the French Church. He could command the reform of monastic orders, the censorship of books and the persecution of heretics if he wished.

The multiple states of the empire did not have such strength, which made them very vulnerable and easy prey for the pope. Huge amounts of money left Germany for Rome every year, from taxes, rents and the sale of dispensations, indulgences and offices. Anti-Italian feeling in Germany was high and the pope was the main target of the anger. This anger was closely allied to a growing self-awareness among Germans that they shared a collective identity and an illustrious past. German national identity was being forged on a fire of xenophobia and anger.

In the late 1490s, the German printmaker Wenzel von Olmütz engraved a cartoon of a monster that had allegedly been washed up on the banks of the River Tiber in Rome in January 1496. The monster had the head of an ass, the breasts and belly of a woman, an elephant's foot in the place of the right hand, fish scales on its arms and legs, and the heads of a dragon and an old man protruding from its back. There were clear references to the papacy: in the background, the papal flag with its keys (representing the keys to heaven) flew from the Castel Sant'Angelo, the papal fortress, while the papal prison was on the right. Like other 'monstrous births' being reported in Germany, this 'Papal Ass' was felt to be an omen of God's anger with Rome and the papacy. Any publication challenging Rome had a receptive audience in Germany. Olmütz probably made a fortune from the sales of his cartoon.

Context is everything.

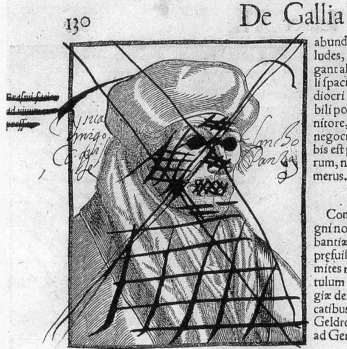

Figure 1.6 Portrait of Erasmus, defaced in the 1550s.

Work in groups.

Take an A3 piece of paper. In the middle of it draw a circle about 20 cm in diameter. Within the circle is the evidence itself, outside the circle is the context.

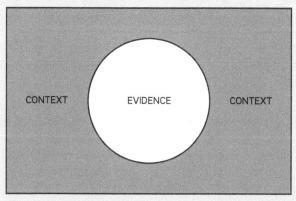

Think of a question that the portrait of Erasmus above could be helpful in answering.

1 Inside the circle, write a set of statements giving information that can be gleaned only from the source itself, without any contextual knowledge.

2 Outside the circle, write down statements of contextual knowledge that relate to the source.

3 Draw annotated lines to show links between the contextual statements and the information from the source. Does context change the nature or meaning of the information?

Now answer the following question.

Explain why knowledge of context is important when gathering and using historical evidence. Give specific examples to illustrate your point.

SOURCE

Celtis' appeal to stop Rome's exploitation of Germany. Conrad Celtis was a German humanist, historian and poet. This is from the inaugural speech that he gave to the University of Ingoldstadt in 1492.

O men of Germany, assume those ancient passions by which you were so often a dread and terror to the Romans, and turn your eyes to the wants of Germany... What a shame to have a yoke of servitude imposed on our nation and to pay tribute and taxes to foreign and barbaric kings. O free and strong people, O noble and brave nation... our land is being emptied of its wonderful natural resources, while we pay from the public treasury to others what we need for ourselves.

SOURCE

Ulrich von Hutten on Rome's exploitation of Germany, from a letter that he wrote to the Elector Frederick the Wise in 1520.

We see that there is no gold and almost no silver in our German land. What little there may be left is drawn away daily by new schemes invented by the council of the most holy members of the Roman Curia. What is thus squeezed from us is put to the most shameful uses. ... Leo X gives a part of it to his nephews and relations. A portion is consumed by a host of the most reverend cardinals (of which the Holy Father created no fewer than one and thirty in a single day), as well as in supporting innumerable referendaries, auditors, protonotaries, abbreviators, apostolic secretaries, chamberlains and a variety of officials forming the elite of the great Head Church.

These in turn draw after them, at untold expense, copyists, beadles, messengers, servants, scullions, mule-drivers, grooms and a countless army of prostitutes and the most degraded followers. They maintain dogs, horses, monkeys, long-tailed apes and many more such creatures for their pleasure. They build houses all of marble. ... In short, a vast number of the worst men are supported in Rome in idle indulgence by means of our money.

A Level Exam-Style Question Section A

How far could the historian make use of Sources 11 and 12 together to investigate the levels and causes of anti-papalism in the empire?

Explain your answer using both the sources, the information given about them, and your own knowledge of the historical context. (20 marks)

Tip

See the Extend Your Knowledge box on the three humanists earlier in this chapter (page 181).

The indulgence controversy of 1517

One of the 'new schemes' referred to by von Hutten in Source 12 was the indulgence issued by Leo X in 1515. Determined to leave his mark in history, Leo X had decided to complete the rebuilding of **St Peter's Basilica**, begun by Julius II and still far from finished.

Leo wanted a magnificent new Basilica to glorify God, revive Rome (sadly dilapidated at the time) and demonstrate the power of the papacy. Huge costs were involved, and Leo decided to raise the money by issuing an indulgence. It was the usual method of fundraising at the time. To organise its sale in the empire, Leo sought the co-operation of the most influential banker in Germany, Jakob Fugger of Augsburg. Fugger decided to link the sale with the needs of another client, Albert of Brandenburg, the brother of the Margrave of Brandenburg, who was one of the seven electors.

Albert was ambitiously accumulating power: aged 23, he was already Archbishop of Magdeburg and Bishop of Halberstadt. In 1514, the Archbishopric of Mainz fell vacant. It was a real prize: whoever became Archbishop of Mainz also became an elector, the primate of Germany and imperial chancellor. Under normal circumstances, Albert would have had to surrender his other positions to get the post, but if he could pay Rome a huge sum, a dispensation would be granted.

So a deal was made: Jakob Fugger would lend Albert the money he needed; Albert would sell the indulgences, and then funnel half the money back to Fugger, and send the rest to Rome. Everyone would win: Albert would be an elector and archbishop twice over; St Peter's would be built; the faithful would gain time off purgatory. Albert hired Johann Tetzel, a Dominican friar, to run the sales campaign in his provinces of Mainz and Magdeburg. This indulgence was to be the most powerful ever sold, as Albert's instructions made clear.

SOURCE 13

The *Instructio Summaria* of Albert of Mainz, 1515. This is part of the instructions that Albert issued to Tetzel and his other indulgence sellers.

The following are the four principal gifts of grace that have been granted by the **Apostolic Bull**; any one of them can be had separately. It is on these four Indulgences that the preachers must concentrate their utmost diligence, infiltrating them one by one into the ears of the faithful in the most effective way, and explaining them with all the ability they have.

The first principal grace is the plenary remission of all sins... Punishments to be undergone in purgatory because of offence done to the divine majesty, are remitted in full, and the punishments of the said purgatory are totally wiped out. ... We lay down the following procedure:

First, let every penitent who has made oral confession visit at least seven of the churches appointed for this purpose and in each church let him say with devotion five **Paternosters** and five **Ave Marias**... If anyone for any reason seeks to be excused the visit to the said churches or altars, the penitentiaries, having heard the reason, may allow it: such a visit may be compounded by a larger financial contribution. ...

The fourth principal grace is the plenary remission of all sins for the souls that exist in purgatory... A contribution placed by the living in the repository counts as one which a man might make or give for himself. ... There is no need for the contributors to be of contrite heart or to make oral confession, since this grace depends (as the Bull makes clear) on the love in which the departed died and the contributions which the living pay.

SOURCE 14

Tetzel's sales technique. This account was written by Frederick Myconius in the 1530s. Myconius became a Lutheran preacher in 1524 and led the reformation of Gotha, a town in Saxony. This account appeared in his brief history of the start of the Reformation in Saxony.

Tetzel gained by his preaching in Germany an immense sum of money, all of which he sent to Rome; and especially at the new mining works at St Annaberg, where I, Frederick Mecum, heard him for two years, a large sum of money was collected. It is incredible what this ignorant and impudent friar gave out. He said that if a Christian had slept with his mother, and placed the sum of money in the pope's indulgence chest, the pope had power in heaven and earth to forgive the sin, and, if he forgave it, God must do so also. Item, if they contributed readily and bought grace and indulgence, all the hills of St Annaberg would become pure massive silver. Item, so soon as the coin rang in the chest, the soul for whom the money was paid would go straightaway to heaven. The indulgence was so highly prized that, when the commissary entered a city, the Bull was borne on a satin or gold-embroidered cushion, and all the priests and monks, the town council, schoolmaster, scholars, men, women, maidens, and children, went out to meet him with banners and tapers, with songs and procession. Then all the bells were rung, all the organs played; he was conducted into the church, a red cross was erected into the midst of the church, and the pope's banner displayed; in short, God himself could not have been welcomed and entertained with greater honour.

Sales were good, but Tetzel's aggressive marketing tactics did not win universal approval. By October 1517, he had reached the borders of Electoral Saxony. The people of Saxony reacted in three very different ways: Frederick the Wise refused Tetzel permission to enter; his subjects flooded over the border anyway, keen to purchase such a powerful indulgence; and Luther wrote a list of 95 Theses (or arguments) against indulgences.

AS Level Exam-Style Question Section A

How much weight do you give the evidence of Frederick Myconius for an enquiry into the impact of Tetzel's sale of the indulgence?

Explain your answer using the source, the information given about it and your own knowledge of the historical context. (12 marks)

Tip

Look carefully at what you learn about Myconius in the information given about the source. Was he likely to be an observant and reliable eyewitness?

Good questions/Bad questions

Below are three contemporaries of Tetzel. Their views are generalisations for the purpose of this exercise.

Frederick the Wise	Ulrich von Hutten	Jakob Fugger
He is a devout Catholic and an elector. He believes in the power of indulgences. He wants nothing to detract from his own indulgence sale.	He is a German nationalist, and interested in keeping foreign influences out of Germany.	He is a devout Catholic and a banker. He is interested above all in recouping the loans he has made to the Archbishop of Mainz.

Work in groups.

1 Devise three criteria for what makes a good historical question.

2 Consider what you know about the indulgences being sold by Tetzel.

3 Each write a historical question based on this subject matter.

4 Put these in rank order, with the best question first, based on your criteria.

5 Using a piece of A3 paper, write the names of the three Germans so they form a large triangle.

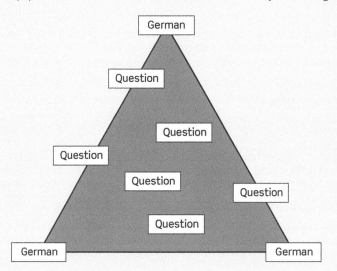

6 Write your questions from (3) on the piece of paper, so that their positions reflect how likely the Germans are to be interested by each question. For example, a question about where the money was going would interest a nationalist like Hutten and a banker like Fugger.

7 Add some further questions. Try to think of questions that only one of the three would be interested in.

8 Take it in turns to try to answer the questions you have created in the style of one of the Germans. See if the other members of the group can guess which one it was.

ACTIVITY
SUMMARY

Conditions for Luther

This chapter started with a statement made by the historian Henry J. Cohn: 'In all eras outstanding leaders require favourable conditions to persuade large populations to change their outlook on the world.'

Write an essay with the title 'How "favourable" for Luther were conditions in Germany by 1517?'

Tip 1: Always notice dates – 1517 precedes the imperial election.

Tip 2: If you are puzzled about how to start, you might consider mind-mapping or a spider diagram. Create a spider with four 'legs', labelled 'Political', 'Socio-economic', 'Religious' and 'Cultural' – the factors that might help to account for Luther's fairly instant popularity. Then, for each factor, add further 'legs'. For example, cultural factors might include the growing sense of national identity. Can you establish links between any of these factors? They exist – in many cases, it is impossible to disentangle one thing from another. Draw on these links. Finally, which factor do you consider the most important?

AS Level Exam-Style Questions Section B

1 To what extent was the German Reformation caused by humanist criticisms of the Catholic Church? (20 marks)

2 How far was the German Reformation caused by hostility towards the papacy within the German nation? (20 marks)

3 How accurate is it to say that corruption within the Catholic Church was the main cause of the German Reformation? (20 marks)

Tip

You will always find it easier to tackle questions on the causes of the Reformation if you can decide ahead of time which factor was the most important and if you can justify your decision. Questions 1–3 each highlight one factor and ask about its importance. Do not rush through that factor, deal with it thoroughly before moving on to what you believe to be the key cause(s).

A Level Exam-Style Question Section B

The controversy over indulgences was merely the trigger rather than the fundamental cause of the German Reformation. How far do you agree with this statement? (20 marks)

Tip

Plan your answer before you begin to write. This should be a three-part essay that might be summed up with three words: agree, however, furthermore. Have an overall judgement in mind before you start so that you can argue from the beginning, and when you tackle the 'agree' section you can do so in an evaluative way. Do you strongly agree? Or is there only limited evidence to suggest this is true?

 WIDER READING

Cameron, E. *The European Reformation*, Clarendon Press (1991)

Kümin, B. (ed.) *The European World 1500–1800: An Introduction to Early Modern History*, Routledge (2009)

Lee, S. *Aspects of European History 1494–1789*, Routledge (1978)

Morris, T.A. *Europe and England in the Sixteenth Century*, Routledge (1998)

Murphy, D., Tilbrook, M., Walsh-Atkins, P. *Europe 1450–1661*, Harper Collins (2000)

Scribner, R.W. *The German Reformation*, Macmillan (1986)

Tuchman, B. *The March of Folly: From Troy to Vietnam*, Random House (1984)

2a.2 Luther's early challenge to the Catholic Church

KEY QUESTIONS

- What shaped Luther's life to 1517?
- Why did Luther write the 95 Theses?
- What influenced the development of his ideas in the years 1517–20?
- Why was Luther excommunicated in 1521?

INTRODUCTION

In 1505, after a completely normal middle-class upbringing and a sound education, Martin Luther suddenly turned his back on training to be a lawyer and became an Augustinian monk. After lengthy training, he was sent by his order to teach in the University of Wittenberg, founded by Duke Frederick the Wise in 1502. His studies and experiences from 1505 to 1517 led him to question the scriptural bases of current teachings on how to achieve salvation. He took particular exception to the claims being made by Johann Tetzel, and in 1517, wrote 95 Theses (or propositions) attacking Tetzel's sale of indulgences. Luther's challenge, unexpectedly, had an extraordinary impact: the Theses were soon the talk of Germany.

Luther was a loyal Catholic in 1517, and he might well have limited himself to denouncing indulgences; indeed the whole affair might even have died down had it not been for the way in which Rome and the Dominican order reacted. Bitter attacks from both forced Luther to defend his own position and think through more deeply the implications of what he had written. Because of his own stubbornness and the strength he drew from the wide support he was receiving, Luther refused to back down. Far from recanting, he became more radical. What had started as a minor challenge to one practice developed into a major confrontation over papal authority and core Catholic beliefs. In 1520, he issued three key pamphlets explaining his new position, and then dramatically burned the papal threat of **excommunication**.

KEY TERM

Excommunication
The most severe discipline short of execution that a pope could give out. If someone was excommunicated, they were expelled from the Church. No Christian could help them. They could not receive the sacraments. Their soul would go to Hell.

1483 – Luther's birth

1505 – Joins the Erfurt branch of the reformed Augustinian order

1508 – Lectures for one semester at the University of Wittenberg

1510–11 – Goes to Rome on business for his order

| 1483 | 1500 | 1501 | 1502 | 1503 | 1504 | 1505 | 1506 | 1507 | 1508 | 1509 | 1510 | 1511 |

1501–5 – Attends the University of Erfurt

1507 – Ordained to the priesthood

1509 – Lecturer in Erfurt

1511 – Transfers to the Augustinian Monastery in Wittenberg

SOURCE 1 This image was made in 1617 when Lutheran Germany celebrated the centenary of Luther posting his 95 Theses on the Castle Church door in Wittenberg.

1512 – Doctor of Theology conferred; begins teaching theology at the University of Wittenberg

1518 – May: Addresses a meeting of the Augustinian order at Heidelberg

October: Interviewed by Cardinal Cajetan in Augsburg

1520 – June: Papal bull *Exsurge Domine*

August–November: Writes the three pamphlets

December: Burns the papal bull *Exsurge Domine*

1512	1513	1514	1515	1516	1517	1518	1519	1520	1521

1517 – October: Nails his 95 Theses to the door of the Castle Church

1519 – January: Death of Maximilian

June: Charles V is elected emperor

July: Leipzig Debates with Dr Eck

1521 – January: Excommunicated

WHAT SHAPED LUTHER'S LIFE TO 1517?

Luther's childhood

Very few facts exist about Luther's childhood. Much of what is known comes from stories relayed years later by Luther himself, which were noted down by his eager listeners and later published in a book known as his *Table Talk*.

> **KEY TERM**
>
> *Luther's Table Talk*
> In 1566, John Mathesius published a volume called *Luther's Table Talk*. Mathesius was a teacher who became a Lutheran minister in later life. In 1540, he spent seven months lodging with Luther during his training, and wrote down everything that his hero said over the dinner table. This formed the core of the *Table Talk*, to which Mathesius added notes made by other students. In one sense, the *Table Talk* is invaluable – it is a rare glimpse of an unguarded Luther.

Unfortunately, memory is a fickle thing. Memories can lapse. For example, Luther was born in the small town of Eisleben in Saxony, but his mother could not remember which year; the rest of the family thought it was 1483. Memories can also be distorted. In later life, Luther projected himself as a man of the people, someone who came from very humble origins and who had endured deprivation, poverty and strict discipline.

- 'I am the son of a peasant. My great-grandfather, grandfather, and father were peasants. I might have become an overseer, bailiff, or some such village official, one servant among others with authority over the rest. Then my father moved to Mansfeld, where he became a miner. This is where I came from.'

- 'In his youth my father was a poor miner. My mother carried all her wood home on her back. It was in this way that they brought me up.'

- 'My father once whipped me so severely that I ran away, and he was worried that he might not win me back again.'

- 'For the sake of stealing a mere nut, my mother beat me until the blood flowed.'

The reality was different. His father's family were actually reasonably successful Thuringian farmers in Electoral Saxony, where they had carefully consolidated land through marriage. The inheritance was not subdivided equally among all sons, as happened elsewhere in Germany, but left to the youngest son. Luther's father, Hans, left because, under Thuringian law, he was not going to inherit.

Luther's reference to his father as a miner is accurate. A year after Luther's birth, the family had moved to Mansfeld, the centre of Saxony's copper-mining industry. However, the phrase 'poor' was far from the mark. Hans did very well indeed: he eventually supervised several mine shafts (the mines themselves being owned by the Counts of Mansfeld) and rented foundries. One can infer a level-headed, hard-working businessman who was clearly respected, since he was chosen as one of four citizens to sit on the town council in 1491, when Luther would have been about eight years old.

Luther's 'peasant background' narrative also completely ignores his maternal roots. His mother's family background was urban, professional and highly educated. The Lindemanns of Eisenach (Luther's maternal cousins) were doctors, lawyers, mayors, magistrates and teachers. One Lindemann relative was chairman of Eisenach's council when Luther started attending school there; another was a professor of medicine at Wittenberg University when Luther arrived there.

Luther's recollections of exceptionally harsh parental discipline can also be viewed with a little scepticism. His mother Margarethe 'possessed all the virtues which are fitting in an honourable woman', according to Melanchthon, Luther's deputy from 1519. 'Other upright women used to take her as an example of virtue.' Honesty and unquestioning obedience to parental authority were expected at the time, and even Luther later said, 'They meant heartily well by it.' There is no reason to doubt that, the odd beating aside, Luther's childhood was anything other than a normal, happy one. He had six brothers and sisters; luxuries may have been few, but the 'deprived childhood' line has little substance, given Hans' success.

Luther's earliest religious education probably came from his devout mother. Luther was baptised the day after his birth and named after St Martin, whose Saint's Day it was, rather than given a family name as would have been usual. Margarethe probably passed on to her children prayers, Bible stories, the importance of good deeds, and the fact that God was a stern judge who would punish sinners just as strictly as their parents did. She also passed on her widely held beliefs in demons, witches and evil spirits, not least that the devil was loose when a thunderstorm broke. The household probably did not own a Bible.

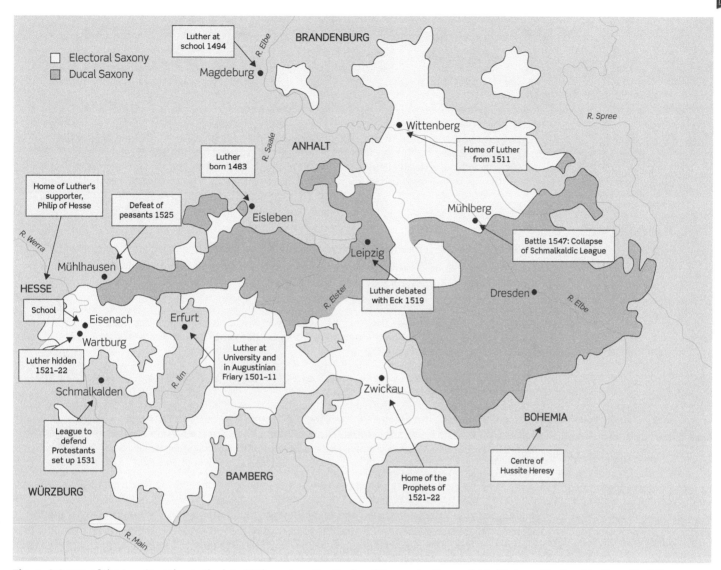

Figure 2.1 Map of the two Saxonies. In the late 15th century, the Duchy of Saxony had been divided in two – Electoral (or Ernestine) Saxony and Ducal (or Albertine) Saxony – and the borders of the two wove in and out of each other in an untidy way. The Luther family was based in Electoral Saxony, ruled by Duke Frederick the Wise.

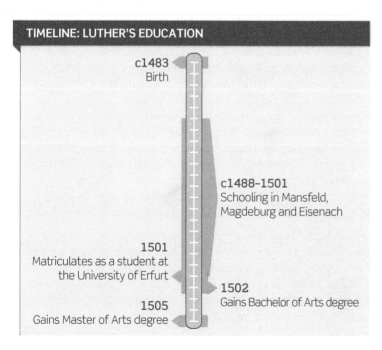

TIMELINE: LUTHER'S EDUCATION

c1483 Birth

c1488–1501 Schooling in Mansfeld, Magdeburg and Eisenach

1501 Matriculates as a student at the University of Erfurt

1502 Gains Bachelor of Arts degree

1505 Gains Master of Arts degree

Luther's education

Hans invested considerable money in his sons' education, so was clearly ambitious for them. From the age of five, Luther attended school. For eight years, he walked daily to a local school in Mansfeld, where the curriculum consisted of Latin and religion and much rote learning. Discipline was tough. Luther later recalled that he once endured 15 beatings in a single day because he had failed to do some homework.

He was then sent to board at a grammar school in the city of Magdeburg, one of the largest cities in the empire. This school may have been one of a number run by the Brethren of Common Life; Erasmus had attended another in Deventer. If it was a Brethren school, Luther was exposed to high standards of scholarship, with an emphasis on inner piety, humility and simplicity of life. It is difficult to gauge quite how much of an impact the Brethren's approach made, since Luther's time with them was short-lived, but in 1532, he defended one Common Life school from closure, writing, 'Your way of life, since you teach and live according to the Gospel, pleases me no end.'

He did retain one clear memory of his time in Magdeburg, which he relayed in 1533, and which is interesting because it resembles Luther's own ideas about how to achieve salvation when he first became a monk.

SOURCE

This account reveals the extent to which men would go to clean themselves of sin, in the hope of achieving salvation through good works. Luther wrote this 35 years later, in 1533, so it had clearly made an impression.

When, in my fourteenth year, I went to school at Magdeburg, I saw with my own eyes a prince of Anhalt, a brother of the Bishop of Merseburg, walk and beg for bread on Broadstreet, with the skullcap of the order of the Barefeet, carrying like a donkey on his back a sack so heavy it bent him to the ground, but his companion walked by him without a burden; this prince alone might serve as an example of the grisly, shorn holiness of the world. He had so castigated himself by going without food and sleep that he looked like the picture of death, nothing but skin and bones. And, indeed, he died soon after, for he could not long bear such a severe life. Whoever saw him could not help gasping with reverence and must needs be ashamed of his own worldly condition.

Within a year, his father transferred him to another grammar school, this time in Eisenach – the fact that his mother's side came from Eisenach was probably the reason, since Luther could now board with relatives. Here he studied Latin for a further four years. In later life, he praised his teacher's talent for presenting grammar 'correctly and skilfully'.

University

Hans Luther's ambitions for his son were high, and in 1500 or 1501, when Luther was 17 or 18 years old, he enrolled at the University of Erfurt, which had been founded in 1392 and was considered one of the best in Germany. Since most students started at about the age of 14, Luther was on the old side, but it is possible that his father had to save for the necessary fees. Today, students choose their degree courses. In Luther's day, everyone had to complete a bachelor's degree and then a master's degree in the Faculty of Liberal Arts. Only then was it possible to specialise in one of the three Higher Faculties of Theology, Law or Medicine. The liberal arts courses that Luther followed were probably predetermined: grammar, rhetoric, logic; and then geometry, arithmetic, music and astronomy. The curriculum was not as random as it seemed, and these courses had formed the grounding needed for those wishing to pursue a career in the Church. Rhetoric, for example, was an exploration in the art of persuasion. Studying geometry and astronomy was a way of understanding God's creation: God had constructed the universe and the planets using geometric principles. The works of the ancient Greek polymath Aristotle dominated all schemes of work, though with changes made to harmonise his views with Christianity. These medieval commentaries on Aristotle formed the core of all learning.

'Scholastic' teaching methods dominated. Students were expected to absorb and regurgitate what they were taught, with an emphasis on memory. Lectures involved dictation; textbooks were written in question-and-answer form. Scholastics also placed enormous emphasis on logical argument. This skill was developed during 'disputations' or formal debates between students, on a preset topic or even a single sentence taken from a medieval commentary or classical text. Ingenuity in arguing was prized above all things. Luther seems to have been rather good at disputing, since he acquired the nickname 'the philosopher'.

Luther achieved his Bachelor of Arts degree in a year, which was impressive (but he was older than usual), and then, in 1505, his Master of Arts, when he came second in a list of 17 candidates. He was now in a position to proceed to one of the three Higher Faculties. Hans decided that Luther should become a lawyer, following in the professional footsteps of the Lindemann relatives, and he gave his son the required textbook on Roman law. Luther's future looked promising. However, two months into his law course, Luther suddenly packed it all in. He decided to become a monk.

The decision to become a monk, July 1505

SOURCE 3

Luther explains why he became a monk, as recorded by a student in July 1539.

On St Alexis day, Luther said, 'Today is the anniversary of entering the monastery at Erfurt.' Then he began to tell the story of how he had made his vow two weeks before when, travelling near Stotternheim, not far from Erfurt, he had been so shaken by a flash of lightning, that he cried out in terror, 'Help me, St Anna, and I will become a monk.' ... 'Afterwards I regretted the vow and others tried to dissuade me. But I stuck to it, and on the day before St Alexis Day I invited my friends to a farewell, that they might accompany me on the morrow. When they would have restrained me, I said, "Today you look on me for the last time." So, with tears, they came with me. My father, too, was angry about the vow, but I stuck with my decision. I never dreamed of leaving the monastery. I had quite died to the world.'

SOURCE 4

A letter from Luther to his father, 1521.

I told you that I had been called by terrors from heaven and become a monk against my own will and desire (to say nothing of the inclinations of the flesh!); I had been beleaguered by the terror and agony of sudden death, and I made my vows perforce and of necessity. Then you said – 'May it not prove an illusion and a deception.' That word penetrated and lodged in the depths of my soul, as if God had spoken through your mouth.

In both accounts, Luther presented his decision to become a monk as a very sudden thing, done reluctantly and in fear. However, it has been suggested that the storm was used to validate a decision already made. For years, Luther had been absorbing the same education traditionally provided for clergy. Recent events then focused his mind more than ever on his own salvation. A serious accident with a knife almost cost him his life and some friends had died from the plague. He later testified that he had also been experiencing acute depression for about six months before his decision. In other words, the storm episode, and especially the 'vow to St Anne' element (since she was the patron saint of miners), may have been used to placate his extremely angry father, who had just purchased a very expensive legal textbook and had other plans for his son. An alternative view is that Luther later used the story to validate his own view that he had been chosen by God: through divine intervention, Luther became God's vehicle for change. He himself drew attention to the fact that in Hebrew 'Anna' means 'grace'. Like her, he was favoured by the grace of God.

Luther's experiences as a monk, 1505–11

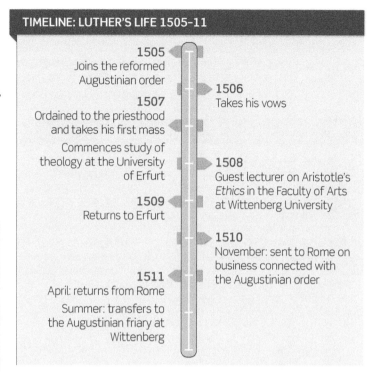

TIMELINE: LUTHER'S LIFE 1505–11

1505 Joins the reformed Augustinian order

1506 Takes his vows

1507 Ordained to the priesthood and takes his first mass

Commences study of theology at the University of Erfurt

1508 Guest lecturer on Aristotle's *Ethics* in the Faculty of Arts at Wittenberg University

1509 Returns to Erfurt

1510 November: sent to Rome on business connected with the Augustinian order

1511 April: returns from Rome

Summer: transfers to the Augustinian friary at Wittenberg

Luther joined the Erfurt branch of the order of St Augustine. The Augustinians had been founded in 1256, and by 1500 had over 2,000 branches in Europe, with 100 in Germany. It was a strict order that had already been reformed. It was not a 'closed' order: Augustinians worked in the community as teachers and university lecturers. (In theory, therefore, they were friars, though Luther referred to himself as a monk.)

Following a year's probation, Luther took the three vows of poverty, chastity and obedience; within two years, he was ordained a priest. If his *Table Talk* is to be believed, Luther could not have been more conscientious as a monk: he subjected himself to severe discipline, even removing blankets in his icy cell; he fasted until he was a skeleton; he prayed for hours at a stretch; he confessed his sins at exhausting length. His acute anxieties about death and salvation threatened his health. Yet nothing he did relieved his sense of utter despair; he would never be able to do enough to merit salvation. God was cruelly demanding. Luther's lengthy confessions must have been exasperating: 'On one occasion, my father confessor said to me when I was constantly bringing stupid sins to him: "You are a fool! God does not rage at you, but you rage at him; God is not angry with you, but you are angry with him!"'

Through all his anxieties, Luther's patient mentor was Johann von Staupitz, head of the Augustinians in Germany from 1503 and first dean of the Faculty of Theology of Wittenberg University, which he had helped to found. Staupitz drew Luther's attention to the works of the order's patron, St Augustine of Hippo, who stressed that man's actions had no effect on whether or not he was saved. God alone decided who would be saved. Luther was putting himself through torment for nothing. Initially, Luther found no relief in this knowledge, it seemed to prove that God was pitiless.

'I hated this just God who punishes sinners', he later wrote. Nevertheless, the Augustinian interpretation was markedly different to Rome's teaching on the issue of salvation. Rome favoured the interpretation given by St Thomas Aquinas (d1274): Thomists (the 'old' school of scholastics) taught that men became righteous in God's eyes (or sin-free and worthy of salvation) by doing righteous things, or good works. The problem here was that one never knew if one had done enough, as Luther had found out. Trying harder had no effect.

EXTEND YOUR KNOWLEDGE

St Augustine of Hippo (354–430)
The patron of Luther's order had been Bishop of Hippo in what is now Algeria. St Augustine argued that nothing that man can do can remove the stain of the Original Sin committed by Adam and Eve. Mankind was hopelessly corrupted by this, and salvation could therefore never be earned through good works. Instead, man must rely on God's grace. God was all-powerful and had already decided who would be saved. Salvation was therefore predestined, or predetermined. St Augustine's views on salvation were much influenced by the Letters of St Paul, and his books, *Confessions* (400) and *The City of God* (412-27), were to be a huge influence themselves on Protestant reformers.

Staupitz also suggested that Luther return to university to study for a degree in theology, perhaps hoping to divert Luther's attention. The Faculty of Theology at Erfurt was dominated by scholastic teaching methods and the study of 'modern' theologians and philosophers belonging to the 'Nominalist School'. 'Modern' was a relative word: the chief philosopher studied was William of Ockham, who had died in 1349. According to Nominalists, one cannot use reason to arrive at a conclusion about God. Religious truth can only be known by faith, in the scriptures as God's word, and in the authority of the Church. The emphasis placed on faith was one that Luther later adopted, though he was to discard the Nominalist emphasis on the authority of the Church, and he certainly discarded their approach to learning.

Studying theology, Luther cannot have been oblivious to a humanist wind of change in the world of higher education. Since the late 15th century, humanists had been mounting a challenge to the scholastic teaching methods dominating universities. Learning by rote, they said, was stifling original thought and creativity. Endlessly disputing single sentences taken out of context was stifling the understanding that can only come from studying entire texts. Humanists argued that the scholastics were uncritically accepting medieval interpretations and commentaries on the Bible. It was time, they said, to cut down this undergrowth and return to original sources. In other words, rather than relying on what medieval scholars had said about the Bible, one should study the Bible itself, and works written by the **Early Church Fathers**.

KEY TERM

Early Church Fathers
The 'Early Church' refers to the first four or five centuries of Christianity following Christ's crucifixion. Protestants viewed the Early Church as a role model, and placed huge importance on the works of the key Christian writers of this period, whom they called the Early Church Fathers. St Augustine of Hippo was one of the greatest of these.

The stress should be placed on understanding the author and thinking about why he wrote what he did, not on memorising what he said. Language skills were essential: in Erasmus' view, 'No one ever understood any other person's opinions without knowing the language in which that opinion was expressed.' The humanists were proposing a new way of learning and a new way of thinking. Though there is little evidence that Luther mixed in humanist circles at Erfurt University, what they said must have made an impact on Luther, since he adopted their approach when he became a lecturer at Wittenberg University.

Luther's visit to Rome, 1510–11

In November 1510, Luther was sent to Rome on business connected with his order, and this is a measure of the trust that Staupitz placed in him. Luther chose to treat the month-long journey there as a pilgrimage, and on arrival he plunged into the usual round of pilgrim fare: he attended services, said confession, visited the seven pilgrim churches, prayed before the high altar of St Peter's (presumably amidst the scaffolding of its ongoing construction) and viewed sacred relics, including one of the 30 pieces of silver paid to Judas to betray Jesus. He climbed the **Scala Sancta** on his knees, saying a prayer at each step to save the soul of his grandfather in purgatory. He toured the catacombs by torchlight. The latter, deep tunnels beneath Rome, were said to contain the bones of 176,000 early Christian martyrs. He was, in other words, a very fervent pilgrim indeed, and certainly still adhering to the Thomist approach to salvation. If he had any doubts about what he was doing, he did not express them at the time. On the other hand, the experience did not bring the spiritual relief he sought, and the trip may well have pushed him towards the Augustinian approach to salvation. Furthermore, though he did not see the pope, the worldliness and insincerity of Rome's clergy did not impress him.

KEY TERM

Scala Sancta
The 'Holy Stairs' to Pontius Pilate's palace in Jerusalem, mounted by Jesus on his way to trial. They were brought to Rome by St Helena in the fourth century and are still 'climbed' in the same way, on one's knees and with a prayer at each step.

SOURCE

Luther on Rome (from several sources).

Rome is a harlot. I would not take a thousand gulden not to have seen it, for I would never have believed the true state of affairs from what other people told me, had I not seen it myself.

The Italians mocked us for being pious priests, for they hold Christians fools. They say six or seven masses in the time it takes for me to say one, for they take money for it and I do not.

The only crime in Italy is poverty. They still punish homicide and theft a little, for they have to, but no other sin is too gross for them.

So great and bold is Roman impiety that neither God nor man, neither sin nor shame, is feared. All good men who have seen Rome bear witness to this; all bad ones come back worse than before.

Luther at Wittenberg

SOURCE
6

This coloured woodcut was made c1558 and comes from the Cranach Studio. It shows the small town of Wittenberg (population 2,000), beside the River Elbe. To the left is the elector's castle ('Das Schlos'), in which was housed Frederick's relic collection. Behind the castle, the spire of the Castle Church can be seen. In the centre are the twin spires of the main town church, St Mary's. The three buildings labelled on the right are, in order, the University of Wittenberg ('Collegium'), Philip Melanchthon's house and the Augustinian friary, the largest building on the extreme right, where Luther lived. Note the defensive walls surrounding the town, built in the 15th century.

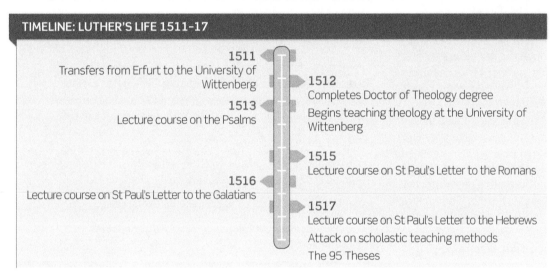

TIMELINE: LUTHER'S LIFE 1511–17

1511
Transfers from Erfurt to the University of Wittenberg

1512
Completes Doctor of Theology degree
Begins teaching theology at the University of Wittenberg

1513
Lecture course on the Psalms

1515
Lecture course on St Paul's Letter to the Romans

1516
Lecture course on St Paul's Letter to the Galatians

1517
Lecture course on St Paul's Letter to the Hebrews
Attack on scholastic teaching methods
The 95 Theses

Three months after his return from Rome, Luther was transferred to Wittenberg to teach in the university there. Wittenberg was a grim town, if contemporary opinions are anything to go by. Luther's later opponents were scathing: Duke George of Saxony called Wittenberg 'a hole', and the Dominican Johann Dietenberger wrote that 'The poor, miserable, filthy little town of Wittenberg isn't even worthy to be called a town in Germany; an unhealthy, unpleasant piece of land; without vineyards; without parks; without orchards; rough; half-frozen; joyless; filled with muck. What's left in Wittenberg, if the castle, monastery, and school were gone? Filthy houses; untidy alleys; all paths, ways, and streets full of mire; a barbarian people which doesn't do anything but farming and small trade.' Even Lutheran supporters were negative. Melanchthon, Luther's deputy from 1519, called Wittenberg 'a hamlet comprised, not of regular houses, but only of little ones, bad huts, built out of clay and covered with hay and straw'.

Luther's new life in Wittenberg was exceptionally busy. He had multiple duties in the Augustinian friary as a reader at meals, an official preacher in the town church, vicar to 11 outlying friaries, and even as an inspector of fish ponds. Meanwhile, at the university, on the retirement of Johann von Staupitz in 1512, he became Professor of Biblical Theology, which involved directing students' studies, giving lectures twice a week and presiding over the disputations held every Friday.

Luther was immediately caught up in the dispute occupying every university theology faculty – whether teaching methods should follow the scholastic tradition, based on studying what medieval commentators had said about the Bible, or the new humanist approach, based on a return to the Bible itself, and the works of the Early Church Fathers. Most Wittenberg lecturers were scholastics, but Luther decided to take the humanist *ad fontes* approach. He based his lectures on his own detailed examination of the Bible and the works of St Augustine.

When Erasmus' New Testament in Greek was published in 1516, he used that, painstakingly teaching himself Greek. In April 1517, he even wrote an attack on the scholastic approach as divorced from reality and artificial, thus seriously annoying his old teachers at Erfurt University. Luther's attack suggests that he already supported the view that the scriptures and works of the Early Church Fathers were more important than medieval thinkers had said. This was later to develop into one of his key beliefs – *sola scriptura* – the scriptures were the sole source of authority on doctrine.

KEY TERM

Sola scriptura
The truth concerning all spiritual matters is in the scriptures alone, which must be translated into the vernacular to make the Word of God accessible to all. Interpretation, however, must be reserved for state-approved preachers.

Luther's studies of early Christian teachings were also gradually changing his view of God. He was moving away from Thomist views about how to achieve salvation. His research initially followed the teachings of St Augustine of Hippo – that man cannot save himself through his own actions; God has already predetermined who will be saved. However, in Luther's eyes, this not only made God seem harsh, but it was not very helpful: people still did not know if they would be saved. At some point, possibly as he prepared for his 1515 lecture course on St Paul's Letter to the Romans, he found a way to make the Augustinian theory palatable. He found relief in St Paul's words, 'The righteous shall live by faith.' Luther interpreted this as meaning that faith, and faith alone, was the key to salvation. God was not harsh, but loving and merciful; he had already sent his Son, Jesus, into the world to save sinners. A person just had to repent and believe in God's mercy. There was nothing new about this view – it had already been expressed by other humanists. In France, for example, Jacques Lefevre d'Etaples used the expression 'faith alone' in 1512.

'Faith alone', or '*sola fide*', was to become the other key belief of Luther. Whether or not he had already reached this belief by 1517 is open to dispute. He did not express the view explicitly until 1520, and in his *Autobiographical Fragment*, written just before he died, he said he only made his 'breakthrough' in 1519. However, if Luther was already moving in that direction, it would explain his objection to Tetzel's sale of indulgences: taken to its logical conclusion, 'faith alone' meant that 'good works' like buying indulgences were useless.

ACTIVITY
KNOWLEDGE CHECK

Luther's influences
Taking each of the following categories in turn, who or what had the most influence on Luther's life to 1517?

People:	Hans Luther, Margarethe Luther or Johann von Staupitz?
Teaching methods:	Scholasticism or humanism?
Ideas on how to achieve salvation:	Thomist or Augustinian ideas?
Places:	Magdeburg, Rome or Wittenberg?

THE 95 THESES OF 1517

In April 1517, Tetzel reached the borders of Electoral Saxony. His marketing of the indulgences was more aggressive than ever. He urged his audiences to imagine the voices of their parents in purgatory: 'We have created you, fed you, cared for you, and left you our temporal goods. Why then are you so cruel and harsh that you do not want to save us, though it only takes a little? You let us lie in flames.'

The Elector Frederick the Wise was furious about the indulgence sale and banned Tetzel from his territories. His anger was based on politics and money. Tetzel's employer, Albert of Mainz, was a member of the Hohenzollern family, Frederick's rivals for influence in the empire – Albert and his brother, the Margrave of Brandenburg, now held two electorships. Also, while the pope's indulgence was being sold, all other indulgences had to be suspended. That would mean a drastic loss in revenue for Frederick, who, over the years, had built up an exceptionally impressive collection of over 17,000 relics, one of the largest in Germany, including a twig from Moses' burning bush, hay from the holy manger, and milk from the Virgin Mary. His collection was next due to be open to the public on All Saints Day, 1 November, and those who paid to see it could obtain merit worth more than 1,902,202 years less in purgatory.

For entirely different reasons, Luther also had objections. On the basis of his intense study of the scriptures, he had had doubts about indulgences for more than a year. Now Tetzel's proximity and outrageous promises, coupled with the flood of excited Wittenbergers over the border to make their purchases, added angry fuel to his beliefs. He wrote 95 Theses (or arguments for debate) about indulgences, which he allegedly pinned to the door of the Castle Church in Wittenberg on 31 October 1517.

In the 95 Theses, Luther argued the following points.

- The theological rationale for these indulgences was very dubious indeed:
  - The pope had no control over purgatory – God alone had that
  - Souls could not therefore be released from purgatory through the purchase of papal pardons
  - Forgiveness was a free gift from God for all truly repentant Christians – it could not be purchased.
- Indulgence selling was harmful:
  - It detracted from the really important thing – preaching the Word of God as revealed in the Gospels
  - It undermined the sacrament of penance and encouraged complacency – sinners did not even need to be contrite to make a purchase, while many seemed to believe they could now sin without fear of punishment
  - It discouraged far more worthy uses for money, like giving to charity
  - The poor could not afford such things – they were giving up all their savings on false premises
  - The pope's reputation was suffering because Rome seemed to be exploiting impoverished Germans.

SOURCE 7 A selection from Luther's 95 Theses, October 1517.

1 When our Lord and Master, Jesus Christ, said 'Repent...', he meant that the whole life of believers should be one of penitence.

2 The word cannot be understood as referring to the sacrament of penance, in other words of confession and satisfaction, as administered by priests.

5 The pope has neither the will nor the power to remit any penalties beyond those he has imposed either at his own discretion or by canon law.

21 Hence those preachers of indulgences are wrong when they say that a man is absolved and saved from every penalty which canon law declares should have been paid in this present life.

22 Rather, he cannot remit to souls in purgatory any penalty which canon law declares should have been paid in this present life.

24 It must therefore follow that the greater part of people are deceived by that indiscriminate and high-sounding promise of freedom from purgatory.

32 All those who believe themselves certain of their own salvation because of letters of pardon, will be eternally damned, together with their preachers.

35 It is not Christian preaching to teach that those who aim to redeem their souls, or to purchase confessional indulgences, have no need of contrition.

36 Any Christian whatsoever who is truly repentant has, as his due, plenary remission from penalty and guilt, even without letters of indulgence.

43 Christians should be taught that one who gives to the poor, or lends to the needy, does a better action than if he purchases pardons.

46 Christians should be taught that, unless they abound in possessions beyond their needs, their duty is to retain what is necessary for their own household, and in no way to squander it in buying pardons.

62 The true treasure of the Church is the holy Gospel of the glory and grace of God.

81 This wanton preaching of pardons makes it difficult even for learned men to redeem respect due to the pope from the slanders or at least the shrewd questioning of the laity.

82 For example: 'Why does not the pope empty purgatory for the sake of most holy love and the supreme need of souls? This would be the most righteous of reasons, if he can redeem innumerable souls for the sordid money with which to build a basilica, the most trivial of reasons.'

86 Again: 'Since the pope's wealth is larger than that of the crassest of Crassi of our time, why does he not build this one basilica of St Peter with his own money, rather than with that of the faithful poor?'

Why did Luther write the 95 Theses?

Luther did not intend to trigger a revolution. He simply wanted to provoke an academic debate about indulgences, hoping to expose their multiple flaws and perhaps thus end the traffic. The preamble to his Theses makes it clear that his aim was limited.

SOURCE 8 Luther's preamble to his 95 Theses, October 1517.

Out of love for the truth and the desire to bring it to light, the following propositions will be discussed at Wittenberg, under the presidency of the Reverend Father Martin Luther, Master of Arts and of Sacred Theology, and Lecturer in Ordinary on the same at that place. Wherefore he requests that those who are unable to be present and debate orally with us, may do so by letter.

He wrote in Latin, so his intended audience was academic: students and members of Wittenberg University (many of the teaching staff there were scholastics) and other theologians and humanists. Pinning the Theses to a church door (if that is what happened) was the equivalent of putting up an invitation on a noticeboard. Theological disputations were a regular part of university life.

Of course, in his choice of date, 31 October, the day before All Saints Day, and the Castle Church door – Frederick's church rather than the town church – Luther was also subtly criticising the indulgence attached to Frederick's relic collection, without actually stating this explicitly. Frederick was his employer, after all. But again, there was nothing unusual in the act. Andrew Carlstadt, his colleague at the university's Theology Faculty, had done exactly the same (only more so – 151 theses against indulgences for dispute) the previous April, when Frederick had last opened his relics for viewing. Frederick had not objected. Debate was what his university was about.

What impact did the Theses have?

Had the Theses remained in Latin, pinned to that church door, little might have happened. However, without Luther's knowledge or permission, they were taken down and printed. Circulation was limited initially to a Latin-speaking audience of perhaps only a thousand, but within weeks, they were translated into German and mass-printed: news spread widely and rapidly. Even Luther was astonished and perhaps a little taken aback at the Theses' reception.

SOURCE

9 Letter from Luther to Christopher Scheurl, March 1518. Scheurl was a German lawyer who had lectured at Wittenberg University from 1506, and was the rector from 1507 to 1509. Luther was replying to a letter Scheurl had sent from Nuremberg, where the artist Albrecht Dürer also lived. The distance between Nuremberg and Wittenberg is about 330 kilometres, over a week's hard journey away, which gives an indication of how the Theses had travelled.

I have received two letters from you, a Latin and a German one, my good Christopher, along with a present from that outstanding man, Albrecht Dürer, and my Latin and German propositions. You wonder I did not tell you of them. But I did not wish them widely circulated. I only intended submitting them to a few learned men for examination, and if they disapproved of them, to suppress them; or to make them known through their publications, in the event of their meeting with their approval. But now they are being spread abroad and translated everywhere, which I never could have credited, so that I regret having given birth to them – not that I am unwilling to proclaim the truth manfully, for there is nothing that I more ardently desire, but because this way of instructing the people is of little avail.

Several factors might explain the immediate popularity of the Theses once they had been translated:

- Their timing – Luther had given a sermon against indulgences exactly one year before, and Carlstadt had posted his theses against indulgences in April. Both were largely ignored. This time, Tetzel's irresponsible salesmanship was causing widespread concern among the educated elite.

- Their tone – Luther wrote the propositions in a hurry and to provoke an academic debate, and his language was theatrical, combative and colloquial. He wrote in a way that ordinary people could understand.

- Their appeal for German nationalists, anti-papalists and the poor – when Luther made the point, several times, that Germans were being tricked into handing over their savings to a foreign power, Rome, he was expressing the frustrations and prejudices of many people. It was a very popular theme.

- Their authorship – Luther was a friar of a reformed order and a respected Professor of Theology at a reputable university founded by one of the electors, no less. His credentials were impeccable.

- Use of the printing press – had the Theses been written a hundred years earlier, at a time when the only means of disseminating them would have meant copying them out laboriously by hand, their spread would have been slower and more local. The fact that the Theses were printed quickly and in such numbers made them difficult to suppress.

EXTEND YOUR KNOWLEDGE

The importance of the printing press to Luther's success

Luther wrote to Scheurl about the 'rapid spread of the Theses' in April 1518. Three years later, in 1521, a papal envoy to Germany, Cardinal Aleander, was astonished at the popularity of Luther: 'Nine out of ten cry Luther.' In an age without good roads, let alone modern electronic communications, what made this possible? The printing press, it has been argued, was crucial to Luther's early success. Invented in the 1460s by Guttenberg of Mainz, by 1500 there were 200 presses in Germany, more than anywhere else in Europe. With the press, work that might previously have taken months to do by hand could now be done overnight.

The role of the press was two fold. The historian Elizabeth Eisenstein argues that the press *precipitated* the Reformation. For example, it led to an increase in the number of Bibles and prayer books in circulation, and the call for a faith more rooted in scripture even before Luther. The press also enabled the circulation of humanist criticisms of clerical abuses and humanist attacks on the way the papacy exploited Germany. In this way, the press had helped to create the anti-clerical, anti-Rome climate in which Luther's protest could thrive. It even enabled the Church to mass-print indulgences – ironically, they were one of the very first things that Guttenberg printed – and so exploit Germany more than ever. Finally, because he did not work in a vacuum, the press gave Luther access to humanist texts from which he drew ideas and even phrases: he used Erasmus' Greek Testament when he translated the Bible, and his opening thesis was drawn from Erasmus' work.

More importantly, the printing press enabled the rapid and widespread circulation of Luther's ideas. The result has been compared to a forest fire that it was impossible to extinguish. The figures are extraordinary. His 95 Theses went through three editions by the end of 1517, and a further 13 in 1518; the first edition of his 1520 pamphlet, 'To the Christian Nobility of the German Nation', sold 4,000 copies in two weeks; 300,000 items by Luther were in circulation by 1521. Between 1518 and 1524, press output went up by 600 percent, and by 1524, 90 percent of all doctrinal works in print were by Luther. His New Testament of 1522 became the best-seller of the day: it sold 200,000 copies in 85 editions over 12 years. Without the press, therefore, Luther's protest might have been a transitory and local phenomenon. Luther fully understood the importance of the press. He called it 'God's highest and extremist act of grace whereby the business of the Gospel is driven forward'. When the reformer Martin Bucer of Strasbourg urged Wittenberg theologians to get out into the world and preach, Luther replied, 'We do that with our books.' He even catered for the fact that 95 percent of the population were illiterate and far too poor to purchase a pamphlet, let alone a book. He deliberately made use of woodcuts and broadsheets – cheap mass-printed images and posters – many commissioned 'for the sake of simple folk' from the Wittenberg artist Lucas Cranach. The number of woodcuts circulating between 1517 and 1521 far exceeded books, and they made skilful use of the fact that this was a very visual period: people were used to *seeing* their faith, painted on church walls, sculpted in images, pictured in stained glass windows.

Proof of the importance of the press lies in the imperial cities, where Luther found his earliest and strongest support. Printing was an urban-based industry, and of the 65 imperial cities, about 51 became Protestant at some stage. Six cities were responsible for two-thirds of the printing output – Augsburg, Basel, Cologne, Leipzig, Nuremberg and Strasbourg – and of these, five became Protestant. The power of the press can be seen in the fact that where effective censorship operated, a city stayed Catholic, which is what happened in Cologne. The structure of the empire made central imposition of censorship an impossibility, so the attitude of individual city or state authorities was important in determining whether censorship was imposed. Cologne was unusual. In Mainz, for example, the printer Schoeffer produced

Lutheran, Catholic and radical literature with impunity: he just wanted to make money, and the city authorities appeared indifferent.

All these facts might suggest that, without the press, there would have been no Lutheran Reformation. However, some perspective is needed. Luther had a receptive audience – people had grievances and they wanted change. That explains his success. No one would have paid attention to him otherwise, printing press or not. Luther was also charismatic and persuasive on paper; a boring writer would have failed to attract an audience, printing press or not.

More crucially, one cannot ignore the fact that 95 percent of the population were illiterate. Literacy was concentrated in the towns, especially in the south-west, but even then only among the higher social classes – the scholars, mercantile elite and clergy. Two-thirds of town dwellers could not read. Furthermore, about 40 percent of *what* was being published in the period 1517–21 was anti-Catholic polemics. Most of the woodcuts, for example, just violently attacked papal greed and clerical immorality, but did nothing to explain Lutheran ideas. At best, this sort of printed material destroyed people's faith in the Catholic Church and created a vacuum, but that vacuum might then be filled with any radical idea, and not necessarily Lutheran ones. Other printed material from this period, the remaining 60 percent of that published, was more serious and did provide positive explications of Lutheran doctrine. However, little of this was intended for a lay audience. Most was in Latin and intended for other clergy to read. If there was a final argument against the importance of the press, it lies in those figures. For example, 4,000 copies of a pamphlet sounds impressive until you realise that meant just one copy per 3,000 people in the empire.

If the printing press was not the key, then what was? Most people did not read about Luther's ideas, they *heard* about them. The historian Andrew Pettegrew has argued that sermons were the key weapon in disseminating Lutheran ideas. Despite his retort to Bucer, Luther was an inspirational preacher. He delivered over 6,000 sermons in his lifetime, and then printed those sermons for other clergy and humanists to deliver. Forty percent of the Lutheran material in print by 1526 consisted of his sermons. In many of the imperial cities that subsequently converted, civic funds were spent hiring in preachers. Over a four- to five-hour period, with a huge and expectant audience standing throughout, a celebrated preacher would cleverly build from a solemn opening to a shattering climax. Sermon-listening was clearly an emotional, transformative experience.

The pulpit was not the only weapon when it came to 'hearing' about Lutheran ideas; word of mouth was just as important. That might explain Luther's support in cities and towns, where large numbers of people lived in close proximity, exchanging news in taverns and marketplaces. Music and theatre were also important when it came to 'hearing'. The pre-Reformation practice of communal singing of ballads and protest songs was later also used by Luther as a way to disseminate his ideas. He wrote hymns set to popular tunes, deliberately setting out to stir men's hearts while delivering his message in a simple way. While Luther did not approve of theatre, some towns had a strong tradition of delivering religious messages via plays. In Nuremberg, the cobbler Hans Sachs wrote over 200 plays, delivering both biblical tales and anti-clerical carnival entertainment.

So, oral communication was the norm among the masses. Printed material, especially the woodcuts, was an addition to this, but not a replacement. Most people never even saw a copy of the Theses, let alone read them. But they did talk about them, and because Luther had a way with words, they remembered them and repeated them. Where the press *was* crucial was in transforming the opinions of the educated elite, and, ultimately, they played the larger role in both the attack on Luther and his survival.

WHAT INFLUENCED THE DEVELOPMENT OF LUTHER'S IDEAS FROM 1517 TO 1520?

Luther was a loyal Catholic in 1517, and he might well have limited himself to denouncing indulgences; indeed the whole affair might even have died down, had it not been for the way in which Rome and the Dominican order reacted.

On the same day that he pinned up his Theses, Luther sent a copy of them, with a covering letter, to his bishop and to Archbishop Albert of Mainz. The letter was polite, but it had an edge. Luther expressed his grave concerns about Tetzel, but he also went further and queried the scriptural basis of indulgences, and then fairly bluntly criticised Albert's own behaviour.

SOURCE 10 Letter from Luther to Albert of Mainz, 31 October 1517.

... With your Electoral Highness' consent, the Papal Indulgence for the rebuilding of St Peter's in Rome is being carried through the land. I do not complain so much of the loud cry of the preacher of indulgences, which I have not heard, but regret the false meaning which the simple folk attach to it, the poor souls believing that when they have purchased such letters they have secured their salvation, also, that the moment the money jingles in the box souls are delivered from purgatory, and that all sins will be forgiven through a letter of indulgence... And, lastly, that through these indulgences the man is freed from all penalties! Ah, dear God! Thus are those souls which have been committed to your care, dear Father, being led in the paths of death, and for them you will be required to render an account. For the merits of no bishop can secure the salvation of souls entrusted to him... Therefore I could be silent no longer.

How then can you, through false promises of indulgences, which do not promote the salvation or sanctification of their souls, lead the people into carnal insecurity, by declaring them free from the painful consequences of their wrong-doing...?

For deeds of piety and love are infinitely better than indulgences, and yet Bishops do not preach these so earnestly...

In addition, Reverend Father, it has gone abroad under your name but doubtless without your knowledge, that this indulgence is the priceless gift of God, whereby the man may be reconciled with God, and escape the fires of purgatory, and that those who purchase the indulgence will have no need of repentance.

What else can I do, Right Reverend Father, than beg your Serene Highness, carefully look into this matter, and do away with this little book of instructions, and command those preachers to adopt another style of preaching... I hope your Serene Highness may graciously deign to accept the faithful service which your insignificant servant, with true devotion, would render you.

> **A Level Exam-Style Question Section A**
>
> How far could a historian make use of Sources 9 and 10 together to assess the gravity of the Lutheran problem for the Catholic Church by March 1518?
>
> Explain your answer, using both the sources, the information given about them and your own knowledge of the historical context. (20 marks)
>
> **Tip**
>
> *As well as identifying and expanding on points from each source in turn, consider them in combination. What points do both sources agree on?*

Albert did not reply to Luther. He had the letter and the copy of the Theses checked for signs of heresy, and then despatched both to Rome on 13 December, asking for action to be taken. Clearly, papal power was being challenged. Underpinning Albert's reaction, of course, was his concern at the reception being given to the 95 Theses. He would be in serious debt to the Fuggers if Tetzel's sales of indulgences collapsed (see page 188). Thirty years later, Luther thought that 'the entire blame' for all that followed rested with Albert. If he had 'at the outset quenched the outbursts of Tetzel, things would not have grown to such a furore'.

The issue now lay in Rome's hands. Over the next two years, four attempts were made to silence Luther:

1 through his own order, the Augustinians

2 through a meeting with the pope's representative, Cardinal Cajetan, at Augsburg

3 through direct negotiation with Frederick the Wise, conducted by the papal chamberlain, Karl von Miltitz

4 through debate with Dr John Eck, a Dominican academic, at Leipzig.

TIMELINE: ATTEMPTS TO SILENCE LUTHER

1517

December: Albert of Mainz forwards Luther's Theses to Rome, requesting that Luther be disciplined

1518

January: Tetzel defends indulgence selling at a meeting of his Dominican order of Saxony

February: Pope Leo requests that the Augustinian order discipline Luther

March: Dr John Eck, another Dominican, attacks Luther in a paper called 'Obelisks'

April: Luther defends his position at a meeting of his Augustinian order in Heidelberg

May: Pope Leo issues orders for Luther to be sent to Rome on charges of heresy

July: Pope Leo's orders reach Wittenberg

August: Emperor Maximilian denounces Luther as a heretic

Luther asks the elector Frederick the Wise to arrange for his case to be heard in Germany, not Rome

Pope Leo sends orders to Cardinal Cajetan, a Dominican and his representative at the Diet of Augsburg: Cajetan is to see Luther, demand that he recant, and then arrest him and deliver him to Rome

Frederick asks Cajetan to meet Luther, but not to arrest him

October: Luther meets Cardinal Cajetan in Augsburg. They row; Luther is not arrested, but has to flee Augsburg

Following the meeting, Cajetan demands that Frederick hand Luther over to Rome or banish him

December: Frederick refuses both options

Karl von Miltitz, a papal chamberlain and Saxon nobleman, arrives in Wittenberg to negotiate with Frederick, bearing a special gift from Pope Leo (a golden rose)

1519

January: Maximilian dies; Leo suspends all action against Luther pending the imperial election

March: John Eck challenges Luther to a public debate at Leipzig

June: Charles V is elected Holy Roman Emperor

June–July: Luther meets Dr John Eck in Leipzig for debate. Eck accuses Luther of being a heretic

1520

January: The case against Luther reopens in Rome

ACTIVITY
KNOWLEDGE CHECK

Attempts to silence Luther

Examine the timeline above showing the attempts to silence Luther.

Some historians believe that Rome reacted too slowly to the Luther affair. Does the evidence agree with this interpretation?
(**Tip**: remember that post from Germany to Rome might take three weeks or more to arrive.)

In what ways does this timeline suggest that Frederick the Wise was important to Luther's survival in the period 1518-19?

Leo X's reaction

When he received Albert's dispatch, which was probably in early 1518 (Albert had sat on the letter for a month), Leo may well have viewed the indulgence controversy as just another squabble between two orders. Rivalry between the Dominicans and the Augustinians was long-standing, and the Dominican order was furious that Tetzel, one of their own, had been attacked. John Eck, a Dominican friar and professor of Theology at Ingolstadt University, was in the process of mounting a fierce campaign against Luther.

At the same time, Leo had other concerns that would have made the Luther affair seem inconsequential: he was as bankrupt as ever, he had recently been at war in Italy, he had thwarted a plot by cardinals to assassinate him (by means of a poisonous bandage to be applied to his anal fistula), and he was trying to pull Christian Europe together to mount a crusade against an increasingly aggressive Ottoman Empire that had almost doubled its size in the preceding decade. Syria and Egypt had just fallen and it looked as though Cyprus would be the next target. Compared with all this, Luther was a minor detail. Anyway, it was not in Leo's nature to get involved: 'The pope is a good-natured and extremely free-hearted man, who avoids every difficult situation and above all wants peace', wrote the Venetian Ambassador in March 1517. So, for all these reasons, Leo took the low-key option. He put his theologians to work preparing a case against Luther, and meanwhile asked the prior general of the Augustinian order to silence the troublesome monk. There would be time later to escalate the discipline if necessary.

The meeting with the Augustinian order at Heidelberg, April 1518

Leo's plan backfired. The prior general delegated the task to the head of the Augustinians in Germany, Johann von Staupitz. Unhappily for Leo, Staupitz knew Luther well as a mentor and friend. He had been Luther's confessor when he was a trainee monk, and had then been Luther's superior as dean of the Theology Faculty at Wittenberg University until 1512. Germany's Augustinians were congregating in Heidelberg anyway for their three-yearly meeting, and Staupitz invited Luther to make a presentation to the gathering. He also asked him to keep away from controversial issues (that is, the indulgences controversy), and instead to explain his views on sin, freewill and grace. Luther was almost the guest of honour. The meeting was a positive one for Luther. He drew strength from the public support he met en route to Heidelberg, and from the fact that his own order did not reject him. He was given an opportunity to develop his ideas and also made converts. At least one of those present, Martin Bucer, was seriously impressed.

AS Level Exam-Style Question Section A

Why is Source 11 valuable to the historian for an enquiry into the reasons why Luther won so much support in the period 1517–20?

Explain your answer using the source, the information given about it and your own knowledge of the historical context. (20 marks)

Tip

This question requires you to do three things. First, to identify evidence in the extract that is of value for the enquiry; some will be explicit and some will have to be inferred. Then use your own knowledge of the historical context to verify that this evidence is accurate. Finally, comment on the ways in which the author and nature of the source add value to the enquiry.

> **EXTEND YOUR KNOWLEDGE**
>
> **Luther's 'Heidelberg Disputation'**
> In the 40 terse, compact theses, Luther presented his 'Theology of the Cross'. Human beings should not speculate about what God is like; the Cross – the crucifixion of God in his human form as Jesus Christ – is the only source of knowledge concerning who God is and how God saves. One can only understand the Cross from studying the scriptures.

SOURCE

11

From a letter by Martin Bucer to Beatus Rhenanus, a German humanist, printer and friend of Erasmus, 1518. Bucer was a Dominican studying theology at Heidelberg when he heard Luther. Following the meeting, he left his monastery, married a runaway nun and moved to Strasbourg, where he played a major part in its reform. Note: Scotus was an important 13th century theologian, and Bucer is making the point that Luther was using the Bible for evidence, rather than medieval Thomist Scholastics.

In giving answers his pleasantness was remarkable, in listening his patience was beyond compare; in his refutation you would have recognised the shrewdness of Paul, not Scotus, and with his replies so concise and so acute and drawn from the store of divine scriptures he easily led them all to admire him. The next day I had a private and friendly conversation with the man, remote from observation, and a meal long prepared and desired, not for its food, but its teachings. Whatever questions I asked, he explained lucidly. All his views concur with Erasmus, except that he seems to excel in this one respect, namely that what Erasmus only implies, Luther teaches more openly and freely. O if I only had time to write to you more about this. He has brought it about that those small-minded writers of Wittenberg have been scorned to a man, while Greek writings – Jerome, Augustine and Paul – are publicly taught.

The intervention of Frederick the Wise, Elector of Saxony

Frustrated, Leo issued orders for Luther to be brought to Rome on charges of heresy, where he would almost certainly have been executed. Frederick the Wise intervened, and requested instead that Luther be interviewed by Cardinal Cajetan, the papal representative to the diet then meeting in Augsburg. Leo agreed to Frederick's request for political reasons: Frederick was the senior elector – his vote would be crucial in the next imperial election. Frederick's role here was crucial. He could easily have ordered Luther to go to Rome. What motivated him to help Luther is open to speculation. He remained a Catholic to his deathbed and showed no open sympathy for Luther's theological ideas. He never talked to Luther, using his secretary Spalatin as a go-between, a sensible move as Frederick did not want to be accused of heresy himself. Nor did Frederick cease adding to his huge relic collection until 1522. Indeed, he added over 1,500 items in the two years after Luther's outburst against indulgences.

THINKING HISTORICALLY   Causation (6b)

Attitudes and actions

Individuals can only make choices based on their context. Prevalent attitudes combine with individual experience and natural temperament to frame an individual's perception of what is going on around them. Nobody can know the future or see into the minds of others.

Action	Context
In 1518, Frederick the Wise refused to send Luther to Rome. Instead, he asked Pope Leo to have Luther interviewed in Germany.	• Frederick was the senior elector. • He was a devout Catholic who collected relics. • He was a very fair man and respected for his sense of justice (hence the epithet, Wise). • He was inordinately proud of the University of Wittenberg. • Luther was making the university famous. • In early 1518, Luther's public views were still limited to attacking the sale of indulgences. • Tetzel's sale of indulgences had undermined Frederick's own annual indulgence sale. • Tetzel was employed by Albert of Mainz, whose family rivalled Frederick for political influence in the empire. • Tetzel had studied at the University of Leipzig in Ducal Saxony, which was ruled by Frederick's cousin George the Bearded – relations between the cousins were not good. • Frederick resented external interference in his state and in the empire, especially from Rome. • Frederick's younger brother, John the Steadfast, and his secretary, George Spalatin, both expressed an interest in Luther's ideas.

Answer the following questions individually and discuss your answers in a group.

1 Why might Frederick have believed that the pope would agree to his request?

2 To what extent was Frederick's protection of Luther self-indulgent?

3 Frederick was a devout Catholic. However, he saved Luther's life, and without his intervention there might have been no Reformation. How reasonable was Frederick's action, given what he understood about the situation at the time?

4 How far should the historian try to understand the context of the beliefs and values of people in the past when explaining why individuals make choices in history?

The meeting with Cajetan at Augsburg, October 1518

Luther went to Augsburg nervously, as Cajetan's reputation preceded him. He was a renowned biblical scholar and Thomist theologian, and the head of the Dominican order. He had taught at three of Italy's best universities. He had been made a cardinal in 1517 and was representing the pope at the diet then meeting in Augsburg. Cajetan was under secret orders from Leo to demand that Luther **recant** in full, and to arrange for his arrest if he refused. Cajetan was not to enter into any sort of debate with Luther.

KEY TERM

Recant
To take back and give up one's views.

In fact, Cajetan did not follow his instructions fully. On arriving in Augsburg, Luther's friends sensibly requested an imperial guarantee of his safety before he would see Cajetan. This prevented any plans of arrest and transportation to Rome. When they finally met, Cajetan also engaged in a brief debate. Luther asked to be shown where he was in error. Cajetan pointed out that Thesis 58 contradicted a papal decree: Luther said that the papal decree in question was 'against the opinion of the whole church'. Cajetan pointed out that Thesis 7 was wrong – no one could ever be certain of obtaining grace. Luther replied that 'Only faith in the word of Christ justifies, makes alive, makes one worthy and prepares one. Anything else is an exercise in presumption or despair.' Cajetan refused to accept either of Luther's arguments, and the interview seems to have degenerated into a shouting match. Luther reported that, 'He will hear nothing from me except, "*I recant, I revoke, I confess that I erred*", which I would not say.'

Despite several further meetings, Luther refused to recant and Cajetan dismissed him. Cajetan's bullying tone made Luther feel his life was in danger, and he was anxious that Cajetan would renege on the promised safe conduct. He fled Augsburg that night, helped by cathedral clergy who arranged a horse for him. Cajetan, meanwhile, wrote to Frederick, informing him that Luther was a heretic and should be surrendered immediately. The whole interview had come to nothing. However, one can learn from it. Luther's belief in 'justification by faith alone' was well developed, even though he might not have used the words; and he had openly expressed his view that the pope could make mistakes.

Negotiations between Miltitz and Frederick, December 1518–January 1519

Leo made one more attempt to get Frederick to hand over Luther in late 1518. The attempt was coloured by politics, as Emperor Maximilian's health was now in decline and, more than ever, this was not the time to offend an elector. Leo acted gently and diplomatically. He sent his chamberlain, Karl von Miltitz, and a gift of a papal **golden rose**. Miltitz was a good choice: he was a Saxon nobleman by birth. As a bribe, the golden rose was also a good choice: it was a papal gift of enormous status, since only one was given each year, to a ruler of outstanding qualities. Whether or not the flattery would have worked is unknowable, since before negotiations could develop far, Maximilian died. Leo suspended all action against Luther, pending the imperial election. He wished Frederick, the senior elector, to stand as a candidate. Miltitz's mission was not completely wasted, though. While in Germany, he took the opportunity to see Tetzel, whom he reprimanded in the severest of terms. Tetzel was retired and died in obscurity in 1519, a broken man.

The Leipzig Debates, June–July 1519

This was the crucial turning point for Luther in mid-1519. For 18 months, the Dominican order had been waging a pamphlet war against the Augustinian Luther, led first by Tetzel and then by Dr John Eck, professor at Ingoldstadt University in Bavaria. A highly educated and respected Dominican friar, he was dedicated to defending the Church from all heresy. Eck was astute. He realised that Tetzel's claims for indulgences were highly questionable. He decided instead to attack Luther from the side – by saying that Luther was challenging papal supremacy. Duke George of Saxony agreed to host a debate between the two sides in Leipzig. George's motives were straightforward on one level: he was a devout Catholic, doing his duty. But on another level, this would be an excellent opportunity to score against his cousin, Frederick the Wise.

Academic disputations of this sort were a popular way to debate disagreements and the rules were straightforward: each side attempted to undermine the other side's argument. George provided the hall of his castle for the occasion, and professors from Paris and Erfurt Universities agreed to act as judges. Eck came with one companion and a letter of introduction from the Fuggers; 200 students of Wittenberg University turned up to support their side. Duke George had refused to issue a safe conduct for Luther to debate, so the Wittenberg delegation was led by Dr Andrew Karlstadt, who had himself anyway issued the initial challenge. Luther went along as an observer. Karlstadt did not have Luther's abilities. One observer from the Wittenberg camp, Peter Mosellanus, said Karlstadt's voice was 'thick and unpleasant, his memory is weaker and his anger more prompt'. Eck had 'a tall stature, a solid square body, a full, German voice, strong lungs as of a tragedian or cryer' and 'a fine memory', though flawed by a lack of judgement: 'he brings together all his arguments and texts of scriptures and quotations from authors without any selection, not considering that many of them are inept and impertinent to the subject, and that some of them are apocryphal or mere sophistry.' Mosellanus, of course, was a biased observer.

KEY TERM

Golden rose
Since at least the 11th century, popes have awarded this powerful symbol of their favour. The rose is made from gold, and in the 16th century it was given to a ruler who had excelled in his work for the Catholic faith and in his loyalty to Rome. Today, the recipient is usually a shrine or a church, and the single rose has been become a bouquet of ten or more roses. They are still made of gold.

For a week, Eck and Karlstadt debated on the issue of free will and its relationship with salvation. Finally, frustrated at not to be able to debate with Luther himself, Eck intervened and persuaded George to grant Luther the necessary safe conduct. In the debate on papal authority that followed, Eck tricked Luther into a corner. He accused Luther of holding the same views as the Bohemian Jan Hus, who had been burned for heresy in 1415. 'Luther at once understood the snare, and raged as though inspired by some spirit at being thus insidiously betrayed on a side issue,' wrote Mosellanus, 'his main effort was to remove far from himself the suspicion of favouring Bohemian schism.'

EXTEND YOUR KNOWLEDGE

Jan Hus (c1372–1415)

Jan Hus was a member of the Theology Faculty at Prague University in Bohemia, becoming its rector in 1409. From about 1402, he preached passionately about the need for reform in the Church. He condemned clerical abuses, including indulgences, and argued the need for the Bible to be in the vernacular. He attacked foreign exploitation of Bohemia, appealing to Czech nationalists who were angry at German and Italian domination. Above all, he argued that only a general council of the Church had the authority to implement much-needed reforms, denying the authority of the papacy. Hus was condemned as a heretic in 1411, but given sanctuary in Bohemia. In 1414, he was persuaded, by the promise of a safe conduct from the Emperor Sigismund, to give his views to Pope John XXIII and the council then meeting in Constance. Despite the safe conduct, he was arrested, tried and burned for heresy in July 1415.

His execution caused uproar in Bohemia, which broke away from Rome in 1420 to form its own national Church, denying Rome, using Czech in services, and distributing the Eucharist in both kinds. The wars to destroy the Hussites caused devastation not just in Bohemia, but also in Saxony. Duke George's antipathy to Luther would have been reinforced by the latter's admission that he was a Hussite sympathiser.

When pressed, Luther said:

- there was no evidence for the papacy in the scriptures

- the papacy therefore had no authority

- the highest authority in the Church lay with a **general council** of the Church.

KEY TERM

General council
This was a meeting of all bishops, archbishops and cardinals to determine important matters of belief and discipline in the Church. Councils, however, represented a challenge for popes. In the first half of the 15th century, many had maintained that a council's authority was higher than the pope's. This 'conciliar theory' was formally condemned in 1460 by Pope Pius II. Councils only met when called by the pope.

Eck pounced: Hus had been condemned by a council; it followed that Luther would be too. Luther was publicly forced to go one step further: even councils were subservient to the scriptures. There was only one authority on what to believe – the scriptures – *sola scriptura*. 'I am sure on this, that many of Hus' beliefs were completely evangelical and Christian.' In arguing that it had been wrong for the Council of Constance to condemn some of Hus' views, since they were based on the scriptures, Luther effectively condemned himself as a heretic.

After almost three weeks, Duke George declared the debate over; he needed his hall back to entertain guests. No winner was declared, since the Erfurt judges refused to give a decision, while the Paris judges demanded a handsome fee before they would give theirs, which George refused to pay. The general view in Leipzig was that Eck had the upper hand, while in Wittenberg they thought Luther had won, and they insulted Dr Eck as 'Dreck', meaning 'dirt'.

The Leipzig Debates were a turning point in three ways:

- Luther had been forced to express ideas well beyond anything he might have contemplated in 1517.

- Luther achieved considerable publicity.

- Eck reported to Rome that Luther was unquestionably a heretic.

ACTIVITY
KNOWLEDGE CHECK

Who was most responsible for the failure to silence Luther between 1517 and 1519?
Make brief notes on the reasons why each of the following could be said to be at fault, and then rank them in order of 'blame' for the failure to stop Luther: Cardinal Albert of Mainz; Pope Leo X; Cardinal Cajetan; Dr John Eck; Frederick the Wise; Emperor Maximilian.

THE THREAT OF EXCOMMUNICATION AND THE THREE PAMPHLETS, 1520

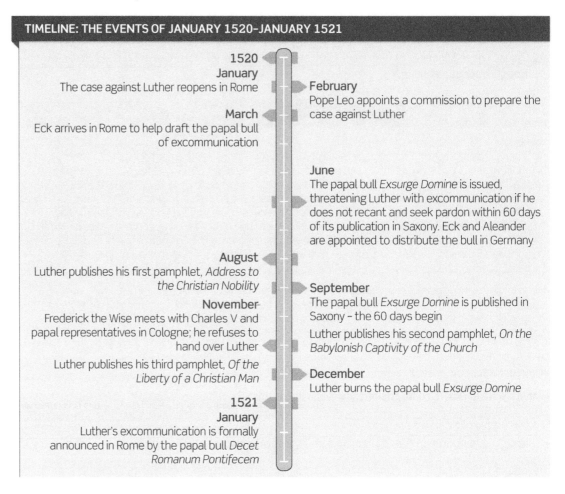

TIMELINE: THE EVENTS OF JANUARY 1520-JANUARY 1521

1520
January
The case against Luther reopens in Rome

February
Pope Leo appoints a commission to prepare the case against Luther

March
Eck arrives in Rome to help draft the papal bull of excommunication

June
The papal bull *Exsurge Domine* is issued, threatening Luther with excommunication if he does not recant and seek pardon within 60 days of its publication in Saxony. Eck and Aleander are appointed to distribute the bull in Germany

August
Luther publishes his first pamphlet, *Address to the Christian Nobility*

September
The papal bull *Exsurge Domine* is published in Saxony – the 60 days begin

Luther publishes his second pamphlet, *On the Babylonish Captivity of the Church*

November
Frederick the Wise meets with Charles V and papal representatives in Cologne; he refuses to hand over Luther

Luther publishes his third pamphlet, *Of the Liberty of a Christian Man*

December
Luther burns the papal bull *Exsurge Domine*

1521
January
Luther's excommunication is formally announced in Rome by the papal bull *Decet Romanum Pontifecem*

The threat of excommunication

In the Leipzig Debate, Luther had openly stated that he agreed with some of the views of Jan Hus, who had been condemned as a heretic and burned in 1415. He had also publicly stated that the papacy had no scriptural basis, and therefore the pope had no authority. Finally, he had publicly stated that the scriptures alone held the truth.

Rome now had no choice; it had to act. In January 1520, the decision was taken to threaten Luther with excommunication. Eck drew up the necessary papers, and in June, Rome issued the **papal bull *Exsurge Domine***, stating that the Church must protect the vineyard of the Lord from the 'wild boar' that had invaded it. Forty-one of Luther's views were condemned as heretical; his books and pamphlets were to be publicly burned; Luther was given 60 days (from the date of publication in Saxony) to recant his views, and in the meantime he was forbidden to preach or write. If he failed to submit, he would be excommunicated.

Two days later, Eck, now promoted to **papal nuncio**, and another papal delegate, Cardinal Aleander, were despatched north to publicise the bull. In areas of strong Lutheran support, the bull was angrily torn down from doors. In Wittenberg, students defiantly published it as a joke in September. The 60 days began.

The three pamphlets of 1520

Luther, meanwhile, was on a mission. In 1520, he wrote and published over 20 pamphlets condemning the errors of the Church, listing its abuses, suggesting reforms, and elaborating the implications of *sola scriptura* and ***sola fide***. Three, in particular, have become known as the Reformation Treatises.

To the Christian Nobility of the German Nation, August 1520

Luther wrote this pamphlet in German, and at the request of legal officers of the elector Frederick the Wise. The purpose was partly political: Luther needed to mobilise some serious support. He addressed everyone in authority in Germany, from the new emperor Charles down, including the princes, nobles, city magistrates and imperial knights. He asked these 'temporal authorities' to start the reform so urgently needed, since spiritual authorities – the Church – had failed to do so. The pamphlet started dramatically: 'The time for silence is gone, and the time to speak has come.'

Luther said that Rome had drawn up three walls to protect itself against reform:

- When temporal authorities requested reforms, they hit the first wall: a refusal to do anything on the grounds that spiritual power was above temporal power.

- When faced with arguments for reform based on the scriptures, the Church put up its second wall: that only the pope could interpret the scriptures.

- When threatened with a council to sort reform, the Church put up its third wall: that only the pope could call a council.

Luther then set out to prove that none of the three walls was true. Not one of them had any basis in scripture, so any 'papists' who continued to defend them were the agents of Antichrist, an imposter put on earth by the Devil. Because of this, it was completely acceptable for temporal authorities to take reform in hand; it was the right thing to do. He then proceeded to provide a comprehensive (if rather disorganised) list of all the reforms needed, which even included what should be taught in universities and schools.

One of the most important theological points to emerge from the pamphlet was in Luther's attack on the first wall. Using the scriptures as evidence, he said that clergy should not enjoy some sort of superior, privileged, irremovable status over ordinary people. Rather, he argued that everyone is equal spiritually, in a 'priesthood of all believers'. The only differences were in office and function: some people were cobblers, some were peasants, others were priests. But everyone was equally accountable to be 'useful and beneficial to the rest'. So if a priest failed to fulfil his office properly, he could and should be demoted. And since priests were not special, there was no reason why they should not marry.

Luther's skill lay in explaining things 'more plainly', and often with very colourful language. He said the 'depths of hell' awaited the pope. When he attacked the third wall, as another example, he compared abuses in the Church with a fire in a city: what if the fire had started in the mayor's house? Surely people would not sit still just because they had not got the mayor's authority to put out the fire? It was everyone's duty to help put that fire out, and the temporal authorities had to take charge.

SOURCE 12

From Luther's work, *To the Christian Nobility of the German Nation*, August 1520.

Let us, in the first place, attack the first wall.

It has been devised that the pope, bishops, priests and monks are called the spiritual estate; princes, lords, artificers and peasants are the temporal estate. This is an artful lie and hypocritical device, let no one be made afraid by it, and for this reason: that all Christians are truly of the spiritual estate, and there is no difference among them, save of office only. As St Paul says, we are all one body, though each member does its own work, to serve the others. This is because we have one baptism, one Gospel, one faith, and are all Christians alike... Thus we are all consecrated as priests by baptism...

And to put the matter even more plainly, if a little company of pious Christian laymen were taken prisoners and carried away to a desert, and had not among them a priest consecrated by a bishop, and were there to agree to elect one of them, born in wedlock or not, and were to order him to baptise, to celebrate the mass, to absolve, and to preach, this man would truly be a priest, as if all the bishops and all the popes had consecrated him. That is why in cases of necessity every man can baptise and absolve, which would not be possible if we were not all priests. This great grace and virtue of baptism and of the Christian estate they have quite destroyed and made us forget by their ecclesiastical law.

On the Babylonish Captivity of the Church, September 1520

Luther wrote his second pamphlet in Latin and addressed it to the clergy and to humanists. This pamphlet was more than a call for the reform of abuses: Luther announced a complete doctrinal revolution. He attacked Rome's teachings on the sacraments, and therefore the whole basis of Catholicism.

He compared the papacy with the Kingdom of Babylon, which, in the Old Testament, had enslaved the Jews. He said that Rome was behaving like a tyrant and was using its tortuously convoluted, fraudulent teachings on the sacraments to enslave people and make them reliant on priests. It was time to liberate the people.

Luther said that only three sacraments – baptism, penance and the Eucharist – could be proved from the scriptures. The other four were pure invention and therefore invalid. Furthermore, the meaning that Rome gave each of the three valid sacraments was wrong. Here, Luther's most controversial points related to the Eucharist. He condemned the idea of transubstantiation. The priest did not transform the bread and wine into the body and blood of Christ. No miracle took place. Instead, Christ was physically present in the Eucharist, just as heat was present in a hot iron rod. Nor was there any scriptural basis for saying that only the priest could take the wine: the laity could take communion 'in both kinds'.

His views on baptism were controversial in a different way, in that he disappointed his supporters with his selective application of *sola scriptura*.

SOURCE 13

From Luther's work, *On the Babylonish Captivity of the Church*, September 1520.

I must deny that there are seven Sacraments, and must lay it down, for the time being, that there are only three, baptism, penance and the bread...

Concerning the sacrament of baptism:
This doctrine ought to have been more studiously inculcated upon the people by preaching... When this divine promise has been once conferred upon us, its truth continues even to the hour of our death; and thus our faith in it ought never to be relaxed, but ought to be nourished and strengthened, even till we die...

We may clearly distinguish between man the minister, and God the Author, of baptism. Man baptises, and does not baptise: he baptises because he performs the work of dipping the baptised person; he does not baptise because in this work he does not act upon his own authority but in the place of God. Hence we ought to receive baptism from the hand of man just as if Christ himself, nay, God himself were baptising us with his own hands. Baptism then signifies two things: death and resurrection; that is full and complete justification. When the minister dips the child into the water, this signifies death; when he draws him out again, this signifies life.

Luther's concluding words:
I charge the pope and all papists that, unless they lift their own laws and traditions and restore to the churches of Christ the liberty which is theirs and see that this liberty is taught, they are guilty of all the souls which perish in this miserable captivity and the papacy is indeed nothing but the kingdom of Babylon and the true Antichrist.

EXTEND YOUR KNOWLEDGE

The reaction of Henry VIII
Luther's second pamphlet was rejected completely by Henry VIII of England. With the aid of Thomas More, he wrote a pamphlet, *In Defence of Seven Sacraments*. Leo gratefully gave him a title, '*Fidei Defensor*' or 'Defender of the Faith'. Regardless of everything else that happened subsequently in England, the monarchy held on to the title, and in its abbreviated form, Fid Def, or FD, it still appears on coins.

This second pamphlet caused division. Moderate humanists and reformers like Erasmus and Thomas More were shocked: Luther had gone too far. They simply wanted reform of abuses. Meanwhile, some hardliners felt Luther had not gone far enough: there was surely no scriptural basis for penance either (Luther did finally drop it from his list of valid sacraments). And why did he not just announce the Eucharist as a purely symbolic act, a sharing of bread and wine done in memory of the Last Supper? (Luther refused to compromise on this, citing that Christ's words at the Last Supper, 'This is my body', should be accepted on faith.) Luther's words on baptism were also to cause controversy. Extremists argued that Luther was being far too cautious. Christ was baptised as an adult, and if *sola scriptura* was applied, then ordinary people should be baptised as adults rather than as infants.

Concerning Christian Liberty, November 1520
Luther's third pamphlet of 1520 was written in German. It was the least combative, the gentlest of the three pamphlets. He was even (a bit belatedly) gentle with the pope, who had clearly just been misguided by evil counsellors.

Luther wanted to share with everyone the sense of liberation he felt in the knowledge that Christ would save all those who truly believed. This was his doctrine of 'justification by faith alone', or *sola fide*. People did not need to spend their lives in perpetual anxiety that they had failed to 'do' enough to merit heaven. A Christian was free of all such things. Faith was the key to true salvation, not being virtuous or performing 'works' like fasting.

If faith alone saved, then what was the point of being good? One might as well be bad. But Luther did not see a problem: *sola fide* did not mean people would stop trying to obey God's laws and the commandments. On the contrary, good works and generously helping others came naturally to a saved Christian as an expression of love and gratitude for God; 'a Christian man is the most dutiful servant of all, and subject to everyone'.

SOURCE 14

From Luther's work, *Concerning Christian Liberty*, November 1520.

As Christ says, 'A good tree cannot bring forth evil fruit, neither can a corrupt tree bring forth good fruit.' [Matthew 7:18] ... So must first a man be good or bad before he can do either a good work or a bad work; and his works do not make him bad or good, but he himself makes his works either bad or good. ...

We do not reject good works; nay, we embrace them and teach them in the highest degree. It is not on their account that we condemn them but on account of this impious addition to them and the perverse notion of seeking justification by them. ... All our works should be directed to the advantage of others, since every Christian has such an abundance through his faith that all his other works and his whole life remain... to serve and benefit his neighbour.

Luther did not convince all of his followers. The pamphlet sparked off a long dispute on the issues of liberty and licence, and whether there was any point in morality.

ACTIVITY
KNOWLEDGE CHECK

The three pamphlets of 1520
Write brief notes on Luther's pamphlets, using a table with five headings: Name of pamphlet; Date; Language used; Intended audience; Key points contained in the pamphlet.

Why did Luther's ideas change so dramatically between 1517 and 1520?

In October 1517, Luther may simply have wanted a debate on indulgences and the way in which they were being marketed by Tetzel. He expressed loyalty to the Church and papacy, and was convinced that the Church authorities did not know about Tetzel's heavy-handedness. He wrote in Latin, asking for an academic debate on the matter. Three years later, he had moved from that position to a full-blown criticism of the Catholic Church, attacking its core teachings on salvation and the sacraments, and its structures, including the papacy and the nature of the priesthood.

Three factors may explain this escalation.

First, the reaction of the Church can explain the development of Luther's ideas. The Church was naturally concerned about Luther's attack on indulgences, and was worried by its theological and financial implications. However, the Church used the wrong tactics to silence him, and that gave Luther the time he needed to think through his ideas.

- Albert of Mainz failed to move quickly enough or in the right direction – if he had simply immediately reined in Tetzel, the affair might have died. (Tetzel was only 'retired' in late 1518.)

- Leo initially underestimated the whole affair, and his decision to rely on the Augustinian order to silence Luther was misjudged.

- The papacy's pace after October 1518 was too slow, but can be explained by Leo's desire not to alienate Frederick the Wise, in light of an imminent imperial election. Politics intervened. However, after the election in June 1519, the papacy's failure then to do anything much at all for six months is hard to explain.

The Church also applied the pressure that forced Luther to think through and expand on his ideas.

- Cajetan, under papal orders, was just too heavy-handed. Rather than discussing matters with Luther, Cajetan simply demanded that he retract and admit that he was wrong. Luther refused, since he genuinely believed he had right on his side. Cajetan's approach backfired in another way: bullying Luther simply made him more popular and a folk hero.

- The Leipzig Debates were a crucial turning point in the expansion of Luther's ideas. The Dominicans and John Eck chose to change the focus of the debate away from indulgence sales and on to the issue of the integrity and authority of the papacy itself. They had hoped, perhaps, to frighten Luther into backing down, but instead widened the scope and focused Luther's attention on much more fundamental issues.

Secondly, Luther almost certainly drew courage from the massive amount of support he received. He was not alone.

- Ordinary people were delighted with Luther's attacks. They were motivated by pre-existing anti-Italian, anti-papal, anti-clerical feelings, and the belief that Rome was milking Germany for money. Many saw Luther as the charismatic fulfilment of a prophecy – the holy man had come to save them, their German hero. One thing is for certain, many did not understand his theological points at all.

- Luther also attracted support from many humanists, especially those of the younger generation, who understood and agreed with his theology. Erasmus was silent, but Melanchthon arrived in Wittenberg in 1518, and Ulrich von Hutten gave Luther his full support by 1520. Martin Bucer was another admirer.

- Equally, if not more importantly, Luther had some powerful protectors, including Frederick the Wise. John Staupitz and the Augustinian order may not have supported him, but they did not reject him. Their motives had little to do with what Luther was saying, but their protection was vital to Luther's survival and morale.

Thirdly, one must look to Luther, and his character and ideas.

- Luther was not the sort of character to have doubts or back down in the face of bullying; on the contrary, he grew bolder. His courage and determination reflected the support he was receiving, but they had been there from the start: his letter to Albert of Mainz in October 1517 has an edge of steel. Equally, it took courage to ignore a papal bull.

- It has been argued that Luther's all-out assault on doctrines and institutions in 1520 was the logical conclusion of beliefs in *sola scriptura* and *sola fide* that he held privately well before 1517, and these beliefs were implicit in his 95 Theses. In other words, though his ideas developed from 1517 to 1520, the core had been there from the start, and that core did not change. Popular support then encouraged him to reveal his beliefs explicitly, and to take them to their logical conclusion.

- An alternative view is that Luther genuinely did just have an issue with indulgences in 1517. Had the Tetzel affair been resolved, that would have been that. External pressure forced Luther to do new research – and that was when he hit upon the doctrine of *sola fide*. His moment of conversion, or 'tower experience', as it is known, may have happened relatively late. Luther himself said it happened in 1519. If this is the case, then pressure from Rome and the Dominicans was to blame for his revolutionary stance in 1520.

EXTRACT 1

From Peter Elmer, *The Renaissance in Europe: A Cultural Enquiry.* Volume 3 *Challenges to Authority* (2000).

Scholars today emphasize the long and often tortuous route by which the scholar from Wittenberg arrived at his radical new approach to issues such as salvation and the scriptures. Increasingly we are being made aware that Luther's journey to spiritual enlightenment encompassed a lengthy process of scholarly introspection – beginning perhaps as early as 1509 – which was informed by a range of intellectual currents then fashionable in northern Europe, including humanism.

EXTRACT 2

From Mark Greengrass, *The Longman Companion to the European Reformation c1500–1618* (1998).

It is highly unlikely that the complexities of Luther's theological development were resolved in a moment of dramatic illumination. [Instead there was a] fruitful period of emerging clarity [which] is now generally taken to have occurred in the year 1515.

EXTRACT 3

From Diarmaid MacCulloch, *Reformation: Europe's House Divided 1490–1700* (2003).

The most likely dating of his Tower Experience is somewhere around [the meeting with Cajetan in August 1518]. Its significance may therefore not be quite what his narrative presents: rather than the definitive breakthrough on justification by faith, it may have represented a moment when the balance between the claims of authority and the claims of faith seen through Scripture began to tilt in his mind.

THINKING HISTORICALLY Evidence (6a)

Arguments and facts
Luther's 'tower experience'

In 1532, one of Luther's keen students noted down a remark made by Luther over dinner, which later appeared in *Table Talk*. Luther said that his theological breakthrough had happened 'in this tower and heated chamber'. His breakthrough is therefore often called the 'tower experience'.

Years later, in an *Autobiographical Fragment* appended to a 1545 edition of his collected works, Luther described his breakthrough in more detail. He had been meditating night and day concerning the true meaning of St Paul's words on 'the righteousness of God' and 'the righteous shall live by faith'. Then, Luther wrote, 'God showed mercy'. He 'began to understand' that the sentences refer to a 'passive righteousness by which the merciful God justifies us by faith'. His new understanding made him feel as though he had been 'born again', and as though he had 'entered through open gates into paradise itself'. Suddenly 'the whole face of scripture changed'. He had been converted to the doctrine of *sola fide*.

When did Luther's 'tower experience' happen?

In his *Autobiographical Fragment*, Luther said his spiritual breakthrough on *sola fide* happened in mid-1519 and rather suddenly, when 'God showed mercy'. However, some historians maintain that the breakthrough happened much earlier in his career at Wittenberg. There is also a view that there was no single and sudden 'tower experience'.

Consider the views of the historians in the three extracts above.

1 Why are facts important in history?

2 Read Extracts 1–3.

   a) How do all three extracts disagree with Luther's own account of his spiritual breakthrough?

   b) How do these extracts disagree with each other?

   c) Which do you think is more important: describing when, or analysing why, Luther reached his views on *sola fide*? Explain your answer.

3 If Luther's account of his tower experience is untrue, should we discount his evidence as being useful? Consider your answer in the light of the following three statements:

   a) Luther may have been confused by old age and ill health, of course, since he wrote his *Autobiographical Fragment* the year before he died.

   b) He may deliberately have been supporting his own interpretation of events: that he developed his more radical ideas unwillingly, and only when he was forced by bitter attacks to defend himself. The Dominicans, and especially Eck, were to blame for the turmoil of the Reformation, not him. Eck's attack happened in 1519, at the Leipzig Debates.

   c) By focusing on a sudden moment of inspiration, Luther may even (egotistically) have been throwing the spotlight onto himself and downplaying his debt to the wide range of writers whom he had been studying for years. Divine inspiration was at work, just as it had been when St Paul was converted.

Burning the papal bull

By the end of November 1520, Luther had committed himself irrevocably on paper. His 60 days were up. On 10 December, surrounded by his enthusiastic students, he solemnly processed to a bonfire built outside the town walls. The students threw on books of canon law defining the legal powers of the Church and all the anti-Luther material they could find, especially the works of Eck. Then, in a dramatic gesture, Luther threw the papal bull *Exsurge Domine* on the fire.

A month later, Leo issued the excommunication, the papal bull *Decet Romanum Pontificem*. In chilling words, Luther and all his supporters and followers were now cast out from the Church. The bull condemned everyone associated with Luther, 'however lofty and dazzling their dignity may be'. It put Frederick the Wise in a very awkward position.

SOURCE

15 From the papal bull *Decet Romanum Pontificem*, January 1521.

Martin himself – and it gives us grievous sorrow and perplexity to say this – the slave of a depraved mind, has scorned to revoke his errors within the prescribed interval and to send us word of such revocation, or to come to us himself; nay, like a stone of stumbling, he has feared not to write and preach worse things than before against us and this Holy See and the Catholic faith, and to lead others on to do the same.

He has now been declared a heretic; and so also others, whatever their authority and rank, who have recked nought of their own salvation but publicly and in all men's eyes become followers of Martin's pernicious and heretical sect, and given him openly and publicly their help, counsel and favour, encouraging him in their midst in his disobedience and obstinacy, or hindering the publication of our missive: such men have incurred the punishments set out in that missive, and are rightfully to be treated as heretics and avoided by all faithful Christians. ...

On all these we decree the sentences of excommunication, of anathema, of our perpetual condemnation and interdict; of privation of dignities, honours and properties on them and their descendants, and of declared unfitness for such possessions; of the confiscation of their goods and of the crime of treason; and these and the other sentences, censures and punishments which are inflicted by canon law on heretics and are set out in our aforementioned missive, we decree to have fallen on these men, to their damnation.

ACTIVITY
SUMMARY

Failure to suppress Luther's challenge

Write an essay with the title 'Why was the Catholic Church unable to suppress Luther's challenge in the years 1517–20?'

Consider: the Church's use of the 'wrong' tactics in 1518; the role played by politics and the imperial election; the reasons why Frederick the Wise did not co-operate; the reasons Luther himself refused to submit; the massive popularity of Luther in Germany, and the reasons for it; the role played by the printing press.

 WIDER READING

Bainton, R. *Here I Stand: A Life of Martin Luther*, Forgotten Books (Classic Reprint, 2012)

Luther, M. *Autobiographical Fragment*, March 1545. In Rupp, E.G. and Drewery, B. *Martin Luther*, Edward Arnold (1970)

MacCulloch, D. *Reformation: Europe's House Divided*, Penguin (2004)

Morris, T.A. *Europe and England in the Sixteenth Century*, Routledge (1998)

Mullet, M.A. *Martin Luther*, Routledge, 2nd edn (2015)

Rice, E.F. and Grafton, A. *The Foundations of Modern Europe*, Norton (1994)

Luther – film starring Joseph Fiennes, 2003

2a.3 The development of Lutheranism, 1521–46

KEY QUESTIONS

- What happened at the Diet of Worms?
- What was Luther's attitude to extremism between 1522 and 1525?
- How did Lutheranism develop in the 1520s?
- Why did Luther's influence on the Reformation decline?

INTRODUCTION

In 1521, Charles V agreed to see Luther, and he was given safe conduct to travel to the town of Worms where the diet was meeting. The meeting is often presented as one of history's great moments – a lone monk defies the emperor in the name of truth – but actually it was something of an anticlimax. Luther was given very little opportunity to express his opinions. Instead, he was declared an outlaw by the Edict of Worms, though Charles lacked the ability to enforce the measure.

To save Luther's life after Worms, Frederick ordered for him to be 'kidnapped' and taken to a safe hideout. Luther's seclusion did not last long, as extremism in Wittenberg forced him to emerge. How he dealt with that extremism, and the more important crises of the Knights' Revolt and then the Peasants' Revolt, was critical in defining Luther as a political and religious conservative, someone whom even princes might find respectable.

Luther devoted the 1520s to enabling others to realise and understand his key messages of *sola scriptura* and *sola fide*. However, he remained reluctant to consider the break with Rome permanent. As a result, he tackled in an unsystematic way the institutional vacuum he had created, often relying on others to define and refine initiatives, and permitting local variations in services and organisation. 'Lutheranism' therefore emerged as a movement united in faith, but rather fragmented in practice. Nevertheless, by 1530, seven princes and about 20 cities had committed themselves as Lutheran.

As priorities shifted from the late 1520s, Luther's input and influence declined, and in the 1540s he was even something of a liability to his own side. His place centre stage had really only lasted for just over a decade.

1520s – Luther translates the Bible and writes hymns
Visitations of Saxony's parishes commence
Writes the two catechisms

1521–22 – Hides in Wartburg Castle
Andrew Carlstadt and the Zwickau Prophets take over Wittenberg
Melanchthon produces *Loci Communes*

1522–23 – Knights' Revolt

1525 – Marriage to Katherine von Bora

1520s	1521	1522	1523	1524	1525

1521 – Diet of Worms
Edict of Worms

1522 – March: Luther restores order in Wittenberg

1524–25 – Peasants' Revolt
Quarrel with Erasmus

SOURCE

Luther addresses the Emperor Charles at the Diet of Worms, painted by Hermann Wislicenus in 1882. Luther is in the centre; Charles V is on his throne; behind him stands Cardinal Aleander. The Archbishop of Trier is seated in his robes on the right. Just beyond Charles' foot can be seen Dr Eck, while on the second row behind him sits Frederick the Wise, with his impressive beard. Luther's books are on the table to the bottom left.

This work was made for the medieval Imperial Palace of Goslar in central Germany when it was restored in the 1870s. Luther's appearance at Worms was a favourite subject matter for late 19th century German artists, reflecting their search for a distinctive 'German' identity once the unification of Germany had been completed in 1871. Luther's faith reflected the Protestant values of the new Second Reich, and he invariably appears as the hero in these paintings.

1529 – Colloquy of Marburg – Luther fails to unite with the Zwinglians

1539–40 – Philip of Hesse bigamy scandal

| 1526 | 1527 | 1528 | 1529 | 1530 | 1531 | 1532 | 1533 | 1534 | 1535 | 1536 | 1537 | 1538 | 1539 | 1540 |

1530 – The Augsburg Confession

What was the new emperor like?

In terms of physical appearance, first impressions would not have been good. Unlike Francis I or Henry VIII, Charles was short and rather puny. Though ugly might be too harsh a term, Charles had a massive lower jaw, bulging eyes and a big nose.

Nor was his health good. Adenoidal problems meant that he could not breathe through his nose, so his mouth was permanently open. He suffered from indigestion and piles caused by excessive gluttony and a tendency to swallow rather than chew his food. Because of his jaw, he dribbled and shyly preferred to eat alone.

More seriously, from his late twenties, he suffered from gout in his hands and feet, swellings of the joints that were so painful that he was sometimes completely incapacitated and unable to focus on work. Always a worrier, by the 1550s he was also suffering from depression. He may well have experienced a complete mental breakdown, since he surrounded himself with clocks, and when the chimes of these did not synchronise, he would obsessively take them to bits and reassemble them.

Nevertheless, the princes would have been impressed by many things when Charles finally arrived in the empire in the autumn of 1520. For his first 15 years, Charles had been brought up by his cultured aunt Margaret of Austria (Philip the Fair's sister), whose Burgundian palaces were a centre of northern Renaissance poetry, art and music. He had been well educated in how to conduct affairs of state. He was an able linguist and spoke French, Spanish, German, Dutch and Latin. He had all the knightly accomplishments: he was chivalrous, he jousted and hunted, and later in life he showed real courage in battle. (Oddly enough, he only seems to have been frightened of spiders and mice.)

Charles was also an exceptionally devout Catholic. He attended mass twice a day, spent hours in prayer, and listened at length to Bible readings. Taught his faith by the honest, prudish Adrian of Utrecht, he believed absolutely that it was his duty to defend Christendom against heretics and infidels.

In his personal life, Charles had such high standards that he was almost dull. Dignified and courteous, he disliked vulgar jokes, drunkenness and ostentatious living, and he remained faithful to his wife, Isabella, while she was alive. He was, in other words, almost the opposite of Henry VIII. He also had a very strong sense of duty. Unless diverted by hunting (or, later, gout-stricken or depressed), he conscientiously applied himself to his paperwork. Though he was neither bright nor a strategic thinker, he did listen to his advisers. He rarely got angry, perhaps because he was a fatalist who believed that God directed human affairs, even when things went badly.

From Frederick's point of view, Charles' greatest virtue was that he had a deep sense of honour, and if he gave his word, he kept it.

WHAT HAPPENED AT THE DIET OF WORMS?

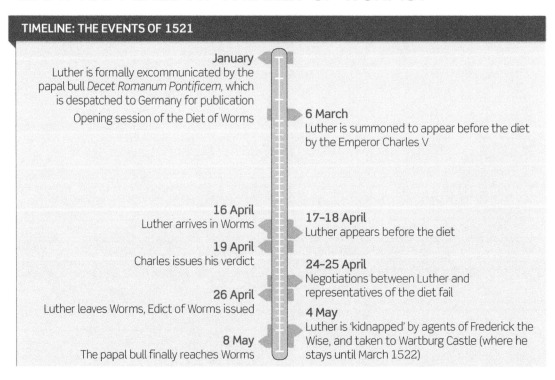

TIMELINE: THE EVENTS OF 1521

January
Luther is formally excommunicated by the papal bull *Decet Romanum Pontificem*, which is despatched to Germany for publication
Opening session of the Diet of Worms

6 March
Luther is summoned to appear before the diet by the Emperor Charles V

16 April
Luther arrives in Worms

17–18 April
Luther appears before the diet

19 April
Charles issues his verdict

24–25 April
Negotiations between Luther and representatives of the diet fail

26 April
Luther leaves Worms, Edict of Worms issued

4 May
Luther is 'kidnapped' by agents of Frederick the Wise, and taken to Wartburg Castle (where he stays until March 1522)

8 May
The papal bull finally reaches Worms

The new emperor Charles V finally arrived in Germany in October 1520. He travelled up the Rhine and summoned his first diet to meet in Worms in January 1521. The highest in the land came, as well as Dr Eck and Cardinal Aleander, the papal representatives.

EXTRACT 1

The writer Heather Cubitt imagines a chaotic scene. From *Luther and the Reformation*, 1976.

The Emperor and his advisers, officials and secretaries, the princes, cardinals and other important clergy, with their servants, crowded into the dingy little town. People thronged the streets, dancing, brawling, drinking in the alehouses, and attending to the business of the Diet. So cramped was accommodation that some visitors were sleeping six to seven in a room. To his vast annoyance Duke Frederick was forced to put up at the Swan Inn, a very third rate place. Even the young Emperor had to share a room with his leading adviser.

Pope Leo's representatives wanted the diet to condemn Luther, immediately and completely.

SOURCE 2

Jerome Aleander to Cardinal de Medici, 8 February 1521. Aleander was the papal delegate sent to Germany in June 1520 in order to publicise the papal bull *Exsurge Domine*. He was writing to Pope Leo's cousin in Rome, the future Pope Clement VII.

The whole of Germany is in full revolt; nine-tenths raise the war-cry, Luther!, while the watchword of the other tenth who are indifferent to Luther is: Death to the Roman Curia! ... I have long known that Erasmus is the source of all this evil which he has scattered around Flanders and the Rhineland. ... A little while ago at Augsburg they were selling Luther's picture with a halo; it was offered without a halo for sale here, and all the copies were disposed of in a trice before I could get one. Yesterday I saw on one and the same page, Luther with a book and Hutten with a sword. Over them was printed in fair letters: To the Champions of Christian Freedom, M. Luther and Ulrich von Hutten.' ... A nobleman showed me such a picture, but I have not been able to get another. So far has the world gone that the Germans in blind adoration press around the two scoundrels, and adore even during their lifetime the men who were bold enough to cause a schism... And I am given up to such people!

However, though Aleander may have wished it otherwise, top of Charles' agenda was the Ottoman issue and a request for the money needed for a crusade. The princes, too, had their own agenda – a list of 102 grievances (or *gravamina*) to do with the Church in Germany, issues that they wanted remedied by a general council. Luther's appeal *To the Christian Nobility of the German Nation* had clearly struck a chord, even though they did not support his doctrinal ideas.

Luther himself was the last item to be considered. On 19 February, the princes persuaded Charles to see Luther, over the protests of Aleander. Charles did not want to alienate the princes and he especially needed Frederick the Wise's support if he was to establish his authority. He also had an excuse, as under the empire's laws, no one of rank could be sent for trial outside Germany without a fair hearing. Luther was summoned to be 'thoroughly investigated by competent persons so that no injustice shall be done, or anything against the law'.

SOURCE 3

A woodcut produced in 1522 in Augsburg, showing Ulrich von Hutten (left foreground) Luther (centre), bowling against the pope (right, wearing the triple crown). The writing in Latin suggests this was commissioned by a humanist.

With the promise of a safe conduct, the emperor's herald as an escort and a carriage provided by Wittenberg town council, Luther set off. His month-long journey was a triumphal procession, and he was cheered and feted in every village they passed through. In Worms, where he finally arrived on 16 April, 2,000 people escorted him to his lodgings in a local friary.

The hearing came the following evening. Luther wore his Augustinian habit; his tonsure was 'large and recently shaved'. However, if Luther had expected to be allowed to explain his views, he was disappointed. Aleander had arranged things otherwise. Luther's books and pamphlets were on a table and their titles were read out. He was asked by an official if he had written them. He agreed that he had. Did he uphold their content, or did he wish to retract? Luther hesitated. He asked for time to consider, to which Charles agreed. Aleander gleefully thought that Luther had damaged his cause.

SOURCE 4

Jerome Aleander to Cardinal de Medici, 17 April 1521.

The fool entered smiling and, before the emperor, kept turning his head continually hither and thither; but when he left he did not seem so cheerful. Many even of his supporters after they had seen him said that he was foolish; others that he was possessed. But many others thought him a pious man, full of the Holy Ghost. In any case he has lost considerable reputation in the regard of all.

The following day, just after 4 p.m., the heralds once more escorted Luther to the imperial court. He had to wait until 6 p.m. to be heard. This time, a more confident Luther addressed the assembly. He spoke, according to one eyewitness, 'like a suppliant, yet without raising his voice – modestly, but with no lack of Christian warmth and firmness'. Many listening thought, and hoped, that he was about to retract. He did not. Rather, he agreed that he had written the books. Some were 'harmless and fit to be read by Christians'.

SOURCE

5 Luther's answer before the emperor and diet, 18 April 1521.

Another class of my writings consists of polemics against the papacy and the doctrine of the papists, as men who by their most evil teachings and example have laid waste all Christendom, body and soul. Nobody can deny or dissemble this: the experience and the complaint of all men bear witness that by the laws of the pope and man-made doctrines, the consciences of the faithful have been most wretchedly ensnared, tormented, tortured; that above all, in this renowned German nation, goods and wealth have been devoured by tyranny unbelievable, and to this day the devouring goes on, endlessly and by most grievous means. Yet the canon law of the papists itself provides that papal laws and doctrines contrary to the Gospel or the opinions of the Fathers should be counted erroneous and rejected. If, then, I revoke these books, all I shall achieve is to add strength to tyranny, and open not the windows but the doors to this monstrous godlessness, for a wider and freer range than it has ever dared before. The memorial of my revocation would be the kingdom of their wickedness, with licence complete and unbridled, exercising over its wretched subjects a sway by far the most intolerable of all, and even strengthened and stabilised if word had gone abroad that I had revoked my books with the authority of your serene majesty and all the Roman Empire. Good God, what wickedness and tyranny should I then let loose!

He agreed that some of his works were overly aggressive, but all were based on the scriptures. If anyone could prove otherwise, he would be the first to cast his books into the fire. Luther was interrupted, and again ordered to give a simple answer: would he take back his beliefs or not? His reply appears in the source below.

SOURCE

6 Luther's concluding remarks at the Diet of Worms, 18 April 1521.

Since your serene Majesty and your lordships request a simple answer, I shall give it, with no strings and no catches. Unless I am convicted by the testimony of Scripture or plain reason (for I believe neither in pope nor councils alone, since it is agreed that they have often erred and contradicted themselves), I am bound by the scriptures I have quoted, and my conscience is captive to the Word of God. I neither can nor will revoke anything, since it is neither safe nor honest to act against one's conscience. Amen.

SOURCE

7 'Written by my own hand', Charles delivered his response the following day, 19 April 1521.

It is certain that a single monk must err if his opinion is contrary to that of all Christendom. According to his opinion, the whole of Christendom has been in error for a thousand years, and is continuing still more so in that error in the present. To settle this matter I have resolved to stake upon this course my dominions and my possessions, my body and my blood, my life and my soul. It would be a disgrace for me and you, the noble and renowned German nation,... if in this our day and generation, not only heresy but even the suspicion of heresy or the diminution of our Christian religion were due to our negligence.

After the impudent reply which Luther gave yesterday in the presence of us all, I now declare that I regret having delayed so long the proceedings against the aforementioned Luther and his false doctrine. I have now resolved never again, under any circumstances, to hear him. He is to be escorted home immediately... He is not to preach or seduce the people with his evil doctrine and not to incite them to rebellion. ... I am resolved to act and proceed against him as a notorious heretic.

Nevertheless, Charles permitted a delegation of eight commissioners to try to reason with Luther one last time. The negotiations failed. On 26 April, Luther was sent home, still under safe conduct. Frederick the Wise diplomatically slipped away as well. On the same day, Luther was declared an outlaw by the Edict of Worms.

All Luther's works were to be burned, the edict went on, and in future all printers had to have the approval of a university faculty of theology before they could print anything even mentioning the Christian faith.

Why did the edict fail?

Had the edict been put into action immediately, then perhaps that would have been an end to the matter. However, it was only promulgated in a few places, including the Habsburg territories, the city of Cologne and Ducal Saxony. What went wrong?

- The structure of the empire meant that Charles had to rely on the princes and on city authorities to enforce the edict.

- However, then, and for the next eight years, the princes said they would only enforce the edict if Charles put pressure on the pope to call a general council to address their 102 *gravamina*. The vast majority did not agree with Luther's doctrines, but they agreed that Germany was being exploited by Rome and that there was a great deal wrong with the Church in Germany. They hoped to use the Luther affair as a lever to achieve their own agenda.

- Charles could not force the princes; he had given his word in the Capitulation he signed in 1519 not to bring foreign troops into Germany. Nor did he have the time to stay and persuade them personally, as other issues were pressing. Spain was in revolt and France was acting aggressively. He left Germany and did not return for nine years. He too wanted the pope to call a council.

- But immediate action would have been difficult. Luther had vanished and no one appeared to know where he was.

Should Charles just have executed Luther at Worms?

With hindsight, it has been suggested that Charles should not have stuck by the safe conduct. He should simply have arrested Luther on 18 April. However, this suggestion ignores several factors:

- Luther was a national hero at the time – executing him would simply have made him a martyr and stirred up even more anti-Rome feeling.

- Nor would executing him have eliminated his ideas. Around 300,000 copies of Luther's works were in circulation, as well as thousands of pro-Luther woodcuts.

- Charles was a man of his word – he had guaranteed Luther safe conduct, and he stuck to his promise.

- Charles also did not want to sour good relations with the princes by backtracking on his word so early in his reign.

Wartburg Castle, 1521–22

On his return journey from Worms, Luther was once again treated as a hero. Despite the edict, the Abbot of Hersfeld treated him as an honoured guest, fed him royally, and even put him up in his own bed. He preached openly. But then, close to home, Luther was 'kidnapped' by five agents of Frederick the Wise. He was taken to the elector's castle at Wartburg, close to Eisenach, and

SOURCE

8   The Edict of Worms 1521, much of which was composed by Aleander.

Charles V... to all the electors, princes etc., one and all, greetings and blessings. ...

Our strict order is that after the appointed twenty days which terminate on the 14th of this month of May, you shall refuse the aforesaid Martin Luther hospitality, lodging and bed; that none shall feed and nourish him with food or drink, or assist and further him by the counsel and help or word or deed, secretly and openly; but wherever you meet him, if you have sufficient force, you shall take him prisoner and deliver him (or cause him to be delivered) to us...

As for his friends, adherents, enthusiasts... we order that you shall attack, overthrow, seize and wrest their property from them...

As for the books of Martin Luther... we order that nobody shall henceforth dare to buy, sell, copy, print or cause them to be copied and printed, or approve his opinions, or support, preach, defend or assert them in any way... for they are impious, foul, suspect, half-baked, the work of a notorious heretic.

put in the care of the castle governor and two servants. For a while, the vanishing act was so convincing that the artist Albrecht Dürer wrote in his diary that he feared Luther had been murdered: 'O God, if Luther be dead who will proclaim the Holy Gospel so clearly to us?'

Safe in Wartburg, Luther grew a beard, dressed in plain clothes, and changed his name to **Junker** George. Boredom threatened; rich food and a lack of exercise caused constipation and piles, and he felt lonely. However, he was not completely isolated from the world. The governor took him hunting a couple of times. He wrote pamphlets and sent and received letters – he even wrote to Albert of Mainz when the latter announced a new indulgence sale. Most importantly, he soon had the materials he needed to embark on a massive project. Armed with Erasmus' Greek testament and Reuchlin's Hebrew dictionary, Luther had decided to translate the Bible into German, starting with the New Testament.

KEY TERM

Junker
A German noble with the status of a squire.

During Luther's ten-month absence, others had taken charge of the Reformation, and by the winter, news was reaching Luther of an alarming level of extremism in Wittenberg. In March 1522, he decided to leave his hiding place and return there.

ACTIVITY
KNOWLEDGE CHECK

The Diet of Worms
In pairs, discuss whether or not you feel Charles made the right decisions in 1521, in summoning Luther for a hearing before the diet, in allowing Luther to leave Worms unharmed, and in issuing the edict of Worms. What alternative course of action might he have taken?

WHAT WAS LUTHER'S ATTITUDE TO EXTREMISM BETWEEN 1522 AND 1525?

Three crises in quick succession absorbed Luther's attention over the four years. His reaction to them determined the long-term success of the Reformation.

Andrew Carlstadt and the Zwickau Prophets, 1521-22

While Luther was secluded at Wartburg, his place in Wittenberg was taken by a senior colleague, Andrew Carlstadt, and by Gabriel Zwilling, an Augustinian preacher. Carlstadt had been a late convert to Luther's ideas, but made up for it with enthusiasm, and he had initiated the debate with Eck at Leipzig. Now he and Zwilling decided to speed up the Reformation and put into practice – as they saw it – everything that Luther had so far put only on paper. The Mass was denounced. The laity in Wittenberg were to be offered communion in 'both kinds', bread and wine. Led by Zwilling, monks denounced their vows, which they decided had been made redundant by the doctrine of *sola fide*. They grew out their tonsures and wore secular clothing. Carlstadt announced his support for clerical marriage, and led the way by marrying a 15-year-old girl.

To Frederick's deep displeasure and anger, Wittenberg was acquiring a reputation for extremism, and worse was to follow when the so-called Zwickau Prophets arrived there in December 1521. These prophets came from the town of Zwickau in Saxony, where they had been radicalised by Thomas Müntzer. In Wittenberg, they announced that they were inspired by direct revelations from God and made bold prophecies: that the Turks would invade; that unmarried priests would be slain; that the end of the world was nigh and 'no impious or wicked sinner would be left alive'. They denounced Luther for excessive caution. They preached that since Jesus had been baptised as an adult, all true believers should be baptised as adults. Swept along enthusiastically, Carlstadt stopped baptising infants, going well beyond anything that Luther advocated. For Luther, infant baptism represented the integration of a child into a community in both its religious and its political sense, while adult baptism threatened to lead to free choice and anarchy. Further radicalism followed. On Christmas Day, the service was delivered in German, and the clergy did not wear the normal vestments. One priest even wore a jaunty feather in his cap. Luther's teachings on the Real Presence were overruled in favour of the Eucharist as purely symbolic. Carlstadt proposed setting up a 'poor relief fund' to relieve social problems and implement Jesus' teachings on charity. Excitement mounted as it seemed that not only church reform, but also radical social reform was being offered.

> **EXTEND YOUR KNOWLEDGE**
>
> Thomas Müntzer and Zwickau
> Zwickau had been radicalised in 1520 by Thomas Müntzer, a well-educated parish priest. An early supporter of Luther, Müntzer was soon disillusioned with Luther's lack of interest in social and political issues, and, in Zwickau, had announced a Kingdom of Christ, to replace all existing authorities. He had preached that the Second Coming would be hastened by destroying the wicked and by confiscating all of the possessions of the rich. The Kingdom did not last, however, and Müntzer had been driven out of Zwickau.

> **KEY TERM**
>
> Iconoclasm
> The destruction of religious images on the grounds that they are heretical.

The pace quickened when Carlstadt and Zwilling then announced that all holy statues and images were the work of the Devil and symbols of materialism, and should be destroyed. Zwilling led the ensuing **iconoclasm**. He lit a fire in the courtyard of the Augustinian friary, and with the help of a mob he threw on to it all of the 'images and banners, crucifixes and candles' of the Church. They then cut off the heads of stone images of Christ, the Virgin Mary and other saints, and stripped the walls of paintings. Zwilling was clearly something of a rabble rouser: in the neighbouring village of Eilenberg, he preached so strongly against the clergy that his listeners stormed the parsonage. What was happening in Wittenberg was not unique, though. Violent anti-clerical outbursts and people taking reform into their own hands were becoming widespread occurrences in Saxony and beyond.

Luther's reaction

In March 1522, Luther decided to return to Wittenberg, both to stop the extremism and to prevent the bloodshed that would ensue if Frederick decided to use force, which was likely, as Frederick did not want to give his cousin George any excuse to invade under the pretext of restoring order.

Luther returned against Frederick's wishes, and in a letter he absolved the elector of blame 'if I am taken prisoner or killed'. It is a measure of Luther's courage, charisma and persuasiveness that he managed to restore order and his authority in just eight days by preaching what are now known as his eight 'Invocavit Sermons'. He deliberately wore his Augustinian habit while he delivered them.

> **SOURCE**
>
> **9** From one of Luther's Invocavit Sermons. The name comes from the fact that the first sermon was delivered on Invocavit Sunday, 9 March 1522. This was one of his gentler sermons. Luther was good at the carrot-and-stick approach to persuasion.
>
> I would not have gone so far as you have done, if I had been here. The cause is good but there has been too much haste. For there are still brothers and sisters on the other side who belong to us and must still be won.
>
> Let me illustrate. The sun has two properties, light and heat. No king has power enough to bend or guide the light of the sun; it remains fixed in its place. But the heat may be turned and guided, and yet is ever about the sun. Thus faith must always remain pure and immovable in our hearts, never wavering; but love bends and turns so that our neighbours may grasp it. There are some who can run, others must walk, still others can hardly creep. Therefore we must not look upon our own, but upon our brother's powers, so that he who is weak in faith, and attempts to follow the strong, may not be destroyed of the devil. Therefore, dear brethren, follow me; I have never been a destroyer. And I was also the very first whom God called to this work. I cannot run away, but will remain as long as God allows. I was also the one to whom God first revealed that his Word should be preached to you. I am also sure that you have the pure Word of God.

In his sermons, Luther insisted on slow, cautious change. Nothing was to be imposed or forced or compelled. Persuasive preaching was the way forward: once 'you have won the heart, you have won the whole man'. Luther took back charge, in Wittenberg at least. The prophets were expelled; Carlstadt was dismissed from the university, and left the town of his own volition in 1524.

The Wittenberg tumults were important in two respects:

- In derailing Carlstadt and the prophets, Luther made clear his conservative approach to change. He opposed all grass-roots activism and extremism. Change was to be slow, and was to be implemented by the authorities in an orderly fashion.

- It also opened Luther's eyes to the fact that he had created a vacuum. He spent most of the rest of the 1520s creating the means by which ordinary people could learn and understand his new doctrines. Immediately, though, he accepted some changes – meat-eating on Fridays, the marriage of clergy (too many monks and nuns had already married for him to undo that change) and taking the Eucharist in both kinds. All of these concessions were already in accordance with his views anyway.

The Knights' Revolt, 1522–23

There was very little Luther could do about the next crisis. It took place on the other side of the empire and involved a social class much higher than his own. Nevertheless, since those involved said they had been inspired by him and were acting on his behalf, some sort of response was required.

The imperial knights were a relic of the Middle Ages, when their role as the military arm of the emperor had given them power and status. Now, however, their position was almost pathetic. They lacked purpose and wealth; their independent enclaves and crumbling castles were threatened by predatory princes and cities, which had also taken over the knights' old roles as the empire's 'policemen'. In 1522, a sizeable group of knights were stirred to take action by Ulrich von Hutten. Hutten was inspired by Luther's reforming ideas, but even more so by his German nationalism, and he wished to accelerate the pace of the change with military force, using his fellow knights as the tool. The knights themselves were genuinely motivated by religious fervour, but equally sought a way to resume their old imperial position.

Led by the formidable Franz von Sickingen, their chosen target was the city of Trier. The Archbishop of Trier ('a truly excellent man', according to Aleander) had played a key role at the Diet of Worms. His assistant had pointed to Luther's books, demanding yes/no answers and interrupting Luther when he was in full flow. Furthermore, the archbishop assiduously burned all heretical texts. He represented Rome, and his vast territories demonstrated Rome's exploitation of Germany. The knights believed that the archbishop's removal would be the trigger to a political revolution and a reforming crusade. Their goal was nothing less than the unification of all German-speaking lands under one national monarch, and the secularisation of all Church property.

Their attack was woefully misjudged. The archbishop refused to surrender. His requests for help were met by local princes, who wished to stop in its tracks this effort to change the political status quo. It was also an opportunity to break the knights for ever. When the attack on Trier failed, Hutten fled to Switzerland, where he died of syphilis, alone and rejected, on an island on Lake Zurich. Sickengen retreated to his strongest castle, which lasted less than a week when besieged by the forces of the Swabian League. He died of wounds the day after he had surrendered.

Luther's reaction

Though Luther had not been involved with the knights' war, it was carried out in his name, and posters linking him and Hutten were widespread. As such, some sort of condemnation might have been expected. Instead, he was remarkably silent, perhaps because of his friendship with his deputy Melanchthon, who had known Hutten well, or perhaps just because of Hutten's reputation as a humanist and author of *Letters of Obscure Men*. However, in the eyes of the establishment, Luther's silence was damaging – it implied he was hostile to princely authority and in favour of governmental reform. How he reacted to the next crisis would be critical if he wished to restore his position with rulers who might be open to Lutheran ideas.

The Peasants' Revolt, 1524–25

From June 1524 to May 1525, much of Germany was plunged into chaos by one of the largest mass revolts of ordinary people ever known. Though urban labourers joined in, this was largely a rural revolt. Peasant discontent had been widespread for decades, and had erupted from time to time in bouts of violence directed against landowners. The difference now was the sheer scale of the event. In 1524, numerous local uprisings started in the south-west – allegedly, the first occurred on the estate of the Count von Lupfen, when, on a public holiday, his wife ordered peasants to collect shells she needed for her embroidery. Within months, uprisings had spread to Austria and into central and north Germany. Armies of peasants up to 15,000-strong roamed the countryside. They were not co-ordinated in any way. There was no central leadership, nor was there any common agenda. The only thing the peasants had in common was a symbol – the *Bundschuh*, or peasant's shoe. The rebels sacked castles and monasteries and plundered towns. Mob rule and terror replaced local authorities.

Causes

In many respects, the revolt reflected mounting hardships. For past decades, increasing financial demands made by landlords had been compounded by legal changes that undermined the traditional ways peasants had made ends meet. The enclosure of common land meant an inability to graze livestock for free, while hunting and fishing were reclassified as poaching offences punishable by death. Yet population growth meant there was more need than ever for access to common land and 'free food'.

The Peasants' Revolt from a contemporary print: a peasant attacks a landlord (back left); a radical preacher attacks a monk (bottom left); a soldier attacks a bishop (bottom centre). God's blessings on the revolt come from the top right, while the goat may symbolise the devil vanquished, in readiness for the end of the world.

Life was even worse for peasants to the east of the River Elbe, where landlords were imposing severe restrictions on movement and demanding more free labour. In other words, serfdom was being imposed.

Increased financial demands and legal changes provided the fuel for the revolt, and recovering lost liberties was the aim of many peasants. However, this revolt was different from previous ones in that grievances now coincided with the spread of new religious ideas. The fact that many priests joined the rebels, some of whom declared that they were followers of Luther, gave the impression that this was also a religious rebellion. So, too, did certain demands that appeared in the many manifestos produced during the revolt: a demand for godly preachers who were elected by the local community, the demand for an end to tithes, an appeal for social justice as revealed in the Gospels.

Inadvertently and indirectly, Luther was a cause. Ambiguity and lack of clarity in some of his theology, his self-promotion as a holy man and his aggressive language were certainly partly to blame.

- Luther's ideas seemed to provide hope. For example, he laid stress on *sola scriptura* and he had burned books of canon law. In the peasants' eyes he was supporting godly law. Since the Bible made no mention of tithes, the peasants thought Luther would support them in denouncing tithes. Luther also stressed the 'priesthood of all believers'. Again he was misinterpreted – the peasants thought he was suggesting the *social* equality of all men, as opposed to the spiritual equality. He had used the story of Christians in a desert appointing one of the group as their priest – the peasants thought he was promoting the right of congregations to elect their own ministers. They also took his emphasis on Christian liberty to mean a licence to act as they pleased.

- From 1519 on, woodcuts circulated showing Luther with a halo and a dove over his head, representing the Holy Spirit, as though he was a prophet sent by God. Luther did not repudiate these – one even appeared on the front cover of one of his 1520 pamphlets. Luther used the prophecy that a holy man would come to save Germany as a means to gain support. The peasants took him literally. They assumed Luther, a self-proclaimed man of the people, would be sympathetic and help them.

- Luther did not hold back from using very aggressive language against his opponents. He referred to papists as the evil instruments of Antichrist, and Duke George of Saxony as 'a tyrant', 'that swine of Dresden', 'a mere bladder'. He was just as rude about other princes: they were 'drunken and mad', 'the biggest fools and worst knaves on earth'. His tone was then reflected in the many thousands of pro-Luther woodcuts circulating at the time, which showed, for example, the pope, cardinals and bishops being thrust into the jaws of Hell. Peasants may have assumed that they were carrying out Luther's wishes.

In most respects, though, Luther can be exonerated from blame for the religious overtones of the revolt. Much of the anti-clericalism was deep-rooted and pre-dated 1517. The Church had been raising tithes and putting a higher 'price' on salvation for a long time, and absentee ecclesiastical landlords were some of the worst offenders when it came to exploiting the peasantry. Also, many peasants were more deeply influenced by wandering preachers like Thomas Müntzer, who preached anarchy and the overthrow of all authority in readiness for the Second Coming of Christ. 'Go to it, go to it, go to it!' urged Müntzer in a letter to the people of Allstedt, 'The time has come, the evil doers are running like scared dogs! … Show no pity!' Luther had already made clear his complete lack of support for such revolutionary incitement in his Invocavit Sermons of 1522. Müntzer called him Doctor Liar, though, suggesting that Müntzer had once interpreted Luther differently.

Luther's reaction

After some initial sympathy and a pamphlet appealing for calm, Luther became horrified at the level of violence and at the way his ideas were being misinterpreted. In April 1525, he toured the Mansfeld valley and Thuringia, his family's home ground, and preached to the peasantry, trying to pacify the revolt with reason.

His peace mission made no impact at all. On the contrary, he was received with hostility, and booed and spat at by peasants. He was shocked to be addressed with the familiar 'du' by his social inferiors. The tour made up his mind: the peasants were 'robbers and murderers', who were using the Gospel blasphemously to cover up their wickedness and insolence. Worse still, they were compelling good people to join them. In May 1525, he wrote one of his most famous pamphlets, *Against the Robbing and Murdering Hordes of Peasants*, calling on the princes to 'stab, smite, slay' the peasants with God's approval and a clear conscience.

SOURCE 11

From Luther's pamphlet, *Against the Robbing and Murdering Hordes of Peasants*, 1525.

I did not venture to judge the peasants, since they had offered to be set right and to be instructed, and Christ's command in Matthew 7, says that we are not to judge. But before I look around they go on, and, forgetting their offer, they betake themselves to violence, and rob and rage and act like mad dogs. By this it is easy to see what they had in their false minds, and that the pretences which they had made in their twelve articles [referring to a popular peasant manifesto], under the name of the Gospel, were nothing but lies. It is the devil's work they are at, and in particular it is the work of the archdevil [Müntzer] who rules at Mühlhausen and does nothing else than stir up robbery, murder and bloodshed; as Christ says of him in John 8, 'He was a murderer from the beginning.'

The peasants have taken on themselves the burden of three terrible sins against God and man, by which they have abundantly merited death in body and soul. In the first place they have sworn to be true and faithful, submissive and obedient, to their rulers, as Christ commands when he says, 'Render unto Caesar's the things that are Caesar's.' Because they are breaking this obedience... they have forfeited body and soul.

In the second place, they are starting a rebellion, and violently robbing and plundering monasteries and castles which are not theirs, by which they have a second time deserved death in body and soul... rebellion brings with it a land full of murder and bloodshed, makes widows and orphans, and turns everything upside down, like the greatest disaster. Therefore let everyone who can, smite, slay and stab, secretly or openly, remembering that nothing can be more poisonous, hurtful or devilish than a rebel. It is just as when one must kill a mad dog; if you do not strike him, he will strike you, and a whole land with you.

In the third place, they cloak this terrible and horrible sin with the Gospel... Thus they become the greatest blasphemers of God and slanderers of his holy Name, serving the devil, under the outward appearance of the Gospel, thus earning death in body and soul ten times over.

Luther said the authorities could execute peasants without trial, and that God was on their side. He wrote the pamphlet when the revolt was at its height, but it was published as the revolt was being crushed. The princes, led by men like Philip of Hesse, and using forces like the Swabian League, defeated the rebels with ease. In the aftermath, about 100,000 peasants were executed out of hand. This sort of repression removed all potential leaders and frightened the rest of the peasantry into submission.

THINKING HISTORICALLY Causation (6a)

Seeing things differently

Different times and different places have different sets of ideas. Beliefs about how the world works, how human societies should be governed or the best way to achieve economic prosperity can all be radically different from our own. It is important for the historian to take these different attitudes into account and be aware of the dangers of judging them against modern ideas.

The suppression of the Peasants' Revolt by the princes

Thomas Müntzer was captured and brutally tortured before being beheaded. Another leader was roasted alive; another flayed. The executioner's bill after the Battle of Frankenhausen read: '80 beheaded, 69 of whom had their eyes put out and their fingers cut off, which comes to 114 florins and two cents.'

Answer the following questions:

1 What sort of attitudes do you think gave rise to this treatment of the leaders of the Peasants' Revolt?

2 If he had known how the Peasants' Revolt would end, do you think Müntzer would have behaved differently?

3 Early modern attitudes to punishment are different from current attitudes.

    a) Are there any other ways in which early modern German attitudes differ dramatically from those current in Germany now?

    b) Why do you think they are different?

4 How important is it for historians to deal with events in the context of the beliefs and values of people in the past?

SOURCE

Luther's reply to Nicholas von Amsdorf, 30 May 1525. Amsdorf was an admiring disciple of Luther. He had written to Luther from Magdeburg, concerned about the bad reputation Luther had gained from issuing his pamphlet against the Peasants' Revolt.

Grace and peace! You inform me of a new honour, my Amsdorf, namely that I am called a toady to the princes. Satan has conferred many such honorary titles on me in these years. But I will not deplore such know-alls, who in judging me only betray their own bloodthirsty and seditious spirit. Rejoice, then, that Satan is indignant and blasphemes whenever I touch him. For what are these but the voices of Satan, by which he tries to traduce me and the Gospel?

Indeed I think it better that all the peasants should be killed rather than that the princes and magistrates should be destroyed, because the peasants take up the sword without God's command. What iniquity of Satan can follow from this but the complete satanic devastation of the kingdom of God and the world. Even if the princes act excessively at least they bear the sword at God's command. However the peasants deserve no mercy or patience, but rather the wrath and indignation of God and Man. For they did not comply when they were warned, nor yield when even the fairest terms were offered to them, but continued to confound everything with the rage of Satan, as those in Thuringia and Franconia did.

A Level Exam-Style Question Section B

'Despite the radical nature of his challenge to the Catholic Church, at heart Luther was deeply conservative.'

How far do you agree with this statement? (20 marks)

Tip

Consider both the political as well as the religious outcomes of Luther's challenge, where he looked for support, his relationship with the princes and his attitude to the Peasants' Revolt of 1525.

ACTIVITY WRITING

Inferences

Aim to include supported inferences in your answers. An inference involves drawing a logical conclusion about the material in a source. It involves reading between the lines, and might seem to be rather risky. However, if you can demonstrate with reasoning or other knowledge that your inference is probably correct, then the risk is fully justified. Inferences do need to be supported – they should not be guesswork. Certain phrases indicate that you are making an inference: 'The source suggests that...'; 'The source indicates that...'; 'The author is likely to...'; 'One can infer that...'; 'It is possible to deduce that...'.

Are the following valid inferences? What evidence would you use from Sources 11 and 12 to support each one?

- The sources suggest that Luther was horrified at the level of violence.
- It is possible to deduce that Luther was very conservative, politically.
- One can also infer that Luther was appalled at the way his ideas were being misinterpreted.

SOURCE

Letter from Herman Mühlpfort to Stephen Roth, June 1525. Mühlpfort was a prominent Lutheran and mayor of Zwickau, one of the earliest towns to adopt religious reforms. Luther had dedicated his 1520 publication on Christian liberty to him. Roth was a translator and publisher in Wittenberg.

Doctor Martin [Luther] has fallen into disfavour with the common people, also with both learned and unlearned... It is true, as Martin writes, that rebellion should be put down, and... that secular authority should punish, though they do it without being asked; but, he conceded too much to one side, for the poor were being strangled. I find that incomprehensible. Martin's remedy is... that the peasants should bear more, while the nobility receive the lion's share and yet concede the least. ... See how violently the nobility will impose all their burdens on the people with the sword and shed the blood of the suffering poor, who cannot protect themselves from hunger because of their poverty. But the nobility will rely on Martin's tract, that this will gain them eternal salvation.

Dear Christian brother, who will now speak out about the need of the commons in town and village? ... Whoever speaks out will be accused of being a rebel and everyone will have to keep silent for fear of tyrants, lest it be said that one is speaking against authority. I know already that in several places more has been imposed on the poor than before and they are told openly: 'You owe me this; if you do not do it, you are opposing me, who am your lord and have sovereign authority over you.'

The consequences of *Against the Robbing and Murdering Hordes of Peasants*

Luther was afterwards blamed for the violence and savagery of the repression and for the imposition of even harsher conditions on the peasants than before. His tone in the pamphlet shocked even close

AS Level Exam-Style Question Section A

How much weight do you give the evidence in Source 13 for an enquiry into the consequences of Luther's stance on the Peasants' Revolt?

Explain your answer using the source, the information given about it and your knowledge of the historical context. (12 marks)

Tip

The 'weight' (or value) you place on the evidence in this source will partly depend on how you rate the author as a witness. Is he likely to have been knowledgeable and reliable?

supporters. His pamphlet played a key role in losing him mass support, certainly from among the peasantry, who saw him as a traitor.

However, the pamphlet also played a role in winning him princely support, at least from those who were already contemplating religious reform. It confirmed the impression that the Invocavit Sermons had given: that Luther was 'respectable' and conservative. He supported rulers' rights and property. In the long term, it was much more valuable for Lutheranism to have the princes' support rather than that of the peasants.

The revolt also ensured that secular authorities fairly immediately started taking the initiative in imposing religious reform, from above. In August 1525, for example, the Margrave George of Brandenburg-Ansbach issued an edict to remove all 'unlearned and unsuitable preachers'. Anyone who had preached rebellion was arrested, 'punished earnestly and remorselessly', and then exiled. The remainder were given clear instructions on what to preach, including their subjects' duty of unconditional obedience.

From then on, there was a clear-cut distinction between a respectable **magisterial reformation** of the Church, and an unacceptable one, the **radical reformation**, which both Catholic and Lutheran princes agreed should be destroyed. The following year at the Diet of Speyer, it was agreed that each prince should enforce the faith 'as he would have to answer to God and to the Emperor'. The choice of faith, though, was limited to Lutheranism or Catholicism.

KEY TERMS

Magisterial reformation
This term refers to reform that was imposed from above by the authorities, the 'magistrates', who were princes or city councils. Lutheranism was considered acceptable and moderate by such reformers.

Radical reformation
This term collectively describes the many groups who promoted their own versions of Christianity in the 1520s and 1530s. There was no unity between these groups at all, and they had little in common, though most demanded the right of congregations to elect their own ministers, and most were Anabaptists: they promoted adult baptism. Most demanded their own right to interpret the scriptures for themselves, relying on guidance from the Holy Spirit. Hardliners rejected the Bible as irrelevant: God spoke directly to his prophets. Some radicals were pacifists, others promoted violence. In preparation for the imminent return of Christ, they said, the elect must declare war on the ungodly, all authority must be overturned, and all wealth redistributed. Some groups practised a form of communal living and secluded themselves from all external authority. Whatever their beliefs, radicals were considered unacceptable and dangerous, and were fiercely persecuted by both Lutherans and Catholics. Luther particularly was anxious to distance himself from radicals, though ironically he probably inspired them in the first place.

EXTEND YOUR KNOWLEDGE

The marriage of Luther
In June 1525, as the Peasants' Revolt reached its climax, Luther married an ex-nun, Katherine von Bora (1499–1552). She had been put in a convent in Ducal Saxony at the age of ten by her stepmother. Unhappy, she and eight fellow nuns escaped and made their way to Wittenberg in 1523. Here Luther found them husbands, marrying Katherine himself when he ran out of other alternatives. Despite his initial doubts, Katherine proved to be an exceptional partner and the marriage was a very happy one. 'I would not exchange my Katie for France or for Venice,' said Luther in 1531. She was intelligent and sensible, and competently managed a huge household including their six children and up to ten lodgers, as well as entertaining Luther's large number of visitors. She also ran a small farmstead, did the books, and administered home-made medical remedies to those in need so competently that one of her sons said later that she would have made an excellent doctor.

Luther's view on sex, marriage and the position of women
In Luther's view, sex was a normal, healthy activity. He rejected all feelings of guilt on the matter. However, sexual relations were only permissible in marriage. Adulterers and fornicators would be damned. Lutheran reformers therefore demanded the closure of all brothels in the interests of creating a godly society. This was a big step, as in many towns, brothels were considered a civic amenity, a necessary evil, and they were often run by salaried civil officials. Young men, said Luther, should get married, and his concerns were not for the prostitutes themselves, whom he loathed as evil 'syphilitic whores'. In Reformation woodcuts, images of evil harlots were often identified with the papacy, and devils were portrayed as whores.

A woman's role was in the home, according to Luther. In 1524, he explained his views to three nuns: 'A woman does not have complete mastery over herself. God created her body that she should be with a man and bear and raise children.' God-given physical differences between men and women indicated their different roles: 'Men have broad shoulders and narrow hips, and accordingly they possess intelligence. Women have narrow shoulders and broad hips. Women ought to stay at home; the way they were created indicates this, for they have broad hips and a wide fundament to sit on.' (In one of his harsher moments, he even said, 'If women grow weary or even die while bearing children, that does no harm. Let them bear children to death, that's what they're here for.')

For Luther, a well-run family was like a well-run society: each member had their duties and their responsibilities. The husband, like the government, held ultimate authority. He was responsible for providing, and for teaching his household core Christian beliefs (the Lord's Prayer, the Ten Commandments, etc.). The wife was in control of all domestic matters, including raising the children. She owed her husband absolute obedience. A good wife and mother was a priceless asset. Women who did not wish to follow this godly road – who might aspire to a single life or paid employment, for example – were unnatural.

Luther's conservative views on women were very much of his time. However, in closing convents where women might become abbesses, in promoting the exclusion of women from paid work, and in rejecting alternative positive images of women (as saints, for example, leaving only a choice between the temptress, Eve, and the perfect mothers, Mary and Anne), he removed choice and made real what many simply thought.

ACTIVITY
KNOWLEDGE CHECK

The importance of the Peasants' Revolt
How was 1525 a turning point in the German Reformation?

HOW DID LUTHERANISM DEVELOP IN THE 1520s?

The crises of the early 1520s called for some emergency measures. People needed to be put right on Luther's key teachings, and the quality of preachers, especially, needed to be checked to avoid another Müntzer. Whether or not further reform or new institutions were needed was another matter. Was the schism with Rome even permanent? As it was felt by many to be the Last Days and that the end of the world would happen shortly, what was the point? Both views were held by Luther, who anyway disliked over-institutionalised churches. As a result:

- Reforms were introduced in a piecemeal and rather random fashion, in reaction to needs as they arose – but because changes were not always well thought through, they did not always succeed.

- There was no central co-ordination from Wittenberg; secular rulers in other states and cities used their own initiative.

- There was therefore a great deal of diversity – a Lutheran church in one state or city was very different from that in another, though all shared the same doctrines.

KEY TERM

Didactic woodcut
This was an image intended to teach the illiterate about true Lutheran doctrine.

Luther himself perceived the immediate priority as getting his message across accurately. Using the printing press as his weapon, he provided a German Bible and the Great Catechism for those who could read. For the illiterate he wrote hymns, commissioned **didactic woodcuts**, demanded schools, and produced a Short Catechism that ministers and parents could use for teaching purposes. For both the literate and the illiterate, he wrote a new liturgy – the German Mass – which put the sermon and preaching the Word at the heart of a service.

The doctrine of the Real Presence

According to Luther, the Gospels had to be taken literally. Since Christ's words at the Last Supper were: 'This is my body' and 'This is my blood', then Christ really was present in the bread and the wine taken at Eucharist. He provided the analogy of an iron poker: if placed in a fire the poker remained iron, but it now had heat. In the same way, Eucharist bread remained bread, but it had the presence of Christ in it. Luther rejected the more radical interpretation that Christ had been simply suggesting that the wine and bread *signified* his body or blood. The debate over how to interpret the Eucharist caused division among Protestants and weakened them, since it prevented an alliance between Lutherans and Zwinglians, followers of the Swiss reformer, Ulrich Zwingli.

Translating the Bible, 1522-34

Spreading the Word of God meant making it accessible to everyone. Luther embarked on his monumental task of translating the Bible into German while he was hidden in Wartburg Castle. He completed the New Testament there. It was smuggled out, illustrated by Lucas Cranach, and printed as the *September Testament*. Two hundred thousand copies were sold over the next 12 years. He spent the 1520s working on the Old Testament, which was completed by 1534, though then endlessly revised by Luther. It was an extraordinary achievement given the other pressures he was under, and it was one of the most important texts of the day. The Wittenberg press alone printed 100,000 copies of Luther's Bible between 1534 and 1600.

Luther went to huge lengths to get it right. He spent days sometimes on just one phrase: he wanted the text to be accessible to everyone and written in simple language that all could understand. The result has been as influential to the German language as the King James Authorised Version has been to English. According to the historian Heather Cubitt, 'His German came bursting out, ringing and clear, with new force and vitality, full of fire, rich poetry and sensitive understanding.'

SOURCE

14 Cochlaeus' views on the impact of Luther's New Testament. John Cochlaeus (1479–1552) was one of Luther's fiercest Catholic critics. He wrote this in 1549, to prove that Luther's work bought chaos not just to the Church, but also to society at large.

Luther's New Testament was so much multiplied and spread by printers that even tailors and shoemakers, yea, even women and ignorant people who had accepted this new Lutheran gospel, and could read a little German, studied it with the greatest avidity as the fountain of all truth. Some committed it to memory, and carried it about in their bosom. In a few months such people deemed themselves so learned that they were not ashamed to dispute about faith and the gospel not only with Catholic laymen, but even with priests and monks and doctors of divinity.

Luther's translation was not, however, without controversy. He wanted to make the Bible 'German', not to provide yet another dull literal translation: 'I aimed to make Moses so German that no one would suspect he was a Jew.' His mission meant choosing exactly the right sort of phrase in his own language. He had a butcher cut up a sheep and describe the entrails so that he could use exactly the right terms in German. He even asked Spalatin, Frederick's secretary, to borrow jewels from the elector's treasury so that he could see what they looked like (he was translating Revelation 21 at the time).

Biblical support for justification by faith alone

Luther was also creative – inventive – with the scriptures when it suited him. He had particular difficulty with two contradictory texts in the New Testament, and resolving the contradiction was crucial if his key doctrine – justification by faith alone, or *sola fide* – was to have scriptural authority. On the one hand there was St Paul: 'the just are saved by faith'. Against that was St James: 'faith, if it hath not works is dead, being alone'. Manipulating the first text and denigrating the second was Luther's solution. He added the crucial word 'alone' to the St Paul text in his translation, and then publicly condemned the St James letter as 'Jewish' in character. His manipulation was spotted by his Catholic opponents: Luther did not care – 'Give these asses no other and no further answer to their blathering about the word *sola* than simply this: "Luther will have it so and he is a doctor above all doctors of the whole Papacy."' Nevertheless, he wrote a lengthy defence of his addition in 1530 for the sake of concerned Protestants: 'I know right well that the word *solum* was not in the Greek or Latin text and had no need of the Papists to teach me that. … At the same time they do not see that the sense is there and that the word belongs there if the translation is to be clear and strong. I want to speak German, not Greek or Latin. … The sense of St Paul demanded it and forced it upon me.'

EXTEND YOUR KNOWLEDGE

The quarrel between Luther and Erasmus over the issues of faith alone and free will (1524–25)
Erasmus and Luther initially appeared to share much in common: a methodology (*ad fontes*), criticism of scholastic theology and criticism of clerical abuses. Luther's stress on inner faith seemed similar to Erasmus' *Handbook of a Christian Soldier* of 1504, and Luther relied on Erasmus' Greek Testament of 1516 for his research and translation work.

However, there were also differences from the start. Erasmus was European in his outlook, whereas Luther was a German nationalist. Where Erasmus was witty and satirical in his attacks, Luther seemed almost to provoke violence. Above all, Erasmus did not agree with Luther's theological interpretations: he remained Catholic in his beliefs and did not wish to destroy the unity of the Church. He wanted reform not revolution, and he believed that the Church would reform itself in time. When other younger humanists flocked to Wittenberg, Erasmus remained silent. In 1520, he let Rome know that 'Erasmus has been and will always be, a faithful subject of the Roman See'. The same year, he drew up a list of 22 statements on how to proceed for the private use of Frederick the Wise: the severity of the papal bull excommunicating Luther and all the other 'bitter hatred' and 'poisonous writing' was counter-productive; the issue would be best resolved by 'the mature deliberation of serious and impartial men'; 'opposition to Luther ought to be without hate'.

Since silence was construed as consent, Erasmus was put under pressure from Rome to make his point of view clear. He finally committed himself publicly in 1524, when he challenged the core of Luther's teachings – *sola fide*. According to Luther's pessimistic view of humanity, nothing that man can do can save him. Faith alone saves, and God has predestined those who will have faith. In contrast, Erasmus believed in the enormous potential of humanity. According to his optimistic outlook, man has free will – he can choose to be good and to do good. He can improve. If free will is taken away, if everything is already predestined, then there really is no point to existence. In the very public pamphlet war that ensued, Luther was biting about Erasmus' views ('rubbish, or dung') and then malicious. Erasmus replied, 'How do your scurrilous charges that I am an atheist help the argument?'

Erasmus died in 1536, and in 1559 the Catholic Church censored all of Erasmus' books, as in its view he was the source of the entire rupture. The books were only officially removed from the 'List of Prohibited Books' in the 1960s.

SOURCE 15

The Difference between the True Religion of Christ and the False Idolatrous Teaching of the Antichrist, an example of the didactic woodcuts that Luther commissioned to educate the illiterate. The image was drawn in 1546 by the Saxon court artist, Lucas Cranach.

EXTEND YOUR KNOWLEDGE

The Difference between the True Religion of Christ and the False Idolatrous Teaching of the Antichrist

In the didactic woodcut shown in Source 15, on the left Luther preaches from the Bible, inspired by texts received directly from God, through Christ and the Holy Spirit. Cherubs approve while the modestly dressed congregation listens intently. The two sacraments are shown: infants are baptised and the laity receive communion in both kinds. John of Saxony turns his head to face us. On the right, a devil inspires the sermon, whispering in the ear of the leering preacher. Cards spill from the hood of one of the monks listening, another has foxes' tails, a symbol of cunning, lining his cloak. 'Good works' are shown: Mass is celebrated; there is a pilgrimage in the distance. The pope, wearing his triple crown, sells indulgences in the foreground. His sign reads: 'When a coin drops, a soul flies to heaven.' In heaven St Francis is shocked, while God is furious.

Hymns, 1524

In 1524, Luther published his first collection of hymns. His love of music came from his mother; he now saw a new opportunity to communicate with the illiterate. He took the folk songs he heard peasants singing in the fields and replaced the often bawdy lyrics with Christian teachings.

EXTRACT 2

The historian Diarmaid MacCulloch, writing on Luther's hymns.

[Luther's hymns] reveal his genius perhaps even more than his Bible, because they transcend the notorious and already the well-established tendency of the German language to pile syllable on syllable in conglomerations of compound-notions. Singers of Luther's verse can revel in strong words of one or two syllables, like his famous 'A safehold our God is still' – *Ein feste burg ist unser Gott, Ein gute Wehr und Waffen.*

The second verse of the hymn cited in Extract 2 could well have been pointed at a peasant audience:

With force of arms we nothing can,
Full soon were we down-ridden;
But for us fights the proper Man,
Whom God himself hath bidden.
Ask ye: Who is this same?
Christ Jesus is his name.

German Mass, 1526

Luther's hesitancy and conservatism when it came to making serious institutional changes can clearly be seen in his approach to the key service of the Catholic Church – the Mass, during which the Eucharist is celebrated. He accepted Carlstadt's fait accompli over communion in both kinds while denying his symbolic interpretation, but then seemed reluctant to go further. He issued broad guidelines in 1523 *Concerning the Order of Public Worship*, but only wrote the definitive German liturgy in 1526. His *Deutsche Masse* set the sermon at the heart of the service, displacing the Eucharist to the second half. Preaching the Word of God was more important. Otherwise, to an outsider, a Lutheran service was often remarkably similar to a Catholic one. Luther even permitted individual churches to retain unimportant 'Catholic' details if their congregation was conservative. It made the pill of Protestantism easier to swallow. It also meant considerable diversity of practice between Lutheran churches. In 1536, for example, a visiting pastor from Augsburg attended a Lutheran service in Eisenach in Saxony and was shocked by the amount of singing in Latin. He was then even more shocked to see the bread elevated while the people sank to their knees, both practices that he deemed to be papist.

How the Eucharist was tackled was a source of bitter contention between Protestants during the 1520s, and caused serious division. Luther believed in the Real Presence of Christ during communion: he interpreted the words 'This is my body' literally: Christ was present as heat was present in a heated iron (a belief known as consubstantiation). This was considered far too 'Catholic', far too close to transubstantiation, by many 'left-wing' reformers. They believed the Eucharist remained simply bread and wine, and that communion was celebrated purely in memory of Christ's Last Supper. A true believer would receive Christ in his heart (a belief known as receptionism). The controversy was important because reputations were at stake – if one was wrong on this, then on what else might one be wrong? It was also important because it was the one issue keeping the two main branches of the magisterial reform movement – Lutheranism and **Zwinglianism** – apart. Division weakened the movement.

KEY TERM

Zwinglianism
This was a Protestant reform movement named after its founder, Zwingli. Based in Zurich in Switzerland, it developed independently of Luther, and was very influential in south Germany. In three respects it was more radical that Lutheranism: no images were allowed in Church; the Eucharist was purely symbolic; and no music was allowed during services.

EXTEND YOUR KNOWLEDGE

Controversy and division over the Eucharist – the Marburg Colloquy (1529)
In 1526, the Landgrave Philip of Hesse converted to Lutheranism, and from then on he played a key role in defending the movement. By 1529, the Catholic threat to the movement looked serious, and in his view it made sense for Luther to ally with the other 'respectable' magisterial reform movement of the time – that of Zwingli, based in Zurich. Reform would then have strength in numbers. He arranged for a discussion meeting (or colloquy) of Zwinglian and Lutheran theologians at his castle in Marburg. Luther led his team; Zwingli led his. On one level the Colloquy was a success: the two sides agreed on 14 out of 15 points under discussion. But on the Eucharist no agreement could be found.

The Catechisms, 1529

Following the death of Frederick the Wise in 1525, his brother John the Steadfast became Elector of Saxony. John had quietly been a supporter of Luther for many years, though he was only openly so from 1526. Concerned about the radical preaching that had played a role in triggering the Peasants' Revolt, he immediately ordered a full inspection of Saxony's churches, effectively re-establishing the Catholic practice of episcopal 'visitations'. Luther and his colleagues devised and published detailed instructions for the inspectors, the sort of things to look for and the questions to ask. The instructions became the role model for inspections that Luther hoped they would be – 'May God grant that it may be and become a happy example which all other German princes may fruitfully imitate.'

Luther did one of the inspections himself. He was shocked by what he found in his own area. Ignorance prevailed even among the clergy: the Reformation might as well not have happened. Traditional, almost pagan, beliefs still held sway in Saxony. Alternatively, of course, what Luther was seeing can be interpreted as a sort of after-effect of the Peasants' Revolt: exhausted apathy, stubborn indifference and an alarming tendency for people to interpret the scriptures as they saw fit and in their own interests.

SOURCE 16 From the 1529 Visitation to the district of Schweinitz in Saxony. Note: householders own property, leaseholders rent property and cottagers are landless labourers.

Aryn (18 householders). The pastor, Rev. Martinus Mauck. We have reports that he teaches untruths, and that he still secretly uses blessed water. In sum, through rumour and reports from the people, he has been found to be still a papist; therefore we have dismissed him.

Stolzenhayn (16 leaseholders, 6 cottagers). The pastor submitted a letter concerning several abominable crimes and blasphemies which the folk in Stolzenhayn demonstrated against the word of God and divine worship. The folk have been earnestly admonished to repentance… The people of Stolzenhayn have also withheld their tithe from the pastor, of which he receives one-third, while two-thirds go to our gracious lord [the elector].

Holzdorf. The pastor complains that the effort he makes in preaching is despised by the people. He had undertaken to preach twice during the week but had to give up because of their indifference. There was more than enough sorcery, adultery and other vices, but the peasants wanted to go unpunished. There was in particular a sorceress called Hermanin, who told the folk where they could find anything they had lost. His churchwarden's wife was an adulteress, and to spite him the peasants took her part. Nonetheless, we have dismissed the pastor, who is to depart by Easter.

Wertho (14 leaseholders, 1 cottager). The peasants here neither pray, nor believe, nor know the Ten Commandments properly, nor have they previously taken the blessed sacrament. So the pastor is to allow no one to take Communion unless he or she has first been confronted with his or her sins and confesses them and can answer the five questions [on the faith].

Wildenau (23 householders, including 17 leaseholders). The peasants can pray quite well and they praise their pastor as someone who is quite learned. The local noblewoman would like to have a different pastor, and has heard an accusation from someone from Tenstedt that he refused to administer the Sacrament under both kinds. But the peasants reported on him rather differently, in the presence of the noblewoman's servants.

In response to the failings revealed by the 1528–29 inspections, Luther wrote two catechisms, or instruction books in the form of questions and answers. The Great Catechism was intended as a sort of manual of instructions for the use of ministers and those who wanted 'a deeper and fuller explanation'. The Small Catechism was a brilliant innovation – it was short, addressing only the key points of faith (the Lord's Prayer, the Creed, the Ten Commandments, the two sacraments), written in simple language, and intended for a minister to use with his congregation, or the master of a house with his household. It was made foolproof. After each Commandment, for example, came the question: 'What does it mean?' followed by a clear explanation. Faith apart, it is possible to detect Luther's conservatism and ongoing concern with public order.

> **A Level Exam-Style Question Section B**
>
> How extensive was the success of Luther's reforms in Saxony by 1529? (20 marks)
>
> **Tip**
>
> *Don't just describe Luther's success, but consider the extent of the success, both geographically and within different sections of society.*

SOURCE 17 From the Preface to Luther's Small Catechism, 1529, which was an instruction manual that he wanted all Saxon ministers and preachers to use from then on.

Martin Luther to all faithful, pious pastors, and preachers…

Merciful God, what misery I have seen – the common people knowing nothing at all of Christian doctrine - especially in the villages! – and unfortunately many pastors are well-nigh unskilled and incapable of teaching; and though all are called Christians and partake of the Holy Sacrament; they know neither the Lord's Prayer, nor the Creed, nor the Ten Commandments, but live like the poor cattle and senseless swine, though, now that the Gospel is come, they have learned well enough how they may abuse their liberty. …

And especially dwell on that commandment that is most neglected among thy people. For example, the Seventh Commandment, about stealing, must be vehemently urged among artisans, tradesmen, and also among peasants and servants, for among such people there is all manner of unfaithfulness and stealing. Again the Fourth Commandment must be especially urged upon children and the common people, that they may be quiet, faithful, obedient, peaceful; and thou must always adduce many examples from the bible of how God punished or blessed such people.

The spread of Lutheranism

By 1530, only seven princes – electoral Saxony, Prussia, Hesse, Brandenburg, Mansfeld, Brunswick and Anhalt – had formally adopted Lutheranism. The princes' motives for converting their states is dealt with in the next chapter. Support for reform, however, was far more rapid and enthusiastic in Germany's towns and cities. Fifty of the 65 imperial cities turned either completely Lutheran or accepted Lutheranism alongside Catholicism, with about 20 imperial cities converting in the 1520s, and a further 30 by the early 1540s.

The reasons why cities converted were as numerous as the cities themselves. Awareness of the Lutheran message was highest in cities with printing presses and important trading links. Those cities with universities had a receptive audience for reform among students and young humanist academics. Some urban authorities harnessed reform to their own aspirations of bringing the Church under civic control, 'domesticating' the Church in the interests of communal harmony and unity. Elsewhere very local social and economic grievances often meant high levels of resentment at clerical privileges, which might be coupled with political frustrations directed at entrenched elitist councils.

There was no single route by which a city turned Lutheran. However, many followed a pattern:

- Pamphlets written by local Lutheran sympathisers prepared the ground.

- Preaching by reforming clergy, either already resident or invited in by the civic authorities, stirred popular demands for change.

- Such demands initially took the form of insulting or mocking Catholic practices (including, for example, anti-papal processions, urinating into holy water, using indulgences as toilet paper, and destroying images), which alienated conservatives and caused disturbances.

- The civic authorities then had the headache of how to keep order, and since resisting change might mean being replaced (which happened in Lübeck in 1533), many decided to hold a public disputation between reforming and Catholic clergy.

- If the result favoured reform (which it usually did) the civic authorities proceeded to denounce papal authority, remove the privileges of the clergy and close monasteries.

- Much more slowly and haphazardly, they issued a Lutheran 'statement of beliefs' and a new order of service. Finally, they introduced a new Church structure. Lacking central direction from Wittenberg, there was an extraordinary variety in practice and implementation.

EXTEND YOUR KNOWLEDGE

Case study - Nuremberg becomes Lutheran

Nuremberg was one of the largest imperial cities, with about 20,000 people living within the impressive city walls and a further 20,000 living in its surrounding 730 villages. The city had a wealthy merchant class and was renowned for its precision work in guns, armour, astrolabes, sundials, clocks and even pocket watches. It was a centre for international trade with reciprocal trade agreements with other cities throughout the empire, and as far away as Spain, Hungary, the Baltic States and England. Nuremberg's importance as a political centre was equally marked: from 1521 the Imperial Chamber Court was located there; the diet met there in 1522-23; imperial regalia for coronations were stored there. The city was run by an inner council representing just 43 patrician families, with day-to-day control organised by an even smaller committee of seven elders. Despite the fact that the vast majority of Nuremberg's citizens were unrepresented, political harmony prevailed. The patrician elite took their duty of promoting public welfare seriously, to the point that all municipal employees were given an hour off every Saturday to go to the public baths. It was a very tightly governed city.

There were early signs that Nuremberg's elite would be favourably disposed to Luther's message. The inner council forbade the sale of the St Peter's indulgence well before Frederick the Wise took a similar line. In 1516, Staupitz, Luther's mentor and head of Germany's Augustinians, was welcomed as a guest preacher. His Advent sermons on predestination and the impotence of free will inspired the formation of a Staupitz Society, which several patricians joined. Other members included the artist Albrecht Dürer; Christoph Scheurl (the city lawyer who had been rector of Wittenberg University from 1507 to 1511 and who corresponded with Luther about the 95 Theses in 1518); and Lazarus Spengler, secretary to the council. The Staupitz Society invited Luther to speak to them in October 1518 as he passed through on his way to meet Cajetan at Augsburg. Spengler was so impressed that he wrote tracts in Luther's defence in 1519 and 1522. In 1521, the inner council dutifully ordered that the Edict of Worms be posted around the city, but then did nothing to enforce it. It also appointed three new preachers, all of whom happened to be reformers. One was Andreas Osiander (1498-1552), who was appointed to the church of St Lorenz.

The ensuing 'pulpit battles' between these reformers and the city's resident conservative preachers caused tension and unrest to spill onto the streets. In February 1522, and again in March 1523, the council issued directives that preachers should only preach 'according to the scriptures' and not attack each other. Such ambiguous instructions, with the emphasis on 'the scriptures', support the view that the councillors leaned in favour of reform. They refused papal requests to arrest the reforming preachers. They also conceded a few changes that indicate their preferences: fast and feast days were simplified; baptism services could be held in German. They turned a blind eye to pro-Luther publications, such as in 1523, when the city's most famous playwright, the cobbler Hans Sachs, wrote a poem, *The Wittenberg Nightingale*, in Luther's honour.

The turning point for the inner council came during the Peasants' Revolt. In 1524, Nuremberg's lower orders rioted in favour of Müntzer, and during the following carnival the clergy were openly derided and a mock procession of the crucifix was held. In March 1525, the council decided that an immediate Lutheran reformation was necessary in order to preserve law and order. Luther's emphasis on obedience to authority was certainly preferable to the anarchy preached by Müntzer. However, they had to tread a delicate path: Nuremberg could not risk falling into imperial disfavour or risk losing important trading links with Catholic states and cities. The council needed to give the impression that it was totally loyal to the emperor and had reluctantly succumbed to overwhelming pressure for reform from below.

The solution was a rigged public disputation between the conservatives and the reformers, represented by Osiander. The ten-day disputation was carefully stage-managed to ensure the right result: it was held in German in the city hall, with the windows open so that the crowds could hear, and it was chaired by Christoph Scheurl, the city lawyer. Not surprisingly, the vote went in favour of reform.

Having secured the decision to reform, the council moved rapidly, at least in terms of removing the old. Catholic preachers were immediately barred from preaching. The authority of the pope was rejected and Nuremberg's clergy were made to swear an oath of obedience to the city. They also lost their right to tax exemption and were made subject to ordinary courts. Monasteries were closed and clerical marriage was permitted. Private masses for the souls of benefactors were abolished. Transubstantiation was denounced. In some things, though, the Nuremberg authorities moved cautiously – there was no image breaking, the interior of churches remained the same, and the convent of the Sisters of Saint Clare was permitted to remain (the abbess' brother acted as legal adviser to the council).

The council's approach to implementing the new was equally cautious and a rather piecemeal and drawn-out affair. It only issued a new 'statement of beliefs' in 1528, and Osiander issued a catechism in 1533 to support it. Confession was retained until 1533 and the liturgy remained in Latin until 1545. The relative moderation of Nuremberg's reformation was diplomatic: it did not wish to harm trade or alienate the emperor. In the 1530s and 1540s, it steered clear of joining Lutheran military alliances; it financed Charles' side openly, and the Lutheran side secretly.

ACTIVITY
KNOWLEDGE CHECK

The development of Lutheranism in the 1520s

Find two pieces of evidence to support each of the following statements:

- Reforms were introduced in a piecemeal fashion, in reaction to needs as they arose.

- There was no central co-ordination from Wittenberg.

- There was a great deal of diversity.

WHY DID LUTHER'S INFLUENCE ON THE REFORMATION DECLINE?

Without Luther there might not have been a Reformation at all, and without his interventions in 1522 and 1525, the Reformation might have taken a very different path. However, from the late 1520s, his importance diminished. The reasons for this sometimes lay outside Luther's hands:

- The Peasants' Revolt prompted reforming princes and city authorities to take the initiative in directing the Reformation.

- The Edict of Worms meant that Luther could not personally put his case to Catholic authorities any more – it was dangerous for him to travel outside Saxony, and therefore he could not be present at important meetings such as that with the emperor in 1530.

- As a result of Luther's enforced absence, other reformers, in particular Philip Melanchthon and John Bugenhagen, became the new public 'face' of Lutheranism.

- Priorities changed: Luther had provided the ideas, but the Reformation now needed to be embedded and physically defended, and here the work of Melanchthon, Bugenhagen and Landgrave Philip of Hesse was crucial.

Nevertheless, Luther himself was also the cause of his own diminishing role:

- His stance on the Peasants' Revolt in 1525 had already lost him a great deal of popular support.

- He continued to alienate and divide: for example, his complete refusal to compromise on the issue of the Real Presence in the Eucharist lost him valuable potential support from other reformers like Zwingli, while his row with Erasmus lost him the support of older humanists.

- He produced little new work after his tremendous output in the 1520s – he focused instead on revising and perfecting his translation of the Bible and on his teaching role in the university. The historian Andrew Pettegree writes, 'There is a strong sense that, having ignited the great movement of reform which bears his name, he had neither the desire nor the intellectual flexibility to harness all of its energies successfully.'

- His role in the Philip of Hesse bigamy scandal of 1540 (see page 237) seriously damaged his reputation.

- In the 1540s especially, as he grew older (and ill, with kidney stones, arthritis, digestive problems and angina), his outbursts became increasingly petulant, cantankerous and vulgar – he had ceased to be an asset to the reforming movement.

Isolating which of these reasons was the most important in explaining Luther's diminishing influence is difficult. The focus below is given first to the work done by two other reformers in embedding the Lutheran Reformation, and secondly to the devastating impact on Luther's reputation of the Hesse bigamy scandal of 1540.

Philip Melanchthon (1497–1560)

Philip Melanchthon was one of the quiet heroes of the Reformation. He was a child prodigy who took his first degree when he was 14 and his master's degree when he was 17. He was well connected to humanist circles, since his great uncle was John Reuchlin, the Hebrew scholar, who had raised him. At Reuchlin's suggestion, he had changed his name from Schwarzerdt to Melanchthon when he was 12. The names meant the same thing – 'black earth' – but the Greek version gave a more scholarly, humanistic impression. In 1518, at the age of just 21, he was appointed Professor of Greek at Wittenberg University by Frederick the Wise. Here he met Luther and was converted to the cause, and from that point he was effectively Luther's deputy, as well as a loyal friend. He accompanied Luther to the Leipzig Debates in 1519 and the Colloquy at Marburg in 1529, and represented Luther at meetings with the emperor's delegates in Augsburg in 1530 and Regensburg in 1541. He helped Luther with his translation of the Bible. He also acted as an adviser to numerous reforming cities – Nuremberg asked him to devise a curriculum for its new training school for preachers in the period 1525–26. Lutherans called him 'the teacher of Germany'.

In many ways, Melanchthon was the perfect balance to Luther. Where Luther could be loud and coarse, Melanchthon was gently spoken. Whereas Luther wrote and spoke in extremes, Melanchthon was a moderate. Luther refused to compromise; Melanchthon was the conciliator. Luther could be egotistical and domineering; Melanchthon was always endearingly modest and courteous (except on the issue of peasants in revolt). He did not have Luther's charisma and magnetism in the pulpit and he stepped back from confrontation. For example, he had been completely bemused about what to do with Carlstadt and the Zwickau Prophets in 1521–22, saying, 'The dam has broken and I cannot stem the waters.' Instead, his strengths lay in his gift for diplomacy and reconciliation. Luther recognised the way they complemented each other: 'I am rough, boisterous, stormy and altogether warlike. I must remove stumps and stones, cut away thistles and thorns, and clear the wild forests; but Master Philip comes along softly and gently sowing and watering, according to the gifts that God has abundantly bestowed on him.'

The contrast between the two can also be seen in the following description, which has the benefit of being written by someone who had met neither man before, and who had been uninvolved in the Reformation to date.

SOURCE 18

Letter from John Dantiscus to John Latalski, Bishop of Posen, August 1523. Dantiscus was a Polish diplomat and humanist passing through Germany. He decided to divert to Wittenberg to see what all the talk was about, and he wrote this letter immediately after his visit.

I found there several young men who were extraordinarily learned in Hebrew, Latin and Greek, especially Philip Melanchthon, who claims the leading position among them because of his knowledge and learning. He is a young man of 26 and was very genial and obliging to me during the three days I spent there. ... I went with Melanchthon to see him [Luther] after a dinner.

Luther stood and offered me his hand – he was rather touched, it seems – and bade me be seated. We sat down and discussed various matters and issues for four hours, well into the night. I found the man witty, learned, eloquent, except that he had little to say of the pope, the emperor and other princes other than abuse, arrogant imputations and snappishness. ... Luther's features are like the books he publishes: the eyes are sharp and have a strange sparkle, as eyes of obsessives are wont to do. His speech is vehement, full of mockery and taunts.

When we were sitting with him, we did not just engage in discussions but merrily drank wine and beer, as is the custom there. He [Luther] seemed to me to be, as the Germans say, 'a merry fellow'. Now as far as the holiness of his life is concerned... he did not seem any different from anyone of us. One can immediately recognise in him haughtiness and great desire for fame; in abuse, mockery and scorn he seems almost frolicsome. He is said to be very well read and to write a great deal. At the moment he is translating the books of Moses from Hebrew into Latin, in which he frequently requires Melanchthon's help. This young man pleases me by far the best of all the scholars of Germany, and also does not agree with Luther in everything.

Loci Communes, 1521

One of Melanchthon's greatest gifts was his ability to consolidate and synthesise Luther's ideas. Between 1517 and 1521, Luther had written dozens of pamphlets and letters, elaborating his doctrine in loud, persuasive language and at sometimes muddling length. Two issues became clear by late 1521: Luther was being wildly misinterpreted, and there was no single short volume of Luther's ideas. What Melanchthon did was to gather together Luther's scattered thoughts into one very clear systematic statement of Lutheran belief, a volume called *Loci Communes*. He wrote it in 1521 in an effort to refute Carlstadt and the Zwickau Prophets intellectually, and in Luther's absence he had to make some unilateral decisions, for example dropping penance from the list of acceptable sacraments. Dantiscus' last point in his letter (see Source 18) – that Melanchthon did not agree on all things with Luther – was very true. *Loci Communes* went through over 50 editions in Melanchthon's lifetime and was considered required reading for understanding Lutheran theology.

The Augsburg Confession, 1530

Melanchthon's other gift was as a conciliator. He wanted nothing more than to repair the breach with the Catholic Church (excluding the papacy) and heal wounds: 'If I could purchase union by my own death, I would gladly sacrifice my life.' He was given the opportunity in 1530, when Charles V finally returned to Germany. Charles was in urgent need of unanimous German support against the Ottomans, and he invited the Lutherans to make a statement of their beliefs to him. Since Luther could not go (the Edict of Worms ensured that), Melanchthon went in his place. He drafted the Augsburg Confession, which was so moderate that even Eck found most of it acceptable.

However, fundamental disagreements remained on the issues of communion in both kinds, the doctrine of transubstantiation, the marriage of priests, and monastic properties that had been taken over by Lutheran states and cities. Though the Augsburg Confession failed to reconcile the two sides, it had enormous influence: many cities converting after 1530 adopted it as their 'statement of belief'.

John Bugenhagen (1485-1558)

Another Lutheran reformer of distinction was John Bugenhagen, a humanist and priest who first came across Lutheran theology when he read Luther's 1520 pamphlet *On the Babylonish Captivity of the Church*. Inspired, he moved from his native Pomerania to Wittenberg, where, in 1523, he became pastor of the main church. Bugenhagen's genius for organisation played a major role in determining how the new church should be structured when it became clear that the split with Rome would be permanent. The end result was the Saxon Model. Though the papacy and higher Catholic offices like cardinals and archbishops were discarded, the Saxon Model was otherwise remarkably conservative. In 1539, Bugenhagen became superintendent of the Lutheran Church in Saxony.

The Saxon Model was copied (with local modifications) wherever Lutheranism established itself. Each ruler took charge in his own territory; each council took charge of its city. The input of lay authorities was therefore essential in setting up, maintaining and defending (if necessary) new Lutheran churches. The system was ideal for Germany, with its politically fragmented structure and particularistic princes, many of whom were naturally delighted to accept new responsibilities if they brought more power.

The Saxon Model

Title	Personnel	Function
The Christian Magistrate or Magistracy	The head of the church was to be the prince in a territory, or the council in a city	To see to the ordering of the church in that territory or city
Ecclesiastical Council	A committee of two lawyers and two theologians, appointed by the Christian Magistrate or Magistracy	Appoints the superintendent, and organises visitations (or inspections) to enforce doctrinal uniformity, maintain high standards among the clergy, and supervise the spiritual and moral welfare of the laity
Superintendent (the equivalent to a bishop)	Appointed by and subject to the authority of the Christian magistrate and the Ecclesiastical Council	To enforce high standards and doctrinal uniformity among parish clergy and preachers

Bugenhagen's organisational genius was in considerable demand: he successfully exported the Saxon Model to eight north German states and cities between 1528 and 1543, earning him the nickname 'second apostle of the north'. His key role lay in creating new church orders – rules and regulations concerning church structures, services, schools and even social welfare. His greatest triumph came in 1537, when the kingdom of Denmark-Norway converted to Lutheranism, and Bugenhagen himself crowned Christian III.

On the negative side, the Saxon Model meant the 'Lutheran Church' of Germany was very fragmented. There was no 'pope', and no two churches were alike, though Luther held the fragments together through voluminous correspondence while he lived. Also on the negative side lay the fact that Lutheranism could not be established where a ruler was unsympathetic: there was no allowance for any sort of independently run congregation. This was a state church; if a prince converted, so did his territory. It was a limiting factor in the growth of Lutheranism outside the empire.

The growing divergence between Lutheran and Catholic beliefs

The table shows the key differences between Lutheranism and Catholicism.

Issue	Lutheranism	Catholicism
Sources of doctrine	*Sola scriptura* – The truth concerning all spiritual matters is in the scriptures alone, which must be translated into the vernacular to make the Word of God accessible to all. Interpretation, however, must be reserved for state-approved preachers.	The Bible, popes, councils and the Church Fathers are of equal importance. The Bible should remain in Vulgate Latin in order to avoid misinterpretation by the ignorant. The pope is the ultimate arbiter on interpretation.
How to get to heaven	*Sola fide* – through faith alone. Faith is given freely to some (the elect) by God. God unconditionally washes away the sins of the faithful.	Through faith with good works, and absolute obedience to the teachings of the Catholic Church.
The role of good works	Good works are a symptom of being saved – a consequence of God's love. Some 'good works' are clearly nonsense, like pilgrimages. But being charitable and neighbourly are 'good works' and a clear sign of God's grace.	Man has free will and can choose to do evil or to do good. Works such as going on pilgrimages and participating in the sacraments are essential in order to earn grace and minimise the time spent in purgatory.
Number of sacraments	Only two – baptism and the Eucharist – are scriptural. They are occasions for the recipient to be reminded of God's saving power.	Seven exist – baptism, confirmation, marriage, Eucharist, penance, last rites, ordination – and they are all a means to salvation.
Eucharist	No miracle takes place during Communion. However, the bread and wine contain the Real Presence of Christ, a belief known as consubstantiation. The laity is allowed to take communion in both kinds.	During Mass, the miracle of transubstantiation occurs: as they are 'elevated' by the priest, and a bell then rung, the bread and wine are literally transformed into the body and blood of Christ. Only those ordained are allowed to take communion in both kinds.
Baptism	Infant baptism only – the ceremony is important in accepting an infant into the community of the church and the state and as a reminder of God's grace.	Infant baptism only. Baptism is a sacrament, removing 'original sin' from a baby.
Priesthood and monasticism	There is no scriptural basis for a privileged priesthood: celibacy and monasticism etc. are nonsense. Rather, a 'Priesthood of all Believers' exists: all men are equal spiritually in the eyes of God. Ministers and preachers are ordinary men who must be trained for the job and appointed and monitored by the state. They can marry.	Priests hold a special and privileged position between man and God. They alone have the right to administer the sacraments. Their unique status is reinforced by celibacy, special clothing and legal privileges. Since they are ordained, their entry to heaven is guaranteed.
Papacy	The papacy is a non-scriptural, man-made institution, the Antichrist sent by Satan.	The papacy has a scriptural basis. The pope is a direct descendant of St Peter and as such is the head of Christendom.
Images in churches	Certain images are idolatrous and detract attention from the Word being preached. However, those that have a scriptural basis have educational value.	Images and statues of saints play a crucial role in educating the illiterate masses and in generating an emotional response. Donating images is a good work.

The Philip of Hesse bigamy scandal of 1540

Luther fully acknowledged his debt to Melanchthon and Bugenhagen. Their importance became all the greater when Luther himself became involved in a scandal revolving around the chaotic personal life of one of Luther's most important princely supporters, Landgrave Philip of Hesse.

In 1523, aged just 19, Philip had married Christine of Saxony, daughter of Duke George the Bearded, the cousin of Frederick the Wise. The purpose of the marriage was political, to forge an alliance between Ducal Saxony and Hesse (though Philip's subsequent conversion to the Lutheran cause did not endear him to his new father-in-law). Philip later claimed the marriage was an unhappy one – he was disgusted by his wife and only shared her bed through duty. Since they had ten children, his protests need to be treated with scepticism. Philip was in fact a serial philanderer who fell from one affair to the next, 'constantly in a state of adultery and fornication' in his own words. In the late 1530s, Philip fell in love with 17-year-old Margaret von der Staal. He turned to Luther for advice, who said divorcing Christine was out of the question. Instead, he reluctantly agreed with Philip's solution: that Philip should take a second wife, in the Old Testament tradition, and thus avoid the even worse evil of adultery.

When news of the marriage leaked out, the reputations of both Luther and Philip were seriously damaged – bigamy was a capital offence. Luther, in particular, appeared a hypocrite. He had ignored his own emphasis on family values; he had ignored the law of the land; he had condoned a practice closely associated with extremists and Anabaptists. Philip lost political credibility as leader of the Lutheran side. The only saving grace to the whole affair was that at least the new marriage was a happy one – the couple had nine children.

ACTIVITY
KNOWLEDGE CHECK

Luther's declining influence

Work in pairs.

Look again at the reasons for Luther's declining influence on the Reformation.

If you had to decide on the three most important reasons for this decline, which would they be? Explain your answer.

If you had to select a single year as the turning point, which would it be? Why?

ACTIVITY
SUMMARY

Write an essay with the title 'How revolutionary was Luther?'

To complete this essay you will need to refer to both Chapters 2 and 3. It is best to decide on your definition of the word 'revolutionary' first. Consider also its opposite, 'conservative', and a third possibility, 'radical', in the original sense of the word as someone who seeks to 'return to roots', the roots being the scriptures in this case.

Dividing the essay into sections makes it more manageable:

- What were Luther's original intentions? Did he intend or plan a revolution in 1517?

- How 'revolutionary' were his religious beliefs as they emerged in 1519–20? This section will require some selectivity. For example, you might include Luther's views on achieving salvation, on the sacraments, on the Real Presence, and on the papacy. Consider also the difference between his intent (often 'radical' in the original sense of the word) and his effect – a 'revolutionary' overturning of Catholic doctrine.

- How 'revolutionary' were his political views? How did he react to the extremism shown in the crises of the early 1520s?

- How 'revolutionary' was the structure of the new Lutheran Church? Was it a complete break with the past?

- How 'revolutionary' were his publications of the 1520s (the German Bible and Mass, the Catechisms)?

- How 'revolutionary' were his social views? Consider his views on the position of women, for example.

In each section, comparison with the views and beliefs of others will help you to place Luther on the 'revolutionary-or-conservative' spectrum. Did Catholics like Aleander or Erasmus see Luther as a revolutionary? Did Carlstadt or Müntzer consider Luther a revolutionary? How far did Lutheranism really diverge from Catholicism?

THINKING HISTORICALLY   Change (6a)

Separately and together – thematic history

Below are some different *types* of history that historians may identify.

Political history	Economic history	Social history
Religious history	Military history	International history

These are thematic histories, where a historian focuses on a particular aspect of change. For example, an economic history of the Holy Roman Empire would focus on trade, whereas a political history of the empire would focus on governance.

Work in groups.

Write a definition for each type of history.

Here are some events from the early years of the German Reformation, all turning points in one way or another.

1518 Pope Leo X sends Cajetan to interview Luther	1520 Luther burns the papal bull	1522 The Knights' Revolt	1524–25 The Peasants' Revolt	1530 Melanchthon's Augsburg Confession	1540 Philip of Hesse's bigamy scandal

Answer the following questions:

1 The first two can be classified as 'religious' events.

   a) Why did Leo agree to Frederick's request for Luther to be interviewed in Germany rather than Rome?

   b) What other *type* of history does this take it into?

   c) Why did Luther burn the bull so publicly?

   d) What other *type* of history does this take it into?

2 Was the Peasants' Revolt religious, social or economic, or all three? Explain your answer.

3 What religious or social changes came about because of the princes' military victories over the peasants in 1525?

4 Did Charles V invite the Lutherans to state their case at Augsburg in 1530 for religious, political or military reasons?

5 What was the political impact of the Philip of Hesse bigamy scandal?

Work in pairs.

6 Write a statement attacking 'thematic history'.

7 Write three statements defending 'thematic history'.

8 Explain why 'thematic history' occurs.

WIDER READING

Cameron, E. *The European Reformation*, Clarendon Press (1991)

Luther Blisset *Q*, Einaudi (1999) this is a novel about the Reformation from the perspective of radical reformers and peasants; it was written anonymously by four left-wing Italian writers, seeking to give a voice to the silenced majority

Mullet, M. 'Luther: conservative or revolutionary?', *History Today*, December 1983

Pettegree, A. 'The execution of Martin Luther', *History Review*, March 1996

Roper, L. 'Luther: sex, marriage and motherhood', *History Today*, December 1983

Scribner, B. 'The reformer as prophet and saint: 16th-century images of Luther', *History Today*, November 1983

Tarr, R. 'The radical reformers', *History Review*, December 2001

Tarr, R. 'Theological debates in the Reformation', *History Review*, March 2005

BBC Radio 4, *In Our Time*, 'The Diet of Worms' (available to download as a podcast)

2a.4 The spread and survival of Lutheranism, 1521–55

KEY QUESTIONS

- Did Charles V use the wrong tactics to eradicate Lutheranism?
- How far were German princes responsible for the spread and survival of Lutheranism?
- How far did conflicting priorities hamper Charles' ability to tackle Lutheranism?
- How did the papacy respond to Lutheranism?

INTRODUCTION

For over 350 years, the city of Augsburg in Bavaria has celebrated a Peace Festival on 8 August, with parades, markets, feasting and interdenominational church services. Prizes are awarded to Peace Makers who promote interfaith harmony. The Festival is a direct link back to the Peace of Augsburg, 1555, by which each prince of the Holy Roman Empire won the right to decide whether his territory was to be Catholic or Lutheran.

No one could have predicted the Peace of Augsburg. Just seven years earlier, in 1547, Charles had defeated the Protestant armies with a resounding victory at the Battle of Mühlberg. Electoral Saxony had been occupied; Charles had entered Wittenberg and allegedly gazed upon the tomb of Luther. If Charles was then unable to capitalise on the victory, he had himself partly to blame: he made errors of judgement that alienated his supporters. However, if the longer view is taken, his failure to crush Lutheranism was largely because of circumstances beyond his control. Throughout his reign, the vast size of his inheritance had meant conflicting priorities. Charles' attention was also demanded by his other territories, especially Spain, and he was forced to devote considerable time to defending his inheritance against French and Ottoman aggression. Even when he could be in the empire, he lacked the power to enforce his will. He had to rely on the princes to enforce the Edict of Worms, yet most princes were unwilling to co-operate until

their grievances with the Church in Germany had been addressed. Lack of immediate support from the papacy for a general council thwarted Charles' attempts to win the Catholic princes' aid, while some princes chose to convert and actively supported and defended Lutheranism.

1521 – Diet of Worms and Edict of Worms

1526 – Diet of Speyer and Recess of Speyer

1527 – Sack of Rome

1529 – Second Diet of Speyer: the revocation of the recess; the Protestation. Ottoman siege of Vienna

1531 – Schmalkaldic League established

1535 – Recapture of Tunis

| 1521 | 1522 | 1523 | 1524 | 1525 | 1526 | 1527 | 1528 | 1529 | 1530 | 1531 | 1532 | 1533 | 1534 | 1535 | 1536 | 1537 |

1522–29 – Charles in Spain

1530 – Diet of Augsburg

1532 – Religious Truce of Nuremberg

1537 – *Consilium de Emendanda Ecclesia*

SOURCE 1

Charles V triumphantly dominates his defeated enemies, from a set of 12 full-page miniatures showing episodes from the reign of Charles V, painted for Charles' son, Philip II, c1556–76 by the Croatian artist Giorgio Giulio Clovio.

1541 – Colloquy of Regensburg; the Algiers campaign

1546–47 – Schmalkaldic War – victory over the Protestants at the Battle of Mühlberg

1548 – Princes reject the Interim of Augsburg

1552 – Protestant princes revive with the aid of French money; French invasion; Peace of Passau

1555 – Ferdinand agrees to the Peace of Augsburg

1538	1539	1540	1541	1542	1543	1544	1545	1546	1547	1548	1549	1550	1551	1552	1553	1554	1555

1545 – Council of Trent convenes

1547 – Armed Diet of Augsburg rejects the Imperial League proposal

1549 – Family quarrel over the inheritance

1553 – Failing to retake Metz, Charles quits Germany, leaving it in Ferdinand's hands

DID CHARLES V USE THE WRONG TACTICS TO ERADICATE LUTHERANISM?

At the Diet of Worms in 1521, Charles V announced his determination to eradicate Lutheranism: 'To settle this matter I have resolved to stake upon this course my dominions and my possessions, my body and my blood, my life and my soul.' A generous interpretation of Charles' reign as Holy Roman Emperor would be that he was an exceptionally devout Catholic who did indeed try to eradicate Lutheranism, using a variety of methods to achieve his goal:

- In 1521, he declared Luther an outlaw by the Edict of Worms.

- In the 1520s and 1530s, he repeatedly requested that the pope call a council to resolve the princes' grievances with the Church in Germany (their 102 *gravamina* or grievances), something the princes demanded as a prerequisite to enforcing the Edict.

- When a council failed to materialise, he attempted to negotiate an end to the schism, in 1530 at Augsburg, and again in 1541 at Regensburg, following the scandal over Philip of Hesse's bigamy.

- When negotiations failed, he threatened Lutheran princes and cities with war unless they recanted, and would have carried out those threats had foreign issues not forced him to defer action.

- Between 1546 and 1547, he declared war on the Schmalkaldic League, and his defeat of the Protestant forces at the Battle of Mühlberg was spectacular, enabling him to recapture south Germany for the Church.

He tried, in other words, to fulfil his vow to eradicate Lutheranism. If he failed to achieve more, according to this sympathetic interpretation, it was largely because he was hamstrung by circumstances beyond his control. The structure of the empire meant his position as emperor was weak, and he was forced to rely on the princes to implement his plans. However, a lack of support from the papacy for a general council in the 1520s thwarted his attempts to win the princes' co-operation. The vast size of Charles' inheritance meant he had conflicting priorities, as his attention was demanded by his other territories, including the Netherlands and Spain. This meant Charles had to absent himself frequently from the empire. Charles also had to defend his territories from attacks by the French and the Ottoman Empire, and these immediate military threats had to be given priority over the internal issues in the empire. These wars drained him of money, which, along with renewed threats from abroad and a lack of support from the princes, helps to explain why he could not capitalise on his victory at Mühlberg.

This sympathetic line, however, has flaws. A cynic might doubt Charles' commitment to his vow, not least because he was hardly ever in the empire. He arrived in Germany over 18 months after his election, missing most of the period 1519–20, years crucial in the development of Luther's ideas. Charles then left the Holy Roman Empire immediately after the Diet of Worms, and he was largely absent in the 1520s and 1530s, decades crucial in the spread of Lutheranism. In all, he spent only about a quarter of his 36 year reign in the empire.

ACTIVITY
KNOWLEDGE CHECK

Charles V – the absentee monarch
Referring to the timeline, calculate exactly how much time Charles spent in the empire in the 1520s, in the 1530s, in the 1540s, and then in the 1550s.

What does this suggest about Charles' views on Lutheranism?

WHEN WAS CHARLES PRESENT IN THE HOLY ROMAN EMPIRE?

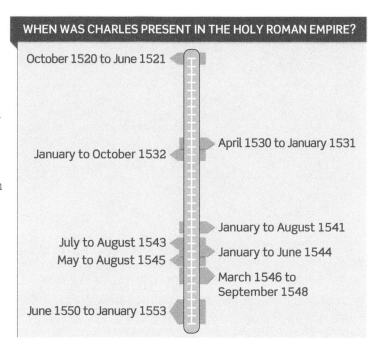

October 1520 to June 1521

January to October 1532

April 1530 to January 1531

January to August 1541

July to August 1543

May to August 1545

January to June 1544

March 1546 to September 1548

June 1550 to January 1553

Charles was not simply a victim of circumstance, endlessly forced to react to events outside his control that took him away from his vow to crush heresy in Germany. There were times when he had choice and when he might have decided to focus on the Lutheran problem and be in the empire. Instead, he chose to pursue Habsburg territorial interests in Europe or his own idealist crusading ambitions against the Turks.

A further reason why he cannot be exonerated completely is that his tactics were flawed. Charles' decision to rely on a general council to resolve the German situation was naive. Until the mid-1530s, the papacy was unlikely to call a council, and when a council was finally called in 1545, it was too late and it focused on the condemnation of Protestantism rather than resolving abuses in the Church. With hindsight, it might have been more fruitful to bypass Rome entirely and call an early national council to resolve German issues, as the princes requested in 1526. In Spain, his grandparents had backed the Archbishop of Toledo's reform of the Church (and banned indulgence selling), so why could Charles not have done so in Germany, given that he had the princes' approval?

Another flawed tactic was Charles' belief that it was possible to reconcile differences between Lutheranism and Catholicism, and end the schism by persuading the Lutherans to rejoin a moderate Catholic fold. He grasped neither the depth of doctrinal division between the two sides nor the princes' depth of faith, and both Catholic and Protestant princes objected to his compromise solutions.

Failing to follow through immediately with his threats of war in the early 1530s, and again in 1541, was also an error, as speedy action might have bought victory. On both occasions, he chose to prioritise other concerns, and made concessions to the Protestants that strengthened their position. Charles also made some ill-judged decisions about the governance of the empire in the late 1540s, which alienated those on whom he relied for support and hampered his ability to capitalise on his victory at Mühlberg.

Hindsight, of course, is a wonderful thing. Charles had multiple concerns and could not isolate the Lutheran problem from these. His difficulties can be seen in his failures to negotiate a settlement.

Charles and the princes: a summary of events, 1521–44

1521	Diet of Worms	Charles issued the Edict of Worms: Luther was placed under the Imperial Ban and Lutheranism was declared a heresy. Except in a few territories (including Ducal Saxony) the Edict was not enforced.
1522–23	Diet of Nuremberg	The princes refused collectively to enforce the Edict of Worms until the pope called a general council to reform the Church in Germany, and address their 102 *gravamina*, or grievances.
1526	First Diet of Speyer and the recess	With Charles absent, the princes once more refused to take any action on the Edict of Worms until a national council was called. In the meantime, the diet passed the Recess of Speyer, effectively saying that each prince could make up his own mind. Ottoman threats to Hungary ensured imperial support for this.
1529	Second Diet of Speyer	Alarmed at the successful spread of Lutheranism, the Catholic princes decided on strong action: the diet revoked the 1526 recess and made the Edict of Worms compulsory, though Ottoman threats to Vienna delayed any action. Six Lutheran princes and 14 cities signed a protestation in response.
	Colloquy of Marburg	The leading Protestant prince, Philip of Hesse, attempted to construct a Protestant alliance between Zwinglians and Lutherans. The attempt failed over the issue of the Eucharist.
1530	Diet of Augsburg	Charles V returned to Germany. Anxious to form a united German front against the Ottomans, he invited the Lutherans to make a statement of their faith. Melanchthon presented the Augsburg Confession which was moderate. However, Charles refused to accept it, and said he would enforce the Edict of Worms. He gave the Lutherans six months to return to the Catholic Church.
1531	Schmalkaldic League	Concerned, Protestants formed the Schmalkaldic League, preparing to defend themselves against Charles' threat.
1532	Religious Truce of Nuremberg	Charles was unable to carry out his threat because of an anticipated Ottoman invasion. Instead, in return for men and money, he offered the League peace. He then left Germany for eight years, dealing with the recapture of Tunis in 1535 and the Third Habsburg–Valois War with France, 1536–38.
1530s	The spread of Lutheranism accelerates	Under Philip's leadership, the Schmalkaldic League acquired new members, money and an internal organisation. Charles periodically denounced heresy, while in practice tolerating it. Simultaneously, he made repeated requests for the pope to urgently call a general council.
1539	Frankfurt Interim	Charles made further concessions: he promised no action would be taken against the Protestants for six months.
1541	Colloquy of Regensburg	Philip was exposed as a bigamist. Charles used the opportunity to insist that Protestants and Catholics sit down and work out their religious differences. Negotiations failed – on some issues, compromise was impossible, while both Luther and the pope condemned the entire venture. Charles at last decided that since peaceable methods would not restore unity, force must be used. However, he deferred war, pending the completion of his campaign to take Algiers, headquarters of the Barbary pirates.
1541–44	The League revives	With Charles absent, dealing first with Algiers and then with French aggression during the Fourth Habsburg–Valois War, Philip of Hesse used the opportunity to spread Lutheranism even further in the empire.

The failure of negotiations, 1521–41

Between 1521 and 1541, Charles pursued three tactics. He relied on the princes to enforce the Edict of Worms; he requested the pope to call a general council; and he tried to negotiate doctrinal compromises that would end the schism between Lutheranism and Catholicism.

The first two tactics were linked. In 1521, the princes, with very few exceptions, collectively refused to enforce the Edict of Worms until the pope called a council to reform the Church in Germany and address their 102 *gravamina*. They reiterated their demands for a general council in 1523 at the Diet of Nuremberg. The princes were genuinely concerned about the state of the Church in Germany. Rome exploited Germany financially, and sold offices to completely unqualified people. The resulting pluralism meant absenteeism, a neglect of duties and lax standards. They wanted these grievances resolved before they would help Charles – they were simply using the Lutheran issue as a lever to effect reforms. Of course, it could also be argued that their demands were not wholly disinterested, since any removal of clerical privileges or papal power would enhance their own positions, while stopping money flowing to Rome would enrich them and their subjects.

The first Diet of Speyer and the Recess of Speyer, 1526

Circumstances had changed by 1526, when the Diet met once more, this time in the city of Speyer. The religious crisis was causing serious instability and mounting tension. The Peasants' Revolt might have been crushed, but it had alarmed everyone in authority. Meanwhile, Germany was dividing into two armed camps. Five hard-line Catholic princes, including George the Bearded of Ducal Saxony, had formed the League of Dessau, and in response, eight Lutheran princes, including John the Steadfast of Electoral Saxony and Philip of Hesse, had formed the League of Torgau. Charles was absent in Spain, busy both with domestic problems there and French aggression in Italy. Deputising on his brother's behalf, Ferdinand opened the Diet with a proposition to enforce the Edict of Worms against Lutheranism, which would eradicate heresy and therefore instability. Given the changed circumstances, Ferdinand might have expected support. However, the diet rejected his proposition. There were various reasons for this. Some princes had already converted. Catholic princes, meanwhile, doubted their ability to eliminate Lutheranism peacefully, but lacked the means to apply force (and possibly doubted their troops' religious affiliations). Applying force would also cause civil war, but Germany had only just emerged from the chaos of the Peasants' Revolt and there was little appetite for further armed conflict. Furthermore, given the Ottoman advance on Hungary that year, plunging Germany into turmoil at this juncture was inadvisable. Unity was needed.

So the princes reiterated the line they had adopted in 1521 and 1523. They hoped to undermine Lutheranism peacefully by tackling the issues that had brought Luther so much support. This was naive, since addressing the causes of anti-clericalism and anti-papalism would not affect the doctrinal appeal of Lutheranism or persuade converts away. Nevertheless, for all these reasons, the princes once again demanded a council, reducing their sights this time from a general to a national council. In the meantime, the diet unanimously passed the rather vaguely worded Recess of Speyer, stating that each prince should enforce the faith 'as he would have to answer to God and to the emperor'. Ferdinand agreed to accept the recess on Charles' behalf. He, too, was anxious for a united front to oppose the Ottoman conquest of Hungary. However, the Recess of Speyer had the effect of encouraging hitherto closet Lutherans to be open about their faith, while encouraging others to convert.

The second Diet of Speyer, and the recess revoked, 1529

In April 1529, the diet backtracked. It revoked the Recess of Speyer and declared the Edict of Worms compulsory. It also banned Zwinglianism and condemned to death anyone convicted of performing adult baptism. The new hard-line approach is easily explained: the majority of princes were Catholic and they were alarmed at the rapid spread of heresy. In response, the Lutheran minority withdrew from the diet: 'We fear the emperor's ban, but we fear still more God's curse.' Fourteen cities and six princes published a 'protestation' (from which we get the word 'Protestant'), which declared that the diet had no right to annul a decision that had been made unanimously.

Fearing an imminent Catholic attack, Philip of Hesse, the leading Lutheran prince, attempted to negotiate a united front between Lutherans and Zwinglians at his castle in Marburg. The Marburg Colloquy failed, leaving Protestants in a very vulnerable position.

However, if Ferdinand had intended to spend that summer imposing the Edict of Worms by force, he was immediately thwarted. In May, a massive Ottoman army departed from Istanbul, bound for Vienna. Ferdinand spent the months following Speyer anxiously monitoring the slow progress of this invading force, which reached Vienna in late September. Poor weather saved the city, and after a three-week siege, the Ottoman armies retreated. The Ottoman invasion of 1529 had diverted Habsburg attention from the Lutheran problem. Almost exactly the same circumstances saved Lutheranism four years later, in 1531–32.

The Colloquy of Regensburg, 1541

Twice during his reign, Charles tried to reunite the Church by negotiating with the Lutherans – at Augsburg in 1530, and at Regensburg in 1541. Since the first attempt failed (Charles rejected Melanchthon's Augsburg Confession), it is curious that he tried again. The doctrinal gulf between Lutheranism and Catholicism seemed too wide to be bridged. After all, either papal authority was acknowledged or it was not, people either believed in transubstantiation or they did not, they either accepted clerical marriage or they did not, and so on.

However, given the pope's difficulties in convening a general council, Charles intended to supervise his own negotiated settlement. He was not alone in believing that reconciliation was possible. Moderates from both sides believed the same. Melanchthon and Bucer were open-minded, and so too, on the Catholic side, were Cardinal Contarini and the Archbishop of Cologne. Furthermore, reconciliation was infinitely preferable to the alternative: the only other way of reversing the Protestant tide by 1540 was by force, but Charles was, as ever, short of funds. In the previous five years, he had conducted expensive campaigns against the French (the Third Habsburg–Valois War) and the Ottomans (Tunis 1535 and Preveza 1538). Overtaxing had already caused a revolt in the Netherlands. Furthermore, any use of force might cause civil war, which would leave the empire vulnerable to attack, unwise given that the Ottomans now occupied Buda, a day's sail down the Danube from Vienna. Finally, Charles held a trump card in 1541: Philip of Hesse's bigamy was a capital offence. Charles was in a position to demand serious concessions on the Protestants' part. For all these reasons, he summoned both sides to a colloquy, a 'friendly meeting of minds', in April 1541. For two months the moderates debated. They achieved some early successes: they agreed on the first five (of 18) points of a draft document, the *Regensburg Book*, and even bridged the divide over how to achieve salvation. Their doctrine of 'double justification' said that faith was fundamental to salvation and the value of good works depended on that faith (which appeased moderate Protestants), but good works were still crucial (which appeased moderate Catholics). Other issues were sadly less open to compromise.

SOURCE 2

Dr Conrad Hel, the Protestant representative from Augsburg, reporting back to his town council from the Colloquy of Regensburg, 1541.

4 May From all the discussions to date, I have come to the conclusion that His Imperial Majesty is anxious above all else for a Christian settlement of religious matters and the maintenance of a just peace and security in the Holy Empire. We must freely thank Almighty God that in these hard times His Godly Majesty has, despite advice to the contrary, ordained our affairs in such a benevolent manner. ... The theologians are applying themselves eagerly in the religious negotiations and have reached agreement on the article concerning justification... Our side is delighted with this. God be eternally praised! Amen!

6 May Yesterday, the theologians hit a crisis. The Catholics want to include transubstantiation in [the article concerning] Our Lord's Supper. Our theologians will not accept this. ... It is to be feared that a split will develop on this issue because the reputation of the papacy hangs on it. Nor are our theologians going to back down, as transubstantiation goes against Holy Scripture.

7 June In the religious discussions, the emperor dearly wishes progress in those articles which cannot be agreed upon. But our theologians have no wish to participate in more talks and therefore agreement cannot be expected. ... I warn you that His Imperial Majesty may perhaps impose his own arrangement. God damn that! ... Granvelle [Charles' Secretary of State] has advised the Landgrave [Philip of Hesse] that war is no more than a hair's breadth away and we should be on our guard.

The Regensburg Colloquy failed when those present could go no further, but it also failed because those not present – Luther and the pope in particular – refused to accept compromises like 'double justification'. The failure made up Charles' mind: war on the Lutherans was necessary.

SOURCE 3

From a letter that Charles sent to his sister Mary, in June 1541. Mary was then acting as governor of the Netherlands. Charles was at the Regensburg Colloquy.

Unless we take immediate action all the estates of Germany may lose their faith, and the Netherlands may follow. After fully considering all these points, I decided to begin by levying war on Hesse and Saxony as disturbers of the peace, and to open the campaign in the lands of the Duke of Brunswick. This pretext will not long conceal the true purpose of this war of religion, but it will serve to divide the Protestants from the beginning. We shall be able to work out the rest as we go along.

However, Charles failed to follow up on his decision immediately; he even granted the Lutherans another 18-month reprieve. Against advice, he had decided to prioritise another concern – the damage being done to his Mediterranean coastlands by Muslim pirates based in Algiers. It was an unfortunate decision; the crusade on Algiers could have waited and was an unmitigated disaster.

THINKING HISTORICALLY   Evidence (5b)

The importance of context

Documents (texts) are like small pieces torn from a larger tapestry (context). Historians have to reconstruct the larger pattern into which documents might fit in order to use them to construct accounts of the past. The problem is that texts can have multiple contexts. Historians often debate how best to contextualise the documents that they interpret.

1   Read Source 3. How does the document indicate that Charles was planning an aggressive policy in the empire? Which states did he expect to be targets? Did he have a timetable and what was it? What were the reasons for this aggression?

The sequence below provides a possible context for Source 3 in the story of Charles' battle against Lutheranism in the empire. Look at this timeline and then answer the questions that follow.

Sequence of events

1521	At the Diet of Worms, Charles passed the Edict of Worms, making Luther an outlaw. He vowed to devote his life to eliminating Lutheranism.
1525	At the First Diet of Speyer, the edict was put to one side. In return for help against the Ottomans then threatening Hungary, Ferdinand (and Charles) agreed to the Recess of Speyer.
1529	The Second Diet of Speyer revoked the 1526 recess and made the Edict of Worms compulsory.
1530	Rejecting the Augsburg Confession, Charles said he would enforce the Edict of Worms, and gave the Lutherans six months to return to the Catholic Church.
1532	Charles was unable to carry out his threat because of an anticipated Ottoman invasion. Instead, in return for men and money, he offered the Schmalkaldic League peace through the Religious Truce of Nuremberg.
1541	Following the failure of discussions at Regensburg, Charles promised his sister 'immediate action' against the Lutherans. (See Source 3.) However, that August, the Ottomans seized Buda and Pest, the twin capitals of Hungary. Unable to match the Ottomans on land, Charles decided to seek revenge by taking Algiers, once again postponing the attack on Lutheranism.

2   In what ways does the sequence suggest a pattern of events in Charles' dealings with the Lutherans?

3 How does Charles' letter to Mary fit into this pattern of events?

So, the document might seem to have one kind of meaning when interpreted in the context of a resolute religious policy (to destroy Lutheranism), repeatedly interrupted by the need to tackle unexpected Ottoman aggression.

A contrasting, more subtle interpretation appears if we locate it in another context: his brother's dynastic ambitions. In 1538, the childless king of Hungary, John Zápolya, agreed to accept Ferdinand as his heir. In July 1540, John Zápolya died, unexpectedly leaving a nine-day-old infant as his heir. Charles was aware that, nevertheless, his brother Ferdinand intended to assert his claim to the Hungarian throne. The campaign was planned for the summer of 1541. Charles would also have been aware that the Ottomans would find Ferdinand's intervention unacceptable, since John Zápolya had effectively been their vassal and they had already agreed to accept the infant, John Sigismund, as king of Hungary, as long as Hungary continued to pay them tribute. In other words, if Ferdinand invaded Hungary, the Ottomans would retaliate.

So despite his letter to Mary, there is good reason to think that Charles never had any intention of declaring war on the Protestant princes in 1541. He knew all along that he urgently needed a united front in Germany – that was the purpose behind the Regensburg Colloquy. The talks there were a genuine attempt at conciliation, but Charles at some point must have realised that they were unlikely to succeed. But even if they failed, he had no intention of declaring war on the Protestants. In July 1541, he agreed to extend the Religious Truce of Nuremberg by 18 months.

A third context emerges if we consider Charles' own ambitions in the Mediterranean. Charles' decision to attack Algiers, the headquarters of Barbarossa and the Barbary pirates, was taken well before the Ottoman attack on Buda and Pest. He had started raising funds for the expedition in late 1540. He had two motives: a need to prove himself after a humiliating defeat at Barbarossa's hands in 1538, and a need to stop the pirate raids. In September 1540, 800 Barbary pirates and Turks had attacked Gibraltar, on the southern-most tip of Spain. The town was plundered and its citizens taken into captivity. Charles' plans in the Mediterranean again reinforce the fact that he had no wish to declare war on the German Protestants in June 1541. He needed peace in Germany.

4 Why might Charles have already decided not to declare war on the Protestant princes?

If this is the case – if he had no intention of taking 'immediate action' on Protestants – *why* did he mislead his sister Mary? It is necessary to look at yet another context.

Context	Mary of Hungary
Fact 1	In the early 1520s, Mary expressed some interest in Lutheranism. Martin Luther even dedicated four psalms to her.
Fact 2	Mary was widowed in 1526, when her husband, King Louis of Hungary, was killed at the Battle of Mohács. The marriage had been happy, but childless.
Fact 3	In 1531, Mary was asked by her eldest brother, Emperor Charles V, to assume the governance of the Netherlands.
Fact 4	She never enjoyed governing the Netherlands and asked for permission to resign several times.
Fact 5	Mary naturally inclined towards lenience in her dealings with Lutherans. Charles suspected her of an overly tolerant approach. In 1531, he even gave her a warning, saying that if his parent, wife, child or sibling became a follower of Luther, he would consider them his greatest enemy.
Fact 6	Charles' policy of harsh repression of Lutherans in the Netherlands was unpopular, and local magistrates were slow to enforce the law. Over-taxation of the Netherlands also caused unrest.
Fact 7	Mary was adamantly opposed to expensive campaigns against the Turks in the Mediterranean, when there were so many issues to tackle at home. She also considered France the greater enemy.

Consider both the timeline and facts concerning Mary.

5 Construct a possible context for Charles' letter to Mary. Why might he have been so adamant about military action against the Protestants at that time?

6 Why is it important for historians to spend time thinking about possible contexts for a document before they start to use it to draw conclusions about the past?

AS Level Exam-Style Question Section A

How much weight do you give the evidence of Source 3 for an enquiry into Charles' determination to eradicate Lutheranism?

Explain your answer using the source, the information given about it and your own knowledge of the historical context. (12 marks)

Tip

The content of this source suggests one thing, but the context another, as the exercises above show. It is important that you tackle both these elements.

HOW FAR WERE GERMAN PRINCES RESPONSIBLE FOR THE SPREAD AND SURVIVAL OF LUTHERANISM?

The princes of the empire had huge power. Seven of them elected the emperor; the princes held almost complete power over their own territories; central government was negligible; there was no imperial army; there was no central executive to enforce censorship across the empire. To get elected, Charles had even augmented princely power (or at least weakened his own position) by agreeing to the capitulation (see pages 171–175). This handicapped him in the long term, since he was unable to bring foreign troops into Germany. Charles' position as emperor was then further weakened by the fact that he owned other territories, which meant that he often had to be absent from the empire.

If Charles was going to crush Lutheranism, therefore, he needed the princes to do the work. Their collective ability was considerable: they successfully crushed the Knights' Revolt of 1522–23 (admittedly, not a difficult task) and the Peasants' Revolt of 1524–25 (thus eliminating the bulk of Luther's early support); and they successfully crushed the Anabaptist stronghold of Münster in 1535. From the start, however, Charles did not have the princes' co-operation on the issue of Luther.

The importance of Frederick the Wise

From 1517 to 1525, Frederick's actions were crucial to Luther's survival. He refused demands to send Luther to Rome; instead, Pope Leo X asked the Augustinian order to discipline Luther. When that failed, Leo asked Cajetan to interview Luther at Augsburg. Frederick also refused papal orders to burn Luther's works in 1520. In 1521, he insisted that Charles V provide safe conduct for Luther for the Diet of Worms, and he was diplomatically absent when the vote on the Edict of Worms took place. Frederick had Luther 'kidnapped' after the Diet of Worms and, given that Luther was now both an outlaw (by the Edict of Worms) and a heretic (by the papal bull *Decet Romanum Pontificem*), he may well have saved Luther's life. Frederick then arranged for Luther to hide in his castle at Wartburg. From Luther's return to Wittenberg in 1522 until Frederick's death in 1525, the elector provided a safe refuge for Luther, refusing to hand him over to the authorities. Throughout this time, he led the princes in their refusal to enforce the Edict of Worms until a council had been called to reform the abuses found in the Church in Germany.

Frederick's ability to protect Luther was linked to his position as the most senior elector. Until his death in January 1519, the Emperor Maximilian courted Frederick's vote to ensure the election of his grandson Charles. For different reasons – to break the Habsburg monopoly – Pope Leo X also sought Frederick's vote. Leo even wanted him to stand as a candidate, and flattered him with a golden rose. Frederick refused to stand. Neither Maximilian nor Leo pushed too hard for Luther to be silenced. Nor, once elected in June 1519, did Charles V put pressure on Frederick: he owed him money and was grateful for the vote, and he did not wish to alienate the princes so early in his reign. So Charles acceded to the request for safe conduct to Worms, he made no effort to arrest Luther at Worms, and he turned a blind eye to the fact that Frederick did not enforce the Edict of Worms.

Frederick's role in Luther's early survival must be put into some perspective. It was all made very easy. He was under no real pressure to surrender his famous professor. He also had very little to do with the spread of Luther's ideas, at least not in any proactive sense. At the most, one could say that he enabled that spread: as Luther's employer, he provided the professor with a respectable platform, Wittenberg University, and he did not censor the press in Saxony nor prevent any Saxon town from reforming.

Frederick's motives for protecting Luther are open to speculation. He remained a Catholic until his deathbed, he showed no open sympathy for Luther's theological ideas and never talked with Luther personally. He only stopped collecting relics in 1522, adding over 1,500 items to his collection in the two years after Luther's outburst against indulgences.

There were probably multiple reasons for Frederick's protection of Luther. He was inordinately proud of the University of Wittenberg, which he had founded in 1502, and its star professor was certainly making the new university famous, drawing in some impressive humanist talent. He also thoroughly enjoyed Luther's attack on Tetzel, not least because the latter's sale of indulgences threatened to upstage Frederick's own indulgence sale on All Saints' Night. Tetzel was also employed by Albert of Mainz, which no doubt added to Frederick's pleasure – the families were rivals for power in the empire. Tetzel had studied at Leipzig University, which was in Ducal Saxony.

Frederick enjoyed anything that irritated his cousin George. The stronger the latter's opposition to Luther, the more Frederick protected Luther. The rivalry between the two sides of the family was notorious, and since George took the Dominican side in the argument, Frederick took the Augustinian side. So, in defending Luther, the elector was initially indulging self-interest.

However, Frederick was also essentially a fair man and respected for his sense of justice (hence the epithet, Wise). He felt Luther deserved a hearing. Frederick also resented external interference in Germany, especially from Rome, and it is very possible that he saw Luther as a lever to force a reform of the Church in the empire. At the very least, he wished the issues to be aired, not smothered. Family probably also played a role: Frederick's brother, John the Steadfast, expressed a serious interest in Luther's doctrines. Finally, Frederick's personal secretary, Spalatin, was an early supporter of Luther and may have been a quiet advocate in his cause.

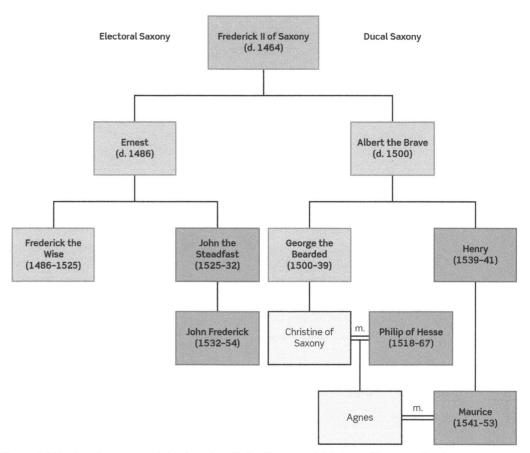

Figure 4.1 The two Saxonies explained: the Wettin family was a divided one. The Ernestine line were the Electors of Saxony (until 1548, when Charles awarded the electorship to Maurice), while the Albertine line were the Dukes of Saxony. Those in blue were Catholic; those in red became Lutheran. The dates each ruled are given.

The importance of the Protestant princes

In 1525, three major princes openly converted to Lutheranism. They held such important positions in the empire that their conversions played a major role in giving Lutheranism credibility and in ensuring the movement's continued survival and growth.

- Albrecht of Hohenzollern was the Grand Master of the Teutonic Order. The Order had been founded in about 1190 to aid Christians on pilgrimages in the Holy Land and to run hospitals for German knights wounded in the crusades – its motto was 'Help, Defend, Heal'. The Teutonic knights had then relocated to the Baltic in order to mount a crusade against pagan Lithuania, but by the early 16th century the Order was much weakened and under the control of Poland. Despite the reduced power and status of the Teutonic knights, Albrecht's conversion shocked Catholic Europe. The fact that he was a cousin of Archbishop Albert of Mainz made his conversion even more controversial.

- Philip of Hesse was a Landgrave. The title made him the empire's third-highest prince in terms of noble status, after the king of Bohemia and the archduke of Austria. Philip's importance was also military: he was an excellent soldier. Aged 18, he had helped to crush the Knights' Revolt in 1522, and he had also played a key role in defeating the Peasants' Revolt in 1525. From 1530 on, Philip played a most crucial role in organising the military defence of the new faith and in negotiating with allies.

- John the Steadfast succeeded his brother Frederick the Wise as Elector of Saxony in 1525. Since Saxony was most senior of the seven electorships, John was politically the second most important man in the empire after the emperor. As Luther lived in his territory, his protection was crucial for Luther's continued survival. Under John's proactive rule, Saxony provided the empire with a role model for the organisation of Lutheranism in a state. For example, the inspections or visitations of parishes in the late 1520s were initiated at his request, and these prompted Luther to produce his catechisms.

Why did these princes convert?

Faith – genuine belief in Lutheran doctrine – must be given a high priority in their reasons for converting, not least because supporting Luther was dangerous. These princes risked losing everything. One could argue, of course, that the Recess of Speyer meant that conversion was comparatively risk-free in the period 1526–29. However, John of Saxony had supported Luther long before that. His influence with his brother Frederick played a crucial role in protecting Luther in the period 1518–25. Albrecht of Hohenzollern had also converted (though not openly) long before 1526. He had heard Luther speak at Worms. In 1522, while attending the Diet at Nuremberg, he met and was converted by the preacher Osiander; he was openly a Lutheran from February 1525, before the Recess of Speyer was promulgated. At the time, both the papal bull of excommunication and the Edict of Worms meant that any supporter could have been condemned as a heretic and outlaw. Furthermore, once the Recess of Speyer had been revoked in 1529 and the Edict of Worms made compulsory, Lutheran princes were once more in a dangerous position. The depth of their faith can be measured by the reason they gave for withdrawing from the Diet of Speyer in 1529: 'We fear the Emperor's ban, but we fear still more God's curse.'

Apart from faith, there were many cynical reasons for converting, and princes stood to gain a great deal personally on conversion. The financial gains were potentially enormous. Confiscated monastic and Church property and treasure enriched princely coffers and multiplied princely landholdings, which meant more rents. Albrecht of Hohenzollern gained the most. He secularised land of the Teutonic Order to create a hereditary Duchy of Prussia for himself and his heirs. He then used confiscated Church revenues to appease local nobles and to pay for the expenses of his court. Königsberg Castle, the order's headquarters, was transformed into his palace. Only a small portion of his new wealth was channelled into providing a school in every town and a Lutheran university, which he founded in 1544. Philip of Hesse was almost as mercenary. He may well have used confiscated revenues to found a new evangelical university in Marburg and a hospital for the poor and sick, but he also kept 41 percent of the money for himself. Monastic lands eventually provided one-seventh of his income. Even John of Saxony does not emerge with his reputation unsullied. He did stop the Saxon nobility from appropriating Church lands, which he left in the possession of the new Lutheran Church of Saxony in order to endow it with the means to pay for maintenance and clerical salaries. However, more Church money was used to pay off the elector's debts than was spent on pious activities. This latter point does highlight the fact that defending Lutheranism was an expensive affair. In other words, any gains made in turning Lutheran were soon spent.

Converting to Lutheranism also enhanced a prince's sovereign powers. He no longer had to share authority with the pope or bishops. The Saxon Model gave the prince the duty of supervising the Church in his state, a flattering responsibility that provided opportunities for patronage and increased control over his own territory. Some Lutheran princes used the occasion to improve their territories and the lives of their subjects, with a particular focus on well-trained and resident clergy, state-endowed education and provision for the poor and sick. Luther's political conservatism was also appealing, with his stress on obedience to authority.

The Schmalkaldic League

In December 1530, Philip of Hesse and John of Saxony convened a meeting in the town of Schmalkalden, in Thuringia between Saxony and Hesse. Five northern princes and representatives from two northern cities attended. They had all signed the Augsburg Confession, and they all believed that an attack on Lutheranism was imminent. Following Charles' rejection of the Augsburg Confession three months earlier, the diet had passed a recess requiring that the Edict of Worms be enforced.

All heresy therefore had to be suppressed, and Charles had given the Protestants six months, until April 1531, to comply, after which he would use force.

After two months of negotiation, those meeting in Schmalkalden agreed to form a league to defend Lutheranism by force if necessary. Southern cities and northern princes made for an unlikely alliance. The formation of the Schmalkaldic League is a measure of both their depth of faith and their concern that the emperor would declare war. The decision was not taken lightly. Luther's views on politics were that 'man must suffer the wicked prince; God will punish him', and he was reluctant to defy the emperor. He only agreed to give his blessing to the League because its aim was defensive. By its charter, any attack on one member was an attack on all, and would be resisted by the League's army. Each member contributed towards the army of 10,000 infantry and 2,000 cavalry. The Augsburg Confession was adopted as the new league's religious statement.

Founded initially for defence, the Schmalkaldic League had considerable success in the 1530s, proactively spreading Lutheranism. In very few cases was force used. Usually, just the League's existence gave waverers the confidence needed to convert. By 1540, almost the whole of north Germany and large swathes of the south had converted, and every Lutheran state and imperial city (except Brandeburg-Ansbach and Nuremberg) belonged to the League. Adding to the sense of unity and strength, most also accepted the Augsburg Confession as their statement of faith. Particularly important additions included Ducal Saxony (previously Charles' most reliable supporter, but now ruled by George's brother Henry) and the Elector of Brandenburg, who converted in 1539.

The league's successes in the 1530s owed a great deal to Philip of Hesse's dynamic leadership. In search of allies, he negotiated with Denmark, England, France and Venice (though he rejected overtures of friendship from the largely Islamic Ottoman Empire). French money helped the Schmalkaldic League to achieve its greatest triumph: restoring Duke Ulrich of Württemberg to his territories in 1534. Whether Ulrich deserved it was another matter: he had been deposed in 1520 by Charles, with the full agreement of the princes, for murdering a man so he could marry his victim's wife. He only converted to Protestantism to get the League's help, and he then greedily helped himself to three-quarters of all the Church's assets, ordering even the gold on altar paintings to be scraped off with a knife. Still, in terms of a morale-raising propaganda coup against Habsburg authority, the taking of Württemberg was unparalleled.

It could be argued, of course, that the League's successes in the 1530s also owed a lot to favourable circumstances. External issues meant that Charles never had the opportunity to follow up on his threat of 1531. In 1532, a massive Ottoman army once again approached Austria, and by the Religious Truce of Nuremberg Charles offered the League peace in return for help. This time, Suleiman's armies stopped two days' march short of Vienna. However, Charles honoured the Truce of Nuremberg for the rest of the 1530s, and was himself absent from Germany, again preoccupied with French and Ottoman threats.

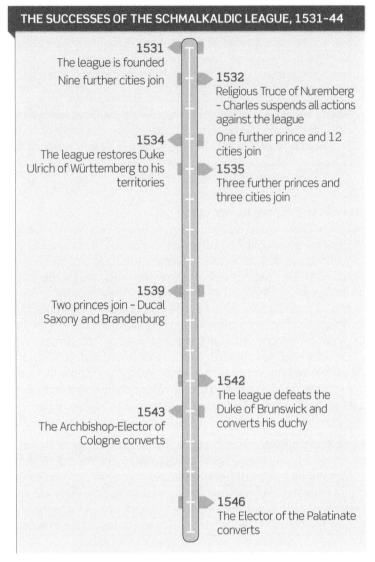

THE SUCCESSES OF THE SCHMALKALDIC LEAGUE, 1531–44

1531
The league is founded
Nine further cities join

1532
Religious Truce of Nuremberg – Charles suspends all actions against the league
One further prince and 12 cities join

1534
The league restores Duke Ulrich of Württemberg to his territories

1535
Three further princes and three cities join

1539
Two princes join – Ducal Saxony and Brandenburg

1542
The league defeats the Duke of Brunswick and converts his duchy

1543
The Archbishop-Elector of Cologne converts

1546
The Elector of the Palatinate converts

External issues helped the Schmalkaldic League in the early 1540s. When the Regensburg Colloquy of 1541 failed to secure the religious compromise that he wished, Charles agreed that the Truce of Nuremberg could be renewed for a final 18 months. Charles had high hopes that a general council was imminent, and he had decided to use the interim to resolve another pressing issue – by taking the port of Algiers on the North African coast, he hoped to end forever the piracy problem plaguing his Mediterranean territories. If the council failed to materialise, he would use force to crush the Lutherans.

Charles' decision to defer war on the Protestants was an error. He missed an opportunity. The Algerian campaign (1541) might have appealed to his crusading ambitions, but it was badly planned and failed dramatically, and on his return he faced new French attacks during the Fourth Habsburg–Valois war (1542–44). The window of opportunity had passed. In Charles' absence, meanwhile, Philip bounced back. Recovering rapidly from his disgrace over the bigamy scandal, he reneged on his agreement to keep the peace, and in 1542 the League defeated the Duke of Brunswick and forcibly converted his territory. In 1544, the Elector of the Palatinate and the Archbishop-Elector of Cologne converted. Four electors were now Protestant. To many, the Protestant tidal wave seemed unstoppable.

The Wettin family and Lutheranism

This chapter includes the roles played by three members of the extended Wettin family of Electoral and Ducal Saxony: Frederick the Wise; his brother John the Steadfast; and the son-in-law of George the Bearded, Philip of Hesse. Find out more about the roles of three further members of this family: Duke George the Bearded, Elector John Frederick and Duke Maurice of Saxony.

Activity – debate and discussion

Decide where you would place these six princes on a continuum that measures the extent to which they helped or hindered the survival and spread of Lutheranism:

Helped ←――――――――――――――――→ Hindered

HOW FAR DID CONFLICTING PRIORITIES HAMPER CHARLES' ABILITY TO TACKLE LUTHERANISM?

The survival and spread of Lutheranism in the 1520s and the successes of the Schmalkaldic League in the 1530s and early 1540s owed a great deal to the fact that Charles was unable to devote his full attention to Germany. Throughout his reign, the vast size of his inheritance meant conflicting priorities. Charles' attention was demanded by his other territories, especially Spain, and he was also forced to devote considerable time to defending his inheritance against French and Ottoman aggression.

Spain

Following his grandfather Ferdinand's death in 1516, Charles inherited Aragon and Castile, the latter jointly with his mad mother, Joanna. Charles arrived in Spain in late 1517, and he spent most of the next 12 years in the country, bar a nine-month visit to the empire in 1520–21. Charles clearly felt it was more important for him to be in Spain than in Germany. His decision can be justified.

Charles' rule in Spain did not start well. He delayed his arrival for 18 months, and when he did arrive, he promptly despatched his much more popular Spanish-born brother, Ferdinand, to Germany. To add insult to injury, Charles did not speak Castilian and he used foreign advisers. His alienated subjects used the opportunity of Charles' departure in 1520 for the empire to rebel. The revolt was centred in towns and was as much about taxes and corruption, but it almost brought down the monarchy until it was suppressed by the Castilian nobility. A key reason why Charles left the empire so promptly after the Diet of Worms was the need to return to Spain and oversee the restoration of order.

Peace was restored by 1522, and it could be argued that Charles' continued presence in Spain for the rest of the 1520s was unnecessary, and that it might have been wiser for him to return to the empire. However, Charles used the decade to strengthen the bond with his Spanish subjects. He learned Castilian; he respected local rights; he worked with the Castilian Cortes (or parliament), which he summoned regularly; he consulted a range of his subjects – the aristocracy, the lesser nobility, professional lawyers – and did not repeat the mistake of relying on foreign advisers. In 1526, he married his cousin Isabella of Portugal, a popular move, and his son Philip was born the following year. By all these means, Charles won the affection of his Spanish subjects.

This was important. Charles needed Spanish resources, which included taxes on New World gold and silver. He also relied on the income from his Crown lands in Spain to pay the interest on loans from the Fuggers of Augsburg. Charles later claimed that Spain alone sustained him. Without Spain, he could not have tackled any of his foreign ventures against the Ottomans or French, nor later declared war on the Schmalkaldic League. In other words, the seven years that he spent in Spain were not wasted.

France

Charles left Germany for Spain so suddenly after the Diet of Worms for another reason too: France had invaded Navarre in the north of Spain. Charles' reign was dominated by war with France. The five Habsburg–Valois Wars of 1521–59 had multiple causes. Antipathy was an issue: Francis I had competed for the title of emperor in 1519 and lost. Pride alone meant that he needed some sort of success against Charles. However, the root cause was land. Rival inherited claims to Navarre, Burgundy, Naples and towns in Flanders fuelled the wars. Dynastic honour ensured that neither side would relinquish its claims, no matter how distant in time the grounds were. Francis demanded Naples, for example, on the grounds that he was the rightful heir to a claim dating back to the 1440s. Charles claimed Burgundy on the grounds that the French had wrongfully seized it from his grandmother, Mary the Rich, in 1477.

Francis also felt encircled by Habsburg land and he feared (wrongly) that Charles intended to add France itself to his dominions. Breaking the circle, and breaking Charles' ability to communicate between his northern and southern territories, became Francis' driving ambition. The key to success lay in retaking Milan, which Charles seized from France in 1521. Francis managed to retake Milan, but immediately suffered a reverse. His armies were utterly defeated at the Battle of Pavia in 1525, and the king himself was captured and taken to Madrid as a prisoner.

Charles was exceptionally magnanimous to his royal prisoner. He did not use the opportunity to demand slices of France – proof, had Francis needed it, that Charles had no expansionist ambitions. Instead, Charles imposed the very moderate Treaty of Madrid. If Francis would promise to desist from aggression, renounce his claims to Burgundy, and pay a massive ransom, he was free to return to France. His two eldest sons arrived in Spain, where they were held as hostages for Francis' good behaviour. The latter promptly reneged on the Treaty of Madrid, and formed an anti-Habsburg alliance. In theory, Charles could have executed his princely hostages. Instead, he demoted them from comfortable house (or palace) arrest to such harsh treatment that the younger prince, Henry, who succeeded his father in 1547, acquired an abiding hatred for Charles.

French aggression, coupled with Charles' pursuit of dynastic claims, played an important role in Charles' failure to tackle the Lutheran issue in Germany:

- Defending his territories against France had to take priority, and Charles was only able to turn to German affairs when he had secured peace. Proof that Charles would have preferred to focus on Germany can be found in the moderate nature of the peace treaties he made with France: all that he asked was that the French desist from attacking and renounce all claims to territories that Charles considered to be Habsburg.

- Francis I attempted to divide Charles' forces by making alliances with the Ottomans. These shocked Christian Europe. No Christian scruple would deter the king of France from bringing the Turks and the devil into the heart of Christendom, commented Thomas Cromwell, if this could help him recover Milan. In 1542, for example, Charles faced co-ordinated attacks on his Italian inheritance from the French and the Ottomans. Dealing with these had to take priority over the Lutheran issue.

- In an effort to undermine his enemy from within, Francis also financed and strengthened the Schmalkaldic League. Fuelled by a hatred for Charles that was so strong that it overrode his devout Catholicism, Francis' son, Henry II, helped the Lutherans even more decisively. He played a major role in reviving the league in the early 1550s. He signed the Treaty of Chambord with the Lutherans, and invaded the empire, taking Metz, Toul and Verdun. Charles was diverted from his efforts to eradicate Lutheranism in an effort to retake Metz. The expense and failure of that attempt led to Charles' decision to abdicate.

The Ottoman Empire

A 'Great Fear' gripped early 16th century Europe. It was a response to the unbelievably rapid and extensive expansion of the Ottoman Empire under its Sultans Selim I and his son Suleiman the Magnificent. In the period 1500–20, the Ottoman Empire had almost doubled in size. Woodcuts showing alleged Turkish atrocities then enhanced the fear. If the Ottomans were going to be stopped, emergency measures were needed, which explains urgent papal pleas for a united front and a crusade. Leo X may have underestimated Luther, but from his point of view, Luther really was a minor issue compared with turning back the Islamic tidal wave that threatened to engulf Christian Europe.

SOURCE 4   A woodcut by Hans Guldenmundt, made around 1540, showing atrocities allegedly committed by the Turkish army. Here a Turkish cavalryman takes two tied-up captured peasants into slavery; on his lance is their speared child.

The Ottoman threat to the empire

Since it was almost on the front line, the Great Fear was especially strong in the empire. One of the reasons Charles had even been elected was because the princes felt he would be in a stronger position to resist Ottoman aggression. At the least, his Austrian territories provided a buffer for the rest of the empire. Charles himself felt the sense of emergency, which explains why he put crusading above Luther on the agenda of the Diet of Worms in 1521.

The fear escalated to panic proportions when the Ottomans invaded Hungary in 1526 and comprehensively defeated the armies of King Louis of Hungary at the Battle of Mohács. The Ottomans were now within reach of the empire itself. The fear provided the princes with an additional reason to propose the Recess of Speyer. Now was not the time to plunge Germany into domestic chaos by enforcing the Edict of Worms. Ferdinand's willingness to accept the recess is explained by dynastic ambition. Louis of Hungary's death left the thrones of Hungary and Bohemia vacant and, as in the empire, both thrones were elective. Ferdinand was the brother-in-law of Louis, and he was elected king of Bohemia. His attempt to claim Hungary, though, was not as straightforward.

The Turks occupied the southern part of the country, and there was a rival candidate – John Zápolyai, the governor of Transylvania, which was the eastern province of Hungary. John was the choice of the Hungarian nobility, but Ferdinand refused to accept this and invaded to take the throne. John responded by striking a deal with Suleiman, whereby he became the puppet ruler of Hungary under the Ottomans, in return for their protection. For the next 15 years, Ferdinand's aggression on 'Turkish' Hungary drew Ottoman retaliation.

In 1529, this retaliation threatened the empire itself when Suleiman launched a campaign against Austria. His army of 200,000, accompanied by 22,000 camels, reached and besieged Vienna. Suleiman had to lift his siege – the weather was atrocious and his supply line was stretched – nevertheless, the fear that the Ottomans would try again was very real. It explains why Charles V tried to negotiate a settlement with the Protestants at Augsburg in 1530. He needed a united German front against the Ottomans. It also explains why Charles agreed to the Religious Truce of Nuremberg in 1532. That year, the Ottomans once more marched on Vienna, though this time, a brave garrison of just 800 men in the fort of Güns stopped their advance two days' march short of Vienna. By then, it was late in the season, and Suleiman decided to turn back.

The campaign of 1532 was the last time the Ottomans came close to invading the empire during Charles' reign. Nevertheless, the Hungarian issue preoccupied Ferdinand almost to the exclusion of everything else for the next three decades. He never ceased laying claim to the whole of Hungary, though the most he managed to acquire was a slice on the west, known as 'Royal Hungary', for which he had to pay tribute in a humiliating truce in 1547. Though a devout Catholic, Ferdinand's later willingness to accept the Peace of Augsburg in 1555 can be explained in part by his preoccupation with Hungary.

EXTEND YOUR KNOWLEDGE

Ferdinand and Hungary (1538-62)

In 1538, Ferdinand reached a secret compromise with John Zápolyai: John recognised Ferdinand as the king of 'Royal' or western Hungary, while Ferdinand recognised John as the king of the rest, provided Ferdinand got it all when John (who was unmarried and childless at the time) died. But then John married and had a son, John Sigismund, before dying in 1540. Ferdinand promptly invaded, determined to claim the lot, as agreed. Unfortunately for him, the Hungarians elected the infant John Sigismund as their king, and asked the Ottomans to defend them. In return, they were prepared to be vassals of the Ottoman Empire. Unhappily for the Hungarians, Turkish troops invaded but took direct control of central Hungary, restoring John Sigismund only to Transylvania. They then pushed west and into Royal Hungary. Faced with total defeat, Ferdinand accepted the humiliating Truce of 1547, whereby he only got Royal Hungary and had to pay tribute for it, while seven-year-old John Sigismund was permitted to be a vassal ruler only over Transylvania. The rest – 'Turkish' Hungary – was fully incorporated into the Ottoman Empire. Despite Ferdinand's best efforts, this was reconfirmed by the peace of 1562.

The threat to Charles' Mediterranean possessions

From Charles' point of view, the threat from the Ottomans was just as great in the Mediterranean. In the east Mediterranean, in 1522, the Ottomans seized the island of Rhodes from a Christian crusading order, the Knights of St John. Charles relocated the knights to his island of Malta. In 1537, the Ottomans laid siege to Corfu, a direct threat to Venetian territory and trade routes, and perilously close to Charles' own territory in Naples. The danger to Christian Europe was such that, for once, enmities were forgotten and a united Venetian–Spanish–papal naval force was launched. It failed. Poor leadership at the naval Battle of Preveza, in 1538, resulted in a permanent Ottoman presence in the central Mediterranean.

In the west Mediterranean, the Ottoman threat was compounded by the presence of their unlikely allies, the 15,000-strong Barbary pirates. These pirates were Muslim and many were refugees from Granada, which had been 're-conquered' for Christianity by Charles V's grandparents, Ferdinand and Isabella, in 1492. From their base in Algiers on the Barbary Coast, the pirates lived by raiding Christian coastal towns and villages. For decades, the Spanish and southern Italian Mediterranean coasts – all Charles' possessions – lived in a state of war-readiness and fear. The Balearic Islands, Valencia and Catalonia especially, were all subject to repeated attacks, while in 1540, 900 pirates attacked Gibraltar. Apart from rape and pillage, the pirates plundered valuables, livestock and, above all, people to be sold in their huge slave markets. They also made money selling back captives to Spain; about 20,000 Spaniards were awaiting redemption by 1550. The pirates also disrupted commercial shipping between Italy and Spain. The situation was made worse in 1533, when Suleiman the Magnificent hired the pirate leader, Barbarossa ('Redbeard') as his Admiral. In 1542, for example, Barbarossa launched attacks on Nice as part of a co-ordinated Ottoman–French campaign against Charles.

On two occasions, Charles made the Barbary pirates his priority. In 1535, he led an expedition to recapture Tunis, which had been seized by Barbarossa the previous year, and in 1541, he attempted to seize Algiers and eliminate the pirates completely. The first expedition was a massive success, the second a humiliating and exceptionally expensive failure, during which Charles lost his fleet. Despite their very different outcomes, both detracted from his ability to tackle the Protestant issue in Germany. In the 1530s, Charles' absence enabled the Schmalkaldic League to grow in strength. He was unable to react to the seizure of Württemberg. In 1541, Charles chose to go to Algiers against advice, when his priority should have been war on the Schmalkaldic League. The Algiers campaign also put him in considerable debt, which helps to explain Charles' inability to later capitalise on his victory over the Protestants at Mühlberg. He had simply run out of money.

Summary

The impact of Charles' wars with France and the Ottomans on his ability to crush the Lutherans was as follows:

- The wars meant that Charles was unable to focus on the Protestant problem. Foreign threats took priority, and time and again he was forced to be absent from the empire. He was only able to turn to Germany when he had achieved peace abroad, but such 'windows' were few and always short-lived. When free of these outside constraints, and present in the empire, he could achieve great things. In 1546–47, for example, he defeated the Schmalkaldic League at Mühlberg and forcibly reconverted most of the south to Catholicism.

- The wars meant that Charles had to make concessions to the Protestants, particularly in order to get their help against the Ottoman threat. For example, with Charles' permission, Ferdinand agreed to the Recess of Speyer in 1526, in order to acquire Protestant support against the Ottoman invasion of Hungary. In 1532, fears of an Ottoman invasion led to the Religious Truce of Nuremberg (or Nuremberg Standstill), by which Charles offered the Schmalkaldic League peace in return for men and money. Both concessions gave Lutheranism the breathing space to grow.

- The wars strengthened the Lutherans in another way: they acquired aid from France. Francis I financed the Schmalkaldic League in the 1530s. His son Henry II signed the Treaty of Chambord with the league in 1552, and provided the money that revived the League. As part of the Treaty, Henry also invaded Germany and took Metz, which diverted Charles' attention (permanently, this time) away from the Lutheran issue. Since both Francis and Henry were devout Catholics, this aid would not have been forthcoming had it not been for the enmity between Charles and France.

- The wars also virtually bankrupted Charles. His Algiers campaign of 1541 was particularly ruinous – he lost an entire fleet. As a result, he lacked the means to follow through the Battle of Mühlberg in 1547, and was forced to ask the diet for aid, which was refused. He spent a year's income trying to retake Metz from the French, and certainly had nothing left to tackle the Lutheran issue. It was one reason why he gave up trying in 1553.

- An incidental impact of the wars was the degree to which Charles' successes, particularly in the 1520s, alienated the papacy. The Papal States were sandwiched between Charles' Italian possessions. When Charles took Milan in 1521 and then crushed French armies in 1525 at the Battle of Pavia, papal alarm at Charles' power was heightened. This helps to explain why Pope Clement VII did not co-operate with Charles' requests to call a general council. This mattered: the Catholic princes in Germany demanded a council to reform the Church before they would enforce the Edict of Worms.

A Level Exam-Style Question Section A

How far could the historian make use of Source 5 and Extract 1 together to investigate the role that Ottoman aggression played in the survival and spread of Lutheranism?

Explain your answer using Source 5 and Extract 1, the information given about them and your own knowledge of the historical context. (20 marks)

Tip

Time spent planning is never wasted. Spend up to ten minutes preparing: read the source and extract and identify relevant evidence in them; look at their provenance and determine what you can about the authors; then plan your answer before you start writing.

SOURCE 5

Charles is advised against a war on Lutheranism by Catholic princes, 1530. This advice – the Protocol of the Diet of Augsburg – was written up by Valentin von Tetleben. At the time, Tetleben was Vicar General for the diocese of Mainz, working for the Archbishop-Elector Albert of Mainz.

Firstly, Charles should know that the sinews of war are money and that he is already in great need of it. Secondly, if the war against the Lutherans and heretics goes badly, the King of France and other rulers will take the opportunity to attack him. Thirdly, if the Turks should by chance make war on the emperor and Germany, and Germany is in strife and inner turmoil, they will be able to destroy everything within it. Fourthly, unless Charles can gain outside help in the war against the Lutherans, he will not be able to complete it satisfactorily. For if he employs German troops, they could defect from the emperor to the Lutherans and he might lose his army. Fifthly, the subjects of the Christian Princes could rebel and rise up against their master, in which case they would have a war on with their own vassals. For these and other compelling reasons, the emperor cannot go to war with the Lutherans for the faith.

EXTRACT 1

The impact of the Ottoman threat on Lutheran fortunes. From Andrina Stiles, *The Ottoman Empire 1450–1700* (1989).

By providing a military threat to the frontiers of the Holy Roman Empire, the Muslim Ottomans enabled the Lutheran Protestants to wring concessions from the Catholic Emperor. From 1526 onwards, all major concessions were the direct result of Ottoman activities in eastern and central Europe. ... It is arguable that Ottoman imperialism was the largest single factor in the consolidation and legitimation of Lutheranism. ... In pursuit of their anti-Habsburg policy, the Ottomans were drawn into an alliance with France. For a while Europe marvelled at the sight of the Catholic King of France making the port of Toulon available to the ships of the Muslim Sultan. This French alliance came to be the cornerstone of sixteenth-century Ottoman policy in Europe. Its intention was disruptive. It was designed merely to foment Habsburg–Valois rivalry.

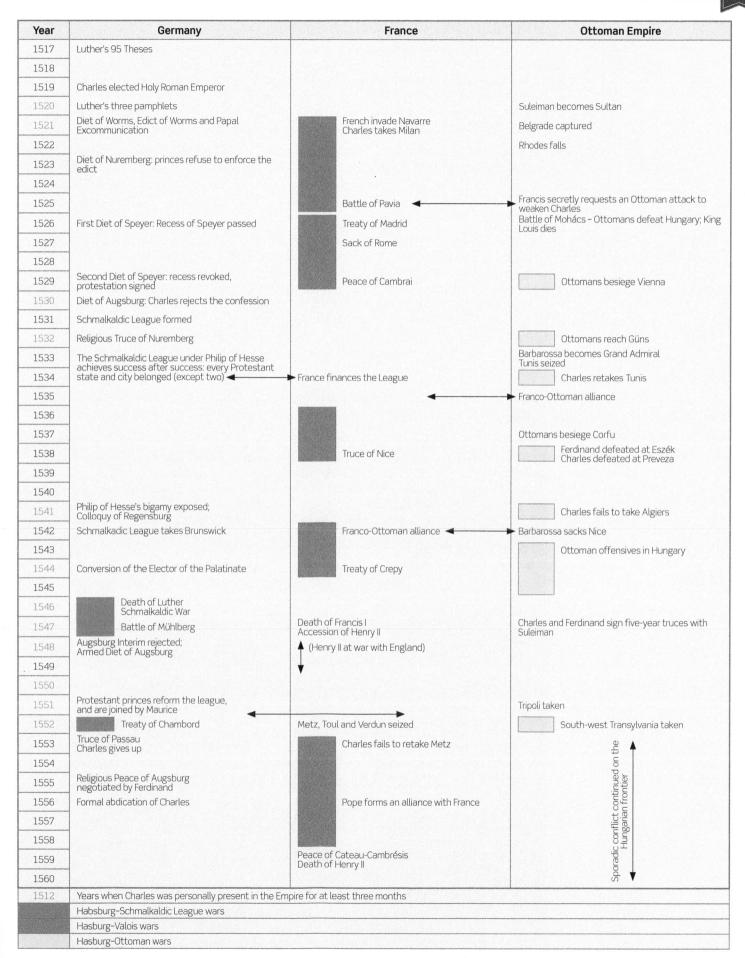

Year	Germany	France	Ottoman Empire
1517	Luther's 95 Theses		
1518			
1519	Charles elected Holy Roman Emperor		
1520	Luther's three pamphlets		Suleiman becomes Sultan
1521	Diet of Worms, Edict of Worms and Papal Excommunication	French invade Navarre / Charles takes Milan	Belgrade captured
1522			Rhodes falls
1523	Diet of Nuremberg: princes refuse to enforce the edict		
1524			
1525		Battle of Pavia	Francis secretly requests an Ottoman attack to weaken Charles
1526	First Diet of Speyer: Recess of Speyer passed	Treaty of Madrid	Battle of Mohács – Ottomans defeat Hungary; King Louis dies
1527		Sack of Rome	
1528			
1529	Second Diet of Speyer: recess revoked, protestation signed	Peace of Cambrai	Ottomans besiege Vienna
1530	Diet of Augsburg: Charles rejects the confession		
1531	Schmalkaldic League formed		
1532	Religious Truce of Nuremberg		Ottomans reach Güns
1533	The Schmalkaldic League under Philip of Hesse achieves success after success: every Protestant state and city belonged (except two)		Barbarossa becomes Grand Admiral / Tunis seized
1534		France finances the League	Charles retakes Tunis
1535			Franco-Ottoman alliance
1536			
1537			Ottomans besiege Corfu
1538		Truce of Nice	Ferdinand defeated at Eszék / Charles defeated at Preveza
1539			
1540			
1541	Philip of Hesse's bigamy exposed; Colloquy of Regensburg		Charles fails to take Algiers
1542	Schmalkadic League takes Brunswick	Franco-Ottoman alliance	Barbarossa sacks Nice
1543			Ottoman offensives in Hungary
1544	Conversion of the Elector of the Palatinate	Treaty of Crepy	
1545			
1546	Death of Luther / Schmalkaldic War		
1547	Battle of Mühlberg	Death of Francis I / Accession of Henry II	Charles and Ferdinand sign five-year truces with Suleiman
1548	Augsburg Interim rejected; Armed Diet of Augsburg	(Henry II at war with England)	
1549			
1550			
1551	Protestant princes reform the league, and are joined by Maurice		Tripoli taken
1552	Treaty of Chambord	Metz, Toul and Verdun seized	South-west Transylvania taken
1553	Truce of Passau / Charles gives up	Charles fails to retake Metz	
1554			
1555	Religious Peace of Augsburg negotiated by Ferdinand		
1556	Formal abdication of Charles	Pope forms an alliance with France	
1557			
1558			
1559		Peace of Cateau-Cambrésis / Death of Henry II	
1560			

Sporadic conflict continued on the Hungarian frontier

1512	Years when Charles was personally present in the Empire for at least three months
	Habsburg–Schmalkaldic League wars
	Hasburg–Valois wars
	Hasburg–Ottoman wars

Figure 4.2 Did external wars prevent Charles from resolving problems in the Holy Roman Empire?

The Schmalkaldic War, 1546–47

By the mid-1540s, Charles was finally free from dealing with foreign affairs. In 1544, he signed the Peace of Crepy with France. Suleiman, engaged in a war with Persia on his eastern front, agreed to a truce over Hungary in 1546. Charles could now deal decisively with the Protestant problem in Germany. He decided on war. The pope had finally called a council, the Council of Trent, which met from 1545, but it was clearly not going to support Charles' aims either of focusing on eradicating abuses in the German Church or of reconciling the two sides. War was therefore the only solution.

Charles laid the ground for victory skilfully, acquiring an ally in the Duke of Bavaria, with the promise of the electorship currently held by the Palatinate. He also lured to his side Maurice of Ducal Saxony, with the promise of the Electorship of Saxony and the land of several bishoprics. Though Maurice was a Lutheran, he held no scruples about betraying the Ernestine branch of his family and his father-in-law Philip of Hesse.

The war was short, sharp and very successful. In 1546, Charles' troops took Ulm, Frankfurt, Strasbourg and the Palatinate. On 23 April 1547, his army decisively defeated the Schmalkaldic League at the Battle of Mühlberg. Maurice occupied Electoral Saxony and Charles entered Wittenberg, where, it is said, he gazed upon the tomb of Luther, who had died in 1546. John Frederick of Saxony was captured at the battle itself; Philip of Hesse was persuaded to surrender; and the Archbishop-Elector of Cologne was forced to resign. Imperial troops then swept through Protestant Germany, forcibly reconverting city after city to Catholicism. Jubilant, Charles commissioned a portrait from Titian to commemorate his victory – the conqueror of heresy triumphant on horseback.

SOURCE

To celebrate his victory at Mühlberg, Charles commissioned this portrait from his favourite artist, Titian. Charles is presented as the calm victor, clad in the same armour he wore for the battle, with lance at the ready, mounted on a lively jet-black charger.

Art as propaganda
The unusual absence of images of corpses or prisoners or fleeing enemies suggests the speed of the victory. The Protestant forces were caught ill-prepared and the 'battle' was more of a cavalry pursuit. Only 55 imperial troops died before John Frederick was captured. (Alternatively, the absence of corpses might suggest Charles' wish now to reconcile rather than gloat.) This was a victory for the Christian faith over heresy. Around his neck Charles wears, as he did in every portrait, the Order of the Golden Fleece. The Order was founded in 1430 by his great-great-grandfather, Philip the Good, Duke of Burgundy, 'for the reverence of God and the maintenance of our Christian Faith'. The reddish sky reflects the popular belief that God had prolonged the day to allow the victory to be won, and that a blood-red sun had risen into the heaven higher than usual. The portrait also subtly suggests that Charles was the saviour of Catholicism in other directions. The use of this particular horse, an Andalusian crossbreed between a Spanish mare and an Arab stallion, suggests a victory over Islam. As a piece of propaganda, the portrait is superb. As evidence for what happened, it is not entirely reliable. Charles directed operations skilfully and his courage inspired the troops. However, he took no part in the fighting itself and it is doubtful that he would have been physically up to controlling such a nervous mount at the time.

The failure to capitalise on victory, 1547-53

By late 1547, Charles was in a superb position to eliminate Lutheranism from the empire completely. The league had been defeated and its leaders imprisoned. Only Magdeburg and a few northern cities held out. However, victory again eluded Charles, for three main reasons: he lacked the money to proceed; he lacked the co-operation of the Catholic princes, whose alienation at this late juncture can be explained by a mixture of alarm and anger; and the French intervened.

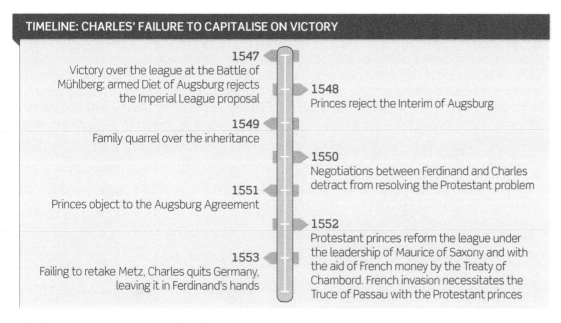

TIMELINE: CHARLES' FAILURE TO CAPITALISE ON VICTORY

1547
Victory over the league at the Battle of Mühlberg; armed Diet of Augsburg rejects the Imperial League proposal

1548
Princes reject the Interim of Augsburg

1549
Family quarrel over the inheritance

1550
Negotiations between Ferdinand and Charles detract from resolving the Protestant problem

1551
Princes object to the Augsburg Agreement

1552
Protestant princes reform the league under the leadership of Maurice of Saxony and with the aid of French money by the Treaty of Chambord. French invasion necessitates the Truce of Passau with the Protestant princes

1553
Failing to retake Metz, Charles quits Germany, leaving it in Ferdinand's hands

Charles' success was so great that the Catholic princes grew alarmed: a strong emperor threatened their own positions. This fear was heightened at the armed Diet of Augsburg of 1547, when Charles announced the creation of an Imperial League. The league would enforce order in the empire; it was to be a standing army, led by the emperor but paid for by the princes. The princes refused his requests for money; they had no wish to strengthen Charles even further. Most viewed Lutheranism as heresy, but if stopping Lutheranism meant augmenting the emperor's powers, they refused to co-operate. As a consequence, Charles was unable to complete the immediate eradication of Lutheranism.

Lacking the money or manpower to impose his will, Charles proposed a temporary settlement of Germany's religious problems pending the final deliberations of the Council of Trent. His 'interim' solution was basically Catholic, with a few concessions to the Protestants on outward matters, such as accepting the marriage of priests and communion in both kinds. The interim solution alienated his Catholic supporters, who had no wish to see their faith diluted in any way, and if he had hoped to win over the remaining Protestant cities, Charles was equally disappointed: most also rejected the interim solution, and leaders like Bucer left for England. Charles had underestimated everyone's strength of faith.

Charles then made another error of judgement, this time one that alienated his brother. In 1549, he announced that his son Philip would succeed his brother Ferdinand as emperor, on the grounds that Spanish money was needed to resolve the German problem. This infuriated Ferdinand, who had assumed his son, Maximilian, would succeed. The ensuing family quarrel took eight months to resolve and weakened the united Habsburg anti-Lutheran front. By the Augsburg Agreement of 1551, it was finally agreed that the succession should alternate between the two branches of the Habsburg family.

News that the Habsburgs were determining the future of the imperial title in this way incensed the princes: the electors' rights were being ignored by the Habsburg family, who were treating the princes with contempt and the empire as their personal property. This compounded the fact that Charles had acquired Duke Maurice of Saxony as an ally by promising to give him the electoral rights of John Frederick of Saxony, despite the fact that switching electorships in this way was completely outside his power. Now he was also presuming to impose a Spaniard as emperor. The princes objected so strongly that Charles was forced to back down. The Augsburg Agreement was retracted.

Charles then faced further setbacks – the French-sponsored revival of the league under the leadership of Maurice of Saxony, and a French invasion. Viewed as a traitor by most Protestants, Maurice was anxious to redeem himself. He had also been angered at Charles' actions: Philip of Hesse had surrendered to his son-in-law Maurice on the condition that he was not imprisoned, a condition that Charles overrode. As a result of the Treaty of Chambord in 1552, Maurice secured French money for the revived Schmalkaldic League. Henry II of France was a devout Catholic, but he was happy to do anything to avenge the humiliations of his imprisonment in Spain as a child, and he was equally happy to expand France. By the terms of the treaty, Henry invaded Metz, Toul and Verdun, which successfully diverted Charles' attention away from his assault on Protestantism. The revived league itself never defeated Charles, but it did succeed in humiliating him into fleeing to Innsbruck.

The Peace of Passau, 1552

The French invasion presented Charles with the old dilemma of conflicting priorities. He decided to focus on evicting the French, and reluctantly allowed his brother Ferdinand to negotiate a peace with Maurice. The Peace of Passau provisionally guaranteed Lutherans the right of worship and released Philip of Hesse from prison. The peace became permanent in 1555. Maurice himself did not live long to enjoy his success; in 1553, he was shot in the back by one of his former Protestant allies and died, aged 32.

ACTIVITY
KNOWLEDGE CHECK

Why did Charles receive such limited support from the Catholic princes?

The structure of the empire rendered the princes powerful and the emperor almost powerless. Charles' failure to harness the princes' power therefore in part explains his failure to crush Lutheranism. Ironically, throughout his reign, the majority of the princes remained Catholic, and had they all co-operated with Charles, Lutheranism would probably have been eradicated.

Write notes summarising why the Catholic princes refused to co-operate:

- in the period 1521–29, when Charles wished to enforce the Edict of Worms
- in the period 1547–53, when Charles wished to complete his victory over Lutheranism.

The failure to retake Metz

Metz was of huge strategic importance to Charles, located as it was between his possessions in the Netherlands and in Franche-Comté. For two months, during a very harsh winter, with two feet of snow, he tried to retake the city. He failed, despite having an army of 80,000 against a defending French force of only 6,000, led by the Duke of Guise (helped, incidentally, by the great French surgeon Ambroise Paré – famous for using ligatures after amputations rather than red-hot cauterisation – who was smuggled into the besieged city to help the wounded). Charles eventually abandoned the siege after losing some 20,000 men to disease and cold. Stricken with gout, he was carried away in a litter.

After 1553, Charles simply gave up. He was ill, tired and disillusioned. The triumph at Mühlberg had been followed by one setback after another: the lack of co-operation from the princes over the Imperial League proposal and the interim solution; the bitter family quarrel over the inheritance; the revived Protestant League and the humiliating flight from Innsbruck; and now the failure to retake Metz. He had no resources to continue; he was ill; his brother distrusted him; and the princes' alienation was so complete that none would assist him. Even the papacy was hostile. Charles felt that God had deserted him. In early 1553, he departed for the Netherlands and never returned. He authorised his brother Ferdinand to resolve the situation in Germany.

The Peace of Augsburg, 1555

Ferdinand was a realist. He recognised, as Charles latterly had not, that the emperor relied on and needed the princes' co-operation. Therefore, the princes' liberties and privileges had to be respected. He also recognised that the Protestants would never return to the Catholic faith, the differences were irreconcilable.

The problem Ferdinand faced was that he had very little room for manoeuvre. He had to deliver whatever the princes wanted since he needed their help to restore order to Germany. A situation of near-anarchy prevailed, with an almost complete breakdown of law and order. Ferdinand lacked the means to resolve the situation by force. He depended on the princes, and their preference was for peace. The situation was also urgent: the French already occupied three German cities and were now threatening the Flemish frontier; the Turks were threatening Naples; in March 1555, a Habsburg-hating pope was elected, Paul IV, who was openly prepared to declare war on Charles in order to evict the latter from the Italian peninsula.

So Ferdinand pragmatically agreed to the Peace of Augsburg, which was effectively a more detailed version of the Peace of Passau of 1552. By this, Lutheranism finally achieved legal status in the empire. Under the principle of '*cuius regio, eius religio*' ('whose region, his religion'), each prince had the right to decide whether his territory was to be Catholic or Lutheran. Subjects who objected to their prince's choice were free to emigrate. In cities with a mixed Lutheran and Catholic population, both were to be tolerated. Ecclesiastical land that had been secularised before 1552 could remain in Lutheran hands, but that date was the cut-off point. Any prelate converting in the future would be required to emigrate, leaving their territories behind with their title.

ACTIVITY
KNOWLEDGE CHECK

How far were external wars with France and the Ottoman Empire to blame for Charles' failures in the empire?

On four occasions, Charles tried to deal with the German Protestant issue decisively: 1521; 1530–32; 1539–41; and 1546–52. On each occasion, he failed. Take these in turn and explain:

- why Charles was so well-placed at that time to deal with the Protestants – look at all his advantages and at what he proposed to do

- why Charles was unable to take advantage of that opportunity, or implement successfully his chosen course of action. Distinguish between external threats, which demanded his attention, and other reasons or problems, including errors on his part, that explain his failure.

SOURCE
7

The Peace of Augsburg, 1555.

15. In order to bring peace to the Holy Roman Empire of the Germanic Nation between the Roman Imperial Majesty and the Electors, Princes and Estates, let neither his Imperial Majesty nor the Electors, Princes, etc., do any violence or harm to any estate of the empire on the account of the Augsburg Confession, but let them enjoy their religious belief, liturgy and ceremonies as well as their estates and other rights and privileges in peace …

16. Likewise the Estates espousing the Augsburg Confession shall let all the Estates and Princes who cling to the old religion live in absolute peace and in the enjoyment of all their estates, rights, and privileges.

17. However, all such as do not belong to the two above named religions shall not be included in the present peace but be totally excluded from it.

18. Where an archbishop, bishop or prelate or any other priest of our old religion shall abandon the same, his… benefices together with all their income and revenues… shall be abandoned by him without any further objection or delay. The chapter… shall elect a person espousing the old religion who may enter on the possession and enjoyment of all the rights and incomes of the place without any further hindrance…

19. Some of the abbeys, monasteries and other ecclesiastical estates having been confiscated and turned into churches, schools, and charitable institutions, it is herewith ordained that such estates which their original owners had not possessed at the time of the Treaty of Passau [1552] shall be comprised in the present treaty of peace.

24. In case our subjects whether belonging to the old religion or the Augsburg confession should intend leaving their homes with their wives and children in order to settle in another, they shall be hindered neither in the sale of their estates after due payment of the local taxes nor injured in their honour.

ACTIVITY
KNOWLEDGE CHECK

The Peace of Augsburg, 1555

This chapter opened with a description of the Peace Festival that is celebrated in Augsburg on 8 August every year, during which prizes are awarded to Peace Makers who promote interfaith harmony. The festival is a direct link back to the Peace of Augsburg, signed in Augsburg 350 years ago.

Activity – debate and discussion

Read Source 7. Decide where you would place the Treaty of Augsburg on a continuum that measures the extent to which it was tolerant (in the sense of celebrating religious diversity and promoting 'interfaith harmony') or intolerant (in the sense of being bigoted and illiberal towards other faiths).

Intolerant ◄─────────────────────────────────────► Tolerant

Charles was a devout Catholic and, in his eyes, the Peace of Augsburg represented his failure to fulfil the pledge to eradicate Lutheranism that he had made 35 years earlier at the Diet of Worms. In January 1556, he abdicated in favour of Ferdinand and retired to a monastery in Spain, where he devoted his time to repairing clocks. (It took the diet two years to ratify Charles' unilateral decision that Ferdinand was the next emperor.)

The Peace of Augsburg was an unexpected success. Ferdinand probably agreed to it as a temporary expedient in a desperate situation, but it kept the peace in Germany for over 60 years. This was remarkable compared to the religious turmoil that convulsed France, for example, in the late 16th century. The treaty really worked. In 1580, the French writer Michel de Montaigne visited Augsburg, and he was genuinely moved to see a happy coexistence of faiths in the city. His excellent landlord at the Linden Tree Inn was in a mixed marriage – he was Catholic and his wife was Lutheran. Their marriage showed how easy it was for the moderate side of each faith to live in ecumenical peace, but Montaigne also saw the extremes of both sides coexisting in Augsburg. He visited the new Lutheran church, walls completely bare of all images except biblical verses, and twice as well attended as the Catholic churches. In the very traditional Catholic Church of the Holy Cross, he was then privileged to see a holy relic, a miraculous host (or Eucharist wafer) that had turned into flesh 'with the redness of skin'.

If the Peace of Augsburg had a flaw, it was that it was insufficiently tolerant. It only permitted Lutheranism and Catholicism; Anabaptism remained anathema and no allowance was made for other versions of Protestantism. This last point was ultimately to be its undoing, but peace prevailed until 1618.

THINKING
HISTORICALLY Causation (5b)

Significant factors behind Charles' decision to agree to the Peace of Augsburg, 1555

Historical events usually have many causes. Some are crucial, while some are less important. For some historical questions, it is important to understand exactly what role certain factors played in causing historical change.

The structure of the empire	Charles' failure to evict the French from Metz, 1552–53	Charles' illnesses and mental breakdown, 1553–55
Luther's pamphlet *Against the Robbing and Murdering Hordes of Peasants*, 1525	Charles' lack of money	The election of a hostile pope, Paul IV, 1555

Answer the following questions on your own.

The timing of the Peace of Augsburg

- In what ways did the French seizure of Metz precipitate the Peace of Augsburg?
- How important was the election of Paul IV in explaining the timing of the Peace of Augsburg?

The nature of the Peace of Augsburg

- Would the nature of the Peace of Augsburg have been different if the Peasants' Revolt had not taken place?
- How far did the structure of the empire affect the nature of the Peace of Augsburg? Would the Peace have been different if the position of emperor had been stronger?

The timing or the nature of the Peace of Augsburg

- Did lack of money affect the *timing* or the *nature* of the Peace of Augsburg?
- Did Charles' fragile health affect the *timing* or the *nature* of the Peace of Augsburg?

HOW DID THE PAPACY RESPOND TO LUTHERANISM?

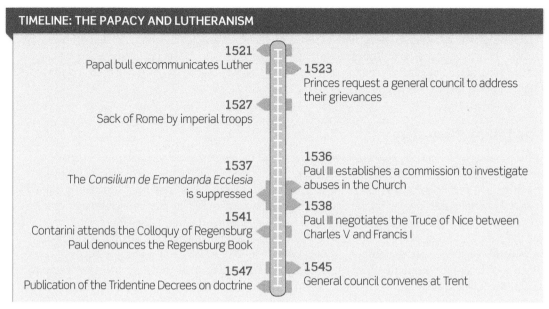

TIMELINE: THE PAPACY AND LUTHERANISM

- **1521** Papal bull excommunicates Luther
- **1523** Princes request a general council to address their grievances
- **1527** Sack of Rome by imperial troops
- **1536** Paul III establishes a commission to investigate abuses in the Church
- **1537** The *Consilium de Emendanda Ecclesia* is suppressed
- **1538** Paul III negotiates the Truce of Nice between Charles V and Francis I
- **1541** Contarini attends the Colloquy of Regensburg Paul denounces the Regensburg Book
- **1547** Publication of the Tridentine Decrees on doctrine
- **1545** General council convenes at Trent

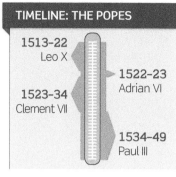

TIMELINE: THE POPES

- **1513–22** Leo X
- **1522–23** Adrian VI
- **1523–34** Clement VII
- **1534–49** Paul III

Throughout the 1520s and 1530s, Charles pursued the princes' request for a general council. He was convinced that reform of abuses in the Church would undermine support for the Lutheran movement; at the very least, it would win the princes' support in enforcing the Edict of Worms. When Charles' old tutor, Adrian of Utrecht, was elected as Pope Adrian VI in 1522, the council proposal looked as though it might happen. Adrian was incorruptible and immediately announced his intention to reform the papal curia. However, within 18 months, Adrian was dead. His successor was Clement VII, Leo X's cousin, and another member of the self-seeking Medici clan. Rather than seeing reform as a way to tackle the Lutheran threat, Clement adhered to Rome's long-held view that a general council was a threat to papal authority. His lack of co-operation also had a great deal to do with politics. He wanted to promote by any means possible the independence of the Papal States. In the early 1520s, he supported the Habsburg forces, but when Charles defeated Francis at the Battle of Pavia, he swapped sides and joined Francis I in an anti-Habsburg alliance, the League of Cognac of 1526. This was an error.

The Sack of Rome

In 1527, without Charles' authority, an imperial army sacked Rome. The 25,000 troops – a motley crew of Spanish, Italian and German mercenaries – were unpaid and thirsty to avenge the death of their commander. Out of control, for weeks they pillaged houses, palaces, convents and churches. Besides money, jewels, gold and silver plate, tapestries and furniture, they took prisoners and demanded ransoms. Clement himself fled from St Peter's through a secret tunnel to the Castel Sant'Angelo, the papal fortress. A month later, he was found hiding in a storeroom and taken prisoner.

AS Level Exam-Style Question Section A

How much weight do you give the evidence in Source 8 for an enquiry into German attitudes towards the papacy during the 1510s and 1520s?

Explain your answer using the source, the information given about it and your own knowledge of the historical context. (12 marks)

Tip

This question requires you to make a judgement, which you then need to justify. Do not sit on the fence in a cautious way!

SOURCE

8 Mercurino da Gattinara, Commissary of the Imperial Army during the Sack of Rome, describes the Sack of Rome, 1527, in a letter to Charles V.

The whole army passed into the city early on that evening of the 6th. As the inhabitants in general relied on it being defended, none of them had fled or removed their property, so that no one of whatever nation, rank, condition, age or sex escaped becoming prisoners – not even women in convents. They were treated without distinction according to the caprice of the soldiery; and after being plundered of all of their effects most of them were compelled by torture or otherwise to pay ransom. ... All the church ornaments are stolen, the sacred vessels thrown about, the relics gone to destruction – for the troops, in abstracting their precious receptacles, heeded these as no more than as many bits of wood; even the shrine of the sancta sanctorum [the 'holy of holies' – possibly a reference to the tomb of St Peter] was sacked, although regarded with particular reverence. St Peter's church and the papal palace have been made into stables. I feel confident that your Majesty as a Catholic and most Christian Emperor will feel displeasure at these gross outrages and insults to the Catholic religion, the Apostolic See and the city of Rome. In truth everyone is convinced that all this has happened as a judgement from God on the great tyranny and disorders of the papal court; but however this may be, there has been vast destruction, for which no redress can be had from your Majesty's arm and authority. This army has no head, no division, no discipline, no organisation, but everyone behaves according to his own fancy. ... The leaders do what they can but to little purpose; for in entering Rome the lansquenets [German mercenary soldiers] have conducted themselves like true Lutherans. ... Most of the troops are enriched by the enormous booty, amounting to many millions of gold. A majority of the Spaniards, it is supposed, will retire to Naples with their spoil.

The Sack of Rome was a turning point. It shocked Catholic Europe. Many interpreted it as a sign of God's displeasure, and that the Church must reform itself. From Charles' point of view, it ensured a marginally more co-operative papacy. Clement VII agreed to crown Charles as Holy Roman Emperor. At Charles' request, he also refused to grant Henry VIII the annulment he wanted from Catherine of Aragon, Charles' aunt, and he sent Cardinal Campeggio to attend the Diet of Augsburg of 1530. However, the Sack of Rome did not immediately result in a council. Clement lacked decisiveness and still feared Charles' power. Once free from the latter's control, he returned to wooing France. His successor was different.

Paul III (1534–49)

In his personal life, Paul displayed all the worldliness of his Renaissance predecessors. He had mistresses and at least five children; he made two of his teenage grandsons cardinals; he enjoyed fireworks and carnivals; he spent lavishly on art. In 1534, he commissioned Michelangelo to paint *The Last Judgement* on the end wall of the Sistine Chapel. The choice of *The Last Judgement* as a theme was revealing. Worldliness aside, Paul was also well aware of the failings of the Church and he could see the need for urgent internal reform. He tried to call a general council in 1536, but was thwarted by the outbreak of the Third Habsburg–Valois War (1536–38). At home he had more success. He ordered 80 bishops living in Rome to return to their dioceses. He gave his support to new religious orders, including the Capuchins (1529), who emulated St Francis in preaching to the poor and caring for the sick, and the Ursulines (1535), who were devoted to girls' education. Most importantly, Paul appointed as cardinals five members of the **Oratory of Divine Love**, including Gasparo Contarini, Pietro Carafa and the Englishman Reginald Pole. Among these there were two views on the best way to move forward with reform – the moderate wing held the upper hand until 1541.

> **KEY TERM**
>
> **Oratory of Divine Love**
> The Oratory was a brotherhood of about 50 high-ranking clerics and noble laymen that had been founded in Rome c1514–17. It pre-dated Luther, in other words. Members devoted their lives to austere living and charity, hoping to regenerate the Church by setting an example.

The moderates – the 'spirituali'	The hardliners – the 'zelanti'
Moderates like Contarini and Pole wanted reform of abuses *and* reform of doctrine. They leaned towards St Augustine's teachings and had some sympathy for the Protestant doctrine of *sola fide*. They believed that a compromise with Lutherans was possible, and they hoped to reunite the Church.	Hardliners like Carafa (who became Pope Paul IV in 1555) wanted reform of abuses only. They accepted Thomist teachings on salvation and wanted no change in doctrine. They rejected any compromise with Lutherans. Lutheranism was a heresy that had to be crushed.

The *Consilium de Emendanda Ecclesia*, 1537

In 1536, Paul set up a nine-man commission to investigate the failings of the Church and to make recommendations. It was chaired by Contarini and included three other Oratory members. After nine months' work, the commission produced its report, the *Consilium de Emendanda Ecclesia* or 'Advice on Reform of the Church'. The report was exceptionally hard-hitting. It sharply criticised low standards in Rome itself, the Mother Church where 'the worship of God and honesty of manners should flourish'. It attacked the abuse of simony, or selling posts to the highest bidder. No care was being taken at all in the appointment of priests, who might be 'totally unlearned, of the vilest of origins and appalling morals, or under age'.

Paul suppressed the report. While he agreed in principle with its findings, in practice the papacy could not afford to lose further income. Since the Sack of Rome, it had relied more than ever on the sale of offices because it had lost everything. Anyway, the report's recommendations would have been impossible to implement. Europe's monarchs might pay attention to a general council, but they would ignore a small Italian committee. Since securing co-operation between Europe's warring Catholic monarchs was going to be essential if a council was even to convene, let alone succeed, Paul assumed a position of political neutrality, the first pope to do so for a long time. In 1538, he sailed to Nice and personally negotiated a ten-year truce between Francis and Charles.

At the same time, Paul III continued to support the moderate reformers' ambitions. In 1541, he permitted Contarini to attend the Colloquy at Regensburg, called by Charles in an attempt to reconcile Catholics and Protestants. However, Contarini exceeded his mandate, especially with the compromise doctrine of 'double justification'. Paul rejected the *Regensburg Book* absolutely and ended the moderates' attempt to reunite the Church. Contarini retired. He died in 1542.

The Council of Trent, 1545

From then on, Paul adopted the hardliners' approach and went on the offensive. He supported Carafa's proposal for a Roman Inquisition modelled on the Spanish Inquisition, to root out heresy in Italy. There would still be a general council, if peace could be achieved, but Paul now held a very different view from that of the emperor on its purpose. For Charles, a council's prime function was still reform of abuses as a preliminary to reconciliation with the Protestants, possible as long as doctrine remained vague; for Paul, the function was now for the sharp definition of Catholic doctrine prior to an all-out war on heresy. Then abuses would be tackled. Paul was the realist here: doctrinal differences between Catholicism and Protestantism were never going to be bridged. The abortive Regensburg Colloquy had proved that.

Nevertheless, Paul did not wish to alienate Charles. When the Treaty of Crepy ended the Fourth Habsburg–Valois War in 1544 and both sides finally agreed to a council, Paul diplomatically suggested that it should meet in Trent – in imperial territory, but on the Italian side of the Alps. The Council of Trent opened in December 1545. However, only 31 bishops attended the opening session (all Italian and just five percent of those entitled) and the agenda soon made clear that the hardliners' approach was dominant. Over the next 18 months, the Council of Trent closed the doors to reconciliation with Protestantism. The **Tridentine Decrees** were just as difficult for moderate Catholic reformers. Doctrines that had previously been slurred or vague were now defined and detailed. Trent labelled as heretics anyone who held beliefs that did not precisely conform. Rome's offensive could now proceed.

> **KEY TERM**
>
> **Tridentine Decrees**
> The decrees of the Council of Trent, 1545-63.

SOURCE

9 The Tridentine Decrees, 1546–47.

[Christian truth is] contained in written books and unwritten traditions, which were received by the Apostles from the mouth of Christ himself, or... at the dictation of the Holy Spirit, and as it were, passed on from hand to hand until they came down to us. ... This Council receives and venerates, with equal pious affection and reverence, all the books of both the New and the Old Testaments, together with the said traditions...

No one, relying on his own judgement and twisting sacred Scripture to his own ends, should dare to interpret sacred Scripture in a way contrary to the sense which Holy Mother Church (whose office it is to judge the true sense and interpretation of the sacred scriptures) has held and now holds...

If anyone should deny that the guilt of original sin is remitted through the grace of our Lord Jesus Christ conferred in baptism... let him be **anathema**.

If anyone should say that justifying faith is nothing other than trust in the divine mercy which remits sins for Christ's sake, or that we are justified by such faith alone, let him be anathema.

If anyone should say that for their good works... the just ought not to expect mercy and hope for an eternal reward from God, through his mercy and the merits of Jesus Christ... let him be anathema.

If anyone should say that the good works of a justified man are so exclusively the gifts of God that they are not also the good merits of the man himself... let him be anathema.

If anyone should say that, in the holy sacrament of the Eucharist, Christ, the only begotten Son of God, ought not to be adored with the worship of divine honour... or that those who thus adore him are idolaters, let him be anathema.

> **KEY TERM**
>
> **Anathema**
> Cursed by the Church.

ACTIVITY
KNOWLEDGE CHECK

The Tridentine Decrees
Taking each of the decrees in turn, state the Catholic doctrine being defined and the Lutheran doctrine that is, by implication, being declared anathema.

Conclusion

Though the Council of Trent continued to meet intermittently until 1563, its opening sessions were probably the most important. In defining so sharply what Catholic doctrine was, the papacy had provided a crucial weapon for Rome's war on heresy. Lutheranism in Italy was persecuted into extinction. However, in the Holy Roman Empire, the Peace of Augsburg prevailed. One-third of the population of Germany is Lutheran to this day.

ACTIVITY
SUMMARY

Who or what was responsible for the failure to eliminate Lutheranism?

Work in groups, each taking responsibility for one of the following factors:

- Charles V
- Protestant princes
- Catholic princes
- the French
- the Ottomans
- the papacy.

Each group should argue the case that their factor bears chief responsibility for the failure to eliminate Lutheranism. The winner of the debate will be the group that not only puts its case, but also successfully undermines other groups' arguments.

 WIDER READING

Atkins, S. 'Charles V and the Turks', *History Today*, December 1980

MacDonald, S. *Charles V: Ruler, Dynast and Defender of the Faith*, Hodder & Stoughton (1992)

Randell, K. *Luther and the German Reformation, 1517–55*, Hodder & Stoughton (1988)

Randell, K. *The Catholic and Counter Reformations*, Hodder & Stoughton (1990)

Richardson, G. 'Charles V – universal soldier', *History Review*, December 2000

Styles, A. *The Ottoman Empire 1450–1700*, Hodder & Stoughton (1989)

Tuchman, B. *The March of Folly: From Troy to Vietnam*, Random House (1984)

Woodward, G. 'The Ottomans in Europe', *History Review*, March 2001

Preparing for your AS Level Paper 2 exam

Advance planning

1. Draw up a timetable for your revision and try to keep to it. Spread your timetable over a number of weeks, and aim to cover four or five topics each week.
2. Spend longer on topics that you have found difficult, and revise them several times.
3. Above all, do not try to limit your revision by attempting to 'question spot'. Try to be confident about all aspects of your Paper 2 work, because this will ensure that you have a choice of questions in Section B.

Paper 2 overview:

AS Paper 2	Time: 1 hour 30 minutes	
Section A	Answer 1 compulsory two-part sources question	8+12 marks = 20 marks
Section B	Answer 1 question from a choice of 3	20 marks
	Total marks =	40 marks

You should familiarise yourself with the layout of the paper by looking at the examples published by Edexcel. The questions for each section are followed by eight pages of lined paper where you should write your answer.

Section A questions

Each of the two parts of the question will focus on one of the two contemporary sources provided. The sources together will total around 300 words. The (a) question, worth 8 marks, will be in the form: 'Why is Source 1 useful for an enquiry into…?' The (b) question, worth 12 marks, will be in the form: 'How much weight do you give the evidence of Source 2 for an enquiry into…?' In both your answers you should address the value of the content of the source, and then its nature, origin and purpose. Finally, you should use your own knowledge of the context of the source to assess its value.

Section B questions

These questions ask you to reach a judgement on an aspect of the topic studied. The questions will have the form, for example, of 'How far…', 'To what extent…' or 'How accurate is it to say…'. The questions can deal with historical concepts such as cause, consequence, change, continuity, similarity, difference and significance. You should consider the issue raised in the question, consider other relevant issues, and then conclude with an overall judgement.

The timescale of the questions could be as short as a single year or even a single event (an example from Option 2C.2 could be, 'To what extent was Russia's involvement in the First World War responsible for the fall of the Provisional Government in 1917?'). The timescale could be longer depending on the historical event or process being examined, but questions are likely to be shorter than those set for Sections A and B in Paper 1.

Use of time

This is an issue that you should discuss with your teachers and fellow students, but here are some suggestions for you.

1. Do not write solidly for 45 minutes on each question. For Section A it is essential that you have a clear understanding of the content of each source, the points being made, and the nature, origin and purpose of each source. You might decide to spend up to ten minutes reading the sources and drawing up your plan, and 35 minutes writing your answer.
2. For Section B answers you should spend a few minutes working out what the question is asking you to do, and drawing up a plan of your answer before you begin to write your response.

Preparing for your AS Level exams

Paper 2: AS Level sample answer with comments

Section A

Part A requires you to:

- identify evidence in the source that is of value for the enquiry; some will be explicit, and some will have to be inferred
- use your own knowledge of the historical context to verify that this evidence is accurate
- comment on the ways in which the author and nature of the source add value to the enquiry.

Read Source 2, Chapter 3, page 219 – Aleander's letter to Cardinal de Medici, February 1521.

Why is this source valuable to the historian for an enquiry into Luther's popularity in Germany by 1521?

Explain your answer using the source, the information given about it and your own knowledge of the historical context. (8 marks)

Average student answer

This is a letter written by the Papal Legate Aleander to the pope's cousin. This source is very valuable because it shows just how popular Luther was by 1521. Aleander says that nine-tenths of the population support Luther. He also says that pictures of Luther are selling out so quickly that even he, the papal legate, was not able to get hold of a copy. He states that Luther is adored blindly by the Germans – the halo on one picture would support this view of Luther being adored. These details are important in establishing the level of Luther's success, which was extraordinary by 1521.

> This is making very good use of the evidence that is actually there. However, more could be inferred from this passage about why Luther was so popular.

Other knowledge confirms that Luther was indeed popular. In this way, this source is valuable because it confirms what other sources say. For example, when Luther arrived at Worms, people touched his robes as though they were touching a saint. Thousands of copies of works written by Luther were on sale. He had caused so much disturbance that the emperor devoted a special session at the Diet of Worms to him.

Aleander is probably speaking the truth for several reasons; as a church man he should not be lying. Furthermore, as papal legate, he would be expected to report accurately back to Rome. He clearly does not like Germany, so the fact that he makes Luther out to be such a wild success suggests that he is telling the truth. Normally one would not exaggerate the success of the opposition. Also, Aleander is writing a letter, not a public document. Therefore he has no reason to exaggerate, unless it was to make his letter more exciting.

> The response is commenting on the author and the source in this paragraph, which is good. Unfortunately, some stereotypical judgements are made. For example, to say that the source is accurate because churchmen do not lie, or to suggest that people always tell the truth in letters, are both points that can be challenged.

In all, I would regard this letter as a very valuable source of information, especially because it was written by one of Luther's enemies.

Verdict

This is an average answer because:

- it has selected evidence that is relevant and valuable for the enquiry, which shows a fairly sound understanding of the source
- it has used some contextual knowledge to confirm that this information is accurate

- it tries to use some reasoning to evaluate the worth of the author and a source of this nature.

Use the feedback on this answer to rewrite it, making as many improvements as you can.

Paper 2: AS Level sample answer with comments

Section A

Part B requires you to:

- assess the 'weight' (or value) of both the author as a witness and a source of this nature
- extract any evidence that the source provides, both directly and by inference, that is relevant for the enquiry specified in the question
- use your own knowledge to confirm that this evidence is typical/accurate, or to challenge it on the grounds that it is of limited use/inaccurate
- make a final judgement about the weight (or value) of the source for the enquiry specified in the question, based on what you have decided about the origin, nature and contents of the source.

Read Source 11, Chapter 2, page 206 – Martin Bucer's letter about his meeting with Luther in 1518.

How much weight do you give the evidence of this source for an enquiry into the reasons why people supported Luther in the period 1517–21?

Explain your answer using the source, the information given about it and your own knowledge of the historical context. (12 marks)

Average student answer

This source is valuable because it has much relevant evidence for an enquiry into why people supported Luther in the period 1517–21. Some people clearly supported Luther due to his charismatic character, with friendly and likeable qualities. For example, Martin Bucer 'left his monastery', suggesting Luther had an immense influence on people. Bucer was a Dominican friar but he speaks positively of Luther who was an Augustinian, giving this source reliability. The letter also says Luther's words were 'drawn from the store of divine scriptures', which 'led them all to admire him'. This is valid because Luther's 'sola scriptura' approach was popular amongst people, as it freed them from indulgences and the Church's other charges.

However, the source may not be reliable and therefore loses value because some of its information is incorrect. For example, it suggests that Luther is making Erasmus' ideas explicit, but in actual fact this was not true. Luther drew his methods from Erasmus ('ad fontes'), but otherwise they did not really remotely have the same views. Erasmus argued that the Church should be reformed and improved, not destroyed. The letter also states that Luther's 'patience was beyond compare'. This statement is false because Luther was known to be 'hot blooded in temperament'. Bucer also said Luther's 'pleasantness was remarkable', but Luther could be very crude: his 1525 pamphlet against peasants was abusive.

In conclusion, the letter does not carry a lot of weight as evidence for why people supported Luther in the period 1517–21 because the personal reasons that Bucer gives for liking Luther do not represent the main views of the nation. The letter does not consider German grievances and financial distress.

> This is a strong opening sentence – it makes a judgement that directly reflects the question. The central part of the paragraph is also good; the weight of the author as a witness is assessed. However, since the paragraph starts and ends by talking about evidence, it seems a little illogical to talk about the author in the middle. Planning is needed.

> Note the outside knowledge here, used to support challenges to the source on the grounds that it is inaccurate. However, that knowledge does need to be accurate: Erasmus was silent on Luther in the period 1517–21.

The first sentence of this conclusion directly contradicts the first sentence of the introduction. It is as though there was a change of mind halfway through writing the answer. Plan the whole answer first, so that you know your judgement before you write, and then stick to it. The last sentence is challenging the source on the grounds that it is of limited use because Bucer's views are atypical, but this point should have appeared earlier.

Verdict

This is an average answer because:

- it demonstrates some understanding of the source and of the question: it selects material that supports relevant analytical points; it selects material to support valid inferences
- it deploys some knowledge of the historical context to support inferences
- it evaluates the source: it explains what weight to give the letter in

light of its content (but it could do so more logically, for example, by keeping all the points about evidence from the source together in one paragraph) and it addresses the value that can be put on Bucer as an author (though not in an entirely logical way: one minute Bucer is reliable, the next he is incorrect).

Use the feedback on this answer to rewrite it, making as many improvements as you can.

Paper 2: AS Level sample answer with comments

Section A

Part A requires you to:

- identify evidence in the source that is of value for the enquiry; some will be explicit, and some will have to be inferred
- use your own knowledge of the historical context to verify that this evidence is accurate
- comment on the ways in which the author and nature of the source adds value to the enquiry.

Read Source 2, Chapter 3, page 219 – Aleander's letter to Cardinal de Medici, February 1521.

Why is this source valuable to the historian for an enquiry into Luther's popularity in Germany by 1521?

Explain your answer using the source, the information given about it and your own knowledge of the historical context. (8 marks)

Strong student answer

This source provides immensely valuable information about the scale and nature of support for Luther by 1521. Support for Luther was clearly very widespread: Aleander explicitly talks about the whole of Germany being in revolt and 'nine-tenths raise the war-cry, Luther!'. The fact that woodcuts depicting Luther were sold out 'in a trice' and that Germans were in 'blind adoration' of him adds to the view that Luther was very popular. Aleander wrote in an exaggerated way, but other evidence supports his view that Luther was very popular: about 300,000 printed items about Luther were in circulation by 1521. His pamphlet 'To the German Nobility of the Christian Nation' sold 4,000 copies in two weeks. Other accounts mention that thousands cheered Luther on his way to Worms. Copies of the woodcuts described still exist and Aleander was clearly observant, since he used accurate detail.

> The opening is strong – it directly reflects the question. Valuable evidence is extracted, with short pithy quotations, placed to support a point. The student uses other knowledge to verify the accuracy of this evidence.

Aleander also provides some indirect evidence about why Luther was popular. The woodcut of Luther 'with a halo' associated him with the fact that a holy man was expected. Another woodcut showed Luther with Hutten, who was a well-known German nationalist. This was a subtle reference to the fact that many Germans thought Luther was standing up to Rome, whose exploitation of Germany was widely resented. Indirectly, Aleander is also suggesting that Luther's doctrines appealed. The phrase 'Champion of Christian Freedom' may be a reference to Luther's 1520 pamphlet 'On the Liberty of a Christian Man', or the fact that he was liberating people from the 'Babylonish Captivity of the Church'.

> Notice the use of language for evidence that can only be inferred – 'indirect evidence', 'suggesting that', 'a subtle reference to' – and the use of 'other knowledge' to support these inferences.

The position that Aleander held adds further value to this source. As the papal delegate responsible for publishing the papal bull excommunicating Luther, he had been travelling around Germany since June 1520. His letter was not just based on his experiences in Worms, since he also referred to his time in Augsburg. In other words, he was probably as aware as anyone in power could be what Germany as a whole was feeling. The other reason for the letter being valuable lies in the fact that it was not in Aleander's interests to exaggerate Luther's support: he had been given the mission to silence Luther, yet this letter is proof that he had failed. The fact that he is so alarmist suggests he was very worried indeed about Luther's popularity and he wanted Rome to know, which is why this letter was sent to Pope Leo's cousin. Alternatively, it is possible that Aleander might be making excuses for his failure, by deliberately making the situation in Germany seem hopelessly out of control. This analysis would explain his over-the-top tone, but it does not undermine other evidence that Luther was very popular indeed by 1521.

> References to the author's position and purpose are used to provide another reason why this source has value.

Verdict

This is a strong answer because:

- it makes direct use of evidence in the source, including the drawing of inferences

- it deploys other knowledge selectively and effectively, to confirm what has been extracted from the source
- it evaluates the source relevantly, by commenting on the additional value brought by the author's position and purpose in writing.

Paper 2: AS Level sample answer with comments

Section A

Part B requires you to:

- assess the 'weight' (or value) of both the author as a witness and a source of this nature
- extract any evidence that the source provides, both directly and by inference, that is relevant for the enquiry specified in the question
- use your own knowledge to confirm that this evidence is typical/accurate, or to challenge it on the grounds that it is of limited use/inaccurate
- make a final judgement about the weight (or value) of the source for the enquiry specified in the question, based on what you have decided about the origin, nature and contents of the source.

Read Source 11, Chapter 2, page 206 – Martin Bucer's letter about his meeting with Luther in 1518.

How much weight do you give the evidence of this source for an enquiry into the reasons why people supported Luther in the period 1517–21?

Explain your answer using the source, the information given about it and your own knowledge of the historical context. (12 marks)

> This is a strong opening that sets forth a judgement. This suggests that the student has planned their answer and has decided on the conclusion. This is far better than a judgement tagged on the end as an afterthought.

Strong student answer

This source carries some value for an enquiry into the reasons why people supported Luther in this period, especially because of its author, but its overall weight is undermined because its scope is so narrow.

Bucer was a Dominican, like Tetzel, so one might have expected him to express antipathy to an Augustinian. The fact that Bucer was in favour of Luther suggests that he is a reliable witness. He also carries weight because he was clearly academic: he refers to Erasmus and Early Church Fathers. Bucer was not reporting gossip or hearsay, since he was present. He was writing a private letter, which again adds weight to the source's value. However, Bucer was not a typical German, since he belonged to the educated elite. He was writing about one event, in early 1518, attended only by other members of that elite, and he makes no reference to other events in the period 1518–21.

> This paragraph provides a balanced evaluation of the weight of the author, and addresses the nature and timing of the source. It also includes some outside knowledge which roots the answer – it makes it more believable.

As evidence for why people supported Luther, the content of this source has some value. It shows that Luther was a charismatic, powerful speaker. Bucer praises Luther's 'lucid' explanations. He 'easily led them all to admire him'. What really attracted Bucer was the depth of Luther's scriptural knowledge and the fact that he seemed to be taking Erasmus to his logical conclusion. One can infer that Luther's popularity in part rested on existing humanist criticisms of scholasticism and clerical abuses. Bucer was already an anti-scholastic humanist since he was delighted that 'those small minded writers of Wittenberg have been scorned to a man'. Bucer was won over by Luther, therefore, because he was leaning in that direction on intellectual grounds already.

> It is best to use very short extracts from the sources. Avoid copying out chunks or even whole sentences. Rather, just select the phrase that you think will support the point you are making. Think of it as precision surgery.

Unfortunately, Bucer makes no reference to the reasons why Luther was so popular with common people: the anti-Italian climate in Germany; the expectation that a holy man would appear; and the 95 Theses. Luther was a hero chiefly for making a stand against Rome's exploitation of Germany. The value of this letter is therefore confined to the reasons why Luther appealed to educated young German humanists. The letter shows how Luther's theological knowledge and skill as an orator drew him support from such men, but also shows the importance of prior humanist criticisms of the Church and scholasticism. Luther could be persuasive, but the audience was already receptive.

> Good use of outside knowledge here to support the judgement that the source has a narrow scope. Though the content is almost certainly reliable, it was probably not typical of the reasons why people supported Luther.

Verdict

This is a strong answer because:

- it extracts evidence that is of value for the enquiry, including inferences
- it deploys other knowledge selectively and effectively, both to confirm the value of the source and to show its limitations
- it makes an overall judgement about the weight of the source for this enquiry, and it provides a balanced insight into the value of the author for this line of enquiry.

Paper 2: AS Level sample answer with comments

Section B

These questions assess your understanding of the period in depth. They will ask you about the content you learned about in the four key themes, and may ask about more than one theme. For these questions, remember to:

- give an analytical, not a descriptive, response
- support your points with evidence
- cover the whole time period specified in the question
- come to a substantiated judgement.

To what extent did hostility towards the papacy in Germany cause the German Reformation in the years to 1521? (20 marks)

Average student answer

Attacks on the papacy were exceptionally popular in early 16th century Germany. The scandalous behaviour of the Renaissance popes was mocked, while Rome's power in Germany and Rome's exploitation of Germany were deeply resented. Without this level of hostility, Luther's protest against indulgences in 1517 might have gone unnoticed. It is therefore accurate to say that hostility to the papacy caused the German Reformation.

The popularity in Germany of anti-papal woodcuts like 'The Papal Ass' and satires like Erasmus' 'Julius Exclusus' demonstrate the low reputation of the papacy in the 30 years prior to the Reformation. This lack of respect was partly caused by the scandalous personal lives of the three Renaissance popes. Self-interest, greed and vice seemed to be their key characteristics: Alexander VI had seven children and a reputation for murder; Julius II shocked Europe by leading his own troops into battle; and Leo X lavished money on his family, art and a luxurious lifestyle. These popes were failing in their duty to lead Christendom; clerical abuses like pluralism, non-residency and ignorance were ignored, or indeed actively promoted. For example, Leo sold Albert of Mainz the dispensation to be Archbishop of Mainz when he was already Archbishop of Magdeburg.

Rome – embodied by these popes – was also a target for hatred because it was so powerful in Germany, probably more so than anywhere else in Europe because of the vacuum of central authority. The Church controlled one-quarter of the land and three of the electorships. The Church had huge legal power, and clerical privileges like exemption from taxes caused deep resentment. In 1513, the craft guilds of Cologne rebelled against their city council and their list of grievances focused on clerical privileges. The power of the Church extended even to everyday life: work was forbidden on 100 Holy Days, a fact resented by employers.

The opening sentences of this introduction are strong because they refer directly to the question, and they steer the essay in a relevant direction. However, as an introduction, there are two flaws. Firstly, the last sentence does not acknowledge that there might be other causes of the German Reformation, nor does it tackle the key issue of whether anti-papalism was the main cause. Ignoring the phrase 'To what extent' will not result in the sort of evaluative judgement required for high marks. The addition of a sentence starting 'However…' would inject a more analytical thrust. Secondly, the introduction ignores the fact that the question requires coverage up to 1521.

The opening sentence in this paragraph is good: the reference here to how the papacy was seen in Germany is clearly relevant.

The use of exact evidence to support points is good practice. However, given the shortage of time and the need to extend the range of the argument, such evidence should be selective and more briefly relayed.

Above all, hostility towards the papacy was based on the widespread belief that Rome exploited Germany financially. Since the empire lacked a strong central government, it was easier for Rome to exploit than anywhere else in Europe. Rents, taxes, the sales of dispensations, indulgences and offices meant huge amounts of money were drained from Germany every year. Anti-Italian feeling was high, and the papacy was the main target for this anger. This anger was felt at all levels of society: Conrad Celtis talked about the 'yoke of servitude' that Rome imposed, and Germany being 'emptied of its wonderful resources' in his inaugural address to the University of Ingoldstadt in 1492.

These paragraphs all open with sentences that refer directly back to the question, which is good practice. So too is the use of the phrase 'above all', because it is evaluative: the *main* cause of anti-papalism has been identified. However, in continuing to support the notion that *only* hostility to the papacy caused the Reformation, the response is missing opportunities to argue and evaluate.

Martin Luther visited Rome in 1510, on business for his Augustinian order. What he saw there appalled him and may have influenced his subsequent denunciation of the papacy. In October 1517, when he was Professor of Theology at Wittenberg University, he wrote 95 Theses attacking the sale of indulgences by Johann Tetzel on scriptural grounds. He wrote in Latin, intending his Theses for debate amongst academics. However, the Theses were taken down, translated into German, and sold.

This paragraph is descriptive: it narrates events and does little to move the analysis forward. It also contains an error, because there is no evidence that Luther was appalled by what he saw in Rome, nor did he see the pope. At the time he behaved like a devout pilgrim.

The immediate and widespread popularity of Luther's Theses can be largely explained by the level of anti-papalism in Germany. Luther's objections to indulgences were theological, but his Theses that a truly Christian pope would help people in purgatory rather than exploit them, or use his own money to build the St Peter's Basilica, caught the popular imagination. Ordinary Germans were being tricked into handing over their savings to a foreign ruler, the pope in Rome. Luther became Germany's new hero, for making a stand against Rome.

When Aleander, the pope's delegate to Germany, arrived in Worms in 1521, he wrote that nine-tenths of Germany 'raise the war cry Luther', while the other tenth cried 'Death to the Roman Curia'. Luther's popularity and the German Reformation would have been inconceivable without the high level of hostility to the papacy that already existed in Germany.

This conclusion provides the sole reference to events after 1517, which is inadequate given that the question requires coverage 'in the years to 1521'. It also simply reasserts that hostility to the papacy caused the Reformation, ignoring a multitude of other possible causes. No effort is made to weigh up the relative merit of these causes.

Verdict

This is an average answer because:

- features of the period that are relevant to the question are analysed, though the wider demands of the question have not been recognised
- it includes accurate, in-depth knowledge, but the answer lacks coverage of the range of causes and material that would help to create an argument

- the final judgement is more of an assertion, repeated from the introduction, rather than the climax to a carefully constructed evaluative argument.
- the answer is organised and communication is clear.

Use the feedback on this answer to rewrite it, making as many improvements as you can.

Paper 2: AS Level sample answer with comments

Section B

These questions assess your understanding of the period in depth. They will ask you about the content you learned about in the four key themes, and may ask about more than one theme. For these questions, remember to:

- give an analytical, not a descriptive, response
- support your points with evidence
- cover the whole time period specified in the question
- come to a substantiated judgement.

To what extent did hostility towards the papacy in Germany cause the German Reformation in the years to 1521? (20 marks)

Strong student answer

By 1521, 300,000 items written by Luther were in circulation in Germany. Luther had moved well beyond his initial criticism of indulgences in 1517: his three pamphlets of 1520 denounced Catholic doctrines and institutions, including the papacy. Huge crowds cheered him on his way to Worms: he was a hero, and this was mostly because he stood up to Rome. In other words, hostility towards the papacy certainly helped to explain Luther's reception. However, the German Reformation owed as much to the social, economic, political and cultural climate of the empire at the time, while Luther himself was not primarily motivated by anti-papalism at all.

Germans did have serious grievances with Rome, which had created a climate of fierce hostility to the papacy. The reputation of the papacy was appalling – Alexander VI, Clement VII and Leo X were all seen as more interested in favouring their families, wealth and war than in leading Christendom. Hostility to the papacy was also about how much power Rome had in the empire: three electors were appointed by Rome; the Church owned one-quarter of Germany. Rome sold offices in Germany to completely unqualified people, and the resulting pluralism meant absenteeism and a neglect of duties. In 1521, at Worms, the princes compiled a list of 102 complaints against the Church – they did not support Luther's demands for changes in beliefs, but they did want changes in practice.

Above all, and the key reason for hostility to the papacy, Germans resented the way that they felt Rome exploited Germany financially. Because of its weak central government, it was being milked for its money in order to pay for the pope's lavish lifestyle and St Peter's Basilica. Everyone resented the financial demands of the Church – the cost of salvation, the payment of tithes, and the fact that they had to pay for everything from baptism to burial. Tetzel's indulgences were typical of this exploitation. A growing sense of German identity lay behind this resentment: how dare Rome exploit the country that had seen off the ancient Romans. (Tacitus' *Germania*.) Hostility to the papacy then mounted in the period 1517–20, partly because of the bullying tactics of Rome, which ineptly attempted to silence Luther with demands that he recant, and threats of excommunication. The more he was bullied, the greater a hero he became in the eyes of German people.

However, the causes of the German Reformation cannot solely be explained by hostility to the papacy. First, lack of respect for individual popes needs to put in some perspective. The reputation of the papacy had been low for decades without causing a crisis. Erasmus' satire 'Julius Exclusus' strongly criticised Julius II, but Erasmus remained a loyal Catholic. Woodcuts like the Papal Ass circulated, but they mocked the papacy rather than demanding its removal. Nor was the level of anti-clericalism that high: the state of the Church in Germany was not uniformly bad. Luther himself belonged to a reformed order, the Augustinian friars. Before

This is a strong opening paragraph, which provides some context and makes clear how far the Reformation had progressed by 1521. The response also challenges the question by suggesting that factors other than hostility towards the papacy were responsible for causing the German Reformation.

The reference to Tacitus' *Germania* needs to be incorporated into a full sentence.

This paragraph shows a very good effort to evaluate the reasons for hostility to the papacy. However, the applicant could do more to show how the resentment at Rome's exploitation of Germany helped to cause the Reformation. Concrete evidence of a direct connection would add weight.

1517, most Germans were content with the teachings of the Church. There had been no heresy trials in Germany since 1470, and there is a great deal of evidence of real devotion: an increase in pilgrimages, the number of confraternities, the building of new churches, the collecting of relics, the buying of indulgences, etc. People were devout, more so than ever. In other words, only one aspect of hostility to Rome – anger at its financial exploitation of Germany – helps to explain the reception given to Luther.

Other reasons besides hostility to Rome might explain the massive support given to Luther's ideas in the period 1517–21. For example, many Germans were anticipating some sort of dramatic change. Omens had been predicting the arrival of a 'holy man', who would change things for the better. The fact that 1500 was a half-millennium added to the air of tense expectation. A Grand Conjunction of the stars was predicted for 1524, and this was interpreted as heralding the end of the world and the Second Coming. The German Reformation was therefore triggered in part because of a coincidence of timing: Luther was 'expected'. Economic and social change also helped to cause the German Reformation. This was a period of inflation, population growth, poor harvests, rising taxes, and the re-imposition of serfdom. There had already been numerous peasant uprisings before the revolt of 1524–25, while the Craft Guilds of Cologne had rebelled in 1515. There is a close link here with religion. The Cologne rebellion was partly to do with resentment at clerical privileges in business and taxation, while merchants resented the power of the Church over their workforce – there were over 50 holy days when no one could work. Anyone who proposed the elimination of unfair clerical privileges in business or taxation, or a less-expensive method of guaranteeing salvation, would have been popular. It is doubtful if Luther would have been as well-received if Germany had been thriving economically.

> These three paragraphs all helpfully point to other circumstances that could have helped to cause the Reformation. However, they do so in a largely descriptive way. They should be weighed up against each other and against hostility to the papacy.

It is equally doubtful if the German Reformation could have happened without the printing press. The power of the printing press was more extensive in Germany than elsewhere, partly because of their number (200), but also because weak central government meant that censorship was ineffective. In 1518–24, press output went up by 600 percent, and 90 percent of it was written by Luther. With the press, his ideas spread quickly and widely. Had the empire had a strong central government and effective censorship, Luther might have been silenced.

However, the most crucial reason why hostility towards the papacy cannot be considered the main reason for the German Reformation lies in the fact that Martin Luther himself was not motivated by hostility towards the papacy, at least initially. His inspiration lay in the *ad fontes* approach of the humanists. Luther used Erasmus' translation of the New Testament (printed in 1515) for his research when he challenged the theological justification for indulgences. Luther remained polite about the pope, and loyal to the idea of a papacy, until 1519. Admittedly, Luther then fanned the flames of anti-papalism. In the Leipzig Debates of 1519, he said there was no evidence for the papacy in the scriptures.

In conclusion, hostility to the papacy helps to explain the reception given to Luther, but only alongside other factors, including the cultural and economic situation in Germany. Furthermore, it does not explain the motivation of Luther himself, who had hoped to open the pope's eyes to a single abuse. Ironically, the papacy's bullying tactics pushed him into expressing more extreme ideas. The hostility of the pope towards Luther was therefore ultimately more to blame for the German Reformation.

> This conclusion has real strengths. It opens with a judgement that directly answers the question, and the references to Luther are interesting and perceptive. However, it would be even stronger if the response weighed up the respective roles of 'hostility to the papacy' and the 'other factors', rather than simply suggesting that they were all of equal importance. There is no right answer here, and it requires courage to suggest that one factor was more important than the others. However, as long as a reason for the choice can be provided, then taking this extra step would be worth the risk.

Verdict

This is a strong answer because:

- the answer analyses and evaluates the role of hostility towards the papacy, and recognises the wider demands of the question by covering a range of other causal factors

- it deploys some sound supporting evidence to meet the demands of the question
- it reaches a final judgement that directly addresses the question, though more could be done to evaluate the role of the other causal factors
- the answer is well-organised and unfolds logically, and communication is clear.

Preparing for your A Level Paper 2 exam

Advance planning

1. Draw up a timetable for your revision and try to keep to it. Spread your timetable over a number of weeks, and aim to cover four or five topics each week.
2. Spend longer on topics that you have found difficult, and revise them several times.
3. Above all, do not try to limit your revision by attempting to 'question spot'. Try to be confident about all aspects of your Paper 2 work, because this will ensure that you have a choice of questions in Section B.

Paper 2 overview

AL Paper 2	Time: 1 hour 30 minutes	
Section A	Answer 1 compulsory source question	20 marks
Section B	Answer 1 question from a choice of 2	20 marks
	Total marks =	40 marks

You should familiarise yourself with the layout of the paper by looking at the examples published by Edexcel. The questions for each section are followed by eight pages of lined paper where you should write your answer.

Section A questions

This question asks you to assess two different types of contemporary sources totalling around 400 words, and will be in the form of 'How far could the historian make use of Sources 1 and 2 together to investigate…?' Your answer should evaluate both sources, considering their nature, origin and purpose, and you should use your own knowledge of the context of the sources to consider their value to the specific investigation. Remember, too, that in assessing their value, you must consider the two sources, taken together, as a set.

Section B questions

These questions ask you to reach a judgement on an aspect of the topic studied. The questions will have the form, for example, of 'How far…', 'To what extent…' or 'How accurate is it to say…'. The questions can deal with historical concepts such as cause, consequence, change, continuity, similarity, difference and significance. You should consider the issue raised in the question, then other relevant issues, and conclude with an overall judgement.

The timescale of the questions could be as short as a single year or even a single event (an example from Option 2C.2 could be, 'To what extent was Russia's involvement in the First World War responsible for the fall of the Romanovs in 1917?'). The timescale could be longer depending on the historical event or process being examined, but questions are likely to be shorter than those set for Sections A and B in Paper 1.

Use of time

This is an issue that you should discuss with your teachers and fellow students, but here are some suggestions for you.

1. Do not write solidly for 45 minutes on each question. For Section A it is essential that you have a clear understanding of the content of each source, the points being made, and the nature, origin and purpose of each source. You might decide to spend up to ten minutes reading the sources and drawing up your plan, and 35 minutes writing your answer.
2. For Section B you should spend a few minutes working out what the question is asking you to do, and drawing up a plan of your answer before you begin to write your response.

Preparing for your A Level exams

Paper 2: A Level sample answer with comments

Section A

You will need to read two sources and then use them in tandem to assess how useful they are for investigating an issue. For these questions, remember to:

- spend up to ten minutes preparing: read the sources and identify relevant evidence in them; look at the sources' provenance and determine what you can about the authors; plan your answer
- use your own knowledge to establish context and to weigh up the typicality of the sources
- use specific references from the sources to show how they could be used for the investigation specified
- come to a substantiated judgement.

Read Sources 16 and 17 in Chapter 3, page 232 (these sources are a little longer than the ones you will have to analyse in the exam. In the exam, the sources together won't total more than 460 words).

How far could the historian make use of Sources 16 and 17 together to investigate the success of the Lutheran Reformation in Germany by the late 1520s?

Explain your answer using both the sources, the information given about them and your own knowledge of the historical context. (20 marks)

Average student answer

The two sources present material that would suggest the Reformation was at risk of completely failing by the late 1520s, though they do so in different ways, for different purposes and to different levels.

Luther does so with passionate language and sweeping generalisations, reflecting both his own nature and his alarm at the situation: 'What misery have I seen – the common people knowing nothing at all of Christian doctrine'. In contrast the Visitation extracts are dry and factual. They use the almost abbreviated style that one would expect from an objective report. Even something scandalous is reported in dry tones: in Holzdorf, for example, 'there was more than enough sorcery, adultery and other vices'.

Differing purposes may explain these different approaches to reporting on the situation. Luther was trying to persuade all Saxony's ministers and preachers to use his Short Catechism, an instruction manual to remedy the ignorance revealed by the Inspections. Naturally, therefore, Luther inflated the situation: hyperbole and persuasive, passionate language might sway an idle minister into using the Catechism. It was their duty to lift these poor people from their lives as 'poor cattle and senseless swine'. If that did not work, Luther ended with a veiled threat: peasants may once again start interpreting the Gospel to suit themselves, in an Anabaptist way. The extracts from the 1529 Visitation, in contrast, are not for public consumption. Inspectors were provided with detailed instructions about what to look for and what questions to ask. They simply had to collect the information and report back, so that a full report on the state of the Lutheran Church in Saxony could then be compiled.

The introduction has some very good points – a judgement, and an awareness of how the two sources differ. What is missing is some acknowledgement of the fact that these two sources refer only to Saxony. Some information on the wider context is needed.

This is interesting stuff, but this paragraph would be improved by substituting the rather vague phrase 'Luther does so…' for something that relates these observations more explicitly to the focus of the question.

The use of these two sources together – moving smoothly from one to another – is good practice. Examining the purpose of each source helps to establish their utility.

The two sources also differ in terms of how grave they feel the situation is. Luther paints a very dire picture: ignorance is so pervasive that so-called Christians 'know neither the Lord's prayer, nor the Creed, nor the Ten Commandments'. These are basic matters, common to all denominations, and it is as though what was failing was Christianity rather than Lutheranism. Perhaps it was a rejection of institutional Christianity, imposed from above, since the peasants were happy with the Gospels. The failure, Luther clearly feels, was due to the many pastors who were 'unskilled and incapable of teaching'.

Luther's preface paints a much blacker picture than the Visitation report. The latter is measured, and provides good news as well as bad. In at least two of the five parishes, the peasants were reasonably good Lutherans: in Wildenau, for example, 'they can pray quite well'. In at least two parishes, the pastors were acceptable: one was quite learned, and another (in Stolzenhayn) had already written in to report about the 'abominable crimes and blasphemies' that his parishioners had been committing. In other words, the failure of the Reformation was not quite as desperate as Luther was portraying. It is, of course, perfectly possible that Luther's preface was based on his reading of all the Visitation reports. This particular report is only from the district of Schweintz in Saxony and it may be untypical.

These sources refer to Saxony only, so they cannot be taken as categorical proof that the Lutheran Reformation was failing everywhere. However, Luther hoped that his guide for inspectors would become a model to be used in all Lutheran states, and the fact that his Catechisms were far more widely published than just Saxony, would suggest that the Reformation had similar failings elsewhere at the time. This situation did not last long. The Ottoman invasion of 1532 earned the Lutherans and the Schmalkaldic League a reprieve, and the Lutheran Reformation was more widely and more firmly embedded in the 1530s.

These are interesting points. This might have been an opportunity to introduce some wider knowledge, relating to the Peasants' Revolt. Such knowledge could be used to support the inference made that what was being rejected was 'Christianity imposed from above'.

The student has rather missed an opportunity here, by dealing with the source on too superficial a level. Digging deeper would reveal that the reception given to Lutheranism depended on the 'class' of peasant. However, at last there is a comment (rather thrown away, at the end of the paragraph) on the typicality of the source.

At last! Some use of background knowledge to establish the wider context and to suggest whether or not these two sources are typical of all of Germany. Such information was needed much earlier.

Verdict

This is an average answer because:

- it shows a very reasonable understanding of the sources and it selects key points that are relevant to the question, though more could have been inferred from the Visitation report
- some knowledge of historical context was used, though more would have helped to confirm the value of the sources for this particular enquiry
- it evaluates the sources on the grounds of their nature and purpose, and on the positions of their authors.

Use the feedback on this answer to rewrite it, making as many improvements as you can.

Paper 2: A Level sample answer with comments

Section A

You will need to read two sources and then use them together to assess how useful they are for investigating an issue. For these questions, remember to:

- spend up to ten minutes preparing: read the sources and identify relevant evidence in them; look at the sources' provenance and determine what you can about the authors; plan your answer
- use your own knowledge to establish context and to weigh up the typicality of the sources
- use specific references from the sources to show how they could be used for the investigation specified
- come to a substantiated judgement.

Read Sources 16 and 17 in Chapter 3, page 232 (these sources are a little longer than the ones you will have to analyse in the exam. In the exam, the sources together won't total more than 460 words).

How far could a historian make use of Sources 16 and 17 together to investigate the success of the Lutheran Reformation in Germany by the late 1520s?

Explain your answer using both the sources, the information given about them and your own knowledge of the historical context. (20 marks)

Strong student answer

By the late 1520s, the Reformation was faltering. Luther's role in the crushing of the Peasants' ◄— Revolt had lost him the support of many common people and, despite the Recess of Speyer of 1526, only six princes and 14 cities had formally converted to Lutheranism by 1529. Catholic forces, meanwhile, seemed to have decided to destroy Lutheranism. In 1529, the diet revoked the 1526 Recess of Speyer and made the Edict of Worms compulsory; abroad, Charles was making peace with France before he returned to the empire to deal with the Lutheran issue. The situation was potentially so dangerous for the Lutherans that the leading Protestant prince, Philip of Hesse, attempted to construct a Protestant alliance between Zwinglians and Lutherans. The attempt failed over the issue of the Eucharist. One could argue that Ottoman aggression alone saved Lutheranism in the late 1520s and early 1530s.

> By using outside knowledge, the introduction has been used here to establish some context to the state of the Reformation in the late 1520s.

Both Sources 16 and 17 support the view that the Reformation had made disappointing progress ◄— by the late 1520s. Even though the prince (John the Steadfast in this case) might formally have converted, his people had not really absorbed Lutheran teachings. Of course, both sources refer only to Saxony, and the Visitation extracts are based on only five rural parishes in one district of Saxony. This restricts the sources' value to the historian if considering the whole of Germany. However, if the Reformation was failing in Saxony, despite the proximity of Luther himself, the press in Wittenberg and a supportive elector in John the Steadfast, it can be inferred that it was likely to be failing elsewhere as well, as least in rural areas. No firm conclusions can be drawn from these sources about the success of the Lutheran Reformation in the towns, but it had probably taken root more firmly there because Luther refers to failures 'especially in the villages', implying that the situation was better in the towns.

> Here the typicality of the sources is weighed up within the context that has been established in the introduction. Notice the tentative language – 'it can be inferred that…' and 'No firm conclusions can be drawn…'.

The sources particularly agree that the Reformation was not fully embedded in rural Saxony. The scale of failure can be inferred from the fact that Luther felt compelled to write his Larger and Smaller Catechisms (the preface of which is Source 17). There was an urgent need to educate people about Christianity. Luther describes the common people 'especially in the villages' as 'knowing nothing at all about Christian doctrine', including its most basic features like the Lord's Prayer, the Creed and the Ten Commandments. His conclusion was based on the evidence provided by the Visitations, including the extract in Source 16 from 1529. In small rural communities like Wertho, for example, the peasants 'neither pray nor believe'. In Stolzenhayn, the pastor reported 'blasphemies' 'against the word of God', and there was 'sorcery' and 'indifference' to preaching in Holzdorf, which hints at paganism. However, where Luther was sweeping in his condemnation, the report is more focused and exact, and shows that the Reformation was not the total failure that Luther presented. The Reformation was clearly least successful among poorer peasants – the leaseholders and cottagers. In comparison, the richer 'householders' were more likely to be good Lutherans. For example, Aryn's 18 householders might have reported on their pastor for teaching 'untruths'. The population of Wildenau was balanced in favour of householders who 'can pray quite well'.

Luther provides a reason for the failure of the Reformation (at least in rural Saxony) when he condemns 'many pastors' as 'unskilled and incapable of teaching'. This judgement is also only partly supported by the Visitation's findings. The pastor at Holzdorf was dismissed because he had given up preaching, but it is also clear that there were some good pastors (the one in Wildenau was learned and praised by his parishioners) while one pastor was just Catholic, rather than 'incapable'. The Rev. Martinus Mauck in Aryn was 'still a papist' and sacked because of it.

Of the two, Luther's preface is of less value than the Visitation report. The report is detailed, exact and objective: the inspectors were noting down what they had found. They seem unbiased, since both good and bad are mentioned. In comparison, Luther uses overly dramatic language and huge generalisations to create a picture of abject failure. Phrases like 'the common people know nothing at all' do not agree with evidence produced by the Visitation itself. Luther had been on an inspection himself, and probably knew that the picture was more mixed, but he was exaggerating for effect because he wanted to emphasise to pastors the need to use the Catechism. Secondly, Luther's preface hints at a political and social purpose. He was harking back to the Peasants' Revolt when he suggested that peasants were using the scriptures to demand their rights – 'they have learned well enough how they may abuse their liberty'. In the Small Catechism, Luther urged pastors to dwell on the Seventh and Fourth Commandments – not to steal and to be quiet, obedient and faithful. This all hints at Luther's fear of a revived Peasants' Revolt.

Nevertheless, despite contradictions between the two sources, and reservations about Luther's motives, both sources do provide an effective starting point for an investigation into the success of the Reformation in Germany by the late 1520s. They agree that: the Reformation was not deeply embedded in Saxony – this was especially so among the rural poor where ignorance and pagan ways prevailed; the quality of pastors was far too variable – therefore a Catechism was needed. If this was all true of Saxony, then it was probably true in other Lutheran states.

> This paragraph shows how specific references can be extracted from the sources. Short quotations only have been selected, and they are always used to support an analytical point. Secondly, notice how the two sources are used here together, to support each other, but also to show differences.

> The conclusion refers back to the question and provides a judgement – these sources are a 'starting point' for an investigation into the success of the Reformation. The judgement is substantiated.

Verdict

This is a strong answer because:

- it interrogates the sources and shows how they could be used, by extracting specific evidence from them

- it deploys some sound own knowledge to establish context and to tackle the issue of how far the sources could be used

- it confidently evaluates the sources, by referring to their typicality and reliability, and reaches a substantiated judgement.

Paper 2: A Level sample answer with comments

Section B

These questions assess your understanding of the period in depth. They will ask you about the content you learned about in the four key themes, and may ask about more than one theme. For these questions, remember to:

- give an analytical, not a descriptive, response
- support your points with evidence
- cover the whole time period specified in the question
- come to a substantiated judgement.

Ottoman aggression hampered Charles V's efforts to crush Lutheranism far more than French aggression.

How far do you agree with this statement? (20 marks)

Average student answer

In 1555, the Religious Peace of Augsburg was signed stating that each prince could choose whether his territory would be Catholic or Lutheran. This is a clear indicator that Charles V failed to defeat the Protestants within the Holy Roman Empire. A key contributor to this failure was the Ottoman threat upon Charles' territory.

War with the Ottomans thwarted Charles' attempts to focus solely on the Protestant issue within the empire. The threat of invasion posed a greater danger and thus was given priority over the Protestant problem, such as in 1541 at the Colloquy of Regensburg, when Charles had the ideal opportunity to stop the Lutherans, but instead he invaded Algiers, the base for the Barbary pirates. The constant threat of war led to Charles being an absent monarch. It can be seen that in times of peace when Charles was able to focus on the empire, such as in 1546, he was able to quell the Protestants, for instance during the first Schmalkaldic War. However, such chances were rare as other threats often loomed.

War with the Ottomans meant that Charles had to ask the Protestant princes for men and money in order to reduce the Ottoman threat of invasion. In order to get their help, Charles was forced to make religious concessions to the Protestants, such as in 1532 at the Religious Truce of Nuremberg. Originally, at the Diet of Augsburg, Charles had given the Protestants six months in which to convert back to Catholicism. However, he was forced to offer them peace under the Truce of Nuremberg when the Ottomans were advancing towards Vienna. Such concessions weakened Charles' ability to crush the Protestant threat and thus allowed them to grow stronger. Ferdinand, Charles' brother, was also forced to concede to the Protestants when the Ottomans were attacking. In 1526, the Recess of Speyer was passed allowing each prince to choose to be Catholic or Protestant. This gave the Protestants a freedom that – without the threat of the Ottomans on Hungary – would never have been granted, thus showing how the Ottoman threat was a reason for Charles not resolving the Lutheran issue within the Holy Roman Empire.

Wars with the Ottomans meant that even when Charles was not fighting abroad, he did not have the money to defeat the Lutherans. In 1547, after the Battle of Mühlberg, Charles should have been able to quell the Lutherans for good: he had captured John Frederick as well as imprisoned Philip of Hesse. But he was unable to defeat the Protestants, as he had little money in order to support an army and thus defeat the Protestant problem permanently. This lack of money was because of the Ottomans: he was almost bankrupt because of Algiers, where he lost an entire fleet. Instead, the Protestants were given time and support from France to challenge Charles again.

> This introduction only considers the Ottomans. The impact of French aggression also needs mention. It is important to remember to address both sides of the question in the introduction, even if you end up dismissing one side.

> This paragraph is rather muddled. It is making some really good points but these are rather lost because they are introduced illogically and not always supported with exact evidence. It is best to devote each paragraph to one point that can be fully explained and then supported with evidence.

> This paragraph has a much better structure: it opens with one point that it develops and then supports with evidence. However, it would have been more logical to tackle the evidence in chronological order. In this case the concessions made in 1526 should come before those made in 1532.

This involvement of France shows that war with the Ottomans was not the only reason for Charles not resolving the Protestant issue. Francis I feared Charles' power and so did very little to support him in tackling this heresy. Indeed he made alliance with both the Ottomans and the Protestants in order to undermine Charles. So did his son Henry, who signed the Treaty of Chambord with the Schmalkaldic League in 1552. This revived the League.

At last, some mention of the French. In practice, this essay should have been more evenly balanced between the Ottomans and the French.

However, Charles clearly felt the Ottomans were the priority throughout his reign. Every treaty he made with the French was lenient, because he hoped to win French support against the Ottomans. This happened even with the 1526 Treaty of Madrid, when Charles had Francis in his control, following his capture at the Battle of Pavia. Charles could have demanded anything, but simply demanded that Francis give up his claims to Milan and other lands, marry Charles' sister, and then join Charles in a crusade against the Ottomans. The same happened in 1529 with the Ladies' Peace. As far as Charles was concerned, the Ottomans were infidels and the proper object of his attentions. As the secular head of Christendom and head of the Order of the Golden Fleece, it was his role to lead a crusade against the Ottomans.

Good use of evidence here to back up the point of the paragraph: that Charles focused his attention on the Ottomans.

In conclusion, Ottoman aggression was far more important than French aggression in Charles' efforts to crush Lutheranism. It played a particularly important role in ensuring the survival of Lutheranism when it was vulnerable and fragile, in 1526 and in 1532.

The concluding paragraph really only considers the Ottomans again. It is a judgement with some substantiation, which is good, but there is no reasoning about why the Ottomans were more important than the French. Simply asserting that they were more important is not enough.

Verdict

This is an average answer because:

- there is some sound analysis of the Ottoman side, but the essay is too one-sided; more was needed on the French in order to create an argument
- mostly accurate evidence is used to back up the points made, though, again, the material lacks range
- the conclusion is an assertion rather than a well-reasoned judgement
- expression is generally clear, though some paragraphs have a rather muddled structure.

Use the feedback on this answer to rewrite it, making as many improvements as you can.

Paper 2: A Level sample answer with comments

Section B

These questions assess your understanding of the period in depth. They will ask you about the content you learned about in the four key themes, and may ask about more than one theme. For these questions, remember to:

- give an analytical, not a descriptive, response
- support your points with evidence
- cover the whole time period specified in the question
- come to a substantiated judgement.

Ottoman aggression hampered Charles V's efforts to crush Lutheranism far more than French aggression.

How far do you agree with this statement? (20 marks)

Strong student answer

In 1521, Charles publicly dedicated his life to crushing Lutheranism; 35 years later he abdicated and permitted his brother Ferdinand to sign the Peace of Augsburg. Of the many factors that hampered Charles V's efforts to crush Lutheranism, arguably the most crucial were foreign threats from the Ottomans and the French. However, while Ottoman aggression was undoubtedly important at key moments, French aggression ultimately had the greater impact.

The impact of Ottoman aggression was considerable in ensuring the survival of Lutheranism at key moments. Twice, Ottoman aggression in Hungary forced Charles to make concessions to the princes in return for support. The 1526 Recess of Speyer, which permitted each prince to choose to be Catholic or Lutheran, was only passed because of the urgent need for men and money in light of the Ottoman victory at the Battle of Mohács that year. The recess resulted in several key princes and cities openly converting to Lutheranism. Secondly, in 1532, Charles was unable to carry out his threat to eradicate Lutheranism because of an anticipated Ottoman invasion. He agreed to the Truce of Nuremberg, suspending action against the Protestants in return for aid – the Ottoman army was within two days' march of Vienna at the time. The truce was renewed with the Frankfurt Interim in 1539. In effect, the Schmalkaldic League was left undisturbed through the 1530s and went from strength to strength.

Ottoman aggression in the Mediterranean, in alliance with the Barbary pirates, also diverted Charles' attention away from the Protestant issue in the empire, as well as proving ruinously expensive to Charles. Constant pirate aggression meant that Charles' Mediterranean possessions lived in a state of fear while trade was disrupted. It was not a situation Charles could ignore. Twice he made the Barbary pirates a priority over the Lutherans: in 1535 he successfully seized Tunis back, and in 1541 he attempted to seize Algiers. Both campaigns detracted from his efforts to tackle Lutheranism. The Schmalkaldic League was able to seize Württemberg in 1535, while in the early 1540s Philip of Hesse was left free to recover from the scandal surrounding his bigamy. Furthermore, the Algiers campaign was a financial disaster for Charles: he lost a fleet and was left in considerable debt. In part, this explains why he lacked the means to follow through on his victory over the Lutherans at Mühlberg in 1546.

However, for several reasons, the impact of Ottoman aggression was less than that of the French on Charles' efforts to crush Lutheranism. The Ottoman threat to the empire itself can be exaggerated: the Ottomans only reached Vienna once, in 1529, and overstretched supply lines coupled with bad weather meant they soon retreated. After 1532, they limited their attention to Hungary, which was claimed by Ferdinand. While this might explain Ferdinand's failure to

This introduction is good in that it confidently states the line of argument that will be taken. By making such explicit use of the words of the question, this introduction is also ensuring a relevant focus.

Both these paragraphs open strongly with analytical points that directly relate to the question. These are then backed up with specific evidence.

This is a good paragraph. Rather than simply describing events in the Mediterranean, the impact of these on the survival and spread of Lutheranism is made clear and supported with exact evidence.

focus on the Lutherans, it does not explain Charles' failure. Furthermore, the threat from the Ottomans was not continuous: Suleiman the Magnificent also faced war on his eastern front with Persia, and he faced succession problems. Once he had secured Hungary to his satisfaction, Suleiman was willing to sign a five-year truce with Charles and Ferdinand in 1547. Tackling the Barbary pirates in Algiers in 1541 appealed to Charles' crusading vision, but he went against advice when his priority at the time should have been the Protestants.

> The last sentence in this paragraph could be more elegantly linked in with what precedes it. It appears a little abruptly.

The impact of the French was greater because, unlike the Ottomans, the French directly helped the German Lutherans in an effort to undermine Charles. Though devout Catholics, Francis I financed the Schmalkaldic League while Henry II signed the Treaty of Chambord in 1552, which revived the League after its defeat in the Schmalkaldic Wars. The Ottomans never provided direct aid in this way. Furthermore, French attacks were more sustained and strategically more damaging than Ottoman aggression. The Habsburg–Valois Wars involved 18 years of fighting over five wars from 1521 to 1559. In contrast, the 1532 campaign was the last time the Ottomans came close to invading the empire; it was just beyond their reach. Like the Ottomans, the French diverted Charles' attention from the Lutheran situation. For example, the 1521 French attack on Navarre was partly responsible for drawing Charles away from Worms and back to Spain, where he stayed for a decade. More critical were French attacks on Milan in the mid-1520s, which Charles saw as a strategically crucial link between his northern and southern territories. The fact that Charles saw the French as the greater priority can be seen in the fact that while he financed the army of 23,000 that defeated Francis I at Pavia in 1525, he ignored Ferdinand's requests for help during the siege of Vienna in 1529. French aggression in the late 1530s and early 1540s drew Charles' attention away from the empire far more than Ottoman aggression. Furthermore, the Ottoman threat in the Mediterranean might not have been as great had not the French colluded with them. In 1542, Barbarossa was permitted to use Toulon as a base from where he launched attacks on Charles.

> By switching between the French and the Ottomans in this paragraph, their relative impact is made clear. However, some assertions are not supported with evidence, and that diminishes their credibility.

French aggression indirectly played another role in Charles' failure to crush Lutheranism. Charles' victories over France in Italy – the taking of Milan in 1521 and the defeat of Francis at Pavia in 1525, in particular – caused alarm in the papal states, which felt threatened by Charles power. This helps to explain why the papacy did not co-operate at the time with Charles' request to call a general council. The Catholic princes of the empire demanded a council to reform the Church in Germany before they would enforce the Edict of Worms, so the lack of papal co-operation was critical. In contrast, the threat from the Ottomans did more to bring Charles and the papacy together.

> This last point is not supported with evidence nor is it explicitly related to the question.

In conclusion, Ottoman aggression played a key role in 1525, 1532 and 1541, particularly in securing concessions for the Lutherans from Charles, in diverting his attention away from the empire, and in depleting his finances. However, the fact that the French not only diverted his attention, but also directly aided the Lutherans, had a greater impact. This was particularly true in 1552, when Henry II revived the league and invaded the empire. When Henry captured Metz, Toul and Verdun, Charles switched his attention from the Lutheran issue to evicting the French. He permitted Ferdinand to sign the Peace of Passau with the Lutherans, while he spent a year's income trying to retake Metz. His failure to do so was a main reason in his decision to give up and abdicate, while permitting Ferdinand to sign the Peace of Augsburg.

> This conclusion is good in that is reaches a substantiated judgement. Unfortunately, this judgement ignores the fact that a key reason why Ferdinand signed the Peace of Augsburg was so that he could turn his attention once more the Hungarian issue.

Verdict

This is a strong answer because:

- it sustains a focus on the question set and argues both sides of the case – both of the key issues – by looking at the Ottomans and French in equal measure
- it uses specific evidence to support the points made, though the level of fear that the Ottomans evoked in Europe is ignored, and more could be said about Ferdinand's preoccupation with Hungary
- it is well organised, the argument is logical and reaches a substantiated judgement, it is coherent, and the expression is clear and precise.

The Dutch Revolt, c1563–1609

This Paper provides an in-depth study of the role of religion and the impact it had on the development of political states within early modern Europe. This in itself is a broad but fundamental focus, since the end of the 16th century marked a shift in the nature of European government. Royal absolutism steadily replaced the medieval system where monarchical power was uncertain and had relied on support from the nobility, and this development saw power become more centralised. Religion was an important feature of this change as the unquestioning belief in God continued to be a significant influence on the way people conducted their lives, and monarchs were able to use this to strengthen their appeal. This influence was a chief component in the political development of nations.

SOURCE 1

The Dairy Cow, oil on panel, produced between 1580 and 1595 by an unknown artist. The cow represents the Low Countries, the rider (who is losing control) is Philip II, the States-General has its hands on the cow's head and is trying to coax Elizabeth I to support it, while William of Orange is underneath the cow fomenting revolt. The figure at the cow's rear is the Duke of Anjou, the proposed successor to Philip II.

1555	Philip II becomes ruler of the Netherlands
1559	Margaret of Parma becomes regent of the Netherlands
1564	Granvelle is recalled to Spain
1567	Duke of Alva arrives in the Netherlands Council of Troubles is established Margaret of Parma resigns as regent
1569	Tenth Penny tax is refused by the States-General
1573	Alva is replaced by Don Luis de Requesens
1577	Duke of Parma takes charge of the Spanish army in the Netherlands
1579	Unions of Arras and Utrecht are formed
1584	William of Orange is assassinated
1588	Spanish Armada is defeated by Elizabeth I's navy
1598	Philip II dies and is replaced by his son Philip III
1609	The Treaty of Antwerp is signed

1556	Philip II becomes king of Spain
1561	Reform of the bishoprics is started under Antoine Perrenot de Granvelle
1566	Compromise of the Nobility is formed Iconoclastic Fury begins Antwerp Accord is agreed
1568	Counts of Egmont and Hoorn are executed Prince of Orange's first invasion and rebel victory at Heiligerlee
1572	Alva starts to use the army to enforce the Tenth Penny tax Flushing and Brill are seized by the Sea Beggars Orange's second invasion
1576	Requesens dies Spanish Fury begins – the sacking of Antwerp takes place Pacification of Ghent is signed Don John becomes governor-general
1578	Don John is replaced as governor-general by Archduke Matthias – Philip II's nephew
1581	Act of Abjuration is passed against Philip II
1585	Treaty of Nonsuch is signed between the northern provinces and England
1592	Death of Parma
1600	Maurice of Nassau's victory at Nieuwpoort

The lens through which this change is viewed in this Option is the successful challenge that the people of the Netherlands directed against their Habsburg masters between 1563 and 1609. During this period, the Dutch-speaking people of the Habsburg Netherlands were pushed into rebellion after the accession of Philip II to the Spanish throne in 1556. More accustomed to the flexibility of his father, the provinces were increasingly alienated by the new king's centralist political system and particularly his overbearing religious policies, which suffocated provincial autonomy. With their highly valued local privileges being undermined by Philip, the independent-minded sections of society grew more rebellious – particularly when Protestantism began to flourish among them only to be met with Habsburg aggression. The combination of religious persecution and the erosion of political freedom inspired people to make a stand against their monarch. The final outcome of this struggle was the creation of one of the era's first republics.

The nature of this struggle is complex, and each of the key themes is carefully established and drawn out in the following chapters in order to provide a well-grounded understanding of the events. Starting with the origins of the revolt, the unusual relationship that the Netherlands maintained within the Habsburg Empire is considered in terms of the accession of Philip II and his own style of control. As heir to the Habsburg throne, Philip inherited control of the Netherlands from his Spanish father, Charles V – the Holy Roman Emperor. The lands themselves had been part of the larger state of Burgundy, which in the 15th century had come into the possession of the Habsburg rulers through marriage. From this point on, heirs to the throne also became 'Duke of Burgundy'. The lands of Burgundy and their people enjoyed special local rights and privileges which Charles had respected, but Philip was more reluctant to do so when he became duke of those lands in 1555. The importance of other individuals is also developed with the start of rebellion under the Prince of Orange, and its attempted suppression by the first of Philip's Spanish governor-generals, the Duke of Alva, whose own policies enhanced Orange's credibility and escalated his small attempt at rebellion into a full-scale civil war. Running through these themes is the continual presence of religious animosities that deepen the schism between Habsburg rule and the Burgundians to the extent that ultimately the Low Countries (the Netherlands) are essentially partitioned along religious lines: Spanish Catholic provinces and the northern provinces where Protestantism enjoyed greater freedom. The impact of religion is considered further as these two regions of the Low Countries are consolidated and the emerging United Provinces of the north begin to secure their position as an independent state in the wake of the Habsburg Empire's wider decline.

The struggle for independence that the Dutch Republic underwent during the last half of the 16th century would have a profound influence upon future political movements. Thirty-three years after its recognition in 1609, England would undergo civil war – temporarily experimenting with its own republic under the auspices of Oliver Cromwell. Additionally, the many constitutional arguments offered against Habsburg rule would later be used to similar effect by Thomas Jefferson in his Declaration of Independence, decrying the tyranny of England. These events themselves are well known, but the groundwork for such republicanism was achieved in the low-lying flatlands of north-western Europe.

2b.1 Origins of the Dutch Revolt, c1563–67

KEY QUESTIONS

- How independent were the Habsburg Netherlands?
- How significantly did Spanish authority affect the Netherlands by 1563?
- How effectively did the Dutch grandees oppose Spanish authority?
- How far did Calvinism impact on the Netherlands?

INTRODUCTION

The Dutch Revolt is the title given to the period when the provinces of the Netherlands undertook to challenge the power of the Habsburg Empire which, since 1505, had acquired an interest in those lands after Philip the Handsome, ruler of the Netherlands, married Juana of Castile and became Philip I of Castile.

The Netherlands – assumed by historians to number around 17 separate provinces – was a prominent part of the Habsburg Empire by the end of the 16th century, and its challenge contributed in no small part to a dramatic decline in that empire's authority. The origins of this revolt lay with the more independent attitudes that existed within the provinces. As the northernmost tip of the empire, a great sense of independence had always existed in the Netherlands, which was added to in the early 16th century when Charles V had been willing to negotiate rather than dictate. This practice changed when Charles' son Philip acceded to the throne in 1556, becoming Philip II of Spain. Unlike his father, Philip adopted a more high-handed approach, which increasingly upset the Dutch **grandees**, who began to resist such governance.

> **KEY TERM**
>
> **Grandee**
> An alternative term used to describe the most powerful of the aristocracy.

> **EXTEND YOUR KNOWLEDGE**
>
> **The 17 provinces**
> These territories sat north of France and nestled between the North Sea and Germany. They were Holland, Zeeland, Brabant, Utrecht, Overijssel, Flanders, Walloon Flanders, Artois, Luxembourg, Hainaut, Mechlin, Namur, Groningen, Friesland, Gelderland, Limbourg and Tournai.

1555 – Philip II becomes ruler of the Netherlands

1556 – Philip II becomes king of Spain

1558 – Philip II proposes reforming the bishoprics

1559 – Philip II leaves the Netherlands

Margaret of Parma is installed as regent

1560 – Antoine Perrenot de Granvelle is appointed principal minister

| 1555 | 1556 | 1557 | 1558 | 1559 | 1560 |

HOW INDEPENDENT WAS THE HABSBURG NETHERLANDS?

The Habsburg Netherlands became known as such when the **Low Countries**, including the lands of Burgundy, came under the control of Maximilian of Habsburg following his marriage to Mary of Burgundy. Her father had previously presided over the lands before being killed at the Battle of Nancy in 1477, whereupon Mary sought to preserve her inheritance through an immediate marriage. By the mid-16th century these lands amounted to 17 provinces, which fell under the control of Philip II of Spain, great grandson of Maximilian.

EXTEND YOUR KNOWLEDGE

Philip II of Spain (1527-98)

Philip II of Spain was the great-grandson of Maximilian of Austria and Habsburg and son of Charles V, the Holy Roman Emperor who officially gave the 17 provinces of the Low Countries independent status after 1548, and then ensured Habsburg control through the Pragmatic Sanction the following year. The Pragmatic Sanction declared that the titles of each of the leaders of the 17 provinces would be inherited by one heir – a Habsburg. Philip was less diplomatic than his father and took a more high-handed approach to ruling the Netherlands, dictating to them rather than working with them in collaboration.

The 17 provinces

Though officially under the control of Philip II after 1555, the geographic location of the provinces at the northernmost tip of the Habsburg Empire meant that the inhabitants of these lands had developed a relatively independent frame of mind. The people of the Netherlands were more used to governing their own affairs than being directed from Spain. Given their location, the nature of the Netherlands was very distinct from Spain. Philip arrived to tour the provinces as early as 1549. This tour was to allow Philip to be acknowledged as Charles' heir and to swear to uphold the privileges of each one. He and his entourage were very impressed by what they saw.

KEY TERM

Low Countries

This term refers to the coastal lands in the north-western part of Europe between the North Sea and the River Rhine – encompassing present day Belgium and the Netherlands.

Geographic considerations

The provinces were very different from what Philip, travelling outside Spain for the first time, was used to. They were also quite different from one another. At the centre there existed a heartland consisting of rich provinces such as Flanders and Brabant that benefited from close proximity to the sea and a dense population. Here there were approximately 30–35 people per square kilometre, and this density of population meant that trade flourished in these areas. The provinces to the north were equally prosperous because of their links to the sea, but they were more difficult to reach, being separated by rivers and lakes that effectively cut them off from the rest of the Netherlands. Just as difficult to reach were the eastern provinces such as Luxembourg and Gelderland, which were separated from the other provinces by boggy moorland and the independent principality of Liège. Given the difficulty of getting to these areas, the population here was more thinly spread than anywhere else.

In total the Netherlands boasted a population of three million people, roughly the same size as that of the slightly larger countries of England and Wales. The majority of this population lived in one of the 200 towns that the territory contained. These mostly lay in the coastal provinces such as Brabant, whose principal city (Antwerp) was home to around 80,000 people.

1561 – Granvelle is appointed cardinal of the Netherlands

Reform of the bishoprics is started

1562 – Huguenot migration into the Netherlands begins

Anti-Granvelle League is formed

1563 – Orange, Hoorn and Egmont leave the Council of State

First Reformed Church Synod is held in Antwerp

1564 – Philip II recalls Granvelle

Orange, Hoorn and Egmont return to the Council of State

Orange speaks in favour of freedom of conscience

1566 – Compromise of the Nobility is formed

Calvinists begin their outdoor services in Flanders

Iconoclastic Fury begins

Antwerp Accord is signed

1566 – Margaret of Parma relaxes the heresy laws

| 1561 | 1562 | 1563 | 1564 | 1565 | 1566 |

Figure 1.1 A simplified map of the territories of the Netherlands in the 16th century.

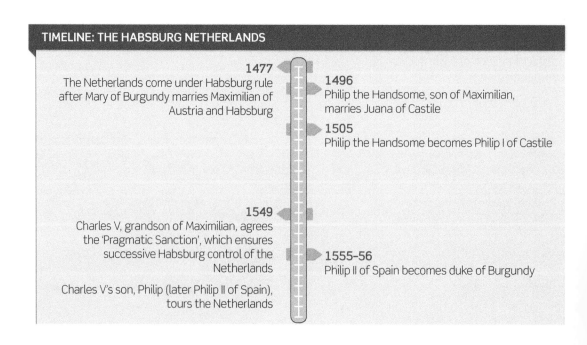

TIMELINE: THE HABSBURG NETHERLANDS

1477
The Netherlands come under Habsburg rule after Mary of Burgundy marries Maximilian of Austria and Habsburg

1496
Philip the Handsome, son of Maximilian, marries Juana of Castile

1505
Philip the Handsome becomes Philip I of Castile

1549
Charles V, grandson of Maximilian, agrees the 'Pragmatic Sanction', which ensures successive Habsburg control of the Netherlands

Charles V's son, Philip (later Philip II of Spain), tours the Netherlands

1555–56
Philip II of Spain becomes duke of Burgundy

Economy

The density of this population was part of the economic success of the provinces. Based on shipping and trading manufactured goods, together with the adoption of some of the most advanced agricultural practices in Europe – including intensive animal husbandry and the development of market gardening – the economy within the provinces was generally very prosperous. Such diversity meant that the Netherlands was better able to withstand fluctuations in economic fortune, while the advanced system of agriculture it pursued was able to take advantage of the 34,000 square miles that the provinces covered. The total value of the Netherlands' exports amounted to 22 million florins during the period of Philip's tour (approximately £2 million), compared with English foreign trade at this time, which amounted to £1 million.

Most of this wealth passed through Antwerp, the commercial heartland of the Netherlands. This city had good trade links with the rest of Europe and also acted as the **clearing house** for northern European countries' public and commercial financial activity. In a day, the city could see ten million florins being exchanged, and this activity encouraged the growth of a prominent banking system. For the Spanish, this was a very impressive sight and as a result the Netherlands was regarded as an important source of income, and a land that could stand higher taxation should the demand arise.

Education

In addition to the financial strength of the provinces, there was a high level of literacy. In Antwerp alone there were 150 schools, while Ghent had 40, including 12 grammar schools. Even the smaller towns enjoyed access to education. For example Veere, which sits on the westernmost tip of Zeeland and had a population of only 2,000, had three schools. These institutions also had regular teachers who were able to provide a consistent level of education to the extent that literacy levels were arguably among the best in Europe. The implication of this degree of learning was that, as a population, the Dutch were more exposed to literature and were also relatively receptive to new ideas that emerged around them. They were also aware of politics and, more importantly, had their own ideas about how they should be conducted.

The extent of local autonomy

The political organisation of the Netherlands was unusual. Since 1506 it had become **sovereign** Habsburg land and this placed it directly under the authority of Charles, who also remained Holy Roman Emperor and king of Spain. Given the extensive responsibilities that Charles had, the Netherlands was left in the hands of a **regent**, initially his aunt, Margaret of Austria, and then his sister, Mary of Hungary. The 17 provinces recognised the authority of both Charles and his regents and willingly negotiated with these rulers directly through a **States-General** and also through the crown-appointed provincial governors, or *stadtholders*.

The assemblies and States-General, together with a national government that operated from Brussels, gave the impression of a unified state. However, in truth the Netherlands was only superficially united. Being so physically divided in terms of geography – the area was criss-crossed by rivers, lakes and marshes – made communication quite challenging. As a result, the provinces had been able to develop practices that had given them much more independent authority. In particular, the provinces had evolved distinct regional differences.

Holland, for example, was tied very closely with the Baltic ports from which its people acquired cereals due to the fact they could not grow their own. Much of the land in this province had been reclaimed from the sea by draining its low-lying areas, and it proved unsuitable for large-scale agriculture. Having developed such ties with the Baltic, it expanded its trade by exploiting the sea and becoming a prominent exporter of salted fish. In contrast, in the more established provinces, such as Brabant, the economy was principally based on financial dealings and trading in Spanish produce.

The regional variance in economy encouraged different cultural sensitivities – including different languages and dialects in some cases. In the Northern provinces like Holland, Dutch was spoken, while in the southern region, which had closer ties with France, a French dialect called Walloon was widely used. Such diversity fomented individualised provincial identities, and this was reflected in the political structure.

At the highest level this diversity was acknowledged in the absence of a single title for the ruler. Charles V and then Philip II were not called 'King' of the Netherlands, but rather 'Duke of Brabant',

'Count of Flanders' and 'Lord of Friesland' among other titles. Although this seems a little superficial in its own right, the lack of an overall title added to the sense of autonomy that the provinces enjoyed. Rather than feeling as if they were subjects, there was a greater feeling among the Dutch upper classes that they were themselves invested with more powers, and certainly more independence.

This was also translated into the manner in which the provinces interacted with one another and the ruler. The individualised titles promoted the idea of a **confederation** of states rather than a single nation, and this was the principle behind the States-General. This body was a parliament that was created from representatives of provincial assemblies (who had already been elected by their provinces). To reach any major decision these assemblies would require the consent of their towns, and therefore decision-making was slow. Any decision also required a unanimous vote among the provinces, such was their degree of autonomy.

The role of the States-General, which had been established in 1427, was to represent the interests of the provinces in their dealings with the prince, while the provincial assemblies could also raise soldiers and collect taxes. The States-General met once every three years and usually to discuss taxation, which often resulted in a degree of unity being achieved between the regular attenders. However, combined with the greater powers of the provincial assemblies, the time delay helped to maintain a more individualised outlook for the provinces.

This was manifested in the vast range of local customs and traditions that existed throughout the Netherlands and produced the 700 or so different legal codes that were in operation there. In Brabant, for example, no one could hold a public office unless they were a native of the province, while in Holland no 'Brabanters' were able to assume office. Furthermore, each province had different rules regarding crime and, just like in the modern USA, people could avoid justice by moving from one province to another. These local laws and customs were very important to the people of the Netherlands as they protected their individuality and also offered some safeguard from the arbitrary use of power by the ruler who, upon accession, had to promise to observe these privileges.

KEY TERM

Confederation
A term often used to describe individually separate states that act together for common aims.

EXTRACT
1
From Geoffrey Parker, *The Dutch Revolt* (1990).

Local laws like these, 'liberties' or 'privileges' as they were called, might seem unreasonable and unnecessary today, but in early modern times they were the life-blood of politics. 'Whoever touches the privileges' wrote the royalist, Maximilian Morillon, 'cuts to the quick'. In a society where government was irresponsible, without restraints, where the subject had no real protection against abusive or arbitrary exercise of power, the existence of guaranteed privileges, however illogical, was of vital importance. They were worth fighting for and rebellion in defence of the privileges was, as the Habsburgs came to realise, nothing new in the Netherlands.

The traditional rights of the Burgundian grandees

The leading social group in the Netherlands was the aristocracy, or grandees, who were the principal landowners. The most prominent among these were the families of **Orange**, Aerschot, Aremberg, Egmont and Hoorn. Orange was the wealthiest family in the Netherlands and owned estates across the provinces as well as in Italy and France. The traditional power of these families led to them having a presence in the central government, particularly within the **Council of State**, which served as a policy-making organ for the Habsburg rulers. As the prominent members of their communities, they were the natural representatives and as such adopted many other public offices. In these roles the grandees assumed the voices of their provinces and were recognised as good sources of advice by the regents whom Charles V had left in charge. As advisers to both Mary of Hungary – Charles V's sister – and Margaret of Parma during their respective regencies, many of the wealthier grandees enjoyed significant influence in the royal house and several were appointed as governors, or *stadtholders*. For example, William of Orange occupied several public offices, including being the governor of Holland, Zeeland, Utrecht and later Franche-Comté. In these roles they could exercise significant **patronage** and oversight of the election of magistrates.

KEY TERMS

Orange-Nassau
This was the principal grandee family in the Netherlands. It was established after the marriage of Henry III of Nassau-Breda in Germany and Claudia of Chalon-Orange in Burgundy in 1515. The title 'Orange-Nassau' was officially founded by William I in 1544 and its lands included: the Burgundian principality of Orange in France; Nassau and Dietz which were in Germany; Vianden in present day Luxembourg; estates in the Low Countries of Holland and Zeeland.

Council of State
This was the policy-making body within the national government. Many of the prominent grandees served in this body, including William of Orange.

Patronage
The power to control appointments and grant rights.

William of Orange (1533–84)
Known as 'William the Silent' due to his careful manner of speech, William was from the wealthiest family in the Netherlands and this position gave him significant political influence. When Philip II of Spain acceded to the throne and took over the rule of the Netherlands, he introduced more Spanish advisers to the court, which William increasingly found unnecessary. As a Dutch grandee he found the increased Spanish influence difficult to accept, particularly as they began to institute changes that challenged the local privileges of the Dutch provinces. He is regarded as the leader of the opposition to Spanish rule, which ignited after 1563.

In effect, the grandees were the political leaders of the Netherlands who worked in unison with the ruling house. As representatives of their provinces, they were invaluable to the regents who relied upon them to help maintain order and support within their respective lands.

In addition to political influence, the grandees were also able to raise a *bande d'Ordonnance*, which was a heavy cavalry troop made up of other noblemen. There were 15 such troops with a combined force of 1,800 men. These men were used to enforce government orders when necessary and regularly undertook military drills together. In essence, these groups served as a social outlet for the nobility, but perhaps more importantly, they also provided a regular forum whereby these members of the Dutch elite could discuss their ideas and air any grievances they might have.

The Habsburg Netherlands was a curious arrangement. Governed by a single ruler but made up of independently minded provinces that guarded their local rights and privileges, the stability of this arrangement depended very much upon the relationship between the grandees and the ruler.

How independent was the Habsburg Netherlands?
Having read about the nature of the Habsburg Netherlands, identify three reasons why it might be described as 'independent' and three reasons that challenge this idea.

HOW SIGNIFICANTLY DID SPANISH AUTHORITY AFFECT THE NETHERLANDS BY 1563?

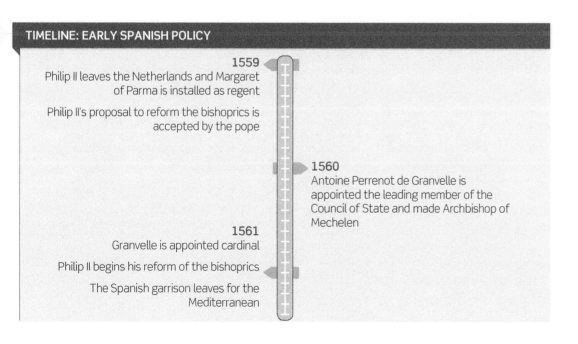

TIMELINE: EARLY SPANISH POLICY

1559
Philip II leaves the Netherlands and Margaret of Parma is installed as regent

Philip II's proposal to reform the bishoprics is accepted by the pope

1560
Antoine Perrenot de Granvelle is appointed the leading member of the Council of State and made Archbishop of Mechelen

1561
Granvelle is appointed cardinal

Philip II begins his reform of the bishoprics

The Spanish garrison leaves for the Mediterranean

Philip II's policy towards the Netherlands and lack of regard for tradition

Disregard for tradition

The relationship between the Habsburgs and the Netherlands grandees came under increasing pressure after 1555, when Philip II replaced Charles V as ruler. Philip II had never left Spain prior to his tour in 1549, and so he was not used to the unusual relationship that his father had established with the provinces. He spoke no Dutch or French, and was disinclined to make the necessary effort to ingratiate himself with the grandees. Observers found him to be a very different person from his father, who had been a careful ruler and sought to negotiate with the grandees and the assemblies.

SOURCE

1 A description of Philip II written by Marino Cavalli in his book *Charles V and his Son* having been a visitor to the Burgundian Court in 1554.

Philip takes excessive pleasure from being revered, and he maintains with everyone, no matter who he may be, a greater haughtiness than his father, a fact which his subjects, except for the Spaniards, are not happy about. And indeed they have good reason, being used to his father, who knows extremely well how to adjust himself by various ways to all kinds of people. It seems as if nature has made the Emperor capable of satisfying the **Flemings** and Burgundians by his habits of familiarity, the Italians by his talents and wisdom, the Spaniards by his reputation and severity. His subjects, who now see the son behaving otherwise, feel not a little displeasure at this change.

The change in leadership created a rift between the grandees and their Spanish masters because the new king was not willing to uphold the existing way of things. The privileges that were so important to the Dutch provinces were given little regard by Philip who did not understand, and was not interested in, these established traditions. His intention rather was to promote a strengthened centralised system of government whereby the autonomy of the provinces was curtailed under a more uniform Spanish system. Such was his disregard for local privileges that on one occasion in 1557 he had threatened to remove these powers from the people of Brussels after its parliament held up the passage of a financial subsidy to him in the States-General. For Philip, these were not inviolable rights, but rather gifts allowed at the discretion of the ruler. Although the Brussels parliament was able to keep its privileges, the threat made the parliament particularly distrustful of Philip and this was increasingly evident in the States-General, which was encouraged by the grandees to demand greater control over the money it voted to him.

The cause of the grandees' growing disaffection lay not only with Philip's failure to respect the existing order, but also his unwillingness to be advised by them. Hailing from the premier families of the Netherlands, these men had enjoyed significant influence in government and had been able to offer advice to the regents, who readily listened to what they had to say. Under Philip's reign, however, this influence was eroded as the new ruler preferred to listen to advice from Spanish tongues. Partly due to his naturally suspicious mind, Philip surrounded himself with a smaller council of advisers who depended upon him personally for their advancement and salaries. To Philip, grandees such as William of Orange or Count Egmont were too independent by virtue of their personal fortunes and therefore could not be relied upon, and he chose instead Spanish advisers whom he could control. The result of this undertaking was that very quickly the grandees saw themselves losing their traditional standing as advisers to the Habsburgs and as a result of being so overlooked they started to become more critical of Philip II's rule, having originally endorsed his position upon Charles V's abdication.

Policy towards the Netherlands

When Philip became ruler, the Netherlands was already subject to strict **heresy laws** so as to dissuade the growth of **Protestantism**. Under Charles V these had infringed provincial privileges as the **Inquisition** was able to arrest and try heretics anywhere in the country, and this undermined the local laws which maintained that local offenders could only be judged by magistrates of the same locality. Under Philip, these laws were extended, as he was a devout Catholic like his father. Just as his disregard of the grandees' positions undermined his relationship with them, the continuance of these heresy laws also pushed the provinces from him as many bristled at the encroachment on their local independence. This manifested itself in various forms, and many local officials protected these free thinkers rather than turn them in to the Inquisition. In adopting such activities, the provinces were already beginning to challenge the rule of the Habsburgs and this continued to be the pattern even after Philip returned to Spain in August 1559.

KEY TERMS

Flemings
The name given to the people who lived in the medieval county of Flanders and spoke the Flemish language.

Heresy laws
These were passed under Charles V to root out heresy – the belief in an alternative concept of God other than that offered by the Catholic Church. After 1550, the death penalty was introduced in the Netherlands for any unremitting heretic.

Protestantism
A different interpretation of Christianity that emerged after 1517, which challenged the Catholic belief in transubstantiation and questioned the importance of papal supremacy over the Church.

Inquisition
A political and religious body whose role was to enforce Catholicism and root out heresy. It was instituted in the Netherlands in 1522.

SOURCE

2 From a letter written by Philip II to his regent, the Duchess of Parma, 17 October 1565.

As to the resentment you have noticed at some of the things which the prince of Gavre [Egmont] says I told him and which didn't seem to correspond with my letters from Valladolid and with the negotiations in progress over the matter of religion, I don't see or understand that I wrote anything different in these letters from what was entrusted to the prince of Gavre. For as the inquisition, my intention is that it should be carried out by the inquisitors, as they have done up till now and as it appertains to them by virtue of divine and human rights. This is nothing new, because it was always done in the days of the late emperor my seignior and father, whom God has in His glory, and by me... You know the importance of this and I command you urgently to do in this matter all that is so necessary and not to agree to any different policy.

THINKING HISTORICALLY   Evidence (5a)

Context is everything

Work in groups.

Take an A3 piece of paper. In the middle of it draw a circle about 18 cm in diameter. Within the circle is the evidence itself, outside the circle is the context.

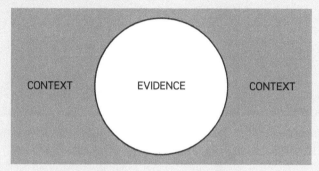

For Source 2:

1 Think of a question that the source could be helpful in answering.

2 Inside the circle, write a set of statements giving information that can be gleaned only from the source itself without any contextual knowledge.

3 Outside the circle, write down statements of contextual knowledge that relate to the source.

4 Draw annotated lines to show links between the contextual statements and the information from the source. Does context change the nature or meaning of the information?

Now answer the following question:

5 Explain why knowledge of context is important when gathering and using historical evidence. Give specific examples to illustrate your point.

In terms of his religious policy, Philip II also proposed a radical overhaul of the religious hierarchy in the Netherlands in 1558, which received the pope's consent the following year. This proposal involved removing the four old bishoprics that were under the singular control of the bishop of Utrecht and replacing them with 14 smaller ones under Dutch archbishops of his choosing. The change was designed to make the Church more efficient. However, it would become a significant feature in the rapid decline of Habsburg control in the country after 1563, having been decreed by Philip two years before.

Essentially the reorganisation of the Church once again undermined provincial privilege. In Brabant, for example, the introduction of a bishop took away the right of many of its monasteries to elect their own abbots as the bishop would assume control of these institutions. Furthermore, the nobility had traditionally been able to exercise their patronage to obtain comfortable Church positions for their younger sons. However, with new bishops, the acquisition of such roles proved to be more onerous as the bishops were more inclined to follow the rules about appointments, and the nobility lost their traditional opportunity to secure good jobs for their children.

Provincial towns also opposed the reforms on the grounds that a tightened religious system promoted accountability. The bishops and archbishops would be living within the area rather than in the province of Utrecht, and this might weaken their trading practices. Antwerp, for example, was opposed to the measures because if there was a local bishop German **Lutheran** merchants would not come to its ports, which in turn would undermine its trading ability.

The grandees also opposed the measures on the grounds that these would give more influence to advisers who owed their allegiance to the Habsburgs rather than to the Netherlands – particularly as the government in that country was weakened considerably after Philip returned to Spain, leaving his half-sister Margaret of Parma as regent.

The regency of Margaret of Parma

Having spent four years in the Netherlands, Philip returned to Spain in 1559, and his half-sister became his regent. Margaret of Parma was an accomplished, if timid, lady but she was politically inexperienced and her governance of the Low Countries was beset with difficulty. Her half-brother had left the country in a position that was becoming less stable. His religious policies had upset many in the provinces, while his own lack of respect towards Dutch traditions – especially the privileges – had begun to alienate the prominent grandees. Fearful that her inexperience might encourage her to rely upon these grandees to help her govern, Philip had established an inner council of three loyal individuals whose task it was to advise Margaret and ensure she performed her duties as her half-brother demanded. Under the growing pressures she faced, notably religious discontent towards the heresy legislation, she was forced to defer to this council, whose chief member was Antoine Perrenot de Granvelle, a man whose loyalty to the Habsburgs was assured by the patronage of Philip II.

Portrait of Duchess Margaret of Parma, oil on canvas in the style of the Flemish school by an unknown artist, dated 1562.

In placing her faith in figures such as Granvelle, Margaret was, however, creating a worse situation. When Philip returned to Spain, the grandees had anticipated that their influence in the Council of State would be restored and that the regent would come to listen to them just as Charles V had done. When she turned to the inner council, the grandees were once again ignored and this gradually became increasingly difficult to overlook. Before Philip's accession they had enjoyed a fair relationship with Charles V, but his son had reduced their influence substantially. For many of these men, notably William of Orange and the Counts of Egmont and Hoorn, the declining political power of their class was a symbol of Philip's intention to reduce the autonomy of the country.

Margaret's regency was further undermined by her half-brother also leaving behind 3,000 Spanish soldiers, ostensibly to garrison the southern border, but their presence was interpreted by many grandees and Dutch citizens as a means of controlling the Netherlands should the need arise. This generated further animosity towards Habsburg rule because it seemed to present a direct challenge to the existing relationship which, given Philip's general attitude towards the country, was already in decline. The reaction of the provincial assemblies to these troops being garrisoned among them was to refuse to release money to pay for them until they were repatriated.

This act in itself was not unusual, as the assemblies had used finance as a means to promote their interests. However, in the more politically heated environment that Philip had left behind, the action became a significant political stand-off. This gave the Dutch a major victory when the soldiers, dissatisfied with not being paid, upset the local people generally through their aggressive behaviour and specifically by taking goods from them. Philip II relented, sending them off to the Mediterranean in January 1561 in return for his subsidy.

SOURCE

4

From a letter written by Antoine Perrenot de Granvelle to Philip II, dated 10 March 1563.

People here universally display discontent with any and all Spaniards in these provinces. It would seem that this derives from their suspicion that one might wish to subject them to Spain and reduce them to the same condition as the Italian provinces which are under the Spanish crown.

Margaret of Parma had a difficult task governing the Netherlands after 1559. Philip II had left a country simmering with disaffection towards its new ruler. Margaret was in one sense an unfortunate choice as she lacked the character to pursue a confident regency and as a result she deferred to others who were seen by the Dutch grandees as Habsburg lapdogs intent on reducing their nation's much-valued autonomy. In another sense, however, she was the right choice for Philip II who, it has been suggested, always intended to govern his northernmost territories himself, with Margaret simply installed as a puppet. In either case, her regency was both the prelude and opening act of the Dutch Revolt.

The influence of Granvelle

In 1560, Granvelle was appointed chief adviser in Margaret of Parma's regency government. As a loyal servant of both Charles V and Philip II, he was a suitable choice as chief adviser to the new regent because he could be relied upon to work in the interests of Philip. His influence was extensive as he conferred with Margaret and was also in correspondence with Philip II. As the principal adviser to the Habsburgs, Granvelle enjoyed significant power, and in his role as Archbishop of Mechelen – with control over all of the bishoprics in the Netherlands – he also acquired great wealth. In 1560, his archbishopric was amalgamated with the Abbey of Afflighem in Brabant and he received the 90,000 florins that were due to the abbot.

This acquisition was part of Philip II's reforms and it was a particularly controversial one as it significantly compromised some of Brabant's political privileges. Within its provincial assembly there were three chambers, in the most senior of which sat the clerical representatives. The spokesman of this chamber was, by traditional rights, the abbot of Afflighem. When this position was taken up by Granvelle there was significant disquiet among many Dutch who thought that the loyal servant of Philip II had been promoted to one of the most influential roles in the province of Brabant – indeed, one of the most powerful in the Netherlands. The promotion of Granvelle to this position was seen as yet another way in which the king of Spain was trying to undermine the autonomy of the provinces, this time by attempting, through his Church reforms, to pack the clerical chambers with loyal servants who would be better placed to subdue the more independent sentiments of the provinces.

Furthermore, when Granvelle was later promoted to cardinal in 1561, his new title also gave him precedence in the Council of State meetings, a precedence that was usually reserved for the most prominent of grandees, either Orange or Egmont. This was not so much a political attack against the grandees but an affront to their heritage. Following so swiftly from the reorganisation of the bishoprics, his appointment was seen as a personal indignity to the principal grandee families who wrote a formal letter of protest to the king, which was eventually posted on 15 August 1561.

In his role as archbishop and then cardinal, Granvelle pursued Philip's religious policy against heretics with great vigour and determination. He supported the establishment of more inquisitors in the provinces. However, this was vociferously challenged by the magistrates and traders of Antwerp in particular because of fears of losing trade and trampling local privileges. By 1563, the idea was dropped as Antwerp was a major financial interest for Spain and the rest of the Habsburg Empire because of its trading potential and banking facilities, and rather than risk further discontent Philip II agreed to suspend any more appointments.

As chief adviser and also head cleric in the Netherlands, Granvelle quickly became an unpopular figure, as he was associated with the perceived attempt to reduce both the autonomy of the provinces and the influence of the grandees. He was also the person who benefited most from the changes – especially the reforms to the Church – and as such it was increasingly felt that he had been a significant advocate for the policy. In combination with the maintenance of the heresy laws, and Philip II's disregard for local traditions and privileges, by 1563 significant numbers of the Dutch elite and increasing numbers of merchants were unhappy about the manner of Habsburg rule and this began to draw them out into open opposition.

ACTIVITIES
KNOWLEDGE CHECK

Spanish domination?

1 Having considered Source 4, can you present any evidence from your own knowledge and reading that supports the view that Granvelle is commenting upon?

2 Why do you think Philip II would want to reduce the autonomy of the Netherlands?

HOW EFFECTIVELY DID THE DUTCH GRANDEES OPPOSE SPANISH AUTHORITY?

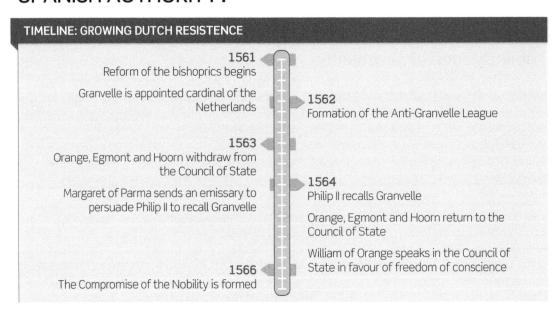

TIMELINE: GROWING DUTCH RESISTENCE

1561
Reform of the bishoprics begins

Granvelle is appointed cardinal of the Netherlands

1562
Formation of the Anti-Granvelle League

1563
Orange, Egmont and Hoorn withdraw from the Council of State

Margaret of Parma sends an emissary to persuade Philip II to recall Granvelle

1564
Philip II recalls Granvelle

Orange, Egmont and Hoorn return to the Council of State

William of Orange speaks in the Council of State in favour of freedom of conscience

1566
The Compromise of the Nobility is formed

The alliance of Orange, Hoorn and Egmont

In response to the marginalisation of their positions, particularly after the creation of Margaret's 'inner council', an alliance was formed between the three most noble of grandees: Orange, Egmont and Hoorn. Like William of Orange, Larmoral, Count of Egmont and Philip de Montmorency, Count of Hoorn were also *stadtholders* (crown-appointed provincial governors) who governed over Flanders and Artois, and Guelders respectively. They each came from wealthy backgrounds with strong ties to the Netherlands, and these men became increasingly upset about the reduction of their own influence over the regent and their replacement with Granvelle, whom they felt to be untrustworthy. Having written in protestation to Philip II in 1561, they subsequently formed the Anti-Granvelle League in 1562 in an attempt to have Granvelle removed.

As prominent figures in the Netherlands, they reasoned that their positions would protect them from any consequence that their action might produce. Each came from an ancient family that had served both the Netherlands and Spain, while William of Orange had also married the Lutheran Anna of Saxony in 1561 and believed his father-in-law would supply him with an army should things go very wrong.

The attack on Granvelle began on 11 March 1563, when they sent to Philip II an ultimatum stating that they would all resign unless the cardinal was removed. While awaiting Philip's response, members of the League sought to ridicule Granvelle by dressing themselves and their servants in a livery of a single colour with badges that mocked his office – including a fool's cap and bell to represent his cardinal's hat. Having so dressed, the League then embarked on a series of meetings and banquets to which friends were invited and where grievances about Granvelle were aired. These banquets evidenced the level of disaffection towards the cardinal: within the elite Order of the Golden Fleece there was widespread support of the league. With the support of such luminaries and given their positions within the court, it was expected that the king would listen more carefully to their request. However, on 6 June his reply asked that one of them come to Madrid to explain the situation, and in the meantime Granvelle was to remain in his post. The response from Philip II was taken as the king's continued support for Granvelle and an unwillingness to listen to what was felt to be a reasonable request by the Dutch grandees. After discussing the letter, each of the three co-recipients resolved to follow through with their threat and sent a letter to that effect in July, after which they each withdrew from the Council of State.

By removing themselves from the Council of State there was a public rift between the king and this group of prominent grandees. In terms of government, despite their perceived marginalisation, the Habsburgs needed the support of their *stadtholders* to maintain good links with the provincial assemblies and States-General, without which they might struggle to raise finances. The rift between them threatened this balance of power and, as anticipated, there were some financial consequences. The wealthy province of Brabant decided to withhold all taxes until the cardinal was removed.

Resistance to the reform of the bishoprics

Philip II's reform of the bishoprics, which had been enacted after 1561, was undoubtedly a significant source of the antipathy felt by the people towards Granvelle. This policy was seen as further evidence of the king seeking to undermine existing privileges and to make the Netherlands more subservient to Habsburg rule. The changes that had been proposed allowed for the creation of 14 new dioceses under new bishops, who would be under the authority of the archbishop of Mechelen. These were to replace the existing four, which came under the supervision of the bishop of Utrecht owing to the provinces' old ties to the Holy Roman Empire.

Ostensibly, these reforms were to improve the management of the Church in the Netherlands. However, they also provided for the usurpation of ancient privileges, and that caused the initial opposition of the provincial assemblies. In particular the new bishops would be paid for by granting them rights over the abbeys, which brought with them an annual income. Also, two canons within the new dioceses would serve as inquisitors for that area. Both of these proposals were anathema to the provinces, as they undermined what autonomy they retained. In the case of the abbeys, this gave the newly appointed bishops seats in the assemblies which potentially gave loyal Habsburg supporters power in these bodies. The example of Afflighem has been mentioned already, and it was feared that this was just the beginning of an attempt to create a majority of loyal supporters and thereby override independent provincial representation.

The significance of this growth in opposition was that it promoted a sense of unity among the provinces. Before this time there had been opposition to the Habsburgs, but it was sporadic and isolated opposition. The reform of the bishoprics provided a clear issue on which consensus could be achieved. The case of Afflighem saw the abbots there promote the dangers of the reforms to others in the provincial assembly, and by the end of 1561 they had won over both nobles and the towns to their cause. This was a significant achievement as there had previously been animosity between these groups on the grounds of taxation: the nobles had often sought exemption, which was opposed by the towns. In binding these groups together, the reforms promoted a more concerted opposition among the Dutch noble grandees and the ordinary people.

Just as the assumption of control over the abbeys was abhorrent, the magistrates and merchants also objected to the suggestion that inquisitors would be placed among them. This not only contravened the established practice whereby local jurisdiction was managed by the local magistrates, but the merchants were fearful that such religious policing by inquisitors in the area would lose them trade with their Protestant commercial interests. In Antwerp this was especially the case, as much of its trade was with the Holy Roman Empire – in which Protestantism was very popular – and England.

The Netherlands relied on Germany for the majority of its metal imports, and by 1550 Antwerp had built up this trade to the point that it was worth two million florins annually.

By 1563, this opposition was finally heard by Philip II who decided to delay the appointment of a bishop to Antwerp until his next visit to the Netherlands – this visit never materialised.

The removal of Granvelle

The impact of this opposition and also the recent exit of Orange, Egmont and Hoorn from the Council of State created a difficult position for the regent, Margaret of Parma. As regent it was her responsibility to ensure the effective governance of the Netherlands for her half-brother. However, with this exit of three prominent Dutch leaders, the government was in danger of being paralysed. Not only were the provinces increasingly combative regarding the religious reforms, but economic considerations were also mounting. The Baltic was closed to Dutch shipping because Fredrick II of Denmark had closed the sea after conflict broke out in 1563 between his country and Sweden, while a trade war with England was also imminent. These were real challenges to the economic performance of the Netherlands and Margaret was keen to address them.

The regent also had personal motives for removing Granvelle. She was very aware of his unpopularity in the Netherlands and that, as regent, she was regarded as a supporter of his. This consequently reduced her own position in the country and drew her some unwanted criticism. Perhaps more tangible, though, was her own resentment of the cardinal, whom she knew regularly corresponded with her half-brother about her and often criticised her performance. Furthermore, she felt that he had not done enough to arrange the marriage of her son, Alexander Farnese, to one of the daughters of the Austrian Habsburgs. Such was her own disaffection with Granvelle that on 12 August 1563 she sent her trusted secretary, Tomas de Armenteros, to Spain with detailed instructions on how to persuade Philip II to recall him.

- Armenteros was to make great play of the affront to royal authority that the Anti-Granvelle League presented.

- He was also to promote the idea that with Granvelle's removal the campaign against heresy would be more effective.

- Finally, he should remind the king of the greater Mediterranean war that Spain had been engaged in since 1560 and suggest that the situation in the Netherlands was an embarrassing footnote to this conflict.

The impact of these instructions is difficult to gauge. Given Philip's close interest in the Netherlands and his unwillingness to let Margaret govern independently, it is unlikely that they persuaded him entirely on their own. However, Granvelle also had enemies in the Spanish court, and when Philip heard other loyal Spaniards in the Netherlands describe the increasing discontent, he reluctantly submitted to Granvelle's recall. On 13 March 1564, Granvelle left his post, never to return to the Low Countries.

SOURCE 5

From an observation made by Viglius, a friend of Granvelle's, soon after the cardinal's recall from the Netherlands in late February 1564. He is writing to the Italian merchant Ludovico Guicciardini.

After the Cardinal departed, those who had been jealous of him became jubilant, acting like schoolboys in the absence of the teacher. Even the duchess was persuaded that she had been delivered from bondage, since previously she had undertaken nothing of importance without the participation of the council and the advice of the cardinal.

Margaret and the heresy laws

The removal of Granvelle saw the power of the inner council destroyed and the return of Orange, Egmont and Hoorn to the Council of State, where they used their newly reacquired influence to moderate the continuing heresy laws that Philip had reinforced prior to leaving the country. These were especially rigid and prescribed the death penalty for anyone who did not recant their belief.

The continuation of these laws and the rigour with which many inquisitors carried out their role had undermined the openness of Dutch society and increased the intervention of the state within people's lives.

Although provinces tried to discourage the Inquisition – Bruges had successfully kept it out and in August 1564 had actually imprisoned two officials of the department – the extent of its power was still felt. Between 1550 and 1566, Peter Titelman, an inquisitor in Flanders, personally managed to try 1,600 cases of heresy at an average of 100 a year.

Such was the impact of the heresy laws that the grandees sought to get them relaxed. The motivation for this endeavour was threefold.

- The excessive persecution of heresy could promote civil war, as was the current state of affairs in France after a long period of similar persecution.

- The use of the Inquisition showed complete disregard for local privileges within the provinces as inquisitors assumed jurisdiction from the rightful local magistrates.

- The grandees, though Catholic, saw no reason to persecute people because of differences in belief.

To an extent, the grandees were supported in their endeavour by the regent. In her letters to Philip II she regularly praised them for the dedication they had exhibited since their return to government. In 1564, and with Margaret's permission, the Council of State agreed to send Count Egmont to Spain to seek approval for the heresy laws in the Netherlands to be moderated. The mission to Spain was a failure, as Philip remained adamant that the challenge to the Catholic faith should be extinguished. Egmont returned to the Netherlands without any doubt as to the mind of the king.

SOURCE

6 From a letter written by Philip II from his residence in the Segovia Woods to Margaret of Parma, dated 17 October 1565.

As to the **Anabaptists**, what I wrote to you about them was in answer to what you asked me about the punishment of some prisoners. This did not differ from what the prince of Gavre [Egmont] reported. For though you have to deliberate about proposals for alternative punishments, this does not mean that they should cease until a resolution is taken. These prisoners must be punished as I told you in my letter from Valladolid. This also answers your representations to me in your letter of 22 July about state-affairs. I cannot refrain from telling you that considering the condition of religious affairs in the Netherlands as I understand it, this is no time to make any alteration. On the contrary, His Majesty's edicts should be executed; I think that the cause of the past evil and its subsequent growth and advance has been the negligence, leniency and duplicity of the judges, about which I shall give you more particulars later. I told the prince of Gavre that since the men condemned to die advance to execution not in silence, but as martyrs dying for a cause you should consider whether they ought not to be executed in secret in some way or other (though it is true that a public execution also serves to set an example).

KEY TERM

Anabaptists
A Protestant religious group that supports the separation of Church and state, and advocates baptism and church membership for adult believers only.

The Confederacy of Noblemen – the 'Compromise'

Although the Council of State had failed in its attempt, it did offer hope to others who were willing to adopt more aggressive techniques to achieve reform of the laws. During the winter of 1565–66, an alliance grew among 400 of the lesser nobles of the Netherlands that became known as the 'Compromise'. These men were predominantly Catholic and were mostly from the outlying provinces such as Gelderland where the government's authority was weakest. These men sympathised with those who were being persecuted for their faith and resolved to do something about the intolerance they felt had become more widespread in the country.

Led by a modest nobleman called John Marnix of Tholuse, the Compromise was intent upon securing more religious freedom on the grounds that intolerance threatened the stability of the Netherlands and also encroached upon the ancient privileges that they enjoyed. With the support of fellow nobles such as Nicholas de Hames, Henry Brederode and Louis of Nassau (the younger brother of William of Orange), the Compromise pressed its case forcefully (see Source 8) and was supported by the grandees, although they did not personally sign the document. Instead, they agreed that they would refuse to enforce the heresy laws in their own provinces. In January, Egmont warned the regent that they would be unable to enforce the heresy laws, while on 24 January 1566, William of Orange asked to be relieved of his post as *stadtholder* for the same reason.

The approach taken by members of the Compromise – confederates, as they were called – differed from the grandees. When they appeared before the regent there were more than 300 of them present, and they had brought pistols with them, which could be seen tucked into their belts. The purpose of this demonstration was to give the regent the distinct impression that should their wishes not be accepted they would resort to force of arms in order to achieve their desired religious reform.

The Compromise sought to:

- end the power of the Inquisition in the Netherlands
- encourage Philip II to withdraw his orders to implement the decrees from the Council of Trent.

EXTEND YOUR KNOWLEDGE

The Council of Trent, 1545–63
This was a meeting, consisting of 25 sessions, of the Catholic Church in Bologna and Trento in Italy.
It was convened to reaffirm the authority of Catholicism in the wake of the growth of Protestantism.
Widely regarded as the embodiment of the Counter Reformation, it also set out the crimes of heresy and demanded that such crimes be actively punished by followers of the Catholic Church.

SOURCE

From the 'Compromise' declaration, which was signed by its leaders in January 1566.

Not only is this inquisition iniquitous and against all divine and human laws, surpassing the worst barbarism ever practised by tyrants, it will also most certainly lead to the dishonouring of God's name and to the utter ruin and desolation of these Netherlands. Under the veil of only a few men's false hypocrisy, it will inevitably destroy all law and order, do away with all honesty, wholly weaken the authority and force of the old laws, customs and ordinances observed from time immemorial. It will deprive the States of this country of all freedom to express their opinion, it will do away with all ancient privileges, franchises and immunities, and not only make the burghers and inhabitants of this country miserable and ever-lasting slaves of the inquisitors, who are worthless people, but even subject the magistrates, officers and all nobles to the mercy of their investigations and visitations, and finally endanger the lives and possessions of all the king's honest and loyal subjects perpetually and openly.

SOURCE

8 From the 'Compromise' request presented to Margaret of Parma on 5 April 1566 by Henry Brederode and 300 supporters.

We are not in doubt, Madame, that whatever His Majesty formerly ordained and now again ordains regarding the inquisition and the strict observance of the edicts concerning religion, has some foundation and just title and is intended to continue all that the late emperor, Charles – blessed be his memory – decreed with the best of intentions. Considering however that different times call for different policies, and that for several years past those edicts, even though not very rigorously executed, have caused more serious difficulties, His Majesty's recent refusal to mitigate the edicts in any way, and his strict orders to maintain the inquisition, and to execute the edicts in all their rigour, makes us fear that the present difficulties will undoubtedly increase. But in fact the situation is even worse. There are clear indications everywhere that the people are so exasperated that the final result, we fear, will be an open revolt.

ACTIVITY
WRITING

Moderating language
Compare Sources 7 and 8.

1 Identify language within each of these sources that demonstrates strong feelings.

2 Compare the sources and offer some brief reasons why one might be more provocative than the other.

The beggars

Henry Brederode, a member of the Compromise, presents their demands to Margaret of Parma on 5 April 1566.

Brederode presente une Requéte à Marguerite de Parme au nom de tous les Conjurez.

The implication of this public demand for reform was significant. Having presented their case so decisively, the 'beggars', as one of Margaret's servants called the deputation, had given Margaret no choice but to consent to their request and in her reply on 6 April she agreed to advocate greater moderation and to instruct the inquisitors to be more lenient when carrying out their duties.

In one sense this was a victory for the confederacy as they obtained what they had sought. However, the resulting document that was circulated regarding the relaxation of the laws was a very moderate proposal, and it still required the approval of the king. It proposed that no one would be persecuted for their private beliefs, but public meetings that promoted alternative religions, or heresy, were still to be forbidden and were therefore punishable. The intention of the government was to appeal to the moderates in opposition, which might then diffuse the growing discontent. To expedite the new legislation, the States-General was not consulted and the individual provinces were forced to acquiesce. In this endeavour, the bishops and several grandees were very influential; the two bishops of Arras and St Omer signed their approval almost immediately, while the Duke of Aerschot and Ernst von Mansfelt, two royalist grandees, also agreed to the terms, which prompted its quick execution.

SOURCE 10

From *The Description of the Events which Happened in the Matter of Religion in the Netherlands* by Jacob van Wesenbeke, an observer of events in 1566. His *Description* was published in 1569.

Embitterment greatly increased and took root in people's hearts when they saw clearly, that some provincial States were ordered to meet separately (according to the aforementioned plan) in the presence of their governors or other knights of the Order or lords of high rank who were sent to persuade them to accept the proposed moderation. Moreover, people's perplexity and despair about the results were complete when it was found that the provincial States were left so little liberty in convoking the meeting that only a few selected members were summoned.

The attempt by Margaret to reduce the growing disaffection was a reasonable effort. However, it did not satisfy the more assertive members of the opposition – particularly the more determined 'beggars' and also William of Orange – who each felt the manner in which people were forced to consent to this new edict was contrary to their established privileges.

The 'beggars' adopted a combative approach and began to dress in grey livery, trimming their beards short in a common style to demonstrate their affiliation with the Dutch people. This activity was, on one level, a modest retaliation to the moderate reforms that disappointed them, but it was also seen as a growing challenge to the Habsburg state. For his part, William of Orange declared he was leaving the Netherlands in protest, and his friends Egmont and Hoorn were leaving with him. This was a clever tactic, as Margaret was reliant upon these men to help her restrain the confederates, and so she was determined to prevent their exit. To secure this she promised to entreat the king to show them more favour and also to give greater importance to the Council of State in which the grandees were dominant.

In securing their support with these promises, Margaret sent them out to confer with the confederates in the hope that they would be quieted. At a meeting in St Truiden in the independent state of Liège, the grandees held their own assembly and then consented to meet with 12 representatives of the confederates in the small town of Duffel. At this meeting they were shown a second Request, which demanded full toleration for Protestants and the calling of the States-General. These demands were more extreme than those imagined by the grandees and as a result the confederates were taken to Margaret to present their request. In demanding these changes, the confederates can be seen as championing religious freedom as well as the independent rights of the provinces. In recent years the States-General had not been called, and in its absence the government had enhanced central control over the provinces – particularly through the use of the Inquisition. In seeking its recall, the confederates arguably hoped to reaffirm provincial privileges in the face of what they perceived as growing centralised, Spanish, power.

Margaret's response to this new request was obvious anger and a demand that they wait 24 days for the expected letter detailing the king's thoughts on their first Request. In the event, this response offered some moderate changes but did not grant full freedom of conscience.

By 1566, the situation had deteriorated significantly. Philip II, having continually ignored the grandees' requests for reform, had encouraged a much more radical opposition in the form of the 'beggars' who were more numerous and less willing to be accommodated by moderate changes. This situation had initially arisen due to fears about Philip's wish to centralise power in the Netherlands and to reduce provincial privilege, but increasingly it took on a more religious tone as Philip II's battle to contain heresy began to spiral out of control with the introduction of a new threat to his religious stance.

> **A Level Exam-Style Question Section A**
>
> How far could the historian make use of Sources 7 and 8 together to investigate the decline in noble support for Habsburg rule?
>
> Explain your answer using both sources, the information about them and your own knowledge of the historical context.
> (20 marks)
>
> **Tip**
> *When answering this question, try to use each source equally when developing your points.*

ACTIVITIES

KNOWLEDGE CHECK

The importance of individuality

1 Identify the main figures involved in promoting the more divided relationship between the Dutch and their Spanish rulers by 1566.

2 For each individual write down two ways in which they contributed to this development.

HOW FAR DID CALVINISM IMPACT ON THE NETHERLANDS?

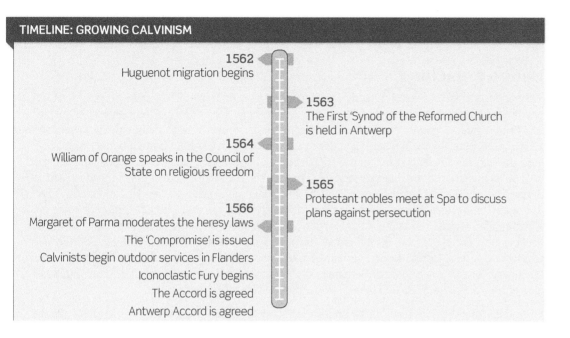

TIMELINE: GROWING CALVINISM

1562
Huguenot migration begins

1563
The First 'Synod' of the Reformed Church is held in Antwerp

1564
William of Orange speaks in the Council of State on religious freedom

1565
Protestant nobles meet at Spa to discuss plans against persecution

1566
Margaret of Parma moderates the heresy laws
The 'Compromise' is issued
Calvinists begin outdoor services in Flanders
Iconoclastic Fury begins
The Accord is agreed
Antwerp Accord is agreed

Philip II, like his father, had always retained a strong personal faith and this was challenged with the growth of **Calvinism** in the Netherlands. Calvinism had been present in the country as early as the 1540s. However, with the repressive heresy laws that Charles had instituted, its followers were forced to practise their faith in secret. After the relaxation of these laws in 1566 following political discontent, Calvinism enjoyed a resurgence and this encouraged further political disagreement that eventually gave way to open revolt.

The Huguenot migration from France

The question of religion had become more pressing since the migration of **Huguenots** into the Netherlands began following the outbreak of religious war in France in 1562. Thousands left France when the war began and many of these people sought refuge in the other parts of Europe, including the neighbouring Low Countries of the Netherlands.

The impact that these migrants had was substantial in terms of promoting political discontent. Arriving in the provinces in 1562, the Huguenots added to the problem of religion there, which had been enhanced following the reform of the bishoprics only the year before. Although this was primarily about reorganising the Catholic Church, the Spanish authorities also wanted to strengthen the Inquisition within the provinces as it was felt that the local magistrates were reluctant to prosecute heretics. For example, in 1562 the pastor at Eeklo complained that he was woken for several consecutive nights by people outside his window singing offensive songs about the sacraments. Similarly, in July 1564, at Ieper there was dancing in the streets to songs about a local Protestant martyr executed the year before. These events evidenced for the authorities the unwillingness of the local magistrates to fulfil their obligations regarding the heresy laws that were in effect.

In truth this was a reasonable conclusion, as the magistrates were the only figures with the power to stop these incidents and yet they were unwilling to commend such action. In this they were perhaps simply reflecting public opinion, which had often sympathised with the heretics. Two 'heretics' were rescued from execution in Valenciennes by the crowd, and in Antwerp two years later there were several attempts to free heretics from local prisons. Public support for the Protestants can in one sense be seen as a religious sympathy – part of a general feeling that people should not be persecuted for a different belief – while in another it could be a symptom of growing disaffection with Habsburg rule which had slowly been eroding local rights. Several of the grandees even voiced this growing sentiment, and in 1564 William of Orange had made a speech in the Council of State maintaining the right that people had to freedom of conscience.

In either case, the Huguenots found ears sympathetic to their plight in the Netherlands despite the heresy laws in place there. The influx of these people gave heart to native Protestants, particularly after 1566 when the laws were moderated, and together they started to practise their faith openly.

Hedge preaching

The sudden growth in Protestant activity alarmed the government in Brussels because it was done so openly and this threatened to attract even greater numbers. The newly arrived Calvinist Huguenots sought to organise open-air services, as had been their custom in France. Although there were some French preachers, the main external influence came from natives of the Low Countries who had gone into exile in England earlier in the 1560s. Some of them were radicalised in exile and returned in 1566 as preachers at the 'hedge' services. The first services took place in Flanders and Hainaut during May 1566, quickly followed by Brabant and Zeeland in June and then Holland on 14 July. The speed with which these services expanded was phenomenal and within two months there were regular services taking place across the south and western Netherlands. The timing of these services was also significant. With the days drawing out as the summer progressed the opportunity for more attendees increased and, combined with a recent economic depression that produced some unemployment, it gave people something to do. An observer in Antwerp estimated that within his area there were perhaps 30,000 people who attended Calvinist meetings.

Since these meetings were still illegal under the heresy laws, they were often organised outside the towns, usually near woods and hedges in the surrounding countryside, away from the authorities. The safest places were on the lands of a sympathetic nobleman whose position prevented government officials from going there. In areas where the local authorities were lacking effective resources or simply did not enforce the heresy laws, these services were often conducted beneath town walls. In most areas, however, this practice was ignored by the local authorities and where there was demand for action, the militia would often refuse to carry out their duty. In Tournai, for example, on 12 July 1566 the militia refused to act on the grounds that their family and friends might be present.

Such was the lack of enforcement against these open-air services that their numbers grew and quickly the Calvinists were in need of more preachers to meet the demand for spiritual guidance. In June 1566, a 'synod' or meeting was held in Antwerp to organise their Church more effectively and to seek more trained preachers from Geneva. The outcome of this meeting was the influx of more ministers, but also the spread of Calvinist literature, which helped to promote the religion even more.

The revolt of 1566

The growing popularity of the Calvinists gave their preachers confidence, and their sermons became more passionate and increasingly began to criticise the Catholic Church. The basis of this criticism lay in Catholicism's use of imagery and idols – the Virgin Mary for instance – within their worship. This was in complete contrast to the Calvinist justification by faith alone and as such they disagreed with what they viewed as **idolatry**.

SOURCE

 From a report written by a government agent in Courtrai and sent to the Spanish court in July 1566.

> The audacity of the Calvinist preachers in this area has grown so great that in their sermons they admonish the people that it is not enough to remove all idolatry from their hearts; they must also remove it from their sight. Little by little, it seems, they are trying to impress upon their hearers the need to pillage the churches and abolish all images.

The Iconoclastic Fury

On 10 August 1566, a Flemish-born Calvinist minister by the name of Sebastian Matte gave a sermon in Steenvoorde, now part of France. Such was the tone of this sermon that many of his audience then proceeded into the monastery outside of which they were standing, and smashed all of the images they found inside. Similarly, three days later in Bailleul, the monastery of St Anthony was sacked after an inflammatory sermon by a Calvinist minister by the name of Jacob de Buzere. These attacks were not isolated and further incidences took place across the provinces in what became known later as the **Iconoclastic** Fury. In west Flanders alone 400 churches were attacked in August, while most of the main towns in the Netherlands witnessed similar treatment.

KEY TERM

Iconoclasm
The destruction of religious images – usually paintings and statues.

SOURCE 12

An example of the iconoclasm that took place in the Low Countries throughout 1566. The engraving is by Frans Hogenburg, c16th century.

Nach wenigh Predication
Die Caluinsche Religion

Das bildens sturmen fiengen an
Das nicht ein bilde dauon bleib sfan

Kap Monstrantz, kilch, auch die altar
Vnd west sonst dort vor handen war:

Zerbrochen all in kurtzer stundt
Gleich gar vil leuten das ist kundt.

Anno Dñj. M. D. LXVI. XX Augusti

The motivation for this religious revolt had its origins in the teachings of John Calvin, the instigator of the new faith, who believed that images should not be used in worship as they undermined a pure faith in God. By adhering so forcefully to this idea the Iconoclastic Fury was a profound event in the Netherlands. It signified the introduction of a new Church and its attempt literally to throw out the paraphernalia of the older, Catholic, faith so as to reclaim the churches for its own use. In this action the established religion was directly challenged in a manner that suggested co-ordination and genuine intent. Indeed, the sacking of the churches in the south of the Netherlands was actually the work of around 50–100 paid iconoclasts. These men were paid for their work by Calvinist ministers in Antwerp and their actions dealt great destruction upon Catholic churches.

Given this professional approach, it is possible that this was a real attempt to dominate the religious arena. However, it is equally possible that the iconoclasts (the people committing the Fury) were motivated to act in this way simply for the opportunity of payment which Calvinist ministers offered.

In 1566, the economy was affected by depression which resulted in unemployment levels increasing and people seeking work wherever it could be found. It might possibly be suggested that many perpetrators of the Fury saw their actions as simply a job rather than the expression of any religious conviction. Despite this implication, the northern provinces saw spontaneous, popular attacks that went much further to promote the idea that there was a political motivation behind the actions, as the north was traditionally much more independently minded and potentially saw the opportunity to challenge the existing political order. After the reform of the bishoprics after 1560, the Church had been explicitly drawn into the political dispute over privilege and was perhaps a victim of that connection.

Whether the intent was to push out Catholicism, challenge the political system, or simply to acquire buildings for their own use, the Fury evidenced a much more confident manner among the heretics in the Netherlands, and the ruling authority endeavoured to address this confidence.

THINKING HISTORICALLY Causation (5b)

Causation relativity

Historical events usually have many causes. Some are crucial while some are less important. For some historical questions it is important to understand exactly what role certain factors played in causing historical change.

Significant factors in the timing and nature of the Iconoclastic Fury

Economic depression	The growth of Calvinism	The relaxation of the heresy laws after 1566
Growing political discontent among the nobles	Many provinces were unwilling to prevent the Calvinist outdoor services	The weakness of Margaret of Parma

Answer the following questions on your own.

The timing of the Iconoclastic Fury

1 How important was the declining economic situation in explaining the timing of the Fury?

2 In what ways did the growth of Calvinism change the state of affairs caused by the relaxation of the heresy laws? How far did this precipitate the Iconoclastic Fury?

3 How could Margaret of Parma have delayed the kind of attack evidenced by the Fury?

The nature of the Iconoclastic Fury

4 How far had the growing discontent among the nobles changed the attitudes of the people who were involved in committing the Iconoclastic Fury?

5 What role did the above factors play in the way that the Fury reshaped the Dutch economy?

6 Would the nature of the Iconoclastic Fury have been the same if the provinces were more authoritative?

7 What roles did each of the above causal factors play in determining the nature and timing of the Iconoclastic Fury?

The restoration of order

The extent of religious discontent stirred the Brussels government into action. Margaret and the grandees within the Council of State were shocked at the turn of events, and the grandees undertook to pacify the situation as best they could. William of Orange and his friends encouraged a conciliatory policy and this was borne out when the confederates used the opportunity to demand more concessions. In August 1566, they presented another petition to the regent, which demanded full toleration of religious views. In light of her weakened position, and entreated by the grandees, she duly accepted this request on 23 August. The Accord, as it became known, stipulated that Protestants could worship openly in places where they had already established services, as long as they also respected the Catholic faith and did not interfere with it.

It was hoped that this would be sufficient to end the Fury. However, in the north, Calvinists continued to smash Catholic imagery – at Groningen on 17 September and Vianen on 25 September among others in that month. The continuation of the destruction was in most cases encouraged by the confederate nobles, many of whom had been won over by the Calvinist faith, while for the grandees it was a source of concern and also embarrassment. They were duty-bound to try to enforce the Accord on the grounds that they had endorsed it, but also they feared for their own properties.

To effect an end to the disturbances, William of Orange chose to grant further concessions to the Calvinists. In September, he issued a compromise in Antwerp that became known as the Antwerp Accord and gave both Calvinists and Lutherans the right to worship both outside *and inside* the city. This had not been granted under the existing Accord, which only provided for these groups to worship outside the towns. Margaret was reluctant to allow worship inside the city in case it encouraged further devotees, and she had neglected to mention this in her offer. The new compromise also allowed for these Protestant faiths to build their own churches – another feature Margaret had omitted from the original Accord. Following the lead of William of Orange, Egmont and Hoorn arranged similar agreements within their provinces, which was then followed in turn by other *stadtholders*.

SOURCE 13

From a letter, explaining his additional compromise to Calvinists, written by William of Orange to Margaret of Parma, dated 4 September 1566.

Whenever such sermons take place 18 or 20,000 persons leave the town through various gates, to listen to them. In Flanders and elsewhere trade as well as industry stagnate, so that the county is full of **vagabonds** and idlers. These might easily mingle with the crowd under the pretext of listening to the sermons, join them (of this we have been warned and are still being warned) and then enter the town together and pillage it. In fact they have said themselves that this is their intention, because it is the richest and most opulent town of the whole country and the one where the most **plunder** is found. They will unite with the great multitude of workmen in this town, who cannot earn wages to sustain themselves, their wives and children because of the troubles and stagnation of trade… but thanks to the new agreement the latter need no longer to go outside the town to hear or attend sermons.

KEY TERMS

Vagabond
A person without a home who wanders from place to place.

Plunder
A term used to describe the stealing of goods, usually by the use of force.

In granting further concessions, the actions of the grandees angered Margaret as she had particularly tried not to promote the new religions in the towns. Her reaction was to denounce the Antwerp Accord and all other agreements made in her name. In addition, she undertook to write to her half-brother to explain how awful the situation had become. She even suggested, erroneously, that half the population was infected with heresy and openly challenging her authority with force of arms.

The letter she sent to Philip II evidences her perceived loss of control over the situation in the Netherlands. Having first been subject to the influence of Granvelle, and always having to keep her half-brother informed, Margaret of Parma was never entirely independent to pursue her own course of action. As the Habsburg representative in the country, she was certainly well placed to appreciate the growing difficulties. However, she was not able to contain it effectively. Her dependence on men like William of Orange, as grandees of the provinces, to help her negotiate with the nation was also problematic in itself. These men were motivated by personal desires for more power and independence from the Habsburgs, while at the same time they were equally fearful of the growing threat of Calvinism – not so much because of what it represented, but rather the threat it created to their own estates and privileges. It was because of this concern that they issued a further compromise that eventually led to them being openly criticised by Margaret in her letter to Philip II.

The effects of Calvinism in the Netherlands

In granting her Accord, Margaret was conceding more than Philip II was prepared to give, and in consequence of its failure to prevent the continuing desecration of Catholic churches, he undertook to restore order in the Low Countries through force of arms. In October 1566, William of Orange received a letter from Spain detailing the king's intentions.

SOURCE 14 From a letter by Montigny, brother of Hoorn, to the Prince of Orange, dated 4 October 1566.

The army His Majesty is raising with which to visit us is thought certain to consist of ten thousand Spaniards (eight thousand veterans from Italy and two thousand recruits ...), six thousand Italians, twenty-four thousand Germans, two thousand light cavalry, one thousand men-at-arms and five thousand heavy cavalry. As for money, I can assure you that it is a long time since a Christian prince was better supplied, even for a greater enterprise.

With Philip II intent on defending Catholicism in his northern possessions, the political situation in the Netherlands became explosive. In creating the immediate justification for the return of his troops, which had been largely absent since 1561, the Iconoclastic Fury is an important marker in the development of open hostilities. By extension, the growth of Calvinism provided the context for this event and therefore is also fundamental to the eventual breakdown in relations.

The introduction of Calvinism was something of a catalyst. In this sense the growth of this religion within the Netherlands created an environment that made worse a political relationship that was already beginning to show signs of estrangement between the Spanish rulers and the Dutch. Evidence of disaffection was present as early as 1555 with the accession of Philip II when he ran roughshod over the ancient privileges of the 17 provinces. More evidence emerged following his attempt to reform the bishoprics and his promotion of the unpopular Granvelle. In these events were sown the seeds of discontent, as the grandees sought to maintain their positions and also to protect the rights of their assemblies. The new religion that came to the fore after 1566 exacerbated these tensions through the demands of the Confederacy of Noblemen, which could be read as a veiled attempt to promote local privilege by undermining the inquisition in the provinces. Furthermore, the Iconoclastic Fury was supported by many of these confederates who used the occasion to extract further reforms from Margaret. In this capacity the religion might well have been thought of as a means to further push ancient rights – or at least gain retribution for their decline. It was an easily used tool with which to attack the government.

Calvinism not only added a new dimension to the existing problems between the Dutch and their Habsburg rulers, it forced a more dramatic solution. Religion was an important feature in the lives of men and women in the 16th century and what a person believed had a significant impact upon the experiences they enjoyed. In the Netherlands, Catholicism was the dominant religion and Philip II was a devout leader who sought to maintain his faith in that country. Calvinism presented a real threat to this faith and so the king was moved to defend it. Initially this was through the existing heresy laws which he could not bring himself to excessively moderate, but by the end of 1566 this was not enough and consequently he decided to take more drastic action.

A Level Exam-Style Question Section B

How far was religion chiefly responsible for the breakdown in relations between the Habsburgs and their subjects by 1566? (20 marks)

Tip
Consider the key phrases in the question. Here the term 'chiefly' is very important, so be sure to address what this might imply.

ACTIVITIES
KNOWLEDGE CHECK

Catalysts

1 Using the material you have just read complete the following activities:

   a) Briefly describe the central feature of Calvinism.

   b) Write down a list of occasions when Calvinism caused discontent between the Dutch and Spanish.

2 A catalyst is something that speeds up a reaction. In what way was Calvinism a catalyst in promoting the decline of Habsburg control by the end of 1566? Remember to justify your answer.

ACTIVITY
SUMMARY

Origins of the Dutch Revolt

1 Create a table using the headings: Role of tradition; Role of individuals; Role of religion. Under each heading write down any evidence you can about how that heading informed the outbreak of revolt by 1567.

2 Using this evidence write a paragraph explaining why you think revolt broke out in 1567.

 WIDER READING

Darby, G. (ed.) *The Origins and Development of the Dutch Revolt*, Routledge (2000)

Parker, G. *The Dutch Revolt*, Penguin (1990)

Rady, M. *From Revolt to Independence: the Netherlands 1550–1650*, Hodder (1990)

Woodward, G. *The Development of Early Modern Europe*, Longman (1997)

2b.2 Alva and Orange, 1567–73

KEY QUESTIONS

- How significant was Alva in promoting further opposition?
- Why did Orange fail in his first attempt to invade the Netherlands?
- How important were the Sea Beggars in challenging Spanish rule?
- Why was Orange able to enjoy greater success by 1573?

INTRODUCTION

The rising level of religious discontent in the Netherlands throughout 1566 was a disturbing prospect for Philip II, whose own faith was absolute. The menace of Calvinism was a challenge he was prepared to meet with force of arms if necessary as he took his role as a guardian of Catholicism very seriously and would not countenance any growth in heretical opinion within his territories. Given the excesses of the Iconoclastic Fury and the pre-existing political discontent that had emerged over the reorganisation of the bishoprics, the Spanish court saw the Netherlands as a troublesome state that needed a stronger line to be taken there. This image was reinforced by Margaret of Parma's letter to Philip in April 1566, in which she deliberately overestimated the level of threat due to the compromise she was forced to concede to the Confederacy of Noblemen that same month. In light of this information, which maintained that Philip II's government was facing an opposition of more than 200,000, the king was moved to take more strident action to ensure his interests. Therefore, he had raised an army with the intention of sending an invasion force both to subdue the growing heresy and to reassert his rule. By the end of 1566, this army had been assembled under the authority of his chief adviser, the Duke of Alva.

EXTEND YOUR KNOWLEDGE

Fernando Alvarez de Toledo, the Duke of Alva (1507–82)
Born into a rich family who loyally served the kings of Castile, Alva joined the Spanish army in 1524 and became a distinguished officer while fighting against the French, where he developed the use of firearms in battle. Having been made the commander of the imperial forces in Italy in 1552 and then viceroy of Naples in 1556, he was recommended to Philip II by his father and became a prominent member of his court after 1559. As a military figure, Alva pushed for a hard line to be taken against the Netherlands, and in 1563 he had recommended that the aristocratic opposition to Philip II in that country should have their heads removed. Although the king did not listen on that occasion, after 1566 he was more inclined towards Alva's aggressive position and charged him with bringing order back to the Netherlands.

1567 – Alva arrives in the Netherlands
Council of Troubles is established
Margaret of Parma resigns as regent
Orange leaves for Germany

| 1567 | 1568 | 1569 | 1570 |

1568 – Egmont and Hoorn are executed
Orange's first invasion
Rebel victory at Heiligerlee
The Sea Beggars are formed

HOW SIGNIFICANT WAS ALVA IN PROMOTING FURTHER OPPOSITION?

Alva's rule

As a principal adviser to Philip II, the Duke of Alva was aware of the growing difficulties within the Netherlands. As a staunch Catholic himself and a loyal servant of the Spanish court, he had often counselled an aggressive policy towards the Netherlanders, preferring a more rigidly centralised political structure there instead of the loose confederation of provinces that existed. This particular attitude was influenced by his own experiences as a military general, who recognised the value of hierarchy and unquestioning obedience to orders. It was on the advice of men like Alva that Philip II resolved to send troops to the 17 provinces, and by the end of 1566 the necessary preparations had been made.

The Duke of Alva arrived in the Netherlands in August 1567 with instruction from Philip II to restore peace and eliminate the heretical opinions that were growing there. Under his command were 10,000 Spanish troops, 4,000 local troops and an array of foreign **mercenaries** from around the empire. In total, the entire force under his direction amounted to approximately 70,000 men, and with this force Alva sought to **pacify** the country. The military heritage of Alva made him a good choice for the king – campaigns in Germany, Italy and France had won him great praise and also given him an aggressive disposition that lent itself to subduing discontent. Having been personally selected by Philip II, the duke regarded himself as accountable only to him and, therefore, upon his arrival in the country he felt able to ignore the authority of the regent and free to pursue his mission as he saw fit.

The replacement of Margaret of Parma

In assuming this stance Alva was quick to alienate Margaret of Parma, who had grown increasingly frustrated by her position in the Netherlands. The lack of independence that Philip granted her when she assumed the role and, more recently, the manner in which she was forced to acquiesce to the demands of the Compromise had undermined her authority. The presence of another who denied her rank further humiliated her and undermined her position, and she grew increasingly hostile towards the duke.

As early as his first day in the Low Countries – 3 August 1567 – Alva had earned the regent's enmity, as the grandees had all turned out to greet him at his camp outside the frontier town of Thionville, leaving Margaret alone in her largely deserted palace in Brussels. The speed with which the grandees attended Alva was suggestive of their desire to ingratiate themselves with the general who, it would seem, was the latest representative of the king.

After presenting himself to Margaret on 22 August, Alva laid out his plans for pacifying the country so that Philip II would be able to return to the lands and reassert his rights as monarch there. To this end he intended to garrison the 10,000 loyal Spanish troops that he had brought with him just outside the capital – the cavalry in Diest and the infantry in the towns of Enghien, Lier, Ghent and

1572 – Alva uses force to collect the Tenth Penny tax

Elizabeth I closes English ports to the Sea Beggars

Seizure of Brill and Flushing

1573 – Alva is replaced by Requesens

1571	1572	1573

1572 – Orange's second invasion

Siege of Mons

St Bartholomew's Day massacre in France

Orange unites the provinces of Holland and Zeeland

Brussels itself. His firmness in this decision illustrates his clear belief that his position was not below that of Margaret in terms of his mission. Margaret was not happy about the idea of billeting Spanish troops in the towns, and she made that clear. In this matter, however, the duke would not tolerate any objections and was less than deferential to the regent.

SOURCE
1 From Alva's reply to Margaret's complaint about billeting troops in towns in August 1567.

I fail to understand how any person of sound mind can be of the opinion that His Majesty should come here with only the mediocre forces at present mobilized. If any moves were made against him from outside or inside the country (where His Majesty has been told that there are more than 200,000 heretics), he would run the dangers and the risks which one can easily imagine.

KEY TERM

Demobilisation
The process of standing down an army - usually because of the end of conflict.

In a high-handed manner similar to that shown in Source 1, Alva was also quick to order the **demobilisation** of troops that Margaret had raised during the recent troubles. The result of this decision in particular was humiliating because loyal troops were summarily dismissed without any form of acknowledgement and, given that they had been employed by Margaret, this treatment reflected badly on her. As well as the billeting of troops in the towns that resulted in public disturbances after several Spaniards attacked the local population, this additional impertinence made it increasingly difficult for Margaret to continue in office.

The final straw for the regent came when, on 8 September 1567, Hoorn and Egmont were summoned to Brussels whereupon they were immediately arrested by Alva's troops. Having fled to Germany with William of Orange, following the realisation that they had all been implicated in the recent troubles, each had been asked to return to the country – Hoorn upon a personal invitation by Margaret at the request of Alva. Orange elected to ignore the summons and remained abroad. The arrest of Egmont and Hoorn made Margaret's position almost impossible, as any credibility she retained was lost, given that it was she who had invited the men back to the Netherlands and therefore she might be viewed as Alva's accomplice. Her position in Brussels was already weak after the Compromise and Alva's arrival, and as a result she was compelled to resign her position, leaving for Italy on 30 December 1567.

In her stead the Duke of Alva was sworn in as governor-general of the Netherlands, and by the end of the year he had already stamped his uncompromising mark on that nation.

The execution of Egmont and Hoorn

The rationale for the arrest of several of the grandees lay in the interpretation of events in 1566 that was adopted in Spain by Philip II. Rather than accept that these individuals were not party to the Compromise or the Iconoclastic Fury that followed, Philip chose to place them at the heart of events, imagining that they were the ringleaders of the challenge to his authority and his faith. For him, such shocking events must have been planned and this could only be managed by the well-resourced grandees who had already opposed his political policies for greater centralised control. Margaret of Parma was better placed to appreciate the finer points of 1566 and had been convinced that these men had not been party to the religious problems that developed and had, in fact, undertaken to minimise the disturbances as much as they could. William of Orange had agreed the Antwerp Accord that allowed greater religious freedoms, and Egmont and Hoorn had agreed similar pacts in their own provinces. After December 1567, however, Margaret no longer held a position of authority and had left the country, therefore removing this line of defence for the grandees.

KEY TERM

Orthodoxy
The only authorised idea or belief permitted.

The Duke of Alva, as the new chief authority in the Netherlands, was quick to establish his authority and set about a more ruthless policy of subjugation, which was based on his principles of Catholic **orthodoxy** and the natural authority of Spain, each of which demanded total obedience. The manner in which he pursued these aims has traditionally been seen as an arbitrarily despotic rule that was designed to force immediate obedience, but actually it only succeeded in promoting further discontent.

THINKING HISTORICALLY   Causation (6a)

Different times, different places

Different times and different places have a different set of ideas. Beliefs about how the world works, how human societies should be governed, or the best way to achieve economic prosperity can all be radically different from our own. It is important for the historian to take into account these different attitudes and be aware of the dangers of judging them against modern ideas.

'One true faith'

Philip II was a devout Catholic and throughout his reign he sought to protect this religion and maintain its position as the 'one true faith'. Like his father before him, Philip II used inquisitors in the Netherlands to root out heretical opinions that challenged the authority of the Catholic Church, and they executed anyone who did not recant their heretical beliefs. Often people did not recant because they believed strongly in their own ideas and felt that through their martyrdom they would receive eternal life.

Answer the following questions.

1 What events had taken place to give rise to the notion that martyrdom was preferable to recanting?

2 If they had known how events would progress, e.g. that the Netherlands would become independent, do you think fewer people would have been martyred?

3 Sixteenth century Spanish attitudes to religion are different from current attitudes in England.

   a) Are there any other ways in which 16th century Spanish attitudes differed dramatically from those that are current in England now?

   b) Why do you think that they are different?

4 How important is it for historians to deal with events in the context of the beliefs and values of people in the past as well as seeing them as part of a greater pattern?

Among the first casualties of this new rule were the grandees Egmont and Hoorn. Having been arrested in September 1567 upon their return from Germany, on 5 June 1568 they were executed on the orders of Alva and in the name of Philip II. The motivation for this action was, in one sense, an assertion of power and desire to make examples of those who challenged the king. As grandees and members of the political opposition – Egmont, for example, had travelled to Spain to petition Philip in 1566 – these men were well known and it was anticipated that their deaths would go some way to silencing the discontent that had been growing. In signing their death warrants, Alva had expected to reinforce his position, but this evidences how little he understood events in the Netherlands. Rather than meekly resigning themselves to what the rebels regarded as a Habsburg occupation, the death of Egmont and Hoorn encouraged resistance and helped to shape William of Orange as the principal opposition to the duke's rule. In this sense, the executions helped to establish clear battle lines within the Low Countries. Until the arrival of Alva, the relationship was arguably salvageable. However, his aggressive tactics alienated many Netherlanders and the execution of these grandees was proof that he intended to assert Habsburg authority vigorously.

The Council of Troubles and the attacks on heresy

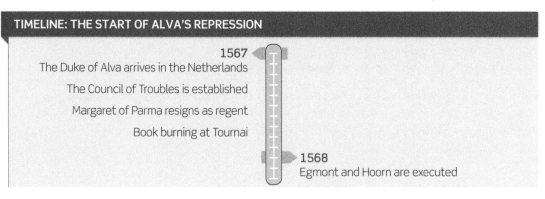

TIMELINE: THE START OF ALVA'S REPRESSION

1567
The Duke of Alva arrives in the Netherlands
The Council of Troubles is established
Margaret of Parma resigns as regent
Book burning at Tournai

1568
Egmont and Hoorn are executed

KEY TERM

Denunciation
The act of informing the
authorities about someone's
actions.

In many ways the execution of Egmont and Hoorn was the spark that set off open conflict in the country. However, the environment was already well adapted to combustion even before this event, and the executions were just another justification for opposing Alva's despotic government. The principal means by which he intended to restore religious and political power was through a judicial body known as the Council of Troubles, which was set up on 5 September 1567. This institution was staffed mostly by loyal Netherlanders under the control of a seven-man tribunal of which Alva was the head, and it was intended that the body would investigate the extent of heresy in the country and then punish any acts that it felt threatened Habsburg interests and particularly the Catholic faith of Philip II. In prosecuting its duties, the Council of Troubles relied on **denunciations** by members of the public, and this method of operation went a long way towards fostering the belief that Alva was deliberately trying to undermine the establishment of a Netherlands unity that might threaten Philip's overall power.

EXTEND YOUR KNOWLEDGE

The Council of Troubles
This was a judicial body that was set up in September 1567 to investigate, and then punish, heresy. It was the conduit through which Alva sought to re-establish Catholicism's dominance in the Netherlands and reinforce the will of Philip II. Such were the excesses of the Council of Troubles that it earned itself the nickname 'the Council of Blood' and between 1567 and 1576 it ordered the execution of more than 1,000 people, having consented to the arrest and torture of more than nine times that number.

In using brutal tactics such as torture and execution, the Council of Troubles quickly achieved an omnipotent presence that terrified the local population as it was very ruthless in following up any accusations. Between 1567 and 1576, 12,000 people were summoned to the courts set up by the Council of Troubles, 9,000 were actually arrested following a hearing and more than 1,000 people were executed after being found guilty of heresy. In addition to arrests, the Council of Troubles also targeted heretical literature and in Tournai, on 16 June 1568, there was a public burning of books following raids on the town's booksellers.

The main intention of these actions was to reinforce Catholic faith. However, the manner in which this was being achieved was also designed to instil fear among the population. So successful was this particular outcome that even innocent people were afraid of condemnation and were driven to extreme action, for example one tax collector called Albert van Loo tried to commit suicide because he felt he might be arrested for failing to stop the Iconoclastic Fury in his area by himself.

In effect, the Council of Troubles established a culture of fear that was further reinforced by the execution of Egmont and Hoorn and the sentence of treason being passed *in absentia* on other grandees (including William of Orange) whose lands were forfeited. In the case of Orange, not only were his estates confiscated by the government, but his eldest son, Philip William, was kidnapped while studying at Leuven. Within this environment, Alva was attempting to construct an unassailable position whereby Habsburg rule would not be questioned again and the Catholic faith would be reimposed without challenge. Anyone who had a connection with the Iconoclastic Fury of two years earlier was implicated and either arrested or forced to flee the country as Alva tightened his grip on the nation. Most left in late 1566 and early 1567.

The Tenth Penny tax

The cost of restoring order in the Low Countries was expensive. By 1572, Alva's army was in excess of 70,000 strong and these men needed paying if they were to remain of use to the duke. The aggressive approach he had adopted made it especially necessary to maintain an effective army. However, by his own reckoning, it would cost just over 1.8 million florins for defence and then another 2.3 million florins for administration each year. In May 1568, he had been informed by Philip II that this money would not be forthcoming from Spain as the country was under financial strain because of its war with the Turks.

SOURCE 2

Executions by the Blood Council (the name given to the Council of Troubles by the people of the Low Countries). A drawing by an unknown artist, c16th century.

EXTEND YOUR KNOWLEDGE

Philip II's war against the Ottoman Empire (1558–80)
The Ottoman Empire was seen as a threat to Catholicism during the 16th century because it was seeking to extend its empire into the Mediterranean and introduce Islam more directly into Europe. After 1558, Spain under Philip II defended the religion against this perceived threat on and off until a peace treaty was signed in 1580. In 1558, the Ottomans invaded the Balearic Islands and Philip saw this as a threat to both Spain and his Church, and therefore he sent troops to the Mediterranean to prevent further Ottoman gains. The war brought Spain to the verge of bankruptcy and not only drew Philip II's attention away from the Netherlands, but also used much-needed resources.

Instead of receiving money from Spain, Alva was told to raise the finance he needed himself, through the introduction of new taxes to be levied on the local population. In March 1569, the duke convened the States-General to vote in the new taxes that he and his advisers had created:

- the Tenth Penny: a permanent ten percent tax on all sales other than land
- the Twentieth Penny: a permanent tax of five percent on all future sales of land-based property
- the Hundredth Penny: a one-off tax of one percent of the value of a person's owned capital.

The Hundredth Penny tax was readily agreed by the States-General because it was not seen as a real threat to their political position since it was a one-off payment, and by 1571 3.3 million florins had been received. The other two taxes, and especially the Tenth Penny tax, were refused because they were permanent and would therefore undermine the power of the assembly, whose greatest power lay with its money-raising authority. If Alva had a permanent source of revenue, then he would have no need to ever call the States-General again, and therefore the demand was denied. However, following intimidation by Alva, the States-General did grant a one-off sum known as an *aide* of four million florins to be collected over two years.

Growing opposition to the tax

This compromise was accepted by Alva as he needed funds to pay for his army. However, he continued to push for the permanent taxes so that he would be financially secure. Initially he tried to negotiate with the assembly: the Tenth Penny would only apply on the first and last sale of moveable goods, which he maintained would not interfere with trade very much. This was also refused and he was told in very clear terms that the assembly would never approve the Tenth Penny. When he sought financial assistance from Spain, once more he was reproached by the king whose commitment against the Turks was sapping the Spanish exchequer. Alva decided to take the tax without the consent of the States-General, and in the spring of 1572 he began to move troops into shops and storehouses to oversee the forcible collection of the money.

The decision by Alva to extract the payment by force was very misguided and it was not popular or successful. Once again the action was interpreted as a Habsburg attempt to reduce the remaining authority of provincial privilege, and in defiance of this act shops closed their doors and trade ground to a halt as taxpayers and local businesses sought to obstruct the collection of the tax. In addition, the provincial assemblies of Hainaut, Flanders, Brabant and Artois sent representatives to Spain to complain in person to the king about the extreme behaviour of Alva and the imposition he now made upon them. Though Philip II was unreceptive to their words, the attempt to force the payment of the Tenth Penny tax met with universal condemnation within the Netherlands. It threatened to stir up further discontent and even, given Alva's unpopular record in that country, a general rebellion.

ACTIVITIES
KNOWLEDGE CHECK

The impact of Alva

The arrival of the Duke of Alva in the Netherlands was intended to reassert Catholicism and consolidate Spanish rule in the country after the unrest in 1566-67.

1 Write a list of points that support his success and a second list of points that challenge it.

2 Briefly answer the following question: How successful do you think Alva was in achieving his objectives?

WHY DID ORANGE FAIL IN HIS FIRST ATTEMPT TO INVADE THE NETHERLANDS?

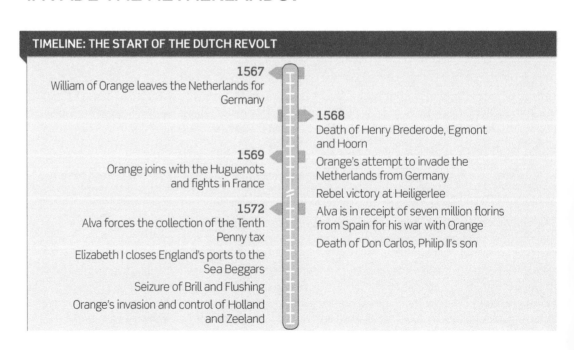

TIMELINE: THE START OF THE DUTCH REVOLT

1567
William of Orange leaves the Netherlands for Germany

1568
Death of Henry Brederode, Egmont and Hoorn

Orange's attempt to invade the Netherlands from Germany

Rebel victory at Heiligerlee

1569
Orange joins with the Huguenots and fights in France

Alva is in receipt of seven million florins from Spain for his war with Orange

Death of Don Carlos, Philip II's son

1572
Alva forces the collection of the Tenth Penny tax

Elizabeth I closes England's ports to the Sea Beggars

Seizure of Brill and Flushing

Orange's invasion and control of Holland and Zeeland

Orange's power and influence in the northern provinces

The execution of Egmont and Hoorn, along with the death of Henry Brederode, the man who had presented the Compromise in 1566, cemented the position of William of Orange as leader of the opposition. However, even before these events he was generally regarded as the only realistic opponent to the Duke of Alva. As the sovereign of the principality of Orange, he was a natural leader to whom people looked for direction, and when the Council of Troubles passed the sentence of treason on him he became a formal enemy of Spain.

Orange had spent his time abroad watching events in the Netherlands with great care, keeping in close contact with friends there and also making new allies. Having embraced Lutheranism in 1567, he had endeared himself to his new co-religionists by supporting the Huguenots in their war against the French Catholics. With allies in Germany and France, Orange set about trying to organise the widespread opposition to Alva within the Netherlands, issuing his 'Warning' to the people of that country in September 1568.

SOURCE

3 From the 'Warning' that William of Orange issued to the people of the Netherlands on 1 September 1568.

It is clear that the inquisitions, executions, mandates, persecutions, innovations and proposals of the cardinal and his men (usurping on the powers not only of the governess but also of the king) damaged and harmed the country very much and alarmed, drove away, robbed and killed a very large number of the inhabitants. At the same time they impaired and hindered the old customary freedom. Nevertheless we see nowadays with great heartache, and it is to be feared that if God does not help us – what we trust He will do and what we are preparing ourselves for to the utmost of our ability – we may see on an even larger scale, how greatly and grievously all the fore-mentioned innovations, proposals, oppressions, inquisitions, persecutions, murders, seizures, executions and tyrannies have increased and multiplied.

The intention of this document was to promote public awareness of the dangers Alva posed and to encourage a broad unity against the duke in the hope that this would help to ensure the success of the invasion of the Netherlands that Orange was planning.

This idea was very ambitious, especially since Orange had lost his estates in the Low Countries and therefore would find it difficult to raise the substantial monies required to fund an army strong enough to challenge Habsburg rule. In Germany there were certainly enough mercenaries willing to fight, but the problem Orange had was limited finances. This was partially remedied by the establishment of a campaign fund into which people could subscribe money that would be used to raise an army. By 1568, he had been able to accumulate 200,000 florins, half of which came from Antwerp, Amsterdam and several towns in Holland and Zeeland and the rest from private donations by other grandees. Orange provided 50,000 florins, having sold some family jewels.

Orange's intention was to attack the Duke of Alva and regain control of the Brussels government so that he and the other grandees might restore their inheritances and also their nation's privileges, which they felt were being eroded more quickly than ever.

The invasions of 1568

To give himself the best possible chance of success, the Prince of Orange intended to invade the Netherlands on four fronts, each at the same time. Having won friends among the French Huguenots after moving closer to Lutheranism, an army of this religion was to invade from the south under the command of the Lord of Hannecamp, while a second force from England would invade Flanders from the west. In the east, troops from Germany would make two separate incursions into Friesland and also Limburg. The prince would provide a reserve force from his base in Cleves. The basis of this attack was essentially to force Alva to split his forces and also to try to raise support from across the whole of the Netherlands. In principle the plan was a good one. However, it was very reliant on effective communication.

KEY TERM

Partisan
An armed group of people who fight an occupying army in secret – often using 'hit and run' tactics rather than open battles.

Early problems

As early as February 1568, the signs were not good for a successful campaign. Hannecamp was captured by Spanish troops while on his way to Flanders to organise additional support from Calvinist **partisans**, who lived in the woods and attacked Catholic priests. Equally unhelpful was that the 3,000 troops marching on Limburg were easily defeated on 20 April after crossing into the country and being unable to stir up public support, which was largely pro-Spanish because of the inhabitants' majority Catholic faith. Without the help of the people in this area the army was easily defeated by a column of veteran Spanish troops and the rebels' leader was either captured or killed. Many of those who were taken prisoner were later interrogated, and under torture gave details of Orange's supporters both inside and outside the country. Further difficulties arose on 24 April when Louis of Nassau, the prince's younger brother, marched into the province of Groningen where it was evident that Orange had miscalculated the degree of anti-Spanish sentiment and, once again, failed to raise public support. Without this assistance Nassau stayed close to the German border so as to be able to retreat if faced with a much stronger force.

The significance of these early problems was that Alva was able to gain important information regarding the planned assaults and therefore formulate his own actions accordingly. Furthermore, they evidenced the extent of reliance Orange placed upon the support of the Netherlanders. Given that he had meagre resources to fund a large army he had assumed – and hoped – that the people would rise in support, which from the early days of the campaign seemed unlikely.

The reason for the lack of public interest is difficult to determine accurately. However, it is likely that the omnipotence of the Council of Troubles was a considerable factor, alongside the small force that Orange had mustered which perhaps did not inspire much hope. Whatever the motivation, the consequence was clear: without public support Orange was unlikely to be able to present a sustained challenge to the Duke of Alva's government.

The rebels' victory at Heiligerlee

Despite early problems, Orange's armies did achieve a notable victory on 23 May 1568 at the monastery of Heiligerlee, outside the town of Winschoten, in Groningen. This was their first victory in the campaign and it offered some hope of further success after early misfortune.

Travelling through Groningen with 3,300 men, Louis of Nassau engaged a mix of Spanish and Netherlandish troops under the command of Count Aremberg, a Dutchman who remained loyal to Habsburg rule. Aremberg had 4,000 troops, many of whom were veterans, but he underestimated his opposition and became overconfident after initial success against Nassau's cavalry, led by his second brother, Adolf, who was killed in a charge. Imagining the force was beaten, Aremberg advanced to the monastery with great assuredness. Louis of Nassau, however, had taken advantage of his surroundings: Heiligerlee was a very wet and marshy area covered with peat holes into which he had placed 400 of his troops. As the Spanish moved past them he was able to trap Aremberg's army in the marshes. In the first two hours of fighting, the Spanish army lost 1,500 men compared with Nassau's 50. Among the dead was Count Aremberg, who became the first Dutch commander fighting for Spain to be killed by his fellow-countrymen during the conflict. The death of Aremberg secured the rebels their first victory in what would later become known as the Eighty Years War.

SOURCE

4 From the testimony of Sybrant Sickes, a soldier who fought at Heiligerlee, given to a court convened to try supporters of Orange on 17 August 1571.

Count Aremberg, riding a gray and white horse, in full armour, tried to jump his horse over a hedge, to escape his enemies; then, while the horse was too close to a tree, it bounced with its chest against the tree, with such vigour the horse sat on the ground; after that, a man called Martin den Taschenmaecker,... shot the Count of Aremberg with his musket in the neck, between the steel collar of his armour and the helmet... He said he heard the man calling, after being hit by the bullet: 'I am the Count of Aremberg, capture me and save my body!' Hearing this, the aforementioned Martin said: 'You are the man I am looking for.' He hit the captured man with his musket on the helmet, with such force it fell from his head. The Count also fell, after the blow, from his horse. And as the captured Count lay on the ground he was hit again, with the same musket, on his head, so the blood came out of his mouth and nose, and they cut him too, after they had taken his armour, and while he was still alive, with a rapier in his leg. After that he died.

The basis of this victory was overconfidence on the part of the Habsburg forces, and Count Aremberg in particular. A consequence of the battle was that Louis of Nassau was able to capture Aremberg's military funds that the Count had been travelling with and use this money to pay his own army, which went some way to offset the financial difficulties of his older brother. Psychologically it would also be reasonable to suggest the victory gave the rebels a reason to be hopeful and raised morale to a certain extent. The reality, however, was that this was only one battle and the war still needed to be won.

SOURCE

5 An engraving by an unknown artist. Count Louis of Nassau defeating Count Aremberg in the Battle of Heiligerlee, 23 May 1568.

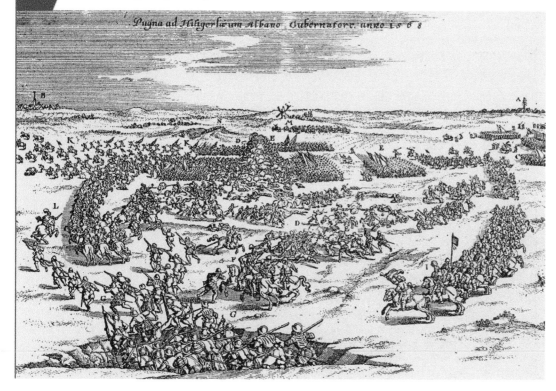

Pugna ad Hiligerlicum Albano Gubernatore. anno 1568

AS Level Exam-Style Questions Section A

1 Why is Source 4 valuable to the historian for an enquiry into the battle of Heiligerlee in 1568?

Explain your answer using the source, the information given about it and your own knowledge of the historical context. (8 marks)

2 How much weight do you give the evidence of Source 3 for an enquiry into why William of Orange invaded the Netherlands in 1568?

Explain your answer using the source, the information given about it and your own knowledge of the historical context. (12 marks)

Tip
In each of these questions it is important to base your answers around the source content and provenance, and then develop them with own knowledge, using the source as illustration.

Disintegration of the rebel forces and Alva's triumph

The victory at Heiligerlee was the high point in an otherwise disastrous campaign for William of Orange. His forces were not as well supported by the local population as he had hoped, and could not make the decisive incursion necessary for success. This was evident from the start. However, even five months into the campaign there was still no support forthcoming. In June, 3,000 French Huguenots were forced to retreat after towns failed to rise up with them. On 18 July, at St Valery, these Huguenots were surrounded and then massacred by French forces sent by Charles IX, honouring an agreement made with Spain in 1565 at Bayonne, which pledged mutual support to defend Catholicism against Protestant threat.

EXTEND YOUR KNOWLEDGE

The conference of Bayonne, 1565
This was a meeting between France and Spain to agree terms regarding the safety of Catholicism following the growth of Protestantism. Each country would support the other to root out heresy within their borders. Together they would work to defeat Protestantism where it existed and challenged their authority and faith.

By the end of the summer, the rebels endured further setbacks after several of their supporters were taken captive while attempting to raid the Netherlands from the sea. These men were funded by refugees who had fled abroad. Having been taken captive, they were then tortured into giving up their accomplices before being executed for their involvement in the invasion. With each of these setbacks, the grip that Alva held over the country tightened, further reducing the likelihood of a popular uprising to the extent that the rebel advance was quickly disintegrating. The final decisive blow came at Jemmigen in Friesland on 21 July, when the Duke of Alva led a force against Louis of Nassau. The day was a bloody affair and no mercy was shown; the defeated Nassau forces were either butchered on the field of battle or tried their luck swimming the two mile wide River Eems to safety.

The significance of Jemmigen

The impact of Alva's victory on the Friesland peninsula was the sudden decline in foreign support for William's campaign. Prior to this defeat, Protestant nations such as England under Elizabeth I and several German states had provided valuable support to the rebels. However, after such a defeat this support disappeared as each benefactor felt discredited. The demise of much-needed support left William of Orange in a difficult situation when, in October 1568, he invaded Brabant with 30,000 men. Without further support, he was unable to advance his cause and was forced to retreat. Gradually his army drifted away and after 29 days of **skirmishing** he crossed back into France, where he paid off the remainder of his forces early in the new year.

The invasion was a complete disaster for William. His forces were totally defeated, but worse was that his supporters now felt compromised and sought to distance themselves from him. Left alone and without funds as he had paid out more than 500,000 florins, the prince wrote a letter which he sent to the States-General as a warning to the people of the Netherlands, and then he temporarily turned his back on the country and went off to fight with the Huguenots in France.

KEY TERM

Skirmishing
A military term used to describe small clashes with enemy forces.

SOURCE

6 From William of Orange's letter to the people of the Netherlands, sent in November 1568.

Do they not want to force you, by putting a rope around your neck, forever to stop speaking not only about your salvation but also about your liberty, rights and customs? Do you not see how they put you at the mercy of officers, provosts and fiscals by confounding all order and justice? Do you still expect any grace, pardon or impunity, when it is so widely known that they had had so many good inhabitants apprehended and killed in divers places simply for having attended sermons, which they say are new, although they were tolerated and permitted by the regent and the magistrates? Therefore my seigniors, brethren and companions, put aside these vain expectations, cease breaking your oaths, recognise the truth, take a firm stand for the maintenance of your own welfare, resist your oppressors with all your might, help by all means those who exert themselves to pull you out of this miserable servitude.

Alva's triumph

The attack by the Prince of Orange had not been executed very well, but it had presented a direct challenge to Alva's rule in the country. The victory Alva was able to secure gave him a great deal of satisfaction as he had been tasked by Philip II to root out heresy and reaffirm Habsburg rule in the Netherlands. The failure of Orange had in part been due to the decision of local people not to rise up in his support either because they disagreed with his rebellion or feared Alva's reprisals. The invasion had also seen the execution of many rebels, including Egmont and Hoorn, who had posed a political threat to Philip II and the defeat of Orange. Furthermore, the duke's victory at Jemmigen had soured foreign support for the Protestant cause in the Netherlands. Orange's supporters felt discredited and fearful of their association with him after this defeat, and this reversal of opinion also reflected well on the Duke of Alva's mission.

In effect, by the end of 1568 Alva had succeeded in his task of securing the country for Philip II, and the duke looked forward to the king's return to the Netherlands and his own hero's welcome in Spain. Unfortunately for the duke however, Philip II was detained in Spain because of an outbreak of rebellion in Granada that was the result of a more strict religious policy recently introduced. More significantly, Philip's only son, Don Carlos, had died in July 1568 after showing signs of insanity. This left Philip II without a male heir and only infant daughters to succeed him. Given this predicament, it was felt to be too dangerous for the king, now 40 years old, to make the long sea voyage to the Netherlands. In lieu of his presence, Philip II did send 2,400 troop reinforcements for Alva, along with a promise to replace him as governor-general so that he might return home. Until that time he was to remain in post and continue his work to secure Habsburg rule and promote the Catholic faith.

To achieve this, Alva looked to the reorganisation of the bishoprics that had been initiated in 1563 but not fulfilled after opposition from the grandees and provincial parliaments. Considering the level of control that the duke had established in the country, the renewed attempt to enforce the bishopric plan was much more successful and by 1570 all 15 had been appointed and were operating effectively. Further to this reform, he also effected legislation – the 'Ordinance of the Penal Law' – which unified the criminal code across the provinces and **codified** many of the customary laws. This included, in 1571, the Customs of Antwerp, which were a series of complicated measures dealing with insuring trade in that city. These have largely been seen as positive changes in recent years. However, in a number of cases, they did override local privileges, which met with only minor opposition because of the power of the duke. It was not until his forcible collection of taxes that Alva was challenged on a national scale that, when combined with a renewed political opposition, was sufficiently strong to present a genuine threat to his position.

By the end of 1569, after less than two years in the country, the Duke of Alva had managed to subdue the Netherlands. His aggressive tactics were unpopular among the people but none dared to challenge his authority despite the opportunity presented by William of Orange. In achieving such acquiescence, Alva had established a strong presence, which seemed to secure Philip II's possession. However, with the new decade came a new challenge that would prove more formidable than Orange's first attempt in 1568.

> **KEY TERM**
>
> Codified
> Writing down laws so that they are organised into a system or code.

THINKING HISTORICALLY　Causation (6b)

Attitudes and actions

Individuals can only make choices based on their context. Prevalent attitudes combine with individual experience and natural temperament to frame the individual's perception of what is going on around them. Nobody can know the future or see into the minds of others.

Context	Action
• Alva was rooting out Protestantism in the Netherlands. • The Council of Troubles was very unpopular. • There was support for the Prince of Orange within Germany, France and England. • The Prince of Orange thought he could inspire a popular revolt in the Netherlands. • The Netherlands had previously opposed Spanish rule in 1566. • The Prince of Orange had become the prominent leader of resistance to Spanish rule.	• In February 1568, the Prince of Orange organised a series of invasions of the Netherlands in order to regain political power and secure greater religious tolerance in the country.

Answer the following questions individually and discuss your answers in a group.

1 Why might Orange have believed that the people of the Netherlands would have approved of his action?

2 Why could he have thought that the people might be willing to rise up with him?

3 What other information would have been useful to him to help him decide on his course of action?

4 How reasonable was Orange's course of action given what he understood about the situation at the time?

5 How far should the historian try to understand the context of the beliefs and values of people in the past when explaining why individuals make choices in history?

ACTIVITIES
KNOWLEDGE CHECK

What accounts for Orange's failure?

1 Using the material you have read, group together evidence for Orange's failure under the following broad headings:

• Strength of Spain

• Weaknesses of Orange.

2 Looking more closely at this evidence, use it to draw out some judgements about why Orange failed. For example, was much of Orange's weakness down to a lack of popular support, or poor military planning? Did Alva's troops defeat Orange on their own?

3 Which of these judgements do you feel is most significant when considering the failed revolt?

HOW IMPORTANT WERE THE SEA BEGGARS IN CHALLENGING SPANISH RULE?

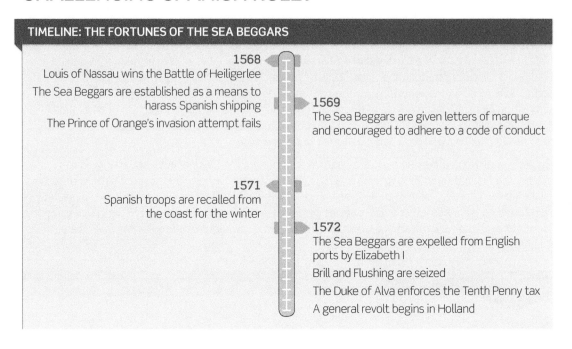

TIMELINE: THE FORTUNES OF THE SEA BEGGARS

1568
Louis of Nassau wins the Battle of Heiligerlee

The Sea Beggars are established as a means to harass Spanish shipping

The Prince of Orange's invasion attempt fails

1569
The Sea Beggars are given letters of marque and encouraged to adhere to a code of conduct

1571
Spanish troops are recalled from the coast for the winter

1572
The Sea Beggars are expelled from English ports by Elizabeth I

Brill and Flushing are seized

The Duke of Alva enforces the Tenth Penny tax

A general revolt begins in Holland

Louis of Nassau and the privateers

To assist in the invasion of the Netherlands, after his victory at Heiligerlee Louis of Nassau sought to establish a link with England in order to draw benefit from Calvinist sympathisers there. They were actively engaged in raising men and money for the cause in the Netherlands, which they saw principally as a religious conflict. The manner in which he achieved this was by organising a fleet of **privateers** made up of fellow noblemen and Calvinist sailors who could then patrol the North Sea and keep this line of communication open between England and the Low Countries. These Sea Beggars as they became known, under the leadership of William II de la Marck, enjoyed some early victories against Spanish ships, including winning an engagement off the coast of Delfzijl on 15 July 1568, which prevented Louis' headquarters there from being forcibly shut down. By offering a means of support from the sea, the Beggars were able to harass Spanish shipping and upset trade with that country which, although only on a small scale, was a defiant action that did not go unnoticed by the Spanish.

The principal motive of this group of seafarers was to provide support for the land-based invasion by maintaining access to England and preventing Spanish reinforcements arriving in the Netherlands from the sea. Despite early victories, however, this group failed to make a significant contribution to Orange's invasion attempt because almost as soon as they had been organised, the attempt collapsed and the Duke of Alva was able to restore his authority.

After the collapse, the Sea Beggars survived through acts of piracy, attacking Spanish as well as neutral shipping and selling these vessels and their cargoes in England for cash. They also raided fishing villages for supplies and even attacked Dutch shipping. Such was the reputation of these men that William of Orange issued **letters of marque** to them in 1569, which clearly set out the rules by which they should operate:

- they should conform to the **Articles of War**

- each ship was to have a minister on board

- all prizes of war should be fairly divided according to established rules

- command of the vessels should be under native Dutch control

- no person of poor standing was to be admitted on board the ships.

The purpose of these rules was to try to establish some sense of order among the Sea Beggars who had, by the end of the 1560s, attracted significant negative attention from Dutch and German merchants as well as the Spanish because of their piracy, and threatened to undermine Orange's relationships with other nations that he was trying to rebuild following his defeat in 1568.

The reputation being garnered by the Sea Beggars was notorious. In one sense they were a useful tool for William of Orange during his invasion of the Netherlands and they had secured several victories on the sea. However, their actions after 1568 threatened his own position as well as that of Spain and the Duke of Alva. Having suffered a disastrous campaign, the Prince of Orange was in need of allies, particularly as many of his erstwhile supporters had distanced themselves from him once news of his defeat was heard. The reason for this reversal was the threat that Spain posed: as the greatest military power in Europe, there was significant reluctance to being seen as a friend of the prince and therefore he found himself alone. The actions of the Sea Beggars further compounded this isolation by alienating even more support for the grandees, and into 1570 his fortunes looked bleak.

The closure of English ports to the Sea Beggars

England had been a sympathetic ally of the Prince of Orange because of the religious context of his cause. Having embraced Lutheranism in 1567, his invasion was seen as an attempt to champion the Protestant cause in the Netherlands against a ruler who was trying to stamp out any challenge to the Catholic faith. This cause resonated with Elizabeth I, whose own country had been the victim of religious division after the growth of Protestantism under Edward VI and the subsequent Catholic backlash that her sister Mary unleashed upon becoming queen. Elizabeth had been locked up for her Protestantism, and 274 of her co-religionists were burned for heresy. As queen, Elizabeth practised greater religious tolerance and created a new more moderate religious settlement in order to secure her throne and promote a more stable nation, so for Elizabeth it was appropriate to support other nations seeking to safeguard her faith. Given that her country was potentially threatened by strong Catholic nations, it encouraged a closer relationship with potential allies, including several of the German principalities.

The support offered by England amounted to providing sanctuary for many Netherlandish Calvinists who chose to flee their country after Alva set about restoring Catholicism. The queen also allowed the Sea Beggars a safe harbour in English ports after they had attacked Spanish vessels in the North Sea. By providing a haven for these privateers, she also kept open a line of communication between the Calvinists in exile and their brethren in the Low Countries, which consequently facilitated the provision of money from the refugee churches to those involved in Orange's campaign. By 1572, there were established communities of Dutch Calvinists in the south-eastern counties of England, and in Norwich these refugees made up 40 percent of the city's population. The presence of such support made England a natural haven for the Sea Beggars and they were secretly allowed by Elizabeth I to make it their home after 1568.

Such was the annoyance generated by their behaviour at the conclusion of the failed invasion, however, that the seaports of England were closed to the Sea Beggars in March 1572 because Elizabeth I feared a Spanish reprisal if she continued to allow them sanctuary. Prior to that decision, they had operated out of several of England's coastal towns, including Dover where they also sold many of their captured prizes. The acts of piracy they committed was in danger of upsetting Philip II and forcing England into a confrontation with an empire that was still the dominant force in Europe. Such was the fragile standing of Elizabeth in her own country that she could not afford to antagonise the Spanish king and therefore she expelled the Sea Beggars from England's ports.

This decision was not simply due to fear of Spain; the Sea Beggars had also been attacking neutral shipping that threatened England's trade with those nations. The queen was continually harassed by members of the **Hanseatic League**, who complained of great losses due to their inability to trade freely because their ships were often attacked by the privateers to whom she had granted anchorage. Such was the need to maintain effective trade relations with these merchants, that for economic motivations as well as political ones, the queen requested the removal of the offending vessels from English ports where they had previously been able to berth.

In denying them a haven, Elizabeth I forced William II de la Marck and his 25 privateers to seek new ports in which to dock and in many regards this refocused their attention on the situation in the Low

KEY TERM

Hanseatic League
A confederation of German merchant guilds that worked together to protect their trades.

Countries. Having contented themselves for more than three years with attacking trade ships and selling them and their cargoes for profit, there was a renewed impetus to restore themselves to their own homeland. With such renewed determination they were able to regain their homes and also contribute in no small part to the Prince of Orange's second campaign which began later that year.

The seizure of Brill and Flushing

SOURCE
7   The seizure of Brill by William II de la Marck on 1 April 1572. A painting by Frans Hogenberg – a Flemish painter who had been banned from the city of Antwerp by the Duke of Alva in 1568.

Having been expelled from England, the Sea Beggars needed to find a new place to anchor their ships. With limited choice they sailed for the province of Holland. However, a storm forced them into the estuary at Meuse, where they discovered that the town of Brill was ungarrisoned by Spanish troops. This was arguably a miscalculation on the part of the Duke of Alva since 1,500 troops were present in Holland, but they were recalled for the winter in November 1571 as the duke did not think any attack would come during those months. Motivated principally by need, but also seeing the advantage of this opportunity to establish a footing in the Netherlands, William II de la Marck and his officers decided to seize the town. On 1 April 1572, with approximately 600 men, they attacked the port. Having captured it, they moved on to seize the unguarded town. Such was the fearsome reputation of the sailors that the inhabitants of Brill put up little resistance, and once inside the walls the Sea Beggars were quick to secure the settlement as a permanent refuge.

The seizure of Brill was initially viewed with little interest by the Prince of Orange, as the town was of limited significance and only very small. In view of the disinterest with which towns across the provinces had greeted his 1568 attempt, he was quite circumspect about the implications of this victory. Despite a few misgivings, however, the Sea Beggars sought to capitalise on their achievement and later in the month they captured the more important town of Flushing, regarded as the key to Zeeland. This gave Orange the confidence for a second invasion attempt. Flushing did not require much threatening since the people there were already upset about the proposed billeting of Spanish troops within their walls. The town had refused entry to the troops, but allowed 14 of the Sea Beggar ships into the town's harbour on 22 April 1572. Although originally a means of securing their own fortunes, the seizure of these towns was a rallying call to the prince because it presented him with a foothold in the region. Also, the successful capture of these towns had been possible in part due to the exploitation of local animosities towards Habsburg rule.

By establishing a foothold in the Low Countries, the Sea Beggars were crucial in progressing the resurgence of opposition to Habsburg rule. Their occupation encouraged the Prince of Orange to consider a new move against the Duke of Alva, and they were able to stir up local support in the area which had been lacking it in 1568.

General revolt in the province of Holland

In fomenting local discontent, the Sea Beggars were helped by the determination of Alva to pursue his economic need to extract the Tenth Penny tax. This was a particularly unpopular action because it was intended as a permanent imposition, which would ultimately undermine what autonomy the States-General still retained. The decision by Alva to forcibly extract this tax was met with a general refusal to trade, and shops closed for business rather than pay the due. This decision resulted in economic decline in the provinces, a downturn that had already started because the Sea Beggars had significantly disrupted trade due to their piracy in the Channel and North Sea. Many traders simply abandoned their attempts to sail to the Low Countries because those that did so were usually attacked and their cargo seized. In this regard the Sea Beggars contributed to the economic problems in the provinces, which Alva's own tax demands then made more acute. The implication of this activity was that Holland and Zeeland in particular, provinces that relied heavily upon shipping to supply them with necessary foodstuffs because their own lands were not suited to growing grains, were already in a difficult economic position. This was made worse by Alva's tax. On the basis of this discontent, the seizure of Brill and Flushing proved to be a call to arms for the local population, who were already opposing Alva on economic grounds.

SOURCE 8 A letter from the vicar-general of the diocese of Mechelen, Maximilian Morillon, to Cardinal Granvelle on 24 March 1572.

People are so incensed that there is talk of changing our prince for another, irrespective of his religion, an act which would plunge the country into a long war which would bring about the death of very many people ... Poverty is acute in all parts ... The money-lenders are closing their doors because they have no more money; all their cash has already been lent out to people. In Holland everyone began by pawning their best items of furniture and clothes, then they pawned the anchors and rigging of their boats, something unseen and unheard of before. There used to be several towns and villages [in Holland] where no beggars were to be found; now they have multiplied in some places to six or seven hundred, most of them sailors and fishermen. The magistrates have had to give them a little bread and money over the past few days, otherwise there would have been disorders.

The level of economic discontent was a key feature for the Sea Beggars' success in capturing further towns and inciting popular support against Spanish rule. By mid-March the vicar-general, Maximilian Morillon, estimated that in Brussels there were between 8,000 and 10,000 unemployed who depended upon poor relief, and this level of despair certainly encouraged greater ill feeling. This was reflected in the growing number of supporters for the Sea Beggars. By 11 April, they had swelled their number to more than 2,000 fighting men.

Many of these people joined with the Beggars simply for the regular meals that military service offered, while others who had become politically more aware since the imposition of the Tenth Penny tax saw them as a means to challenge the Spanish government. In either case, Brill became a magnet for those who sought change, and with every day that passed it became harder for the government to retain control in the province. Rioting broke out in Enkhuizen towards the end of April and this delayed the departure of 20 government ships from that town that were intended for attacking the Beggars in Brill. Although order was eventually restored and 11 ships were able to set sail in May, rioting broke out again almost immediately and this time it was the Beggars who were invited by the local authorities to provide help. Also in April, supporters from Flushing were able to capture the arsenal at Veere where they took possession of 2,000 naval guns, powder and shot. This was an especially valuable haul that also strengthened the Beggars' position in Holland.

Part of the success they enjoyed was undoubtedly the result of Alva's demand for his tax: this clearly turned many people against him, particularly since trade also slowed down because of the acts of piracy that were committed. This created the necessary environment for local support, which had been absent in 1568, but what also gave them the time to consolidate their position was the location of the province and its general topography. Holland was a coastal province, almost cut off from the others by a number of lakes and rivers that covered its landscape. It was difficult to reach by land because much of it was below sea level and therefore it often became waterlogged, particularly during difficult winters when storms would damage the many dykes and water channels. This made it difficult to travel quickly by land and therefore there was a much greater reliance upon the sea, which was well marshalled by the Beggars. Furthermore, because of the difficulty in getting to Holland there was a much greater sense of autonomy and many Calvinists could be found there simply because it was less accessible for religious enforcement. With a greater number of Calvinists, the province was therefore more tolerant and favourably disposed towards the Sea Beggars, which almost certainly added to the success they enjoyed.

The general unrest that ensued after the spring of 1572 was the result of a collection of factors, not least economic difficulties brought about by the action of both the Sea Beggars and the Duke of Alva's desire to claim the Tenth Penny tax. The declining economic situation, which had put so many people out of work, cultivated a renewed bitterness towards Habsburg rule which overrode fear of the 'iron duke' – a name Alva acquired during his bloody, early repression. This bitterness was then unintentionally manipulated by the Beggars' need to find a new port, and having taken the town of Brill it became a rallying point for a renewed campaign against the government.

> **A Level Exam-Style Question Section B**
>
> 'The actions of the Sea Beggars were chiefly responsible for the outbreak of general revolt in the province of Holland in 1572.'
>
> How far do you agree with this opinion?
>
> Explain your answer. (20 marks)
>
> **Tip**
> *Consider the phrasing of the statement and look for clues to help answer the question – why would it say 'chiefly'?*

ACTIVITIES
KNOWLEDGE CHECK

The Sea Beggars

Having read about the actions of the Sea Beggars complete the following tasks.

1 Write down three reasons why they could be regarded as being important in causing the general revolt in Holland in 1572.

2 Identify three other reasons that might have promoted this general revolt.

3 Bearing in mind your reasons above, summarise the significance of the Sea Beggars in fewer than 20 words.

WHY WAS ORANGE ABLE TO ENJOY GREATER SUCCESS BY 1573?

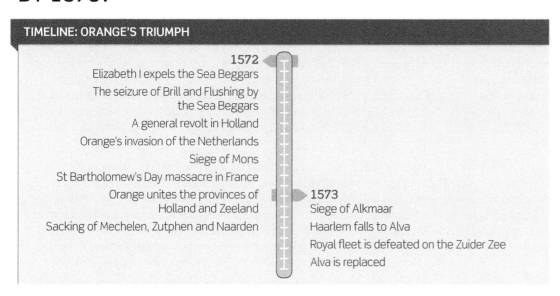

TIMELINE: ORANGE'S TRIUMPH

1572
Elizabeth I expels the Sea Beggars
The seizure of Brill and Flushing by the Sea Beggars
A general revolt in Holland
Orange's invasion of the Netherlands
Siege of Mons
St Bartholomew's Day massacre in France
Orange unites the provinces of Holland and Zeeland
Sacking of Mechelen, Zutphen and Naarden

1573
Siege of Alkmaar
Haarlem falls to Alva
Royal fleet is defeated on the Zuider Zee
Alva is replaced

The invasion of 1572

The revolt in Holland marked the beginning of the Prince of Orange's second campaign to remove the Duke of Alva. Having sent a letter to the people of the Low Countries encouraging support for the revolt in Holland, he also hoped to capitalise on the events in the north by invading the southern provinces in May 1572.

SOURCE 9

From a pamphlet written by the Prince of Orange to the people of the Low Countries calling upon them to rise up against the Duke of Alva, dated 16 June 1572. It was printed in Dutch and circulated throughout the provinces by agents of the prince.

But as the tyrant will not deviate from his course as long as he is not certain of being able to keep his possession, to your utter ruin, all those rights and privileges of yours which he holds now as if they were withdrawn and obsolete, I pray you once again, because of the loyalty which you and I owe to our dearest fatherland, that with my help you rescue, take back and protect what you don't want to lose for ever. If you do not do so, then I assert most solemnly that it will not be my fault if severer measures are taken. But if you take my admonition to heart (and I sincerely hope you will do this for your own sake) then swear allegiance firstly to Christ the only God our Saviour, next to the king who takes delight in sworn laws, finally to me as patron of the fatherland and champion of freedom. You must keep your promises and help me to make peace in religious, legislative and judicial affairs, without wronging any class. You must appropriate God, you must see to it that the king is given back his authority and that peace is restored to the state. Then alone may you expect to regain that trade with free transit through Germany, England, France and Poland, which the tyrant, that inhuman destroyer, impeded, causing without any justification enormous damage to you, and to conduct it without being hindered by taxes, pillage and servitude.

The invasion was better organised than that of 1568 and it enjoyed greater resources. Since his first failed attempt the Prince of Orange had carefully prepared himself for a second; he had gone to great lengths to present himself as the national leader of the Netherlands and had utilised significant amounts of **propaganda** in the form of pamphlets that listed the evil deeds of Alva to promote this image. He had also fought in France alongside the Huguenots, where he was able to win the support of their leader, Admiral Coligny, who was the most influential figure in the court of Charles IX by 1571. This relationship allowed the prince to rely upon French support and it also caused great concern to Alva who anticipated a French invasion of the Netherlands.

The invasion began in the southern province of Hainaut, with Louis of Nassau riding into the town of Mons on 24 May after being reliably informed by Protestants in the town that its defences were very limited. With more than 1,000 local supporters in the town and 1,500 French troops, Louis of Nassau set up a provincial government and legalised Calvinist worship. The ease of this victory was

KEY TERM

Propaganda
Information that deliberately presents one particular view in order to influence opinion.

emulated in the town of Valenciennes and also Zutphen in June, where each local population came out in favour of the rebel army and opened their gates to them. Within six weeks most of Friesland and Overijssel was under the control of Orange's supporters. The speed and peaceful nature of these occupations testified to the growing hostility of the local population towards Alva's rule, although the rebel forces were also helped by the duke's decision to withdraw all his available troops to Mons where he sought to restore government rule. This decision was primarily tied to the belief that the southern provinces were more important to Philip II. There were a greater number of Catholics in the south and the cities there played a greater part in Spain's wealth generation. Antwerp, for example, was the city where Spain's gold bullion from the Americas was traded. By comparison, the northern provinces had always been more independently minded and harder to control because of their geographical locations and even different languages. In this sense, Alva was making an informed decision based on Habsburg priorities.

Alva's main focus was therefore Mons, as to retake this city would crush any further potential for revolt in the south, and having put down this threat he could then focus entirely on the northern provinces under Orange's control. The decision to move south was therefore a strategic one. It was influenced by his fear that France would support Orange in his invasion, given the good relations he now enjoyed with Admiral Coligny, one of the king of France's influential advisers. This fear was fully justified. In July, the king had consented to support the Protestant rebels, sending an initial, small, force of 6,000 Huguenots to relieve the town of Mons, which had been encircled by Alva's troops and was under siege. This force was easily defeated at St Ghislain, six miles from Mons, discrediting France and particularly the Huguenots who had pushed for French support for the Netherlands. This event did not end France's involvement in the Low Countries; it precipitated a chain of events that changed the king's mind. As a result of the weakened positon that Charles IX found himself in, Catholics in France felt there was an opportunity to reduce the Huguenots' influence in the country and consequently they arranged for prominent Huguenots, including Coligny, to be assassinated. On 23 August, in what would become known as the St Bartholomew's Day massacre, more than 3,000 Huguenots in Paris were murdered, and it is claimed that more than 100,000 nationwide were killed by the end of the month.

EXTEND YOUR KNOWLEDGE

St Bartholomew's Day massacre, 1572

In 1572, the French king, Charles IX, had both Huguenots and Catholics at his court. By August, the Huguenot Gaspard de Coligny enjoyed the greatest influence, and this upset the Catholics. The king's mother, Catherine de Medici, felt this influence undermined her own and would draw France into war with Spain. She therefore supported the removal of prominent Huguenot supporters. On the night of 23 August, Coligny and 3,000 others in Paris were murdered; by the end of the week more than 100,000 Huguenots were killed as the massacre fanned religious conflict throughout the country. Coligny had promised French support for the Prince of Orange, but as a result of this event the king did not send the French troops that had been promised and therefore the Dutch were essentially left on their own.

The impact of the assassinations was crucial to the Netherlands as they effectively ended France's support. With the death of Coligny, the king fell under the influence of his Catholic advisers and subsequently lost interest in the Low Countries. The result of this development was that Alva was able to rest assured that no French troops would be coming to reinforce Orange's supporters and he could focus on his task against the Netherlanders.

For the Prince of Orange, the events in France were received with dismay as he had entered his homeland in July with 20,000 and had secured several towns for his cause. The news of the massacre undermined his hopes of further support and, therefore, a better chance against Alva. More immediately, it also meant that Mons would not be relieved, and therefore on 27 August the Prince of Orange invaded Brabant with the intention of achieving this himself. His army arrived on 12 September but failed to engage Alva's troops, who chose instead to wait for the prince's soldiers to drift away due to lack of pay, as they had done four years before. This duly happened and the prince was forced to withdraw, leaving Mons to fall to the Spanish on 19 September.

With the collapse of the town and the absence of a French threat, the Duke of Alva had gained the upper hand and was free to restore his rule in those areas that had supported the rebels. In the autumn he retook the town of Mechelen and **sacked** it as an example to other towns that had sided with Orange. Such was the devastation of this action that other towns quickly surrendered to Alva to avoid the same fate, and by October much of the land occupied by Orange supporters was reclaimed. To emphasise his power, Alva put two more towns to the sword: Zutphen in November and Naarden the following month. Both of these towns were razed to the ground and their inhabitants mercilessly killed.

With Alva's advance, the Prince of Orange fled to Holland – one of only two provinces still in revolt – and there he sought to capitalise on the solid body of Calvinist support. He also sought to take advantage of the success that the Sea Beggars enjoyed in keeping open the North Sea. This particular development meant that better communications would be available and offered hope of effective resupply of arms and food from his friends abroad.

Orange's control over Holland and Zeeland

In travelling to Holland, the Prince of Orange was returning to familiar territory having been the *stadtholder* under Margaret of Parma. Such familiarity would strengthen his cause, but he had also prepared the ground having sent a missive to the towns in July when they had resolved to organise a meeting to decide how to proceed in the current climate. The meeting was held in Dordrecht and attended by the province's nobility and 12 out of 18 of its principal towns. The purpose of the meeting was to agree a plan of action and they discussed the letter from the Prince of Orange.

SOURCE

 From a letter read by Philip Marnix on behalf of the Prince of Orange to the delegates of the Dordrecht meeting in July 1572.

They shall discuss and ordain the best and most suitable means of restoring and re-establishing in their own form and full vigour all the old privileges, rights and usages of the towns, which may have been suppressed and taken away by Alva's tyranny… His Highness has no other purpose than to restore under the lawful and worthy reign of the King of Spain the power, the authority and reputation of the estates to their former condition in accordance with the privileges and rights which the King has sworn to maintain. And without the estates, His Highness shall not endeavour to do or command anything that concerns the provinces or that may be harmful to them… His Highness binds himself to undertake or command nothing without the advice or consent of the estates or at least the majority of them, and without consulting these estates and countries if and when they desire this. To this end, the estates and the delegates of the towns shall swear to His Highness to be faithful to him for ever and not to desert him, but to assist him in every possible way.

The content of this correspondence essentially set out the basis for greater unity among the states. The prince was keen to bring them together in a common goal against the duke and he asked them to do three things to achieve this.

- To recognise the authority of the Prince of Orange; to fight with him to regain their rights and privileges and to not make separate agreements without his consent.

- To pay for the military fighting Alva.

- To support freedom of worship in the province.

For his part, the Prince of Orange would reciprocate and not enter into any agreement without first talking with the states, and military command would lie jointly with himself and the states. In essence, this agreement sought to establish power sharing between the prince and the province. In one sense this was a return to the old system of provincial power that Charles V had allowed, but in another it was also a much greater step towards constitutional reform. By clearly setting out the authority of each participant, there were defined rules that governed their actions. This not only safeguarded their own positions, but also bound them more closely together in a common interest.

Binding the province together, along with Zeeland, which also agreed to these terms, the Prince of Orange was forging a united front against the Duke of Alva. It could be argued that he was deliberately creating a more equal partnership in order to stiffen resolve in the face of potential aggression, such as that witnessed in Naarden and Zutphen, but there was also a financial incentive. The prince needed funds to maintain his army, and only the provinces had the power to raise money for him. Under the new agreement, the parliaments acknowledged the authority of the prince and

KEY TERM

Sacked
This is a term used to describe the actions of an army having taken control of a town and then looting it, attacking and even murdering its inhabitants for their personal goods and also destroying property. Often this tactic was used by successful commanders to make examples of their enemies.

accepted his request on 23 July, voting him taxes worth 500,000 florins. With this extent of finance, the prince could afford to maintain his army and thereby ensure its continued support.

Alva's failure to reconquer the northern provinces

The agreement between Orange and the provincial assemblies strengthened his position in the north of the Low Countries and gave his revolt a broader basis of support. Despite this development, however, his position was still far from secure, and the Duke of Alva was still intent on subduing these last rebellious provinces. After moving against the towns in the north-west, Alva marched towards the remaining provinces of Holland and Zeeland where the prince had fled. To withstand the duke's threat, Orange was dependent on several factors.

The geography of Holland and Zeeland

The geography of these two provinces was hugely significant for the defence of Orange's revolt. Such was the positioning of the territories along the coast of the country that they enjoyed the natural defence provided by the sea. Also, the south and eastern sides of the provinces were naturally blocked by lakes and rivers, which made them challenging to travel to and through. In 1573, these physical attributes were used to great advantage by Orange and his supporters to relieve the besieged town of Alkmaar by breaking the dykes, cutting off the supply route for Alva and his men while allowing a ship to sail to the aid of the town.

The determination of the local populations

The Duke of Alva also struggled because of the increased resolve of the population to resist his occupation. In many cases, this was because of the actions employed by the duke after the surrender of towns to him – Mechelen, Zutphen and Naarden in 1572 and Haarlem in July 1573 – when, although promised **clemency**, 2,000 people were executed and the town forced to pay 200,000 florins for its defiance. Intended as a warning to other towns, these actions had the opposite effect and actually encouraged more determined action.

SOURCE

From the legendary reply by the town of Leiden after it was called upon to surrender by the Duke of Alva in 1573. This response was first published in a contemporary account of the siege by J. Fruytiers in 1574.

> You heare that in our Toune are both dogges, kine and horses. And if wee should in the end want these, yet hath every one of us a left arme to eate, and reserve the righte arme to beat the tyrant and the rest of you which are his blooddy ministers from our walles: but if at the last, our force shall not bee strong enough ... we will never ... give over the defense of the libertie of our countrie, choosing rather when wee are at the verie word [sc. end] to set our Towne in fier, then that it shold [in] any way be gainefull unto you and we become your slaves.

The reply from the town of Leiden, when asked to surrender in 1573, is a clear indication of the extent to which the northern provinces were prepared to resist Alva. A local official declared that the citizens of the town would prefer to eat their own arms than let him through their gates, which offered quite an indictment of the duke, while their willingness also to burn their town to the ground before letting the Spanish in is equally determined. This level of opposition was also evident in the siege of Alkmaar between August and October 1573.

EXTRACT

From Peter Geyl, *History of the Dutch-Speaking Peoples 1555–1648* (2001).

> A great crowd of citizens had assembled in front of the town hall, waiting for the resolution of the magistrates. When this had gone on for a long time, Ruyschaver [the Orangists' leader] said with anger in his heart: 'this is not the time to deliberate any longer. Tell us briefly what you will do or will not do.' Upon which Floris van Teylingen, one of the burgomasters, said: 'with Prince and citizens I live and die,' and immediately he went with Captain Ruyschaver out of the town hall. Many citizens crowded in front and behind, Meerten Pietersen van de Mey, the town carpenter, among them, with axes and sledge hammers, and they hacked the Friesland gate open and let in the men of the prince of Orange, and the next moment the Kennemer gate was opened so that these soldiers could make a sally against the Spaniards.

SOURCE 12

The siege of Alkmaar, August–October 1573; a drawing made in September 1573 by Frans Hogenberg.

The resolve of these towns was very different from that of many earlier ones, which had capitulated to the duke often before a siege was organised. It could be suggested that this was because many of the earlier towns in the southern provinces were Catholic and therefore had a greater affinity with Habsburg rule, while in the northern provinces Calvinism was much stronger because royal authority was harder to enforce there. By this line of argument, the stiffened resolve was not only the result of Alva's atrocities, but also a greater sense that his restoration of power would result in far greater consequences for them – notably the reimposition of the Inquisition and attacks on their faith. This particular analysis is difficult to substantiate completely. However, it would offer some indication as to the position taken by the clutch of towns in Holland and Zeeland that offered a greater challenge to the duke.

In addition to the physical and personal strengths evidenced by the Netherlanders in the north, the Duke of Alva was in a more challenging position than he had anticipated and this also contributed to his failure to secure the rebellious provinces.

The cost of Dutch resistance

The rising level of defiance that greeted the Spanish as they attempted to restore Habsburg authority also began to affect their financial reserves. The longer it took to subdue a town the greater the cost, as soldiers still needed to be paid throughout a siege. Given that one of the main influences in the outbreak of this new revolt was the imposition of the Tenth Penny tax, because of Spain's stretched financial burdens, the rising costs into 1573 became prohibitive.

Not only did it cost more to maintain an army, but the revenue coming into the Netherlands treasury was significantly less in 1573 than it had been in 1571, as many towns continued to refuse payment of the Tenth Penny tax.

SOURCE 13 Income of the Netherlands treasury.

Year	Local taxation	Money from Spain
1571	8.8 million florins	1.1 million florins
1573	1.8 million florins	6.9 million florins

The implication of such a dependence upon Spain was that Philip II was financially stretched beyond his own capabilities, especially since he could not bring himself to abandon his war in the Mediterranean, which was consuming significant amounts of his income. This had very real consequences for Alva, as he relied totally upon Spain for his financial backing. Even before the revolt had begun in 1572, the Spanish troops in the Netherlands were owed 18 months' wages and they were increasingly disinclined to fulfil their duties if they did not receive payment. Without guaranteed funds from Spain, Alva's own army was vulnerable to mutiny. The siege of Alkmaar had in fact ended because the troops refused to attack the town initially, thereby forcing the commander to adopt siege tactics instead.

Alva was increasingly discredited

The financial reliance of the duke upon Spain was a source of great annoyance for Philip II. As early as 1571, he had informed the duke that he should raise his own funds for the pacification of the Low Countries and yet, two years later, he was still requesting money. Not only was this problematic in itself because of Spain's ongoing war with the Turks, but his attempt to raise funds actually encouraged the current situation in the Netherlands that he was struggling to contain. These failures were not well received in Madrid and increasingly Alva was losing support there.

Augmenting this decline was also the evident failure of Alva to restore Habsburg authority in the northern provinces. The siege of Alkmaar was a failure, while in Haarlem, although it was a technical victory, the duke had lost 10,000 of his own soldiers during the siege. These were not the only difficulties he endured. Other towns were lost to Orange, and on 11 October 1573 the royal fleet was defeated on the Zuider Zee and its commander taken prisoner. In all, the performance of Alva was no longer as promising as his early arrival had suggested.

To a great extent, the Duke of Alva was unable to reconquer the provinces of Holland and Zeeland because the Prince of Orange had initiated a constitutional revolution there, which offered the people far more than that which the duke was prepared to grant. This, in combination with the atrocities the Spanish committed in Mechelen and other towns, encouraged greater public support for the prince and his revolt. The consequent resolve of both Holland and Zeeland therefore made his attempts much more difficult than he initially anticipated, and as the resistance continued, the cost of the campaign rose. Facing the expense of war with the Turks, Philip II was not prepared to absorb this cost and therefore he sought to replace the increasingly discredited Alva with a more suitable candidate.

AS Level Exam-Style Questions Section A

1 Why is Source 11 valuable to the historian for an enquiry into the failure of the Duke of Alva to end the revolt of 1572?

Explain your answer using the source, the information given about it and your own knowledge of the historical context. (8 marks)

2 How much weight do you give the evidence of Source 10 for an enquiry into why William of Orange's revolt in 1572 was successful?

Explain your answer using the source, the information given about it and your own knowledge of the historical context. (12 marks)

Tip
In each of these questions you should demonstrate clear critical awareness of the source material – does it only evidence the weaknesses of Spain in 1572?

ACTIVITIES
KNOWLEDGE CHECK

Changing fortunes

1 Considering the failure of Orange's first invasion in 1568, what had changed by 1572? Draw up a list of factors that allowed for Orange's more successful invasion.

2 Which of these factors do you think played the greatest role?

ACTIVITY
SUMMARY

Alva and Orange

1 Using the material you have read and your own knowledge, draw up a list of points that summarise the actions of both Alva and Orange.

2 Can you add a third column to this list that identifies the actions of third parties such as the role of Elizabeth I?

3 Using these lists, address the following question: How significant were the actions of others for the performance of Alva and Orange?

WIDER READING

Limm, P. *The Dutch Revolt, 1559–1648*, Longman (1989)

Maltby, W. *Alba: A Biography of Fernando Alvarez de Toledo 1507–1582*, University of California Press (1983)

Parker, G. *The Army of Flanders and the Spanish Road*, Cambridge University Press (1972)

Swart, K. *William the Silent and the Revolt of the Netherlands*, Historical Association Pamphlet (1978)

van der Hoeven, M. (ed.) *Exercise of Arms: Warfare in the Netherlands 1568–1648*, Brill (1997)

2b.3 Spain and the re-conquest, 1573–84

KEY QUESTIONS

- Why was Requesens unable to secure a Spanish victory?
- Why did Parma enjoy more success than Requesens?
- How important was foreign intervention to the Prince of Orange's success?
- How successful were the northern provinces in becoming more independent?

INTRODUCTION

The rebellion of 1572 was a much more organised affair than that of four years earlier. The Prince of Orange was better financed and, crucially, the local population was more willing to support his attempt to oust the Duke of Alva. In this regard the better fortune that met the prince's second invasion was indicative of a shifting attitude towards Habsburg rule, which would encourage further confrontation. The motivation for such a transition lay both with the actions of the duke, whose attempt to enforce the unpopular Tenth Penny tax gave rise to widespread hostility, and the fortuitous actions of the Sea Beggars, which gave Orange a footing in the Netherlands. These particular changes, in tandem with Orange's efforts abroad to promote himself as a national leader, helped to give heart to and motive for greater local support that ultimately undermined the position of Alva within the country.

In weakening the duke's position, the rebels in the northern provinces were able to take advantage of the greater sense of autonomy in existence there. They were able to consolidate a heartland, which proved increasingly difficult for Alva to subdue. As the costs of pacification escalated, the duke lost credibility, and on 29 November 1573 he was formally replaced by Don Luis de Requesens, who had until then been the governor of Lombardy. As a naturally moderate individual, the new governor-general presented a chance for reconciliation. However, his position was made difficult by an uncompromising king and also a rebellion that had gained sufficient ground to make greater demands of the government in Brussels.

EXTEND YOUR KNOWLEDGE

Don Luis de Requesens (1528–76)

Born in Barcelona in 1528, Don Luis de Requesens was a career diplomat and had first gained Philip II's attention for being a trustworthy servant when acting as his representative to Rome in 1563. Requesens was generally a figure of moderate views and preferred to negotiate with Orange and the rebels. However, despite issuing a general pardon in 1574 he was restricted by the unconciliatory king and also the Duke of Alva who continued to recommend an aggressive approach in the Netherlands.

1573 – Alva is replaced by Requesens

1574 – Louis of Nassau is killed in the Battle of Mook

1575 – Philip II suspends payment of his country's debts
Peace negotiations fail at Breda

1576 – Requesens dies in office
Don John of Austria becomes governor-general of the Netherlands
Spanish Fury – sacking of Antwerp
Pacification of Ghent is signed

1577 – Parma takes charge of the Spanish forces in the Netherlands

| 1573 | 1574 | 1575 | 1576 | 1577 |

WHY WAS REQUESENS UNABLE TO SECURE A SPANISH VICTORY?

Requesens was appointed to replace the discredited Duke of Alva. However, the new governor-general still found himself in the position of having to rely on similar tactics to those employed by his predecessor. This was largely due to the difficult situation he inherited. Such was the entrenchment of the rebels within the northern provinces of Holland and Zeeland that they were difficult to negotiate with, while his relationship with his Spanish backers was also challenging. Philip II was unwilling to offer any significant terms to the rebels as he was intent on preserving the Catholic faith in the Low Countries and many of their demands involved recognising Protestantism. Furthermore, he was hampered by the outgoing duke, who stayed on in the country until late December to counsel his replacement. This was particularly challenging and certainly made the new governor-general's first month a difficult one. Advising the continuation of the military campaign he had begun, Alva was quick to promote the potential threat of adopting a lenient approach and as a result two Spanish officials – Julian Romero and Baron Noicarmes – were disavowed because they were seeking to determine on what terms the rebels would settle. The particular difficulty with this overlap in policy was that the new representative had an opportunity to offer an alternative approach but instead adopted the existing policy, which arguably gave a poor first impression to the rebels, and one that would continue to make his position almost impossible.

Requesens' failure to defeat the northern provinces

Upon the advice of Alva, Requesens continued to wage war against the rebels, and his first action resulted in a defeat at sea in the Scheldt estuary in January and then the collapse of Middelburg, which until 18 February 1574 had been the last Spanish stronghold in Walcheren. The immediate significance of these defeats was to emphasise the poor position in which the Spanish now found themselves. In the case of Middelburg, with this defeat the royal government lost its footing on the strategically important island of Walcheren, which offered some control over the shipping into Zeeland. Rather than asserting power, the action gave away more territory to the rebels, which actually helped to consolidate their hold over the region. In this regard the new governor-general therefore added to, rather than alleviated, the problems facing his country's government.

The difficulties facing Requesens were also compounded by the constitutional position taken up by the rebels. In promoting their cause and to encourage further support from other provinces, they emphasised that their rebellion was designed entirely to restore the ancient rights and privileges that the provinces had enjoyed before Philip II had begun his attempt to centralise the governing system in the Netherlands and to enforce the Catholic faith via his inquisitors. Attacking Requesens himself, they also maintained that the Prince of Orange had a more legitimate claim to rule the provinces, as his **lineage** was of greater nobility than the governor-general's and therefore he was a more appropriate ruler. By focusing on the broader rights of the states, and specifically the privileges of the provinces, the rebels were careful to convey the idea that they were not fighting the currently loyal provinces, but rather the growth in Habsburg authority over the rights of all the provinces.

KEY TERM

Lineage
Another term for 'ancestry'.

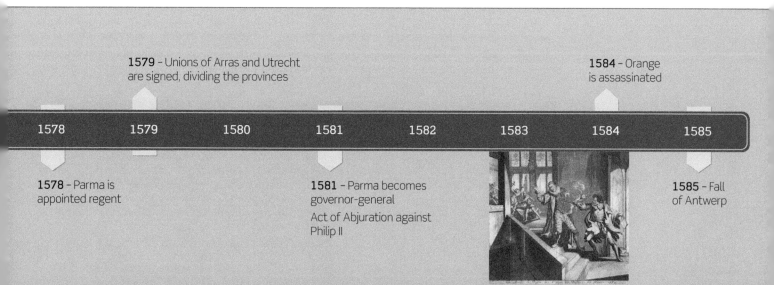

1579 – Unions of Arras and Utrecht are signed, dividing the provinces

1584 – Orange is assassinated

| 1578 | 1579 | 1580 | 1581 | 1582 | 1583 | 1584 | 1585 |

1578 – Parma is appointed regent

1581 – Parma becomes governor-general

Act of Abjuration against Philip II

1585 – Fall of Antwerp

In this manner, the northern provinces were portrayed as defenders of the Low Countries in their entirety and not simply a rebellious few seeking personal gain. The benefit of this stance was that it extended the appeal of the rebels' cause and gave credibility to both Holland and Zeeland – the only two provinces then opposing Habsburg rule.

SOURCE

1 From a letter sent by the rebel states of Holland and Zeeland to the loyalist states of the southern provinces early in June 1574.

But is it necessary to dwell upon this any longer? It is clear to all the world that what has been done in these provinces in the last eight years on behalf of the king, and is still being done, is not the work of the king, but of the inquisitors and the pope. Those who protect the dear fatherland from the despotism and tyranny of foreign lords, cannot be the enemies of their legitimate and true lord and of their dear fatherland. But those who aid and adhere to the foreign lords are indeed enemies and traitors of both. The inquisitors have the king with them in person, and we have the king with us by oath. The oath remains the same and does not change and is not subject to accident; quite the contrary is the case with the person of the king. And as the person of the king is all but imprisoned by the inquisition and as he cannot act according to his own will, it is his oath that gives us the right to use the name of the king in our struggle for the protection of his honour and of the dear fatherland. It is certainly wrong for the common enemies to use the king's name so boastfully, because they do so neither with the king's unqualified consent nor by virtue of his promises and his oath.

By calling into question the legitimacy of Requesens, and more importantly the legitimacy of the existing government, the rebels were able to justify their own cause and even claimed the support of the king on the grounds of the ancient privileges that had been the basis of their acceptance of Habsburg rule under Charles V.

Collectively this constitutional claim, alongside the unpopular policies begun by Alva and continued by Requesens, strengthened the hand of the rebels and solidified their presence in the north. As a result they became even more resolute in their actions and this not only made conciliation more difficult, but also placed a significant weight upon the Spanish army, which was already beginning to groan under the existing pressure it faced – both militarily and, more pressingly, financially.

Difficulty paying the army

The effort to subdue rebellion in the north was an expensive affair. The Duke of Alva had struggled to raise sufficient funds to maintain an army and this was arguably a significant contributing factor to the existing troubles facing Requesens. The unpopularity of the Tenth Penny tax had stirred up widespread discontent that had strengthened the hand of Orange and his rebels. Since Requesens was forced to adopt a similar policy upon his arrival, he faced the same financial problems as the duke. Only 10,000 troops were actually Spanish, the majority of the other 75,000 or so troops were made up of foreign mercenaries who had no national allegiance and fought only for payment. The consequence of this was that if payment was not made, these fighting men had no incentive to remain in the Netherlands and therefore Habsburg authority would quickly melt away.

This problem was well recognised by the new governor-general, whose own estimate of the cost of maintaining an army, calculated in March 1574, ran to 1.2 million florins a month since it had been expanded to counter the growing Dutch forces. This sum ignored the back pay owed to the troops, and it did not take into account government debts. The implication of such a vast sum was that Spain would struggle to fund this campaign, especially since Philip II was also concerned about the threat from the Turks and had been engaged in war with them in the western Mediterranean. Money was therefore scarce and without it the Habsburg army was likely to abandon him.

EXTEND YOUR KNOWLEDGE

Spain's war with the Ottoman Empire
As a devout Catholic and a monarch of the strongest European empire, Philip II took his responsibilities as a 'defender of the Catholic faith' very seriously. After the Ottomans invaded the Balearic Islands in 1558, he was determined to stop Islam from spreading into Europe and undermining Catholicism, which was already being challenged by the growth of Protestantism. He sent an army to the Mediterranean in order to prevent the Ottomans from gaining more territories. After 1571, when the pope called on all Catholic states to defend the faith, a Holy League was formed and the war took on even greater importance for Philip. In 1578, he signed a truce and then in 1580, a peace treaty was signed, ending 37 years of war.

Mutinies within the Spanish forces

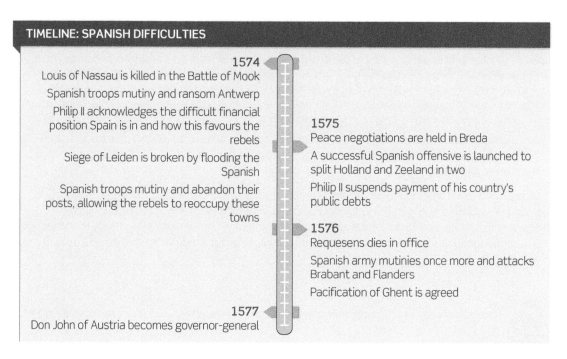

TIMELINE: SPANISH DIFFICULTIES

1574
Louis of Nassau is killed in the Battle of Mook

Spanish troops mutiny and ransom Antwerp

Philip II acknowledges the difficult financial position Spain is in and how this favours the rebels

Siege of Leiden is broken by flooding the Spanish

Spanish troops mutiny and abandon their posts, allowing the rebels to reoccupy these towns

1575
Peace negotiations are held in Breda

A successful Spanish offensive is launched to split Holland and Zeeland in two

Philip II suspends payment of his country's public debts

1576
Requesens dies in office

Spanish army mutinies once more and attacks Brabant and Flanders

Pacification of Ghent is agreed

1577
Don John of Austria becomes governor-general

The political difficulties facing Requesens were certainly challenging, but his more immediate issue was the economic fragility of Spain. This was especially dangerous because the growing expense of the Netherlands campaign was affecting Spain's ability to pay for its forces there, which in turn began to undermine the loyalty of both the Spanish army and the mercenaries employed within it, who were growing tired of deferred wages. This was a very real problem for the governor-general, because without the support of this force the position of Spain was increasingly untenable.

EXTRACT

1 From Geoffrey Parker, *The Dutch Revolt* (1990).

On 31 May 1574 Philip II confided to his private secretary, Mateo Vázquez, that he considered 'the loss of the Netherlands and the rest [of his monarchy] to be as certain as, in this situation, anything that can be … It is a terrible situation and it is getting worse every day.' On 20 June he returned to his despondent refrain: 'I believe that everything is a waste of time, judging by what is happening in the Low Countries, and if they are lost the rest [of the monarchy] will not last long, even if we have enough money.' The financial situation of the Castilian treasury had become the key to the situation. 'We must do everything we can to succour the Netherlands,' he wrote on 4 July, '… because if we have no money, our position at the conference table will prove even more difficult.' On 14 July the king's financial advisers warned him that the coffers were empty and that the only way to avoid bankruptcy was to repudiate all public debts and abandon the war in the Netherlands. Four days later Philip lamented: 'I think that the Netherlands will be lost for lack of money, as I have always feared … We are in great need and our enemies know it well, so that they will not wish to make a settlement …' 'We are running out of everything so fast', the king concluded, 'that words fail me.'

Philip II's finances were in a bad way by 1574: his extended war against the Turks was consuming money very quickly and the escalating costs in the Netherlands were emptying Spain's purse at an alarming rate. The immediate consequence of this financial challenge was that the Habsburg forces in the Low Countries, sick of their employer's failure to pay them, **mutinied** in April and attacked the city of Antwerp with the intention of sacking the city for the money owed to them – approximately one million florins.

Although this mutiny was ended with the soldiers eventually being paid off by the beginning of June, it had significant consequences for the rebellion. It weakened the position of Spain, particularly as it came just after a military victory in the town of Mook, where Louis of Nassau was killed in battle on 14 April. That a very capable general, and the Prince of Orange's own brother, was killed should have given the Spanish a greater opportunity to pacify the rebellion, but rather than capitalising on this

KEY TERM

Mutiny
Personnel refusing to obey their orders and taking actions that serve their own interests rather than those of their state.

fortune, the mutiny effectively nullified the event and arguably left the rebels in a stronger position than they had anticipated.

This position was made more secure with further mutinies in the spring. The town of Leiden had been under siege since March, given only temporary respite when Louis of Nassau had engaged the Spanish in a battle that had resulted in his death. After April, the town was besieged once more until October when the dykes holding back the sea were destroyed in order to drive the Spanish away and allow a ship to help the beleaguered town. This action reminded the Spanish how inhospitable the landscape in the north could be. A month later, just as winter was beginning to set in, there were further mutinies as Spanish garrisons left their posts, not wishing to spend any more time in the frozen and waterlogged lands of the northern provinces. By abandoning their positions, these troops were in effect handing control to the rebels, who quickly reoccupied the vacated towns, further consolidating their position and strength.

The loss of so many troops was also a blow for the morale of the Habsburg authorities, who increasingly began to question the likelihood of their continuing presence in the Netherlands. Requesens himself began to doubt the success of his campaign (see Source 2), and with the tangible loss of more than 24 towns in the north, his natural inclination for moderation motivated him to try to negotiate peace.

SOURCE

2 From a letter written by the governor-general, Luis de Requesens, to Philip II in December 1574.

Many towns and a battle have been won, each of them a success enough in itself to bring peace, and even to win an entire new kingdom elsewhere; but here they have been to no avail because after each victory came the mutinies … I believe that God for my sins has chosen to show me so many times the Promised Land here, as he did to Moses, but that someone else is to be the Joshua who will enter therein.

The peace negotiations at Breda, 1575

Such was the reduced state of the Spanish treasury by 1575 that Philip II gave his permission for Requesens to arrange a meeting with the rebels and empowered him to make some concessions that might end the war between them. At the subsequent peace negotiations, held in the town of Breda in March 1575, the governor-general was able to offer the withdrawal of Spanish troops from the Netherlands in return for the cessation of hostilities and a return to order. Since some of the local discontent was the result of poorly behaved Spanish troops who were garrisoned in their towns, this concession was felt to be a welcome offering which, it was hoped, would encourage Dutch agreement. Although this compromise did raise expectations for a peace settlement, Philip II was unwilling to compromise on matters of religion. His own faith would not allow him to accept Protestantism in the Low Countries, and therefore all he was prepared to allow his governor-general to permit on this issue was six months' grace, allowing the Protestants to leave the Netherlands unharmed.

For their part, the rebels were equally resolved to maintain their religion and would not countenance any limitation to Calvinism. They were willing to accept the authority of the king, but on the issue of religion they would not be moved. Since they were in a strong position, the rebels felt able to dig in their heels, and faced with an equally intransigent king, Requesens had no choice but to dissolve the peace negotiations in July after three months of diplomacy.

The result of this failure was the recommencement of fighting, which saw the Spanish make some useful gains in their attempt to divide Holland and Zeeland by seizing the islands of Schoonhoven and Schouwen-Duiveland, which sat between the provinces. Despite these victories, the problem of finance was quick to undermine Spanish control and in September 1575 Philip II formally suspended payments of the country's public debts and declared bankruptcy. This action effectively ended his ability to pay for the troops serving in the Low Countries as this was usually undertaken by means of a **bill of exchange**, which no bank was now willing to honour. The consequence of this action was once again the loss of their advantage, as mutinies in the army occurred once more in early July 1576.

AS Level Exam-Style Question Section B

To what extent was Luis de Requesens' failure to achieve agreement at the peace negotiations in Breda during 1575 the result of Spain's weak financial position? (20 marks)

Tip

When answering questions like this you should think about other factors that might also have influenced Requesens' failure – military and political influences for example.

KEY TERM

Bill of exchange
A written order, requesting the recipient to pay out on the author's behalf. Also known as a promissory note or cheque.

The Spanish Fury of 1576

Writing as early as November 1575, Requesens had anticipated the collapse of the military once Philip II had declared his bankruptcy, and he was right. With the government's inability to pay its troops, the soldiers sought their own solution to the financial settlement they were due. This plan involved marching on Brussels and demanding the money owed to them which, by mid-1576, amounted to 24 months' pay each. While en route to the capital, they also sacked towns they passed through as a means of compensating themselves and strengthening their bargaining hand. The manner in which they set about this task was ferocious – in the loyal southern province of Brabant alone, the soldiers sacked more than 170 towns. Such was the extent of the violence that it became known as the Spanish Fury and it had very significant consequences for both Spain and the Netherlands.

SOURCE

3 From a letter written by the governor-general, Luis de Requesens, to his brother, dated 12 November 1575.

Such a blow to the Exchange here [in Antwerp] that no one in it has any credit ... I cannot find a single penny, nor can I see how the king could send money here, even if he had it in abundance. Short of a miracle, the whole military machine will fall in ruins so rapidly that it is highly probable that I shall not have time to tell you about it. And all this has to come at a time when, if the king could have delayed for three months, I hold it certain that in that time we could have captured all the rest of Zealand and even the other provinces.

Among the first towns to be attacked was Aalst in Flanders. This had always been loyal to the Habsburg crown and its sacking was met with great surprise. Being only 16 miles from Brussels, news of the event was received there very quickly and since the attack was rightly felt to have been unprovoked, the people of Brussels took up arms to defend their city from a similar fate. This action evidences the growing divide between the Spanish and their Netherlandish supporters. While the northern provinces were ostensibly rebellious, the southern provinces, given their closer ties with Spain and Catholicism, were more disposed towards loyalty. In this sense, therefore, the actions of the mutineers not only caused excessive violence within the Low Countries, but also alienated the ruling authority from its loyal citizens.

The sacking of Antwerp

Perhaps the most shocking example of the Fury was the course of events that befell the town of Antwerp in November 1576. As one of the richest towns in Europe, Antwerp was an appealing target for the mutineers, and when they entered the town they set about looting it with such ferocity that after three days of violence more than 8,000 citizens had been killed and substantial amounts of property destroyed. Although towns had been sacked before – Alva had allowed similar undertakings at Mechelen, Zutphen and Naarden – these had not been on the same scale as the events in Antwerp. So great was the extent of the savagery that news of the atrocities there was heard across the Low Countries.

The sacking itself, and the public awareness of the atrocity, had a profound effect on the country. Prior to the outbreak of the mutinies, the majority of the southern provinces had remained loyal to Philip II. As primarily Catholic citizens they were less motivated by the defence of Protestantism, which had become central to the Prince of Orange's rebellion, and therefore they were more favourably disposed towards Spanish rule. Although they had been displeased with the attempt to enforce the unpopular Tenth Penny tax, the removal of Alva had moderated their opposition, and when rebellion had broken out the majority of towns decided to remain neutral rather than take a specific side.

Such was the extent of terror waged on Antwerp, and other loyal southern towns, that the inhabitants of these areas began to reconsider their position. In essence, the sacking of the town had helped to sate the troops' desire for payment and it had offered a means for them to vent their frustration, but in the process it had ruined any hope of reconciliation between the southern provinces of the Netherlands and their Habsburg rulers.

The Sack of Antwerp, November 1576. A coloured copper engraving by Frans Hogenberg, depicting the citizens of the town climbing the walls to escape the Spanish atrocities being committed, created c1576–90.

The Pacification of Ghent in 1576

During the war against Holland and Zeeland, the remaining 15 provinces largely remained neutral or, at least, generally sympathetic towards Spain. With the Spanish Fury enacted by the unrepentant and unpaid soldiers of that country, these provinces were increasingly encouraged into an alliance with their rebellious northern neighbours.

In many regards, however, the Spanish Fury was only the latest motivation in a gradually growing list of reasons to oppose Habsburg rule. The old concerns about receding privileges and excessive taxation had already raised whispers of discontent, and the general behaviour of Spanish soldiers while billeted in the towns had also always been a source of animosity. In this sense the Fury that was unleashed simply gave greater resolve to the leadership of these provinces and, in November 1576, they signed what became known as the Pacification of Ghent, which achieved the following objectives.

- The rebel and obedient states agreed to temporarily set aside their disagreements over religion and government.

- In unison they would make a determined effort to eject the Spanish mutineers from their lands.

The significance of this agreement was that for the first time the provinces had asserted a national consciousness. In this regard the Spanish Fury, and particularly the sacking of Antwerp, was especially significant because such a consciousness had not been forthcoming between the rebel and obedient provinces. Certainly the southern states had been willing to assist one another – Hainaut had invoked the mutual support clause from the **Pragmatic Sanction** on 27 August 1576 and sought help against the mutineers from Brabant, but officials from Brabant did not seek help from Holland and Zeeland. The Pacification of Ghent (formally signed on 8 November 1576) was therefore a very progressive step in forging a common opposition to the excesses of Spanish rule.

The consequence of this arrangement was that the provinces were more empowered, and this was reflected in the States-General. This organ of government had been divided since the rebellion began. However, it was now reunited and this gave greater opportunity to demand terms with the Spanish – especially given that country's financial position. In this undertaking they were also the benefactors of unforeseen circumstances. Requesens died in office in March 1576 and his replacement was slow to arrive, which gave the assembly time to make its own arrangements. The governor-general was eventually replaced by Philip II's half-brother, Don John of Austria. When the Spanish prince was addressed by the States-General in January 1577, he had no choice but to agree to the request by the strengthened States-General to withdraw the mutinous Spanish troops and he was asked to sign the **Perpetual Edict** to this effect. The provinces of Holland and Zeeland objected to this edict and withdrew from the States-General in protest on the grounds that they did not trust the king's word.

Despite the opposition of the two provinces, the States-General was certainly helped by the reduced position that Philip II had found himself in because of his ongoing war with the Turks. His subsequent acceptance that concessions would have to be made to maintain his rule in the Low Countries was therefore presenting an improved opportunity for the provinces, even before the agreement was formed. However, Philip II's willingness to consider concessions was not publicly known and therefore the Pacification of Ghent formalised a renewed union between the provinces, which strengthened their hand when negotiating with the new governor-general. This enhanced position enabled them to assert their ancient privileges more effectively and attempt to redress the balance of power.

SOURCE

5 From a letter written by Philip II in 1576 to his brother, Don John of Austria, acknowledging the need to offer concessions in order to maintain authority in the Low Countries.

If matters are in such a state that the States demand unilateral concessions before they will recognize your authority, it seems that, safeguarding religion and my authority as much as may be ... we shall have to concede everything necessary to bring about a conclusion and save what we can. This is the ultimate solution to a problem like this, and we shall have to trust these people, in spite of all the risks involved.

ACTIVITIES
KNOWLEDGE CHECK

The decline of Habsburg authority
Using the material you have read and your own knowledge, complete the following activities.

1 Produce a list of factors that contributed to the decline of Habsburg rule between 1573 and 1576.

2 Number them in order of greatest significance.

3 Offer a brief reason for this judgement.

The advance of Calvinism in the southern provinces

The agreement signed at Ghent offered the chance of an improved relationship between the provinces. However, the issue of religion had been carefully avoided in the interest of securing the removal of the mutineers.

With the acquiescence of Don John of Austria, the States-General had been able to achieve this objective and in the process assert their own autonomy more than they had been able to previously. The impact of this latter development was that the question of religion was soon in need of addressing, as the rebel states were very motivated to promote Calvinism across the Low Countries, while the southern provinces were determined to maintain the dominance of Catholicism.

The issue of religion was contentious, and many of the southern provinces did not trust the Prince of Orange and his Calvinist sympathisers. At a meeting held in St Geertruidenberg in early 1577, the prince and his followers openly stated that they would never renounce their new faith, regardless of whether it was Philip II or the States-General that asked them to do so. It was this determined attitude that led to the distrust of them among the southern provinces, particularly since the Spanish mutineers had been paid off. Now that threat had passed there was the opportunity for the rebels to promote their faith.

The first so-called Calvinistic republic was established in Ghent, where there was further iconoclasm, suspension of the mass and expulsion of Catholic clergy. This triggered similar changes in other Flanders' towns, such as Oudenaarde, and later in Antwerp and Brussels. In June 1578, the Calvinist Church sent a petition to the States-General demanding that their faith be freely allowed in any town wherever 100 families asked for it. This demand was being pushed through the States-General by Orangists. However, in July it was successfully blocked by Catholic opposition.

Known as the Religious Peace, this demand would have provided for freedom of worship in the Low Countries, but instead it was returned to the individual provincial parliaments and towns to decide their own position on religion. The implication of this decision meant that the brief unity that the Pacification of Ghent had achieved was coming under significant strain, as religion encouraged provinces to ally with one another in order to defend their faith from attack. In October 1578, Hainaut and Artois sought a partnership to defend Catholicism from the Calvinist threat emanating from Flanders and Brabant, which were already allied themselves. Such was the immediacy of the Calvinist threat for Catholics in the south that each side looked for help abroad: France for the Catholics and Germany for the Calvinists.

WHY DID PARMA ENJOY MORE SUCCESS THAN REQUESENS?

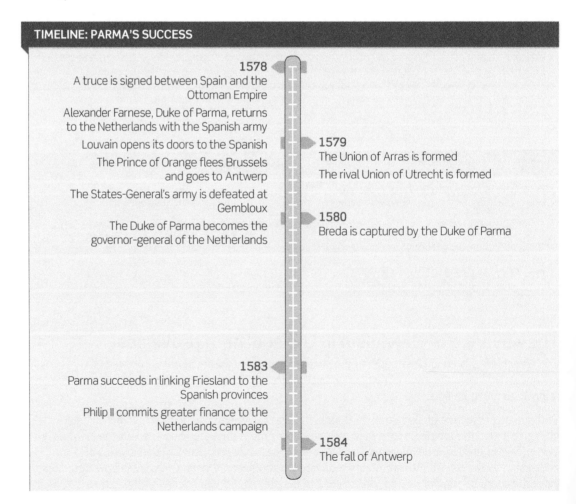

TIMELINE: PARMA'S SUCCESS

1578
A truce is signed between Spain and the Ottoman Empire

Alexander Farnese, Duke of Parma, returns to the Netherlands with the Spanish army

Louvain opens its doors to the Spanish

The Prince of Orange flees Brussels and goes to Antwerp

The States-General's army is defeated at Gembloux

The Duke of Parma becomes the governor-general of the Netherlands

1579
The Union of Arras is formed
The rival Union of Utrecht is formed

1580
Breda is captured by the Duke of Parma

1583
Parma succeeds in linking Friesland to the Spanish provinces

Philip II commits greater finance to the Netherlands campaign

1584
The fall of Antwerp

Re-establishing Spanish rule in the south

Just as the issue of religion was threatening to split the union established by the Pacification of Ghent, Don John of Austria grew impatient with the States-General, and particularly the Prince of Orange who was suspicious of his motives and had refused any overtures from the Spaniard. Intent on reasserting his half-brother's power, he broke the Perpetual Edict and in July 1577 had recalled the Spanish army to the Netherlands. This was only possible because the Turks had signed a truce with Philip II and therefore he was free to resume his war in the Low Countries. This action was seen as a betrayal of the agreement signed between the provinces and the governor-general. It served the Prince of Orange very well as he was proved right in his suspicion of the king's brother, and was asked by the States-General to come and defend Brussels from this enemy. In effect the redeployment of Spanish forces allowed Orange to be recognised as the **_de facto_** leader of the Netherlands – the man called on to save them from the Spanish threat. It also undermined the position of Don John as the governor-general of the country, since many of the provinces would not trust him again.

The Spanish army entered the Netherlands at the end of 1577 under the command of the Duke of Parma, Alexander Farnese – the only son of the last regent, Margaret of Parma. In January 1578, it defeated the States-General's forces at Gembloux and was also able to occupy the town of Louvain, which had willingly opened its gates to the army. The action taken by this town evidences the strained relationship that had developed between north and south since the issue of religion had emerged, and the re-entry of the Spanish army gave each side a greater sense of clarity about their priorities in this matter. With the advancing Spanish force, the Prince of Orange and States-General moved to Antwerp as more southern, Catholic-dominated towns opened their doors to Farnese. Such was the ease with which the returned army was able to reoccupy these provinces that many began to consider ways of **seceding** from the States-General and making their own independent peace with Philip II.

KEY TERMS

De facto
A Latin term meaning 'in reality' or 'in fact'.

Secede
To withdraw formally from an organisation.

EXTEND YOUR KNOWLEDGE

Alexander Farnese, Duke of Parma (1545–92)
Alexander Farnese was the only son of Margaret of Parma, regent of the Netherlands after Philip II's return to Spain in 1559. Born into such an influential family – a relative of his was made Pope Paul III in 1534 – Alexander enjoyed an indulgent upbringing and spent much of his time learning the skills of leadership. An active person, Farnese enjoyed hunting, riding and warfare. In 1571, he fought at the Battle of Lepanto against the Turks, where he acquitted himself very impressively and earned the respect of his commanders. Appointed command of the Spanish army returning to the Netherlands in 1577, he showed the same talent for war in that country where he was able to assert Spain's authority once more and became the governor-general upon the death of Don John of Austria.

The Union of Arras, 1579

The reoccupation of the southern provinces and the demonstration of Habsburg authority encouraged the provinces of Hainaut, Walloon Flanders and Artois, to secede from the States-General and establish their own confederation – known as the Union of Arras – in 1579. Though encouraged by the reassertion of Spanish power, this action was primarily motivated by the growing religious difficulties between the rebels and the remaining 15 provinces. Since the exit of the mutinous Spanish troops after the signing of the Perpetual Edict, the Calvinists had taken full advantage of the new-found freedom afforded to their faith in the absence of Spanish oppression. With the influence of the Prince of Orange behind them, they had sought to spread their religion and this had begun to alienate some of the Catholic-dominated towns and provinces. With the reintroduction of Spanish troops, these provinces saw an opportunity to defend their faith from the spread of Calvinism and therefore abandoned the States-General which, they felt, was increasingly under the influence of the Protestant rebels.

The significance of this union lay in the implications it had for the Low Countries. The Pacification of Ghent had offered the opportunity of unity among them, united against the common enemy of Spain. However, the agreement signed in Arras destroyed this comradeship and gave the advantage back to Spain – even more so when the northern provinces later signed their own pact in the Union of Utrecht (see pages 351–352).

From the agreed principles of the Union of Arras, signed on 6 January 1579. The Union required the acceptance of the following requests before the participating provinces would recognise the authority of Spain and its new governor-general.

In order to maintain an appreciably better confidence among the subjects of His Majesty by means of a good union and accord in the service of God for the preservation of the Roman, Apostolic and Catholic religion, and obedience to His Majesty, together with the repose and prosperity of the country, both parties consent to a perpetual amnesty for all things that may have been said or done since the beginning of hostilities, or in consequence of them... His Majesty shall send out all Spanish, Italian, Burgundian and other foreign troops not acceptable to the country within six weeks of the publication of the present treaty or earlier... During the time until the departure of the said foreigners, His Majesty and the United Lands will raise an army of natives of this country and others acceptable to His Majesty and to the estates of the provinces... His Majesty will choose for his Council of State ten or twelve persons, including lords and nobles as well as men of learning, all natives of the country, of which two-thirds shall be acceptable to the estates of the said provinces... All correspondence and dispatches shall be drawn up according to the advice and decisions of the councillors of state... These provinces shall henceforth not be burdened in any way with taxes, tributes or impositions other than those which were in force during the time of the late Emperor Charles, and with the consent of the estates of each province respectively. Each and all of these shall be maintained in their privileges, usages and customs, in general and individually. And in the event that any be infringed, it shall be made good and restored.

The union itself sought guarantees from Philip II and required more autonomy than previously allowed, but in effect it tied the participating provinces to Spain and redrew the battle lines once more. This time the prominent motivation was religion – the southern provinces did not feel that Catholicism was safe under the pact they had signed with their northern neighbours. However, the political consequence of this undertaking was also greatly significant. The union polarised the Low Countries once more and dispersed any notion of a unified state as long as the issue of religion was not settled. In effect, it cemented religion as the single most divisive force in the Netherlands, strong enough to divide the native population and encourage the Catholic-dominated provinces to reassert their support for their traditional foreign rulers.

The immediate effect of this support was seen in the help offered to Farnese's army by his new allies. Using troops supplied by the Union of Arras, he was able to capture Maastricht and 's-Hertogenbosch in 1579 and then Breda in 1580 and Courtrai in 1581. These victories enabled him to quickly move further north, and by the early 1580s much of the rebel-held land had been retaken.

Parma's diplomacy, military tactics and strategy

Diplomacy

The Duke of Parma, son of the last regent of the Netherlands, was an astute leader. His diplomatic ability meant he was effective in dealing with his opponents in the Netherlands once he became governor-general in October 1578. As a shrewd individual, he was aware of the religious discord among the northern and southern provinces and was able to exploit this by making overtures to those who sought to defend Catholicism. His diplomacy helped to secure the Union of Arras in May 1579 and also, one month earlier, a treaty with the discontented soldiers of the Netherlands who had mutinied after the States-General had fallen into financial debt and could no longer afford the 50,000 men it had been able to raise. These malcontents, as they became known, were reconciled to Philip II by the Treaty of St Moi, whereby their force of approximately 7,000 men were paid 250,000 florins between them and in return joined the royal army.

Such diplomacy proved very successful for reasserting Spanish Habsburg authority because it enabled the Duke of Parma to exploit the States-General's financial weaknesses by buying off its soldiers. This action reduced his opposition and effectively ripped apart the Pacification of Ghent.

The defection of these men, together with the weakened position of the States-General following the Union of Arras, encouraged others to seek a deal with Philip II. Since the resumption of hostilities upon the return of Spanish troops, the southern provinces were in a difficult position. Having fallen out with Holland and Zeeland over the matter of religion and also with Spain having signed the Pacification of Ghent, their position was increasingly weak, and so to preserve any of the rights they had secured they needed to secure guarantees. These were discussed at a conference held in Cologne in May 1579.

Evidence (5b)

The importance of context

Documents (texts) are like small pieces torn from a larger tapestry (context). Historians have to reconstruct the larger pattern into which documents might fit in order to use them to construct accounts of the past. The problem is that texts can have multiple contexts. Historians often debate how best to contextualise the documents that they interpret.

The Union of Arras, signed in 1579, is an agreement between the southern provinces of the Netherlands to recognise the king of Spain as their sovereign ruler.

1 Summarise some key points from Source 6. Does the document indicate what the motives for the union were? Were provinces looking for protection? Were they hoping to enhance their own powerbase?

As well as noting the contents of the union, it is important to consider who signed the union: the conservative and Catholic noblemen of Hainaut, Walloon Flanders and Artois.

The timeline below provides a possible context for the document in the wider story of Netherlandish domestic policy. Look at this timeline and then answer the question that follows.

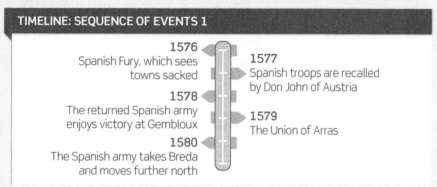

TIMELINE: SEQUENCE OF EVENTS 1

1576 Spanish Fury, which sees towns sacked

1577 Spanish troops are recalled by Don John of Austria

1578 The returned Spanish army enjoys victory at Gembloux

1579 The Union of Arras

1580 The Spanish army takes Breda and moves further north

2 How does the Union of Arras fit into the pattern of events? Why might conservative leaders of these provinces want to support the king of Spain?

The document might seem to have one kind of meaning when interpreted in the context of domestic policy. A contrasting interpretation appears if we locate it in another context.

There is good reason to think that the conservative leaders of the southern provinces were afraid that Catholicism would be destroyed because of the spread of Calvinism into their lands.

TIMELINE: SEQUENCE OF EVENTS 2

1576 The Perpetual Edict is signed requiring the Spanish mutineers to leave the Netherlands

1577 The Prince of Orange declares he will never renounce Protestantism

1578 Calvinism spreads into the southern provinces and towns are forced to accept this faith

The Religious Peace is being considered in the States-General, which would allow the establishment of Calvinist churches

1579 The Union of Arras is agreed

1580 The Spanish army is able to take Breda and push into the north

3 Why might the leaders of the southern provinces have been motivated to sign the Union of Arras? Consider both timelines together and answer the following questions:

a) Use information from both timelines to construct a possible context for why the Union of Arras might have been signed.

b) Why is it important for historians to spend time thinking about possible contexts for a document before they start to use it to draw conclusions about the past?

Military tactics and strategy

In addition to his diplomatic skill, the duke was also an effective military figure, and in June 1579 he laid siege to Maastricht. His capture of this town strengthened the hand of Spain during its negotiations at the Cologne meeting and it was therefore more able to be intransigent with regard to the terms discussed. Catholicism was to be the exclusive religion in all the provinces with the exception of Holland and Zeeland, where Calvinism would be allowed to continue for a temporary period, and there was also to be a return to the political relationship that existed in 1559 – essentially no constitutional restrictions upon the power of the monarch. This was an uncompromising set of demands, but given the military success enjoyed by Farnese it was anticipated that several more, if not all of the provinces, would actually agree to these terms. In this manner the military skill exhibited by the duke was able to place Spain back in the dominant position in the Low Countries.

This position was further improved when the duke was able to win over the town of Mechelen. This he achieved in a similar fashion to that which had acquired him the loyalty of the malcontents – he bought them. In the case of Mechelen he paid the governor of the town 5,000 florins to open the gates, which the man duly did on account of personal greed. The timings and manner in which Farnese was able to achieve this struck hard at the States-General, discrediting an already weakened assembly that subsequently began to fracture as provinces started to look to their own defence.

The conference at Cologne was abandoned in November 1579 as the rebels – calling themselves patriots – hardened their resolve against Philip II, whose demands suggested he would never accept Calvinism. By pushing this religion, however, they drove more towns into a new alliance with the Spanish, and by December many Catholic-dominated areas had signed a peace treaty with the Duke of Parma. By March 1580, the northern province of Groningen had also settled with the Spaniard.

The success he was able to enjoy lay in part with the loyal provinces that had signed the Union of Arras. Part of this agreement had been the removal of foreign troops, but by 1581 this had been abandoned as the provinces recognised that the king would struggle to defend them with so few native troops and therefore withdrew this stipulation. By 1582, Parma controlled 60,000 men as new men were raised throughout Europe and sent by Philip II to the Netherlands. With these men Parma was able swiftly to capture further towns, and by 1583 he had been able to link the northern province of Friesland with the rest of the loyal provinces – an achievement that won Philip II's admiration and secured the king's financial commitment. From the summer of 1583, he promised to pay a monthly stipend of 500,000 florins, and this income allowed the duke to begin his campaign against the larger towns, with the intention of encircling the rebel areas.

The fall of Antwerp in 1584

The city of Antwerp was one of the most important in Europe. Were the Spanish to reclaim its loyalty it was anticipated that this would significantly strengthen Philip II's authority in the Netherlands and reduce the influence of the rebels. To this end the Duke of Parma, having enjoyed so much success by 1584, turned his attention to this great city and its impressive fortifications.

It was the intention of the duke to starve the town out, and to achieve this he first built a bridge across the River Scheldt to enable his troops to cut the town off from the sea. Completed in February 1584, the bridge (which was almost 750 metres long) was an impressive achievement and the avenue down which Parma sought to capture Antwerp. Although defended by 200 siege guns, the rebels sought to destroy this construction and in April sent **fire ships** down the river, blowing up a 60 metre section and almost killing the duke. This success was not quickly followed up, however, and the weakness was resolved before anyone could help the besieged city.

As approximately one-third of the population were Catholic, the city's leaders came under increased pressure to submit to the Spanish and by August an agreement was signed.

The success of this venture lay in the skills of the Duke of Parma. His understanding of military strategy combined with a strong grasp of the geography of the Low Countries – particularly the importance of the rivers and the sea links – enabled him to raise sieges and effectively starve towns into submission without having to engage in drawn-out battles. His success was also dependent on the obedient troops he marshalled. The duke was well aware of his predecessor's difficulties with maintaining loyal troops, and he had been very careful to keep up payments to them. He was greatly helped by Spain's improved financial security following the truce with the Turks in 1578, but he also made sure the troops were looked after. When Antwerp fell, he immediately ordered their arrears to be paid in full and the city handed over more than one million florins for that purpose.

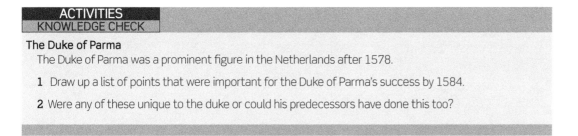

ACTIVITIES
KNOWLEDGE CHECK

The Duke of Parma

The Duke of Parma was a prominent figure in the Netherlands after 1578.

1 Draw up a list of points that were important for the Duke of Parma's success by 1584.

2 Were any of these unique to the duke or could his predecessors have done this too?

HOW IMPORTANT WAS FOREIGN INTERVENTION TO THE PRINCE OF ORANGE'S SUCCESS?

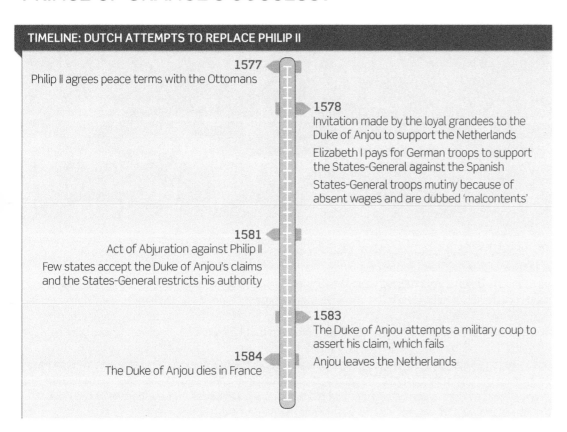

TIMELINE: DUTCH ATTEMPTS TO REPLACE PHILIP II

1577
Philip II agrees peace terms with the Ottomans

1578
Invitation made by the loyal grandees to the Duke of Anjou to support the Netherlands

Elizabeth I pays for German troops to support the States-General against the Spanish

States-General troops mutiny because of absent wages and are dubbed 'malcontents'

1581
Act of Abjuration against Philip II

Few states accept the Duke of Anjou's claims and the States-General restricts his authority

1583
The Duke of Anjou attempts a military coup to assert his claim, which fails

Anjou leaves the Netherlands

1584
The Duke of Anjou dies in France

Orange's decision to seek foreign help and the invitation to the Duke of Anjou

The return of Spanish troops and their early success under the Duke of Parma encouraged the Prince of Orange to take measures to protect the gains he and his faith had made by 1578. The States-General was divided on the issue of religion and the Spanish had an opportunity to exploit this. To counter the renewed threat posed by the Spanish, Orange sought to attract foreign support for his cause. He anticipated that this would not only fortify his opposition to Spain but also provide a greater sense of centralised control within the States-General. This decision was quite astute, as in many ways the prince himself can be seen as part of the division within that parliament: his personal association with the Protestant faith and its more radical proponents had raised suspicions among

Catholic members of the assembly and therefore they maintained a wary attitude towards the prince and his activities. By looking to a neutral third party for support, it was anticipated that perhaps a greater unity could be maintained among the provinces in the face of Spain's resurgence.

SOURCE 7

An etching by the Antwerp-based French publisher Christophe Plantin in 1582. It depicts the ceremony that marked the acceptance of the Duke of Anjou as the 'Defender of the Liberties of the Low Countries', which took place in August 1578.

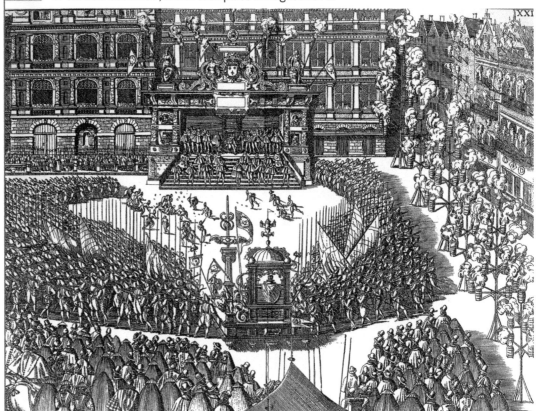

The decision to seek outside support, however, was essentially forced upon him by the other grandees, who were suspicious of his intentions. Since 1576, the Catholic provinces had been courting the Duke of Anjou (brother to the king of France), hoping to be able to call on his support should Catholicism need defending. In 1578, they approached the duke once more via Count Lalaing, the governor of Walloon Flanders. Anjou was invited to the Netherlands to reign as an alternative, and hopefully more popular, monarch. It was intended that he would be a bulwark against the rising Calvinist threat. However, the Prince of Orange sought to use the duke as a means to promote the power of the States-General in the resistance against Spain, and therefore he undertook to draw him away from the distinctly Catholic intentions of the Walloon Flanders governor. After considerable debate, the provinces agreed that Anjou would become the Defender of the Liberties of the Low Countries, and that he would provide 12,000 men to reinforce the States-General.

SOURCE 8

From a pamphlet to John Marnix written on 1 June 1578. The author poses as a German nobleman from Cologne.

You need fear neither the desires nor the designs of Monsieur Anjou who would never have conceived of becoming your lord had you not asked him first, and, who, employing all his means to free you from a great evil, can have no other power than that which is conferred upon him by respect for him personally and by your laws.

SOURCE

9 From the negotiations between the States-General and the Duke of Anjou between July and August 1580, in which the terms of the duke's authority were determined.

His Highness and his successors will not only swear a general oath to the States that they will keep to this treaty but also swear the usual solemn oath in each province. In case His Highness or his successors infringe any point of this treaty the States will *de facto* be relieved of their duty to obey him and of their allegiance to him and will be allowed to take another Prince or arrange matters differently as they think best.

The motivation for the title Defender of the Liberties of the Low Countries rather than 'sovereign' arguably lies with the intentions of the provinces to retain greater authority for themselves, but it also evades the issue of religion and Anjou's own Catholicism. In addressing this concern, albeit indirectly, the arrangement between Anjou and the provinces highlights the political motivations of the Prince of Orange to give the Low Countries a stronger degree of autonomy and also greater religious freedom.

The overtures made to Anjou also encouraged support from England, since Elizabeth I was unhappy with the influence that Anjou was acquiring in the Netherlands and felt that such influence would make the Low Countries a satellite of France. For Elizabeth this was unacceptable because it would give France a stronger hand in Europe. To counter this threat she undertook to support the States-General by funding a German mercenary army under the command of John Casimir – the ruler of the Rhine Palatinate and, from 1583, regent for his nephew.

This army amounted to 12,000 men and arrived in the Netherlands in August 1578. The Prince of Orange helped to broker this arrangement as he also hoped that Elizabeth I would eventually send her own force to support him and with this he hoped to secure an independent and religiously tolerant state. In the meanwhile, however, the troops under Casimir's command were gratefully received although they proved to be less effective than the prince had hoped.

As a devout Calvinist, Casimir was more interested in supporting his faith's struggle against the Catholics. Therefore, rather than support the States-General as instructed, he led his men to Ghent where they engaged in religious conflict with the Catholics. Instead of reinforcing the States-General, this army actually added to the assembly's difficulties and encouraged many Catholic towns to seek protection from the Spanish Crown, resulting in the Union of Arras in 1579.

EXTRACT

 From G. Parker, *The Dutch Revolt* (1990).

On the 13th August, after much bitter wrangling, the States agreed to recognize Anjou as 'the Defender of the Liberties of the Low Countries.'

EXTRACT

 From M. Rady, *Revolt to Independence: the Netherlands 1550–1650* (1990).

The next month the States-General granted the French prince the title 'Defender of the Liberties of the Netherlands.'

EXTRACT

 From E. Kossman and A. Mellink (eds), *Texts Concerning the Revolt of the Netherlands* (1974).

After long negotiations and morose hesitations on the part of the individual provinces Anjou was at last offered a treaty (August 1580) which would promote him to the quality of 'prince and seignior of the Netherlands – not to that of sovereign'.

EXTRACT

 From G. Parker and C. Martin, *The Spanish Armada* (1999).

Deliverance was, however, at hand. The prince of Orange persuaded Francois de Valois, duke of Anjou and heir apparent to the French throne, to become 'prince and lord of the Netherlands'. In 1581 the States-General declared Philip II deposed from all his Netherlands titles.

Arguments and facts

Work in groups.

1 Why are facts important in history?

2 Read Extracts 3 and 4.

   a) How do these extracts disagree?

   b) Which one do think is correct? Explain your answer.

3 Read Extracts 2 and 5.

   a) How do these extracts disagree?

   b) What do you think is the significance of Anjou being recognised? Do you think that these authors, whose accounts differ in terms of the facts, would have viewed the significance of Anjou's recognition differently from the way you would view it? Explain your answer.

4 All these extracts give detailed arguments about the significance of Anjou's recognition by the States-General, but they only briefly mention the dates of the decision to do this. Which do you think is more important?

5 If we accept that Extract 5 is wrong about the date of recognition, do we discount Extract 5 as being useful? Explain your answer.

The Duke's unpopularity and withdrawal in 1583

Despite being granted the title of Defender of the Liberties of the Low Countries by the States-General, to which he added Duke of Brabant in July 1581, the Duke of Anjou was not universally accepted. Although under the Act of Abjuration (see pages 352–354) the duke had formally been recognised as the Low Countries' own choice as a replacement for Philip II, the provinces of Holland and Zeeland refused to recognise his authority. The reason for their opposition was religion: as a Catholic, the two provinces did not trust Anjou to keep his word. Also, as their populations were mostly Calvinist, they did not wish to be under the authority of someone whose faith they fundamentally disagreed with. The implication of this opposition was that the powers granted to the duke were tightly restricted to the extent that he essentially had to seek permission from the States-General whenever he wanted to make any significant decision.

The limited nature of Anjou's power was not just a consequence of his religion. The particularisms of provincial individuality meant that the Netherlands was also reluctant to accept another centralised authority and therefore they had adopted the same wariness towards Anjou as they had done towards the Habsburgs. In this sense the provinces were simply looking to safeguard their ancient privileges as they had always done.

The difference in the 1580s, however, was that religion was a much greater dividing influence than it had previously been, and therefore his new acquisition was a very challenging nation to govern: it was divided against itself and also fighting a war against Spain. Perhaps worse for the duke was the popularity of the Prince of Orange. Both Holland and Zeeland had refused to accept the duke's authority, but they were very pleased to acknowledge their Protestant co-religionist, Orange, so much so that in August 1582 he was offered the title Count of Holland. Although he initially hesitated over receiving this title, the prince accepted graciously as it was an honour that the people were very happy to grant.

The duke's attempted coup and his eventual withdrawal

Anjou was effectively stifled by the limitations on his power, and he greatly resented them. In January 1583, therefore, he embarked on a course of radical action to free himself from these restrictions by force of arms. He reasoned that the only way to assert his authority was to seize the major towns in Flanders and establish a clear base of support. Throughout January, his men seized control of many of the coastal towns, including Dunkirk and Ostend, but the major towns of Bruges and Antwerp resisted his attempts and in the case of the latter city, extracted an expensive price for the duke's ambitions – 2,000 out of the 3,500 troops he commanded there were killed.

Known locally as the French Fury, the aggression of Anjou significantly undermined his credibility in the Netherlands and also weakened the opposition to Spain. Although several of the towns he controlled undertook to form a religious alliance with the Spanish, and Orange brokered a deal between the States-General and Anjou in March 1583, the duke's position was effectively untenable and by the summer he left the Netherlands, dying the following year in France.

ACTIVITIES
KNOWLEDGE CHECK

The significance of foreign intervention
Answer the following questions.

1 How did the Duke of Anjou enhance the position of those opposing Spain?

2 What was the significance of Elizabeth I's intervention?

3 Why do you think foreign intervention failed to secure real advances for the Netherlands?

A Level Exam-Style Question Section A

How far do you agree that the failure of the Duke of Anjou to be accepted by the states in 1583 was because of his religion? (20 marks)

Tip
When answering this question you should consider why Anjou was being suggested as a replacement for Philip II.

HOW SUCCESSFUL WERE THE NORTHERN PROVINCES IN BECOMING MORE INDEPENDENT?

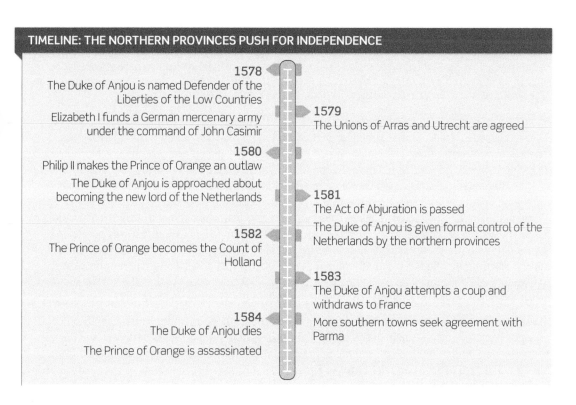

TIMELINE: THE NORTHERN PROVINCES PUSH FOR INDEPENDENCE

1578
The Duke of Anjou is named Defender of the Liberties of the Low Countries
Elizabeth I funds a German mercenary army under the command of John Casimir

1579
The Unions of Arras and Utrecht are agreed

1580
Philip II makes the Prince of Orange an outlaw
The Duke of Anjou is approached about becoming the new lord of the Netherlands

1581
The Act of Abjuration is passed
The Duke of Anjou is given formal control of the Netherlands by the northern provinces

1582
The Prince of Orange becomes the Count of Holland

1583
The Duke of Anjou attempts a coup and withdraws to France
More southern towns seek agreement with Parma

1584
The Duke of Anjou dies
The Prince of Orange is assassinated

The Union of Utrecht, 1579

The failure of the Duke of Anjou to unite the provinces against Spain was in many ways unsurprising. By the end of the 1570s, the Netherlands was a deeply divided collection of states that were suspicious of one another. Indeed, this was actually one of the reasons that he was invited to the country in the first place. These provinces had always asserted their individuality when they were taken under Habsburg rule after 1549. Protecting local autonomy was an accepted practice in the years that followed, but agreement on significant decisions could always be arrived at through negotiation and debate. During this time, however, the growth of Protestantism had injected a new dimension into the relationship, and as this faith matured, the problem of religion drove a more permanent wedge between them.

Evidence of the split can first be seen with the Union of Arras (see pages 343–344) when the provinces of Hainaut, Walloon Flanders and Artois combined in a Catholic union to protect their faith. Reflecting this move, and perhaps because of it, the northern provinces also formed a more formal alliance which became known as the Union of Utrecht and was signed in January 1579.

SOURCE

10 From the Union of Utrecht, signed in January 1579, which united the northern provinces in a confederation that would promote their traditional privileges and secure freedom of religion.

The aforesaid provinces shall ally, confederate and unite to hold together eternally in all ways and forms as if they were but one province and they shall not separate from each other... However this is agreed without prejudice to the special and particular privileges, freedoms, exemptions, laws, statutes, laudable and traditional customs, usages and all other rights of each province and of each town, member and inhabitant of those provinces. Not only shall the provinces not hinder each other from exercising these rights nor impair, nor prejudice them in anyway, but they shall help each other by all proper and possible means, if necessary with their lives and with their property, to maintain and strengthen them, and they shall protect and defend them against all and everyone who may actually design to encroach upon them.

... Concerning the matter of religion, Holland and Zeeland shall act at their own discretion, whereas the other provinces of this union may introduce (all together or each province separately), without being hindered or prevented from doing this by any other province, such regulations as they consider proper for the peace and welfare of the provinces, towns and their particular members and for the preservation of all people, either secular or clerical, their properties and rights, provided that in accordance with the Pacification of Ghent each individual enjoys freedom or religion and no-one is persecuted or questioned about his religion...

The deputies who are responsible for and have concluded this union declare that it has never been and is not now their purpose and intention to exclude from the union and alliance any towns or provinces which want to maintain the Catholic religion exclusively... for it is not their opinion that one province or town should lay down the law to others in the matter of religion, as they want to further peace and unity among the provinces and to avoid and take away the main occasion for quarters and discord.

The significance of this union is similar to that of the Union of Arras in that it bound provinces together in common cause. The Union of Utrecht in particular united many of the northern provinces including Holland, Zeeland, Utrecht and Groningen. Others joined the following year and by the end of 1581 there was a clear division between these and the southern provinces, which increasingly sided with Spain once more. This division was predominantly based upon religious belief and although the union proclaimed religious freedom, in reality this was difficult to achieve as Catholics left the provinces and travelled south in the wake of anti-Catholic legislation that was passed in several areas. In many cases this was simply the denial of leadership roles to Catholics, but in some areas there were violent attacks on them and their property was either confiscated or destroyed. In Utrecht itself the provincial parliaments outlawed Catholic services in June 1580, while Holland began to censor religious texts in 1581, having proscribed the Catholic mass in 1573.

These discriminatory policies hardened the resolve of the Catholic majorities in the southern provinces against Protestantism in the north. They also encouraged civil war between the Netherlanders, and in the States-General unity was almost impossible, which consequently gave further advantage to Spain and the Duke of Parma.

The Act of Abjuration, 1581, and the establishment of the Republic of the United Provinces

The military successes of the Duke of Parma were very worrying for the Prince of Orange and therefore he had sought support from foreign sources. Much of his challenge to Philip II revolved around the king's treatment of the Netherlands and particularly the high-handedness of his approach to governing and adjudging the matter of religion. To this end the prince had taken advantage of the provincial concerns for their ancient privileges and consequently had been able to win more support from surrounding provinces. Having been effective at undermining the authority of Philip II, he now sought to bind the states together under an alternative, centralised, leadership that could offer a more robust defence than the existing loose confederation of provinces that currently existed. The prince sought to achieve this by offering the sovereignty of the northern provinces to another on the grounds that Philip II had forfeited his claim to them by virtue of his unpopular actions. The person who was selected was the Duke of Anjou. As the Defender of the Liberties of the Low Countries since 1578 he was a natural choice and therefore was approached by the Dutch provinces. In 1580, he was formally accepted as the successor to Philip II by the States-General in the Treaty of Plessis-les-Tours.

Having established the successor, it was now necessary to legitimise the removal of Philip II so that the people would accept the decision. This was achieved by the creation of the Act of **Abjuration** in 1581, which sought to explain the failings of the Spanish king and justify his replacement by Anjou.

Abjuration
A solemn renunciation of something or someone by oath.

SOURCE

From the States-General's Act of Abjuration, issued in 1581.

We have declared and declare herewith by common accord, decision and agreement that the king of Spain has, *ipso jure* [by operation of law] forfeited his lordship, jurisdiction and inheritance of these provinces, that we do not recognise him in any matters concerning him personally, his sovereignty, jurisdiction or domains in these countries, nor to use or to permit others to use his name as that of our sovereign. Consequently we declare all officers, judges, lords with lower jurisdiction, vassals, and all other inhabitants of these provinces whatever their condition or quality, to be henceforward released from all obligations and oaths they may have sworn to the king of Spain as lord of these countries.

This undertaking had a significant impact on events in the Netherlands. The Act of Abjuration was intended to bind people to a new sovereign lord and therefore unite them against the ongoing challenge presented by the Duke of Parma and Spain, but instead it not only drove more loyal provinces into Spanish arms, it also divided the north.

The southern provinces' rush to rejoin Spain was not entirely surprising, but the split created in the northern provinces was more disturbing as the intention had been to bring them closer together. In effect, by declaring themselves independent of Philip II, the Act of Abjuration required the people of the northern states to accept Anjou as their leader, but this opened up religious problems that threatened to splinter their alliance. The issue was in one sense the requirement that people swear a new oath as this affected the religious groups occupying the northern lands. Firstly, in most areas, the Catholics were still the majority and they were reluctant to turn their backs on Philip II, who was seen as the staunch defender of the Counter-Reformation. Also, many of the Protestant faiths renounced the use of oaths and did not feel happy swearing obedience to someone other than God.

EXTEND YOUR KNOWLEDGE

Counter-Reformation, 1545–1648
The Counter-Reformation was a Catholic reaction to the growth of Protestantism in the 1500s. It began with the Council of Trent where the Catholic Church sought to reassert its doctrines and encouraged its loyal congregations to defend their faith against all challenges that Protestantism created. It saw an increase in seminaries for the education of more priests and also the extended use of the inquisition to root out heresy across the Christian world. As a devout Catholic, Philip II took his responsibilities to defend his faith very seriously, becoming embroiled in war with the Ottoman Empire and also maintaining his strict religious policies in the Netherlands.

In Woerden, a small town in Holland, the Lutheran minister had to be expelled for preaching against the Act, while across the provinces officials chose to resign their posts rather than swear allegiance. The case of Woerden is particularly telling as Holland had been the first to rebel against Philip II in 1572 and yet ten years later it was questioning the very States-General that it sought to promote. Furthermore, because each religion objected for different reasons, the Act also encouraged greater discord among them. This was manifested in the slew of anti-Catholic legislation that had already begun following the Union of Utrecht and continued in the aftermath of the Abjuration.

By opening up a rift between the States-General and the religions of those it served, the Act of Abjuration promoted the outbreak of further religious discontent that threatened to weaken the self-named United Provinces.

The declining influence of the Prince of Orange

In the wake of growing religious and political fragmentation, the Prince of Orange began to lose credibility. Throughout his political career he had always maintained that the rights of the provinces and freedom of religion were paramount. However, neither seemed achievable in 1583. In several quarters, people were beginning to question both his leadership and his motivations. Even as early as 1582, when debating whether or not to confer the title of Count of Holland on the prince, a group of powerful merchants were sceptical of his worthiness.

SOURCE
12
From an essay by Cornelius Pieterszoon Hooft, an Amsterdam magistrate, voicing his concerns about the Prince of Orange in 1582.

If at the beginning of the war His Excellency had said or shown that he was working to this end [to become count], it is my belief that he would have achieved little and that the people who everywhere opened the town gates for him would not have been so willing to do this. But people were doing everything at that time with the fine words *Pro Lege, Rege et Grege* [For the law, the king and the people] and everyone was worked up about the liberties of the provinces without a single mention being made, as far as I remember, of the idea of making His Excellency the hereditary lord of these provinces.

In one regard, this could be considered the discontent of those who found themselves in a state of conflict that almost certainly had an adverse effect upon their trades. The years of resistance had taken their toll on the economy, and business was disrupted. However, there was also a sense that the prince had failed to secure what he had promised to the states, and in this regard he was rightly challenged. The United Provinces of the north were without an effective governing body since the people did not universally accept the Duke of Anjou, and in trying to promote this course of action the prince had instead opened up greater religious problems that not only undermined the faint promise of religious freedom, but also threatened to undermine their unity in the face of a resurgent Spain.

The subsequent seizure of power that the duke attempted further discredited the prince, who had placed so much faith in him that when his perceived treachery was known, some blame was also attached to Orange. The position that he found himself in towards the end of 1583 was not an enviable one. He had gained doubters in Holland and in 1580 he had become a wanted man when Philip II had him declared an outlaw. As the leader of armed resistance against the authority of Philip, and given his efforts to replace him with the Duke of Anjou, this was not an unexpected turn of events – he and his late friends Egmont and Hoorn had been denounced years earlier – but being declared an outlaw was to have significant consequences in the future.

The assassination of the Prince of Orange, 1584

In March 1580, Philip II had outlawed the Prince of Orange and offered a reward for his capture or death. Philip felt that the prince had incited treason against his lawful king and encouraged the Low Countries to abandon Catholicism. Given these crimes it was felt that the prince should be brought to justice.

The proclamation was published in June 1580 and in December of that year the prince issued his own defence, known as the Apology, which he addressed to the States-General rather than Philip II. Within the document Orange set out the justification for his actions by reference to his own standing as a sovereign prince, whose status gave him the right to declare war on another sovereign. Furthermore he criticised Philip II for Philip's failures. The greatest of these was to honour the solemn oath between a sovereign and his subjects, and in particular to uphold the ancient and protected rights and privileges of the Low Countries.

SOURCE
13
From the Prince of Orange's Apology, which he sent to the States-General in December 1580 to justify the actions for which Philip II had declared him an outlaw. By sending it to the States-General he was acknowledging that this body was the one he recognised and that could legitimately hold him accountable.

You know, gentlemen, the obligations which bind him, and that he is not free to do what he likes as he can in the Indies. He may not by force compel any of his subjects to do anything unless the customs of the local courts of justice, which have jurisdiction over him, permit it. Nor can he change the general state of the country in any way by ordinance or decree. He must be satisfied with his customary and regular income. He cannot levy and demand any taxes contrary to the privileges of the country or without its consent. He cannot have a subject arrested until the local magistrate has examined the case, nor can he send a prisoner out of the country.

When you hear even so brief a summary, gentlemen, do you not realise, that if the barons and nobles of the country entrusted with its defence by virtue of their prerogatives, did not rise in opposition, when these clauses are not only broken but tyrannically and haughtily trodden under foot – not one single clause, but all of them, not once but a million times, and not only by the duke himself but by barbaric foreigners - ; if I say, the nobles did not honour their oath and obligations and force the duke to make reparation for his misdeeds, would they not then themselves be convicted of perjury, disloyalty and rebellion against the State of the country?

This Apology was shared publicly across the Netherlands and was intended to stir up public support for the prince by referencing his determination to protect provincial rights, and reminding the people of all the controversy that Philip II's reign had encouraged: his uncompromising position on religion and particularly his attempt to remove the privileges so beloved by the Low Countries. In effect the document, like the later Act of Abjuration, can be read as a declaration of independence whereby the prince and the States-General were making their case for the challenge to Philip II. The basis of this argument lay with the strong emphasis upon Philip's own failings to the people and hence their opposition to him.

Despite the approval of the States-General and the overall support of the public, the price attached to the prince by the king of Spain was attractively high – 25,000 crowns – and as such there were several who conspired to murder him. On 10 July 1584, a young French assassin by the name of Balthasar Gerard, a graduate in the law, was able to gain access to Orange's home in the town of Delft, Holland, where he then shot the prince.

SOURCE 14 Balthasar Gerard assassinating the Prince of Orange in 1584. The 17th-century engraving is by R. de Hoge, and was made to commemorate the deed.

De Moordt des Prinsen van Oranje, tot Delft, in den Jaare 1584

Having been shot twice in the chest, the prince died where he fell, and with his passing the United Provinces lost their universally accepted leader. Philip II was so grateful for the sacrifice of Gerard, who was caught and subsequently executed in an overly brutal manner by his captors, that he paid the reward to Gerard's family and even raised them into the peerage. The impact of the prince's death for those in the Low Countries was equally transformative: as the popular leader of the Dutch resistance he had been a controversial figure, converting from Catholicism to Lutheranism and seeking to attract foreign support for his campaign. Orange had converted to Calvinism in 1573 and appointed his own Calvinist chaplain, Jean Taffin. Though he drew critical attention for his action, he was generally regarded as the driving force behind the push for independence. In death, his vitality and drive were sorely missed and quickly the push ran out of momentum in the face of Habsburg power. Parma was able to secure more towns and it looked like the country would succumb to the will of Philip II once more.

THINKING HISTORICALLY Change (6a)

Separately and together

Below are some different types of history that historians may identify.

Political History	Economic History	Social History
Religious History	Military History	International History

These are thematic histories, where a historian focuses on a particular aspect of change. For example, an economic history of the British Empire would focus on trade and the economic reasons for the expansion of the empire, whereas a political history of the empire would focus on governance of the colonies and strategic reasons for its expansion.

Work in groups.

1 Write a definition for each type of history.

Here are some events in the period covered by this Paper that relate to the Spanish reconquest of the Netherlands.

1577	1578	1578	1579	1581	1584
The Spanish army returns under the control of the Duke of Parma	The States-General's army is defeated at Gembloux	Elizabeth I pays for a German army of mercenaries to go to the Netherlands in support of Orange	The Unions of Arras and Utrecht are signed	The Act of Abjuration is issued	The Prince of Orange is assassinated

Answer the following questions:

2 The first two changes can be classified as 'military' events.

a) Why was the second event so important?

b) What other area of history does this take it into?

3 What political changes came about because of the military victories in 1578?

4 Was Elizabeth's action of paying for an army either a 'military history' action, a 'political history' action, an 'international history' action or all three? Explain your answer.

5 What was the social impact in the Netherlands of the Unions of Utrecht and Arras?

6 Was the Prince of Orange assassinated for political or religious reasons?

Work in pairs.

7 Write a statement attacking 'thematic history'.

8 Write three statements defending 'thematic history'.

9 Explain why 'thematic history' occurs.

AS Level Exam-Style Question Section A

1 Why is Source 12 valuable to the historian for an enquiry into the declining influence of the Prince of Orange by 1584?

Explain your answer using the source, the information given about it and your own knowledge of the historical context. (8 marks)

2 How much weight do you give the evidence of Source 13 for an enquiry into the Prince of Orange's motivation for establishing the United Provinces after 1579?

Explain your answer using the source, the information given about it and your own knowledge of the historical context. (12 marks)

Tip

When answering these questions remember to include in your response some judgement about the provenance of the sources.

ACTIVITIES
KNOWLEDGE CHECK

The growing independence of the northern provinces

Write a brief summary about how independent the northern provinces were. Use the prompts below to help focus your writing.

1 What affected the independence of these states?

2 What might have given them a better chance of unity by 1584?

ACTIVITY
SUMMARY

The state of the Netherlands by 1584

Having read about the emerging independent spirit of the northern provinces and Spain's resurgence after Alva was replaced, and using two different colours:

1 Plot a graph that represents the progress made by each of these groups.

2 Briefly explain the trend represented by your graph, acknowledging any significant changes that appear.

 WIDER READING

Darby, G. (ed.) *The Origins and Development of the Dutch Revolt*, Routledge (2000)

Gelderen, M. *The Political Thought of the Dutch Revolt 1555–1590*, Cambridge University Press (2002)

Israel, J. *The Dutch Republic: Its Rise, Greatness, and Fall*, Oxford University Press (1998)

Limm, P. *The Dutch Revolt, 1559–1648*, Longman (1989)

2b.4 Securing the independence of the United Provinces, 1584–1609

KEY QUESTIONS

- Why was Maurice of Nassau so important to the United Provinces?
- Why did the Spanish fail to conquer the United Provinces?
- How did the United Provinces enhance their power?
- Why did Spain's influence in the Netherlands decline?

INTRODUCTION

The death of the Prince of Orange signalled a transitional moment in the northern provinces' war against Habsburg rule. In one sense it was an obvious tragedy that robbed the resistors of their emblematic leader, the man who had stood against Spanish power and offered the opportunity for greater freedom. In this interpretation, the assassination was a high point in Philip II's attempt to restore his authority, coming at a time when provincial cohesion was breaking down and religious animosities were threatening to split the United Provinces of the north apart. The circumstances surrounding the death of the prince were certainly wrought with difficulty, and his assassination did not make things any easier.

Despite the bleak outlook of 1584, Spain's re-conquest of the 17 provinces did not happen. Instead, over the next 25 years, the northern provinces continued to resist Habsburg authority and eventually, in 1609, they were officially recognised as independent of this rule. This achievement would be at a cost: ten of the original provinces that made up the Netherlands would remain bound to Spain on the basis of religious sympathies, but the remaining seven were free to manage their affairs as they saw fit. In these states, the ancient rights and privileges so beloved by the provinces were enshrined and religious tolerance was granted, finally fulfilling the wishes of the fallen prince.

The journey to this better world was arduous, however, and it required a determined leader to offer clear direction – first to maintain the momentum of the rebellion, and then to exploit the opportunities that emerged because of it. Between 1584 and 1609, the United Provinces had several leaders, each of whom offered useful direction, but none more so than the Prince of Orange's son, Maurice of Nassau, who was able to conduct a very effective military campaign against Habsburg rule through effective military strategy and taking advantage of favourable circumstances, which included the fact that Philip II ended by fighting both England and France in addition to the Dutch rebels. Foremost, his contribution offered the necessary stability that the United Provinces needed in order to get organised. Once this was achieved they never looked back.

1585 – Treaty of Nonsuch is signed between England and the northern provinces

1588 – Spanish Armada sets sail for England

1592 – Death of the Duke of Parma

1596 – Philip II declares bankruptcy

1584	1586	1588	1590	1592	1594	1596

1587 – Maurice of Nassau is appointed as head of the Dutch armed forces

1590 – Start of the Ten Glory Years, which sees the Dutch achieve a number of victories over Spain

The States-General declares itself sovereign over the United Provinces

1593 – A year-long mutiny in the Spanish army begins

WHY WAS MAURICE OF NASSAU SO IMPORTANT TO THE UNITED PROVINCES?

Nassau's military reforms and changes in strategy and tactics

The death of the Prince of Orange came at a very difficult time for the United Provinces. Since the Union of Utrecht in 1579, religious discord had threatened to destabilise all that he had achieved, and even the attempt to bind the provinces under the leadership of a new monarch, the Duke of Anjou, after 1581 had failed to create the necessary unity to successfully withstand the Spanish advance.

In 1585, the prince's son, Maurice of Nassau, aged 16, was chosen to replace Orange as *stadtholder* of Holland and Zeeland. Then, in 1587, he was appointed by the States-General as the Captain and Admiral of the Union – a post that effectively gave him control over the armed forces of the United Provinces. The decision to promote Orange's second son (his first, Philip William, was a captive of Philip II) could be seen as an attempt to maintain the influence of the dead prince by continuing with his son – a symbolic act to retain some presence of the man many regarded as the guiding light of the rebellion. Whether it was a symbolic act or not, Maurice proved to be a fine choice. Despite being so young, he proved himself to be an able military leader and his knowledge of siege tactics especially was much admired. Under the direction of this young man, the forces of the United Provinces were soon able to match the quality of the Spanish troops who were still under the leadership of the Duke of Parma. As a result of this improvement, the anticipated victory by Spain following the dark days of 1584 was delayed indefinitely. Rather than consume the northern provinces, during the 1590s Parma's army was pushed back into the south during what became known in the Netherlands as the Ten Glory Years.

EXTEND YOUR KNOWLEDGE

Maurice of Nassau (1567-1625)

Maurice was the second son of William of Orange and his wife Anna, daughter of the Elector of Saxony. When his father was killed, Maurice was studying at Leiden University but was named *stadtholder* of Holland and Zeeland despite being only 16. Over the next two years he keenly studied military tactics and strategy and quickly became known for his considerable knowledge about how to lay sieges. This particular skill would serve him very well when, in 1587, he was given command of the United Provinces' military forces. He flourished in this role and, alongside Johan van Oldenbarnevelt as head of the civil government, Maurice helped to secure the independence of the United Provinces in 1609. This truce with Spain led to internal discord among the newly independent states and as a consequence Nassau fell out with his long-time friend, Oldenbarnevelt, who was beheaded in 1619 after trying to encourage Holland to push for independence from the United Provinces.

The Ten Glory Years

This was the period beginning in 1590 when Maurice of Nassau, as military leader of the United Provinces' army, was able to retake towns and cities in the northern provinces that had been captured by the Spanish. His first victory was his family seat in the town of Breda in 1590 and the period culminated in his success at Nieuwpoort in 1600.

1607 – An armistice is signed between the United Provinces and Spain

1600 – Maurice of Nassau's victory at Nieuwpoort

1604 – Peace between England and Spain

1609 – Treaty of Antwerp is signed

| 1598 | 1600 | 1602 | 1604 | 1606 | 1608 | 1610 |

1598 – Philip II dies and is replaced by Philip III

1602 – Dutch East India Company is founded

1605 – Gunpowder Plot in England undermines Anglo-Spanish relations

Military reform

Maurice was able to transform the rebel army into a force capable of challenging the veteran Spanish troops under Parma by instigating a series of military reforms. When he took over military control, Maurice was keen to reorganise his troops so as to remove any potential weaknesses and ensure that the provinces had an effective fighting force. An immediate reform that was introduced was to standardise the weaponry and equipment of his army. This allowed for efficient resupply via a series of supply depots, and also familiarisation among the men with regard to the weaponry they were given. This was a simple reform that went some way to addressing minor issues within the army, but there were more serious issues with which to contend.

By far the most significant problem facing all armies was the threat of mutiny – both the fortunes of Spain and the States-General in recent years had borne testament to this – and therefore Maurice's first task was to ensure that this did not happen to him. To achieve this he arranged for the troops to be properly paid on a regular basis, and he created a standing army rather than continuing the practice of disbanding troops at the end of the campaigning season. The regular payment was a clear means of maintaining loyalty, but so too was the establishment of a permanent force. This created a greater sense of identity, and also **camaraderie** among the troops, which helped to build a cohesive body of men willing and more determined to fight together. Many of the problems in the past had been because troops fought for whoever paid them, and this was often on short contracts, whereas the creation of a permanent force generated a sense of belonging for those taking up arms.

Apart from this welcome development, a permanent force also allowed Maurice to introduce greater discipline and an effective training regimen for his soldiers. In the case of the latter this was especially noticeable on the battlefield, where his modern tactics proved to be very effective. In 1590, he was able to recapture the town of Breda and then follow this up with another quick victory at Zutphen in 1591.

SOURCE

From a plea by a nobleman of Flanders to the States-General for the maintenance of the State of the Netherlands made in August 1584 – one month after the assassination of the Prince of Orange.

It is already a month, or rather almost six weeks ago since our wise prince departed this life. He was the true father and protector of our fatherland and by his unique wisdom and deliberation he was able to steer our vessel like a good and sure helmsman in the midst of the terrible thunderstorm and tempest in which we are in danger of being shipwrecked. With God's help he was able to protect us from being lost. Now the body is without a head, the ship adrift without a helmsman. We will inevitably perish unless in your wisdom you take the necessary measures as soon as possible.

You know, gentlemen, that nowadays every one has his eyes fixed on you. You must put the helm right in its place again, and appoint another helmsman. You must ensure that the ship is navigated into a good port in spite of this tempest and that Ghent is relieved, and that Antwerp and Dendermonde are set free from the fetters of the enemies and that wherever necessary everything is put in order. The way to do this is to establish immediately a good Council of State, made up of honourable God-fearing men, who understand political and state-affairs as well as warfare, and whose election is not brought about by any sort of favouritism or nepotism. It will be vital too to establish a good council of war of reputable, properly qualified persons, noblemen, colonels, captains as well as other commanders, who are skilled in warfare, as the well-known proverb goes: *Ut tractent fabrilia fabri* [Let smiths perform the work of smiths]. This council must be entrusted with full power and sovereign authority, so that it will no longer be necessary to report back each time to the provinces for this is one of the chief reasons of our present decline. The council of war must restore strict military discipline, for the soldiers have become intolerably disorderly because of the protracted wars, and reform is urgently required.

Strategy and tactics

The basis of Maurice's military success in the early 1590s lay firstly with his well-drilled and disciplined modern fighting force. It was also the product of a change in the traditional manner of Netherlandish military tactics. Originally this had amounted to large and unwieldy battalions, but Maurice reduced these units to no more than 550 men per battalion, which allowed them to operate more effectively as a unit. Employing a combination of **musketeers** and **pikemen,** these battalions would arrange themselves in ranks where the musketeers would fire their weapons once at the front and then move to the back to reload, being replaced by the rank behind. If charged by cavalry they would fall in behind the pikemen, who could then fend off the enemy. These particular tactics, known as 'pike and shot', allowed Maurice's army to maintain a constant volley of fire for as long as their ammunition lasted. As a tactic it was very effective, but it depended on well-drilled soldiers who knew the formation and methods and could maintain these under fire.

In addition to military tactics, Maurice also took advantage of the natural landscape of the northern provinces. The lakes and bogs offered a natural line of defence, as it was very difficult for armies to cross these barriers quickly and efficiently. In this way Maurice's smaller, more mobile force was better suited to the environment and this attribute also promoted his success. He was able to move against the Spanish and then withdraw much more easily than his enemy, which gave him greater opportunities to attack without conceding heavy losses.

To take further advantage of the natural defences, he also built a line of fortifications to complement these obstacles and make it difficult for Parma to resupply his men and bring up reinforcements. Collectively these barriers, together with the newly instilled discipline and well-trained soldiers under his command, gave Maurice the opportunity to offer an effective opposition to the Habsburg forces and provided for a much better organised defence of the United Provinces.

Siege warfare against fortresses and border towns

The pike and shot tactics could certainly be very effective. However, the greatest technique that Maurice developed was the use of **sieges**. These were a traditional way of doing battle during the 16th century, and Maurice became an expert in this particular strategy.

At Leiden University he came under the tutelage of Simon Stevin – a mathematician and engineer who also had a keen interest in military tactics and used his expertise to improve upon the traditional texts on the subject. As his student, Maurice was able to read widely about siege tactics and became well acquainted with the techniques – and particularly how to use the natural environment to greater advantage. These skills allowed the young commander to develop a very successful campaign against the Spanish, which saw him retake many towns and fortresses.

> **KEY TERM**
>
> **Siege**
> A military tactic whereby an army surrounds a settlement – usually a town or fortress – and cuts off any supply lines to and from that settlement. The objective is to starve out those inside so that they surrender their position to the army outside.

EXTEND YOUR KNOWLEDGE

Simon Stevin (1548–1620)
Simon Stevin was born in Bruges to the Mayor of Veurne and his wife. He received a good education and was employed as a bookkeeper in Antwerp until 1577 when he accepted a job working for the local government in its financial department. In 1583, he enrolled at Leiden University after moving from Bruges because of his Calvinist sympathies and the anti-Calvinism of the Duke of Alva who had undertaken to restore the Catholic faith in the 17 provinces. It was while at Leiden that he became friends with Maurice and was able to develop his interest in mathematics, and he is associated with the introduction of decimal fractions. He was also able to experiment with engineering theories that Maurice would later use to great effect in his campaign against the Spanish.

Siege warfare

The first town to fall to Maurice was his family seat in Brabant. Breda had been under the control of the Spanish since 1581 and in 1590 he laid siege to the town, garrisoned by 500 Spanish soldiers. As an example of his modern style of operation, Maurice had sent one of his men, Charles de Heraugiere, to scout the town for potential weaknesses that he could exploit. Having found his way into the town by concealing himself on a peat barge, de Heraugiere found that the garrison did not inspect the vessel and therefore concluded that a similar undertaking with armed soldiers might yield some advantage. Maurice was happy to approve such an opportunity, which proved very successful as the concealed troops were able to take the city almost single-handedly from the inside while Maurice then attacked the gates. The surrender of Breda was an embarrassment to Parma and the Spanish, who had assumed that the town was loyal and therefore safe. The three captains charged with garrisoning the town were executed as a result because their failure had given the United Provinces a notable victory that also gave Maurice a strategic base for further operations.

Having inherited 10,000 men upon his assumption of command, Maurice, by applying his reforms, was able to build a formidable army. The following year they were able to capitalise on their success at Breda when they captured the town of Zutphen in May 1591, after only five days of siege. The following month they took Deventer after only ten days' siege. Such was Maurice's effectiveness and

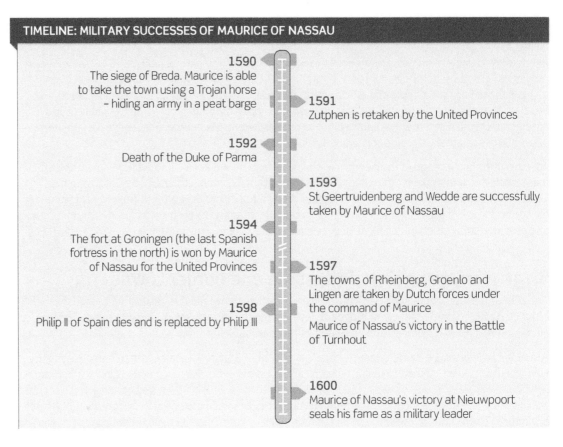

TIMELINE: MILITARY SUCCESSES OF MAURICE OF NASSAU

1590
The siege of Breda. Maurice is able to take the town using a Trojan horse – hiding an army in a peat barge

1591
Zutphen is retaken by the United Provinces

1592
Death of the Duke of Parma

1593
St Geertruidenberg and Wedde are successfully taken by Maurice of Nassau

1594
The fort at Groningen (the last Spanish fortress in the north) is won by Maurice of Nassau for the United Provinces

1597
The towns of Rheinberg, Groenlo and Lingen are taken by Dutch forces under the command of Maurice

Maurice of Nassau's victory in the Battle of Turnhout

1598
Philip II of Spain dies and is replaced by Philip III

1600
Maurice of Nassau's victory at Nieuwpoort seals his fame as a military leader

speed in taking these towns that the Spanish army could not counter very easily and therefore he was able to gain the upper hand. These early successes were swiftly followed up in 1593 with successes in St Geertruidenberg and Wedde during the summer months, and in 1594 when the United Provinces' army was able to take the last Spanish fort in the north when Groningen capitulated on 23 July.

These successes were testament to the effective training that Maurice had given to his Dutch soldiers, who were able to lay a siege and then remain a compact unit during the waiting time. This was due to good discipline and also the regular payments they received. Success also came because the sieges worked against the psyche of the Spanish soldiers, who were not well known for their discipline. Many garrisons simply gave up their posts when confronted by Maurice. Nijemegen, for example, did not even wait for the siege guns to arrive before submitting in 1591. Furthermore, since Maurice had been able to establish an effective **blockade** in the north by taking key positions and thus being able to cut off Spain's ability to resupply itself, those who did resist were so ill or weak through lack of food that their opposition was often not difficult to defeat.

KEY TERM

Blockade
A means of sealing off access to a place so that no people or goods can either enter or leave it.

The border towns
Having re-established greater control in the United Provinces, in 1597 Maurice extended his campaign to the border towns of the south. Once again sieges proved very effective, and he was able to starve out the towns of Rheinberg, Groenlo and Lingen during the autumn of that year. These towns safeguarded what he had already achieved as they were some of the more accessible access points to the north, and therefore under Dutch control they facilitated a greater chance of protecting the United Provinces from further Spanish invasion. As a result of this new-found feeling of security, Maurice was able to give the north some breathing space after the suffocating presence of the Spanish. By establishing reasonably secure borders, the United Provinces would be free to start to develop a clear national identity without fear of immediate attack.

The victories at Turnhout and Nieuwpoort
Many of Maurice's victories came through his use of classic siege tactics. However, two of his most significant successes came from open battle with the Spanish: Turnhout in 1597 and Nieuwpoort in 1600. These were very prominent engagements that underlined the young commander's military prowess and brought him European recognition as a military leader.

The Battle of Turnhout, 1597

Turnhout was significant because of its location: it lay on the border with the Spanish-controlled southern provinces and therefore it was strategically important. Garrisoned by a Spanish commander by the name of Varax, the battle that ensued on 24 January saw Maurice place his troops in open field. The town itself had no walls despite its strategic significance. His well-drilled troops were more than a match for the Spanish cavalry, who were defeated very comprehensively. Given the location of the town, the battle was primarily a tactical victory that served two purposes for Maurice:

- it pushed the Spanish out from a strategically significant position, which allowed him to consolidate the United Provinces' borders with the south

- it evidenced to the Spanish that his army was as effective in open battle as it was in siege warfare.

In this last sense, the victory was especially important since the Spanish forces, under the control of Archduke Albert VII of Austria (husband of Philip II's daughter Isabella since 1596) had enjoyed a small resurgence of fortune with victory over the Dutch in the town of Hulst on the river Schelde. By turning the tide of this fortune at Turnhout, Maurice was able to reaffirm his own position and prevent Albert from capitalising on his victory. Consequently, although the battle itself was a small engagement and Maurice did not maintain a presence there after his victory, it had symbolic importance while also pushing the Spanish out of the immediate area.

SOURCE

2 An engraving by the artist D.A. Peduzzi commemorating the victory of Maurice of Nassau at the Battle of Turnhout in August 1597. The date of production is unknown.

The Battle of Nieuwpoort, 1600

Of greater significance than Turnhout was Maurice's second open engagement on the battlefield. This took place in Nieuwpoort in July 1600.

Having been asked by the States-General to capture Nieuwpoort and Dunkirk – two seaports known to accommodate those who engaged in piracy – the intention was to reduce attacks against Dutch shipping and therefore strengthen the United Provinces' economic footing. Maurice led 10,000 men into Flanders to seize these towns, confident that the people of the area would support his efforts. Such was the level of confidence, however, that Maurice did not adopt his usual caution and there was no substantial reconnaissance of the area to ascertain enemy positions or the feeling among the local population. These omissions allowed Archduke Albert VII to trap the Dutch and force them to fight an open battle on the beaches of Nieuwpoort. The battle itself was a bloody affair: at its conclusion more than 2,500 Spanish troops lay dead, while Maurice lost 2,000 men. The victory went to the Dutch commander and cemented his reputation as a military leader, but it was a **pyrrhic victory**. The loss of so many troops meant the Flanders **campaign** could not continue and later that month Maurice led his men back into the United Provinces.

The failed campaign was arguably the result of the confrontation at Nieuwpoort. This battle, like Turnhout, did not result in any significant advantage for either side except that, for Maurice, it evidenced the realistic fact that the south and the north of the Netherlands could not be reunited. The people of Flanders did not rise in support of his army, and despite his victory the Spanish were still able to match him in open battle to great effect. For the southern provinces the Battle of Nieuwpoort also had significance. It proved to the States-General in the south that they should raise more money to defend themselves against invasion from the north, and in July 1600 they agreed to raise a regular monthly stipend to fund the garrisoning of 21,450 troops in towns across the border.

The conclusions reached by the southern and the northern provinces after the Battle of Nieuwpoort underlined the growing divide between them, and in this sense the battle itself was the point of no return. After this engagement it was clear that each side had chosen its future and was therefore unlikely to be reconciled to the other.

Maurice as *stadtholder*

Following his victory at Nieuwpoort, Maurice of Nassau was recognised as an effective military leader throughout Europe. Having been appointed *stadtholder* of Holland in 1585, however, his political skills did not match his military abilities. The responsibility of this position was extended when similar titles were granted to him from Zeeland, Utrecht, Gelderland and Overijssel, but perhaps because of his role as a military leader and the assassination of his father he was not a tactful politician or a natural diplomat. He therefore relied on more able politicians to help him govern. His principle advisers included Johan van Oldenbarnevelt, who was the legal counsel of Holland, and the *stadtholder* of Friesland, William Louis. With these men he formed a successful **triumvirate** that set about administering the United Provinces and formed a more unified bond between each member state.

EXTEND YOUR KNOWLEDGE

Johan van Oldenbarnevelt (1547–1619)
After studying law in Louvain and Heidelberg, Johan van Oldenbarnevelt converted to Protestantism and upon his return to the Netherlands became the legal counsel for the province of Holland. In 1572, when the province successfully resisted Spanish rule, he decided to remain in the province while his colleagues in the Court of Appeal fled to Utrecht. In 1576, he helped to relieve Leiden and Haarlem and was awarded the position of chief counsel in Rotterdam, which gave him a place in the provincial parliament. As one of the negotiators at the Union of Utrecht, Oldenbarnevelt was intent on securing for Holland the largest share of power, as it had been the original province to resist the Spanish. When Maurice replaced his father, Oldenbarnevelt took charge of the political organisation of the provinces while Maurice concentrated on the military campaign. The two men worked well together. However, following the Twelve Years Truce in 1609, their friendship soured on the issue of religion and in 1619 Oldenbarnevelt was executed after being accused of attempting to encourage Holland to undermine the United Provinces.

The selection of Maurice as the new *stadtholder* for Holland in 1585, and then additional provinces within two years, was never really challenged. It was seen as a natural succession from his father and the appropriate choice in the absence of his elder brother. Though young, his selection suggests an attempt to imbue Maurice with dynastic rights and to establish his family as the *de facto* rulers of the United Provinces. In the mid-1580s, this still seemed an ambitious objective as the provinces retained the services of a Council of State wherein policy decisions were made by a majority vote which meant that no one state could veto a decision. This model preserved the idea of autonomy among the states and, in promoting individual power, the body was effective.

In this regard, the appointment of Maurice as the head of several provincial administrations perhaps better suggests the wish to promote a greater sense of unity among the United Provinces. As the governor of several provinces, Maurice was invested with significant influence within the Council of State and therefore he was able to present a better impression of unity among them. This was in one sense a necessity, given they needed to co-ordinate an organised defence against Spain, but it also helped to foster a more united identity around which the seven provinces could rally.

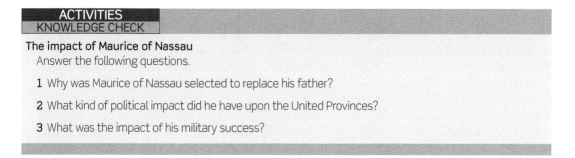

ACTIVITIES
KNOWLEDGE CHECK

The impact of Maurice of Nassau
Answer the following questions.

1 Why was Maurice of Nassau selected to replace his father?

2 What kind of political impact did he have upon the United Provinces?

3 What was the impact of his military success?

WHY DID THE SPANISH FAIL TO CONQUER THE UNITED PROVINCES?

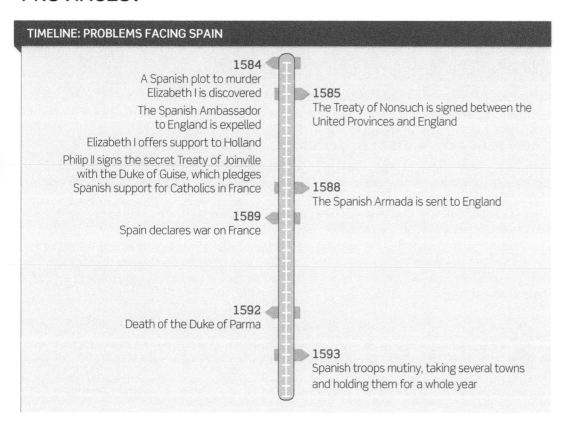

TIMELINE: PROBLEMS FACING SPAIN

1584
A Spanish plot to murder Elizabeth I is discovered

The Spanish Ambassador to England is expelled

Elizabeth I offers support to Holland

Philip II signs the secret Treaty of Joinville with the Duke of Guise, which pledges Spanish support for Catholics in France

1585
The Treaty of Nonsuch is signed between the United Provinces and England

1588
The Spanish Armada is sent to England

1589
Spain declares war on France

1592
Death of the Duke of Parma

1593
Spanish troops mutiny, taking several towns and holding them for a whole year

Support for the United Provinces by Elizabeth I of England

Elizabeth I of England watched the development of the Dutch resistance to Spanish rule with interest. As a Protestant herself, she was sympathetic to the religious demands made by the Confederacy of Noblemen as early as 1566, and favoured supporting her Protestant co-religionists. Despite this opinion, however, the extent of tangible support she offered was very limited. A few hundred soldiers were sent to help the Prince of Orange during his rebellion in 1572 and then, in 1578, she sent one million florins to aid his cause. In neither case was this support openly given, since she had no wish to anger Philip II, whose empire was the greatest threat to England at the time. Such was her fear that public support for the rebellion would draw the Spanish king to attack her kingdom, that she even expelled the Sea Beggars from her ports in 1572 so as to not draw Spanish hostility against England.

In this regard, Elizabeth's relatively conservative religious sympathies had to be overridden by political expediency. However, in 1584 this changed. The success of the Duke of Parma in retaking many of the towns and cities occupied by the rebels greatly alarmed the queen since a strengthened Spanish Netherlands presented an even greater threat to her borders as she was encircled by Catholic Spain, France and, increasingly, the Netherlands. From a strategic perspective, the maintenance of a Protestant foothold in the Low Countries was very advantageous as it not only retained a religious ally, but also allowed for better access to the Protestant German states. Reinforcing this strategic concern was the awareness that Philip II, as a devout Catholic, was openly critical of the Protestant English queen. Indeed, in 1583, a plot to murder her was uncovered, involving a gentleman by the name of Throckmorton who had received Spanish support in his attempt. The consequence of this specific action was that the Spanish ambassador, Bernardino de Mendoza, was expelled from England and Elizabeth became more publicly willing to support the Dutch in their campaign against Spain. This decision was sealed following the deaths of the Duke of Anjou and the Prince of Orange, and in October it was formally agreed in the **Privy Council**.

The decision by Elizabeth I to support the United Provinces was therefore not explicitly motivated by religion, but was rather born from a need to secure her own throne. Certainly her Protestantism made her sympathetic to the cause, but this particular feeling had to be dulled out of political necessity given the power of Spain and her own position in England, where there remained some residual anti-Protestant feeling among Catholics. By 1584, however, the situation was different and Spain's successes in the Netherlands presented a greater threat; the death of Orange was perceived as weakening the rebels' chances of withstanding the momentum of Parma. Furthermore the **Treaty of Joinville (1584)** raised the spectre of a Spanish–French alliance, which alarmed the queen. Under these conditions she was more prepared to risk the anger of Spain and therefore consented to support her co-religionists in the Low Countries.

The Treaty of Nonsuch, 1585

In effect, the treaty signed between the English Crown and the United Provinces on 20 August 1585 was tantamount to declaring war on Spain. Known as the Treaty of Nonsuch, the agreement pledged English military support for the Dutch whereby, in return for the towns of Flushing, Rammekens and Brill which were to be placed under English control for the duration of the war, England would provide 6,000 men and pay the States-General 600,000 florins a year for the duration of the campaign. England would also provide a governor-general who would be advised by a new Council of State and direct the military campaign. The Treaty offered a real chance to check the growing power of Spain. However, it did not strengthen the rebels' position in quite the manner that was anticipated.

SOURCE

3 From the Treaty of Nonsuch, signed between Elizabeth I and the United Provinces on 20 August 1585, which pledged England's military support to the Dutch in their war with Spain.

The Queen of England should send to the United Provinces an aid of 5000 footmen and one thousand horse, under the conduct of a Governor-General who should be a person of quality and rank, well-affected to the true religion, and under other good chiefs and captains, all of whom shall be paid by the Queen as long as the war lasts.

The United Provinces, individually and collectively, bind themselves, when, by God's grace and her Majesty's assistance, they shall be re-established in peace and repose, to repay all that her Majesty shall have dispersed, as well for the levy of troops and their transportation, as for their wages...

For greater assurance of the repayment the town of Flushing, the castle of Rammekens, in the isle of Walcheren, and the town of Brill, with two fortresses in Holland shall within one month of the confirmation of the Contract be placed in the hands of such governors as it shall please her Majesty to appoint until she shall be completely repaid.

The person selected to be governor-general was Robert Dudley, the Earl of Leicester, who landed in Flushing in December 1585 with money and more English troops so that their military presence in the Low Countries amounted to 8,000 men at arms. His powers were wide and largely undefined – all the Treaty had called for was a central authority to offer clear direction to the military campaign and the details were to be arranged by Leicester and the provinces. The lack of definite instructions made the task of co-ordinating a cohesive response more difficult. The provinces each wanted different things: the inland provinces sought a stronger administration that could effectively protect them from attack, while the peripheral states of Holland and Zeeland preferred to retain greater independence. Even within these two provinces there was disagreement, since some towns supported Leicester's intention to create a stronger authority and others did not. In 1586, Leicester set about organising a separate tax for the war and also proposed an **embargo** on all Spanish and southern provincial shipping to the north. However, this was blocked by Holland which objected to the potential negative impact it could have on its own trade. The immediate difficulty, therefore, was that rather than binding the states in strong defence against Parma, the efforts of the Earl of Leicester actually divided them.

Adding to his difficulty, two of Leicester's commanders could not prevent Deventer from being captured by the Spanish in 1587 while the earl was in England at the request of the queen. The bad feeling that this created among the Dutch was only compounded on his return in March, since he was required by Elizabeth to engage in negotiations with Parma. For the Dutch provinces this was seen as a sell-out, and they were reluctant to consider the demand by the queen requiring Leicester to negotiate. In spite of this disaffection, formal talks were arranged in February 1588, and in May of that year Elizabeth ordered her troops in the Low Countries to return to England in order to help defend their country against potential Spanish attack – a possibility that was increasingly likely after England had openly sided with the Dutch against Philip II.

The involvement of English troops in the Netherlands offered some significant gains for the rebels. Although Leicester withdrew after two years having failed to make any progress, his replacement, Sir Francis Vere, was a skilled commander and was able to give effective support to Maurice – including around 1,600 men at the Battle of Nieuwpoort.

> **KEY TERM**
>
> Embargo
> An official suspension or ban on trade with another country.

The diversion of Parma's troops to support the Spanish Armada in 1588

Perhaps the greatest impact of England's alliance with the United Provinces was in the diversion it offered to the Dutch. In effect, the Treaty of Nonsuch was a declaration of war against Spain by the English, and therefore Philip II was inclined to attack Elizabeth I in addition to his ongoing war with the rebels. This new dimension to the revolt arguably had a much greater impact for the Dutch than the troops sent by England to directly support them. This was because it meant that Philip II was now intending to fight on two fronts, just as he had done against the Ottoman Empire the previous decade. That particular conflict had brought Spain to bankruptcy and allowed the rebels to increase their control of the Low Countries. Consequently Philip's decision to raise an invasion force against England, taken in January 1586, offered some prospect of a repeat impact.

The Spanish Armada, 1588

The decision to attack England was motivated by several factors: Elizabeth's Protestantism; the acts of piracy committed by her sea captains Francis Drake and John Hawkins in the West Indies that targeted Spanish vessels; but mostly the fact that the Treaty of Nonsuch had reinvigorated the Dutch resistors. This last point had resulted in the moderate members within the rebel town councils (who had been increasingly disposed towards appeasement) being removed from office, and in 1586 the states could deploy their largest army yet.

The result of this new determination was that both Philip and his governor-general in the Netherlands (the Duke of Parma) were of the opinion that any further advancement of their own campaign would only be effective if England was forced to give up its support. To this end a large invasion force was assembled which, by spring 1588, amounted to more than 150 ships under the command of the Duke of Medina-Sidonia. Carrying 30,000 men, these vessels were to support Parma's own voyage to England where he was to seize London and force England out of the Netherlands.

The intention was well conceived, but the execution was less effective. England took the initiative and attacked the Armada with guns and fire ships, which wrought significant destruction on the Spanish. The smaller, quicker English vessels could manoeuvre more effectively than the larger Spanish ships, and that also gave the English an advantage. Further benefiting from fortuitous weather, many of the Armada ships were blown north to Scotland where several were shipwrecked. The attempt by Philip II to force England out of the Netherlands by force of arms resulted in a victory for Elizabeth and humiliation for the Spanish forces.

SOURCE 4

Defeat of the Spanish Armada off the coast of England on 30 May 1588. The source is an engraving by the Flemish artist Frans Hogenberg who was banned from the city of Antwerp by the Duke of Alva in 1568 and had subsequently travelled to London before settling in Hamburg in 1585. The engraving was made around the late 16th century.

The decline of Parma

The defeat of the Armada in 1588 marked a turning point in the Dutch conflict with Spain. Foremost, it marked a humiliating defeat for Philip II – the biggest fleet ever assembled, at a cost of two-thirds of the entire yearly revenue of the Habsburg Empire, was defeated. Not only was this a decisive blow to his finances and personal credibility, but it also had military repercussions.

Having been diverted to support the Spanish Armada, the Duke of Parma had to suspend his campaign in the Netherlands, which at once gave the rebels time to organise. Consequently, when he returned to this campaign he was increasingly frustrated by the more determined opposition he faced. In late 1588, he tried to lay siege to Bergen-op-Zoom, the last major town in Brabant that he had not taken, but despite the siege lasting more than a month he was forced to retreat in the face of the town's resolute defenders. This was the first major failure Parma had suffered in the war and it was quickly followed by others – most importantly, the failed invasion of the Island of Bommel, which was his main objective throughout 1589. This was not only significant in that he wasted many resources trying to take this island, but also because of the manner in which he failed: his troops mutinied on 30 August and this was the first of over 40 mutinies that would frustrate Spain's military efforts in Flanders between 1589 and 1607.

The re-emergence of mutiny was a bad omen for Parma who, until 1587, had enjoyed strong support within the army and in many respects his success was a result of that loyalty. A successful army in the 16th century was content because it was able to receive regular payment and **bounty**. However, when defeat started to follow defeat, morale dropped and rewards were less frequent. Given the cost of the Armada (which affected the timing of the troops' pay) together with the ebbing fortune of Parma in the face of greater opposition, Parma's troops became less buoyant and mutiny was the product of this decline.

The slow destruction of the Spanish army because of growing disaffection within it was a significant factor in Spain's failure to subdue the United Provinces after 1588. This was obviously because a well-disciplined army is essential for success, but also, and perhaps most importantly, it gave the Dutch greater hope for their own ambitions.

SOURCE

From a private letter written in 1589 by Sir Roger Williams, a captain in Elizabeth's navy. He is writing in the aftermath of an English and Dutch attack on Lisbon in 1589 and is commenting on the reduced state of the Spanish forces.

What makes the Spaniards' discipline to be so famous as it is? their good order; otherwise it is well knowne, the Nation is the basest and [most] cowardlie sort of people of most others; so base, that I perswade my selfe, ten thousand of our Nation would beate thirtie of theirs out of the field, let them be chosen where they list; saving some three thousand which is in the Low Countries.

The defeated armada, together with the subsequent failures of Parma, added to the resolve of the United Provinces because they evidenced the limitations of Spain's power. In the wake of the defeat at sea, Spain's military began to crumble on land too. This gave the advantage to the Dutch, who then became more unwilling to consider any form of peace negotiation with Spain – even when Parma made overtures to them in late 1589 in an attempt to resolve the deadlock and perhaps restore his waning prestige.

Intervention in France, 1589

The growing Dutch advantage over Spain received a further welcome boost after 1589, when Spain could not ignore the strengthened position of Protestantism in France following the death of Henry III. Having failed to leave a natural successor, the claimants to his throne were Charles of Bourbon and his nephew, Henry of Navarre. Though Henry's claim was greater, he was a Protestant, and therefore Catholics in France were reluctant to recognise him. The result was that France again descended into civil war upon the king's death and Navarre enjoyed the greatest success – defeating the **Catholic League** at Aques in September 1589 and then at Ivry in March the following year.

Just as the intervention of England on the side of the Dutch rebels affected Spain's abilities to subdue the United Provinces, so too would these events in France since Philip II, by virtue of his own devout Catholicism, could not allow the French succession to pass to a Protestant. This would leave Spain vulnerable in Europe and also allow a stronger footing for the faith he had committed himself to defeating since the Council of Trent. Given the position he perceived himself in – that of defender of Catholicism – in April 1590 he ordered the Duke of Parma to invade France with 20,000 men and to seize Paris in order to prevent Navarre from being crowned. The duke duly achieved this, which in the short term stopped the spectre of a Protestant France. However, the action obliged Philip II to continue to support the claims of Charles Bourbon and the Catholic League.

The significance of this obligation was to divert the Duke of Parma from his campaign in the Low Countries for a second time. Not only did this diversion deprive Parma of his momentum, it also contributed to the growing disaffection among his troops. The cost to Spain of Philip's support of the Catholic League amounted to three million florins from 1582 to 1587. Between 1588 and 1590, he added a further two million florins, and then from 1591 to 1595 another 2.5 million florins. In addition to this commitment, he also paid a 15,000 florin subsidy to the Duke of Savoy for allowing him to accommodate Spanish troops in his state for the benefit of the Catholic League. This was a tremendous sum of money which almost certainly impacted on his ability to maintain regular wages to the army in the Low Countries, precipitating the growing number of mutinies that took place there after 1589. Indeed, the army in Flanders had received 18 million florins in 1590 but two years later received only 4.5 million florins – clear testimony as to the king's new priority.

Despite the evident distraction that the war in France offered Spain, the Dutch rebels did not seize great advantage themselves and chose instead to consolidate their position. In this sense, the real significance of the French campaign was to undermine the effectiveness of Parma. Having been a genuine force in the Low Countries upon his arrival, the demands placed upon him by Philip – first his requirement that the duke invade England, and then his wish that Parma push into France – reduced the duke's well-achieved advantage against the Dutch rebels. The gains he had painstakingly made were almost all lost. Zutphen fell to Maurice of Nassau in May 1591, Deventer was lost in June the same year. Having spent long campaigns achieving these victories, Parma's own morale declined and, after a little less than 20 years fighting in the Netherlands, he died in Arras in 1592.

SOURCE

6   From the recollection of Oldenbarnevelt of a statement made by the States-General of the United Provinces. It explains their decision to consolidate their position rather than go on the offensive against Spain in 1589 after the *stadtholder* of Friesland suggested a more aggressive policy during a meeting of the states.

[They preferred] to use the cessation of hostilities and rest that the enemy had given them to their advantage, with the building of necessary fortifications and putting everything in good order; contenting themselves with retaining what they still had and preventing the enemy's further invasion. They said also that by doing otherwise and seeking out the enemy they would rouse a sleeping dog and bring the war, now averted, upon themselves again.

ACTIVITIES
KNOWLEDGE CHECK

Why did Spain struggle to defeat the United Provinces?
Having read this section about the difficulties of Spain's campaign in the Netherlands:

1 Produce a spidergram of reasons why Spain struggled.

2 Arrange the points in the spidergram in order of which you think was most important.

3 Briefly explain why you chose this order.

A Level Exam-Style Question Section B

'Elizabeth I's decision to openly support the Dutch rebels in 1585 was the decisive reason for Spain's inability to subdue the United Provinces in the years 1584–1600.'

How far do you agree with this opinion? (20 marks)

Tip
Try to cover the whole time period mentioned in the question. Why might the examiner have chosen these dates?

THINKING HISTORICALLY Interpretations (5c)

Good questions/Bad questions

Below are some criteria that would be of particular importance to three monarchs who were in power during the 1580s. They are generalisations for the purpose of this exercise.

Elizabeth I	Philip II	Henry III of France
She is particularly interested in safeguarding England from Spanish aggression and protecting her throne.	He is interested in promoting Catholicism and subduing the United Provinces.	He is interested in securing his own throne from internal discontent.

Work in groups.

1 Devise three criteria of what makes a good historical question.

2 Consider what you know about the Spanish Armada.

   a) Each write a historical question based on that subject matter.

   b) Put these in rank order, with the best question first based on your criteria.

3 Using a piece of A3 paper, write the names of the three monarchs so they form a large triangle.

   a) Write your questions from 2a on the piece of paper so that their positions reflect how likely the monarchs are to be interested by that question. For example, a question about the defeat of the Spanish Armada would be more important to Elizabeth I and Philip II than to Henry III and so would be somewhere between Elizabeth I and Philip II, but nowhere near Henry III.

   b) Add some further questions. Try to think of questions that only one of the three would be interested in.

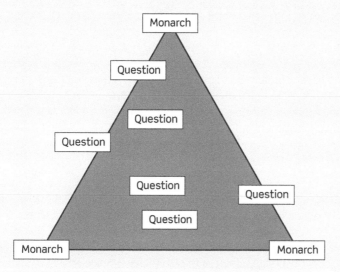

4 Take it in turns to try to answer the questions you have created in the style of one of the monarchs. See if the other members of the group can guess which one it was.

Answer the following questions individually using the examples created by the above activity.

5 Does one method of constructing history lead to better reasoning than the others? Explain your answer.

6 Explain why all views, if well considered, are to an extent useful sources for the study of the past.

HOW DID THE UNITED PROVINCES ENHANCE THEIR POWER?

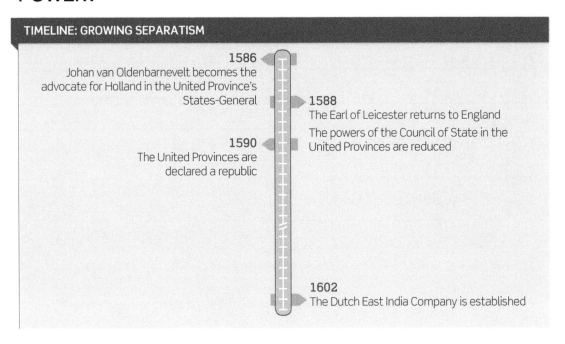

TIMELINE: GROWING SEPARATISM

1586
Johan van Oldenbarnevelt becomes the advocate for Holland in the United Province's States-General

1588
The Earl of Leicester returns to England

The powers of the Council of State in the United Provinces are reduced

1590
The United Provinces are declared a republic

1602
The Dutch East India Company is established

Oldenbarnevelt's reforms

The military successes enjoyed by Maurice of Nassau reflected the changing priorities of Philip II, but they were also the product of a much more stable relationship between the members of the United Provinces. In 1584, they were very much divided and even the presence of the Earl of Leicester until 1588 did not elicit any greater bond among the states. What continued during this period was something that had always existed: individual provinces acting in accordance with their own interests, occasionally supporting one another when the interest was mutual, for example the war against Spain. Outside of these common aims, the provinces looked to their own borders and this had both slowed the creation of a collective identity and also undermined the broader defence campaign through disagreement and internal disputes.

After 1588, however, the United Provinces underwent a series of political changes that helped to overcome the individual antagonisms between states and streamlined the decision-making process, giving the collective state a better chance of mutual growth and success. The chief architect behind this transformation was Johan van Oldenbarnevelt, the legal adviser of Holland who, after 1586, was appointed that province's **advocate** in the States-General. Under his guidance political reforms were introduced that allowed the provinces to bind together more effectively, and this facilitated the military success of Maurice and also provided for a stable platform that subsequently encouraged greater economic success.

The basis of his reforms was to promote a stronger States-General. As both the advocate for Holland – the most dominant province, which contributed more than half of the United Provinces' federal budget – and also the holder of several smaller offices that put him in close contact with a wide number of influential people within that province, he was able to promote a more centralised role for the assembly. This began with the appointment of Maurice of Nassau as *stadtholder* of five of the seven provinces between 1585 and 1590. In the remaining two provinces his cousin William Louis was appointed, and therefore the administrative leadership of the collective state was unified by his family. Further to this reform, Oldenbarnevelt continued to press for greater centralisation and in 1588 was successful in reducing the powers of the Council of State, which had been established following the Treaty of Nonsuch. By reducing the authority of this body more decisions were taken in the States-General and it began to enjoy a more integral role within the country. This increased authority was confirmed in 1590 when the States-General declared itself to be the sovereign institution of the United Provinces. In making this declaration the United Provinces officially

KEY TERM

Advocate
Another term for 'representative' or 'deputy'.

promoted themselves a republic. However, the reality was that the States-General was still reliant upon the provincial assemblies since it was these who elected the advocates sent to it.

What the declaration did achieve, however, was an improved sense of identity among the provinces and this offered the republic much-needed stability that would yield further benefit for the state.

The Dutch East India Company and the development of overseas trade

The improved political system in the United Provinces also facilitated the growth of a strong economy, which itself contributed to the state's successful resistance to Spanish rule. The Netherlands had always relied on international trade. For example, many of the cereals consumed in the north came from the Baltic, while the coastal regions in Holland and Zeeland operated profitable shipping industries. The United Provinces were therefore very aware of the importance of trade for their survival.

Trade also served other purposes besides fulfilling economic needs – it could help to promote the political agenda of the United Provinces, offering another way for the international community to recognise them as a republic. This independence had only been declared by the state in 1590 and had not yet been accepted by the wider world. Enhancing trade opportunities with other nations could help to foster better relationships with the world generally and therefore add further credibility to the provinces' claim to autonomy.

The Dutch East India Company

Throughout the 1590s, trade expanded in the United Provinces. They saw significant growth internally as the population multiplied with the arrival of Calvinist immigrants from the south who sought work and, crucially, brought their capital with them to help establish new businesses. They also witnessed burgeoning trade at an international level, which saw the traditional Baltic–European trade routes develop, and also the creation of new commercial routes in the Atlantic and Pacific as Dutch shipping sought new markets to help sustain their new state. In 1598–99, the first Dutch vessel circumnavigated the world, and one sea captain from Rotterdam arrived back from a voyage to Indonesia with a cargo of spices. These events evidenced the growing confidence of the Dutch and also their eye for commercialism: the interest in spices made the captain a rich man and others sought to emulate his success; in the pursuit of profit, further voyages were made to the Philippines, Malacca (Malaysia) and India and each yielded a good return.

In 1602, the United Provinces granted a 21-year **monopoly** of the Pacific trade to the Dutch East India Company which had quickly been established by raising private capital amounting to 6.5 million florins in less than a month. The Company was among the first of such large international ventures and the first to issue shares. Using this model it quickly became the dominant interest in the Pacific and between 1602 and 1796 when it was liquidated, it had traded more than 2.5 million tonnes of goods from Asia.

KEY TERM

Monopoly
Exclusive control of trade.

The money that the Company was able to generate (it could yield an annual 18 percent dividend for its shareholders) introduced significant wealth into the United Provinces, which could then be reinvested in other projects or even to support the military effort against Spain. In 1592, expenditure on the province's army was 3.2 million florins, but by 1607 the States-General was able to spend 8.8 million florins because of its ability to raise state loans for this purpose. This was an alternative way to raise capital rather than increasing taxes, and it offered a ten percent interest rate for those with spare money to invest. The success of ventures like the Dutch East India Company certainly offered the opportunity to bring in more income, which was taken up by the business-minded and increasingly patriotic members of the United Provinces.

Further development of overseas trade

In addition to the East India Company's trade in the Pacific, other markets were also opened up. Between 1598 and 1605, 25 ships were sailing to West Africa, 20 to Brazil and more than 150 to the Caribbean each year, and this helped to develop Dutch colonies. This was particularly the case in Indonesia, where they were able to establish two outposts: the first in 1605 in Amboina and then a second in Ternate two years later. These developments reinforced opportunities for the provinces

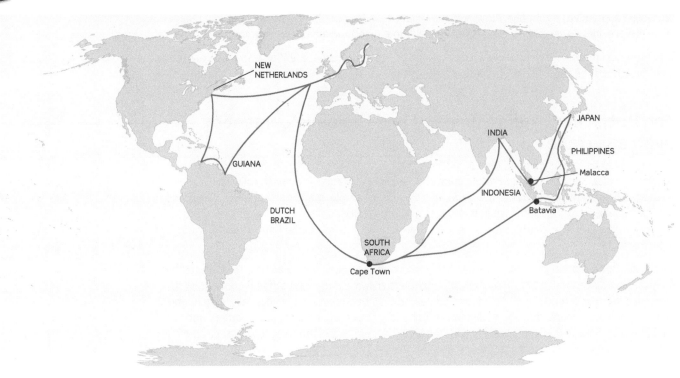

Figure 4.1 Map of the trade routes of the Dutch East India Company.

as trading posts, and businesses were then set up in these areas that created guaranteed markets for Dutch exports and also imports.

The development of international trade had significant effects on the United Provinces. It enhanced their economic position by opening up new markets for their produce and also stimulated new enterprises that could generate substantial profits by exploiting the growing world markets. In terms of the war with Spain, the economic success this brought underpinned the military campaigns of Maurice and ensured that his troops did not mutiny in a similar fashion to those of his enemy. It also offered the possibility of long-term sustainability that attracted more people to the country, thereby strengthening its position, and, more importantly, presenting itself as a distinct state separate from its southern counterpart.

The growing divergence of north and south

SOURCE

7

From a diary entry of an Englishman recording his thoughts about the difference between the northern and southern provinces following his visit to the Netherlands in the early 17th century.

The care [shown by the north Netherlanders] in government is very exact and precise, because everyone has an immediate interest in the State. Such is the equality of justice here that every man is satisfied; with such care are regulations drawn up that a man may see the laws as a guide, not as a means of entrapment; such their exactness in calculating the expense of an army, as that it shall be equally free from superfluity and want... The largest part of the income of the United Provinces comes from trade, in which business they are nowadays the wisest. For all the commodities that this part of the world wants, and the Indies have (as spices, silk, jewellery, gold), they convey – as the Venetians did of old. And all those commodities that the northern Baltic countries abound with and the southern countries stand in need of, they likewise convey thither, which was the ancient trade of the Eastlings [Germans]. And this they do, having little export of their own, buying and selling at their own prices.

As soon as I entered the southern country, I beheld the results of a land distressed by war. The people forlorn, and more reproachful of their governors than revengeful against their enemies. The bravery of what was left of the nobility and the industry of the merchants were both decayed. The towns were ruinous and the people here were growing poor with less taxes than they seem to flourish with in the United Provinces.

The northern provinces

The economic prosperity of the north, together with the increased political and religious freedoms enjoyed there, enabled those provinces to flourish. Maurice's victories during the 1590s had driven the Spanish out and secured the border, and as a result the United Provinces were able to start looking to the future and to safely remodel their states into a more unified collective that could effectively coexist. Such thinking was only possible because they were now reasonably secure and distanced from the war that continued in the southern provinces.

The result of this newfound security was that the population grew substantially. For example, in 1514 Holland had a population of 273,000 and by 1622 this had swelled to 670,000. For many people the prospect of religious toleration was especially attractive and therefore many Calvinists and other Protestant groups chose to relocate from the southern provinces. The greatest consequence of this movement was that the new immigrants brought with them essential skills and also their own money, which contributed effectively to the ongoing development of the nation. Before the rebellion the southern provinces had been the most prosperous – Antwerp was regarded as the pre-eminent city. However, by the late 1590s Amsterdam was becoming the new dominant centre of commerce and much of this was because of the new money arriving in the city from those leaving the south – by 1611, out of the 320 largest depositors in the Amsterdam Exchange Bank, more than half were southern migrants.

In addition to the money that poured into the north, new skills also contributed to the overall enhancement of the region: 442 teachers from the south moved to the north between 1575 and 1630. Many of these were experts in their fields and therefore added considerably to the intellectual acumen of the country. In terms of practical skills, over the same period in Leiden more than 10,000 people arrived from the cloth-weaving towns of Flanders to increase that city's productivity.

In every way the United Provinces were expanding at a fast pace. Economically, politically and intellectually they were becoming far more prosperous than they had been at any other time and this was reflected in their growing confidence and greater sense of identity. Although the war years remained difficult – financing the war was always a challenge – the fortunes of the north were certainly improving.

The southern provinces

By contrast, the southern provinces under Spanish control did not fare so well. Having lost significant sections of its population to the north, and being the main theatre of battle, these provinces suffered and struggled to retain the prosperity they had enjoyed in the 1560s.

The governor-general of the ten remaining Spanish provinces was Archduke Albert VII of Austria who, in 1596, had replaced his brother Ernst. When Philip II died two years later, Albert was granted full sovereignty of the Spanish Netherlands and jointly with his wife (Philip II's daughter Isabella) he governed the state with the support of Philip III who acceded to the Spanish throne. Despite being sovereign of the lands, Albert relied heavily upon his brother-in-law for money and troops. Therefore, just as his father had done, Philip III was able to exercise significant influence over the administration of the land and he also retained military control.

The implication of this arrangement was that Spain continued to determine the nature of government in the ten provinces and so the state remained highly centralised as per the policies of the late king. In effect, the provincial assemblies were little more than tax-raising institutions for the Brussels government, which retained the decision-making powers. Even here, however, there was little opportunity for the Catholic nobles to offer opinions, as the Council of State was reduced to an advisory body and the real decisions were taken by the Spanish ministry. This was an informal group of Spanish advisers who held influence over the archduke and directed policy in line with that proposed by Philip III.

The consequence of this arrangement was that the grandees gradually stopped attending the Council of State, returning to their estates and therefore allowing the government to adopt a distinctly foreign air that diminished the idea that the provinces were able to contribute to their own governance. One important product of this state of affairs was the migration of so many people to the north: between 1570 and 1600, the population of Antwerp declined by one-third while those of Mechelen and Louvain reduced by half. The loss of so many people significantly undermined the prosperity of these provinces, and this naturally affected the ability of the Spanish to raise sufficient money from the population.

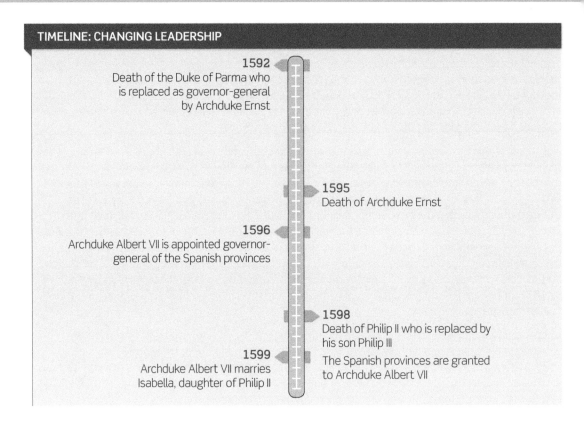

TIMELINE: CHANGING LEADERSHIP

1592
Death of the Duke of Parma who is replaced as governor-general by Archduke Ernst

1595
Death of Archduke Ernst

1596
Archduke Albert VII is appointed governor-general of the Spanish provinces

1598
Death of Philip II who is replaced by his son Philip III

The Spanish provinces are granted to Archduke Albert VII

1599
Archduke Albert VII marries Isabella, daughter of Philip II

Oldenbarnevelt's success in curbing Calvinist excesses

The growth in the population in the north was in one sense a great source of economic prosperity, but it also brought with it some difficulties as many of the immigrants were Calvinists who, upon their arrival in the north, expected there to be a triumphal Protestant state.

Religion had destabilised the provinces during the 1570s and 1580s. Following the Union of Utrecht (see pages 351–352) for example, Protestants sought to pass laws that discriminated against Catholics, and this had upset the relationship among several provinces who each had different ideas about the question of religious practice. Given the potential for fragmentation that religion presented, the leading political figure in the United Provinces, the Holland advocate Oldenbarnevelt, undertook to promote a greater sense of religious toleration and sought to reduce the more strident opinions of the Calvinist adherents.

The growth of Calvinism in the north brought with it greater demands from that faith to be involved in the decision-making process of the state and in particular for their hierarchy to have greater control over public affairs. In this demand there was the potential for the same religious instability of previous decades and therefore Oldenbarnevelt was reluctant to grant such a measure.

Sharing his reluctance were the local authorities of the towns, who felt that any changes would negatively affect their own authority as the Calvinists would look to their Church for guidance and leadership rather than the civic authorities. With this understanding the local authorities anticipated that what could emerge would be a religious state within a state that could potentially disrupt the cordial relations currently enjoyed between the religious groups. Acknowledging the potentially ruinous consequences of such a request, Oldenbarnevelt took the side of the civic authorities and helped to empower the local town councils with the authority to dismiss any ministers who were deemed to be attempting to disrupt the peace. He also made it a requirement that all churchmen in his own state of Holland had to swear an oath of allegiance to the local authorities.

By raising civic authority, the advocate for Holland was attempting to enforce a common loyalty. The different religious groups had only really been governed by their own consciences and religion was the only guiding principle. By empowering the town councils to dismiss unruly ministers, a clear signal was being sent that even spiritual authority had an obligation to obey common laws. In promoting this idea Oldenbarnevelt was attempting to remove the potential threat of religious extremism in the United Provinces.

The power of the United Provinces

1 Using your own knowledge and what you have read here, write down a list of reasons that explain the growing power of the United Provinces.

2 Which of these do you think is most important?

WHY DID SPAIN'S INFLUENCE IN THE NETHERLANDS DECLINE?

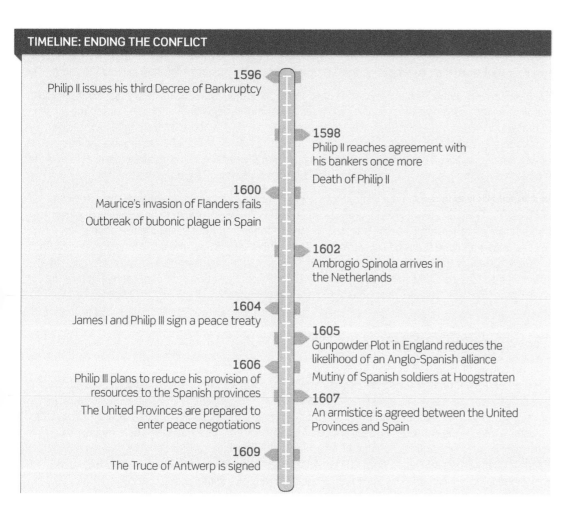

TIMELINE: ENDING THE CONFLICT

1596
Philip II issues his third Decree of Bankruptcy

1598
Philip II reaches agreement with his bankers once more

Death of Philip II

1600
Maurice's invasion of Flanders fails

Outbreak of bubonic plague in Spain

1602
Ambrogio Spinola arrives in the Netherlands

1604
James I and Philip III sign a peace treaty

1605
Gunpowder Plot in England reduces the likelihood of an Anglo-Spanish alliance

Mutiny of Spanish soldiers at Hoogstraten

1606
Philip III plans to reduce his provision of resources to the Spanish provinces

The United Provinces are prepared to enter peace negotiations

1607
An armistice is agreed between the United Provinces and Spain

1609
The Truce of Antwerp is signed

Spain's inability to pay its troops

The expanding foreign policy of Philip II took a huge toll on the financial strength of Spain and this had significant consequences for the ongoing war with the United Provinces. His campaigns against the Ottoman Empire had been a great advantage to the Dutch as many vital resources were diverted to this campaign, which had afforded the rebels time and opportunity to improve their own forces. Similarly, his undertaking against England in 1588 was equally advantageous – the cost alone of the Armada that was amassed was two-thirds of the entire Habsburg Empire's annual revenue, and its failure resulted not only in his humiliation but also the mutiny of his troops who were denied payment because of the lack of funds.

This continued to be a recurring theme into the 1590s, when Spain continued to pursue its war in France. The religious context of this war essentially robbed Philip II of perspective and he diverted vast sums of money into this conflict and also demanded that troops in the Netherlands be used to secure Paris in 1590. The consequences of this level of involvement were that the campaign against the United Provinces was delayed, and his troops there were required to participate in two separate wars but were denied regular payment since money was in increasingly short supply.

The Duke of Parma had fallen victim to the disaffection of his troops as early as 1591, when 2,000 of his best troops mutinied because of excessive wage arrears. The result of this action was that Maurice of Nassau was able to achieve some notable victories – recapturing Zutphen and Deventer without the Spaniards being able to stop him. Further mutinies took place in 1594 under the new governor-general, Archduke Ernst: 4,000 veteran troops abandoned their duties in Flanders and were joined in 1596 by other soldiers after Philip II had once more declared state bankruptcy. These acts of defiance from the Spanish troops undermined the prestige of Spain just as the failed armada had done. Once feared for their ferocity in battle, increasingly the Spanish army was becoming discredited by its own ill-discipline. This not only affected the resolve of their Dutch enemies, but also began to lose them ground in the campaign. Perhaps the most glaring consequence of this was Spain's failed invasion of the Island of Bommel in 1599, where its troops once more mutinied and the towns they had captured were then sold back to the Dutch for cash by the troops who had garrisoned them.

The constant instability of Habsburg resources was a perennial issue for those trying to conduct the war against the north. Without regular payments it was increasingly difficult to guarantee the loyalty of the troops, which gave Maurice of Nassau the upper hand. The issue of funding became even more acute in 1599–1600 when Spain suffered an outbreak of bubonic plague and around ten percent of its population died. The loss of so many people naturally reduced both the taxes available and the productivity of the country so that once more there was a delay in payments to the troops.

In effect the failure to maintain a consistent supply of finance to the southern provinces drew the conflict out. The gains that Spain had made under the Duke of Parma were generally lost, either through mutiny or resources being diverted to other conflicts. In both cases the underlying issue was finance, and it allowed the rebels to make significant advances during the late 16th century. Maurice was able to secure the borders of the United Provinces and this in turn allowed the state to build an effective infrastructure that promoted both internal unity and also international trade. Each of these developments made the task of subduing the north much more challenging and expensive.

The armistice of 1607

The fortunes of Spain

Despite the arrival of a new and very capable military commander in 1602 – Ambrogio Spinola, who was able to win the siege of Ostend in September 1604 – the resources of Spain were increasingly being exhausted. Spinola brought renewed hope of a possible victory for Spain following his success at Ostend and then a short but equally successful campaign in 1605 that saw Spain retake the fortresses of Wachtendock, Lingen and Oldenzaal in the province of Flanders. This success rekindled Spanish fires, particularly since Philip III had been able to conclude a peace treaty with England the previous year, which offered a greater chance of resupplying the Spanish occupied Netherlands. However, there was little available cash to fuel this ambition. When a request for more finance came to Philip III's ministers, they responded with a long list of other commitments that also needed to be supported, and therefore the request was refused.

EXTEND YOUR KNOWLEDGE

Ambrogio Spinola (1569–1630)
Born in Genoa to one of the city's most powerful families, Ambrogio Spinola was a supporter of Spain and Habsburg rule. To further his family's fortunes, he raised 9,000 troops and marched them to serve under Philip II's army in the Netherlands. As a military commander, Spinola was equal to Maurice of Nassau and is best remembered for his successful siege against Ostend in 1604. He also served as a financial backer for Philip II in 1606 but was never repaid by Spain and later suffered financial ruin.

As many as the commitments cited were, they did not acknowledge the personal costs of Philip III. Unlike his father who had run a very restrained court with running costs amounting to 500,000 florins a year, Philip III required more than four times that amount. With personal costs of two million florins, in addition to the many other costs of running a vast empire, the Spanish treasury was drying up.

Without finance from Spain, Spinola's early successes were, like Parma's, undermined. His army, also like Parma's, mutinied in December 1606 and more than 4,000 troops abandoned their posts only to return when their arrears were paid at a cost of one million florins. The following year – on 9 November 1607 – Philip III, like his father, issued a decree of bankruptcy.

The United Provinces

The States-General was also growing tired of the conflict. The costs they were incurring had risen from an average of five million florins in the 1590s to ten million florins between 1604 and 1606. Despite a growing economy these figures were a significant burden on the provinces and therefore there was increasing discussion between them about negotiating some respite from the conflict.

Voices for this course of action grew louder after Spain's conclusion of a treaty with England in 1604, since this ended any chance of support from that nation. Furthermore, it also raised the spectre of an Anglo-Spanish alliance, which could significantly undermine the security of the United Provinces' borders and affect their shipping. This fear increased after Spain also concluded a peace treaty with France that effectively left Spain free to pursue its interests in the Netherlands without complication. Despite the fragile relationship with England being undermined in 1605, following the failed Gunpowder Plot (in which some plotters had fought in Spanish armies, while others were Catholic gentry), the threat from Spain remained a potent one that the United Provinces could not ignore.

EXTEND YOUR KNOWLEDGE

The Gunpowder Plot, 1605

This was an attempt to blow up the Houses of Parliament in England in 1605. It was orchestrated by a small group of disaffected Catholic soldiers, including Guy Fawkes, who had served in the Habsburg Netherlands for ten years. The intention was to kill the Protestant King James I as he opened parliament so that he could be replaced by his daughter Elizabeth whom the conspirators had hoped they could capture and raise as a Catholic.

On both the Dutch and Spanish sides, therefore, there was motive to seek an agreement, and in February 1607 a negotiator was sent from Brussels to the United Provinces after the latter announced their willingness to talk. This negotiator was empowered to convey the willingness of Spain to accept the independence of the United Provinces as a basis for a permanent settlement in return for a ceasefire for eight months that would come into effect a month after 29 March when the deal was struck. This effectively ended more than 30 years of fighting between the two sides.

The Truce of Antwerp, 1609

Having accepted the ceasefire, the two protagonists met at The Hague in Holland to discuss a settlement of the conflict. The Spanish delegation was led by Spinola, while the United Provinces were guided by Oldenbarnevelt and Maurice of Nassau (who was opposed to any kind of deal that did not imply victory).

The negotiations were naturally quite strained as each side wanted to secure a good deal for themselves. In return for recognition the Spanish required:

- an explicit guarantee for the Catholics living in the new Dutch Republic

- that the blockade of the Schelt and Flemish coast be lifted so that Spanish shipping could resume trading more effectively

- the end of all Dutch trade with the East and West Indies.

A commemorative engraving by Palas in 1609 depicting the Dutch celebrating the Truce of Antwerp between the United Provinces and Spain.

These requests were rejected out of hand by Holland and Zeeland, especially since they were the main beneficiaries of the trade with the Indies. Other provinces within the Dutch state were more willing to consider these terms, but as the dominant province Holland in particular was able to maintain its objection and therefore the offer was formally rejected on 25 August 1608. Despite the tiredness of each participant and their equal reluctance to resume hostilities, there was no loss of focus with regard to the importance of their potential agreement.

To prevent the complete failure of these talks, however, intermediaries from France and England proposed a different offer, which deliberately ignored the issue of religion and allowed both parties to continue their overseas activities. Under this solution, which was explained as a long truce rather than a formal treaty, both the United Provinces and Spain could continue to trade in the disputed Indies, but in Europe they would seek each other's permission to trade in their respective waters. The terms meant that the potential for conflict overseas was accepted, but an agreement was made stating that any such conflict would not affect the European arrangement. These terms were agreed to by each party after some further discussion, and on 9 April 1609 the Truce of Antwerp was signed, pledging the cessation of hostilities between Spain and the United Provinces for the period of 12 years.

SOURCE

9 Taken from the Truce of Antwerp, which ended the war between Spain and the United Provinces for a period of 12 years.

II. To wit, that the said truce will be in force and observed strictly, faithfully, and inviolably for the time of twelve years, during which there will be a halt to all acts of enmity between the said king, archdukes, and States-General, at sea and in other waterways as well as on land in all their realms, provinces, lands, and lordships, and between all their subjects and residents of all conditions and qualities, with no exception of places or persons.

III. Each party will remain in occupation and effective possession of the lands, cities, places, lands and lordships which he holds and possesses at present, without being disturbed or troubled therein during this truce: and this is understood to include the boroughs, villages, hamlets, and countryside dependent upon them.

IV. The subjects and inhabitants of the lands of the said king, archdukes and States will keep on good terms of friendship and understanding with each other during this truce, without resentment for offenses and damage already suffered; and they shall also be able to travel and stay in each other's countries and conduct their businesses and trade in them with full security, both at sea and on land. However, the king understands these conditions to be restricted and limited to the realms, countries, lands, and lordships which he holds and possesses in Europe and other places and seas where the subjects of other princes who are his friends and allies engage in such business by mutual agreement; and as for the places, cities, ports, and harbours which he holds outside these limits, the aforesaid States and their subjects cannot engage in any business in them without the express permission of the aforesaid king.

A Level Exam-Style Question Section B

How accurate is it to say that the successes of the northern provinces in the years 1585–1609 were due to the economic frailty of Spain? (20 marks)

Tip
When answering questions like this remember to relate additional factors that you come up with to the factor stated in the question. For example, how might the northern provinces' relationship with England have influenced Spain's economic frailty?

The signing of the Truce of Antwerp formally ended more than 30 years of conflict between the northern provinces of the Netherlands and their former Spanish rulers. It was a culmination of many different forces that had each further divided the two. However, fighting broke out again in 1621 and peace between Spain and the Netherlands was not formally achieved until the Peace of Westphalia in 1648. Religion and political disagreements had been the initial point of rupture, but as the dispute wore on it was financial constraints that eventually forced them to seek better relations. The consequence of such an achievement redrew the political map in Europe.

Spain's *de facto* recognition of the independence of the United Provinces

In signing the Truce of Antwerp, Philip III was in reality accepting the fact that his possessions in the Netherlands were now reduced. By formally acknowledging the United Provinces and concluding terms with them, he was recognising the independence of these lands and allowing other nations formally to do that too.

Immediately following the signing of the truce, diplomatic recognition was granted to the new state by the rest of Europe, and the States-General's **envoys** to these countries were elevated to the status of **ambassadors**. James I of England reciprocated in October 1609 by raising his envoy in The Hague to the same status in recognition of the new state. Though a simple act, the United Provinces' acceptance by the European community marked a great moment in its history and arguably underlined the real significance of what they had achieved: independence from Habsburg rule and the birth of their own **republic**.

The recognition afforded to the United Provinces was the reward for such a determined attempt to preserve the privileges of their states and to safeguard the right of religious toleration. This determination had been stirred up by a high-handed King Philip II who, unlike his father, had failed to appreciate the sensibilities of those he governed. This political discontent was fanned by the growth of Protestantism and Philip's hatred of any challenge to his own Catholicism. Intent on crushing any hint of this alternative faith, his actions in the Netherlands, which included the extensive use of the Inquisition, exacerbated already existing tensions and this led eventually to open confrontation. In this regard, religion was a fundamental cause of the final separation: it was the fuel that kept the fires alight for 30 years and demanded each side dig deep into their respective pockets, which, when they were empty, saw the suspension of hostilities.

KEY TERMS

Envoy
A messenger or representative.

Ambassador
An accredited person sent by a state to a foreign country as its permanent representative. They retain formal negotiation powers and also immunity from harassment while serving abroad.

Republic
A state that does not have a hereditary monarch but rather has an elected head of state.

ACTIVITIES
KNOWLEDGE CHECK

Why did Spain lose power?

Consider what you have just read and, using your own knowledge, offer five justified reasons why Spain lost its power in the Netherlands.

ACTIVITY
SUMMARY

How did the United Provinces secure their independence?

Having read about the fortunes of the United Provinces, write a 500-word explanation about why they were able to secure their independence. In your explanation you should consider the following ideas:

- the impact of finance
- military performance
- the role of individuals
- the role of religion.

WIDER READING

Duke, A. *The Reformation and Revolt in the Low Countries*, Bloomsbury (2003)

Imperato, T. *An Introduction to Early Modern European History 1450–1610*, Hodder (2000)

Lotherington, J. (ed.) *Years of Renewal: European History 1470–1600*, Hodder (1999)

Parker, G. *The Dutch Revolt*, Penguin (1990)

Woodward, G. *The Development of Early Modern Europe*, Longman (1997)

Preparing for your AS Level Paper 2 exam

Advance planning

1. Draw up a timetable for your revision and try to keep to it. Spread your timetable over a number of weeks, and aim to cover four or five topics each week.
2. Spend longer on topics that you have found difficult, and revise them several times.
3. Above all, do not try to limit your revision by attempting to 'question spot'. Try to be confident about all aspects of your Paper 2 work, because this will ensure that you have a choice of questions in Section B.

Paper 2 overview:

AS Paper 2	Time: 1 hour 30 minutes	
Section A	Answer 1 compulsory two-part sources question	8+12 marks = 20 marks
Section B	Answer 1 question from a choice of 3	20 marks
	Total marks =	40 marks

You should familiarise yourself with the layout of the paper by looking at the examples published by Edexcel. The questions for each section are followed by eight pages of lined paper where you should write your answer.

Section A questions

Each of the two parts of the question will focus on one of the two contemporary sources provided. The sources together will total around 300 words. The (a) question, worth 8 marks, will be in the form: 'Why is Source 1 useful for an enquiry into…?' The (b) question, worth 12 marks, will be in the form: 'How much weight do you give the evidence of Source 2 for an enquiry into…?' In both your answers you should address the value of the content of the source, and then its nature, origin and purpose. Finally, you should use your own knowledge of the context of the source to assess its value.

Section B questions

These questions ask you to reach a judgement on an aspect of the topic studied. The questions will have the form, for example, of 'How far…', 'To what extent…' or 'How accurate is it to say…'. The questions can deal with historical concepts such as cause, consequence, change, continuity, similarity, difference and significance. You should consider the issue raised in the question, consider other relevant issues, and then conclude with an overall judgement.

The timescale of the questions could be as short as a single year or even a single event (an example from Option 2C.2 could be, 'To what extent was Russia's involvement in the First World War responsible for the fall of the Provisional Government in 1917?'). The timescale could be longer depending on the historical event or process being examined, but questions are likely to be shorter than those set for Sections A and B in Paper 1.

Use of time

This is an issue that you should discuss with your teachers and fellow students, but here are some suggestions for you.

1. Do not write solidly for 45 minutes on each question. For Section A it is essential that you have a clear understanding of the content of each source, the points being made, and the nature, origin and purpose of each source. You might decide to spend up to ten minutes reading the sources and drawing up your plan, and 35 minutes writing your answer.
2. For Section B answers you should spend a few minutes working out what the question is asking you to do, and drawing up a plan of your answer before you begin to write your response.

Preparing for your AS Level exams

Paper 2: AS Level sample answer with comments

Section A

Part A requires you to:

- identify key points in the source and explain them
- deploy your own knowledge of the context in which events took place
- make appropriate comments about the author/origin of the source.

Why is Source 4 (Chapter 2, page 318) valuable to the historian for an enquiry into the Battle of Heiligerlee in 1568?

Explain your answer using the source, the information given about it and your own knowledge of the historical context. (8 marks)

Average student answer

Source 4 is a testimony about the death of the Count of Aremberg which took place at the battle of Heiligerlee in 1568. It is very graphic about the manner of his death, which gives a good impression of possible attitudes that were present and the extent of feeling that might have influenced the battle itself. It says that the count was knocked off his horse and then shot, and once wounded he was beaten to death by his enemies. This was a brutal death which suggests that the battle generated a great deal of animosity between the participants. Given the religious and political nature of the battle – the Dutch rebelling against Spanish rule – this was likely to be fierce and this is certainly how the source presents the battle.

> This paragraph offers some awareness of the source and how it might be valuable, but it does not really explain why.

The source is also valuable because it offers the opinion of someone who actually fought in the battle and therefore could give a realistic account of what took place. This would be very useful to the historian as they would be able to get a clear idea about what happened from a first-hand account rather than having to imagine what might have taken place. Sybrant Sickes was an Orangist supporter and this would therefore give the historian a more accurate picture of the motivations of this particular side. The killing of Aremberg signalled the victory of Louis of Nassau over the Spanish force and therefore the source offers good evidence of this conclusion.

> The paragraph considers some of the source quality but then makes a general comment about the relevance of the source. This could be more thoughtful and specific to the question, perhaps using own knowledge to develop the point.

Overall the source and the associated information about it clearly evidence how brutal the battle of Heiligerlee was and also the extent of animosity between the two sides. The nature of Aremberg's death was a clear indication of the extent of anger between the protagonists.

> This conclusion offers some judgement, but it would be stronger if own knowledge was included in support.

Verdict

This is an average answer because:

- it demonstrates some understanding of source quality and tries to integrate this within the overall response to the question focus
- it deploys some knowledge of the historical context but this could be developed more throughout

- there is some overall evaluation of the source but it needs more specific explanation to add substance.

Use the feedback on this answer to rewrite it, making as many improvements as you can.

Paper 2: AS Level sample answers with comments

Section A

Part B requires you to:

- interrogate the source
- draw reasoned inferences
- deploy your own knowledge to interpret the material in its context
- make a judgement about the value (weight) of the source.

How much weight do you give to the evidence of Source 3 (Chapter 2, page 317) for an enquiry into why William of Orange invaded the Netherlands in 1568?

Explain your answer using the source, the information given about it and your own knowledge of the historical context. (12 marks)

Average student answer

Source 3 is a deliberate attempt to encourage popular support by the Prince of Orange for his revolt in 1568. It offers his justification for rebellion and therefore is quite valuable as an indication of what his intentions and motivations were. In particular he criticises Philip II for his authoritarian policies that have deliberately undermined the rights and privileges of the 17 provinces and as such this would offer a good idea of why William of Orange invaded the Netherlands.

> This paragraph offers some explanation of the source's intent and shows some general awareness of the context.

Since it is entitled the 'Warning' however, it is reasonable to suggest that this document is deliberately seeking to scare the population into siding with the prince against Spain, and therefore as propaganda it could also be challenged in terms of its weight of credibility. Propaganda is intended to encourage a particular attitude and as such it might be exaggerated so as to elicit this response – in this case an anti-Spanish reaction. Consequently, even though it offers some clear reasons for Orange's invasion, these may not be entirely true and therefore although it offers some useful evidence, it should not be totally relied upon.

> This paragraph starts to consider the quality of the source and tries to use this to reach a judgement, but the material is a little simplistic and could show more balanced awareness of the source.

In support of the questionable quality of this source, it is also written by the prince himself who would have a natural interest and, therefore, in support of the need to be wary of the evidence, perhaps the material is quite limited despite offering clear motivations.

> This point needs to be better developed – perhaps own knowledge could be used to enhance the point being made.

Overall the source presents some good reasons behind why the prince invaded the Netherlands, but it is a propaganda piece of writing designed to create a particular response and therefore it needs to be considered with care.

> A judgement is reached here which addresses the question asked, but it could be fleshed out a little more – perhaps, again, with reference to own knowledge.

Verdict

This is an average answer because:

- some analysis is offered, but this is not made explicit throughout
- there is focus on the question asked which could be extended more using relevant own knowledge

- a judgement is offered, but this is quite general in scope.

Use the feedback on this answer to rewrite it, making as many improvements as you can.

Paper 2: AS Level sample answer with comments

Section A

Part A requires you to:

- identify key points in the source and explain them
- deploy your own knowledge of the context in which events took place
- make appropriate comments about the author/origin of the source.

Why is Source 4 (Chapter 2, page 318) valuable to the historian for an enquiry into the Battle of Heiligerlee in 1568?

Explain your answer using the source, the information given about it and your own knowledge of the historical context. (8 marks)

Strong student answer

The source is very valuable for an enquiry into the battle of Heiligerlee which was fought in 1568 against Louis of Nassau and the Count of Aremberg. Nassau was a commander in the rebel army and Aremberg, though a Netherlander himself, was the commander of the Spanish forces. The battle took place because the Prince of Orange – a grandee and stadtholder of Holland – felt that Philip II was trying to centralise power in the provinces and override their rights. As a source commenting on the battle, the testimony of Sickes offers a clear indication of the brutality and therefore significance of the battle. The fact that it was so brutal suggests that it was a very serious affair with severe consequences for those involved. Such was the level of intensity that people reacted in excessive ways, which the source evidences nicely. Although this can only be implied, the source has credibility that supports this idea since it was a testimony given to a court investigating the battle. Going to the effort of an investigation corroborates the idea that the battle was particularly significant.

There is some deployment of own knowledge here and it is well focused on the question demand. Some obvious source development is also present.

Considering this is a testimony there is some need to be wary of the evidence as perhaps the witness would be quite subjective towards his side. Supporting this point is the agenda of the piece, which might be deliberately moderated by its speaker so as to secure a better outcome for himself. Consequently while what he says certainly has value in terms of what might have happened, it must also be remembered that it is potentially diluted and therefore can only offer value to a point. Having said that, however, it is a first-hand account of the battle by someone who participated in it and in this sense his view still has validity. Sybrant Sickes was a pro-Orangist supporter and therefore he fought against the count of Aremberg. In this sense his evidence can be said to be quite accurate because he was actually present on the field and, as an individual, his testimony could be very useful for an enquiry into the actions of those present. However, he offers only a snippet of the battle – the death of Aremberg – and therefore his evidence is only useful to a point, offering his own interpretation of individual actions, how Aremberg met his death and some indication of his murderer's actions.

This is a better paragraph as it considers the quality of the source and then tries to explain the significance of this with regard to the question demand. Material could be a little more developed, but overall this is well focused on the quality of the evidence.

Although the source only offers a small window into the battle and the actions of individuals, it does give a lot of information about a particular, and important, event which involved individual action and therefore it is quite valuable to an enquiry into people's actions. As a first-hand account by someone actually present it is certainly reasonably credible and its evidence can be ascribed some authority.

There is some judgement here, which addresses the question demand.

Verdict

This is a strong answer because:

- it has a clear understanding of the question demand and interrogates the source material with confidence to develop points of argument
- in developing an argument, the response uses effective

knowledge of the historical context to inform and enhance the points made from the source material

- it concludes with a clear and well-justified evaluation of the source material that has been consistently developed in the body.

Paper 2: AS Level sample answer with comments

Section A

Part B requires you to:

- interrogate the source
- draw reasoned inferences
- deploy your own knowledge to interpret the material in its context
- make a judgement about the value (weight) of the source.

How much weight do you give to the evidence of Source 3 (Chapter 2, page 317) for an enquiry into why William of Orange invaded the Netherlands in 1568?

Explain your answer using the source, the information given about it and your own knowledge of the historical context. (12 marks)

Strong student answer

The source is very useful to an enquiry into the motivations of William of Orange's invasion because it is essentially the prince setting out his justifications for doing so. Being produced just before the invasion in 1568 it is especially significant because it offers an indication of motive and also intent. Motive on the basis that it talks about the injustices perpetrated by Philip II – particularly his efforts to undermine the privileges of the provinces and the States-General, such as his efforts to reform the bishoprics in 1562. Given these unpopular policies the motive behind the document can arguably be seen as being to incite local support for his rebellion that was being organised for later that year.

> This has good own knowledge in support of the explained points, drawn from the source material.

This idea is given further credibility when you consider that the prince was actually in exile at the time because of his resistance of Philip II's rule – he was seen as being a ringleader during the 1566 Compromise and also as vacillating during the Iconoclastic Fury. On this basis, although it would be reasonable to suggest he has a particular motive (to win back his homeland and attack the person who essentially forced him out), this only enhances the light that the document sheds about why he invaded in 1568. Having said that, however, the fact that he clearly sets out his objectives and justifications also suggests that he was perhaps trying to promote his cause, suggesting that his intentions would not actually be met with widespread support. In this sense although the document makes out that he has noble goals for the country – evidenced by his focus on the tyrannical nature of the Spanish regime – it could also suggest that his motives were entirely self-motivated and that the document was intended to push this one objective.

> This paragraph continues to develop the point made above, offering further own knowledge in support, and also introduces some awareness of quality.

Coming from William himself also grants the document great weight in terms of why he chose to invade. However, it is certainly a reasonably subjective view on the grounds of his own motives. In this sense the document needs to be considered with some care – to assume it is a genuine intention to raise awareness of Spanish injustice and incite a popular rebellion is only one interpretation. Considering the context of the material (Orange's exile and personal standing as a result of Philip II's policies) also offers a more personal motivation that needs to be considered. In either capacity, however, the document is a useful signifier of motivation and therefore can be ascribed real value.

> A thoughtful paragraph that offers clear judgement based on a good consideration of the context and source material.

Verdict

This is a strong answer because:

- it evidences a strong understanding of source quality and uses this effectively to address the question demand

- it makes effective use of a range of accurate own knowledge to develop reasoned points about the source material
- the response offers effective evaluation based upon a critical consideration of the source material.

Paper 2: AS Level sample answer with comments

Section B

These questions assess your understanding of the period in some depth. They will ask you about the content you learned about in the four key themes, but they may not ask about more than one theme. For these questions, remember to:

- give an analytical, not a descriptive, response
- support your points with evidence
- cover the whole time period specified in the question
- come to a substantiated judgement.

To what extent was Requesens' failure to pacify the northern provinces between 1573 and 1576 the result of financial difficulties? (20 marks)

Average student answer

To a great extent Requesens' failure to defeat the rebels was the result of economic problems because the Spanish were financially very poorly off during this period. However, there were many other factors that also contributed to the continuation of the rebellion after 1576.

> This is a weak opening as it does not offer particular argument and nor does it really consider the overall debate in the question.

In 1573 the Spanish government was struggling financially because Philip II had been at war with the Ottoman Empire since the 1560s and this was draining his economic resources to such an extent that the rebellion in the Netherlands was a costly addition which Spain could not really afford. Requesens had estimated the cost of maintaining the army as being more than one million florins a month and that was without including the debt that had been accrued and the arrears that the soldiers were owed. This cost was so great that it was really difficult to keep the soldiers happy, which then also made it difficult to continue fighting the rebels as the troops could not be relied upon to do their duty effectively.

> This paragraph has some clear thoughts about the role of Spain's finances, but it does not really develop the arguments very far and instead drifts into some narrative. The comment about soldiers not being happy and therefore less reliable is a reasonable point with more focus.

The economic difficulties of Spain were therefore very important, but the way Requesens behaved was significant too. He was naturally a very moderate person, but when he came to the Netherlands he was strong-armed into behaving just like the unpopular Duke of Alva who stayed on in his post until December to advise the new governor-general. The Duke himself was a very unpopular person because he had tried to enforce the Tenth Penny tax after 1571 which sought to undermine the power of the States-General by giving him a permanent source of revenue. Being advised by such an unpopular person meant that Requesens was also unpopular and this made his job difficult. Since a lot of the problems caused by the rebellion were because people felt unhappy with the Duke of Alva, Requesens struggled and this was maybe more important than economic problems.

> This paragraph considers some debate and offers a valid alternative point about the difficulties Requesens faced. Once again there are narrative passages that undermine the overall analytical development. There is an attempt to relate back to the question towards the end, but more could be made about how Requesens behaved and the impact this had upon the rebellion.

Also important was the role of the military. The Spanish army was very upset about the fact they were owed so much money and this meant they were not motivated to be loyal to the governor-general. Between 1573 and 1576 there were several mutinies within the army and one reason that the town of Leiden was besieged in 1573 was because the commander of the Spanish forces could not get his troops to attack due to their own displeasure about their lack of payment. This shows that the army was very important to the failure of Requesens to bring the rebellion under control by 1576.

> There is a relevant point being made here but it is not developed very well. The idea of military weakness is very good, but there is a missed opportunity to link this clearly with the financial situation facing Requesens. The evidence is appropriate and there is an attempt to link back to the question at the end.

In addition to the problems in the Spanish army, the prince of Orange was also a contributing factor to the continuation of the rebellion. He had been the main reason for the outbreak of conflict in the first place and by 1573 had been able to unite the provinces of Holland and Zeeland. His conversion to Lutheranism in 1567 had helped to achieve this by promoting the issue of religion and helping the rebellion to adopt a religious focus in addition to the anti-Spanish authority cause. This was especially important because it was able to win more sympathetic supporters in the northern provinces which increased his army there and therefore made it more difficult for the Spanish to regain complete control over the Low Countries.

> This is a reasonable paragraph that starts to consider further relevant ideas. There is a greater degree of explanation here, although the comment on religion could be explained more, and some specific examples would make the paragraph stronger.

Overall, the economic problems facing Spain and their consequent impact on Requesens' ability to end rebellion was very important, but also important were other factors that generally made things even more challenging, and therefore these were of greater significance.

> There is an attempt at a judgement here although it is fairly general and lacks real explanation in the body of the essay.

Verdict

This is an average answer because:

- there is some attempt at analytical explanation, but this is sometimes undermined by narrative passages
- the answer is generally well organised and focuses on the question. However, a couple of paragraphs, though accurate and broadly relevant, are fairly freestanding and could be improved with sharper links to the question overall

- a judgement is reached, but this is quite general and needs greater corroboration in the body.

Use the feedback on this answer to rewrite it, making as many improvements as you can.

Paper 2: AS Level sample answer with comments

Section B

These questions assess your understanding of the period in some depth. They will ask you about the content you learned about in the four key themes, but they may not ask about more than one theme. For these questions, remember to:

- give an analytical, not a descriptive, response
- support your points with evidence
- cover the whole time period specified in the question
- come to a substantiated judgement.

To what extent was Requesens' failure to pacify the northern provinces between 1573 and 1576 the result of financial difficulties? (20 marks)

Strong student answer

To a great extent the failure of Requesens to restore order to the northern provinces can accurately be attributed to the financial difficulties of Spain because the military commitment required was considerably more expensive since the 1572 revolt enjoyed much greater public support and was much better organised. In this regard it is evident that the governor-general was facing strong opposition, but this was generally exacerbated by the economic frailties of Spain.

In many ways the financial problems facing Requesens were fundamental to his difficulties in pacifying the rebellious northern provinces. This is because funding was central to anything his government could do, and when he took over after the unpopular Duke of Alva there was considerable work to be achieved which would require a constant and reliable supply of income. The most significant demand for money came from the military commitment that had built up in the Low Countries as a result of rebellion in 1572. Although a large military presence had existed prior to this event, in 1572 the Spanish military presence amounted to more than 70,000 men who each needed paying. This was singularly the greatest impact on Requesens' failure to re-establish order because the army was increasingly unwilling to fight or even obey orders if they were not going to be paid. Given the economic problems in Spain because of Philip's war with the Ottoman Empire, money was not readily forthcoming from this purse and therefore funding the army in the Netherlands fell into arrears. The immediate result of this was mutiny in that army and in 1576 this disaffection culminated in the Spanish Fury, which saw towns violently sacked – the worst of which being Antwerp where 8,000 people were killed. Not only was this event significant in hardening the resolve of the population to Spanish rule, but it also resulted in the dismissal of Spanish troops from the land which made it very difficult for Requesens to then establish order.

The Fury itself was certainly the product of Spain's financial difficulties, but its impact encouraged a strong reaction to Philip's rule that arguably made Requesens' objective even harder. In this sense the economic problems were both a direct challenge and an indirect one. Since the 1572 rebellion had enjoyed greater support among the local population because of Spain's increased unpopularity – the result of Alva's attempt to enforce the Tenth Penny tax – the atrocities committed by the Spanish troops only vindicated this unpopularity and went even further in alienating public support for their traditional rulers. This increased alienation was very important to the governor-general's failure as an earlier rebellion in 1568 had easily been pacified because of a lack of public support, suggesting that this could make a considerable difference. By actually encouraging local discontent the Spanish were themselves undermining their own chances of pacification. This could be seen as a separate factor in Requesens' failure, but in reality this was generally fostered by underlying financial problems.

This is a strong introduction because it offers a clear argument that includes some broad awareness of debate relevant to the question demand.

This is a well-developed paragraph that addresses the question effectively using strong evidence to support the points made. The points are clear and logically explained, culminating in an explicit link back to the question at the end.

This paragraph offers some further discussion of the question by broadening the debate to consider other factors that might explain Requesens' failure. It is well-conceived and explicitly linked to the stated factor of financial difficulty, which therefore maintains a direct focus on the question demand while offering clear evaluation of it.

As important as the failings of Spain are, the strength of the prince of Orange and his followers was also central to the failure of Spain to re-establish order. In this regard the prince was much better organised than he had been in 1568 and was able to secure foreign support. Furthermore he was able to present himself as a national leader of the northern provinces by emphasising his concern for the ancient privileges of the states themselves. This enabled him to secure greater sympathy among the population because each town was fiercely protective of their rights and so was more willing to support the prince. This was certainly enhanced by the Spanish demand for taxes and greater centralised control, but it particularly meant that he could take advantage of the naturally independent proclivities of the provinces.

> This is a relevant point that is quite well developed. It could be explained a little more – possibly by referring to the financial need for greater taxes. It could also be illustrated with some specific examples of towns' support, but overall, clear direction is evident.

The prince's support was also strengthened by the religious dimension to his rebellion. The Spanish authorities were heavily associated with Catholicism while the northern provinces were generally seen as a haven for Protestantism, and therefore this religion thrived better there. The issue of faith was hugely divisive in the Netherlands and therefore this also hardened the resolve of the local population. Since the Prince of Orange had converted to Lutheranism, this issue at once contributed to his portrayal as the national leader of the northern states, clearly demarking the choice available to the people. While this was not necessarily a clear choice since many people in the north were Catholic, it helped to formulate loyalties that undoubtedly made Requesens' job harder.

> This paragraph could be more developed in terms of analytical judgement but the points are valid, if a little general.

Overall, therefore, the difficulties facing Requesens were many. The position of Spain was well challenged by a more organised opposition that played on the support of the local population. However, much of this support was the result of growing discontent with Spanish rule and this was primarily the result of increased demands made on the people as a consequence of financial difficulty. In the immediate term this was also the most significant reason behind the governor-general's failure as his army was unreliable.

> This is a well thought out conclusion that offers a clear judgement to the question.

Verdict

This is a strong answer because:

- clear and sustained analysis is presented that focuses on the key features of the question
- the material is well supported by good knowledge that evidences a clear understanding of the question demand and a confidence to address this requirement
- a clear and well-informed judgement is reached that has been developed in a logical manner.

Preparing for your A Level Paper 2 exam

Advance planning

1. Draw up a timetable for your revision and try to keep to it. Spread your timetable over a number of weeks, and aim to cover four or five topics each week.
2. Spend longer on topics that you have found difficult, and revise them several times.
3. Above all, do not try to limit your revision by attempting to 'question spot'. Try to be confident about all aspects of your Paper 2 work, because this will ensure that you have a choice of questions in Section B.

Paper 2 overview

AL Paper 2	Time: I hour 30 minutes	
Section A	Answer I compulsory source question	20 marks
Section B	Answer I question from a choice of 2	20 marks
	Total marks =	40 marks

You should familiarise yourself with the layout of the paper by looking at the examples published by Edexcel. The questions for each section are followed by eight pages of lined paper where you should write your answer.

Section A questions

This question asks you to assess two contemporary sources totalling around 400 words, and will be in the form: 'How far could the historian make use of Sources 1 and 2 together to investigate…?' Your answer should examine each source separately, and you should make three points on each source: the value of its content: its nature, origin and purpose; and then you should use your own knowledge of the context of the source to assess its accuracy and value. Finally, you should make a few concluding points on the two sources taken together as a set.

Section B questions

These questions ask you to reach a judgement on an aspect of the topic studied. The questions will have the form, for example, of 'How far…', 'To what extent…' or 'How accurate is it to say…'. The questions can deal with historical concepts such as cause, consequence, change, continuity, similarity, difference and significance. You should consider the issue raised in the question, then other relevant issues, and conclude with an overall judgement.

The timescale of the questions could be as short as a single year or even a single event (an example from Option 2C.2 could be, 'To what extent was Russia's involvement in the First World War responsible for the fall of the Romanovs in 1917?'). The timescale could be longer depending on the historical event or process being examined, but questions are likely to be shorter than those set for Sections A and B in Paper 1.

Use of time

This is an issue that you should discuss with your teachers and fellow students, but here are some suggestions for you.

1. Do not write solidly for 45 minutes on each question. For Section A it is essential that you have a clear understanding of the content of each source, the points being made, and the nature, origin and purpose of each source. You might decide to spend up to ten minutes reading the sources and drawing up your plan, and 35 minutes writing your answer.
2. For Section B answers you should spend a few minutes working out what the question is asking you to do, and drawing up a plan of your answer before you begin to write your response.

Preparing for your A Level exams

Paper 2: A Level sample answer with comments

Section A

You will need to read and analyse two sources and use them in tandem to assess how useful they are in investigating an issue. For these questions, remember to:

- spend time, up to ten minutes, reading and identifying the arguments and evidence present in the sources. Then make a plan to ensure that your response will be rooted in these sources
- use specific references from the sources
- deploy your own knowledge to develop points made in the sources and establish appropriate context
- come to a substantiated judgement.

How far could the historian make use of Sources 6 and 7 (Chapter 1, pages 299 and 300) together to investigate the decline in noble support for Habsburg rule?

Explain your answer, using both sources, the information given about them and your own knowledge of the historical context.
(20 marks)

Average student answer

The two sources offer useful insights into why the nobles came to challenge the Habsburgs' rule. In Source 6 there is a clear indication of the religious priorities of Philip II and his desire to force this faith upon the 17 provinces, while in Source 7 a clear message of intent is being presented by the nobles. Each of these sources therefore offers some motivation for the declining popularity of the Habsburgs' rule in the Netherlands.

Source 6 offers a good indication as to why the nobles might have lost faith in the rule of Philip II because it is a letter from Philip to his sister, Margaret of Parma, who was his regent in the Low Countries which sets out his attitude toward that country. In the document he asserts the need to remain vigilant and maintain the assertive policies that have begun to make his reign unpopular. He talks explicitly about the role of the Inquisition which had become more active after 1562 when the bishoprics were starting to be reorganised. He says very clearly that this organisation is to continue with its work despite the representations of the Prince of Gavre (Egmont). By not listening to the demands of the prince it is reasonable to suggest that this would have helped to speed up the decline in support for his rule.

This idea of not listening to the nobles is also present in Source 7 which is the Compromise demanded by the nobles in 1566. It essentially criticises the existing government and seeks changes – particularly religious toleration for Protestantism which had grown in recent years. Considering the views expressed in Source 6 there is some justification for these demands, and therefore when used together the sources help to paint a picture of why support for Habsburg rule was in decline. The comments about religious toleration implied by the comment 'freedom to express their opinions' are especially useful as they go a long way to explaining the growing rift between some of the Netherlanders and their Spanish rulers as the latter were seeking to drive out Protestantism and this was a major issue in the 1560s.

Furthermore the two sources together offer some illustration of the kind of ruler Philip II was. The Compromise is critical of his leadership, while his own letter to his sister suggests a person who has a specific idea about what he wants and how it should be achieved. In this sense it could

This opening paragraph considers broad points from the sources and offers some judgement on the question demand, but there needs to be some explanation of the final sentence's assertion.

This is a reasonable paragraph that uses some broad own knowledge in conjunction with the source material, but it does not really go beyond making an assertion and could be more effectively explained.

These paragraphs have a lot of merit as they use the sources together to draw inferences. However, some more own knowledge to help develop these ideas would strengthen the response here. Also it would be a stronger response if there was some more critical thought about the quality of the sources to help promote a more focused response regarding 'how far'.

be suggested that the declining support of the nobles was perhaps the result of his unwillingness to compromise, or in fact listen to anyone else. Source 6 is particularly good evidence of this as the nature of the letter even suggests he was dictating to his own sister. As nobles of the Low Countries, the authors of the Compromise would almost certainly have expected their opinions to be considered – especially the grandees who served in the Council of State which was the policy-forming body for the Habsburg government. If Philip II was so arrogant that he would not allow his sister any real power, then it is likely his treatment of the nobles would have been even worse, as evidenced by Source 7, and therefore clear reasoning for their declining support.

Overall the sources are very useful to a historian looking into the decline of noble support for Habsburg rule because they offer clear motivation and reasoning for this decline by showing how Philip II could have created resentment among the nobles.

This conclusion offers a clear judgement but it is a little general and could be developed further.

Verdict

This is an average answer because:

- it shows some good understanding of the source material and uses this to address the question demand by selecting some key points to develop
- it deploys some knowledge of the historical context to support its ideas, but this sometimes lacks precision or clarity

- an overall judgement is offered, but this is quite limited and could be more developed.

Use the feedback on this answer to rewrite it, making as many improvements as you can.

Paper 2: A Level sample answer with comments

Section A

You will need to read and analyse two sources and use them in tandem to assess how useful they are in investigating an issue. For these questions, remember to:

- spend time, up to ten minutes, reading and identifying the arguments and evidence present in the sources. Then make a plan to ensure that your response will be rooted in these sources
- use specific references from the sources
- deploy own knowledge to develop points made in the sources and establish appropriate context
- come to a substantiated judgement.

How far could the historian make use of Sources 6 and 7 (Chapter 1, pages 299 and 300) together to investigate the decline in noble support for Habsburg rule?

Explain your answer, using both sources, the information given about them and your own knowledge of the historical context.
(20 marks)

Strong student answer

The two sources certainly provide different perspectives on the nature of Habsburg rule. Source 6 (a letter by Philip II setting out his instructions for the governance of the Netherlands) offers some insight into the manner in which he ruled the country. Source 7 on the other hand offers some direct motivation by the nobles themselves as it is the Compromise of 1566 that was presented to the regent by the confederacy of noblemen as a result of growing discontent among them. Offering the views of both protagonists in the decline of popularity therefore offers the chance to draw effective conclusions as one can be used to corroborate the other and this would be especially useful to a historian.

The tone of the letter suggests quite a determined approach by Philip and his belief that strong government is necessary there – particularly in terms of religious policy and the use of the Inquisition, which he feels is absolutely critical. Given the king's own strong religious faith (Philip II was a devout Catholic to the extent that he would wage war on behalf of the Church against the Ottoman Empire), this particular attitude offers some useful commentary about (and possible motive for) reasons for the decline of noble support. If Source 7 is also looked at, then the inferences of Philip's manner of government can be drawn out further. The Compromise of 1566 was an attempt by the lesser nobles to address the issue of religious toleration that they felt was lacking in the Netherlands. After 1562, Catholicism was being deliberately tightened up through the reorganisation of the bishoprics and increased use of the Inquisition to offset the growth in Calvinism. This was just one clear example of the high-handedness of Philip II who would not countenance any religion other than Catholicism. Although this would not necessarily undermine the nobles specifically as many were Catholic themselves, it is a good example of the broader attempt at centralisation that Philip employed after he took power in 1555. As leaders of Low Countries and members of the Council of State, the nobles would have objected to these changes and therefore this perhaps was the motivation for Source 7's creation.

> This is a good paragraph because it focuses explicitly on the source material and draws comments based on this.

> This is a strong paragraph because the source points are well developed using own knowledge to offer context and justification. There is also some effort to link the sources and use them together.

This idea is given more credibility in Source 6 which talks specifically about the 'punishment of prisoners' and the criticisms of the 'prince of Gavre'. Despite the representations of this man, Philip II clearly ignores what he has said and this offers clear motive for the nobles' possible decline of support. This is supported in Source 7 when it talks of 'barbarism… practised by tyrants', which leaves the reader in no real doubt as to what the authors feel about Philip II and Habsburg rule. Although each source evidently offers comment from different perspectives – Source 6 from Philip and Source 7 from the nobles – there is sufficient similarity that can be drawn from them to offer a reasonably secure understanding of why there might have been decline in popularity.

Overall therefore, the sources offer the opportunity to consider motivation for declining support from two disparate backgrounds and this provides the chance to effectively judge one against the other. This is very useful to a historian as it offers the opportunity to draw a balanced viewpoint by considering the motives of both sides.

These paragraphs are well focused on the question demand and draw some useful conclusions. The judgement is sound and well supported in the body of the response.

Verdict

This is a strong answer because:

- it is rooted in the sources and interrogates them with confidence to develop an argument

- it deploys a good knowledge of the historical context to discuss the quality of the sources
- it evidences a good level of evaluation by sustaining a clear and consistent argument.

Paper 2: A Level sample answer with comments

Section B

These questions assess your understanding of the period in some depth. They will ask you about the content you learned about in the four key themes, but they may not ask about more than one theme. For these questions remember to:

- give an analytical, not a descriptive, response
- support your points with evidence
- cover the whole time period specified in the question
- come to a substantiated judgement.

How far do you agree that the success enjoyed by the Duke of Parma before 1584 was the result of his military power? (20 marks)

Average student answer

The success enjoyed by the Duke of Parma before 1584 was mostly down to the military power of Spain. This is because they had a very sizeable force of veteran troops who knew what they were doing. The size of the Spanish army was about 70,000 and Parma was able to rely on this numerical advantage to secure most of the territories lost to the Prince of Orange. Although this was certainly the most important reason, there were some other factors that also contributed to the duke's success.

It is reasonable to suggest that military power was most important to the success of the Duke of Parma because he was able to capture lots of rebel towns during the 1580s which had been acquired by the Prince of Orange's men. Following the rebellion in 1578 Orange had been much more effective as he had greater local support and as such he had captured a lot of towns from the Spanish. Parma was able to re-take these because he was a clever tactician and his army was more responsive to his orders. With a greater army than the rebels, and also an able leader at the helm the Spanish under Parma were therefore much more effective and this was because of their increased military capability.

Although military power was very important to Parma's success, he was also a very clever tactician, which meant he could manipulate his enemy quite effectively. This was really apparent by 1579 when he was able to exploit the tensions between the individual provinces who disagreed over particular rights and the issue of religion. Here Parma was able to drive a wedge between these groups by being willing to sign agreements with them which promised them what they wanted. In the case of the southern provinces they wanted Catholicism to be protected and Parma was able to offer this. The result of Parma's scheming was the Union of Arras in 1579 which saw many of the southern Catholic provinces bind together in support of their faith and agree terms with Parma. By contrast, the northern provinces signed their own union called the Union of Utrecht in the same year which bound them together in mutual support. The outcome of these unions was that the Netherlands became divided almost along religious lines and this played into the hands of Parma as he was able to reduce the level of opposition he faced.

This is a typically average start that offers some awareness of the question demand and answers the question, but in a general way – only acknowledging the debate in brief terms.

This paragraph offers some explanation that is reasonably focused on the question demand but it is a little limited in its analysis and could be more developed using own knowledge in support.

This paragraph has some very good points in it that are relevant to the question demand. The own knowledge is accurate but the explanation is quite narrative and this undermines its analytical qualities.

Not only were Parma's political tactics very important to the success he enjoyed before 1584, the financial security offered by Spain at the time was also significant. Before 1584 the rebels struggled to finance their army and as a result of this they often struggled to pay their troops, which could result in mutiny, for example when the malcontents rebelled. Since Parma had the backing of the Spanish empire he was able to use his financial security to bribe the opposition. He paid 250,000 florins to the malcontents and in return they joined his army. Also, he could bribe the leaders of towns to open their gates to him, which many did. Without his ready supply of money this might not have been possible and therefore his success was also because of his financial strength and not simply his military might.

> Here is another relevant paragraph, but once again it lacks really focused analysis. The evidence is a little general but there is some attempt at a judgement towards the end.

Overall, therefore, the military power of Parma and the Spanish empire was certainly very important to the success that the duke enjoyed before 1584, but so too were other factors like his financial security and clever politicking. Without these contributing factors Parma may not have been quite so successful.

> There is a judgement here although it is a little general.

Verdict

This is an average answer because:

- it uses some accurate knowledge in support of its points but this could be more thoughtfully developed overall
- there is some evidence of analysis being developed but this is sometimes undermined by narrative passages

- the judgement reached is broadly developed in the body of the essay but it lacks decisiveness.

Use the feedback on this answer to rewrite it, making as many improvements as you can.

Paper 2: A Level sample answer with comments

Section B

These questions assess your understanding of the period in some depth. They will ask you about the content you learned about in the four key themes, but they may not ask about more than one theme. For these questions, remember to:

- give an analytical, not a descriptive, response
- support your points with evidence
- cover the whole time period specified in the question
- come to a substantiated judgement.

How far do you agree that the success enjoyed by the Duke of Parma before 1584 was the result of his military power? (20 marks)

Strong student answer

To a certain extent it is very appropriate to suggest that the success enjoyed by the Duke of Parma before 1584 was motivated by his military power. This is because the threat posed by the rebels required a military presence to subdue it, and without his army, Parma would have been unable to check this challenge. In this sense it is right to point out the value of military might. However, such might is not just about the number of muskets you have. Parma also had other resources that complimented his army's physical size and these allowed the duke to take full advantage of his strength.

> This is a well-conceived introduction that offers a broadly explained, balanced, argument.

Given the nature of rebellion it is very reasonable to suggest that military strength is the decisive influence upon success. The rebellion in 1568 failed because it lacked sufficient numbers for the Orangists, while the prince's second attempt in 1572 was much more potent having acquired greater numbers because of the unpopularity of the Duke of Alva. On these grounds it is clear that military success can rest on numerical strength. In the case of Parma, he controlled more than 60,000 men compared with the rebels' more modest figure of 10,000 and so he was always likely to be successful, particularly in any open field confrontation. Under these circumstances the plethora of victories he achieved, including the seizure of Maastricht in 1579, were certainly influenced by physical power.

> These two paragraphs offer a well-developed argument that evidences a good understanding of the question demand. Material is explained and also supported effectively by accurate own knowledge.

Having said that, however, it is also appropriate to consider the choices that Parma made in selecting his targets. Rather than randomly attacking any rebel town, instead the duke conducted a systematic approach that sought to encircle the rebels and eventually cut them off from possible support. In this manner the military power was not so much physical as tactical, and this attribute is equally appropriate to the overall power of Parma. The best example of his tactical awareness is the way in which he sought to take advantage of the religious animosities among the provinces. Since many of the southern states were Catholic and the northern ones were heavily Protestant-dominated, Parma was able to apply 'divide and conquer' tactics by appealing to the religious fears of the south who consequently signed the Union of Arras in 1579. This agreement essentially wedded the southern provinces to Spain once more and established a clear division between them and the north who signed their own Union of Utrecht a few months later. By exploiting the religious weakness among his opponents Parma was able to neutralise much of the threat and this secured him great success without simply relying on physical power.

Central to his success was also the financial backing he received from Spain. Throughout the rebellion money was a crucial factor to the success of either side and although the Spanish army had succumbed to mutiny in 1576, under Parma they enjoyed regular wages which minimised the likelihood of this reoccurrence. In contrast the rebel forces at this time struggled to fund themselves, relying on patchy support from England or funds raised in the north. The importance of this factor is evident as late as 1581 when troops under the command of Orange's captains rebelled and were then 'bought' by Parma for 250,000 florins. This particular example is significant for two reasons: firstly it evidences the fragility of the rebel forces and secondly it shows how Parma could actually strengthen his own hand by exercising his financial superiority.

In conclusion, it is perfectly reasonable to suggest that Parma enjoyed considerable success because of his military power, but this does not completely satisfy the complexity of Parma's success. Certainly he wielded physical power, but he also used tactics, finance and religion to great strategic effect. Collectively these attributes inform a broader interpretation of 'military power' and therefore only when these are also considered is it accurate to say his success was based on military power.

> This judgement is well considered and directly addresses the question demand.

Verdict

This is a strong answer because:

- it directly addresses the question demand using well-informed analysis throughout the essay
- it employs a good range of accurate own knowledge in support of its well-drawn arguments and this is evenly spread throughout the response

- a clear and well-substantiated overall judgement is reached, which is based upon the material discussed.

Index

Acknowledgements

The authors and publisher would like to thank the following individuals and organisations for permission to reproduce photographs and text in this book.

Photographs

(Key: b-bottom; c-centre; l-left; r-right; t-top)

akg-images Ltd: 166, 167, 192, 193, 199, 230, Quint & Lox 284, Schadach 177, 217; **Alamy Images:** Classic Image 42, 104, FALKENSTEINFOTO 315, Heritage Image Partnership Ltd/E&E Image Library 95, Heritage Image Partnership Ltd/Guildhall Library & Art Gallery 92, Imagestate Media Partners Limited – Impact Photos 73, Ivy Close Images 103, Lebrecht Music and Arts Photo Library 9t, Masterpics 286, 294, National Geographic Image Collection 6, PearlBucknall 88, 89t, Pictorial Press Ltd 224, The Art Archive/Museo del Prado Madrid 256, The Art Archive/University Archive Geneva 305, 368, Tracey Whitefoot 110, World History Archive 45, 287, 301, 310, 311, 319, 324, 331, 348; **Bridgeman Art Library Ltd:** Akademie der Bildenden Kunste, Vienna, Austria 179, National Trust Photographic Library/Andreas von Einsiedel 108, Pinacoteca Nazionale, Siena, Italy 89b, 112, Private Collection 10, 98, 102, 107, 130, Private Collection/Photo © Bonhams, London, UK 114, 123, Private Collection/The Stapleton Collection 9b, 72, Woburn Abbey, Bedfordshire, UK 63br, 86, 124; **British Library Images Online:** CC0 1.0 Universal Public Domain Dedication 241; **Mary Evans Picture Library:** 335, 355, 363, Grovsenor Prints 359, 380, INTERFOTO/Sammlung Rauch 334, 340; **The Masters of the Bench of the Inner Temple:** 19; **TopFoto:** Heritage Images/Fine Art Images 168, 171, The Granger Collection 219, ullsteinbild 252

Cover images: *Front:* **Getty Images:** Palace of Westminster, London, UK/Frank Cadogan Cowper

All other images © Pearson Education

Figures
Figure 1.1, p.16 from Tudor family tree, http://englishhistory.net/tudor/tudortree.bmp. Reproduced by permission of EnglishHistory.net c/o Clever Bytes Ltd; Figure 1.4, p.175 from Charles V's territories, http://en.wikipedia.org/wiki/Charles_V,_Holy_Roman_Emperor, CC BY-SA 3.0; Figure 2.1, p.195 adapted from *The Oxford Illustrated History of the Reformation* ed. Peter Marshall, Oxford University Press, 2015, p.52, copyright © Oxford University Press, 2015. Reproduced by permission of Oxford University Press, www.oup.com; Figure 1.1, p.288 from *ATH From Revolt to Independence – Netherlands 1550–1650* by Martyn Rady, Hodder Education, 1990, p.4. Reproduced by permission of Hodder Education.

Tables
Table p.25 from *Source: Parliament under the Tudors* by Jennifer Loach, Clarendon Press, 1991, p.x, Oxford University Press; Tables on pages 32, 69, 97 from *Source: Tudor England* by John Guy, Oxford University Press, 1988, pp.38, 310, Oxford University Press; Table p.94 from *Source: The Population History of England, 1541–1871: A Reconstruction* by E.A. Wrigley and R.S. Schofield, Cambridge University Press, 1981, pp.531–533, Cambridge University Press; Table p.135 from *Source: The Later Tudors, 1547–1603* by Penry Williams, Clarendon Press, 1995, pp.360–363, 172–173, Oxford University Press; Table p.332 from *The Dutch Revolt* by Geoffrey Parker, Penguin Books Ltd, 1990, p.162. Reproduced with the kind permission of the author.

Text

Extracts pp.20–21 from 'Elizabeth I: exception to the rule' by Helen Castor, *History Today,* Vol. 60 (10), October 2010, http://www.historytoday.com/helen-castor/elizabeth-i-exception-rule. Reproduced with permission of History Today Ltd; Extract pp.25, 142 from *The Elizabethan Puritan Movement* by Patrick Collinson, Clarendon, 1967, p.27. Reproduced by kind permission of the Estate of Patrick Collinson; Extract p.28 from *England and Europe 1485–1603* by Susan Doran, Routledge, 2013, p.31. Reproduced by permission of Taylor & Francis; Extract p.43 from *The Tudors* by Richard Rex, Amberley, 2012, p.108. Reproduced by permission of Amberley Publishing; Extract p.48 from *Politics and the Nation, 1450–1660* by D.M. Loades, Fontana/Collins, 1974, pp.253–254. Reproduced by permission of Professor David Loades; Extract p.54 from *The Church, Catholics and the People* by Christopher Haigh, Palgrave Macmillan, 1984, p.202. Reproduced by permission; Extracts pp.57, 121, 148–151 from *The Later Tudors: England 1547–1603* by Penry Williams, Clarendon Press, 1995, pp.115–119, 348–349. Reproduced by permission of Oxford University Press, www.oup.com; Extract p.70 from *New Worlds, Lost Worlds: The Rule of the Tudors, 1485–1603* by Susan Brigden, Penguin Press, 2000, pp.81–82, copyright © Susan Brigden, 2000. Reproduced by permission of Penguin Books Ltd; Extracts pp.111, 128, 164–165 from *Tudor England* by John Guy, Oxford University Press, 1988, pp.439–440, 450. Reproduced by permission of Oxford University Press, www.oup.com; Extracts pp.122, 148–151 from *The Tudor Years* ed. J. Lotherington, Hodder Education, 1994, p.266. Reproduced by permission of Hodder Education; Extracts pp.128, 162, 164, 165 from *Politics and Nation: England 1450–1660* by David M. Loades, Blackwell, 1999, pp.263–264, copyright © 1999, John Wiley and Sons. Reproduced with permission of Blackwell Publishing; Extract p.133 from *Studies In Tudor And Stuart Politics And Government. Papers And Reviews 1946–1972*, Volume Two, by G.R. Elton, Cambridge University Press, 1974, p.164. Reproduced by permission of Cambridge University Press; Extract p.134 from *Elizabethan Parliaments, 1559–1603* by M.A.R. Graves, Longman, 1987, pp.48–49. Reproduced by permission of Taylor & Francis Books UK; Extracts pp.168, 191 from *The European World* by Henry J Cohn, ed. Beat Kümin, Routledge, 2009, p.97, copyright © 2009. Reproduced by permission of Taylor & Francis Books UK; Extract p.180 from *Imperial Cities and the Reformation: Three Essays*, ed. & translated by H.C. Erik Midelfort and Mark U. Edwards Jr., Fortress Press, 1972, p.36. Reproduced by permission of Augsburg Fortress Publishers; Extract p.181 from *The Penguin History of the Church: The Reformation* by Owen Chadwick, Penguin Books, 1964, 1969, 1972, 1990, p.32, copyright © Owen Chadwick, 1964, 1969, 1972. Reproduced by permission of Penguin Books Ltd; Extracts pp.182, 214 from *The Renaissance in Europe: Challenges to Authority* by Peter Elmer, Yale University Press in association with The Open University, 2000, pp.21, 26–27. Reproduced by permission of Yale University Press and The Open University; Quotation p.184 by Dr Alister E. McGrath in 'Religion on the eve of the Reformation', History Sixth, No. 6, March 1990. Reproduced with kind permission; Extract p.184 from *The German Reformation* by R.W. Scribner, Palgrave Macmillan, 1986, p.7. Reproduced with permission of Palgrave Macmillan; Extract p.184 from *Years of Renewal*, 5th edition, ed. John Lotherington, Hodder & Stoughton, 1992, p.136. Reproduced by permission of John C. Lotherington; Extracts on pp.189, 194, 197, 201, 204, 214, 215, 220, 221 from *Martin Luther* by E.G. Rupp & B. Drewery, Edward Arnold, 1970, pp.1, 2, 3, 15–17, 19–25, 58–60, 61–62, 64–65, 178–179. Reproduced by kind permission of the Estate of Benjamin Drewery; Extracts p.194 from *Martin Luther*, 2nd edition by Martin Luther, Routledge, 2014, pp.37, 43, 44. Reproduced by permission of Taylor & Francis Books UK; Extract p.195 from *The Pastoral Luther: Essays on Martin Luther's Practical Theology* ed. Timothy J. Wengert, Wm. B. Eerdmans Publishing, 2005, p.350. Reproduced with permission of Wm. B. Eerdmans Publishing Co.; Extracts p.199 from 'How Did the Town of Wittenberg Look at the Time of Luther?' by Gottfried Krüger, Wittenberg, translated by Holger Sonntag, http://thewittenbergproject.org, Hermann Böhlaus Nachfolger. Reproduced by permission of J.B. Metzler; Extract p.203 from *Reformation and Society in Sixteenth Century Europe* by A.G. Dickens, Thames & Hudson, 1971, p.86. Reproduced with permission; Extract p.209 from *Documents on the Continental Reformation* by William G. Naphy, Palgrave Macmillan, 1996, p.127. Reproduced with permission of Palgrave Macmillan; Extracts pp.214, 244 from *The Longman Companion to the European Reformation c.1500–1618* by Mark Greengrass, Longman, 1998, pp.44, 245; Extracts pp.214, 230 from *Reformation: Europe's House Divided 1490–1700* by Diarmaid MacCulloch, Penguin Books, 2003, pp.126–127, 133, copyright © Diarmaid MacCulloch, 2003. Reproduced by permission of Penguin Books Ltd; Extracts p.219, 228 from *Luther and the Reformation* by Heather Cubitt, Longman, 1976, pp.53, 64; Extracts on p.223 from *Luther's Works (Vol. 51: Vol. 1 of 2 of collected sermons) 'The First Sermon, March 9, 1552, Invocavit Sunday'* By Jaroslav Pelikan and Helmut T. Lehmann, Fortress Press, 1943, p.71. Reproduced by permission of Augsburg Fortress Publishers;

Extracts pp.226, 227 from *The German Peasant's war: A History in Documents* by Tom Scott and Bob Scribner, Humanity Books, 1994, pp.322–324, 330–331. Reproduced by permission of Prometheus Books; Extract p.229 from *Desiderius Erasmus. Christian Humanism and the Reformation. Selected Writings with The Life of Erasmus by Beatus Rhenanus*, ed. John. C. Olin, Harper Torchbooks, 1965, pp.147–149. Reproduced by permission of HarperCollins, Inc.; Extract p.234 from 'The Execution of Martin Luther' by Andrew Pettegree, *History Review*, Issue 24, pp.20–25, March 1996, http://www.historytoday.com/andrew-pettegree/execution-martin-luther. Reproduced with permission of History Today Ltd; Extracts pp.235, 276 from 'Johannes Dantiscus von Höfen. Ein Diplomat und Bischof zwischen Humanismus und Reformation (1485–1548)' by Inge Brigitte Müller-Blessing. Translated by Elisabeth Feist Hirsch, *Renaissance Quarterly*, Vol. 22 (4), pp.390–392, copyright © 1969, The Renaissance Society of America, Inc.; Extract p.242 from *The Trial of Luther* by James Atkinson, Batsford, 1971, p.178. Reproduced with kind permission of B.T. Batsford, part of Pavilion Books Company Limited; Extract p.245 from *The Emperor Charles V* by Martyn Rady, Routledge, 1988, pp.108–109, copyright © 1988. Reproduced by permission of Taylor & Francis Books UK; Extract p.257 from *The Knights of the Crown* by D'Arcy Jonathan Dacre Boulton, Boydell Press, 1987, p.361. Reprinted by permission of Boydell & Brewer Ltd; Extracts pp.290, 295, 304, 308, 312, 325, 330, 337–339, 341, 349, 354, 370 from *The Dutch Revolt* by Geoffrey Parker, Penguin Books Ltd, 1990, pp.34, 46, 76, 84, 104, 126, 160, 165, 166, 169, 177, 191, 207, 227. Reproduced with the kind permission of the author; Extracts pp.293, 299, 300, 302, 307, 317, 320, 329, 336, 344, 348, 349, 352, 354, 360, 397 from *Texts Concerning the Revolt of the Netherlands*, ed. by E.H. Kossman and A.F. Mellink, Cambridge University Press, 1974, pp.33, 54, 55, 60, 63, 66–67, 76, 85, 88, 118, 154, 212, 261–262. Reproduced by permission of Cambridge University Press and the estate of E.H. Kossman; Extract p.298 from *Margaret of Parma: A Life* by Charles R. Steen, Brill, 2013, p.104 and Extract p.318 from *Exercise of Arms: Warfare in the Netherlands (1568–1648)* ed. by Marco van der Hoeven, Brill, 1997, p.64, copyright © Koninklijke BRILL NV; Extracts pp.327, 353, 381 from *The Low Countries in Early Modern Times* by Herbert H. Rowen, Macmillan, 1972, pp.41, 102. Reproduced by kind permission of the Estate of Herbert Rowen; Extract p.330 from *History of the Dutch-Speaking Peoples 1555–1648* by Peter Geyl, Phoenix, 2001, p.134, copyright © 1932, 1961, Sebes & Van Gelderen Literary Agency; Extract p.349 from *Representative Government in Western Europe in the Sixteenth Century* by Gordon Griffiths, Oxford University Press, 1968, pp.495–496, Reproduced by permission of Oxford University Press, www.oup.com; Extract p.349 from *ATH From Revolt to Independence – Netherlands 1550–1650* by Martyn Rady, Hodder Education, 1990, p.48. Reproduced by permission of Hodder Education; Extract p.349 from *The Spanish Armada* by Colin Martin and Geoffrey Parker, Manchester University Press, 1999, p.52. Reproduced by permission; Extract p.366 from The Treaty of Nonsuch, http://www.historylearningsite.co.uk, copyright © 2000–2015 HistoryLearningSite.co.uk; Extract p.369 from *The Works of Sir Roger Williams* ed. by J.X. Evans, Oxford University Press, 1972, p.12. Reproduced by permission of Oxford University Press, www.oup.com.

Every effort has been made to contact copyright holders of material reproduced in this book. Any omissions will be rectified in subsequent printings if notice is given to the publishers.